The Intellectual Property of Textiles and Fashion: From the Medieval Loom to the New York Fashion Week

The Intellectual Property of Textiles and Fashion: From the Medieval Loom to the New York Fashion Week

A Sourcebook

Nuno Pires de Carvalho

Wolters Kluwer

Published by:
Kluwer Law International B.V.
PO Box 316
2400 AH Alphen aan den Rijn
The Netherlands
E-mail: international-sales@wolterskluwer.com
Website: lrus.wolterskluwer.com

Sold and distributed by:
Wolters Kluwer Legal & Regulatory U.S.
7201 McKinney Circle
Frederick, MD 21704
United States of America
E-mail: customer.service@wolterskluwer.com

ISBN 978-94-035-3784-9

e-Book: ISBN 978-94-035-3785-6
web-PDF: ISBN 978-94-035-3790-0

For Ana (for ever)
For André, Hugo, and Carolina
For Theo, Felipe, Pedro, Sofia, and Mateo

Mr. von Mitzelben. The whole question of fashion enters here. A fashion is only what is substantially imitation anyway. If one person alone wore a thing you could not call it a fashion. To make it a fashion it has to be communicated through some journal like ours, so that a great many people get to wearing it. I think that this raises the objection to this registration. ...

Mr. Gotlesby. ... However, I think you are not giving proper credit to our American designers. I know a couple of young ladies who sell hundreds of dozens of dresses and negligee dresses of different kinds that are advertised as being imported direct from Paris. Neither of them have ever been across the water, but their dresses give just as much satisfaction as if they did come from Paris.

Mr. Gotthelf. That is right, but they are all as nearly stolen as these are, because everybody steals from everybody else, and you [can] not get away from it. That is what constitutes fashion. Let [me be] frank about it.

Gotthelf and von Mitzleben represented fashion journals at the hearings on a proposed act on the registration of designs, promoted by the Committee on Patents of the House of Representatives, USA, 1916. Gotlesby presided the Committee.

It can be rightly maintained that, obliged to be inspired by Fashion, i.e., the taste of the moment, in the need to obey, therefore, to a fleeting conception of lines, shapes or even colours, hats, like all the other objects of women's dressing, ... it cannot however be disputed that certain hats made with a deeper science, a more sure taste, a choice and an assembly still unsuspected of the raw materials that compose them or serve as ornaments to them, thus affirming by a succession of original and personal notes, much more than by a perfection which does not have to be envisaged, and thus the creative talent of the house that launches them, escapes the public domain and must be classified among the number of the objects whose reproduction, when it results in the slavish or quasi-slavish copy of the essential specificities and details from which their personality derives, constitutes an infringement as understood by the law, which justly punishes it; ...

It suffices to note that while the plaintiffs are obliged to incur in considerable expenses to ensure the development of collections whose development requires not only long months of research and combinations, [and] the collaboration of a large staff, but also and above all renowned makers of outfits, the counterfeiters, without high general costs, without any merit of invention, resort not to the creative brain but to the copying hand. ...

Paris Court, 9th Chamber of Appeals, Demoiselle Jacquet v. Caroline Roux, Rose Descat et autres, July 18, 1934.

Table of Contents

List of Figures xxiii

Preamble xxvii

CHAPTER 1
The Business Identifiers of Textiles and Fashion 1

§ 1.01 An Early Statute Setting a Mark of Origin: The By-Laws of the Weavers of Canvas of Douai—1261 1

§ 1.02 By-Laws of the Woollen Clothmakers and Merchants of Saint-Omer—1268, 1285 2

§ 1.03 Regulation Concerning the Profession of Tailors, Paris—1323 3

§ 1.04 Upon Their Request, Clothmakers and Merchants of Châlons, France, Are Authorized to Adopt a Seal Certifying the Origin of Woollen Cloth—1339 4

§ 1.05 Edward III, of England, Determines That No Cloths Should Be Sold Between Merchants Without Being Previously Inspected and Sealed—1348 5

§ 1.06 In Abbeville, France, the Use of a Mark of Origin by the Cloth Industry Becomes Mandatory and Exclusive—1352 6

§ 1.07 Edward III Approves Another Statute Imposing the Inspection and the Sealing of Imported Cloths—1353 8

§ 1.08 The Emergence of a New Industry in Tournai—The Manufacture of Velvet Cloth—Was Accompanied by Rules on the Mandatory Use of Marks of Origin as Well as Individual Trademarks 8

§ 1.08.1 The First Regulation on Tournai's City Mark and Individual Marks for Carpets Made of Velvet—1380 9

§ 1.08.2 Statute Amending the Regulations of the Tapestry Industry of Tournai—1397 9

§ 1.09 A Contract on the Assignment of a Trademark Between Two Merchants from Milan—1383 10

§ 1.10 The Use of Certification and Individual Marks Is Made Mandatory for the Leather Workers of Amiens—1383 12
§ 1.11 Following the Example of Other Cities, Lille Regulates the Textile Industry and Adopts Provisions on the Mandatory Use of the City's Seal and Individual Marks—1384 13
§ 1.12 Arras Passes a Statute on the Establishment of a Cloth Manufactory—1394 14
§ 1.13 By-Laws of the Tanners, Shoemakers, and Cobblers of Amiens—1407 16
§ 1.14 Ordinances of Tournai Concerning the Tapestry Industry—1408 17
§ 1.15 The Aldermen of Amiens Approve an Ordinance Concerning the Cloth Industry—1413 19
§ 1.16 Regulations of the Cloth Industry of Chartres—1418 20
§ 1.17 Regulations of the Cloth Industry of Dijon—1425, 1435 22
§ 1.17.1 Regulation of 1425 22
§ 1.17.2 Amendment to the 1425 Regulation—1435 23
§ 1.18 By-Laws of the Carpet Makers of Paris—1465 24
§ 1.19 Edward IV Approves a Statute on the Making of Worsteds in the County of Norfolk—1467 25
§ 1.20 Louis XI Establishes the Manufacture of Cloth in Montpellier—1475 26
§ 1.20.1 Establishment of the Manufacture of Cloth in Montpellier—1475 26
§ 1.20.2 Charles VIII, of France, Complements and Details the Regulations of Drapery of Montpellier—July 1493. 27
§ 1.21 By-Laws of the Woollen Clothmakers of Amiens (1480, 1494, and 1511) and Paris (1481) 28
§ 1.21.1 By-Laws of the *Sayeteurs* of Amiens—1480 29
§ 1.21.2 New By-Laws of the Clothmakers and Tailors of Amiens—1494 30
§ 1.21.3 New By-Laws of the *Sayeteurs* of Amiens—1511 30
§ 1.21.4 By-Laws of the Sayeteurs of Paris—1481 31
§ 1.22 By-Laws of the Cloth Shearers of Paris—1483 31
§ 1.23 Reunion of Various Professions Dealing with Carpets under the Same Corporation—Paris, 1490 32
§ 1.24 By-Laws of the *Saieteurs* of Lille—1500 33
§ 1.25 Fernando and Isabel, of Spain, Approve a General Regulation on the Cloth Industry, Including Detailed Provisions on Certification and Individual Marks—1500 34
§ 1.26 Several Statutes Concerning the Woollen Cloth Industry Approved by Henry VIII of England—1511, 1513, 1523, 1535, 1541—and by Edward VI—1549, 1551 36
§ 1.26.1 An Act Against Deceitful Making of Woollen Cloth—1511 37
§ 1.26.2 An Act for the True Making of Cloths in Devon, Called *White-Straits*—1513 37

§ 1.26.3 Statute That Concerns the Draping of Worsteds Sayes and Stamyns for the Town[s] of Great Yarmouth [And Lynne]—1523 38
§ 1.26.4 An Act for True Making of Woollen Cloths—1535 39
§ 1.26.5 An Act for the True Making of Kerseys—1541 40
§ 1.26.6 An Act for the True Making of Woollen Clothes—1549 40
§ 1.26.7 An Act for the Making of Woollen Cloth—1551 40
§ 1.27 By-Laws of the *Saieteurs* of Abbeville—1518 42
§ 1.28 Ordinances of Seville—1519 44
§ 1.29 By-Laws of the *Sayeterie* of Lille—1524 45
§ 1.30 An Ordinance Settles a Dispute Between the Masters and the Companions of the Guild of Carpet Makers of Brussels—1528 45
§ 1.30.1 Ordinance of 1528 Set by a Magistrate Settling a Dispute Between the Masters and Jurors of the Corporation of Carpet Makers of Brussels, on the One Hand, and the Companions, on the Other 46
§ 1.30.2 Edict on the Manufacture of Tapestries in Flanders, Approved by Charles V—1544 46
§ 1.31 Statutes of the Knitwear Makers of Paris—1550 47
§ 1.32 By-Laws of the Workers in the Industry of Gold and Silver Cloths of Lyon—1554 47
§ 1.33 A French Statute on Technical Standards for Wool Cloth, and Their Marks of Origin and Certification—1571 50
§ 1.34 Patent Letters Confirming the By-Laws of the Shoemakers of Paris—1573 51
§ 1.35 Two Master Carders Dispute in Court the Ownership of a Trademark; Rennes, France—1578 52
§ 1.36 The First (?) English Court Dispute Involving Cloth Trademarks: The *Sandforth's Case*—1584-1585 53
§ 1.37 An Act Approved by Elizabeth I on the Regulation of the Making and Selling of Kersies—1593 55
§ 1.38 By-Laws of the Makers of Fustians of the City of Lyon—1595 56
§ 1.39 Henry IV Approves the General Regulation of French Manufactories, Including Provisions on Silk Cloth Dyers' Trademarks—1601 57
§ 1.40 By-Laws of the Community of Shoemakers of Paris—1614 59
§ 1.41 Administrative Provisions Putting an End to the Passing Off of Trademarks in the Commerce of Wine from Bordeaux and of Pastel from Loragnes—1614 59
§ 1.42 Judge Doddrige Cites, as a Precedent, a Court Decision Dealing with the Counterfeiting of a Cloth Merchant's Trademark: *Southern v. How*—1618 60
§ 1.43 By-Laws of the Guild of the Makers of Cloth on the High Loom—Paris, 1627 60
§ 1.44 Statute Regulating the Industry of Worsteds of Norfolk and Norwich—1662 61

§ 1.45 Josse van Robais, a Dutch Clothmaker, and His Successors Resort to Various Intellectual Property Mechanisms to Secure Competitive Advantages—1665 Onwards 62

§ 1.45.1 Industrial Privilege Granted to Josse van Robais with Exclusive Rights in the Making of Fine Cloths in Abbeville in the Manner of Spain and Holland—1665 63

§ 1.45.2 In a Letter to the Intendant of Rouen, Colbert Refers to a Trade Secret Owned by van Robais on a Method of Dyeing Cloths—1683 64

§ 1.45.3 A Historical Account of van Robais Heirs' Long Struggle in Obtaining Exclusive Rights in a New Business Identifier: The Dawn Colored Selvage of Their Cloths 64

§ 1.45.4 Report on the Complaint by the Heirs of van Robais Concerning the Infringement of Their Selvage—1773 65

§ 1.45.5 Van Robais Advertises the Manufacture's Exclusive Rights in the Selvage—1749 66

§ 1.46 Regulations of the Making of Cloths in the Manner of Spain and Holland in Sedan—1666 66

§ 1.47 By-Laws of the Corporation of Woollen Clothmakers of Amiens—1666 69

§ 1.48 General Regulations of the French Cloth and Dyeing Industries—1669 71

§ 1.48.1 Regulations Concerning the Dyeing of Cloths—1669 72

§ 1.48.2 Regulations on Mandatory Technical Standards for Cloths 74

§ 1.48.3 Regulation on the Dyeing of Fine Cloths and Thread 75

§ 1.49 Ordinances Concerning the Seals to Be Affixed to the Cloths Made in Lille—1673 75

§ 1.49.1 Ordinance Concerning the Pieces of Lead, Seals, and Tokens to Be Affixed to the Pieces [Of Cloth] 76

§ 1.49.2 Ordinance Concerning the Tokens, Stamps, and Pieces of Lead That Must Be Affixed to the Articles of *Sayetterie* and *Bourgeterie* 77

§ 1.50 A Court Dispute Concerning the Similarity of Two Cloth Merchants' Shop Signs Is Cited in a Judgment of the Parliament of Aix-en-Provence—1678 78

§ 1.51 The Regulation of Cloth Manufacture of Portugal—1690 79

§ 1.52 A Late Portuguese Sumptuary Law—1690 81

§ 1.53 The State Council Prohibits the Use of Foreign Marks to Designate Cloths Made in France—1692 and 1723 82

§ 1.53.1 The State Council Prohibits the Use of Foreign Marks to Designate Cloths Made in France—1692 82

§ 1.53.2 The King's State Council Reiterates the Prohibition of 1692—1723 83

§ 1.54 The French State Council Settles the Dispute Between the Makers of Knitwear and the Makers of Socks—1707 84

§ 1.55 Letters Patent on the Community of Shoemakers—Paris, 1705 85

§ 1.56 Regulation of the Corporation of Carpet Makers of Paris—1719 86
§ 1.57 Lille Adopts a Regulation on the Manufacture of Cloths and *Pinchinas*—1732 87
§ 1.58 In the Eighteenth Century, in England, Exclusivity in a Trademark Was Not Unconditional—1742 88
§ 1.59 England Establishes Rules of Origin for Preventing the Exportation of Foreign Linens under English or Irish Marks and Seals—1744 88
§ 1.60 Two Disputes Between the Community of Shoemakers of Paris and "Privileged" Shoemakers—1749, 1758 91
§ 1.60.1 Decision of the Grand Council Against the Widow of a Privileged Shoemaker—1749 92
§ 1.60.2 Decision of the Grand Council Against a Privileged Shoemaker—1758 93
§ 1.61 French Authorities Prohibit Competition Among Master Tailors, Including Their Advertising of Low Prices—1760, 1761, 1782 93
§ 1.61.1 A Judgment of the Court of Parliament Prohibits Tailors from Announcing Their Articles at Low Prices—1760 94
§ 1.61.2 Ordinance Prohibiting Cloth Merchants from Competing with Each Other, Including Announcing Their Articles at Low Prices—1761 95
§ 1.61.3 The Provost of the Community of Clothmakers Is Denounced for Infringing the Ordinance and Inserting on His Signboard Indications of Articles' Prices—1761 96
§ 1.61.4 A French Jurist Defends the Practice of Distributing Cards Advertising the Name and Address of Merchants—1782 96
§ 1.62 Fashion Law's Birth Certificate?—1728, 1779 98
§ 1.62.1 The Sayetteurs of Lille Are Authorized to Make New Cloths According to Whatever Taste and Design They Deem Convenient and Following the Fashions—1728 98
§ 1.62.2 Louis XVI Acknowledges the Incompatibility of Existing Rules on Textiles with the Fleeting Nature of Fashion and for the First Time Admits a Duplicity of Legal Regimes for Trademarks Certifying Cloths' Quality and Origin—1779 99
§ 1.63 Patent Letters Confirming the Previous Text in Connection with Linen Cloths—1780 101
§ 1.64 Two French Cities Dispute the Ownership and Use of Colored Selvages—1782 102
§ 1.65 Decision of Louis XVI's Council Concerning the Marks of Woollen Cloths—1783 104
§ 1.66 New Regulation of the Marks of Linen Cloths (Canvases)—France, 1785 105
§ 1.67 Decision of the Louis XVI's Council on the Trademarks of Canvases—1787 105
§ 1.68 *Burberrys v. Raper and Pulleyn*: When Misbranding Deceives the Customer—1906 106

§ 1.69 *Société Anonyme Valisère v. Tinet-Claverie and F. Claverie*: The Protection of Prestige and Reputation Against Unfair Competition—1935 108
§ 1.70 *Mark Foy's Ltd v. Davies Coop & Co Ltd ("Tub Happy Case")*: An Australian Court Defines the Essence of Trademarks—Establishing Empathy Between the Consumer and the Article (Or Service) They Designate—1956 110
§ 1.71 The *YKK* Case: A Brazilian Court Defines the Essence of Intellectual Property's Role—To Serve Honesty in Trade—1982 114
§ 1.72 Where Does Parody Stop and Infringement Start (Or Vice-Versa)? *Louis Vuitton Malletier S.A. v. Haute Diggity Dog, LLC and Others*—2007 116
§ 1.73 Where Does a Fashion Design Stop and a Trademark Start (Or Vice-Versa)? The Opposing Views of the European Union General Court and of the United States Court of Appeals for the Ninth Circuit 125
§ 1.73.1 *Rosenruist—Gestão e serviços, Lda v. Office for Harmonisation in the Internal Market (Trade Marks and Designs) (OHIM)*—In Case T-388/09—2010 127
§ 1.73.2 *Levi Strauss & Company v. Abercrombie & Fitch Trading Company*—2011 132
§ 1.74 A Legal Drama in Various Episodes: Louboutin's Trademark: The Red Sole of Women's Shoes—2012, 2017, 2018, 2020 135
§ 1.74.1 Christian Louboutin Obtains Protection for His Red Shoes' Sole Trademark in the United States—2012 136
§ 1.74.2 The Switzerland Federal Supreme Court Refuses to Acknowledge Louboutin's Red Sole as a Trademark—2017 144
§ 1.74.3 The EU Court of Justice Holds That Louboutin's Red Sole Is Independent of the Shape of the Sole—2018 148
§ 1.74.4 The Court of Milan Takes Louboutin's Red Sole European Trademark for Granted and Enforces Exclusive Rights in It—2020 152
§ 1.75 The Problem of Converting Designs and Patterns into Trademarks 154
§ 1.75.1 *Louis Vuitton Malletier v. OHIM*—2015 156
§ 1.75.2 *Birkenstock Sales GmbH v. European Union Intellectual Property Office (EUIPO)*—2016 163
§ 1.76 The Dispute Over the New York Fashion Week Trademark: Another Case of *Turpis Causa*?—2016 175

Chapter 2
Appropriation of Knowledge and Creativity in Textiles and Fashion 183
§ 2.01 The City of Bordeaux Grants an Industrial Privilege to a Clothmaker—1236 183
§ 2.02 England Inaugurates a System of Industrial Privileges to Lure Foreign Clothmakers—1331 185

§ 2.03 The Cloth Act—1337 186
§ 2.04 Edward III Grants Another Privilege to a Flemish Clothmaker—1343 186
§ 2.05 The Struggle Between Guilds' Strict Standards and Innovations Dictated by Fashion—1398 187
§ 2.06 Siena Grants an Industrial Privilege to a Flemish Clothmaker—1438, 1439 189
§ 2.06.1 Rinaldo Di Gualtieri Obtains a Privilege for Two Years—1438 190
§ 2.06.2 Gualtieri's Privilege Is Extended for an Additional Six-Year Term—1339 190
§ 2.07 Siena Offers Privileges to All Silk Workers Willing to Settle in the City and Invest in the Industry—1439 191
§ 2.08 On Industrial Espionage, Sabotage, and Dumping by Florence, Against the Silk Industry of Siena—1440 191
§ 2.09 The Municipality of Siena Lures Another Flemish Tapestry Maker and Orders Three Carpets from Him—1442, 1447 193
§ 2.09.1 Agreement Between Master Giachetto di Benedetto and the Municipality of Siena—1442 193
§ 2.09.2 The Municipality of Siena Orders Three Carpets from Master Giachetto—1447 194
§ 2.10 Pedro of Portugal, Regent, Grants an Industrial Privilege to Prince Henry, the Navigator, for Establishing a Factory of Pastel Dye—1445 194
§ 2.11 Edward IV Authorizes Two British Merchants to Hire Twenty Foreign Clothiers Knowledgeable in the Art of Making Cloths Not Known in the Country—1483 195
§ 2.12 Industrial Privileges Concerning the Textile Industry Granted by the Senate of Venice, under the Statute of 1474—1497 Onwards 196
§ 2.13 The First Statute Providing for the Protection of Designs Against Copying? By-Laws of the Guild of Tapestry Weavers of Brussels—1525 197
§ 2.14 François I, of France, Extends the Period of Apprenticeship of Clothmaking from Two to Three Years—1531 198
§ 2.15 A Contract of Apprenticeship Containing a Secrecy Clause—1535 199
§ 2.16 Two Privileges Granted by the Municipality of Amiens, France, for Inventions in the Textile Industry—1539, 1543 200
§ 2.16.1 Privilege Granted by the City of Amiens to the Inventor of a Furnace That Could Be Used for Dyeing Cloths and Making Beer—1539 200
§ 2.16.2 Privilege Granted by the City of Amiens to the Inventors of a Machine That Reduced the Costs of Satin Calendering—1543 201
§ 2.17 The Municipality of Lille Passes an Ordinance Settling a Dispute Between Two Categories of Clothmakers—1544 201
§ 2.18 Several Industrial Privileges Granted by Elizabeth I—1561 Onwards 202
§ 2.18.1 Privileged Granted to Several Dutch Clothmakers—1561 203

§ 2.18.2 Privilege Granted to the Inventors of a Method of Obtaining Oil to Be Used in the Cloth Industry, Including the Right to Plant and Sow Plants Used in the Making of Such Oil—1565 203
§ 2.18.3 Privilege Promised to All Persons, Either Foreigners or British, to Be Appointed by the Municipality of Coventry, for the Making of Certain Cloths of *Great Estimation in Foreign Realms* and Unavailable in England—1568 204
§ 2.18.4 Privilege Granted to a Spanish for an Imported Method of Dyeing Cloths—1568 204
§ 2.18.5 Privilege Granted to the Introducer of a Method of Making Certain Cloths in the Manner of Holland—1569 205
§ 2.18.6 Privilege for the Introduction of Imported Techniques Concerning the Making of Cloths and Earthenware—1570 205
§ 2.19 An Indirect Method of Appropriation of Technology: A Spanish Tailor Writes about Certain Tailoring Techniques and Obtains a Privilege for the Exclusive Printing of His Book—1589 206
§ 2.20 The General Regulation of the Factories of France Promises a Number of Privileges to Foreign Skilled Cloth Workers, in Particular to Those Who Bring New Inventions—1601 208
§ 2.21 Henry IV Sets a Factory of Fine Cloths in Paris—1603 209
§ 2.22 Industrial Privilege Granted to Olivier de Serres on a Method of Extracting Fibers from the White Mulberry Tree for the Making of Canvases and Cloths—1603 212
§ 2.23 A Carpet Maker and Upholsterer Receives an Industrial Privilege for the Introduction in France of a New Technique of Making Carpets in the Manner of Spain—1604 215
§ 2.24 The Trade Council of Henry IV, of France, Approves the Granting of a Privilege for the Making of Turkey-Style Carpets—1604 217
§ 2.25 The Municipality of Lille Settles a Dispute Concerning the Exclusivity of Making Certain Cloths Between the *Sayeteurs* and the *Bourgeteurs*—1610 219
§ 2.26 Privileges Granted by the Municipality of Tournai, Belgium, to Inventions in the Tapestry Industry—1615, 1684 221
§ 2.26.1 Privilege for Simon Bedoret—1615 221
§ 2.26.2 Privilege for Jean Duquesne—1684 221
§ 2.27 Ordinances of the Art of Silk of Toledo—1616 221
§ 2.28 Judgment Settling the Dispute Between the Carpet Makers and the Turners of Paris on the Exclusivity of Making Parasols—1638 222
§ 2.29 The Invention of the Knitting Machine: Jean Hindret Obtains in France the Patent That Was Denied to William Lee in England; Disruptive Technologies and the Proverb "One Man's Loss Is Another Man's Gain"—1656 224
§ 2.29.1 Patent Granted to Jean Hindret and Léonard Blaise for Lee's Invention of the Knitting Machine—1656 226

§ 2.29.2 William III Prohibits the Export of Knitting Machines from England—1696 227
§ 2.30 The Demands of New Fashions Have Led the Guild of Hat Makers of Paris to Apply to the King for His Approval of New By-Laws—1658 228
§ 2.31 France Determines, for the First Time, the Exclusivity of Industrial Designs Applied to Tapestry—1664 229
§ 2.32 Louis XIV Grants an Industrial Privilege for a New Invention Concerning the Tanning of Leather—1666 231
§ 2.32.1 Patent Granted to Ellie Bonnet—1666 232
§ 2.32.2 Patent Letter Interpreting the Privilege Granted to Ellie Bonnet—1667 233
§ 2.33 Some Inventors from Poitiers Ask for a Privilege, Concerning a Loom for the Making of Braid and Ribbon—1666 235
§ 2.34 Privileges Granted to Foreign Clothmakers Who Brought Secret Knowledge to Lyon and Were Willing to Communicate It to the Guild Authorities—1667 236
§ 2.34.1 By-Laws Concerning the Manufacture of Fine Cloths of Lyon—1667 236
§ 2.34.2 Amendment to the By-Laws Concerning the Manufacture of Fine Cloths of Lyon—1700, 1702 237
§ 2.35 Louis XVI Grants a Printing Privilege for the Publication of *the Sincere Tailor*—1670 237
§ 2.36 Acts and Ordinances Concerning the Tailors' Trade of Aberdeen—1678 239
§ 2.37 Printing Privilege for Le Mercure Galant, the First Fashion Journal Published in France—1678 240
§ 2.38 The Aldermen of Lille Decide in Favor of Preserving the Trade Secrets of Three Clothmakers—1692 242
§ 2.39 The Social Construction of Inventions: Jean Marius, Inventor of the Folding Parasol/Umbrella, Obtains an Industrial Privilege, But Social Pressure Creates Resistance to ITS Use—1710 and Onwards 243
§ 2.39.1 Industrial Privilege Granted to Jean Marius for the Invention of the Folding Parasol/Umbrella—1710 245
§ 2.39.2 Le Mercure Galant Praises (And Advertises) Marius' Invention—1711 247
§ 2.39.3 The Folding Parasol/Umbrella Becomes a Fashion Item and, at the Same Time, a Sign of Social Division—1768 247
§ 2.39.4 In 1769 a New Business Model Was Born in Paris: The Commercial Rental of Umbrellas at the Entry and Exit Points of the Pont Neuf 248
§ 2.39.5 Regulation on the Business of Renting Umbrellas at the Bridges and Main Streets of Paris—1769 249
§ 2.40 In Another Initiative Linked to the Tapestry Industry (Aubusson), France Reaffirmed the Exclusivity of Industrial Designs—1730 250
§ 2.41 Regulation of the Industry of Woollen Cloths of Lille—1732 251

§ 2.42 Louis XV, of France, Cancels an Industrial Privilege on Grounds That It Harms Imports—1736 252
§ 2.43 The Protection of Industrial Designs Is Confirmed and Strengthened in Respect of the Fine Cloth Industry of Lyon and Later Extended to Other Cities—1744 Onwards 253
§ 2.43.1 Regulation of the Industry of Fine Cloths of Lyon—1744 254
§ 2.43.2 A Lawsuit Involving the Infringement of Industrial Designs in Lyon—1749 254
§ 2.43.3 Decision of the King's Council Extending the Protection of Industrial Designs to the Fine Cloth Industry of France—1787 255
§ 2.43.4 A Formal System of Registration of Fashion Designs Is Established in Lyon—1806 257
§ 2.44 Great Britain Awakens for the Importance of Protecting Industrial Designs for Cloths—1787 258
§ 2.45 The Invention of the Cotton Gin and the Affliction of Its Inventor, Eli Whitney—1794 Onwards 259
§ 2.45.1 Eli Whitney's Cotton Gin Patent Specification 260
§ 2.45.2 Message from the Governor of Georgia, James Jackson, Attacking Whitney's Patent—1800 260
§ 2.45.3 Eli Whitney and Phineas Miller Respond to Governor of Georgia's Letter—1800 261
§ 2.45.4 Confronted with Rampant Infringement, Whitney and Miller Advertise Their Intention to Sue All Infringers and Offer Settlement 262
§ 2.45.5 Denison Olmsted, One of Whitney's Attorneys, Speaks of His Determination in Enforcing His Patent Rights 263
§ 2.46 In a Case Involving a Textile-Related Invention, the British Court of Chancery Holds That the Invention Disclosure Requirement Is Embedded in the Rationale of the Patent System—1816 264
§ 2.47 A British Court Enforces a Non-competing Covenant and a Trade Secret in Dyeing—1822 265
§ 2.48 The Sewing Machine: A Disruptive Invention That Has Given Rise to the Emerging of the Fashion Industry—1830 267
§ 2.48.1 Specification of the Patent Obtained in England by Thimonnier and Magnin for an Improved Sewing Machine—1848 268
§ 2.48.2 Patent Obtained by One of Thimonnier's Assignees in the United States—1850 269
§ 2.48.3 Public Charity Comes to the Rescue of Thimonnier's Widow 270
§ 2.49 In a Case Involving Trade Secrets Concerning the Japanning of Leather, a Scottish Court Condemns the Undue Interference in a Labor Contract—1836 272

§ 2.50 Competition for Foreign Markets with Other Trade Powers Spurs Great Britain to Increase Protection for Industrial Designs—1839 Onwards 274
§ 2.51 An Act regulating Labor and Commercial Matters in the English Textile Industry—1843 277
§ 2.52 The Debate on How to Best Protect Fashion Designs Starts in French Courts—1857, 1860 278
§ 2.52.1 *Lafont et Davasse v. Durst, Wild et Cie.*—1857 278
§ 2.52.2 *Erhardt v. Durst-Will et autres.*—1860 279
§ 2.53 British Patents for Fashion Designs—1857 Onwards 280
§ 2.54 French Patents for Industrial Designs—1864 281
§ 2.55 The Supreme Court of Massachusetts Protects a Trade Secret Concerning a Process of Making Cloth—1868 283
§ 2.56 From Function to Ornament: Levi Strauss' Jeans Riveted Pockets—1873 283
§ 2.57 The United States Supreme Court Raises the Bar for the Notion of Inventiveness and Refuses Patentability to New Uses of Known Looms and Textile Materials—1875 285
§ 2.58 England Unifies the Protection of Designs for Ornamental Purposes with Those for the Shape and Configuration of Useful Articles—1883 288
§ 2.59 A French Court Denies Protection to Fashion Designs under the Act on Industrial Designs Due to Their Ephemeral Nature—1895 289
§ 2.60 The English High Court of Justice Refers to the Basic Element of Cloth-Related Industrial Design Protection: The Appeal to the Eye—1897 291
§ 2.61 A French Court Changes Course, and Takes the First Step Towards Modern Fashion Design Law—1899 293
§ 2.62 An English Court Discusses the Tension Between the Design of Fashion and the Mode of Manufacture—1906 294
§ 2.63 The French Parliament Enacts a Statute on Industrial Designs with Express Coverage of Apparel and Accessories—1909 299
§ 2.64 The Building of Case Law in France Involving the Protection of Fashion Designs—1911-1913 300
§ 2.64.1 *Béchoff, David et Cie v. Galeries Lafayette:* Oral Arguments of Master Maurice Bernard, for the Plaintiff—The Fashion Wars in Paris, in the Early 1900s 301
§ 2.64.2 *Béchoff, David et Cie v. Galeries Lafayette.* The Opinion of the Civil Court of Seine, 3rd Chamber—1911 303
§ 2.64.3 *Rodier frères v. Galeries Lafayette*—1911 306
§ 2.64.4 The Protection of Industrial Designs Extends to the Unauthorized Publication in Fashion Journals: *Callot soeurs v. Finkelstein et Gruenwald*—1911 310
§ 2.64.5 A Court Acknowledges That Certain Designs Serve as Identifiers of Origin—*Chamussy et Cie. v. Favier et Beurrier*—1911 313

§ 2.64.6 *Bachwitz et autres v. Société Paquin limitée*—1913 316

§ 2.65 In the United States, Fashion Journals Oppose the Enactment of a Law on Industrial Designs—1916 317

§ 2.65.1 H.R. 6,458, on the Registration and Protection of Designs—1916 318

§ 2.65.2 Statement of Mr. B. von Witzleben, Representing S. T. Taylor Co., Publishers of *Le Bon Ton*, a Fashion Journal, New York City 319

§ 2.66 Madeleine Vionnet's Relentless and Influential Struggle in Favor of the Protection of Fashion Designs—1934 322

§ 2.66.1 Under an Ironic Heading, Madeleine Vionnet Advertises in the Press the Measures Taken by Her House for the Sake of Ensuring Authenticity of the Garments She Designed and Sold—1921 324

§ 2.66.2 Madeleine Vionnet Offers a Reward to Who Provides Information on a Stolen Mannequin 326

§ 2.66.3 Vogue, a Fashion Magazine Publishes a Long Article Celebrating the Landmark Court Opinion (In an Action in Which Madeleine Vionnet Was the Plaintiff) That for the First Time Held That Fashion Designs Were Protected under Copyright 326

§ 2.66.4 Illustrating Its Importance, the Same Judgment Was Reported in Other Newspapers of a More General Nature 328

§ 2.66.5 Madeleine Vionnet Advertises a Patent She Obtained for a Secret Invention, *Jalousement Gardé (Jealously Kept)*—1923 328

§ 2.66.6 A Fashion Magazine Claims That Enforcement of Copyright in Fashion Designs Has Led to Excesses and Abuses—1933 328

§ 2.66.7 *Dames Segall et Dodu v. Société Vionnet*—1934 329

§ 2.66.8 *Société Madeleine Vionnet et Demoiselle Chanel v. Dame Laniel*—1934 332

§ 2.67 The United States Court of Appeals for the Second Circuit Acknowledges That Fashion Designs Are Unprotected—1929 334

§ 2.68 The Protection of Fashion Designs by French Courts Reaches Maturity: *Demoiselle Jacquet v. Caroline Roux, Rose Descat et Autres*—1934 336

§ 2.69 French Case Law Assumes That the Mere Possession of Unauthorized Sketches Is Counterfeiting—1937 340

§ 2.70 The Creative Fashion Industry of the United States Reacts and Takes Collective Action Against Rampant Counterfeiting, But Hits an Antitrust Wall—1941 343

§ 2.71 United States Case Law Moves Forward: Copyright Protection Is Available for Fashion Designs, But the Requirement of Ensuring That a Notice of Copyright Is Affixed in Each Garment May Be an Obstacle—1960 347
§ 2.72 The Only International Agreement That Has Adopted Language with Fashion Designs as a Special Target: The TRIPS Agreement—1994 350
§ 2.72.1 Austria Proposes the Adoption of a Special Regime for the Protection of Fashion Designs—1989 352
§ 2.72.2 Switzerland Proposes the Adoption of a Special Mechanism of Registration for Textile Designs—1990 352
§ 2.72.3 The TRIPS Agreement—1994 353
§ 2.73 The Conundrum of the Protection of Fashion Designs: Their Conversion into Business Identifiers and the Need to Prove Secondary Meaning—2000 353
§ 2.74 Fashion and Traditional Textiles: Cultural Inspiration or Cultural Appropriation?—2000 Onwards 358
§ 2.74.1 Panama Adopts a Statute Protecting the Collective Rights of Communities in Traditional Designs (And Other Creations)—2000 361
§ 2.74.2 Regulation on the Use of the Kuna People's Collective Right—2001 365
§ 2.74.3 Proposal for a Requirement Concerning the Disclosure of Origin of Traditional Designs (To Be Introduced in a Future WIPO Design Law Treaty)—2015 366
§ 2.75 United States Congress Receives a Bill (But Does Not Submit It to Vote) Aimed at Providing Special Protection for Fashion Designs—2011 368
§ 2.76 The United States Supreme Court Holds That Some Two-Dimensional Fashion Designs Are Copyrightable—2017 371
§ 2.77 The Superior Court of Justice of Brazil Accepts the Application of the Doctrine of Dilution to Industrial Designs—2019 376
§ 2.78 An English Court Opens Another Avenue for the Protection of Fashion Designs: Certain Figurative Elements of Apparel Can Assume a Branding Function and Thus Be the Subject of Passing Off—2020 380

Credits and Sources of Texts and Illustrations 387

Index 401

List of Figures

Figure 1. The medieval loom. Illumination depicting the horizontal or low loom, used for weaving most types of cloth.

Figure 2. Two clothiers' workshops in the fourteenth century.

Figure 3. The seal of Tournai, Belgium.

Figure 4. "The History of Abraham," carpet made in Tournai, sixteenth century.

Figure 5. The trademarks that Pietro de Preda assigned to Petrolo Tanzio, in 1383.

Figure 6. The vertical or high loom, used mainly for the making of carpets.

Figure 7. Cover page of the booklet containing the general regulation of the cloth industry, as approved by the king and queen of Spain, in 1500.

Figure 8. A sixteenth-century wool weaver working at a high (vertical) loom.

Figure 9. Marks from Brussels.

Figure 10. The cover of a book published in Lyon, between 1515 and 1535, containing designs and patterns of cloths embroidered and woven with gold, silver, and silk threads.

Figure 11. Example of the use of the rampant lion and the greyhound as business identifiers in the cloth industry.

Figure 12. Detail of the shop sign of a tailor's workshop in the sixteenth century, Fribourg, Switzerland.

Figure 13. The workshop of a sixteenth-century tailor.

Figure 14. The two lead tokens of Josse Vanrobais.

Figure 15. The stocks, a device used in the Middle Ages for the punishment of certain sorts of crimes, such as counterfeiting.

Figure 16. The "gallantry shop" in 1678.

Figure 17. The pillory, a medieval instrument of punishment.

Figure 18. Trade cards (*cartes d'addresse*) of two tailors of the eighteenth century.

Figure 19. Ads of the Valisère trademark.

Figure 20. Louis Vuitton's multicolor monogram Speedy and two of its imitations.

Figure 21. Levi Strauss' trademarks.

Figure 22. Detail of Christian Louboutin's *Guerilla* model

Figure 23. LVM's "Neverfull" bag.

Figure 24. Birkenstock's slippers, with its original innersole.

Figure 25. A snapshot of one of the fashion shows organized by IMG in the course of the NYFW.

Figure 26. Map of Bordeaux in 1229.

Figure 27. Portrait of a noble man wearing socks garnished with *aiguillettes*.

Figure 28. Carpet from Brussels, sixteenth century, made of wool and silk.

Figure 29. Cover and plate of the second edition of Libro de Geometria.

Figure 30. Cover page of the technical memoir that Olivier de Serres submitted to the King's trade commission.

Figure 31. William Lee's knitting machine, invented in 1589

Figure 32. Tapestry of wool and silk, from Beauvais, *Psyche at the Basketmakers*.

Figure 33. Cover page of Le Tailleur Sincère.

Figure 34. Plate from Extraordinaire du Mercure Galant.

Figure 35. Drawing of Marius' original invention of the folding parasol/umbrella.

Figure 36. Illustration of a woman carrying a parasol.

Figure 37. The rental of umbrellas on Pont Neuf.

Figure 38. Armchairs with upholstery from Aubusson, Paris, 1760.

Figure 39. Eli Whitney's cotton gin, patented in the United States in 1794.

Figure 40. The original model of Thimonnier's sewing machine.

Figure 41. Drawing annexed to the patent granted in the United States, in 1750, for an improvement to Thimonnier's invention.

Figure 42. Poster of 1855 advertising the sewing machine improved by Magnin.

Figure 43. Drawing accompanying the specifications of the 1873 US patent letter for the application of rivets to the seams of pockets in pantaloons.

Figure 44. A coat designed by Béchoff and the Galeries Lafayette at the beginning of the twentieth century.

Figure 45. Fashion designs published by the journal Le Grand Chic Paris, in 1908.

Figure 46. Advertisement of Madeleine Vionnet's fashion house published in the Vogue Magazine of June 1, 1924.

Figure 47. Dress designed by Madeleine Vionnet.

Figure 48. Madeleine Vionnet at work. The salon of her fashion house.

Figure 49. Hat designed by Lucien Lelong.

Figure 50. Tory Burch's creation, and a traditional woollen sweater from Póvoa de Varzim, Portugal.

Figure 51. Drawings accompanying the two registrations of the industrial designs concerning tennis shoes.

Preamble

In 2020, Wolters Kluwer published two sourcebooks on the past and present of intellectual property (IP). The first one[1] covers a broad spectrum of IP and shows that IP has emerged quasi-spontaneously in the context of the struggle of artisans and merchants in luring or retaining clients against their rivals. IP has been regulated and used since immemorial times, and the general principles that preside over it today are not dramatically different from those that were in force six thousand years ago.

The second sourcebook looks at the evolution of IP from a specific angle: that of medicines and, more generally, of access to health.[2] Also starting from the perspective of the merchants and manufacturers of medicines, and their efforts to make a living from their trade, that book gives clear evidence that IP is not neutral as regards the way it treats its subject matter. In other words, the IP that applies to medicines is not the same that applies to toys or furniture. The main reason is the interference of regulation in the pharmaceutical sector. IP being essentially a market tool—a tool that permits the differentiation of products based on their intangible features—it follows that what impacts the market also impacts IP.

This third sourcebook looks to IP from another specific angle: that of the textile industry and, in particular, that of fashion. And again, this book confirms that IP is not indifferent to the peculiarities of the subject matter it covers. Here, the reason may not be the same that cause the IP of medicines to be extraordinary, and yet the markets for textiles and, particularly, for fashion have developed characteristics that have required lawmakers and courts to treat the IP that applies in their context in ways that vary from other industries.

In the beginning, human society created the textile industry. The social (and commercial) phenomenon of fashion appeared much, much later—in the seventeenth

1. Nuno Pires de Carvalho, From Babylon to the Silicon Valley: The Origins and Evolution of Intellectual Property—A Sourcebook (Wolters Kluwer, 2020) (hereinafter, From Babylon to the Silicon Valley).
2. Nuno Pires de Carvalho, From Antiquity to the COVID-19 Pandemic: The Intellectual Property of Medicines and Access to Health—A Sourcebook (Wolters Kluwer, 2020) (hereinafter, "From Antiquity to the COVID-19 Pandemic").

century, to be more precise. This does not mean that before the seventeenth century, human beings, influenced by collective taste, did not make choices about what they dressed. This is easy to demonstrate: a simple visit to the British Museum, for example, shows that men and women in Ancient Greece or Rome dressed themselves differently from their contemporaries that lived in Egypt or in Byzantium, even if the climates were not that contrasting, and thus could not explain alone differences in garment designs and fabrics.

Fashion, broadly speaking, has always existed, but until the seventeenth century, when consumerism started to become predominant in the organization of society, it changed very slowly and did not impose legal, technical, and economic pressures, as it does today. In addition to the absence of a social force that might push individuals to constantly adopting changes in the way they consumed, there were two other factors in medieval Europe acting against an early arising of fashion, as we understand it today: the strict technical standards that applied to the manufacture of fabrics and cloths by corporations; and the frequent enactment of sumptuary laws. The first factor will be abundantly reflected in the texts included in this book. Technical standards and IP generally operate in opposite ways because while the former searches for uniformity, the latter depends on and operates in favor of differentiation. However, the adoption and enforcement of technical standards were and continue to be frequently entangled with IP rules—IP ensures the differentiation between those products that are in compliance with the standards. Compliance with standards was mandatory for guilds' members; lack of compliance was almost invariably sanctioned with harsh measures; and one of the manners to assess compliance with those standards was through the use of business identifiers—certification marks, geographical indications, trade names, and trademarks.

As an illustration of the strict imposition of technical standards, we will see that in 1398, the sock makers of Paris had to appeal to the king in order to obtain authorization to make socks with *aiguillettes*, a new fashionable ornament with a useful purpose (that of fastening the socks to the doublet) that consumers looked for, but which the guild's rules prohibited them from making. It was only in the sixteenth century that guild regulations, on a regular basis, permitted the introduction of cloths of new invention and design, but on the condition that their making and sale were previously approved by the authorities. This reveals that in that period, social demands dictated by the imperatives of fashion were already in operation, and yet the guild regime was not yet ready to receive them—and would never be, really.

The second factor was related to the layered organization of medieval society. Under the pretext of protecting the poor, sumptuary laws reserved the use of certain luxury fabrics and garments to the royal family or to those with a minimum level of income. The sumptuary laws concerned certain fabrics, namely those more expensive, because they were imported, such as silk, or because they were made with rare materials, such as gold and silver thread. Besides religious motivations in the pursuance of humility, behind those laws there was also a financial and political motivation, which was to avoid that noble classes, in their pursuit of luxury and ostentation, fell into excessive debt. Indebted feudal lords would normally seek to increase their financial resources by increasing the exaction of taxes from their vassals, and this could cause social unrest. Those sumptuary laws operated against the early rising of fashion because they implied a certain uniformity in the garments worn by individuals. Sumptuary laws were not an isolated phenomenon. They have been enacted in most European countries.

So, in the beginning, what existed was the textile industry, an extremely important segment of human economic activities, perhaps only overshadowed by the businesses associated with our constant search for food.

And yet, unlike the preparation of food, in Sybaris, a Greek colony in Southern Italy, in the sixth century BC,[3] or the extraction of medicinal earth, in Lemnos, a Greek Island, in the second century BC,[4] the making and the trading of textiles seem not to have attracted the early use and/or regulation of related intangible assets. Of course, it is possible, if not probable, that several of the trade secrets confided by artisans to their apprentices in Babylon, corresponded to knowledge acquired in the field of clothmaking. Law 89 of the Code of Hammurabi prohibited the apprentices' families to reclaim those apprentices to whom the artisan had taught his trade. This was a provision of family law but, indirectly, an early IP rule because it led to the indirect appropriation of knowledge.[5] The same rule still prevails today as a matter of contract law and unfair competition. But even if that is true, those rules of family law did not have trade secrets concerning textiles as a special target.

It is in the Middle Ages that we see the first expressions of statutes and regulations dealing specifically with the businesses of textile making and trading. In this regard, rules on the use of business identifiers and on the appropriation of knowledge developed in parallel, as the grasp of the corporative regime expanded, on the one hand, and, on the other, industrial policies aiming at promoting the importation of textile-related technology were adopted throughout Europe.

As a systematic mechanism of differentiation in the textile industry, intellectual property started developing in the Middle Ages, towards the end of the Commercial Revolution (tenth to the thirteenth century). At that time, the textile industry had already become the main engine of economic growth of the most powerful European political entities, such as France, England, Milan, Florence, and Flanders. The need for ensuring quality in the making of textiles and the growing competition over their sales in distant markets, led national authorities, in the context of guilds, to impose the use of certification marks. Those marks would certify compliance with the technical standards set out by guilds' by-laws. They would also certify the origin of cloths, given that the masters would not compete with their colleagues within the same guild, but they would definitely compete with the masters of other cities. In this token, we will see that authorities were several times called to regulate the use of business identifiers specifically linked to certain cities, namely marks, seals, colors of selvages, and strings.

With the expansion of the European economy, individual marks started gaining relevance, and in the sixteenth and seventeenth centuries, we see the first rules being adopted in their regard, still in the context of guild by-laws. In that same period, the

3. *See* From Babylon to the Silicon Valley, *supra* note 1, at 8.
4. *See* From Antiquity to the COVID-19 Pandemic, *supra* note 2, at 2.
5. *See* From Babylon to the Silicon Valley, *supra* note 1, at 157.

first court disputes also started to emerge, thus revealing an increasingly competitive environment. From that period onward, the relevance of individual business identifiers gained importance, in tandem with the growth of economic freedom and rivalry among national and international traders.

But it was at the end of the eighteenth century (in 1779, more precisely) that, along with the birth of fashion law, certain trademarks were released from mandatory controls—those trademarks that corresponded to cloths and garments newly introduced and did not obey the guilds' standards. The corresponding regulation—we may call it the certificate of birth of fashion law—permitted clothmakers and merchants to adopt their own trademarks, as they saw fit, in order to designate such cloths. Even more strikingly, that same regulation adopted rules on what today we call well-known trademarks.

A few years later, the French Revolution would erupt, with its general ideas of individual freedom and respect for private property. From that date onward, the use of individual business identifiers for fashion only expanded and followed the same patterns of evolution as those that applied to other sectors of business.

In recent years, however, fashion imposed certain special constraints on the law of business identifiers. Those constraints result from the essentially visual nature of fashion, which, in the eyes of consumers, causes certain designs to acquire the function of business identifiers. But the contrary may also be true, and certain business identifiers are used by fashion houses as ornaments. This aspect is a true transboundary that brings trademark issues into the realm of designs, such as dilution, secondary meaning, and passing off, as well as distinctiveness.

This is the most important topic of fashion law that is yet to be solved, and that is reflected in both chapters of this book, because of its multi-layered legal implications. Of course—and this should go without saying—fashion law is more than just IP applied to fashion. Fashion law covers other matters, of no less importance, such as those concerning labor, gender discrimination, taxes, international commerce, and others, and much work has been done in that regard by a number of specialized institutions. In this book, however, the term "fashion law" is limited to the IP-dimension of fashion.

As regards the appropriation of knowledge and its expressions, in parallel with the first norms of certification marks, the constraints dictated by competition among nations caused by the interest of national authorities in having access to new technologies have given rise to the grant of industrial privileges to foreign artisans who were willing to move to other countries with their families, apprentices, working tools, and, most importantly, their knowledge.

In the Middle Ages, the mechanism of industrial privileges spread quickly through Europe. But the protection of designs took much longer to emerge. The absence of a concept of fashion did not make it necessary. Concerns with such protection were expressed in the sixteenth century onward, and it concerned tapestry in particular. The increasing competition in supplying the castles and palaces of the wealthy citizens, eager to adhere to the new fashion of adorning the floors of the walls of their homes with luxurious carpets, displaying intricate designs, has led to the adoption of rules protecting in a certain way the exclusivity of those designs. It seems that such a solution was first introduced in the tapestry industry of Brussels, at the end of the sixteenth century, but in the next century, it would become a common practice in France, where the privileges accorded for the opening of new factories would be accompanied by rules protecting new designs against unauthorized copying.

Strikingly, there was one early case in which design protection was specifically accorded to cloths. That was the case of the manufacture of cloth of Abbeville, which was established in 1665, by a Dutch entrepreneur, Josse van Robais. But that was not a trend. And this is shown by the fact that in 1743 when Robais' privilege was again renewed (it was renewed several times), his descendants acquired the right to introduce a blue stripe at the edge of each cloth they made. This sort of trademark protection confirms that the interest of van Robais was more in the process of making the cloths itself than in designs and patterns they might be commanded to print by their customers.

At that time, as said, the notion of fashion had not yet reached the cloth industry. The affluent sectors of society were not strange to fashion, but only as regards other objects of consumption, such as silverware and porcelain. In the matter of cloths, fashion was *collective*, in the sense that the designs of cloth used by the wealthy were very similar. The evolution of those designs was very slow. It could take more than one generation for the whole appearance of the way people dressed to change significantly. And yet, the changes were accompanied by those who could afford it in an indistinct manner.

It was at the end of the seventeenth century that, very hesitantly, fashion in cloths started to acquire an individual tone—that is, when wealthy women and men started to have the desire to distinguish themselves from their peers, in a new mode of consumption, which has been very aptly coined by Thorstein Veblen as *conspicuous consumption*. On the one hand, fashion is a response by the human being to a natural inclination for the beautiful. But, on the other hand, fashion speaks to the human desire of impressing those who are around us, causing admiration and envy. In this manner, consuming is not only an intimate action—it is also an action that projects ourselves among those human beings who surround us.

This was the period in which the Industrial Revolution spread through Europe and beyond. With it, industrial production grew exponentially, giving rise to a great increase in the comfort of the living of the well-off, and the emergence of a segment of laborers dedicated to producing the superfluous for the consumption of those well-off. It was in this period that the first magazines specialized in fashion started being published. And it was at this time also that society began experimenting with tools of intellectual property to promote and protect the business interests of those entrepreneurs and creators engaged in producing fashion.

For a certain time, while a specific regime covering fashion designs was developing in France, in the eighteenth century—patents were applied for and obtained for certain fashionable cloths. This was the time when the new modern patent system emerged. However, fashion is inherently fleeting. Because of its nature, fashion invites imitation, and once the object of desire is imitated, its owner is irresistibly inclined to move forward and create new models—which will generate further imitation; imitation will cause the source of admiration to move forward again; and so forth. The fact that fashion in garments is in constant motion makes the patent system intrinsically inappropriate to protect it. Here we need to make a distinction between the makers of cloth and the designers and creators of garments. The former may also be affected by movements in fashion, such as the creation of new patterns that are printed on the fabrics, but other than those patterns, which may change from season to season, machinery and processes of making cloth tend not to change so swiftly. So, the patent system is an apt mechanism for the makers of fabrics, but not for the tailors and dressmakers who transform fabrics into fashionable garments.

In the nineteenth century, three factors pushed garment fashion to new heights. One was the growth of the middle class, with the impulse of their own to consume fashion. The second factor was the invention of the first sewing machine, by Barthelemy Thimonnier, in 1830. As a consequence, setting small shops and boutiques to design and make garments has become accessible to a myriad of entrepreneurs. This naturally has generated more competition, and more competition has generated the need for intellectual property. A third factor was introduced in the United States at the end of the nineteenth century—the emergence of the massive ready-to-wear fashion (*la mode prête-à-porter*)—under the influence of the system of mass production, born from the Industrial Revolution. Actually, the first stores where ready-to-wear garments were on sale to customers were opened in Paris, in 1830, in the middle of a crisis of the textile industry, where many workers were unemployed. A few entrepreneurs had then the idea of hiring some of those workers to finish the fabrics that they would consign to them and transform them into finished garments, ready to wear, which would be sold at reduced prices. The two first outlets with finished garments on sale were "Le Bonhomme Richard," at Place Victoire, Paris, and "La Belle Jardinière." (Pierre Vidal Pierre Vidal, HISTOIRE DE LA CORPORATION DES TAILLEURS D'HABITS, POURPOINTIERS, CHAUSSETIERS, DE LA VILLE DE PARIS, at 199 (1923). Source: <gallica.BnF.fr>.) This rising trend coincided, as noted, with the invention of the sewing machine, and its transforming power of the whole industry. Therefore, *la mode du prêt-a-porter* was invented in France, but it was in the United States that it acquired the significant dimension it has today.

In the nineteenth century, a new phase of fashion law started, which consisted of the accommodation of the jurisprudence to this complex new reality, where lawmakers and courts struggled with the application of industrial design law and copyright to protect creative shapes of garments and accessories. Initially, courts struggled with the possibility of applying the law of industrial designs—originally created for tapestry, as said, and later expanded to objects made by the industry—to garments.

Later in the nineteenth century, French courts would apply the laws on industrial designs to garments, and in the twentieth century, they agreed that such protection could accumulate with copyright. This would not settle the matter, however. The very nature of fashion makes it inherently incompatible with certain traditional forms of intellectual property. A fashion house that produces hundreds, even thousands, of new designs for one single season, will not achieve the level of originality in each new model that could justify protection under design or copyright laws. Even if for copyright the level or originality required is low, it is not that low as to encompass thousands of garments that present modest changes from one season to the next. Moreover, a number of fashion houses affirm their individuality based on some iconic elements, which are repeated through their entire collections, as a sort of a figurative leitmotiv that operates as a general artist's signature and speaks for their originality.

Examples of these leitmotivs are the Burberry's checkboard fabric, with its Scottish flavor; the Versace's medusa, with its Greek motivations; and the Missoni's waves, a stylized form of the initial M. Those elements are designs, and can even be (or have been) protected as such, but once their term of protection ends, they fall into the public domain. So, they are trademarks, with the caveat that they are not used always in the same form. The creators of those three houses do combine the iconic motives with different colors and shapes and apply them to different materials—something that trademark law does not cover.

Moreover, copyright law, once applied to fashion, prevents the reproduction of the drawings that serve as the templates for the garments, but not the making of the garments. So, without a serious adaptation as to its scope of protection, copyright law does not cover fashion. By contrast, the protection of designs does not extend to the mere reproduction of the designs—it is limited to the making and selling or offering for sale of articles embodying the protected designs. Copyright protection is about expressions. Design protection is about expressions embodied in articles—i.e., about ideas.

It was this sort of considerations that led to a new phase of fashion law, in the first part of the twentieth century, and in which we still find ourselves: the intellectual property that applies to fashion is a combination of rights that better respond to the specific needs of entrepreneurs, this meaning a combination of industrial design law, patents, copyright, trademarks, trade names, trade dress, and, of course, repression of unfair competition. And yet, this combination of legal regimes does not answer all the most difficult questions raised by the need for differentiating the products of fashion.

We can summarize these three questions, which reflect fashion as a hybrid of function and aesthetics: (i) how to protect the small *nuances* that are introduced in fashion articles that do not have enough originality or novelty to be seen and protected as industrial designs or as artistic works, but nevertheless cause a distinctive impression on consumers—or, as the French would say, have a special *cachet*? (ii) how to convert a particular ornament that becomes the identifier of a product and of its maker into a trademark? and (iii) how to overcome the argument that luxury fashion houses cannot prove damages in the face of cheap knock-offs, given that the persons who buy those cheap imitations could never afford the original products?

This book comes with several proposals to address all these three questions. They are not the definitive answers, however, because fashion law is still under construction. In 1989, during the negotiations of the GATT Uruguay Round, which led to the adoption of the Agreement on Trade-related Aspects of Intellectual Property Rights (the TRIPS Agreement), the Austrian delegation emphasized the need for having a debate on fashion law, which deserved a sui generis regime of its own. That was a serious proposal, which, however, did not receive much attention. The WTO is made of consensus, and at that time (as well as today), the issue was not mature for receiving the full attention it deserves. Moreover, and that adds to the problems of fashion law, as the Austrian delegation has stated, not only the fashion industry has become global: counterfeiting of fashion has also become global. Thus, only a global regime, or at least one globally harmonized, could produce significant results in protecting the legitimate rights of fashion houses and consumers.

This book is structured in two main chapters, which correspond by and large to the avenues taken by intellectual property to develop in connection with textiles and fashion. It should be noted, however, that such categorization is to a large extent arbitrary, given that, when it comes to the protection of fashion's differentiating assets, very often the borders separating the various branches of IP are blurred, if not completely inexistent. That is, by the way, how this book ends: by showing that, when it comes to fashion, trademarks become designs, and designs become trademarks.

Anyway, as I have done for the two preceding sourcebooks, instead of describing the evolution of fashion-related IP with my own words, I have given the voice to those who make IP: the artisans, the merchants, the lawmakers, and those who construct and enforce the law. These are testimonies of IP as it should be always seen—an IP at the service of those who make a living from their creative brain and not from their copying hand, to paraphrase the 1911 French court opinion cited in the epigraph.

Before I give the voice to those who have made (and continue making) the intellectual property of textiles and fashion, four preliminary editorial notes are in order.

First, all sections are preceded by notes that explain the contexts of the selected sources. I have tried to keep those notes as succinct as possible, so as to give preeminence to the sources. Hopefully, the sources selected will be able to speak for themselves.

Second, the sources are particularly focused in France, with a number from the United Kingdom (indifferently designated in the book as Britain, or Great Britain, even if that is not correct), Italy, and the United States also included. The reason is that the law of fashion is, basically, a French concept. It was in France that fashion emerged first as a phenomenon deserving particular legislative attention, and it was there, in the nineteenth and twentieth centuries, that courts have started building a consistent body of jurisprudence opening the way for its protection under IP. Other countries have only followed France in that regard, with the United States, the largest world economy and a thriving center of the fashion industry, still lagging far behind in the making of adequate, encompassing, and effective fashion IP law.

Third, many of the sources in this book have been translated (with, in some cases, the assistance of Google Translation—an increasingly superb tool), and thus a word of caution is appropriate: given that translation is (re)creation, eventual inaccuracies in those translations are entirely my fault. I only hope they are not too many.

Finally, the selection of sources is exactly that: a selection. The criteria for choosing one particular text and not another have been exclusively dictated by my belief that the former could be more illustrative of the way intellectual property has developed in association with textiles and fashion. Moreover, as a selection, the collection of sources is not, nor is it intended to be, exhaustive. My choice has focused on those sources that appeared to me as being of more relevance, as stones in a road's pavement. I did not include all the stones, but just those that, as I view them, are sufficient to permit one's walking the road, without having to jump over deep gaps. This book has been structured in the same manner as the two aforementioned sourcebooks that Wolters published in 2020. Actually, it may be seen as a spin-off of the first one, in that it follows the same logical arrangement of sources, in accordance with the types of intellectual property involved and, as much as it is possible, in chronological order.

In the last years of my professional life, the belief that many of the current debates on intellectual property are mere repetitions of discussions maintained by the generations that preceded ours has grown in me, along with the idea that it might be useful to learn how arguments and counterarguments have been absorbed or discarded by the laws. This puts things in perspective, which is always useful.

I have again included a few pictures and drawings that illustrate some aspects of the peculiarities of intellectual property as applied to textiles and fashion. The reason for that is well known: a picture is worth one thousand words, as the saying goes. Well, frequently it is worth more than one thousand words.

To me—and, I hope, to the reader too—these texts and the accompanying figures are not just literary and artistic expressions of frequently conflicting interests in trade and fashion, but also, and mainly, expressions of human beings trying to make a living from their work. It is true that not all those human beings have pursued their interests in an honest manner, but that is life—and imposing honesty in trade is, after all, IP's ultimate goal.

I cannot close the presentation of this book without thanking my wife, Ana, for her care and her almost infinite patience while I, confined with her in pandemic times, went through a lot of reading, searching, browsing, and looking for expressions of IP in association with textiles and fashion. Ana, moreover, has assisted me through the making of this book with her vast knowledge of fashion and acute insights on taste and trends.

Through this journey, Ana has been by my side, always interested in listening to the fascinating stories I found in some of the selected sources. With her inquiries and comments, Ana has greatly contributed to this book. But more than her patience, care, and suggestions, once again this new book has greatly benefited from her companionship and love.

Porto, Portugal, June 4, 2021 (Mateo's 13th birthday)

CHAPTER 1

The Business Identifiers of Textiles and Fashion

§ 1.01 AN EARLY STATUTE SETTING A MARK OF ORIGIN: THE BY-LAWS OF THE WEAVERS OF CANVAS OF DOUAI—1261

The text that follows is an excerpt from a statute enacted by the municipality of Douai, France, adopting the city's seal as a mark of origin for cloths. As the medieval economy grew—manufacture and trade of cloth being important economic activities—and corporations were established both as institutions for the social protection of workers and as structures of organization of labor and regulation of industry, marks were initially adopted with two purposes: to certify compliance with guild by-laws' technical standards and to certify geographical origin. Certification of geographical origin was, at that time, more important than the differentiation of individual manufacturers. The reason was that because of the way corporations were organized, commercial rivalry among the masters of the same city was extremely reduced. Rivalry would be exercised against the articles (and their manufacturers) of other cities, which would be sold either in the trade halls of each city or in local or regional fairs.

Therefore, to a large extent, the city's marks, still serving as signs of certification of geographical origin, served also as collective marks, because they indicated to potential buyers the common affiliation of those masters and merchants.

Subsequently, as trade continued to grow, collective (guilds') marks and individual (artisans') marks gained relevance and were the subject of particular attention by statutes and by-laws. However, through the Middle Ages, those marks would still serve the main purpose of certifying compliance with the technical standards imposed by the guilds, and attributing liability in the event of flawed cloths.

October 1261

Weavers of canvas.

In the beams of the VIII men [the eight wardens of the profession]

...

2. And that there be no weaver so bold in all this city who dare to weave cloth that is not marked with the mark of the cloth of the city of Douai, under the penalty of L pounds and his banishment for one year from the city and the loss of the cloth. ...

Figure 1 The medieval loom. Illumination depicting the horizontal or low loom used for weaving most types of cloth.

§ 1.02 BY-LAWS OF THE WOOLLEN CLOTHMAKERS AND MERCHANTS OF SAINT-OMER—1268, 1285

Following what had already become an administrative practice as regards the regulation of the textile industry, the by-laws of the makers and merchants of woollen cloth of Saint-Omer (north of France), of 1268, amended in 1285, provided for the mandatory printing of the city's seal and individual marks on the fabrics. In addition, these by-laws provided for the registration of individual trade names and marks at the city hall.

Significantly, the concern with avoiding the risks of confusion and passing-off was already expressed in these by-laws (albeit with the same purpose of ensuring compliance with standards and assigning personal liability).

These are the ordinances and the regulations of the city of Saint-Omer.

> 199. It is ordered that every piece of cloth including woolen cloth, when dyed, shall be marked with the city's mark and whoever delivers cloth, including woolen cloth, without being marked with the city's mark shall lose the cloth or woolen cloth and his profession for one year and one day. ...
>
> 573. It is ordered that those who make cloths shall mark them with their own mark and not other's and who makes cloth longer than xv *paus*, [shall pay] the penalty of xv *sols*; and that no one use the sign of the commune or use linen in woolen cloth or green thread or other mark by which he may be known and not another and in a way of concealing the merchant's mark, on the penalty of lx *sols* and losing his profession for one year and one day.
>
> 574. It is ordered that every merchant who has purchased white woolen cloth at the halls shall have the mark of the cloth maker woven so that he may be known, on the penalty of lx. *sols*.
>
> XVII.
>
> [Regulation of cloth making]
>
> 595. All those who make cloths must swear that they will make fair cloths, on the penalty of lx *sols* and of losing their profession for one year and one day. And each cloth maker must have his name and his mark written at the hall.

§ 1.03 REGULATION CONCERNING THE PROFESSION OF TAILORS, PARIS—1323

The setting and enforcement of technical standards in the Middle Ages was not only a matter of consumer protection but also an issue that had to do with unfair competition. Indeed, those masters and workers who abode by those standards might have to compete with dishonest rivals who would not offer the same quality as required by guilds by-laws. Therefore, guild members—like today's entrepreneurs—were the first to ask the authorities for the adoption of measures that enabled them to differentiate their articles from those of dishonest competitors. In the case of the tailors of Paris, in the fourteenth century, those measures were the requirement of affixing of marks to all garments made by the city tailors. If those marks were different from today's, in the sense that they did not merely differentiate articles and their makers but also, and mainly, identify the liability of those makers as regards compliance with the required standards, they were nonetheless an expression of the repression of unfair competition. Today, in several countries, entrepreneurs' failure to comply with various sorts of legal obligations, such as labor laws and quality standards, may be denounced in court by rivals as acts of unfair competition.

Regulation of the profession of tailors[6] of Paris, approved on June 20, 1323.

> To all those who will see these letters, Jehan Loncle, guard of the provosts of Paris: greetings. As the good tailors of the city of Paris have come to us and begged us and required that, because every day more and more a great quantity of people have interfered and interfere with the tailors' profession, more frequently than it used to be, and therefore many frauds, falsehoods and malice are committed that cannot be well perceived, and by this the people are greatly deceived and harmed, because thus far no ordinance or regulation has been made containing rules on that interference or on the will to interfere ... we have made, ordered and established, make, order and establish the points and articles that follow hereafter. ...
>
> *Item* that on all the garments that will be made from now on, each worker of the said profession shall put the mark at the collar and at the stoles that will be inside them, by which the good people cannot be deceived. ...
>
> In testimony of the things said above we have put in these letters the seal of the provosts of Paris, the year of grace of one thousand three hundred twenty-three, on Monday, the twentieth day of the month of June.

§ 1.04 UPON THEIR REQUEST, CLOTHMAKERS AND MERCHANTS OF CHÂLONS, FRANCE, ARE AUTHORIZED TO ADOPT A SEAL CERTIFYING THE ORIGIN OF WOOLLEN CLOTH—1339

Following the same trend revealed by the previous text, clothmakers of the city of Châlons, France, in 1339, asked the king for the adoption of measures to protect them against competition of poor quality, cheaper fabrics made in other cities. In response, the king granted them the right to use a mark identifying the geographical origin of the cloths they made. This regulation implies that exclusivity in the use of Châlons' seal to mark cloth made in the city was enforceable under the same strict rules that applied then to counterfeiting—including seizures, fines, and corporal punishment.

Philippe [VI], by the grace of God, King of France, make known to all, present and future.

> That as by our loved wardens of the cloth industry of Châlons, we had been formerly informed on their behalf as well as on behalf of the cloth makers of the said city, that the cloth industry of this city being older than all others and having introduced a certain pattern and great beauty, which caused the cloths to be usually sold better than the cloths from other common cloth industries; and that after a short time, many [persons] of our kingdom and outside undertook to counterfeit their cloths, and sold them for cloths made at Châlons, and by such fraud and malice the people and the good persons who bought them for their uses and believed to have real cloths from Châlons, were badly damaged and fooled, when they found the falseness of short duration in those false and counterfeited cloths, and that for this reason the cloth industry was very impoverished and defamed, and that so few cloths were made presently, because those who bought

6. In French, *pourpointiers*. The term referred to one special category of tailors—those workers who designed, cut and sewed doublets—but eventually it was used to mean the generality of the profession.

them, because of the said counterfeit and defamation, found that it was convenient for the said cloth industry to come to naught, if remedy was not properly put in soon; and we were required by those named above that we should give them leave and license to put some seal of lead on their cloths.

So that the malice and deceit of the people were removed, and the cloth industry were retained in its good and first state, which seal was taken and held by the hand of the said wardens to whom belonged the inspection and the government of the cloth industry, so that everyone may know henceforth the true cloths of Châlons against counterfeits and those falsely made; ...

Let them have a seal of lead, as it pleases them, to hold forever and perpetually, to put on their cloths, which seal shall be taken and held by the hand of the said wardens to whom the wardenship and the government of the cloth industry belongs, as said. ...

Given at Maubuisson lès Pontoise, the year of grace of 1339, in the month of April.

Figure 2 Two clothiers' workshops in the fourteenth century. Left: a tailor shows a piece of woollen cloth to a client while a colleague takes the measures of another client. Right: While two seamstresses sew a dress, two other dressmakers cut a piece of linen cloth.

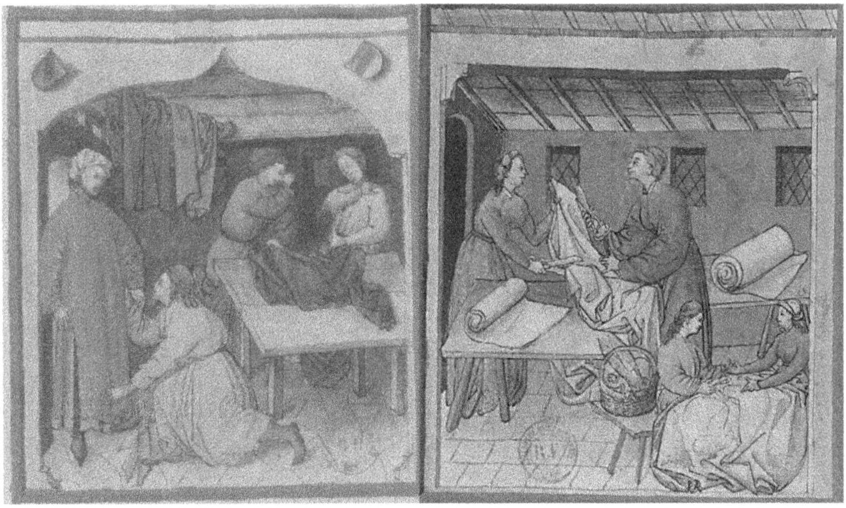

§ 1.05 EDWARD III, OF ENGLAND, DETERMINES THAT NO CLOTHS SHOULD BE SOLD BETWEEN MERCHANTS WITHOUT BEING PREVIOUSLY INSPECTED AND SEALED—1348

Through the Middle Ages, the inspection of cloths for ensuring compliance with technical standards—concerning the quality of raw materials, length, weight, colors—and the payment of taxes was mandatory. Such inspection would result in the printing or stamping of seals on the cloths. There were different seals for approved cloths and for those cloths that did not pass the examination. Those seals were not trademarks as we see them today. The stamping of artisans' individual marks was also required, but as complement to the seals of certification, and with the main purpose of designating their liability in the case they sent faulty products to the market.

In this regard, the practices of France and England were very similar. In France, perhaps, there was a somewhat differentiated legal custom that consisted of using the city's coat of arms as the certification seal. With this, besides serving as an element of quality certification, the sign served also the purpose of designating the article's origin and supporting its competitive standing against similar products from other cities. In England, cities' seals were also employed for the same purpose, but their mandatory use does not appear so frequently in statutes dealing with the textile industry.

The following text is an early expression of England's practice in sealing cloths with a public mark.

February 12, 1348

> Appointment for life of John Marreys, king's yeoman, to hold the office as well of the alnage of canvas, linen web, napery made as well in England as elsewhere, "wadynekk," "haydok," "mendeps," kerseys, serges of Louthe, Worstede, Norwich, Ireland and Causton, and of all other serges and scarlets, and all kinds of cloths of London, York, Winchester, Bristol, Lincoln, Essex, Norfolk, Suffolk, Kent, Staunford, Beverley, St. Osyth, Devon and Cornwall, as also of all other cloths made in England, as well as of the seal ordained for the office of the alnage and all that pertains to the office, in the same manner as others have held the office of the grant of the king's progenitors. Also it is the king's will, and he charges that all such cloths for sale between merchant and merchant, which shall be of the right assize, shall be sealed before being exposed for sale, under the penalty hitherto accustomed.

§ 1.06 IN ABBEVILLE, FRANCE, THE USE OF A MARK OF ORIGIN BY THE CLOTH INDUSTRY BECOMES MANDATORY AND EXCLUSIVE—1352

The following text concerns an act granting the exclusive right in the commercial use of Abbeville mark and strings, which would be attached to the cloth made in that city and its suburbs. These particular regulations provided for an exception in the case the cloths were made to be used by the artisan and his family—i.e., without a commercial purpose. This is an anticipation of a rule that prevails today under some national statutes, which exempts from trademark infringement the making and using of articles for a non-commercial purpose. A bill introduced in United States Congress, in 2011, aiming at amending the Copyright Act so as to provide for special protection to fashion designs, also included this sort of "home sewing exception."

Strings in particular shapes and colors, as well as the selvages of some cloths, such as carpets and bed sheets, have also been used as signs of differentiation.

The fact that this text employs the term etc. several times, thus suppressing language of a legal nature, indicates that in the fourteenth century France had already developed a template for granting this sort of privileges. The applicants of the privilege themselves make reference to similar acts granted in favor of the draperies of other cities, like Rouen.

June 1352

Charles etc. we make known etc. We have received the humble request of our beloved makers and weavers of the cloth industry of our city of Abbeville stating that for a long time, for the preservation of said industry, which is one of the beautiful and good of our kingdom and to obviate the faults and abuses that might have been caused to them, they had been given by our predecessors, kings and counts of Ponthieu, several fine privileges, formerly advised and concluded by the mayor and aldermen and those [enforcers] of the law of our said city, which privileges they have always enjoyed and still do, but they doubt that without having confirmation from us, others may wish to impede them, requesting for this reason our provision, and with it, in amplifying their privileges, that henceforth no other people of the trade having good style and way of life, may use the said manufacture of drapery, unless it is for dressing them and their family only, or commercialize it as do those supplicants who live only from said industry, and moreover that in the city and suburbs of Abbeville be not and cannot be sold any cloths from towns, cities and neighboring places which do not bear or have a different mark or strings, so that they may not be surreptitiously countermarked, taken out, or sold in the city in retail or in any other way by concealment under the sign of the supplicants, under pain of confiscation of those cloths, corporal punishment and arbitrary fine, and all this as it is used to do in our city of Rouen and other good and great draperies of our kingdom, etc. because etc. to the supplicants we have confirmed, ratified and approved, confirm ... etc. their privileges as they were granted to them by our predecessors and that are contained in the letters on this [matter] granted to them and which are registered in the book of the law of the city of Abbeville and that they and their successors enjoy them from now on in the same manner as their [predecessors] have well and duly enjoyed and used them. And with this, of our greater grace, amplifying their privileges, we accord and grant that they enjoy the two points and articles said above, namely that no person other than the supplicants, having other way of living, residing in the city and suburbs of Abbeville will engage in the trade of cloth making from now on and for the time the manufacture of the commodity of cloths remains, unless it is for the dressing of them and their family, and also that in that city and its suburbs cloths from the surrounding cities and places may not be sold unless they display or have different marks or strings, so that they are not surreptitiously countermarked for and instead of the cloths of that city, under the penalty of confiscation of the cloths and of punishment of prison and arbitrary fine, and all this in the form and manner that it is above provided for, and that is contained and provided for by the ordinances of the city of Abbeville. Therefore we command the municipality of Ponthieu and all our other etc. who, by our grace, make confirmation and ampliation, obey and permit the supplicants and their successors to enjoy and use, without doing to them etc. and in doing and obeying this they oblige all those who for this will be compelled etc. And therefore etc. And so that etc. Except etc. Given in Paris, in the month of June of the year one thousand and one thousand CCC IIII and twelve, and of our reign the ninth. Thus signed by the king. ...

§ 1.07 EDWARD III APPROVES ANOTHER STATUTE IMPOSING THE INSPECTION AND THE SEALING OF IMPORTED CLOTHS—1353

The following text concerns a statute that dealt with imported cloths that did not comply with mandatory standards (the cloths "were not of the Assise"). In order to avoid the fraud, the King ordered those cloths to be inspected and sealed, on the same penalty that applied to counterfeits. The seal's purpose was to certify the length of the cloths and the payment of taxes.

> *Item*, Whereas the Great Men and Commons have shewed to our Lord the King, how divers Merchants, as well Foreigners as Denizens, have withdrawn them, and yet do withdraw them, to come with Cloths into England, to the great Damage of the King and of all his People, because that the King's Aulneger surmiseth to Merchant Strangers, that their Cloths be not of Assise, that is to say, ...
>
> "Our Lord the King, upon such Condition hearing their Supplication, hath released and excluded him [the Aulneger] of all the said Forfeitures, and he willeth and granteth for him and for his Heirs, that there shall be no Cloths forfeit, although they be not of the same Assise, but the King's Aulneger shall measure the Cloth, and mark the same, by which Mark a man may know how much the Cloth containeth; ...
>
> (14) So always, that of no Cloth which containeth not half a Cloth, nor of Cloths which a Man maketh for his own Use to clothe him and his Meiny, nor of Cloth sealed with the Seal of the Collector of the said Subsidy was once paid by the Seller, to whose Hands that such Cloths shall come after to sell, or in any Manner, nothing of the said Subsidy shall be paid and demanded.
>
> (15) And that such Manner of Cloths which be put to Sale before that they be sealed with the said Seal, shall be forfeit to the King, and taken into his hands by the said Collector or Aulneger, or by the Deputy of one of them, or else by the Bailiffs of the Town where such vendible Cloths not sealed shall be found."

§ 1.08 THE EMERGENCE OF A NEW INDUSTRY IN TOURNAI—THE MANUFACTURE OF VELVET CLOTH—WAS ACCOMPANIED BY RULES ON THE MANDATORY USE OF MARKS OF ORIGIN AS WELL AS INDIVIDUAL TRADEMARKS

Corresponding to what had already become a legal standard, a new industry that was being established in the city of Tournai (today, in Belgium) triggered the passing of rules on the mandatory use of marks for purposes of ensuring competition with other cities as well as of designating the liability of individual artisans in the case of failure to comply with quality standards. Although the two regulations that are here partly quoted and translated have general language as regards the cloth industry, they refer specifically to the tapestry industry, which achieved great technical and commercial success in the fourteenth and fifteenth centuries. Also in accordance with what had already become a practice, both the city's mark of origin and the artisans' individual trademarks were registered with the wardens, so that the latter could identify counterfeits as well as those liable for manufacturing cloths below mandatory standards.

§ 1.08.1 The First Regulation on Tournai's City Mark and Individual Marks for Carpets Made of Velvet—1380

August 7, 1380

Regulations made and approved by the three Consuls, on Tuesday, the seventh day of August, year one thousand three hundred eighty, for the public good, as regards the cloth of velvet that from now on will be made in Tournai.

... *Item* there will be some wardens knowledgeable about this matter and appointed by the magistrates as well as a certain seal with which the velvet cloths shall be sealed so that, once they are dyed, there will be no better way of, during their inspection, having full knowledge of fraud that has been committed. ...

Item that each worker put his mark on each cloth he will make, and likewise the master to whom the cloth belongs put his mark, so that there is knowledge of those who make good work or otherwise. And also that the fuller shall not full those cloths, and the dyers shall not dye them until they have the mark written, on the penalty of c *sols*. ...

Item that merchants, workers, or others do not attach seals of lead to the mentioned cloths except the seal or mark of the city, on the penalty of c *sols*.

Figure 3 The seal of Tournai, Belgium, the affixation of which was mandatory on carpets made in the city. The tower appears in the city's coat of arms.

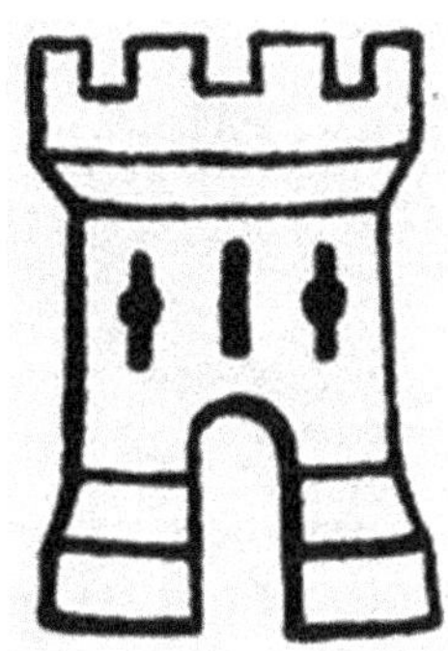

§ 1.08.2 Statute Amending the Regulations of the Tapestry Industry of Tournai—1397

March 26, 1397

Ordinance made and passed by the Counsels of the said city [of Tournai] for the benefit of the public good on the matter of the high looms and articles of tapestry and velvet cloths made in Tournai; Tuesday the twenty-sixth day of March one thousand ccc. iiii^{xx} and xvii and published the following Friday. ...

11. *Item* that no merchants, workers or others of the said city who, from now on, buy or have bought, or have in their houses or elsewhere, in the said city, any velvet cloths that have been made outside that same city without, before they are

made, having been seen and approved by the wardens who will be appointed for that purpose, i.e. that they will be good for being sold in the said city and burgh, and in the case [any cloth] is found without the city's mark, but [with] a mark different from and not similar to the mark of the velvet cloths made in Tournai; and if they are found not good, the cloths will be cut lengthwise, as it is done in the said city of Tournai, and condemned under the laws of justice.

Figure 4 Left: "The History of Abraham," carpet made in Tournai, sixteenth century. Right: detail of the same carpet, displaying Tournai's mark of origin on the border of its down right corner.

§ 1.09 A CONTRACT ON THE ASSIGNMENT OF A TRADEMARK BETWEEN TWO MERCHANTS FROM MILAN—1383

In medieval Europe, marks were mainly symbols of certification, both of quality and origin. Marks could also serve the function of differentiating artisans and the articles they produced, but those signs would basically associate the artisans with the quality of their products, i.e., their purpose was to designate personal liability. This situation was due to the way in which corporations operated. Masters and workers were supposed to obey principles of solidarity, and thus they were not expected—or even authorized—to compete against each other. Commercial rivalry would normally erupt between cities and their respective corporations, but not within the cities.

There were a few exceptions, however, particularly in certain activities and under exceptional circumstances in which a certain artisan or merchant operated beyond the constraints of guilds, or when, even within the guild, a certain artisan or merchant acquired exceptional reputation. In From Babylon to the Silicon Valley, *we included a patent letter by which, in 1364, Charles V, of France, authorized the transfer of ownership of a trademark that belonged to Jean de Saint-Denis, merchant of knife blades, who had passed away without heirs or successors, to a certain Evard de Boessay, who had used the same trademark for some time. As we said there, it is not impossible that the assignee had been a partner of the deceased merchant.*[7]

*Bartolo da Sassoferrato, the medieval jurist who wrote about coats of arms (*De Insigniis et Armis, *published posthumously by his son-in-law in 1358), mentioned the possibility of one of the partners, upon the dissolution of the company, acquiring the trademark that was associated with the business in question.*

> *There are also certain insignia that belong to some partnerships of merchants; and in this context, since the partnership does not pass on to the heirs, transmission of such insignia by inheritance does not have to be considered. But with whom will the trademark remain when the partnership has been dissolved? It is not fair that all the partners have the right to use the same trademark, as has been said. I respond that, if there were someone in the company who was the head and very close to being the master of the company, he should keep the trademark, since it should remain with the one who was in the position of greatest honor. But if there were not such a person, then it should remain with the one who had the greatest share in the partnership. Osvaldo Cavallar* et al., A Grammar of Signs—Bartolo da Sassoferrato's Tract on Insignia and Coats of Arms, *at 148-149 (Univ. of Cal. at Berkeley, 1994).*

The text that follows is another example of a trademark being dealt with as a business asset. The text refers to a public record of a contract of assignment of figurative trademarks between two cloth merchants of Milan. It is worth noticing that the record refers to trademarks "approved for use by the guild of the trade of wool of Milan." This does not mean that those were not individual trademarks, otherwise, Pietro de Preda could not have assigned them. The meaning was that, as it happened in other guilds, the magistrates of the corporation approved the trademarks individually used by members.

> On 10 June of the year 1383, Pietro de Preda, son of the late Gaspare, residing in the parish of St. Simpliciano, assigns to Petrolo Tanzio, son of the late Nicola, residing at St. Cipriano, at Porta Comasina, the signs copied below approved for use by the guild of the trade of wool of Milan, recorded in the book by the provosts of the society and community of the Art of wool trade of Milan, and they are sketched and designed below [*see* Figure 5], with the right and the possibility of using the said marks, or any of them, or similar ones, and marking wool cloths or similar with them, at the will of Petrolo Tanzio himself. And likewise [he sells] all rights, suits, and advantages in and from these marks, and on account or by reason of them, which belong to the seller, Pietro himself. ...
>
> And for the sale, for the price and the agreed payment of the price and transaction concerning all and each of the aforesaid signs, the seller has acknowledged and acknowledges, and gives receipt that he has received from the said Ser Petrolo, buyer, 100 florins in silver coins of the Milanese currency in course, ...
>
> Made in the Broletto Nuovo of the Commune of Milan, ...

7. From Babylon to the Silicon Valley, *supra* note 1, at 91.

Figure 5 The trademarks that Pietro de Preda in 1383 assigned to Petrolo Tanzio, which appear annexed to the contract.

§ 1.10 THE USE OF CERTIFICATION AND INDIVIDUAL MARKS IS MADE MANDATORY FOR THE LEATHER WORKERS OF AMIENS—1383

As trade increased and competition became more intense in the Middle Ages, the adoption of formal mechanisms of protection of business identifiers expanded—not only as designations of origin and quality but also as tokens of direct differentiation and commercial rivalry. The text that follows consists of excerpts from the by-laws of the guild of cobblers of Amiens, of 1383, approved by the city's aldermen in 1407.

The rules and ordinances for the shoemakers, leather workers, and tanners follow.

> ...
>
> 21. *Item*, any shoemakers, leather workers of old or new, tanners, saddlers, glove makers or any other, outside of the city of Amiens, who purchase or order the purchase and bring to Amiens any pieces of tanned leather, notwithstanding that they are marked with the sign or mark of the city from which they will be brought, the person who has purchased them, as soon as he brings them to Amiens, shall be required to bring them to the place of the Pont de Baudri, and there they shall be controlled by the inspectors of the tanners of Amiens; and if they are found well made, they shall be marked with the sign of the tanners of the

said city of Amiens, and, if they are not controlled and marked, they cannot be sold, purchased, or transformed, or resold afterwards. And if it happens that, in any of the said trades, the leathers that would be purchased and brought from outside the city, and which were not controlled or marked with the sign of the city, were found for sale or for finishing ... they shall be sanctioned with a fine of XX *sols*. And all this shall be brought before the mayor and the aldermen, and by judgment shall be condemned to burn before the house of the one who made such mischief. ...

23. *Item*, it is ordered and forbidden to all tanners of leather of the said city, that they do not dare to put in black or to make any pieces or whole leathers, hides and prepared leathers, pieces which will belong to them or which will be consigned to them, if, before any work is done, they do not send them to be marked with the sign of the city of Amiens and with the countermark of the shoemaker, and leather worker of Amiens to whom the leathers will belong, upon the said fine. And the inspectors of the shoemaking trade shall be required to inspect the leathers in the house of the leather workers and shoemakers aforesaid, and those that they will find badly tanned shall be brought to the mayor and the aldermen, to take such punishment as above is declared.

24. *Item*, that the leather workers may be leather workers and merchants at the same time, among which there will be ten trades of good inspectors of the tanners, shoemakers and leather workers, that is to say two for each of the said trades, and there will be an iron determined for such marking as the mayor and the aldermen will see fit. Which iron the inspectors of the shoemakers will control, and will not be able to sell or deliver any leathers whatsoever, if that have not passed by the said inspectors and marked with the mandatory iron as said above, on the fine of xl *sol parisis*. ...

25. *Item*, and furthermore that, if any shoemaker wants to buy any leathers tanned in Paris, Compiegne, Beauvais, Noyon, Arras, Lille, Abbeville, they may do it; but they will not be allowed to put them in their houses, unless they are controlled and marked with the previously mentioned mark and brought in the place determined for that purpose, on the fine of XX *sols parisis*. ...

§ 1.11 FOLLOWING THE EXAMPLE OF OTHER CITIES, LILLE REGULATES THE TEXTILE INDUSTRY AND ADOPTS PROVISIONS ON THE MANDATORY USE OF THE CITY'S SEAL AND INDIVIDUAL MARKS—1384

Confirming what had already become practice, the Council of prud'hommes (a sort of a modern Chamber of Arts and Trade, composed of artisans and merchants, which in some cities provided notarial services and operated as a commercial and labor court) of Lille also adopted rules providing for the mandatory use of the city's seal and artisans' individual marks. The reference to the uses and customs of the textile industry as well as of those of the council suggests that these regulations are just a confirmation of previous practices.

The temporary nature of these regulations (one year and one day) implies that they were supposed to be confirmed by a higher authority.

Regulations concerning weavers and fullers

1. That no weavers of cloths, both in this city and outside, whoever they may be, be so bold that, after the coming day of Pentecost, weave or have woven in their workshops either whole cloths or pieces thereof, that are not woven and finished with the quantity of thread as they should be, according to the use and custom of the cloth profession and of the council of prud'hommes of this city; and that, as soon as the said cloths leave the looms, they shall bring them or have them brought to the council of prud'hommes, so that they are sealed with the council's sign in the customary manner, on the penalty of a fine of 10 lb. every time that someone does the opposite.

2. And that no fullers, both from this city and outside, whoever they are, be so bold that, after the said coming day of Pentecost, treads or cause to be treaded in their workshops either whole cloths or pieces thereof that are not sealed with the seal or lead of the council of prud'hommes, and which shall not be reported and be brought to the council for receiving the said seal, with which it has been the use and custom to mark the cloths of this city, and bring or have brought the cloths to where they have to be woven, or to the workshop of the weaver who shall mend them, on the penalty of 10 pounds of fine, every time that someone does the opposite.

3. And that no tailors or seamstresses of this city, whoever they are, be so bold that, after the said coming day of Pentecost, sew or permits to be sown either whole cloths or pieces thereof that are not to be reported and brought to the council of prud'hommes for receiving the seal of the said council, with which it has been the use and custom to mark the cloths of this city, and the said cloths or pieces thereof be brought or made brought by the said weavers and tailors who have woven or mended them to the council of wardens of the masters, for sealing them, if they are found good, in the usual manner, on the penalty of a fine of 10 pounds, every time that someone does the opposite.

These rules shall apply for one year and one day. Done on the XXIIIth day of May, the year of one thousand III IIII^{xx} and IIII.

§ 1.12 ARRAS PASSES A STATUTE ON THE ESTABLISHMENT OF A CLOTH MANUFACTORY—1394

The following text presents a number of early expressions of law policies that later would become common through France. First, it is an instrument of industrial policy. The duke of Burgundy has approved the establishment of a new textile industry in Arras with the explicit purpose of creating jobs and therefore stopping the depopulation and reducing the poverty of the city. There was also a mercantilist rationale in that measure, to the extent that the statute prohibited the importation of textiles that might compete with those made in the city. Henry IV and Louis XIV, several centuries later, would make mercantilism the main rationale of their industrial policies. We will see several expressions of that through this book.

Also, besides the usual instruments of differentiation of the cloths made in the city for the sake of certifying quality and origin, this statute also provided for the use of colored selvages and threads as an element of differentiation. We will see through this book that specific and exclusive colors of selvages were considered by artisans and merchants an important intangible asset—eventually, as much important as individual trademarks.

This practice of resorting to colored selvages as elements of differentiation remained through the late Middle Ages until the late eighteenth century, as we will see below, in connection with Vanrobais' manufacture of fine cloths in Abbeville (see § 1.45).

> Phelippe [the Bold], son of the King of France, Duke of Burgundy. … We make known to all … that it has been humbly exposed to us by our beloved mayor, aldermen, bourgeois, and inhabitants of our city of Arras, which has always been the most important and notable city in our county of Artois, greatly populated, and adorned with several wares and crafts; and that so much by the great natural mortalities, which have occurred several times in our said city, as for other causes, this city is very greatly depopulated, diminished and reduced, both from large numbers of people and from capacities and properties, in consequence of which it is in great peril of falling into desolation and destruction, taking into consideration the great burdens of rents and other things with which it is charged, [and thus] without rescue and help there will be no provision and remedy, as they say; and in order to provide for this necessity, and to find some remedy for the maintenance of our city and our subjects and its repopulation, they have advised that a profitable thing would be to establish, build, and organize a cloth manufactory in our city, in the manner … they have advised; concerning which our subjects who for this have assembled, agreed and assented, without there being anyone contradicting; which advice and manner they have reported to us for having our authority and consent on this. …
>
> *Item*, other cloths can be made in the said city, i.e., grayed out, white drapery or towels … ; and these cloths will have two cotton threads outside the selvage in [the shape of] a grid, and in each *diquedune*[8] in the center of the selvage, so as that there be awareness of it.
>
> 6. *Item*, that all the cloths above mentioned will have such selvages as one wants to put in them, provided that, for every four threads of the mentioned selvages there will be two threads all along those selvages, so that it can be perceived and there be awareness that those cloths will have been made in the city of Arras.
>
> 7. *Item*, in city of Arras cloths of wool from little lambs will be made by whoever wants to make them . … And in order to make it known that it is cloth made of wool from little lambs, the selvage shall be dyed of blue and have at its selvages two threads of cotton, for making it known that they have been made in the city of Arras. …
>
> 37. *Item*, and so that the said cloth industry may be erected and can support itself, and that the merchants, who will begin [to deal with] those cloths and the industry, may have deliverance and start again and pursue it, and that the large amounts of money that are daily sent out may remain in the city, it is advised upon mature deliberation by the mayor, aldermen, bourgeois and inhabitants of the city of Arras, without any division or contradiction whatsoever, that all residents in the said city and subject to the law and its enforcers cannot, to dress themselves, buy any cloths other than those that will be made and manufactured in the city, by the time and space of 3 continuous years, beginning on the date of these letters, except cloths from Brussels, Liège, Monstierviller and Ypre, bearing the signs of the mentioned good towns and places; and who would do the opposite, he would lose the cloth, and in the event of recidivism, he would be punished at the will of the bailiff and aldermen of Arras, half of the said cloth [to be] delivered to us, a quarter to the profit of the town and the other quarter at the profit of the whistleblower.

8. *Diquedune*: a sort of cloth with the threads irregularly distributed along its length.

And so that this may be a firm and stable thing, we have had put on these presents our seal in a ribbon of silk and green wax. ...

Given at Neufcastel-en-Boulenois, in the month of May, the year of grace one thousand three hundred and ninety-four.

§ 1.13 BY-LAWS OF THE TANNERS, SHOEMAKERS, AND COBBLERS OF AMIENS—1407

The following excerpts of the by-laws of the leather workers and shoemakers of Amiens, France, approved by the aldermen in 1407, deal with the organization of those professions into a single corporation, thereby organizing their trade, setting quality standards, and contributing to appease the disputes among masters that frequently arose concerning their exclusive right to produce certain articles.

These by-laws, following the examples of the rules organizing other professions, have paid great attention not only to quality standards but also to matters of competition. Indeed, it provided for certain mandatory conducts that avoided commercial rivalry among the members of the same guild. In particular, clause 19 speaks eloquently on this issue. That clause prohibited the guild member to sell any articles if he was not inside his stall, at the market. Therefore, he could not come out to the street to proclaim and sell his articles. Nor could he call from his stall a merchant (i.e., a potential customer) standing in front of another artisan's stall. In other words, diversion of a competitor's clientele or its attempt was prohibited.

In such a scenario of restrained competition, intellectual property had its importance reduced as far as the trade by guild members in the city was concerned. But particular attention was accorded to the use of the city's seal, as it was of significant relevance in boosting the competitive advantage of the masters and workers of a city vis-à-vis those living and working in rival cities.

By-laws of the Tanners, Shoemakers, and Cobblers of Amiens

... 3. *Item*, every tanner and also every shoemaker shall have a sign and mark, with which each of them will mark the leathers that will be brought and consigned for tanning, and also their own leathers, in order that those who would make poor tanning be known; and each sign shall be [formed by a] countermark different from each other, on the penalty mentioned. [the fine of xx *sols parisis*, of which the wardens will have v *sols*, and the city, the surplus]. ...

19. *Item*, that no one of the mentioned artisans may sell his works, him being in front of his stall, nor call a merchant who is at another's stall, on the said fine. ...

21. *Item*, any shoemaker or cobbler, tanner, yoke maker, purse maker or any other, from outside the city of Amiens, who will have purchased or caused to be purchased and brought to Amiens any tanned leathers, notwithstanding that they are marked with the sign or mark of the city from which they will be brought, whoever has purchased them will be required, immediately after they have brought them to Amiens, to have them brought to the Square du Pont de Baudri, and there they will be inspected by the wardens of the tanners of Amiens, and if they are found to be correct, they shall be marked with the sign of the tanners of the city of Amiens, and, if they are not so inspected and marked, they cannot be

sold, purchased, or worked upon, or resold afterwards. And if it were to happen that, in any of the aforesaid professions, the leathers that would thus be purchased and brought from outside the city, and that would not be inspected or marked with the sign of the city, were found on sale or being worked, by sock makers, boot makers, yoke makers, tanners, purse makers, will be fined in xx *sols*. And all that shall be brought before the mayor and aldermen, and by judgment will be condemned to be burnt in front of the house of the one who will have done wrong.

...

23. *Item*, it is ordered and forbidden to all tanners of leather of the said city, that they do not dare to put in black or to make any garments or whole leathers, skins and *hastereaux*,[9] which either belong to them or that will be consigned to them, if, before any work, it appears to them that they are not marked with the sign of the city of Amiens and the countermark of the shoemaker and tanner of Amiens to whom the leathers belong, on the penalty of the same fine. And the wardens of the profession of shoemaking will be required to inspect the leathers in the workshops of the above-mentioned tanners and shoemakers, and those that they find badly tanned shall be brought before the mayor and aldermen, to take such punishment as stated above.

24. *Item*, that the tanners may be tanners and merchants concurrently, among which professions there will be good wardens for the tanners and shoemakers, i.e., two of each profession, and there will be a stamp with such mark as the mayor and aldermen will see fit; which stamp the wardens of the shoemakers will inspect, and the latter shall not be permitted to sell or deliver any leather whatsoever, unless they have gone through said wardens and stamped with the established stamp, on the penalty of a fine of xl *sols parisis*.

25. *Item*, and moreover, if some shoemakers want to buy any leathers tanned in Paris, Compiègne, Beauvais, Noyon, Arras, Lille, Abbeville, they may do so; but they shall not bring them to their workshops unless they are inspected and marked with the above-mentioned mark and brought to the local determined for that purpose, on the penalty of a fine of xx *sols parisis*. ...

35. *Item*, that no tanners may sell or deliver leather from their workshops, unless it is inspected and marked with the city's stamp, such as will be determined by the mayor and aldermen. ...

Which ordinances above declared were and are made at the will and confirmation of the said mayor and aldermen, by Sire Frémin Piédelieu, mayor of Amiens; present. ... aldermen, the eighteenth day of July, the year one thousand four hundred and seven.

§ 1.14 ORDINANCES OF TOURNAI CONCERNING THE TAPESTRY INDUSTRY—1408

Confirming what had already become the general rule in the textile industry, in 1408 the magistrates [counselors] of Tournai ordered carpet makers to print their individual marks on the articles they produced. They also established that those marks should be distinctive, i.e., different from each other, so that liability in the event of some faulty work could be easily asserted.

9. *Hastereaux*—a special treatment given to leather and skins.

Interestingly, the ordinances declared the objective of contributing to the growth of the local tapestry industry and justified its provisions with the pursuit of the public good. This latter formula would be frequently repeated from that date on.

August 7, 1408

> Ordinances made, passed and granted by the Counselors of the city and town of Tournai concerning the profession, the works and the goods of the cloths named *hautelisse*[10] in the said city for the common profit and the utility of the public interest of the city, on Tuesday, vii^{e} day of August, in the year one thousand cccc and viij, as follows. ...
>
> 1. First, so as to increase the said industry it is ordered to have wardens for the said cloths, and a seal with which the wardens will mark the cloths [made on the vertical looms] that will be deemed good and sufficient, which will display the said seal as it will please the said Counselors to order; for their trouble to go around by the artisans' workshops, where the cloths will be inspected and approved, and for marking them, the wardens will have each ii *deniers tournois* for their salary; ...
>
> 6. *Item*, that all masters and workers who will work or will have worked on the said vertical looms shall put their mark on each cloth and each shall have a mark different from one another, which will be thus put and in such a way that the said wardens will be able to see and recognize them, so that no fraud can be committed and that each one's work be known, on the penalty of a fine of xx *sols*; ...
>
> 14. *Item* that no workers or merchants of the said city may have in their workshops or elsewhere in this city and jurisdiction carpets made or worked outside Tournai, if they have not been inspected and sealed by the wardens and [have not been deemed] valid for having said [mark], on the penalty of a fine of c *sols*.

10. *Hautelisse*—term designating the high or vertical loom, mostly employed in the making of carpets.

Figure 6 The vertical or high loom, used mainly for the making of carpets.

§ 1.15 THE ALDERMEN OF AMIENS APPROVE AN ORDINANCE CONCERNING THE CLOTH INDUSTRY—1413

Although in a different city, the same purpose and political justification of the previous statute were mentioned by the mayor and aldermen of Amiens in regulating the local textile industry. As far as the marks are concerned, the rules adopted followed the same legal pattern as set in other cities and countries: on the one hand, signs certifying quality and origin, and, on the other, individual marks for setting liability.

Complementary ordinance of the aldermen concerning the cloth industry

October 18, 1413

Know all those who will see what is written that, by the mayor and aldermen of the city and town of Amiens, in accordance with the opinion and deliberation of the majority and healthier part of the dyers, tailors and weavers of cloths of the city of Amiens, it has been and it is ordered in the matter of the said cloth industry, for the common good and profit, according to the will and consent the said mayor and aldermen, the following: ...

4. *Item*, that each piece of cloth dyed of dark green in the manner Amiens, when well dyed, will wear the seal of said city.

5. *Item*, that each cloth weaver residing in the said city and suburb of Amiens shall have sign and mark different from each other, and shall put on each piece of cloth woven by him his sign and mark, whereby one has and it is possible to have knowledge of the weaver who has woven the cloth, and that, if there is a fault due to him, so he be and may be punished according to reason.

§ 1.16 REGULATIONS OF THE CLOTH INDUSTRY OF CHARTRES—1418

The adoption of rules concerning the use of marks of origin and certification in France, originally aimed at fighting counterfeiting, soon became tangled with fiscal policies. The clothmakers of Chartres, harmed by dishonest practices, requested the King to pass a regulation that, following the example of other French and Flemish cities, imposed sanctions on counterfeiting. The text that follows confirmed such regulation-imposed sanctions on counterfeiting and set a fee for each piece of cloth that, upon inspection, was marked with the city's seal of quality and origin.

Charles [VI], by the grace of God, King of France: We make known to all present and future and see the Letters in the form that follows.

To all those who see the present Letters, Etienne Deprez, Esquire, cupbearer of the King our Lord, his Bailiff at Chartres, and Esquire of the Stall of Monseigneur the Duke of Burgundy: Greetings.

As the Masters and Jurors of the trade and making of cloth of the city of Chartres, called Cloth's trade, had come before us a long time ago in Judgment, and had exposed to us that among the other trades of the city, the trade of Cloth was one of the most remarkable, ancient, and chief trades of the city, and by which more people of this city were supported and had their lives; and in the course of which trade the city of Chartres was renowned at the [fair of] Lendit, at the fairs of Châlons and other fairs of this Kingdom, one of the seventeen sworn cities of this Kingdom, where the trade is carried out; and preserving this in good policy, upon the antiquity of several statutes, ordinances and impositions that exist on the manners of cloth, which the Jurors and Workers of that trade are obliged to hold and to observe, for whose compliance the cloth industry of Chartres has been and is well renowned at the fairs and places above mentioned and others of this Kingdom, and the cloth that in its manner have come, reputed as good, fair and of trade value, and all foreign Merchants are well pleased with it when they know that they come from the manner of cloth making of Chartres; nevertheless, in other towns of smaller authority, and in several villages of the country of Chartain, the making of several cloths of the same kind or similar manner, like that of Chartres, had become usual for some time, and that their vendors, or some of them, at fairs and markets, affirmed they were made in the manner of Chartres, or at least occasionally the buyers thought they were so; in regard of which cloth the inspection and compliance with the Statutes that existed and applied in the city of Chartres had not been observed, and the buyers could not notice that in good faith, because the cloth made in the manner of that city did not have a mark or a public sign, by which it is possible to discern with certainty the cloth that had passed by the inspection and approval of the city, in which the buyers had been several times defrauded, and the cloth industry of the city blamed; for these reasons the said Masters and Jurors said that, to obviate the frauds and inconveniences that by the means above mentioned as well as other means could happen to the manufacture of cloths of Chartres, for keeping it under good governance, for increasing its reputation, and for removing all suspicions that foreign merchants might have in its regard, it was expedient that the merchants of cloth that from now on came out in that manner, and were the work of Chartres, had a mark and sign of lead, to be printed and attached after the cloth is inspected and approved by the Jurors instructed to do so, and passed by the sworn cloth inspection of the King, which exists in that city, put in the perch, and signed by the Jurors, of a wax imprint to this specially ordered; and that no cloth be made in the city, nor delivered to the party to which it would belong, until after its inspection and approval, the printing of the mark and public sign of lead in the manner that is described; and that for the trouble of doing so, and for the interest on the lead [used] to make the mark, there be certain fees that the Clerks may, in this regard, charge and levy on each piece of cloth thus passed, approved and signed; about which fees the Masters and Jurors said to be quite adequate and without grievance to any, in the sum of two *deniers tournois* for each mark thus attached; and furthermore the Masters and Jurors said that such was the practice in several good cities of this Kingdom, such as Rouen, Evreux, Saint-Lo, Bernay, Monsliervillier, the good cities of Flanders, and several others of this Kingdom; and that in order to better reinforce the Ordinance and its good compliance, and to retreat the bad intentions of those who would fraudulently remove their cloths from that approval, it was expedient to impose a penalty by way of a fine, on each person doing the opposite, that is to say, that for each cloth made in that manner that would have been found folded and prepared, the person with whom it would have been found, would be obliged to pay a fine of ten *sols tournois* to the King our Lord and suffer the penalty of the seizure of the cloth and otherwise; ... For the causes and reasons above mentioned, and also taking into consideration the reports and the agreement of the Prosecutor of the King, and all that is worthy of consideration and that can persuade us to move in this direction; by leaning on the request of the Masters and Jurors, and particularly on the public favor, we have ordered and determined, order and determine by way of perpetual Statutes and Ordinance:

(1) That all the cloths that will henceforth be made in the said city, for being put in commerce, in the manner and the work of that city, shall have a mark and public sign of lead; which mark shall have on one side of its imprint, the image of Notre-Dame, and below it shall have written Chartres, and on the other hand of that mark, it shall have an imprint of a Chartain containing the arms of the city; which mark and piece of lead shall be printed on and fastened to such piece of cloth, after the cloth is inspected and approved by the Jurors instructed to do so, and passed by the sworn cloth inspection of the King, which exists in that city, put in the perch, and signed by the said Jurors, of a wax imprint to this specially ordered;

(2) *Item.* We order that from now on in the city of Chartres, no such cloth will be passed or delivered to the party to whom it will belong, until after its inspection and approval, the mark and public piece of lead be printed and attached, in the manner that is said.

(3) *Item.* We order that for the trouble of making and placing and attaching the lead, and for interest on the lead and other that the Jurors may have, by those Jurors or whoever will be committed by them to do so, may take and levy on each cloth thus passed, approved and signed, the fee of two *deniers tournois* for each mark and lead thus attached.

(4) *Item.* We order that whoever passes or carries cloth of that manner and type, and which will be found or that one may show to have been folded or finished without having the said mark and lead, will be held to pay to the King a fine of ten *sols tournois* for each piece of cloth thus found or shown; and the Jurors of that trade and others to whom it will concern may take and cease all such cloths that they will find or will be able to prove or show to have been passed without that approval and without lead; and their task is to constrain those who have them to pay the mentioned fine, as well as to inspect those cloths so as to check whether they are bad, and, as regards those cloths and the persons to whom they belong, to punish them according to the by-laws of the art; and if they are good, according to the said by-laws, to mark them with the mark and lead, according to what is said; and where, as the case may be, those

pieces of cloths passed without the lead may not be found so that the fine can be exacted for the King, through the seizure of the cloth, those to whom such pieces of cloth belong, and who shall be guilty of having them passed, may be fined before us at the request of the Jurors. ...

Given in testimony of this, under the Seal of Affairs of the Municipality of Chartres, Friday the xvi[th] day of September, the year of grace of one thousand cccc & eighteen. Signed Cadou.

Approved by patent letters of Charles VI, in Paris, June 1419.

§ 1.17 REGULATIONS OF THE CLOTH INDUSTRY OF DIJON—1425, 1435

The following two texts—excerpts from the regulation passed by the municipality of Dijon in 1425, and amended in 1435, concerning the cloth industry—bear witness to the fact that the combination of the city's mark of origin with weavers' individual marks had become a standard rule by the end of the Middle Ages.

However, the 1435 statute has a new aspect that is noteworthy because it would become a practice: the city marks, the wardens' seals, and the artisans' marks were kept in a safety box for the eventual necessity of conferring the authenticity of the marks printed on or woven in the cloths. That safety box could only be opened with the combination of three keys. One of the keys was held by the mayor; another was in possession of certain merchants (who had knowledge about the specific case and were appointed for that purpose); and the third key was with the fuller and the weaver. This suggests a sort of an administrative procedure, requiring the participation of the three professional categories.

§ 1.17.1 Regulation of 1425

April 22, 1425

Ordinances made by Our Lords the mayor and aldermen of the city and commune of Dijon, on the xxii[th] day of April after Easter, the year one thousand CCCC twenty-five, at which time was mayor Sire Étienne Chambellan, concerning the manufactures and professions hereafter declared, for the good, honor, profit and utility of the said city, and its public good, published through the said city with its horn and yell.

And first of all concerning the cloth industry. ...

VI. *Item.*—That all cloth workers and others who have been accustomed to making cloths in their workshops and elsewhere and who henceforth will make woolen cloth, shall henceforth be required to bring them to the Town Hall or the office of the officials appointed for this, three days during the week, namely: Monday, Wednesday, and Friday, at eight o'clock before noon on said days, and likewise those who want to dye them will bring them before they are dyed or immersed in dye, so that they are seen and inspected [to verify whether] they are good and admissible for dyeing, and in the case they are good they will be marked with one of the seals of the said city. And in the event that they are not good and admissible for dyeing, said clerks will pull one of the selvages of those cloths throughout, and they will not be approved for dyeing.

VII.—And when those cloths are dyed, those to whom the cloths belong shall bring them to the said chamber, so that they are seen and checked whether they are well dyed, and then they shall be marked with the other city's seal and shipped for display and sale. ...

X.—And the said clerks or others may not put and exhibit for sale those cloths until they are inspected by the clerks for this appointed and marked with the said seal, on the penalty of a fine of forty *sols* for each cloth and for each time they are caught doing the opposite, [from which fine] half will be applied to the said city and the other half to the said clerks, and that all the said cloths that are found on sale or exposed and put up for sale unmarked and unsealed shall be cut through.

§ 1.17.2 Amendment to the 1425 Regulation—1435

Ordinance on the cloth industry and its inspection.

I.—Cloths spun by the spindle: they will be of the size and thickness as their makers will see fit, and those cloths will have the selvages such as it will please the master to whom they will belong, outside or inside, in accordance with the selvage reserved to Rouen. And the said cloths will be marked with two seals and will be double-checked well and loyally by the jurors appointed for this, and if there is fault, the master to whom the cloth belongs shall amend it, or the workers or fullers or the one who has made the fault and one of the selvages shall be removed throughout or, if necessary, [the cloth] will be destroyed. ...

XII. *Item.*—For their review and work, said jurors and reviewers will have half of the cloth that they will seal and half of the fines. And there will be three keys of the small safety box: the mayor, [will keep] one; the merchants for this chosen because of their having knowledge of this [matter], the other; the fuller and the weaver, the other. ...

XIV. *Item.*—The weaver and fuller will not have with them the keys of the clerks' seals for sealing any cloths of the manner of Dijon, as provided; [the clerks are] who will carry the keys of the said seals.

XV. *Item.*—That as regards whole and half cloths that will be made in the city of Dijon, both cloths spun with a spindle and *auversins*,[11] no merchants to whom the aforementioned cloths belong will be so daring to have them in their stores or their stalls, or bring them or have them brought outside the said city, without their being marked with the seal of the said city and the said license of the said jurors, on the penalty of a fine of sixty *sols* and the city will dispose of the cloths. ...

XIX. *Item.*—That henceforth no shearers be so daring to shear or fold any cloths of the manner of the city of Dijon, before they are seen and inspected and also sealed by said clerks, on the penalty of a fine of twenty *sols tournois*.

XX. *Item.*—That no dyers dye any cloths of the manner of Dijon without their being inspected and sealed on penalty of a fine to be applied as above.

Witness the manual signature of Jehan Balier, clerk, here put in the month of December, one thousand and CCCC XXXV.

11. *Auversins*: cloths not made of wool.

§ 1.18 BY-LAWS OF THE CARPET MAKERS OF PARIS—1465

Tapestry manufacture and trade acquired great relevance in the European economy through the Middle Ages and thereafter. Carpets were not only seen as utilitarian objects that protected the walls of palaces and houses from humidity and extreme temperatures but also served as ornaments and expressions of political and religious interests. Besides ornamenting wealthy homes and palaces, carpets were also used for decorating streets and squares of some cities, welcoming illustrious visitors, or celebrating religious ephemera. Thus, since early in the Middle Ages, the tapestry industry has become an engine of economic growth and job creation. Therefore, it is not surprising that carpets were a matter of careful regulation on the use of marks (of origin as well as collective and individual marks). In tapestry, we can also devise the remote origins of the protection of industrial designs, which, in some convoluted ways, would later give rise to the first debates on the protection of fashion.

By-laws of the Merchants and Master Makers of Carpets, Blankets, Serges, and *Tiretaines.*[12]

February 15, 1465

Excerpt from the Royal Records registered at the Parliament.

> To all those who will see these present Letters, Louis Seguier, Chevalier, Baron of Saint Brisson, Lord of Ruaux and Saint Firmin, Counselor to the King our Lord, Ordinary Gentleman of his Chamber, and Guard of the Provosts of Paris: Greetings. We make known today, on the date of the Presents, We had extracted from the Second Register the pages sixty-five and sixty-six, being in the Chamber of the King's Prosecutor the following:
>
> New ordinance on the local Carpet Makers
>
> To all those who will see these present Letters, Robert d'Estouteville, Knight, Lord of Beine, Baron of Ivry and Saint Andry en la Marche, Counselor Gentleman of our Lord's Chamber, and Guard of the Provosts of Paris: Greetings . ... and also because on behalf of the Jurors and Wardens of the profession of the local Carpet Makers of Paris we were given to understand that as regards the products and the goods of the said Profession of Tapestry in the said City, it was indeed necessary to make and increase certain points and articles; for that purpose, they have given us [those points and articles] in writing, requesting that we should see and examine these articles, and add to and incorporate them into said old Ordinances and By-Laws, and order that they shall be followed, kept and observed from now on in respect of all that may be concerned, under the penalties, fines and conditions declared in the said articles, whose content follows. ...
>
> XIX.
>
> *Item.* Each Local Master Maker of Carpets shall put in each piece of work of the said Craft made by him, his mark and his sign, so as that who will have made the said

12. *Tiretaine*: a thick woollen fabric.

> piece of work will be known, on penalty of a fine of ten *sols parisis* fine to be applied as above.

§ 1.19 EDWARD IV APPROVES A STATUTE ON THE MAKING OF WORSTEDS IN THE COUNTY OF NORFOLK—1467

A statute approved by Edward IV required that the makers of worsteds print their individual marks on them so that in case of a defect, they could be identified. Following the practice, those individual marks were to be designated by the wardens, i.e., the officials in charge of inspecting and approving the cloths. The statute also provided for the affixing of a mark of certification, to be chosen and used by the wardens, "so that all Buyers may well know which Piece is sufficiently and rightfully searched and wrought."

As already noted, the statutory treatment of business identifiers in the textile industry in France and England was very similar in general, but we can nevertheless find two main differences. One has already been noted: France would put more emphasis on the use of the city's seals as collective marks than England, although this practice was not unknown to the English authorities. The second difference is that, in general, France would attribute to wardens and jurors the power to collect fees from their affixing of seals on the cloths they approved. Those officials would extract their wages from the fees they collected. By contrast, the majority of regulations dealing with English textiles established that the inspection and sealing of cloths were free of charge.

For the making of Worsteds

> First, For that there be as well within the City of Norwich, as elsewhere within the County of Norfolk, divers Persons which do make untrue Wares of all Manner of Worsted, not being of the Assise, in Length nor in Breadth, nor of good Stuff and right making as they ought to be, and of old time were accustomed, and the Sleyes and Yarn pertaining to the same not well made and wrought, in great Deceit as well of Denizens as of Strangers inhabiting or repairing to this Realm, which have used and do use to buy such Merchandises, trusting that they were within as they seemed without, where indeed it is the contrary: ...
>
> (3) Our said Lord King, by the Assent of the Lords Spiritual and Temporal, and at the Request of his Commons being in the said Parliament, and by the Authority of the said Parliament, for the Wealth of his People, and the perpetual Amendment of the said Worsted, and eschewing and avoiding all Manner of Deceits to be done and wrought in Worsteds by them that work the same, and are the Means thereof, hath ordained and established, ...
>
> V. And if any Man, before the said Mayor and Steward, or either of them, be thereof found defective, by their Discretion shall be corrected; ... (3) And that no Man of the said Craft make any Worsted, unless he put his proper Mark fixed or woven upon the same, by the Ordinance to the said Wardens, or else the said Worsted shall be forfeit to our said Lord the King.
>
> VI. Moreover, for the full reformation of the Deceits and Falsehoods above rehearsed, by Authority aforesaid it is ordained and enacted. ... (2) And if the said Wardens find the said Worsteds by their Search well and lawfully made, that then such a Mark or Token shall be set by the said Wardens, or by one of them, without Fine or Fee upon the same, so that all Buyers may well know which Piece is sufficiently and rightfully searched and wrought; and that the said Search shall as

well extend to the Stuff of the same, as to the sufficient making; (3) And such as they shall find defective, that the Mayor of the said City, and Steward of the said Duchy, or one of them for the time being, by the Assent of the said Wardens and Twelve Artificers, shall, have Power by this Act to set therein such Correction as to them shall seem reasonable; and for every Piece of Worsted sold, not marked after the Form aforesaid, That the first Seller thereof shall forfeit the Price of the Piece so by him sold, to our Lord the King; ...

§ 1.20 LOUIS XI ESTABLISHES THE MANUFACTURE OF CLOTH IN MONTPELLIER—1475

The textile industry being a powerful economic engine for growth and job creation, public authorities did not hesitate in promoting the establishment of new cloth industries. The reasons invoked by French and English sovereigns would coincide: the setting of new textile manufacturers created wealth, generated jobs, and avoided the depopulation and decay of cities.

This was again the case of the cloth industry that Louis XI authorized to be established in Montpellier, in the fifteenth century. Importantly, instead of determining the rules on the use and protection of business identifiers, the king empowered the local masters to set them and provide for their enforcement.

§ 1.20.1 Establishment of the Manufacture of Cloth in Montpellier—1475

Louis, by the grace of God, King of France, to all those who will see these letters, greetings.

We have received the humble request of our dear and well-loved consuls, bourgeois, residents, and inhabitants of our city of Montpellier, containing that our city, which sits in very good and fertile country, used to be very populous and inhabited by several remarkable merchants, and other people of various states, abundant in wealth and goods, and presently, and since some time, on the occasion of mortalities that have taken place in our kingdom and especially in our country of Languedoc, and of the wars, divisions, and passages of men-at-arms who have been in the said country, and also of the great burdens that they have agreed upon, and that each one agrees to bear, in order to provide for the very great and urgent business of ours of and our kingdom, such city is so diminished and impoverished, both of people and of means of subsistence, that half of its houses are not inhabited, and each day it diminishes and impoverishes greatly; and for which it cannot be comfortably reassured or repopulated without a large attendance of people, which they could not reach without having any new art or profession in the said city, those supplicants have advised among them to have established in our said city of Montpellier the manufacture and the art of cloth making, which seems to them the most suitable to help and restore that city, with the intention to order and conduct in it the manufacture and art of cloth making, and to keep in it the police, justice and other matters, as those that are kept by the cloth industries of our cities of Rouen and Bourges, but they would not dare to do it, nor to proceed without having our leave and license in that regard, as they say, by humbly requesting us that, since the surrounding country is furnished with good and fine wools in great abundance, and that near and joining the said city there is a small river where there is water very clean and good for said profession and art of cloth making and that, by the means of that art, the inhabitants of this city, among which there are many idle people, will exercise and occupy themselves to make it, and others will come, by whom our city will be able in any way to populate and enrich, for the good of us and the public thing of it and its surroundings, it pleases us to grant them our leave and license, and on this we shall give them our grace.

It is because of this that we, these things considered, wishing the good and growth of our said city, to the said consuls, residents and inhabitants of Montpellier, for these causes and considerations, and other motivations, we have given and granted, give and grant, by special grace, by the present [letters] leave and license that they can and decide to erect and establish in it the trade and art of sworn cloth making in our city of Montpellier, to be used and exercised, both in police and justice and in other way and manner of doing, exactly in the same manner it is used and exercised and it will be used and exercised from now on in our said cities of Rouen and Bourges. And to better conduct and maintain the said policy and in order, we have granted and accorded that they can make and write articles and chapters, in which shall be contained and written the form and order of how the work shall be performed in the manufacture and exercise of drapery, and what seals or marks, selvages, length and width the cloths must have, so that the cloths that will be there made and crafted may be known, as [it is done] in the other good sworn cities of our kingdom, where the manufacture and exercise of cloths had its course; and also that they may appoint and authorize a certain number of remarkable and knowledgeable men in that art, as many and who as they will see fit, who have the authority to visit the cloths that will be made and crafted in the said drapery, and to correct the defects that they will find in them, either by burning the cloths that will not be good and as they should be, or otherwise, and sentencing the offenders. ...

Given at Plessis du Parc les Tours, the XXIIIth day of January, the year of grace one thousand IIIIth seventy five, and of our reign the fifteenth.

On behalf of the king, master Guillaume Picart, ...

§ 1.20.2 Charles VIII, of France, Complements and Details the Regulations of Drapery of Montpellier—July 1493.

We, Charles, by the grace of God, King of France, make known to all present and to come, having received the humble supplication of our dear and well beloved consuls, bourgeois, residents and inhabitants of Montpellier, containing that, both by our late dear lord and father, may God absolve, and by us, license, and permission has been given to the said supplicants to establish in the said city the profession, art, and sworn exercise of cloth making, as well as in some of the other good cities of our kingdom, as it appears more plainly by the letters of donation to them on this granted by us as well as by our said late lord and father, by means of which, among other things, we have given them leave and license to make certain by-laws, articles and ordinances, for the good, profit and utility of the said city and the said profession, as well as of the public affairs of the country, and to prevent the faults, frauds and abuses, which, in the absence of establishing and ensuring order and compliance, could be practiced and perpetrated. For these reasons, the said supplicants, in pursuance of our leave, license and permission, and by the advice of several remarkable cloth merchants, and other persons knowledgeable of the matter, both of the city of Montpellier, and of our city of Paris, as well as others, have advised, deliberated among them, and put in writing the said by-laws, articles and ordinances, in the form and manner that follows: ...

Item, it has been ordered that, after the cloth is woven, it will be duly finished and cleaned; and, once this is done, it will be brought to the house of those who will be appointed to the inspection of the cloths, by whom those will be inspected, before they are sold and delivered to the fuller or miller. And, if it is found that they are well woven and cleaned, two small stamps of green and red wax will be placed in the middle of the top of the said cloth. And the fuller or miller shall not dare to take the said cloth for strengthening it if it has not been previously sealed, under the penalty of a fine of sixty *sols tournois*, the third party [to be applied] to the king, the other third party to the offenders' charity and fraternity, and the other third party to the said clerks' pension fund, to be received by their clerks as well as for the measuring, as it is provided next. And the sealed cloth will be brought by the fuller or miller, for completing his duty; and it will be brought by the fuller or miller to the house of the appointed persons or jurors; and the cloth shall be sealed with a seal of lead at the end of the top of the said cloth, which seal shall be on one side the majesty of the king, and on the other the arms of the said lord. ...

Item, and after the cloth is set and finished well and duly by the master, as it belongs and is the custom of the city of Perpignan, the master shall be required, before he brings the cloth to the controller, to bring the cloth again to the house of the clerks and jurors; and it will be visited by them, and at least by three clerks, provided that one of them is a master, a weaver, a citizen or a merchant, who will pass the cloth by the perch, in the place for this determined; and if it is acknowledged to be of good quality, well woven and finished to their knowledge, it shall be ordered that a small sign be placed on the city's arms, which lead will have, as a mark, the city's arms on one side, and Our Lady on the other side, for which seal one *denier tournai* shall be paid, which seal will be named Seal of license, and afterwards, when it will please to the cloth owner to have it sealed with another seal of square lead, there it will have Fy as sign, and on the other side it will be Our Lady, having at her feet the coat of arms of the city, for which he will pay nothing. And if it happens that the cloth is found to be of not enough quality or poorly woven, instead of the seal of license [it will be sealed] with another small seal of lead, which on one side will be Our Lady and on the other side will have no impression; and, instead of the Fy sign, it will be sealed, under the city arms, with another small seal of lead, which will be named Seal of megem, which will have on one side for sign L., which will mean Loyal, and on the other side Our Lady. ...

And if the cloth owner feels grieved, he may appeal to the eight counselors, so that they decide what in accordance with God and their consciences should be done. ...

Item, it has been ordered that no cloth, no matter how good it is, shall not be sealed in the city, if it is not woven and finished by the masters of that city, and bearing theirs marks. ...

Given at Paris, in the month of July, the year of grace, one thousand IIII ninety-three, and of our reign, the tenth.

§ 1.21 BY-LAWS OF THE WOOLLEN CLOTHMAKERS OF AMIENS (1480, 1494, AND 1511) AND PARIS (1481)

The introduction of a new industry in France, known as sayetterie (this term meaning the manufacture of cloths—saies or sayes—made of Spanish wool, and lighter than the traditional cloths), before the end of the fifteenth century, led to the setting of specific rules. As a matter of course, these new cloths did not observe the technical standards then in force, hence the need for imposing new ones. As it had already become the practice, the new cloths had to be inspected, certified, and distinguished by means of business identifiers.

The following texts mirror the legislative practice that had already been developed and settled as far as the regulation of the textile industry was concerned. They show, however, a few aspects that are worth noticing. The by-laws partly transcribed in the first text provided that in case someone bought a flawed saie, the customer was entitled to recover the loss directly from the seller. This contrasts with the general rule that a faulty cloth would generate the payment of a fine, whose beneficiaries could vary: the wardens, the king's treasury, the poor members of the corporation, or the whistleblower. Moreover, the first by-laws mention the mandatory registration of the masters' marks, prior to their use. It is not clear whether this implied some sort of examination of the masters' signs, but at least the statute was unequivocal in that the marks would be chosen by the masters themselves, not by the magistrates of the guild.

The third text, from the standing of trademark law, is surprisingly modern. First, it implies that in the city hall of Amiens at the beginning of the sixteenth century, there existed a centralized register of trademarks. Second, the use of trademarks by clothmakers and shearers was under the condition that they should be absolutely identical to those that were filed with the city hall (a requirement that applies today; failure to comply with this requirement leads to the cancellation of the trademark registration). Third, the compensation for defective cloths was to be paid directly to the merchants who had consigned the materials to be worked upon by the artisans.

Of course, the modernity of these statutes stops here. Those trademarks were still basically aimed at ensuring compliance with technical standards, not of simply distinguishing products and appropriating reputation, as of today's trademarks.

The fourth text provides an interesting example of the prohibition of passing-off.

§ 1.21.1 By-Laws of the *Sayeteurs* of Amiens—1480

Whereas on behalf of Regnault Hanon, Pierre Parent ... all merchant workers in the profession of *sayeterie* in the said city of Amiens, we have been presented in our municipality with some requests, containing certain articles in respect of the said trade, so as to make us maintain the said trade and merchandise in such recommendation and honesty as it had long been in the incorporated city in which they have lived, it pleases us to cause them to have stamp and sign to put and affix to the *saies* that would be made in this city, along with briefs and ordinances to maintain and keep it in good order and justice, as we will see to be done for the good of the said city and its trade; ...

7. *Item*, no one shall put the *saies* of the trade on sale, unless they are not signed with the small seal set for this purpose, displaying the arms of the said city, proving that they will have been made in this city; and if they work on some [*saies*] brought from the outside, they will not carry the said stamp. ...

22. *Item*, no master of the said trade shall make or cause to be made *sayes*, unless they have first put and brought their marks to the public register [*papier*] of

the said city of Amiens, so that, if fraud is found in any *saies* sold or otherwise, that the buyers can recover from the one whose *saie* will bear the mark.

§ 1.21.2 New By-Laws of the Clothmakers and Tailors of Amiens—1494

... To all those who see these present letters, the mayor and aldermen of the city and town of Amiens, greetings. ... we make known that, having seen the said request and the advice given on it in the council of aldermen, we, for the good of the said supplicants [the masters and companions of the trade of cloth making], and for the sake of the said cloth industry and the public good, have ordered and order to those supplicants, in the form of briefs and ordinances, the points and articles hereafter declared: ...

15. *Item*, we have also ordered, in addition to and in conformity with the points above declared, that henceforth no master tailor of the said city shall receive any cloths from the weavers of that city, unless those cloths are appropriately marked with the marks of the weavers who have delivered them, so that those tailors can resell good, strong, fair, and well-finished cloths, with two aunes[13] in white and dyed, on the penalty for each infringement of a fine of sixty *sols parisis*, to apply as follows: forty *sols parisis* of the fine to the said city, ten *sols parisis* to the guild and ten *sols parisis* to the wardens of the said trade.

§ 1.21.3 New By-Laws of the *Sayeteurs* of Amiens—1511

January 19, 1511

To all those who see these letters, the mayors and aldermen of the city and town of Amiens, greetings. We make known, as usual, on behalf of Regnault Talmant, Huchon Malapart, ... upon mature deliberation of this council, that we have ordered the said *saieteurs* to keep, maintain, observe, and use [these new regulations] from now on, in addition to their ancient regulations, for the sake of the aforesaid trades and the public good, in the form and manner that follows: ...

11. *Item*, the said merchants, dyers and fullers shall put in each piece of satin that they will dye and full a mark, for which purpose they shall have in their possession two small engraved iron wedges to be used for the underside, in which there will be a large A engraved, for the meaning of Amiens, and above it such a mark as of their name or sign they will want, to put above, in the other corner, on a small lead that the said dyers and fullers shall put at their expense in each of the said pieces, before returning them to the merchants or other persons, on such penalty and fine as above.

12. *Item* that, before any one can use said methods of dyeing and fulling or be received[14] by or work in the said trades, they shall take for that purpose their mark as it said and have it registered at the city hall, along with their names and surnames, so as to make it possible to identify those who have used the said methods and may have made a mistake as regards those satins and be found negligent in failing to comply with the said ordinance, on the same penalty as above.

---

13. *Aune (aulne* or *anne)*: old length measurement.
14. *Reception* was the passage of an apprentice to the grade of companion or of a companion to that of master.

13. *Item*, also that henceforth all those, be they men or women, who may wish to deal with the aforesaid satins, before they can exercise the said profession, shall register with the registry of the said city and file in it the mark or sign they will want to use, exactly identical to those they shall sew to the other side of the seal of each satin by them sheared, which will give knowledge of whether any mistake has been made by the aforesaid shearers in their shearing, so as to return the interest to the merchant as reasonable, on such penalty and fine, to be applied as above. ...

§ 1.21.4 By-Laws of the *Sayeteurs* of Paris—1481

September 20, 1481

Letters from the Provost of Paris concerning the by-laws of the *sayeteurs*, in twenty-four articles.

To all those who will see these present letters, Jaques d'Estouteville, in the presence and with the consent of all the workers of the said trade above named, and of several others in large number, by these present [letters] before us, whose content that follows they have promised and sworn by oath to maintain and observe, without infringement, on the penalties which ensue, we have ruled, ordered, and established, rule, order, and establish: ...

10. *Item*, and so that the aforesaid defects can be more obviously noticed and that no one can be excused, each master will be held to have his mark different from the others', and which will be known by the jurors; which mark they shall put at the bottom of their works as well as of those [cloths] they will cause to be worked, so as to punish the infringers according to the circumstances of the case and [shall] not seal nor put on sale the *sayes* that will be found unmarked or wrongly marked.

11. *Item*, and no worker of the said trade shall take the mark of another worker and mark [with] other signs or marks, on penalty of a fine of ten *livres parisis*, from which eight pounds shall apply to the King and the forty *sols* to the jurors.

§ 1.22 BY-LAWS OF THE CLOTH SHEARERS OF PARIS—1483

The following text, which applied to another specialized profession within the textile industry—the shearing of wool—contains provisions similar to those of the previous texts, as far as business identifiers are concerned. Remarkably, its language shows that this regulation was an addendum to existing by-laws, dealing specifically with business identifiers. This gives a good measure of the significant importance that the proper use of distinctive signs in the textile industry had acquired at the end of the fifteenth century.

September 24, 1483

Letters from the Provost of Paris homologating four statutes for the shearers of cloth

To all those who will see these present letters, Jacques d'Estouteville, guard of the Provosts of Paris, we make known that we have seen some of the articles submitted by the shearers of cloth, whose content is as follows: ...

3. *Item*, that henceforth every master of the said trade shall have a mark, with which they shall mark each piece of cloth that they will shear or cause to be sheared, on the penalty above.

4. *Item*, that no master of the said trade shall henceforth shear or cause to be sheared any cloth marked with the mark of another master of the said trade, on the said penalty of a fine of sixty *sols parisis*, to be applied as provided.

And they agree that these articles be adjusted and added to their by-laws, so that they be fully kept, maintained, understood and observed.

This was made on Wednesday, the twentieth-fourth day of September, the year one thousand four hundred eighty-three.

§ 1.23 REUNION OF VARIOUS PROFESSIONS DEALING WITH CARPETS UNDER THE SAME CORPORATION—PARIS, 1490

One of the characteristics of the corporatist regime was the fierce defense that each profession made of securing exclusivity in its trade. Frequently, disputes between workers whose skills were complementary ended up in court, when they did not result in physical fights. Most guild by-laws were carefully drafted so as to specifically identify who could make what. It has already been suggested that, to a large extent, certain court disputes concerning the boundaries of each profession were not very different from today's lawsuits involving the interpretation of patent claims.

The choice of the professions that gathered under one single guild depended on a variety of factors, and particularly on the type of technology used, but political pressure also played a dominant role. In obedience to those pressures, and with the main purpose of avoiding disputes between masters and companions, the mapping of the borders between professions could vary.

Anyway, as in the case that follows, the organization or reorganization of labor could not do without rules on the certification of compliance with technical standards.

Incorporation of Master Carpet Makers and Local Workers of Carpets, with Carpet Merchants—Workers of Tapestry, Tents, and Pavilions, etc.

March 25, 1490

To all those who will see the Present Letters, Jacques d'Estoureville, Knight, Lord of Beyne and Blainville, Baron of Ivry and of Saint Andry in the March, Counselor, gentleman of the Chamber of the King our Lord, and Guard of the Provosts of Paris: Greetings. We make known that, having seen the request made to us in writing and submitted on behalf of the Jurors Workers-Carpet Makers and of the Jurors Workers of Tapestry, Tents and Pavilions, Merchants of Tapestry of this city of Paris, whose contents follow.

To Monsieur the Provost of Paris or his Deputy, the Jurors Tapestry Workers and the Jurors Workers of Tapestry, Tents and Pavilions, Merchants of Tapestry of the city of Paris, given that thus far they have moved and started several court disputes between the said Supplicants concerning the said Trades and the Inspections and masterpieces of the said gentlemen, as well as concerning the inspection and approval of every article of Tapestry, Serges and Blankets that are brought from outside this city of Paris, and so as to avoid court disputes and debates between the said Parties, and that each of the said Masters, and their workers may henceforth live in peace, without disputes, debates, or challenges; and for the sake of the public good, they have gathered and agreed, if it pleases you, in the form and manner that follow, that is to know: ...

III.

Item. As far as the Products and Goods that come and are brought from outside the city of Paris to this city are concerned, they shall not be approved, seen or inspected unless there are two Jurors [of the Carpets makers], and two Jurors of the Workers of Canopies, Tents and Pavilions, and Merchants, at least one from each of those Trades, which Jurors [of those two Trades], when they see and inspect them, and find them good, fair, and tradeable, they shall mark them with a seal of lead marked with the arms of the city of Paris, on one side, and on the other it will be written PARIS.

§ 1.24 BY-LAWS OF THE SAIETEURS OF LILLE—1500

The following text is an excerpt from another regulation concerning the sayeteurs that comes to us from the Flanders, a region whose manufacture and trade of woollen cloths were of enormous importance. According to the practice then in force across Europe, cloths were marked with individual marks as well as with certification signs. The former were registered with an official body of inspectors—another early instance of trademark registration.

February 27, 1500

Ordinances and constitutions made by the very honorable lords, gentlemen of accounts and aldermen of this city of Lille on the matter of the new *saieterie* erected and established in this said city, followed by the grant by our very dreaded lord and prince the Duke of Austria and Burgundy, earl of Flanders. ...

XXXI.—*Item* that all those men and women of the said trade of *saieterie* who will make or cause *saies* to be made in the said city shall have a mark for marking the said *saies*, which will be different one from another, so as to acknowledge from whose hands those *saies* will originate; they shall register those marks at the register of the *vingtaine*,[15] for which they shall pay to the clerk XII *deniers* for the registration as said, and if any of those makers of *saies* fail to adopt a mark and to register it as said and to mark the *saies* that they made or caused to be made, they will be fined on XL *sols* of the said currency each time they do so and in addition they shall be arbitrarily punished. ...

XXXIV.—*Item* and for the sake of the said trade there shall be a stamp and seal with which the *saies* shall be sealed at the looms, which stamp or seal shall be bailed and put in the hand of the officials of the said *vingtaine* on the day they will be sworn, which seals or stamps shall be printed and marked as follows: one with the lily flower, and the other with the word "vingtaine," written as "vingtaine."

15. The "vingtaine" is defined by Article 1 of the by-laws as a body of six men, namely, two wardens to be designated each year under the law; two bourgeois merchants of *saies* of Lille; and two masters of the city's guild of *saieterie*. The six men "will be designated [collectively] as *vingtaine* and will be renewed every year under the law of the city." Later, the number of the members of the *vingtaine* was increased to eight.

XXXVI.—*Item* and likewise there will be two other stamps or seals with which the *saies* shall be stamped or sealed when they are brought to the market, which will be larger than the stamp and seal above mentioned, on whose edge a lily flower and a little lion shall be printed, and to the other stamp or seal the said word "vingtaine" and the Sunday letter of the year shall be imprinted; and the stamp bearing the said Sunday letter will be broken every year and renewed according to each year's Sunday letters, in order to recognize in which year the said *saies* are stamped and sealed by those officials.

XXXVII.—*Item* there shall be yet another stamp or seal with which the *saies* that will be inspected by those officials of the *vingtaine* shall be marked in the cases they have not been approved as good by those officials; those stamps or seals shall bear the same marks mentioned above except that the lily flower shall be stricken through and the said seal or stamp shall be smaller than the large stamp mentioned above.

§ 1.25 FERNANDO AND ISABEL, OF SPAIN, APPROVE A GENERAL REGULATION ON THE CLOTH INDUSTRY, INCLUDING DETAILED PROVISIONS ON CERTIFICATION AND INDIVIDUAL MARKS—1500

The wealth that Spain acquired from its maritime expansion in the fourteenth and fifteenth centuries was partly used in promoting the growth of its industry and trade in cloths. Spain was the origin of merino wool, a raw material that was avidly sought after by clothmakers across Europe. As we have seen, its use has even given place to the emerging of a specialized category of industry and its artisans: the saieterie (or sayeterie or sayetterie) and the sayeteurs. Some regulations were passed both by national and local authorities with the purpose of organizing the growing textile industry. The following text provides for excerpts from a regulation on Spain's cloth industry, as approved by the Catholic kings, Fernando and Isabel.

The regulation's long preamble is interesting to the extent that, in mentioning the usual acts of counterfeiting as regards cloths made in different cities, it reveals the intense competition among cities in their exportation—thus emphasizing the importance of geographical indications as elements of differentiation. Also interesting is an element that appears in similar statutes of other countries: the reference to the public good as the justification for the measures and sanctions.

From today's standing, it is worth noticing that this statute admitted some flexibility as to the apposition of collective and individual trademarks (and the prohibition of passing off), provided that potential customers could distinguish the cloth's real geographical origin and maker.

The cover page of the booklet containing this regulation shows a summary of the industrial privilege obtained by the printer, Niculoso de Monardis Ginoves (see Figure *7).*

Royal ordinances made by the king and queen our lords on cloths: printed with movable types in the city of Seville by Niculoso de Monardis Ginoves; with the privilege from their highnesses that no one else can print or sell the said ordinances in all their kingdoms and lordships within three years under a certain penalty contained in the letter of privilege from their highnesses: and orders that the price of the said ordinances be ten and seven *maravedís*.

Don Fernando and doña Isabel by the grace of God King and Queen of Castile, Leon, Aragón ... To those of our council and magistrates of our chamber; mayors; sheriffs; officials; members of the council of twenty-four; aldermen; jurors; knights; squires; officials and good men of all the cities and towns and places of our kingdoms and lordships, both those who now are and those who will be henceforth; and to the merchants and weavers and shearers and dyers and fullers and other any people our subjects and to any of you, health and grace. Be informed that because it has been reported to us that in some parts and places of our kingdoms where cloths were made and worked on behalf and at the charge of the masters who made and sheared and dyed them and that several of those [cloths] that they caused to be made, because of their malice and malpractice, presented certain defects; and that in each city or town or place of our kingdoms where the said cloths are made, these cloths were made in accordance with standards and techniques different from what they should have been, not in pursuance of the technique and art according to which they should have been made, but because they were not made in the manner as they should be; and existing, by the grace of our lord, in our kingdoms many looms both of fine wools and of dyes and masters for making the said cloths perfect and that each one who wove the said cloths has made the signs and selvages that they wished in a manner that caused them to be unknown and that those who bought them for dressing did not know what kind of cloths they were buying; therefore the public good of our kingdoms has been greatly deceived; and we, caring for and wishing the public good of our kingdoms and of our subjects and natural of them, have brought masters from some cities and towns and places of our said kingdoms and lordships where cloths are worked and made; and we have ordered to those of our council that they talked and communicated with those masters about the manner that they thought it should be from now on, so that the cloths were well and perfectly made and those who would buy them knew what they were buying and there would be no place for deceits or for one [cloth] being sold for another. And all this having been seen and discussed in our council it has been agreed that we should order that from now on all the cloths that are made in our kingdoms, since the first day of January of the coming year of one thousand and five hundred and one onwards, shall be made, sheared, worked, and fulled in accordance with the following ordinances and form. ...

Weavers

Moreover, we establish and order that each weaver shall put on the cloth he weaves, whatever its type or quality, regardless of it being his own or of another, the sign of the city or town or place where he weaves it, on the penalty of sixty *maravedis* for each cloth that he weaves without putting the said sign; and that no weaver dare to put or weave the sign of another city or town or place ...; and the weaver who does it willingly shall pay one thousand *maravedís* of penalty for each cloth that he makes, from which penalty one third [goes] to our chamber, and the other third to the accuser, and the other third to the said magistrates; and if there is no accuser, let it be split in half between our chamber and the said magistrates. Furthermore, that besides the sign of the city or town or place where the cloths are woven that each weaver has to put on the cloths that he weaves, he shall put his own mark on the cloth; and that no weaver dare to put on the cloth he weaves the mark of another and to put his sign on the cloth that another weaves, unless each weaver puts his mark on the cloth that he weaves in such a way that those who look at it can clearly and recognize in which city the cloth has been made and which weaver has woven it, under the penalty of sixty *maravedís*, for each cloth on which he fails to put his mark or for each mark of his own that is put on the cloth that another weaves; which [penalty] shall go to the said magistrates. ...

Given in the very noble, renowned, and great city of Granada, on the fifteenth day of the month of September, Year of the birth of our savior Jesus Christ of one thousand and five hundred.

Figure 7 Cover page of the booklet containing the general regulation of the cloth industry, as approved by the king and queen of Spain, in 1500.

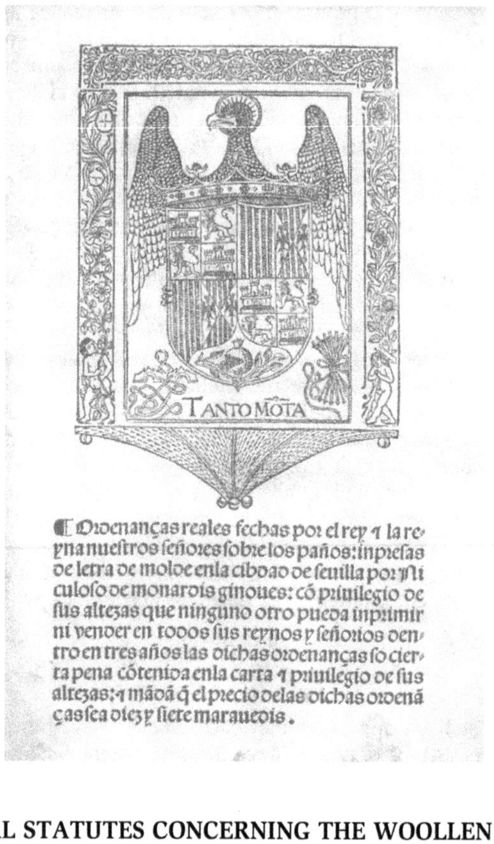

§ 1.26 SEVERAL STATUTES CONCERNING THE WOOLLEN CLOTH INDUSTRY APPROVED BY HENRY VIII OF ENGLAND—1511, 1513, 1523, 1535, 1541—AND BY EDWARD VI—1549, 1551

King Henry VIII, of England, has approved several statutes regulating the woollen cloth industry. Six samples follow. Four of them concerned the industry in general throughout the realm and contained the normal rules ordering the use of seals of certification, which was to be affixed by the alnager (the civil servant in charge of inspecting cloths) as well as individual marks. The other two texts are specific to certain cloths made in specific cities, some of which contain detailed provisions on the use of individual marks, which should be distinctive, and explicitly prohibiting the passing-off.

Interestingly, the second text implies that the cloths in question (white-straits) had been invented in Devon, and that was the reason why the city had specialized itself in making and selling them. Perhaps because of such uniqueness, the statute does not make reference to the mandatory use of certification seals.

The four last texts associate seals with labels, to the extent they should contain the true measure of the cloths, so as to inform buyers and sellers. Significantly, the fourth text is unequivocal in attributing greater importance to those labels than to individual trademarks. In its last paragraph the owners of cloths—be they their makers or the merchants who had ordered their making—are dispensed from the obligation to put their individual seals on the cloths.

The last text shows that, under Edward VI, the Parliament's patience with counterfeiting had run thin: the penalties were significantly increased. In the case of recidivism, the counterfeiter, besides other penalties, would sit on the pillory—a penalty at that time usually reserved for thieves.

§ 1.26.1 An Act Against Deceitful Making of Woollen Cloth—1511

For the deceitful draping and making of woollen clothes made and draped within the Realm, And also for measuring in sale the same, Our Sovereign Lord the King by advice and assent of his Lords spiritual and temporal and the Commons in this present parliament and by authority of the same hath ordained, established, and enacted divers ordinances and statutes for the true making and draping of such woollen clothes and for measuring in sales the true content of the same in manner and form following; ...

Item that the Alnager or Seller after the said feast of Midsummer next coming reasonably required shall put to every Woollen cloth made and draped within the circuit or precinct of his office to be sold by the King's Seals of lead and not put to any such clothes any seals of wax in any wise upon pain of forfeiture for every cloth sealed otherwise than with lead iij s. iiij d. ...

§ 1.26.2 An Act for the True Making of Cloths in Devon, Called *White-Straits*—1513

Prayen the Commons and Inhabitants (Cloth makers, and Buyers of the Same) within the County of Devon, that where divers and many Cloths, called *White-Straits*, be and have been continually made within the said County, to the great Profit of the King's Subjects there, the which Cloths were wont to be well and sufficiently made, and bear their Breadth Yard broad and half Quarter raw, and fifteen Yards of Length, and that no Man in Times past hath used to make them, but that the Maker thereof hath set his special Mark upon every of the said Cloths so by him or them made, whereby every Man may know their own Cloths from other Men's by reason of their said several Marks; (2) so it is, that nowadays the said Cloths be not sufficiently made, nor bear their Length and Breadth according as they should do, neither marked with every Man's own Mark, whereof great Inconvenience doth daily ensue and increase, to the impoverishing and hurting, as well of the King's Subjects, Buyers and Sellers of the same, as of Merchant Strangers; (3) Wherefore, the Premises considered, that it may be therefore enacted by the King our Sovereign Lord, by the Assent of the Lords Spiritual and Temporal, and the Commons, in this present Parliament assembled, and by the Authority of the same, That from the Feast of Pentecost next coming, no Person make no such Cloths (called *White-Straits*) to sell, without that he be when he is raw ready to be toked, of the Breadth of a Yard and Half a Quarter, and of Length fifteen Yards; (4) and that no Person make no such Cloths, but if he set his special Mark upon every of the said Cloths, so by him or them made; (5) And that no Person use no Mark on his Cloths such as any other Person doth and hath used before him, upon Pain of Forfeiture of every of the said Cloths, the one Half to the King, and the other Half to him that so seized the said Cloths, so made or marked contrary to the Form and Effect afore expressed; (6) and this Act to endure unto the next Parliament.

§ 1.26.3 Statute That Concerns the Draping of Worsteds Sayes[16] and Stamyns[17] for the Town[s] of Great Yarmouth [And Lynne]—1523

Because it is discretely considered in this present parliament that the true making and draping of Worsteds Sayes and Stamyns is one of the most profitable occupations of this Realm, And that the same Worsteds Sayes and Stamyns truly and substantially made and wrought been right acceptable and commodious merchandises as well in this Realm of England as in other foreign regions and countries; For establishment and good order whereof divers good and laudable statutes, acts and ordinances have been made and enacted, ... And because the Towns of Great Yarmouth and Lynne in the said County [have] been incorporated, and the inhabitants of the same Towns now daily practice and use the making and draping of the said Clothes of Worsteds Sayes and Stamyns more busily and diligently then they have done in times past, to whom it is painful and costly to transport and convey the said Clothes to the City of Norwich or to places within the said County of Norff which [are] far distant from either of the said Towns, to be searched and sealed by the Wardens of the Worsted Weavers of the same City of Norwich or County ...

And that the said Warden of the said Town of Great Yarmouth for the time being so elected and sworn, may ordain and appoint a seal whit this letter Y to be graven in the same seal, and may have full power and authority to view, search, cease, and seal in lead, with the same seal so to be appointed and engraved and none other, all Worsted Sayes and Stamyns within the said Town of Yarmouth and suburbs of the same made or to be made and not elsewhere ... .

And that no person inhabited within the said Town, except he be an Englishman born and have been apprentice to the said occupation, and without he weave therein such proper mark as shall be limited and appointed by the said Warden of the said Town for the time being elected and sworn as is aforesaid, upon pain of forfeiture thereof to the King our Sovereign Lord; And that every Warden of the said Town shall limit, distinct, and several marks to every of the said

16. Here the term *sayes* does not have the same meaning as in French statutes. *Sayes*, here, means blankets.
17. Worsteds of a larger size.

Worsted Weavers of the same Town of Great Yarmouth, and the same marks by the said Warden to be registered in a Book.

[Identical provisions as regards the Town of Lynne follow, except that the Warden's seal for Lynne contained the letter L, instead of Y].

§ 1.26.4 An Act for True Making of Woollen Cloths—1535

Forasmuch as great infamy and slander hath risen of late years in sundry outward parties beyond the Sea of the untrue making of Woollen Clothes within this Realm, to the great derogation of the Common well of the same and to the no little hindrance of the sale of the said commodity; For remedy whereof be it ordained and enacted by the King our Sovereign Lord, the Lords spiritual and temporal and the Commons in this present Parliament assembled and by authority of the same, that after the feast of Saint Michell the Archangel next coming all and every Clothier within this Realm shall weave or cause to be woven his or their several token or mark in all and every cloth kersey and other cloths whatsoever they be, made and wrought to be uttered and sold; and when any such cloth shall be ready made and dressed to put to sale every of the same Clothiers shall set his seal of lead unto every of the same his or their Clothes and Kerseys, in which seal of lead shall be contained the true and just length of every of the same Clothes or Kerseys, as it shall be duly found by every buyer of the same upon due proof thereof to be tried by water; And in case upon any such proof to be made by any buyer of them at the water there shall be found less or smaller content than is contained and specified in every of their said seals, than every of the said Clothiers making such default shall lose and forfeit unto every such buyer of the same the double value of so much cloth as shall want and lack of his said content and length, at the only sight and judgment of any two indifferent persons that shall measure the same Clothes and Kerseys; And every Clothier sending or putting any of their Clothes to sale, before such time as all and every of the same Clothes shall be sealed by the Aunager of the same Counties where it shall chaunce any of the said Clothes so to be made, and also to be ordered and sealed by every of the said Clothiers in form aforesaid, shall lose and forfeit his cloth or clothes whatsoever they be; the one half thereof shall be to the King's Highness, his heirs and successors, and the other half to him or them that will sue for the same by bill plaint action of debt or otherwise, in which action no wager of Law or protection shall be allowed. ...

And be it further enacted by the said authority that the aunager of any County shall not seal any of the said clothes with the King's seal, until such time as they and every of them shall be first ordered and sealed with their contents according to the true meaning of this present act in form aforesaid, upon pain of leasing of his office; And that no buyer of any of the said clothes or kerseys marked and sealed in form aforesaid presume by any manner of slight means or engines to draw pull or to stretch out any of the same cloths or kerseys, otherwise than to make them even after they be wet, and to agree with the contents specified and contained in the seal of every of the same clothes and Kerseys as near as they can; upon pain to forfeit the double value of every cloth or Kersey so misused to the true intent and meaning of this present act, to be levied to the use of the King's Highness and of any other that will sue for the same in like manner and form as is before declared.

Provided always that all Cloth hereafter made to be sold within the City of Worcetour, the Towns of Droitwiche, Evesham, Kedermynster, and Bromesgrove, in the County of Worcetour, shall be sealed with the seal of the Searchers there, according to an act of parliament in that behalf provided and made the xxv. year of the reign of our said Sovereign Lord; And that the Owners of the Clothes made within the said City and Towns shall not be compelled by this Act to put their own seals to any clothes there made or hereafter to be made.

§ 1.26.5 An Act for the True Making of Kerseys—1541

Where at the Parliament at London in the third day of November in the one and twentieth year of our most dread Sovereign Lord the King most gracious reign that now is, and from thence adjourned to Westminster and there continued by sundry prorogations unto the fourth day of February in the xxviith year of his reign, It was ordered and enacted ... that every Clothier within this Realm should set his seal of lead unto every Cloth and Kersey that should be ready made and dressed to be put to sale, in which seal of lead should be contained the true and just content of the length of every of the same Cloths and Kerseys as it should be duly found by every buyer of the same upon due proof to be tried by water; And in case upon any such proof to be made by any buyer of them at the water there should be found less and smaller content in length than should be contained and specified in every of the said seals, then that every such clothier making such default should lose and forfeit unto every such buyer of the same the double value of so much cloths as should want or lack of his said content in length, at the only sight and judgment of any two indifferent persons that should measure the said Cloths and Kerseys.

§ 1.26.6 An Act for the True Making of Woollen Clothes—1549

Forasmuch as by the slate and subtle making of Clothes and Colors within divers parts of this Realm, now of late practiced and used, not only great infamies and slanders have grown to the same Realm, but also the King's Majesties faithful and true Subjects have sustained great loss in the use and wearing of the same Clothes so slightly and subtly made: For remedy and reformation whereof, be it ordained and enacted by the King's most Excellent Majesty with the assent of the Lords spiritual and temporal of the Commons in this present Parliament assembled and by authority of the same: That every Clothier and Clothes maker shall from the feats of the Annunciation of our Lady next coming set his seal of lead to his Cloth, declaring thereby the just lengths thereof to be tried by the water; ...

§ 1.26.7 An Act for the Making of Woollen Cloth—1551

We are heretofore advised and many goodly Statutes have been made for the true making of Cloth within the Realm, which nevertheless, Forasmuch as Clothiers, some for lack of knowledge and experience and some of extreme covetousness, do daily more and more study rather to make many than to make good Clothes, having more respect to their private commodity and gain than the advancement of truth and continuance of the commodity in estimation according to the worthiness thereof, have and do daily instead of truth practiced falsehood, and instead of substantial making of Cloth, do practice slight and slender making, some by mingling of Yarns of divers spinnings in one Clothe, some by mingling Fell Wool and Lamb's Wool or either of them with Fleece Wool, some by putting too little Stuff, some by taking them out of the mill before they be full thicked, some by overstretching them upon the tentor and then stopping with flocks such bracks as shall be made by means thereof, finally by using so many subtle sleight and untruth as when the Clothes so made be put in the water to try them, they rise out of the same neither in length or breadth as they ought to do and in some place narrower then some, beside such cockling, banding, and divers other great and notable faults as almost cannot be thought to be true; And yet nevertheless neither fearing the law in that case provided, nor regarding the estimation of their Country, do not only procure the Alnager to set the King his seal to such false and untrue Clothe, but do themselves weave into the same the likeness and the similitude of the King His Highness most noble and imperial Crown, and also the first letter of his name, which should be testimony of truth and not a defence of untruth, to the great slander of the King our Sovereign Lord and the shame of this land, and to the utter destruction of so great and notable commodity as the like is not in any foreign Nation; Our said Sovereign Lord the King therefore minding to advance all truth and to abandon falsehood, and also to provide for the continuance of the said commodity of Cloth making to his honor and the common profit of the Realm ... It is enacted as hereafter follows, ...

And be it further enacted by the same authority, that as well the said Mayor of the City of London as every other Mayor, Bailiff, Portreeve, or other head Officer of every City, Borough, Town corporate, or Port Town, shall on this side [of] the said Feast cause to be prepared a seal of lead, wherein as well the Arms as the name of every such City, Borough, Town corporate, or Port town shall be graved, which the same Searchers shall cause to be fixed to every Cloth that they shall find after the said Feast well and sufficiently dressed, died, and pressed with the cold press without any [of] the deception aforesaid, and shall have for their pains and travails therein to be taken by the Owner thereof for the sealing of every Cloth two pence.

And be it further enacted, that if any Searcher or Searchers so to be appointed do after the said feast, find any of the Clothes being colored or died so made after the said feast either cockely, pursy, bondy, squally, or rowy, or evil burled or wasted in the mill, or full of holes or bracks, then the same searcher or searchers shall besides the seal of the City, boroughs, or town corporate where the same Clothe shall be found, put another seal of Lead at every end of the said Clothe, wherein shall be graven the letter F. and shall also set a mark in the list right against such place where any of the faults aforesaid shall be, with the print of a letter or mark of an inch compass at the least, whereby every buyer may well know what and where the fault is. ...

And be it further enacted, that if any person or persons but such as are appointed, assigned, and permitted by this Act, do at any time after the said feast counterfeit, set or take away from any of the Clothes, Kerseys, Frocks, Rugs, or Cottons aforesaid any of the Seals so to be fixed as is above recited, that then every person so offending shall for the first Offence, being thereof duly convicted by verdict of twelve men by two sufficient witnesses, or by confession of the party, forfeit and lose ten pounds, and for the second Offence being likewise thereof convicted, shall sit on the Pillory, and lose and forfeit to our Sovereign Lord the King all such his goods and chattels his debt being duly and truly paid without fraud or covyn, as he had or shall have at the time of his conviction. ...

Figure 8 A sixteenth-century wool weaver working at a high (vertical) loom. Engraving by Jost Amman, 1568.

§ 1.27 BY-LAWS OF THE *SAIETEURS* OF ABBEVILLE—1518

As another expression of the importance that the saieterie gained in the sixteenth century in France, excerpts from another regulation, this time concerning the industry of Abbeville, follows. The rules on the use of business identifiers by that industry were already consolidated by then, namely the mandatory use of the city's seal to be affixed upon inspection and approval by the wardens; and the use of individual trademarks. The example now given has two aspects that later would become practice: individual trademarks were not a matter of free choice by the masters, but they were chosen by the wardens; and the city's seal was to be kept in a locked safe, with its corresponding keys being assigned to certain officials under detailed rules. We have seen above a somewhat similar scheme, but in that case, the safe received all marks, both certification and masters' individual marks (see § 1.17.2). Later, this system of control of trademarks would be replaced by a system of registration in centralized offices, either with the guilds or with the municipalities.

> To all those who will see or have these letters, the mayor and aldermen of the city of Abbeville, greetings. Because several masters of the trade of *saieterie*, provided with 24 looms, tools of the said trade, have come to live in this town to use and work in the said trade where they have already started working, and supplicated us for granting them some briefs, ordinances, and by-laws concerning that trade, to avoid the frauds and abuses that might be committed according to the articles presented to us, which we have seen, inspected and corrected in our council, we inform that we, considering the said request to be fair and reasonable for the sake, profit, and utility of the public good of the city, which could be better populated and from which trade several poor people could earn their living, have made in respect of the said profession the edicts, ordinances, and by-laws that follow, which nevertheless, by using our authority, justice and privilege, we may correct, increase or decrease for the sake of the said city and of the said guild any time that we will deem convenient, by ordering them to keep and maintain the said ordinances and statutes, on the penalties and fines and by paying the duties as hereafter will be declared. …
>
> 11. *Item*, at the place set for the inspection of the said *sayes* or satins there will be a safety box with five locks, where the stamps and seals of the said city will be locked, of which the provost or clerk for the city will have one of the keys, without which it will not be possible to open the safe: two aldermen appointed for this purpose, each [one will have] a key, one of which will be able to open two locks, and at least two of the guards, and in the absence of the others, the other two different keys.
>
> 12. *Item*, the said masters shall not work in a workshop in the said city, unless they first come to seek and take their sign or mark at the city hall, and in doing so they shall call for the wardens, who will find out whether they are [qualified] enough to have their signs, and comply with the rules above, and to pay xii *deniers* to the clerk. …
>
> 14. *Item*, no shearers or fullers shall shear or full either *saye* or satin that has not been manufactured in the said city and that it is not marked with the small seal specific to the trade; and, if another strange article brought to them for shearing or fulling is found, the said article would be lost and the shearer or fuller who has received it would have been fined for lx *sols* at our will.
>
> 15. *Item*, no one shall sell in this city other than good and fair articles, and marked with the seals of the good cities of the said guild.
>
> 16. *Item*, that all manglers, once the articles are mangled, shall put their seals on them; and the mangler shall not make packages or loads without calling the said wardens to check whether the seals are good and there are no foreign articles stuffed among the said packages; and if one of those is found, he would incur in a fine of forty *sols*, to be applied half to the said city and the other half to the said wardens and guild, which wardens for their inspection will have two *sols* for each package. …
>
> 19. *Item*, the said masters shall not make a piece of *saye* or satin without their mark or sign being woven to them with thread of linen, hemp or another, except *sayette*, on the said penalty.
>
> 20. *Item*, if any counterfeit mark or sign was found, whoever did it would be deprived of the profession and punished corporally, at the will of us, mayors and aldermen.

§ 1.28 ORDINANCES OF SEVILLE—1519

In the sixteenth century, Seville had adopted the same rules of other European cities in respect of business identifiers for clothing: after being inspected, the cloths received the city's seal; this mark represented that the cloths complied with the technical standards in force, and identified the geographical origin of the manufacture. Moreover, masters were requested to put their individual signs on certain cloths—signs which were attributed to them by the inspectors of the trade. The following text is an excerpt from the Ordinances of Seville, which were a codification of a vast number of loose statutes and regulations enacted in that city from the thirteenth century onwards. Those laws were codified between 1515 and 1519 by determination of Fernando and Isabel.

Title: About the Weavers of Velvet.

> Moreover, we order, and command, that none of the said merchants, and officials, and people of the said art, dare to iron any silk cloth, or sell it ironed in this city, upon the penalties contained in the first chapter: and because in the said city there are some ironed silk cloths, we let them be finished, so that they be sold within three months: and that they be sealed, so that they be known, and thereafter other silk cloths shall not be ironed to be sold along with the former: and that henceforth, they keep, and maintain this chapter, according to what is contained in it. Moreover, we order, and command, that any person of the said trade, who would sell any silk cloth to any public merchant of this city, that he must sell it sealed with the seal that the inspectors of the said trade have for that purpose, and not in any other way: and if they have outside the loom, in their houses, and stalls, some piece larger than five yards, they shall not have it without it being sealed with the said seal; upon the penalty of losing it, and paying a fine of two thousand *maravedís*, for each time it is found unsealed. ...

Title: About the cap makers.

> Moreover, we order, and command that no officer cap maker, from now on, makes any caps, or opens up a store, without first being examined by the said inspectors of the said profession, and that the latter examine them while making two folded caps, and two singles, and two *carmellonas*,[18] and another double folded cap, and a folded bonnet ... And if the examined work is found sufficient, and made by a master, that the said inspectors may give him his examination certificate, and his mark, so that he can put it on the said caps and bonnets that henceforth he makes; ...
>
> Moreover, we order, and command, that all caps and bonnets that are made and dyed in this city, be marked with a thread of the master who makes them; and if the said caps and bonnets, or any of them, are found without the said thread mark, they are to be lost: and if any worker, or master, or other person puts another's mark on any clothing, that the said clothing be lost, and [the person] pay a thousand *maravedís*, as a counterfeiter, and spend thirty days in jail.

18. *Carmellona*: a special type of cap that men used in the Middle Ages.

§ 1.29 BY-LAWS OF THE *SAYETERIE* OF LILLE—1524

The following text is one of the earliest sources that refer explicitly to the differentiating function of individual trademarks. Indeed, if the mandatory distinctiveness of the signs had the mere purpose of identifying the clothmaker for the purposes of designating his/her liability in the case of flawed work, there would be no need to make it clear that the signs to be adopted by the saieteurs of Lille had to be capable of distinguishing the saies of one maker from those of another. The simple linkage between the defective pieces of cloth and their maker would have been enough.

By-laws of the *sayeterie*

December 22, 1524

> Ordinances and constitutions done by the very noble gentlemen, messeigneurs the presidents, provosts, and aldermen of the city of Lille, on the matter of the industry of *sayeterie* erected and established in said city, following the granting letters from our very dread lord and prince, Monseigneur the archduke of Austria, duke of Burgundy, earl of Flanders. ...
>
> 44—That all men and women of the said trade of *sayeterie* who will want to make *saies* or cause them to be made in the said city and county, shall have a mark to show that the *saies* are different from each other, and to make known from whose hands they will be originated, and they shall register those marks at the register of the *vingtaine*, in respect of which registration they shall pay to the clerk twelve *deniers*; and if any of the aforesaid fails to do this, i.e., to adopt a mark, to have it registered as it is provided, and to have marks that differentiate the *saies* that they have made or caused to be made, that will be upon the penalty of forty *sols* in the said currency, with arbitrary punishment.

§ 1.30 AN ORDINANCE SETTLES A DISPUTE BETWEEN THE MASTERS AND THE COMPANIONS OF THE GUILD OF CARPET MAKERS OF BRUSSELS—1528

The enormous importance that the tapestry industry of Brussels acquired in the sixteenth century led to significant developments in the way intellectual property addressed differentiation in that industry. One of those developments will be shown in Chapter 2: for the first time explicit reference was made to exclusivity in designs. This took place by means of the adoption of new by-laws of the local guild of carpet makers, adopted in 1525 (see § 2.13). Another development, which in this case reflects a practice that was followed in other sectors of textile manufacture, was the mandatory adoption of a mark of origin, which should be apposed on the selvage of each carpet made in the city.

The first of the following texts is the trademark-related portion of a summary given by a historian of the tapestry industry, Alohonse Wauters, on the dispute between the jurors and masters of the respective guild, on the one hand, and the companions, on the other.

The second text reproduces an excerpt from an edict signed by Charles V, in 1544, providing for the mandatory apposition of masters' individual trademarks to carpets in addition to the collective city's mark.

§ 1.30.1 Ordinance of 1528 Set by a Magistrate Settling a Dispute Between the Masters and Jurors of the Corporation of Carpet Makers of Brussels, on the One Hand, and the Companions, on the Other

Every piece made in this city, measuring more than six yards, must henceforth bear at the bottom: on one side, the mark of the manufacturer or of the person who caused it to be made, and, on the other, a small escutcheon between two Bs. Every master and worker had to present his mark to the jurors, to have it copied in a special register. With regard to smaller pieces, these would be marked only if the makers deemed it appropriate. But, as regards large pieces, the failure of marking was punished with a fine of 6 *florins carolus*. If the Brussels mark was affixed to a piece not made in this city, it was confiscated and the counterfeiter was banned from the trade for a year.

§ 1.30.2 Edict on the Manufacture of Tapestries in Flanders, Approved by Charles V—1544

It is forbidden to manufacture tapestries outside of Brussels, Louvain, Anvers, Bruges, Oudenarde, Alost, Enghien, Binche, Ath, Lille, Tournay, and other free towns where the craft is organised and regulated by ordinances. In pieces worth more than twenty-four *sous* an ell, the warp should be of the worsted thread of Lyons, of Spain, or of Aragon, of spun thread, or of similar material, thoroughly cleaned and dyed in fast colours. Each cloth should be in one single piece.

The master-worker making, or causing to be made, such a tapestry, is bound to have his mark or ensign woven in one of the corners at the base of the said tapestry; and, near to this, such ensigns as the town shall order, so that, by means of these ensigns and marks, the work shall be known to be of that town and made by that master, and to be worth twenty-four *patards*, or more, the ell.

Figure 9 Left: origin marks from Brussels, printed on the selvages of carpets made in the city, under the ordinance of 1528. Center and right: master carpet makers' personal trademarks, sixteenth century.

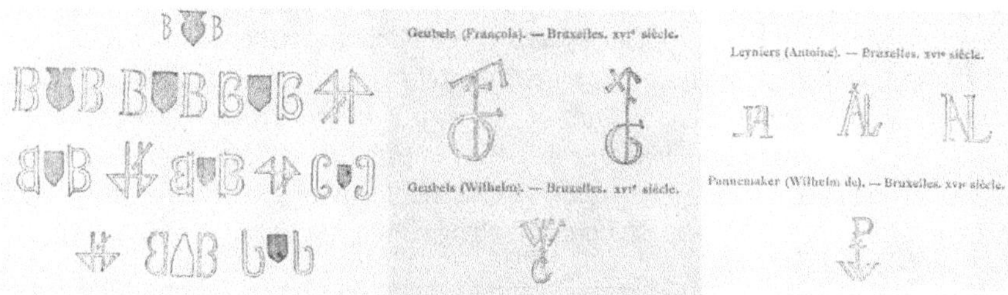

§ 1.31 STATUTES OF THE KNITWEAR MAKERS OF PARIS—1550

The following text reveals a new step in the evolution of textile-related trademark law: the requirement to have the masters' individual marks registered with a centralized office, at the Châtelet of Paris, where the notarial, court and administrative services of the city of Paris were provided and recorded. Even though the registration of clothmakers' trademarks had already become a practice, such registration was generally done with the office of the magistrates that supervised and inspected the trade. Here, by contrast, we see a practice that can be deemed as a precedent of the modern trademark office.

Statutes of the knitwear makers in 40 articles and patent letters of Henry II, which confirm them

January 1550

These are the articles of the statutes and ordinances that the masters of the trade of the makers of knitwear, almuces, and mittens, in the City of Paris, beg and very humbly request that the good pleasure of the King be to grant, approve, ratify and confirm by edict, statute and royal ordinance, for their keeping and maintaining, to avoid the poor workmanship and embezzlements that are done in that trade and are committed each day in the said trade and professions of knitwear making, to the great interest, prejudice and damage of the public good and of the trade: ...

20. The said master makers of knitwear may also have their knitwear and laces dyed in the said City and suburbs of Paris, in good dye of pastel and madder and good scarlet; likewise they may also dye the small kinds of knitwear and laces in Brazilian red, in small black and other kinds and colors of dye, because it is permitted to do so, on the condition, however, that the said knitwear of the small kind will all be marked with a single countermark, of which a sample will be placed in the chamber of the King's prosecutor, like the others, so that those knitwear and laces of a small kind be countermarked, for avoiding the abuses, thefts and deceits that might be done in its regard, upon a similar fine of ten *livres parisis*.

21. The said masters shall have a distinct and separate mark, with which they shall mark their knitwear, as much of wool as of other cloths and other articles made by the same profession, so that they are recognized when they are dyed and everywhere else as appropriate; which marks they shall bring to the office of the King's prosecutor, at the Châtelet of Paris, within fifteen days after the publication of these presents, to be kept and locked in a separate place. And said masters are prohibited from counterfeiting each other's marks, upon penalty of an arbitrary fine.

§ 1.32 BY-LAWS OF THE WORKERS IN THE INDUSTRY OF GOLD AND SILVER CLOTHS OF LYON—1554

The gold and silver cloth industry of Lyon was born from the immigration of Italian artisans, who were lured to leave their cities with promises of privileges and rewards. Soon Lyon specialized in the making of fine, luxury cloths, and the industry became a powerful engine for the city's growth. As with other industries, intellectual property mechanisms were introduced to ensure quality. But the increasing importance of the cloth industry in Lyon led to the adoption of new mechanisms ensuring, to a certain extent, competition between artisans and merchants. As we will see in the Second Chapter, subsequently the industry of Lyon would trigger the development and the consolidation of the protection of industrial designs, which started in the textile industry and later extended to other fields of industry.

In the sixteenth century, as we will see in the following text, a statute approved by Henry IV (a king that would not spare incentives for the promotion of the French industry) required the adoption of individual trademarks by the masters of the fine cloths made in Lyon. Those marks were to be affixed to the cloths before they went sent to the artisans for finishing.

Letters that confirm the by-laws of the workers of gold and silver cloths of the city of Lyon.

Paris, April of 1554; registered in the parliament on December 4.

> Henry [IV], etc. As our late and very honored lord and father, whom God absolves, being well aware of the great *deniers* that were drawn and put outside our kingdom to buy gold, silver, velvet, and other kinds of silk cloths from foreign nations, and very often from our enemies, who by this means have made themselves strong against us, and exhausted the gold and silver of our kingdom, in order to attract, establish, and communicate among our subjects the art of manufacture of the aforesaid cloths of gold, silver and silk, which is the only means of avoiding said inconvenience and transport of said *deniers*, had given and granted several fine privileges, liberties, franchises, immunities, and exemptions to all masters or workers, both foreigners and our subjects, unemployed and working currently at the aforesaid manufacture in our good city and town of Lyon.
>
> Which privileges on our accession to the crown we have likewise confirmed, and ordered them to be peacefully and inviolably kept and maintained, as they have been and are still at present, from which has ensued so great a fruit that our said city of Lyon has withdrawn and ceased to depend upon the nations of Italy and elsewhere, and such a [large] number of masters, workers, linen weavers, dyers, millers, spinners, and other persons [have engaged in] making the said manufacture of cloths of gold, silver and silk, [and consequently] a good part of the aforesaid cloths that were brought from Genoa and Italy are today made in our city and suburbs of Lyon: and there is an opportunity to hope that, if the growing of said manufacture continues, in brief all our subjects will no longer have to buy them from said foreign nations, and by this means the *deniers* that [those nations] used to raise will remain in our kingdom: and besides that, several poor people, young girls and children of our said city of Lyon will work in the aforesaid manufacture and trades that depend on it, and will easily gain their life without falling into idleness and begging.
>
> But because hitherto no ordinances, laws and statutes have been made in our city on the ways and manufactures of the aforesaid cloths of gold, silver, and silk, [and] on the regulation of masters and workers, and on the punishment and coercion of faults and abuses that can be committed there, our dear and beloved counselors and aldermen of our city of Lyon, have since advised us that by the malice of men and time there are several faults, defects and deceits in the said cloths of gold, silver, and silk made in our said city of Lyon: and usually several complaints are made by some of the said trade against another, and by the masters

against their companions, workers, millers, dyers, spinners, upon which they enter into various lawsuits against each other, and distract themselves from their vocation. Because of those abuses, defects, quarrels, and lawsuits, the said manufacture of cloths of gold, silver, and silk so well started in our said city of Lyon could be lost and discontinued to the great damage of the city and of all of our kingdom, if a remedy were not provided for. ...

(7) That the dyers, millers, and spinners will return to the masters the silks received by them, well dried and conditioned, without wetting them, loading, suffocating or keeping in damp places, or doing anything else to them, as a result of which the weight, when they return them, might be bigger than it was when they received them: and the said spinners in charge of spinning the silks, both raw and dyed according to the specifications that will be communicated to them by the said masters, which [silks] will be for this purpose marked with the marks that each master will have, different from each other, the said spinners not being allowed to put anything that can increase the said weight: and in returning the said silks spinned by them, they shall also return the respective samples to said masters, everything upon penalty of punishment as above.

Figure 10 The fine cloth industry settled in Lyon in the fifteenth century with the contribution of Italian artisans who migrated to France lured by privileges and financial incentives. In the sixteenth century, the industry was already thriving and the technology was in the hands of French masters and designers, as these illustrations show. Left: the cover of a book published in Lyon, between 1515 and 1535, containing designs and patterns of cloths embroidered and woven with gold, silver, and silk threads. The book is a collection of the creations of three masters, Jehan Mayol, Jean Troveon, and Anthoine Belin. The title of the book reads: "The flower of the patterns of lingerie, in gold thread, in silver thread, and silk thread or another, in whatever work, comprising the art of embroidery and weaving." Right: the last of the 119 plates contained in the book, designed by Anthoine Belin.

§ 1.33 A FRENCH STATUTE ON TECHNICAL STANDARDS FOR WOOL CLOTH, AND THEIR MARKS OF ORIGIN AND CERTIFICATION—1571

In the sixteenth century, the requirement of the affixing of cities' seals as proof of origin was still a common practice. The manner trade was carried out, although greatly expanded by comparison with the Middle Ages, had not yet evolved significantly. Cloths were still chiefly sold at the halls and fairs, and competition between individual artisans within the same city and guild was still strongly discouraged. One had to wait for the emergence of liberal ideas, by the end of the sixteenth century, to see things change in that regard, and for cities' seals and other certification marks to lose part of their importance.

Nevertheless, as we will see in the next texts, soon lawmakers and guilds' magistrates, although hesitantly, started to understand the importance of individual signs as elements of differentiation and health competition between artisans and merchants, even within the same guild, or profession, or city. The reason was the almost imperceptible, but effective, departure from the constraints of the corporatist regime, which would remain in place, but highly eroded, until the eighteenth century.

Edict of the King (Charles IX) for the reformation, police, and regulation on the ways and dyes of the cloth, small wool cloths [*estamets, sarges*], and other fabrics of wool, which are made in this Kingdom.

March 19, 1571

> And for compelling the weavers, workers and clothiers to do their duty in the manufacture of said cloths, small wool cloths [*sarges et estamets*], and in order to punish those who will contravene it, and also to prevent the abuse of the names of the places where the best cloths are made:
>
> We have ordered and order that in each piece of cloth, small wool cloths [*estamet, sarge, camelot de laine*], and other cloths that will henceforth be dyed in our Kingdom, country and lands of our obedience, of any color whatsoever, on its top and first end, after it is dyed, a mark or seal of lead will be printed, containing the place where the dying is made.
>
> Likewise, all the woolen cloths and small cloths in wool, and the cloths, all together, that are whitened so as to be used and left white, will be sealed on its top and first end, when they leave the hand of the fuller.
>
> Making express prohibitions and inhibitions to all dyers, fullers, and shearers, to give, consign or deliver any cloths, small wool cloths or other cloths and any product of wool of any kind, to the merchants and other persons who would have consigned it with them for dyeing, finish or whitening respectively, unless firstly the said seal in the manner that is said has been put on and affixed to each piece, under the penalty of a fine of twenty pounds for each piece: prohibiting also all merchants of whatever quality they are, to buy, put on or display for sale the aforesaid cloths, unless they are previously sealed, as it is said, on the similar penalty of a fine of twenty pounds for each counterfeit and of confiscation of the piece sold or purchased. ...
>
> Made at the King's Council, held in Paris on the nineteenth day of March, the year M. D. LXXI.

§ 1.34 PATENT LETTERS CONFIRMING THE BY-LAWS OF THE SHOEMAKERS OF PARIS—1573

While the previous text is still an explicit manifestation of the medieval regime of business identifiers, clearly more focused on certification than on differentiation, the following one serves as an example that things had started to change in the second half of the sixteenth century. Coexisting with corporatist rules that trumped competition among masters and merchants, some signs of evolution, albeit hesitantly, started to appear, by means of statutes and court disputes focusing on individual trademarks.

The following text speaks to this issue. The amendment of the by-laws of the shoemakers of Paris, approved by Charles IX, of France, does not make any reference to certification marks but contains a short and explicit reference to individual trademarks. These could, of course, be used as tokens of individual liability in the case of defective products, but such a reference does not appear in the text, which could mean that something was in the process of change.

Patent letters of Charles IX confirming the by-laws of shoemakers, in 41 articles.

April 1573.

35. Each shoemaker shall have his mark.

§ 1.35 TWO MASTER CARDERS DISPUTE IN COURT THE OWNERSHIP OF A TRADEMARK; RENNES, FRANCE—1578

This text—a report of the judgment of the Parliament of Bretagne settling a dispute involving similar trademarks owned by two wool carders of Rennes, France—serves as a good illustration of the notes preceding the two previous sources: in the second half of the sixteenth century, individual trademarks were gaining importance as signs of differentiation and means of appropriation of personal prestige, rather than as mere signs certifying quality and identifying the artisans for the purposes of product liability.

September 12, 1578

There was a dispute between Guillaume Jolif, one of the master carders of Rennes, and Pierre Baimer, also master carder, which Baimer had as his mark a rampant lion, he complained that Jolif, who should have in his mark a Greyhound, had ordered one that resembled a lion, which disguise caused him serious damage. He concluded by pleading the reform of the mentioned Greyhound trademark.

The parties were taken out of the court and procedure, and nevertheless it was decided that the mentioned mark of the greyhound should be reformed, and that it will be engraved lying down, the feet together & the tail lowered.

Figure 11 Example of the use of the rampant lion and the greyhound as business identifiers in the cloth industry. The figure shows a trade card (carte-addresse) of Pere, Fils & Co., manufacturer of fine gold and silver thread at Lyon, France, in the seventeenth century. The card shows the manufacturer's trademark, with a rampant lion holding the balance of justice, and a greyhound, meaning loyalty—symbols of Lyon's textile industry. These were symbols inherited from heraldry, very commonly used by merchants and manufacturers of many sorts.

§ 1.36 THE FIRST (?) ENGLISH COURT DISPUTE INVOLVING CLOTH TRADEMARKS: THE SANDFORTH'S CASE—1584-1585

The texts that follow—abstracts of an English lawsuit (known as the Sandforth's case)—confirm that in the second half of the sixteenth century, clothmakers and merchants were already seeing their trademarks as assets that permitted to secure any competitive advantage they had resulting from prestige and reputation.

It seems that Sandforth's case is the first reported case in England involving a dispute over the infringement of a trademark.

> (i) J.S., being a clothier who made good cloth, used a mark; and J.D., being also a clothier but who made bad cloth, used another mark; then J.D. set J.S.'s mark on his [own cloth], and by means thereof obtained good business (utterance); but [J.D.'s] cloth was found upon trial to be bad, and by reason thereof J.S's cloth was discredited and he could not have as good business afterwards as he had before. Upon all this matter J.S. brought an action on the case against J.D. Anderson C.J. said it seems the action lies, because J.S. is damaged by J.D. using his mark. Peryam J. said there was no law against anyone using whatever mark he wished; and when J.D. used the mark which J.S. used he did no wrong to J.S., it being a

lawful act. And even though J.S. was thereby damaged, he shall not have an action on the case for it, because it is *damnum absque injuria*. Anderson C.J. said if someone has a house he may lawfully burn it if he wishes; but if by its being burned someone else's house is burned, the latter shall have an action on the case; and yet it was a lawful act.

(ii) Note, by Fletewoode, that an action on the case lies by the custom of London for counterfeiting another's mark. And he put this case when the following matter was moved by Fenner: "a clothier did give the mark of another clothier, but with a little difference hardly to be perceived, and set that on bad and false cloths, whereby the cloths of the other (which made good) were after discredited." And it was demanded whether an action on the case lay. Anderson C.J. said it did. Wyndham J. agreed, if the statute enacted that no clothier shall give the mark of another. Fletewoode. In 5 Mar. it was adjudged in one Longe's case accordingly in parliament, and the counterfeiter was [a member] of the house and for this reason was put out and paid the other 300 pounds. Peryam and Mead JJ. said that anyone may give what mark he will, and it is *damnum absque injuria* to the other, and deceit does not lie against him who does a wholly lawful act for his own profit. Id. at 617-18 (citing manuscript HLS MS. 5048, fo. 118v. (formerly HLS MS. Acc. 704755, fo. 118v.)).

Figure 12 Detail of the shop sign of a tailor's workshop in the sixteenth century, Fribourg, Switzerland.

§ 1.37 AN ACT APPROVED BY ELIZABETH I ON THE REGULATION OF THE MAKING AND SELLING OF KERSIES—1593

This text is another example of the introduction of mandatory marks in order to avoid frauds and malpractices in the making of kersies (and to identify those artisans who would be liable for the defective cloths). The kersey was a sort of coarse woollen cloth.

Even though this Regulation is not much different from several texts previously transcribed, it contains two interesting aspects. First, it does not refer to artisans' seals, but to their shop-marks. This suggests that trademarks and shop signs were being used as if they were just a single sign—which was not uncommon. Many artisans would adopt as their trademarks the signs they put on the entrances to their shops. Today, the custom is the reverse: most merchants use their trademarks as shop signs.

The second point is the reference to the "new inventions and devices" introduced by master weavers, tuckers, and artificers, which were changing the cloths, their weight, and thickness, and thus justified these rules that aimed at getting back to old practices. This shows that in such a period, the cloth industry was already responding to customers' changing demands and modifying cloths and garments in response. However, it would still take some time for lawmakers to accept such constant changes in the manufacture and design of cloths. This is, actually, the basis of fashion, which only many years later would appear in the radars of lawmakers (of French lawmakers, first, as it will be shown in § 1.63).

Moreover, this statute shows concern with the possibility that the working on cloths after their being marked might eliminate the seals and the information they provided. That is why it deals with the marking in a way that is specifically aimed at avoiding such risk. We will see this same concern reflected in other legal texts not only in England but also in France.

An Act for the Reformation of Sundry Abuses in Clothes, called *Devonshire* Kersies or Dozens, according to a Proclamation of the thirty-fourth year of the Reign of our Sovereign Lady the Queen that now is.

In their most humble and dutiful wise shown and beseeched your Highness, your true and faithful Subjects, the Clothiers, Merchants and Chapmen of your County of Devon, and of the Counties adjoining, That where in the Month of January in the four and thirtieth Year of your Majesty's most happy Reign, as well as the humble Suit and Petition of sundry your said Subjects, as upon Certificate of divers Justices in your Highness said County of Devon, and upon Complaint of the States of Holland, it pleased your Highness, with the Advice of your most honourable Privy Council, by your Highness Proclamation, for the Reformation of the Insufficiencies grown in the Clothes called *Devonshire* Kersies or Dozens, (a Commodity heretofore in great Request, Price and Estimation, both among your natural Subjects, and in Foreign Nations and Countries), but of late marvelously (and not without Occasion) discredited by the Inventions and new Devices of the Weavers, Tuckers and Artificers, To command that the Laws before that Time made, and standing in Force not repealed, for and concerning the Premises, should be duly accomplished in all Things: And that every Officer should diligently perform his Office accordingly: (2) And that the Weight of the said Kersies or Dozens, being raw, and wrought, with clean Stuff, without any deceitful Addition, should weigh fifteen Pounds, and contain in the Market at least between fifteen and sixteen Yards in Length, and that the same should be sewantly woven throughout of like sorted Yarn, forbidding all other Deceits in weaving, and all diminishing and unreasonable drawing, stretching and other Deceits in Tuckers: (3) And that each Weaver should weave his Shop-Mark in each Dozen, and a Purrel in each End thereof: (4) And that Officers should be appointed in Market-Towns, to view, weigh and try the same Kersies whether they were in Length, Weight or Goodness, according to the Rate and Proportion set forth in the same Proclamation: The same Proclamation to endure till the first Day of this present Parliament, as by the same more at large may appear. ...

V. And that it may be further enacted by the Authority aforesaid, That each Weaver shall weave his Shop-Mark of some coloured Yarn in the End of every Kersie which he shall hereafter weave or make, and shall also at each End of every the same Kersies weave one Purrel likewise of coloured Yarn, of the Breadth of three Quarters of an Inch at the least, whereby the deceitful cutting and diminishing of such Clothes by Tuckers or Fullers heretofore used, may henceforth be prevented: (2) And if any Weaver shall use any deceit in mingling his Yarn, or shall omit his Shop-Mark, or shall not weave in every Kersie two Purrels, according to the Tenor of this Act, he shall forfeit and lose for every Offence to the contrary, ten Shillings.

VI. And to the End that the Weight and Goodness of all the said Kersies called Dozens, being raw, may be the better and more certainly known, it may be further enacted, That no Weaver, nor any other Person whatsoever, shall offer or put to Sale any of the same raw Kersies called Dozens, before the same have been viewed, weighed and marked in some City, Town Corporate or Market-Town used and appointed for that Purpose; (2) upon Pain to forfeit and lose for every Cloth sold or offered to be sold to the contrary, ten Shillings: ...

§ 1.38 BY-LAWS OF THE MAKERS OF FUSTIANS OF THE CITY OF LYON—1595

Due to its importance, the cloth industry of Lyon was, from the sixteenth century onwards, subject to intense regulation. We have already seen some expressions of that (see § 1.32). The following text deals with a specialized branch of clothmaking—that of fustians, a type of thick cloth. The remarkable aspect of this text is that it reveals that the examination and registration of trademarks had already become a practice at the end of the sixteenth century. In this particular case, the registration was not made by a public authority, such as the King's prosecutor sieged at the Châtelet, in Paris (see § 1.31), but by the fustian makers and merchants themselves, which could be seen as a sort of self-regulation of the acquisition and use of trademarks.

Henry [IV], by the grace of God, King of France and Navarre: To all those present and to come, greetings. Our dear and beloved fustian merchants, workers and doing business in our city of Lyon, and its surroundings, have humbly said and demonstrated to us, that to avoid the abuses and wrongdoings that are committed in the said trade, they would have done and drawn up among them certain articles, which, having begged us to confirm, we would have sent to the Seneschal of Lyon, for informing on the content of the request and articles, and giving and sending us his opinion: which having been seen, and after the said Seneschal having been heard, and upon the consent of the Aldermen of the said Lyon, he is of opinion, under our good pleasure, of the maintenance and observation of the said articles, as being for the good, profit and utility of the said city, of all the said trade, and of the public.

The said merchants begging and humbly requesting us that we wish to confirm said articles, statutes, and regulations, in accordance with said advice.

We make known that, inclining liberally to the supplication and request of the supplicants, and wishing to put an end to all abuses and wrongdoings that could be committed in said trade, and profession of fustian making: We hereby have the articles, statutes, and ordinances, and all the contents therein, along with the said advices attached under the countersign of our chancellery, praised, ratified, confirmed, and approved, and with our certain knowledge, full power, and royal authority, we praise, confirm, ratify, approve, and deem very pleasant, to be enjoyed by said supplicants according to the contents of said articles. ...

Articles proposed and drawn up by the merchants and makers in the trade and profession or manufacture and business of fustians in the city of Lyon, for the police and regulation of said trade and profession, set and granted between them and its Consulate, under the good pleasure of his Majesty, to obviate the abuses, wrongdoings, and undertakings that are committed daily as much by those of the said city as by foreigners, to the great prejudice of both the public and private interest. ...

Firstly, that in order to obviate such abuses, and to avoid the complaints that arise therefrom, at least that the aforesaid wrongdoings be known, and from where they proceed, all kinds of fustians whatsoever shall be marked with the mark of whoever causes them to be made and manufactured. And to this end each one will submit his mark, which will be examined among them and afterwards registered, so as to have recourse to it: and all pieces that will not be marked, will be confiscated, as it is provided below. ...

§ 1.39 HENRY IV APPROVES THE GENERAL REGULATION OF FRENCH MANUFACTORIES, INCLUDING PROVISIONS ON SILK CLOTH DYERS' TRADEMARKS—1601

Between the beginning of the sixteenth century and the end of the seventeenth century, France developed and consolidated a trademark system in connection with the cloth industry that acquired complexity and sophistication, mainly in respect of the combination of certification seals and individual artisans' marks. The system can be summarized in this way: cloths of all kinds had to be inspected before they were put on the market, or, in the case they served as ingredients for finished garments or useful articles, such as hats, handkerchiefs, towels, etc., they had to be inspected before they were handed over to the artisans for their finishing. The inspection (with approval) was certified by the affixing of seals or marks on the cloths, which could be of several types: the city's seal (the main certification mark in the fourteenth and fifteenth centuries, until channels of commercial distribution changed, and distant cities became easier to reach—which led to a reduction in the importance of geographical indications as tokens of prestige and reputation in the cloth industry); collective marks adopted by the jurors or inspectors of a given trade; and individual marks specifically attributed to individual inspectors. These were called "marques de visite" (inspection marks). In certain cases, the inspection marks were affixed temporarily, subject to periodical renewals (i.e., the cloths would be periodically inspected until they were sold to the final consumer). Temporary marks, upon each renewal, would be destroyed (they had the form of pieces of lead). These temporary marks were designated as "marques de grace". In the seventeenth century, many French cities had their own "bureaux de marque", or mark offices, where these certification marks were registered, and where they could be checked at any time by inspectors to verify the quality of goods.

Artisans had their own individual marks, mostly formed by their initials, but in many cases, they also resorted to figurative elements. Eventually, individual trademarks were chosen not by the artisans but by the inspectors or wardens of the trade. This practice was common in the first years of the cloth industry and was abandoned later when the industry grew too large and thousands of artisans spread through France, to permit such a practice. They were required to affix those marks to the cloths they worked upon (or to the cloths they sold, in the case they were merchants), in a manner that, if the cloths were transformed in a subsequent phase of manufacture, the signs would remain visible. These marks were, of course, distinctive signs—the requirements that the mark of an artisan should be different from those of his/her competitors and that he/she should not use another's mark as if it were his/her own, were common. But they had, from the authorities' point of view, a purpose of assigning liability in the event of defective cloths. As time went by, a system of registration of these individual marks—"marques de fabrique" or "marque de fabriquant"—was established, with, in certain cases, certificates of registration being issued to the artisans.

This evolving mechanism will be illustrated in the texts that follow. We have selected only a few, which we believe to be more representative of the most significant elements of the system, but the certification of cloths through marks was the subject matter of hundreds of regulations, decrees, and court judgments, between the sixteenth and seventeenth centuries. Sometimes, certification marks were an incidental topic to the regulation of industry, but in many cases, they were the central focus of legislative action.

Evidencing that the use of trademarks had become a matter of tax, administrative, and commercial practices, the general regulation on France's manufacture, approved by King Henry IV, of France, contains several provisions dealing with the mandatory use of those signs in the context of clothmaking as proof of individual origin and ground for liability in the case of defective works.

Henry, by the grace of God, King of France and Navarre, to those all present and to come, greetings.

VII. Policy of the dyes of the silk and woolen cloths

> And as regards the policy of dyeing, each dyer shall affix his lead mark on the dyed woolen cloths and all other fabrics, which will contain, on one side, the mark of the place where the dyeing will be done, and on the other side the name of said dyer, so that where pieces poorly dyed are found, we want and are pleased that

said dyer be condemned to the arbitrary fine of ten crowns; and likewise, it shall be taken care that the dyeing of the silk cloths is neither overdone nor counterfeited, especially the black silk cloths, and that they are made according to the ordinances, and that they have their number of threads, weight, length and width, under penalty of confiscation of the said goods and large fines, a quarter to the whistleblower.

Given at Fontainebleau, the 13th day of April, the year of grace of one thousand six hundred, and the twelfth of our reign. *Signed*: Henry. *On the king's behalf*: Potier. And sealed with the great seal of yellow wax.

§ 1.40 BY-LAWS OF THE COMMUNITY OF SHOEMAKERS OF PARIS—1614

In the seventeenth century, the examination and registration of individual trademarks had already become a common practice and was found in most statutes and regulations dealing with the organization of professions. The by-laws of the shoemakers of Paris, of 1614, was not an exception.

By-laws of the Community of Master Shoemakers of the City and Suburbs of Paris, Confirmed by Louis XIII and presented to the King, and to Our Lords of his Privy Council, in 1614

XXXV

Item, That each leather currier have his sign or mark, and likewise the shoemaker his own, with whose signs or marks all the leathers or hides of all kinds that will be bailed for the purpose of being curried will be signed and marked, in order to recognize the one who will do wrong; that collation will be made of the aforesaid marks, so that they do not look similar in figures.

§ 1.41 ADMINISTRATIVE PROVISIONS PUTTING AN END TO THE PASSING OFF OF TRADEMARKS IN THE COMMERCE OF WINE FROM BORDEAUX AND OF PASTEL FROM LORAGNES—1614

This text, extracted from a law treatise elaborated by the famous French jurist Antoine de Mornac, is about the counterfeiting of French wine and pastel (blue dye). Pastel was a dye intensively used, and this explains that it was the matter of specific rules on the protection of geographical indications, as the following text suggests, as well as, as we will see in the Second Chapter, of an industrial privilege granted in Portugal to Prince Henry the Navigator (see § 2.09).

On the 5th of August 1614, prohibitions were imposed on certain inhabitants in the north of Orleans, to have their barrels hooped like those of the said city of Orleans; which is likewise followed at Bordeaux, for it is not possible to hoop the barrels in the manner of Bordeaux. It is also the same for the pastel of Loragnes; for it is forbidden for all other than those who are of the said country, to put pastel in bags which are of the mark of those of the said country of Loragnes.

The reason for all this is that one does not sell under such disguises wine as if it were from Orleans or Bordeaux, and yet they are not; nor of pastel as if it were of the said country of Loragnes, and yet it is not.

§ 1.42 JUDGE DODDRIGE CITES, AS A PRECEDENT, A COURT DECISION DEALING WITH THE COUNTERFEITING OF A CLOTH MERCHANT'S TRADEMARK: SOUTHERN V. HOW—1618

In Southern *v.* How *(a case heard in 1618, involving the counterfeiting of jewels), Judge Doddridge made a reference to another court dispute (unreported) concerning the counterfeiting of a merchant's cloth trademark. For some time, this was thought to be the first court dispute over a trademark in England, but it was not (see* Sandforth's *case, § 1.36).*

Southern v. How

1618

... Doddridge cited a case to be adjudged 33. Eliz. in the common Bench: A clothier of Gloucestershire sold very good cloth, so that in London if they saw any cloth of his mark, they would buy it without searching thereof; and another who made ill cloth put his mark upon it without his privity; and an action upon the case was brought by him who bought the cloth, for his deceit; and adjudged maintainable.

§ 1.43 BY-LAWS OF THE GUILD OF THE MAKERS OF CLOTH ON THE HIGH LOOM—PARIS, 1627

The Parliament of Paris having gathered a number of cloth-making professions under one single guild, with the natural objective of eliminating the many disputes between them concerning professional exclusivity, had to enact new by-laws, which necessarily contained provisions on the marking of the cloths with the artisans' individual marks. The following text concerns the makers of tapestries.

By-laws and Regulations of the Masters and Merchants Carpet Makers, of the High Loom—Makers of oriental carpets and *entraitures* [cloths with invisible sewing], of patchworks, tailors and seamstresses of this City, Municipality and Vice county of Paris, united and incorporated in accordance with the Decrees of the Court of Parliament, Judgments, Sentences of the Provost of Paris, of the twentieth of May one thousand six hundred and twenty-two, sixth of August one thousand six hundred and twenty-five, and the third of July one thousand six hundred and twenty-seven. ...

LV. *Item.* The blankets called eight quarters will be two ells long and one and a half wide marked by the corner of two points with the worker's mark by the other corner in the usual manner, and the common, fine, and crossed ones, in the usual way, and will be worked with good, hairless wool, on the penalty of a fine of twenty *livres parisis* as above.

Figure 13 The workshop of a sixteenth-century tailor. Engraving by Jost Amman, 1568.

§ 1.44 STATUTE REGULATING THE INDUSTRY OF WORSTEDS OF NORFOLK AND NORWICH—1662

In the following text, we can see another expression of the impact that the increasing pace of invention in the seventeenth century had on the regulation of the cloth industry. As it was the practice then—still inspired by medieval corporatism—the imposition of new standards was accompanied by the adoption of rules on certification and individual marks.

An act for regulating the making of stuff in Norfolk and Norwich

May 15, 1662

> Whereas divers abuses and deceits have of late years been had and used in the making of worsteds, and other stuffs commonly called Norwich stuffs, and in the reeling of yarns, whereof the said stuffs are either wholly or in part made, which tends to the debasing of the said manufacture, unto the prejudice of the public; (2) which said trade of weaving of stuffs hath of late times been very much increased, and great variety of new sorts of stuffs have been invented; so that the power given in by the statute of the seventh of Edward the Fourth, chapter the first, is not sufficient for the regulating of the same; (3) and that the number of the wardens by

the same act appointed, being but eight, are too few for the governing and ordering the same trade; by which means the same manufacturer will soon be lost, if not prevented, and carried into foreign nations, to the great diminution of his Majesty's customs, and turning out of work many thousands of poor people: ... (2) and that all stuffs made and to be made under the regulation aforesaid, before the same shall be offered or put to sale, shall be brought to weavers-hall for the time being within the county of the city of Norwich, to be viewed and searched by the said wardens or any of them; (3) and if the same shall be found to be well and sufficiently made and wrought according to the rules and ordinances of the said trade, then all stuffs shall be by the wardens, or any two of them, sealed and allowed accordingly, without any sum of money paid or to be paid for the same; ...

XII. And be it further enacted by the authority aforesaid, That it shall not be lawful for any person or persons to buy any piece or pieces of stuffs before the same be sealed by the wardens of the said trade: saving to the King's majesty, his heirs and successors, all such right of customs, subsidies and aulnage of Norfolk and Norwich stuffs or worsteds or any of them, as he or they might lawfully have claimed before the making of this act: (2) and that if any piece or pieces of stuffs shall be found in the possession of any person or persons unsealed, except in the possession of the first owner or maker thereof, the person or persons in whose custody the same shall be found, shall be adjudged guilty of deceit, and shall forfeit for every piece of stuff which be so found in his or their possession unsealed as aforesaid, the sum of four shillings; (3) and the maker or seller of the same who shall deliver the same out of his or their possession before the same be sealed, shall likewise forfeit for every such piece, other fours shillings, to the use of the poor of the said trade and manufacture.

XIV. And that if any person shall counterfeit any seal of the said trade, or shall seal any piece of stuff under the regulation with any counterfeit seal, or shall remove a seal off one piece, and set it unto another piece which hath not been sealed by the wardens, every person so offending and being thereof convicted by his own confession, or by the oath of two or more witnesses, to be taken before the mayor of the said city or his deputy, or any one justice of the peace of the city of Norwich or county of Norfolk, who respectively have hereby power to administer an oath for that purpose, shall forfeit for every such offence the sum of twenty pounds of lawful English money, to the use of the King's majesty. ...

XVI. And that every person under the said regulation shall weave his proper stuff-mark into every piece of stuff which he shall weave or cause to be woven, at the head-end of the same piece; upon pain of forfeiting three shillings for every piece that shall be woven without such mark, to the use of the poor of the said trade and manufacture.

§ 1.45 JOSSE VAN ROBAIS, A DUTCH CLOTHMAKER, AND HIS SUCCESSORS RESORT TO VARIOUS INTELLECTUAL PROPERTY MECHANISMS TO SECURE COMPETITIVE ADVANTAGES—1665 ONWARDS

In the second half of the seventeenth century, Josse van Robais (also referred to as Vanrobais), a Dutch industrialist, was lured into setting a cloth manufactory in Abbeville, France, by certain privileges, including a prohibition of the counterfeiting of his trademark "and manufacture," expression with a very vague and broad meaning, comprising the industrial process and the machinery, as well as the designs and cloths he manufactured. This privilege was prorogated several times, namely in 1708, 1725, and 1743. As the following texts show, van Robais and his heirs had a keen interest in protecting the reputation of the cloths they manufactured through the exclusive right in the use of a blue selvage. Indeed, van Robais did not consider the exclusivity stemming from the trademark sufficient for the protection of his business interests. Perhaps as an anticipation of today's struggle of the fashion sector to find a specific intellectual property mechanism that protects adequately the core of their business, van Robais for several years insistently requested—and finally obtained—the privilege of differentiating and certifying the origin of his cloths by having four blue selvages ("lisières bleues") woven in them. Later, he would publish ads announcing his privilege on the use of the selvages and would enforce such privilege rather than the trademarks.

Besides securing a privilege, trademarks, and exclusive selvages, van Robais successfully persuaded French authorities, namely Colbert, to enforce his exclusivity in a trade secret.

§ 1.45.1 Industrial Privilege Granted to Josse van Robais with Exclusive Rights in the Making of Fine Cloths in Abbeville in the Manner of Spain and Holland—1665

Louis [XIV], by the Grace of God King of France and Navarre, to all those present and to come, Greetings. The knowledge that we have of the great advantages that the establishment of factories in our Kingdom brings to our subjects, makes us willingly listen to the proposals made to us, and treat favorably those whose proposals are deemed to bring to the public some utility in their execution. Moreover, considering the unrestricted protection that we give to trade and manufactures by inviting foreigners to come and receive their benefits, our beloved Josse Vanrobais, Dutch merchant, informed us of his intention to reside in the city of Abbeville and to establish there a manufacture of fine cloths in the manner of Spain and Holland, and for this purpose to transport a number of cloth looms and fulling mills and to bring with him forty or fifty Dutch workers to be employed in the said Manufacture, which proposal, with the conditions thereof having been seen and examined by our beloved and chief Counselor in our Royal Council, Lord Colbert, Counselor in our Councils, Commander and Grand Treasurer of our orders, superintendent and general comptroller of our buildings, industries, and manufactures of France, said Vanrobais would have presented himself to us and would have very humbly begged us to grant him permission to establish the said manufactory and our letters to that necessary. For these reasons, wishing to treat the said Vanrobais favorably and to attract by his example those who excel among foreigners in some sort of manufacture to come and establish factories in our kingdom, with our special grace, full power, and royal authority, we have allowed and granted, and through these present [letters] signed by our hand, allow and grant to the said Vanrobais [the authorization] to come to and reside in the said city of Abbeville with fifty Dutch workers and to establish therein a manufactory of fine cloths, in the manner of and as they are made in Spain and Holland, and for this purpose to transport and erect there thirty cloth looms with fulling mills and all kinds of other tools used in the said Manufactory. ...

And so that the supplicant may freely enjoy the fruits of his labor, we have defended all workers and other persons of whatever quality and condition they may be, from imitating or counterfeiting the mark and manufacture of said cloths for the time of twenty years, as well as from erecting in the said city and within ten leagues in its vicinity similar cloth looms and from building any mill, without the permission of the said Entrepreneur and his associates, on the penalty of a fine of fifteen hundred pounds, applicable to the hospitals of Abbeville, and all costs, damages and interest to the said Entrepreneur, to whom we have allowed and allow to associate in the said manufacture with such people as he sees fit, without for this reason his associates being supposed or deemed to have derogated from nobility under the pretext of engaging in the trade of goods which, as necessary, we have exempted and exempt them. ...

Because such is our pleasure and so that it be always firm and stable, we have had our seal put on these present [letters] ... . Given in Paris, in the month of October, the year of grace one thousand six hundred and sixty-five.

Signed: Louis.

§ 1.45.2 In a Letter to the Intendant of Rouen, Colbert Refers to a Trade Secret Owned by van Robais on a Method of Dyeing Cloths—1683

Paris, June 27, 1683

To Mr. Méliand, Intendant of Rouen.

The named Van Robais whom the King has transferred from Holland to Abbeville to establish the manufacture of cloths of Holland and England, having sent a number of pieces of these cloths to the named Guillotin, merchant of Rouen, the wardens of the cloth guild have seized those pieces of cloth, and intend to confiscate them because they are not *garancées*,[19] in accordance with the regulations that apply to the manufactures. As the said Van Robais has a particular secret for black dyes, which has been acknowledged as very good by the experiments which have been made of them in the presence of the most skillful merchants of Paris, he has been authorized to sell his dyed cloths by the means of his trade secret, and the merchants of this city have not opposed any obstacle.

That is why it is necessary, for the maintenance of this manufacture, that you promptly release the seizure of those cloths, and that you give the merchant in charge of them the freedom that is necessary for him to carry them out. I beg you to let me know what you have done to execute this letter.

§ 1.45.3 A Historical Account of van Robais Heirs' Long Struggle in Obtaining Exclusive Rights in a New Business Identifier: The Dawn Colored Selvage of Their Cloths

In 1718 it is mentioned in a letter from Mr. Barague, of Darnetal, that the Vanrobais would have requested the exclusive privilege of putting a red selvage on their cloths. [note omitted] The Deputies of Trade to whom this letter is addressed state that they were not aware of the fact. They are moreover quite hostile to this innovation, because, according to them, a trademark denotes neither the quality nor the place of manufacture and [for that purpose] the name of the manufacturer at the head of the piece of cloth is sufficient. In 1724, upon a request from the

19. Dyed in red.

Vanrobais in the same direction, they replied that the Vanrobais, having previously marked their cloths like other manufacturers, i.e., with their name and a piece of lead with these words: "Manufacture Royale d'Abbeville," the public have recognized their merit and given them preference. A golden piece of lead and a selvage would deceive the public, which judge by appearance. The makers of Abdelys and Louviers could be discouraged and forced to start using less fine wools. Finally, in England and Holland, fine cloths are distinguished only by the name of the manufacturer and their beauty. [note omitted] By virtue of all these fine reasons which were to cease to be valid thereafter, the Vanrobais obtained only the following addition in the privilege of 1724: "We want that on all your cloths and terry cloths which will be made in the said factory, the names of the said Vanrobais and that of the said town [Abbeville] be embroidered both on the head and on the tail of said cloths and terry cloths and that on the head of each piece, a piece of lead be affixed, on one side of which our arms will be engraved, and on the other, these words: 'Manufacture Royale d'Abbeville'."

But the Vanrobais did not desist and were the first to introduce the use of a special mark in factories. In 1733, they proposed, as one of the remedies for the mediocre state of their affairs, to distinguish the cloth of each factory by the manufacturer's name and mark, "but also by a more striking mark, less easy to alter and which would be accessible and known to everyone." They ask, if this project is adopted, to continue using for their fine cloths "Swiss-red selvages with two blue threads placed between the selvage and the cloth, which they are in the habit of putting on said cloths."

At the same time that this request was brought to the Board of Trade, one of the Vanrobais went to see the Commissioner rapporteur, Mr. de Hauteroche, and proposed to adopt "a new blue selvage with four dawn color threads woven between the border and the cloth." The Council did not consider it advisable to extend the measure to all factories, but was of the opinion that a judgment should be given granting the Vanrobais the exclusive ownership of their mark. Consequently, a decision of the Council of September 12, 1733 gave them the right to put on their cloths a blue selvage with four dawn color threads, with prohibition from infringement. [note omitted].

The use of this distinctive mark had good results only, considering that the Deputies of Trade, examining the Vanrobais' requests for a new privilege in 1743, thought that such a distinction did not harm anyone and that, on the contrary, it would be desirable that the use of a particular selvage became generalized in order to force retailers not to sell one kind of cloth for another. [note omitted]

A mention to the selvage was included in the letters patent of 1743 and 1768. The Vanrobais have held to this privilege, given that in 1773 we see them complaining that Messrs. Homassel, manufacturers of Abbeville, imitated their selvage. The Subdelegate, at their request, visits the accused establishment; he notices in the cloths' selvages a slightly dawn color, and on October 18 an Ordinance of the Intendant appears forbidding Messrs. Homassel from using "any dawn color or yellow thread or any other shade whose colors may have an analogy." [note omitted]

§ 1.45.4 Report on the Complaint by the Heirs of van Robais Concerning the Infringement of Their Selvage—1773

1773.—Industry.—Report on the investigation made by Mr. de Braulicourt, subdelegate in Abbeville, on the request presented by Messrs. Van Robais and nephews; in order to be maintained in their privileges, "in particular that of putting in the cloths of their factory a particular selvage ... in result of which, visit and inspection would be ordered to the premises of Messrs. brothers Homassel, who have established in the same town some clothing looms, in order to elaborate a report on the cloths that would be in their workshop in violation of said privilege. Attached the samples of the selvage of Messrs. Van Robais and that of Mr. Hommassel. September 15.—Report by Mr. de Branlicourt, in the sense of prohibiting the widow Hommassel and son from using in the future in the selvage of the cloths of their manufacture any dawn or yellow thread and other colors the nuances of which may have some relation with them." Abbeville, September 20; with order of the Intendant rendered in consequence of the said report. October 18.

§ 1.45.5 Van Robais Advertises the Manufacture's Exclusive Rights in the Selvage—1749

As there is always great abuse, both in France and in foreign countries, in the distribution and sale of the fine cloths and terry cloths from the manufacture of Messrs. Van Robais and Nephews, established in Abbeville, which is extremely prejudicial to them and to the public, we are obliged to inform again those who wish to use said cloths, that by privilege of S.M.T.C. [*Sa Majesté Très Chrétienne*], exclusive to all others, all the cloths and terry cloths of said manufacture are distinguished, and can be easily recognized; 1. by the selvages which are blue with four 4 dawn threads, woven between the blue of the selvage and the cloth or terry cloth; 2. by the words *Van Robais & Neveux à Abbeville*, embroidered in wool and in large characters on the head and tail of each piece; and in 3rd. place, by 2 large tailless pieces of lead, affixed one at the beginning of the piece, and the other at the end of one of the two selvages, which are engraved on one side with the arms of France, with the name *Van Robais* below the escutcheon, and on the reverse are written these words: *Manufacture Royale des Draps fins d'Abbeville.* This notice was published in 1749.

Figure 14 The two lead tokens of Josse Vanrobais that were affixed to the two extremes of each cloth that left his factory.

§ 1.46 REGULATIONS OF THE MAKING OF CLOTHS IN THE MANNER OF SPAIN AND HOLLAND IN SEDAN—1666

Since the middle of the sixteenth century, the treatment of business identifiers for the cloth industry had reached a sort of harmonization, as the many regulations dealing with that industry reveal. The text that follows is an expression of the legal standard that resulted therefrom. One peculiar aspect of this regulation was its concern with the possibility of corruption of the inspectors ("jurors"), who might be influenced or biased in favor of or against certain masters. The latter were, therefore, required to conceal the individual marks they sewed to the cloths under a fold. Supposedly, that fold would be undone after the inspection, so that the mark could become visible. In subsequent regulations, other ways of preventing jurors' malpractices will be shown. The most common way was the attribution of individual signs to jurors so that they, like the artisans, could also be identified in the case some error in certification was found.

Decision of the Council, which confirms the Minutes of August 24, 1666, containing Regulations for the Manufactures of Cloths, in the manner of Spain and Holland, established in Sedan

September 16, 1666. Registered in Parliament, on January 8, 1667

> The King [Louis XIV] having had himself represented in his Royal Council of Trade, the Minutes of the general assembly of Magistrates, Aldermen, Mayor, principal Residents of the city of Sedan, held, following the orders of His Majesty, on 24 last of August, 1666, in the presence of Thomas Renart de Fustemberg, Advisor to His Majesty in his Councils, Commissioner by Him appointed, for the general and sovereign reformation of Waters and Forests in the department of Champagne and dependent Countries, containing the Statutes and Regulations, in the number of sixty-six articles, by which the said Residents have unanimously declared that their opinion was that the factories and manufactures of cloths, in the manner of Spain and Holland, which were established 20 years ago in the said city of Sedan by Mr. Nicolas Cadeau,[20] in consequence of the privilege that has been granted to him by His Majesty, and afterwards to several Residents of the said City, could be greatly increased and improved, and that the fulfillment of the said Statutes, if it pleased His Majesty to order their homologation, would be of great utility for the said Residents, and very advantageous to trade. His Majesty willing to provide it; Heard the report of Lord Colbert, Advisor in his Royal Council, Comptroller-General of Finances, Superintendent of His Majesty's Buildings, Arts and Manufactures of France. ...
>
> X. The Jurors-Wardes and Merchants will meet twice a week, namely, on Tuesday and Saturday, at the place to be agreed by the Corporation of the said trade, on which days all the pieces of cloths that will have been made in the said City will be brought to be inspected and marked there with a mark that will be made for this purpose, namely, once, when they will be in canvas, the other, on their return from the mill, and the other, after being dyed and finished.
>
> XI. When the Jurors find that the cloths that will be presented to them are well-conditioned as far as the material and the manner [of making] are concerned, if they are of the first quality of very fine cloths, they will be marked with a mark of lead, having on one side the effigy of the King, with these words, *Louis XIV*,

20. Nicolas Cadeau and two partners received in 1646 an industrial privilege for the exclusive making in the city of Sedan of cloths in the manner of Spain and Holland. The privilege had the term of twenty years, and included several benefits, including the grating of nobility to Cadeau. This new Regulation, twenty years later, reflects the expiry of the exclusivity term. Nevertheless Cadeau continued receiving favorable treatment, to the extent that his cloths were excluded from the inspection as well from the obligation to give accommodation to members of the military (*see* Article xxi of the Regulations).

Restaurateur des Arts & du Commerce, and on the other, the arms of the said city of Sedan, around which will be written, *Draperie Royale de Sedan*, and on top of the piece, before it is brought to the fuller, the name of the worker shall be put. ...

XIV. If the cloths are not of the required quality, they will be cut and torn in pieces, and will be marked by the Wardens with a particular mark, and returned to the master for being used by him, his workers and servants only, and the master or worker, who has made the flawed piece, shall be fined in at least ten pounds.

XV. Each master of the said trade will have his particular mark, which will be placed and written on the register of the said Corporation, with which they shall mark their cloths, before bringing them to the said Chamber, and without their being allowed to apply the said mark except to the cloths of their own making, upon penalty of confiscation, and a fine of three hundred pounds.

XVI. And so that the Jurors shall not be biased in favor or against any [master], those marks shall be hidden in a fold of the cloth, which will be sewn for this purpose.

XVII. In order that the inspection be more accurate, there will be three samples of cloths of the first, second, and third kinds in the said common Office, with which the pieces of cloths that will be brought will be compared, in order to know by which marks they must be marked, be they of the first, second or third kind. ...

XX. If any manufacturer or another [ab]uses the mark of a city other than Sedan, or applies, or causes to be applied that of Sedan or his own to any foreign cloth, he will be tied to the stocks, for six hours, in the middle of the public square, with a poster displaying the falsehood committed by him; and for this purpose, the fuller is prohibited from receiving any cloth without the inspection's mark, in writing, as stated above, on the penalty of a fine of twenty pounds for each piece of cloth.

XXI. And whereas Mr. Nicolas Cadeau has established in the City of Sedan the first manufactures of fine cloths in the manner of Spain and Holland, and has given sufficient proofs of his capacity and loyalty in the said Manufacture, taking this into consideration, all the cloths of his factory, and of his Successors, and the premises of his Manufactories shall not be subject to any inspections, or to the obligation to give accommodation to Persons of War [members of the Military]. ...

Figure 15 The stocks, a device used in the Middle Ages (and afterward, as the previous text shows) for the punishment of certain sorts of crimes, such as counterfeiting.

§ 1.47 BY-LAWS OF THE CORPORATION OF WOOLLEN CLOTHMAKERS OF AMIENS—1666

The following by-laws summarize the rules that applied to certification and trademarks through the sixteenth and seventeenth centuries. The difference that can be found here by comparison with other regulations dealing with the same subject is that these ones do not contain detailed provisions on the registration of trademarks with the City Hall—but they still require such registration.

The rule (CI) that admitted the introduction of works of new invention by the clothmakers is also worth noticing. At that time, the freedom to offer articles produced under the pressure of fashion was not yet entirely available, because the introduction of those articles on the market was still dependent on superior approval. However, it was a significant change in the way that the cloth and fashion business was being carried out.

Also interesting are the two rules imposing restrictions on the way masters competed with each other (CLII and CLIII).

By-laws and Regulations adopted by the Council, for the *Sayeteurs, Hautelisseurs* [workers of the high loom], Combers, Fullers and other workers forming part of the Manufacture d'Amiens

August 23, 1666

> In Assembly held in the Council Chamber of the common Town Hall of the City of Amiens, on the fourth day of November, 1665, and on the days of the week, and on Monday, Tuesday, Wednesday and Thursday of the following [week], and again on Tuesday and Wednesday of the one after, in order to reply to the letter from Lord Colbert, Counselor to the King in all his Councils, Superintendent of Buildings and Manufactures of France, Commander and Grand Treasurer of his Orders, by which he decides to send Messrs. Correur and Chenard to examine, with the Company, the means of putting the Trade and Manufacture of *Sayeterie* in this Town back to the state it should be, and to see what can be done for its growth ... And after having made known to all the aforementioned the obligations of which this City will be eternally indebted to the King's kindness, and to Lord Colbert's particular care for the increase of the Trade: And having read to them the letter with which he has honored the Company, and having informed of the intention of fulfilling it with all the zeal and respect possible; the By-laws, Regulations and Ordinances concerning the Manufacture of the said *Sayeterie* were read, examined and reformed as follows, after having heard all the aforementioned on the Articles concerning the profession of each of them in particular, and carefully deliberated on the whole. ...
>
> CI. And where some *Sayeteur* decides to make some piece of new invention, he shall not put it at the loom[21] without asking the permission of the Aldermen, so that they specify the number of threads and the length, after having heard four Merchants and four former *Sayeteurs*. ...
>
> CII. So that the Worker or Master who will have produced a piece of *Sayeterie* in the said City can be recognized, with the purpose of recovering from that Master the damage and the sanctions of the defects that might be found there, each Master *Sayeteur* shall have a mark, which he shall bring and register, within eight days after the publication of the present [letters], on a Register that will be established for this purpose at the Secretariat of the Town Hall; from now on, in addition to having entered the said mark in the said Registry, they shall renew it, on the penalty of a fine of sixty *sols*, applicable as above.

21. The original term is "estile." This term (also spelling as "étile" and "stile") was used in ancient French with several possible meanings, the two most important being "loom" and "trade or profession." So, here, the expression "mettre sur l'estile" means to put it at the loom, i.e., to make the new cloth. More broadly, it also means to include the new cloth in the catalogue of products manufactured by the guild (and offering them for sale).

CIII. The said Masters shall weave or cause to be woven the said mark at the beginning of each piece [of cloth], which will be warped and mounted in their workshops; they shall not be allowed to use each other's mark, and modify their ordinary marks, on the penalty of a fine of ten pounds, applicable as above.

CIV. Each Master will have a stamp on which his mark will be engraved, with the name and surname around it, with which he will imprint his mark, and his aforesaid name and surname on one side of the stamp on the Warden's loom; who will engrave on the other side the arms of the City: And the said Masters shall have the said stamps within eight days from the publication of the Present [letters], on the penalty of a fine of sixty *sols*, to be applied as above.

CV. The six Wardens-sealers are ordered to fulfill their duties, and to incessantly inspect the workshops of the said Master *Sayeteurs*, and to apply the stamp at the loom to all the pieces of *Sayeterie* that are mounted there; the mark with the name and surname of the Master will be engraved on one side of that stamp, and on the other side, the arms of the City, as provided above; so that there can be certainty about the place where the piece will have been worked, and the said Wardens shall not apply the said stamp to pieces other than those that have the mandatory number and count of threads, according to and in conformity with the present By-laws, on the penalty of a fine of ten pounds, and of answering for damages and interests on their behalf, for the first time, and for the second time, of a greater fine, and deprivation of their Offices; the said fine being applied half to the City, and the other half to the accusers: And in the event of a default in the number of said threads, the said Wardens shall seize the piece in which the defect will be found, counter-seal it and denounce it immediately to the Town Hall, on penalty, in case of collusion, of a similar fine, to be applied as above. ...

CVIII. The Master *Sayeteurs* shall not offer for sale any pieces of *Sayeterie* if they are not sealed, in accordance with the Articles above, on penalty of confiscation of the articles; and the Merchants [shall not] buy them, without the said seal, upon the penalty of a fine of twenty pounds, half applicable to the city, and the other to the accusers. ...

CLII. There shall be only one Master in each workshop, even though several looms may be operated there, on penalty of a fine of ten pounds, half to the City, and the other half to the Wardens or accusers.

CLIII. Two or more Masters shall not associate nor profit in common from their works, in order to avoid monopolies, frauds and collusions that could arise, on penalty of a fine of sixty *sols*, applicable as above for the first time, and an arbitrary fine for the second.

§ 1.48 GENERAL REGULATIONS OF THE FRENCH CLOTH AND DYEING INDUSTRIES—1669

The cloth industry being the main economic activity of France between the Middle Ages and the Industrial Revolution, it naturally attracted a great deal of laws and regulations, aimed at organizing it. However, that did not prevent the eruption of a vast amount of controversies and challenges among manufacturers and merchants, and between them and authorities. Failure to comply with mandatory standards and counterfeiting of trademarks were also very common. By the middle of the seventeenth century, the situation had reached such a critical point that, by inspiration of Colbert, his main advisor and ministry of finance, Louis XIV was obliged to abrogate all statutes, regulations, and by-laws then in force, and replace them with a few new regulations, with the purpose of bringing some coherence, consistency, and harmony to the manufacture and commerce of cloths.

The texts that follow are just a few excerpts from those regulations, which included detailed norms on the use of certification, collective and individual marks. These excerpts deal specifically with the norms on business identifiers, but the regulations also provided in detail specific methods of manufacture, materials to be used, lengths, weights, colors, etc.

In these excerpts, a few aspects are particularly worthy of notice: in the first text we can see several examples of the most common frauds committed in order to avoid inspections and taxes; in the second text, there is a special rule prohibiting the "débauchage"—i.e., the prohibition to interfere in a contract of apprenticeship held by a competitor, which is today seen as a matter of unfair competition;[22] *besides, the texts provide for a few rules in which intellectual property and competition intersect, such as the one that prohibited masters and merchants from having more than one shop as well as from licensing their names and trademarks to outsiders; we can also find interesting rules on how artisans and merchants could visually advertise the articles they sold in their shops, including mandatory limits on displays' sizes. This provision may be seen as a precedent of the rules that would be enacted one century later in Paris (and subsequently in the whole country) curtailing the excesses of signboards, which had become so large and heavy that they put the life of bypassers in danger.*[23]

§ 1.48.1 Regulations Concerning the Dyeing of Cloths—1669

Statutes, Ordinances, and Regulations that His Majesty wishes to be observed by the Merchant Master Dyers, in the great and good Dye of Cloths, Woven and other Woolen Cloths, of all the Towns and Boroughs of his Kingdom

July 13, 1669

> VII. … And by the said Police Officers, or the one who will be by them appointed, assisted by the Masters and Wardens of the Haberdashery, and the Juror Dyer, a similar inspection and marking will be made of all the Dyed and Woven Woolen Cloths, which will be in the Stores and Workshops of the Merchant Haberdashers, and Privileged Merchants[24] following the Court, without exception; And afterwards the figure of the said mark will be imprinted in the Register of the Community of the said Cloth Merchants, Haberdashers and Dyers, then torn apart,

22. The prohibition of *débauchage* was the matter of one of the first rules on intellectual property ever to be enacted—law no. 89 of the Code of Hammurabi, of *circa* 1,750 BC. *See* From Babylon to the Silicon Valley, *supra* note 1, at 157.
23. *See* From Babylon to the Silicon Valley, *supra* note 1, at 127.
24. The term "privileged" refers to those professional makers and merchants who, in spite of not being admitted as members of corporations, were allowed to carry out the profession as a result of their personal (i.e., privileged) position. For example, the personal tailors of the King and the Queen were "privileged" to make cloths, even if they did not follow any apprenticeship or joined the guild of tailors.

put into pieces in the presence of all those who will have made the said Inspections, which will be mentioned in the said Registers. ... [25]

XXXIV. And to give an obvious testimony that all the Cloths will be dyed with good color and good ingredients, in the manner previously expressed, all Dyers will leave at the end of each piece of said Cloths a Rose of the size of a silver *écu*, in blue or yellow color, and all the other colors that will have served as a base and in depth for the dyeing of the said cloths, and if the said pieces of fabric are not entirely dyed in depth, in accordance with the said roses, they will be confiscated, and the Dyer condemned to a fine of five hundred pounds, and forever banned from Mastership, as a public Counterfeiter. ...

XXXVIII. To further oblige the Master Dyers of the good Dye to do their duty and perfect their Dyes, the Merchant Clothiers will appoint one among them (starting with the oldest one, who has been promoted to Warden) for visiting the said Master Dyers in their workshops, including the Jurors in charge, every working day, during fifteen days, to see and examine the Ingredients from which they will compose their Dyes, and the Articles dyed by them, and whether these will be of the same quality of the samples put in the Office of the Community: for the purpose of which Inspections, the Masters and Wardens of Cloth Making will cause five Marks to be made at the expense of the said Community, and on each of [those marks] the name of the City where the said Dyes will be made will be engraved, and around it the following words, as follows: on the first [mark] *Guesde* [Pastel] for passing to *Garence* [a bright red dye]; on the second, *Guesde and Garence* for passing to Black; on the third *Blue* for passing to Black; on the fourth, *Gaude* [a type of plant from which a yellow dye is extracted]; and on the fifth, *Cramoisi* [crimson]: which marks will be placed along with pieces of the said samples in the hands of the person appointed by the said Masters and Warden of Cloth Making to the said Inspections, in order to mark on a piece of lead the Articles that will be dyed with the said qualities in conformity of the samples. And in order to know the names of those who will have dyed the said Articles, all Master Dyers shall have in their workshops a small anvil on which their name and surname will be engraved, so that the Merchant in charge of the Inspections apply a piece of lead to the top of the dyed pieces, the name of the Dyer who will have dyed them be printed on them from below at the same time as the Mark of the said Cloth makers will be printed from the top, when it will be placed on the said piece of lead, and struck with a stroke of hammer on that Anvil. ...

XL. And all the more so as it is to be feared that several of the Merchants who would be in charge of the Inspections of the Dyers not being sufficiently aware of their defects, the Master Dyers who would not intend to comply with these Regulations, could make false dyes, or, for depriving them of the knowledge of it, they would hide the poorly dyed cloths during the Inspections that would be made in their workshops; and afterwards to better cover their counterfeits they would deliver them secretly to the Merchants for whom they would have dyed them, and with whom they would be in agreement as regards the low prices of the said false dyes, or to have less risk of being surprised in the trade in said false dyes, they would dye for Merchants [in] Cities other than that of their residence, or the Merchants in the trade of said false dyes, or the Merchants of the Kingdom's Border Cities, in order to reduce the costs of dyeing of their Articles, could send them to dye false dyes in foreign neighboring countries; or even foreign merchants could send falsely dyed Articles to France; and by these means all those kinds of false dyeing would remain in trade, and would prevent the success and the perfection of

25. This was a standard provision, and was repeated in respect of the other sorts of cloths dealt with by the other regulations that will be partly transcribed and translated below.

the good dyeing, to the great prejudice of the business of the Manufactures of France, of which the past and the present provide only too many examples of similar abuses: For remedying which all the Dyed Cloths and Woolen Cloths that will not be marked with the mark of the Merchant Clothiers and of the Dyer Juror, as said above, will be confiscated; said Merchants shall receive or display them for sale; and all persons shall buy them only after the aforesaid marks have been affixed thereon, upon the penalty of a fine of two hundred pounds against each of the offenders, to the payment of which they will be compelled without deportation. And to know whether the Foreign Articles will have been marked, and whether the mark of the good Dye will have been faithfully put together with those that will have been dyed in Foreign countries [and whether these] are of good Dye, both Articles, without exception, shall be seen and inspected by the Masters and Wardens of Drapery, who will be accompanied, if they deem it convenient, by the Dyer Juror of the said Cities where the said Articles will be brought to be sold, and by them marked with their mark, if the Dye is good; and if it is false, they shall be seized and placed in sequestration, and the confiscation judged by the Judge of Police, and the selvages torn. ...

XLVIII. The Masters of the said Community shall not deviate or attract to their workshop the Apprentice or Companion of another Master, nor give him employment directly or indirectly, on the penalty of a fine of sixty pounds. ...

LVI. None of the said Masters nor their Widows may occupy more than one Shop, Stall or Dyeing Workshops, and may put Canvases, Carpets, Showcases associated with that Trade in front of said Workshops, and shall not be allowed to lend their name to anyone whatsoever, under pretext of kinship or otherwise, nor associate with anyone who is not a Master of the Community, on the penalty of a fine of five hundred pounds: And they may also attach to the said Workshops Poles so as to display over the Street the Cloths and Works that they will have dyed, which shall not extend beyond half the Street, and the Cloths and Works that they will have dyed shall not go down more than three fathoms from the ground, according to the Decree of the Parliament of Paris, of the tenth of March one thousand six hundred ten. ...

Our opinion is, under the good pleasure of His Majesty, that the said Articles are useful to the Public, and very necessary for the restoration and perfection of the Dyes of the Woolen Cloths, Articles, and Manufactures that are made in France, both for use and consumption in the Kingdom, and to increase sales in Foreign Countries. Made at Paris on the thirteenth day of July, one thousand six hundred and sixty-nine.

§ 1.48.2 Regulations on Mandatory Technical Standards for Cloths

Statutes, Ordinances and Regulations, on the lengths, widths and qualities of Cloths and other Wool Fabrics and Thread, which His Majesty wishes to be observed by all the Master Cloth Makers, Workers and Finishers of the Cities, Burghs and Villages of His Kingdom

LI. The name of the Masters, Workers and Finishers will be placed on the top and first end of each piece of said Articles, made at the Loom, and not with the needle, upon the penalty of a fine of twelve pounds for each piece where the said name will not have been put.

§ 1.48.3 Regulation on the Dyeing of Fine Cloths and Thread

Statutes, Ordinances and Regulations, which His Majesty wishes to be observed by all the Merchants, Master Dyers in Silk, Wool and Thread of the Towns and Suburbs of his Kingdom

July 22, 1669

> LXXXIV. Each one of the Master Dyers of Silk, Wool, and Thread, shall have in their Workshops, Shops, and Stalls, a stamp and mark, where on one side the name and arms of the City where they reside will be engraved, and on the other, the surname, the said Stamp and mark to be applied and engraved on a piece of lead that will be attached with a Thread to the bundles of Silk, Wool or Thread, and to the body and top of the Cloths by them Dyed when they deliver them: So that the said Thread and Piece of Lead cannot be separated and removed from the place where they will be applied without a visible severance, so that those by whom the said Fabrics, Silk, Wool, and Thread have been Dyed be known, of which Dyes' goodness they will remain guarantors and liable: And for this purpose each of the said Master Dyers will provide an imprint of their mark both to the Office of their Community and to those Merchant Haberdashers and Master Workers in Gold, Silver, and Silk Cloths, in the hands of the Master Wardens or Jurors of the said Communities in Charge, who shall make mention of it in their registries, to have recourse to them when necessary: The said Dyers may not sell or deliver the said Cloths, nor the Silks, Wools, and Threads in bundles, and no person shall buy or receive them without their being marked as said; moreover, the Dyer shall not put any mark other than his own, the whole upon the penalty of a fine of hundred pounds for each counterfeit, and the confiscation of the said unmarked Cloths Silk, Wool and Thread Fabrics. ...
>
> XCIV. The said Masters and their Widows shall not occupy more than one Shop, Stall or Dyeing Workshop, and may place in front of said shops, such carpets as they deem necessary and other things associated with said Trade, and shall not lend their names to anyone else whatsoever, under any pretext or otherwise, upon the penalty of a fine of one hundred pounds, and will be exempt from the right of high ban.[26]

§ 1.49 ORDINANCES CONCERNING THE SEALS TO BE AFFIXED TO THE CLOTHS MADE IN LILLE—1673

As in other French cities, by the middle of the seventeenth century, the manufacture and commerce of cloths had acquired such an important role that authorities would not hesitate to take measures to avoid their importation. In 1673, Lille adopted such a regulation. About one decade later, that regulation had to be reinforced due to lack of compliance. Both regulations dealt essentially with the sealing of cloths made in Lille, with both the city's seal and the clothmakers' marks.

26. *Le droit de ban* was the right that certain feudal lords had to enroll their subjects in certain public services.

§ 1.49.1 Ordinance Concerning the Pieces of Lead, Seals, and Tokens to Be Affixed to the Pieces [Of Cloth]

April 8, 1673

The aldermen, council and eight men [the *vingtaine*][27] of this city of Lille, because it has come to their knowledge that several persons both from this city and outside, notwithstanding the prohibitions several times made by their predecessors in Law, published on 26 of May and 6 of October, 1568, and 27 of October, 1570, interfere and engage in causing to be brought or bringing into this city a large number of foreign Articles of *sayeterie* and *bourgeterie*[28] and not made in this said town, for being sold and worked upon, to the great damage, prejudice and interest, and even the obvious ruin of the said corporations of *sayeteries* and *bourgeterie*, and of several residents and inhabitants of this city living out from the said professions, and generally of the public good, the said aldermen, wishing in their power to remedy it, have, upon mature deliberation, and in the form of a solution to last as long as it pleases them, starting on the twentieth of April next, ordered and order what follows. ...

Item that, as from the said day onwards, each of all the Master *sayetteurs* and *bourgeteurs* of this city shall have a token on which his/her sign is printed, such as and in conformity with the one they took when passing their masterpiece and registered in the registers of the community, and that alongside such a sign be also printed the first two letters of the name and surname of such *sayetteur* or *bourgeteur*, at the risk [on penalty] that if any difference were found, of incurring for each time and in each of the mentioned cases, in the fine of six pounds applicable as it is provided below, and other punishment at the discretion of the aforesaid communities of *sayetterie* and *bourgeterie*. ...

The aforesaid *sayetteurs* and *bourgeteurs* shall not bring or send the articles to be inspected nor the sealer appointed to seal shall inspect them unless they are sealed with the stamp and token of this city, set to be stamped at the loom, and that the articles have the signs of the master *sayeteurs* or *bourgeteurs* to whom they will belong with pins at each end of another very different and visible color than that of the said pieces, at the risk of paying by the offenders for each piece and each fault a fine of six *livres parisis*, applicable one third to the accuser, another third to the profit of the chapels of the patron saints of the aforesaid communities, and the other and last third to the profit of the aforesaid communities of the *vingtaine* and *bourgeterie*, and moreover the appointed sealer to be suspended from his office and declared disqualified to continue being so, or as the aldermen at their discretion may decide otherwise.

27. *See supra* note 15.
28. *Bourgeterie* was, in addition to *sayetterie* (*see* § 1.21), the other large industrial sector of Lille, and consisted in the making of cloths mixing wool with linen.

§ 1.49.2 Ordinance Concerning the Tokens, Stamps, and Pieces of Lead That Must Be Affixed to the Articles of *Sayetterie* and *Bourgeterie*

July 28, 1684

The wardens, mayor, aldermen, council and eight men of the city of Lille, being informed that their ordinance of April 8, 1673, enacted with the purpose of avoiding that articles of *sayetterie* and *bourgeterie* that have not been made in that city be brought to it, has not been observed in all its points; and whereas what has been ordered is very useful for the maintenance and growth of the communities of the trade of *sayetterie* and *bourgeterie* established in this city; have prohibited and prohibit, as before, all master *sayetteurs* and *bourgeteurs* from cutting or putting at the loom any articles from their trade if they are not sealed and marked with the token of this city by those who have been appointed for this purpose by the officers of the office of the *vingtaine* and *bourgeterie,* and this on the penalty that the articles that will be found at the looms without said mark will be deemed as foreign articles, and adjudged as such, unless they are provided with the seals of this city affixed upon inspection by the appointed sealers.

And so that the manufacturers be not harmed by the delay, those who will be appointed for sealing [the cloths] at the looms shall go twice per week, and more frequently if necessary, to the workshops of the *sayetteurs* and *bourgeteurs,* to seal at the looms all the articles that are manufactured there, and will have as wage five *deniers parisis* for each piece, [which will be paid] by delivering at their expense the lead seals that they are required to collect at the offices of the *vingtaine* and *bourgeterie.*

The token of the city that will be affixed at the loom shall have as a countermark, the token of the makers of *saies* and *bourges*; and because each of them shall have one token, on which their marks will be imprinted, as such as they have taken when they passed their masterpiece, and registered at the register of the *vingtaine* and *bourgeterie,* and by the side the marks, the first letters of their names and surnames, on penalty, in case of default, or in the case there is a difference, of paying a fine of six *livres parisis,* or other arbitrary punishment.

And because the lead seals that are affixed at the loom serve only the purpose of proving that the article in question has been manufactured in this city, and it is of sufficient quality as [it] has passed the inspection, and that the appointed sealers have affixed to them the lead seals and the mark of this city, We command those appointed sealers that they leave in the articles that they will inspect and seal at the loom with the city's token the said lead seals, and to break them in such a way that they can no longer be used; and anything that might result from that shall be to the profit of the chapels of the said trades.

If it happened that someone were so bold to lift and extract the lead seals from the articles of *sayetterie* and *bourgeterie,* either at the loom or at the inspection, and to affix them to another article not sealed nor inspected, he will incur in the fine of fifty *livres parisis* and in addition he will be punished and sanctioned as a counterfeiter, at the aldermen's discretion.

The fines in which they will incur in result of this ordinance shall be applied one third to the accuser, another third to the chapels of the said trades, and the remainder to the profit of the offices of the *vingtaine* and *bourgeterie,* which will be accounted for along with the other fines which are attributed to the said offices.

Made at the Halle, the twenty-eighth of July in thousand six hundred eighty-four.
Signed: B. Herreng.

§ 1.50 A COURT DISPUTE CONCERNING THE SIMILARITY OF TWO CLOTH MERCHANTS' SHOP SIGNS IS CITED IN A JUDGMENT OF THE PARLIAMENT OF AIX-EN-PROVENCE—1678

As noted above, in the seventeenth century, the use of business identifiers as tools for ensuring competitive advantages in an environment of commercial rivalry was already a common matter. This results not only from the assiduous presence of rules on trademark examination and registration, as shown above, but also from the increasing number of court disputes between competitors alleging trademark infringement.

The text that follows is the judgment of the Parliament of Aix-en-Provence that, acting as a court, settled a dispute between two medicine makers and sellers concerning the Orvietan trademark for an antidote. The decision was based on principles of Roman law as well as on case law, as set by a number of French Courts and Parliaments. This opinion is of great significance, not only because of the breadth of its arguments and analysis but also because it touches upon several areas of intellectual property, namely copyright, patents, trade names, and trademarks. Its main conclusion was based on the fundamental principle of honesty, which cuts across the whole spectrum of intellectual property, and buttresses the meaning and the purpose of differentiation. As far as trademark law is concerned, this opinion reiterated the principle of first in time, first in right.

One of the precedents drawn from French case law in this opinion was a case involving the shop signs of two cloth merchants.

Two merchant knitwear makers from Paris, neighbors of one another, had the Pavilion as a shop sign. He who had taken this sign first having caused the other to take away his own, the latter, decided to have painted in his sign, instead of a Pavilion, a large butterfly, with wings wide spread, so that he represented, or at least imitated, the figure of a Pavilion. By a second judgment this knitwear maker was ordered to change the sign.

Figure 16 The "gallantry shop" in 1678—a shop where fine cloth, wigs, and knitwear, such as socks, were on sale. At the end of the seventeenth century, fashion was still very far from the "ready-to-wear." Women and men acquired the fabrics and resort to the services of tailors and seamstresses for getting finished apparel. Engraving by Jean Lepautre, upon a drawing by Jean Berain, published in Le Mercure Galant, the first fashion magazine ever published.

§ 1.51 THE REGULATION OF CLOTH MANUFACTURE OF PORTUGAL—1690

As shown in all the preceding sources, the use of trademarks as tools of certification, or of origin, or of mere differentiation, became a normal practice in the cloth industry through the Middle Ages and onwards. Gradually, some guild by-laws added another requirement: that of inscribing the trademarks that were assigned to (or chosen by) the masters in a public, centralized registry, so that those signs could be publicly known and consulted, in case of disputes over product quality and trademark ownership.

This early requirement for legal security is also found in another industry, which also depends on trust and precision: gold and silversmithing.

This new requirement of registering trademarks has rapidly spread through Europe. The text that follows is a compilation of excerpts from the Regulation of the Cloth Industry (Regimento da Fábrica dos Pannos), of Portugal, of 1690, which can be seen as a synthesis of the rules concerning the business identifiers used at that time in the textile industry: marks of quality certification, marks of origin certification/geographical indications, and individual trademarks, as well as the duty to register the latter with the Municipality.

Regulation of the Manufacture of Cloth of Portugal, 1690

Chapter IX

About the Letters, Marks and Signs that shall be affixed to the *Dozeno*[29] when weaving.

As he begins weaving the Dozen, the Weaver shall put on its top, in woven letters and signs, the weight and mark of the cloth, as follows: to the Dozen he will affix a Cross, and before it, two risks, these meaning Dozen; and so he will add a *B*, meaning *Berbim*, and he will further add the mark of the place, where the said cloth is made, and the stamp or sign of the weaver who weaves it: and the weaver who fails to affix these Letters, Marks and Signs, shall pay for each piece devoid of them four hundred *reais*; and by putting more or less than what corresponds to such a cloth, he will lose its value, in addition to the crime penalty, in which he will also incur, because it is a case of counterfeit.

Chapter XVII

About the penalty of the Weaver who on the cloth puts the mark of another weaver or place.

No weaver will put another weaver's mark on the cloth he weaves, or the mark of any other place, other than that of the place in which he weaves, under the penalty to anyone who changes the said mark, or sign, of paying twenty *cruzados*, in addition to the crime penalty, and he will be exiled for two years to one of the Places beyond; and the same penalty will be applied to the Ragman, who does not put the same mark on his cloth.

Chapter LXXXV

There shall be two Books, on which signs and seals be printed.

I also order and command that in each of the Cities, or Villages, where cloths are made, there shall be two bound Books, on which the signs and seals of the fullers and ragmen shall be printed, so that one may see who has fulled and woven the cloths; of which two books one will always remain in the Notary of the Municipality, so that all the signs of the Officers who come anew will be placed on it, and from it they will pass to the other Book, which will have an Inspector, to whom it will be delivered at the time of his election; and the sign and mark of each Ragman and Officer who will come anew shall be different from the others; no other person shall be able to take the sign of that who dies, nor his son, with suspension from his office, until my mercy; and for this very reason, the sign and seal of each City, Town, or Locality, be also different from the signs and seals of the other Localities, so that through such signs and seals one may see and know in what Locality the cloths have been made, because the cloths from some Localities have advantage over those from others.

29. *Dozeno* (*dozen*): a fabric with 1,200 woven threads.

Chapter LXXXVIII

What the Inspector of Cloths will do at the beginning of the year about the cloths that will be made in the County.

> The Inspector of cloths, at the beginning of each year, will provide that the cloths that are to be made within the County of the City or Village where he resides and lives, coming to be fulled in the said Village and City, have his mark; and the Weavers, who weave the said cloths, will be obliged to show them, to be inspected whether they are well woven and finished, under the penalty of two thousand *reais*, which will be incurred by those who fail to do so, half to [be applied to] the said Inspector, and the other half to whoever accuses him.

Chapter XC

That the said wool officers have marks and signs, to put on their cloths.

> All the wool officers, Ragmen, Weavers, Fullers, and Shearers, will have marks and signs to be put on the cloths that they manufacture in their workshops so that at all times it be possible to know by those signs who made and wove, fulled, carded, and sheared them; which marks shall have been registered in the books of the Chambers, in accordance with Chapter Eighty-five; and failing to do so, they will incur a penalty of two thousand *reais*, half to the Inspector, and the other half to anyone who accuses him.

§ 1.52 A LATE PORTUGUESE SUMPTUARY LAW—1690

As noted in the Introduction, sumptuary laws were a common legal feature in many European countries through the Middle Ages, inspired by religious, political, and economic reasons. As the economy grew and the merchant and artisan classes were empowered, sumptuary laws lost meaning. In the seventeenth century, they were already very rare. However, in 1686, D. Pedro II, King of Portugal, approved a sumptuary law, imposing restrictions on the use of certain pieces of apparel and accessories, such as garments and hats. But because citizens were circumventing those restrictions by importing the restricted articles, four years later—in 1690—the King ordered that only hats made in Portugal could be used. As proof of compliance, the new regulation required the printing on hats of certification marks (the Royal Arms) as well as the masters' individual marks.

Decree in which a declaration is made on the *Pragmática*[30] of August 9, 1686, concerning hats, commanding that they be marked with certain marks, so that there would be no mistake in the introduction of those from the outside

1690

> I, the King, make known to those that see this Decree, that whereas the insistent orders issued for better compliance with the *Pragmática* that I ordered to be enacted concerning the ban on dresses and hats have not been sufficient; and

30. In Portuguese, *Pragmática* (as a noun) is an old term for designating a statute.

because the said Act is infringed because many people wear hats from outside, saying that they are made in the Kingdom, and it is not possible to examine the truth because the similarity that one has with the others: it is my pleasure and I command that it is not permitted to buy or sell hats of Beaver hides, Feathers and Wool (which are the three qualities of hats from outside), unless they are made in the Kingdom, and marked at the outside of the band by the Inspector, who has been appointed for this effect, with two marks of the Royal Arms imprinted on wax, with the stamp that has been ordered to be made. And moreover they will also be marked with the particular mark of the Master who makes them, imprinted with fire on the hat's band, also on the outside, under the same penalties imposed in the said *Pragmática* to offenders. Therefore, I command all Ministers, Officers and people to whom the knowledge of this matter concerns that they comply with it, and have it fully complied with and kept, thus and in the way it provides for. And in particular I order the Curator of the Kingdom's manufactures to oblige the Masters of the hat manufactures that each one has in his workshop the said particular mark, so that they mark the hats they make in their manufactories, as provided. ... João Cardoso made it in Lisbon on November 15, 1690. Sebastião da Gama Lobo has recorded it. King.

§ 1.53 THE STATE COUNCIL PROHIBITS THE USE OF FOREIGN MARKS TO DESIGNATE CLOTHS MADE IN FRANCE—1692 AND 1723

Consumers have always tended to let themselves be influenced by idiosyncrasies that eventually do not accept a rational explanation. Two Decisions by France's State Council, under Louis XIV and Louis XV, speak to that. It seems that in that period, French consumers had a preference for cloths of foreign origin, and were ready to pay a higher price to obtain them. Because of the difficulties in importing those cloths, due to protectionist measures, French cloth merchants and manufacturers reacted by cheating: they would put foreign trademarks on the products of their making, thus misleading consumers as to their true origin.

The following texts are not only a matter of intellectual property but also an issue of consumer law.

§ 1.53.1 The State Council Prohibits the Use of Foreign Marks to Designate Cloths Made in France—1692

Extracted from the Records of the State Council

February 5, 1692

The King having had presented to him the Decision rendered in his Council, His Majesty being there, on March 16, 1688, by which prohibitions were made to all Workers in Woolen Cloths, and particularly those of Carcassonne, to put on the pieces of cloth they will manufacture in the future, any mark of foreign England, for whatever cause and pretext that it might be, under penalty of confiscation: And His Majesty, being informed that to the detriment of the aforesaid prohibitions, the same abuse that had slipped into the Manufactories of Carcassonne, has since been imperceptibly introduced into other significant Manufactories of the Kingdom, and that several Entrepreneurs, Workers, on the most beautiful pieces of cloths they make, add to their names and to their ordinary marks other foreign marks of Spain, or England, and of Holland, which they have affixed or embroidered on the heads of pieces of Cloth woven with gold or silk, so as to permit the Merchants to sell them for a higher price, and as foreign goods, to those who are not familiar with them; which is implemented all the more easily, that several of the aforesaid Merchants, after having withdrawn from the inspection the pieces of Cloths thus marked and embroidered on the heads, remove the name of the French Worker, with the inspection's seal, and leave the only marks with which those of Foreigners have been imitated: Because it is necessary to deal with these matters, and to remedy an abuse so prejudicial to the Public, so contrary to the good faith of Commerce, and to the most important Manufactories of the Kingdom: His Majesty being in His Council, has made very express prohibitions to all Entrepreneurs of Manufactories, to Workers working in Woolen Cloths, and generally to all other persons, to apply or put to any articles and pieces of woolen cloths, any letters or foreign marks, even any letters, characters, figures, or shapes, of whatever quality they may be, without exception, besides the name of the Worker, and marks established by the Regulations; all on penalty of confiscation of the said articles, and a fine of fifteen hundred pounds in the event of infringement. And His Majesty also makes very express prohibitions to all Cloth Merchants of Paris, Rouen, Lyon, and other Cities of the Kingdom, to have any of the aforesaid marks put on the Woolen Cloths, to have any of those Cloths thus marked in their shops and warehouses, and to offer them for sale, upon the same penalties. And for this purpose this Decision shall be read, published and posted in Paris, and elsewhere where necessary, so that it is not claimed there is a cause of ignorance. His Majesty instructs Lord de la Reynie, Ordinary Councilor in his State Council, Lieutenant General of Police of the City of Paris, and the Lords Intendants, Commissioners designated in the Provinces, according to their attributions, to support the execution of this Decision, which will be executed notwithstanding any opposition or appeal, and without prejudice to them. Done in the King's State Council, His Majesty attending, held at Versailles on the fifth day of February, one thousand six hundred and ninety-two. Signed, Phelypeaux.

§ 1.53.2 The King's State Council Reiterates the Prohibition of 1692—1723

Decision of the King's State Council

April 26, 1723

Prohibits all Entrepreneurs of Manufactories, Workers working in Woolen Cloths, and generally all other persons, from applying or putting on any Articles and Pieces of Woolen Cloth, any Letters or Foreign Marks, including any Letters, Characters, Figures or Shapes, of whatever sort they may be, without exception, besides the name of the Worker and the Marks established by the Regulations; and all Cloth Merchants from having pieces of Cloth so marked in their Shops and Warehouses, on the penalty of confiscation and a fine of Fifteen hundred pounds.

Extracted from the Records of the State Council

The King being informed, that although His Majesty has, by a Decision of his Council of February 5, 1692, forbidden all Entrepreneurs of Manufactures, Workers working in Woolen Cloths, and generally all persons, from applying or putting to any Articles or pieces of Woolen Cloth, any Letters or Foreign Marks, including any Letters, Characters, figures, or shapes, of any sort whatsoever, without exception, besides the name of the worker and Marks established by the Regulations; and also all Cloth Merchants of the Cities of the Kingdom, from causing to put any of the said Marks placed on the Wool Cloths, and from having any of those so marked in their Shops and Warehouses, and from offering them for sale, all on penalty of confiscation and a fine of Fifteen hundred pounds: And yet, under the pretext that during the time of war there was the obligation to tolerate a similar abuse to facilitate to the Merchants the commerce of their Cloths in the Foreign Countries, several of them continue using the same Marks, apparently with a view to making a greater profit on the sale of their Goods ...; so that at the Fair held in Reims, several pieces of Serges in the manner of London were seized from the manufactory of Donchery, namely, four pieces in the Shop of the named du Rieu, Merchant in Amiens, and five pieces in that of the named Berthelin, Merchant in Troyes, wrapped in canvases with the arms of England printed on them: And all the more so as the reasons that for some time justified this tolerance, no longer subsist; That, moreover, the attention that His Majesty continually gives to obtaining all possible perfection for the cloths that are manufactured in France, give them a superiority over all those of the Foreign Manufactories; That therefore such an abuse no longer could be practiced without causing considerable damage to the commerce of the Kingdom: To which His Majesty desiring to provide a solution: Heard the Report of Mr. Dodun, Ordinary Counselor of the Royal Council, Comptroller of Finances. His Majesty being in His Council, has ordered and orders that the said Decision of February 5, 1692 will be executed according to its form and content; And in accordance with it, makes very express prohibitions and inhibitions to all Entrepreneurs of Manufactories, to Workers working in Woolen Cloths, and generally to all other persons, from applying or putting to any Articles and pieces of Woolen Cloth, Foreign Letters or Marks, including any Letters, Characters, figures or shapes, of any sort whatsoever, without exception, besides the name of the worker and the Marks established by the Regulations: And also to all Cloth Merchants of all the Cities of the Kingdom, from causing those Marks to be put on the Wool Cloths, from having any of those pieces so marked in their Shops and Warehouses, or to offer them for sale, all on the penalty against the infringers of confiscation of the said Articles and a fine of Fifteen hundred pounds, which cannot be waived or reduced for any cause and under any pretext whatsoever: And nevertheless His Majesty orders the return of the Warsteds, in the manner of London, seized to the aforesaid du Rieu and Berthelin, no consequence being drawn from this grace. His Majesty instructs Mr. d'Argenson, Lieutenant-General of Police of the City of Paris, and the Intendants and Commissioners in the Provinces and Generalities of the Kingdom, to carefully ensure the execution of this Decision, which will be read, published and posted wherever it belongs, so that no one is unaware of it. Made at the King's State Council, His Majesty attending, held at Versailles on the twenty-sixth day of April one thousand seven hundred and twenty-three. Signed Fleuriau.

§ 1.54 THE FRENCH STATE COUNCIL SETTLES THE DISPUTE BETWEEN THE MAKERS OF KNITWEAR AND THE MAKERS OF SOCKS—1707

This was already the eighteenth century and gradually France had started to release itself from the strictures of the guild regime. In the example that follows, a reference is made to private citizens that, even though their not being members of the corporation of the makers of knitwear of Paris, had received royal permission to engage in the making and selling of those articles, and even to have their own trademarks.

May 17, 1707

1. The master makers of knitwear of the suburbs of Paris may continue, depending on the customs and use of their location, selling and trading socks and other articles of knitwear made in the loom manufactured by the masters of the community of master makers of socks at the loom of Paris, or by private citizens having express permission and letters of privilege from His Majesty to make socks and other articles of knitwear made at the loom in Paris, and marked with the particular mark of the said master makers of knitwear or of the said privileged individuals in accordance with the said decision of the Council of March 30, one thousand seven hundred. ...

3. Nor shall the said master makers of knitwear buy or bring socks and other articles made at the loom of the other cities and localities of the kingdom, or of foreign countries, on penalty of confiscation of the knitwear articles made at the loom that will be found at their stores, without the mark of a master or a privileged maker of socks at the loom of Paris, on penalty of a fine of three hundred pounds and having their shops closed for three months.

4. The said Master makers of knitwear shall not keep in their stores socks and other knitwear articles made at the loom marked with a mark other than that of one of the masters or privileged persons of Paris, under the penalties above, unless the said articles belong to merchants of knitwear and have been given by them for fulling and finishing to the master makers of knitwear of the suburbs, and that these articles as well as the names of the merchants or others who have given them for fulling and finishing jointly be entered in the register that the said master makers of knitwear of the suburbs must keep, according to the sentence of the lieutenant general of police, of the tenth of January, one thousand six hundred and ninety-eight.

§ 1.55 LETTERS PATENT ON THE COMMUNITY OF SHOEMAKERS—PARIS, 1705

Louboutin, the famous French luxury women's shoemaker who in recent years has been engaged in a struggle to have the red color of his shoes' soles recognized as a trademark (see § 1.75) might find some comfort in realizing that very early in the eighteenth century, master shoemakers were under the obligation of printing their trademarks (the first two letters of their name) in the soles of the slippers they made. In today's trademark law jargon, this rule might be seen as a precedent, albeit remote, of "position marks."

Letters Patent or Declaration of the King, which confirms the Community of Master Shoemakers in the inheritance of the Offices of Accounts Auditors, and of Jurors in title, and which reunites the office of the Provost with that Community. Registered in Parliament on September 4, 1705

> VIII. Each of all Masters and Privileged ones who sell articles to the said Halliers [31] shall mark them with the mark of the first two letters of their name, which will be applied inside, over the quarter of the show, and inside the knee pad of the boots, and inside of the slippers, on the first sole above the heel. ...
>
> IX. The Articles that will be found with the said Halliers will be marked with a special mark that the Trustee and Jurors in Charge will affix to them within fifteen days from the publication of the Present [letters].

§ 1.56 REGULATION OF THE CORPORATION OF CARPET MAKERS OF PARIS—1719

The following text is an interesting testimony of competition for the market of Paris for carpets. In a Regulation dealing with the makers of carpets of Paris, one provision has been introduced giving the makers of carpets of Aubusson the right to enter that market, but under special conditions on the use of trademarks. In this case, the idea was that the mandatory use of the origin/collective mark of Aubusson actually protected the carpet makers of Paris against counterfeits (and cheap articles) falsely identified as being originated in Aubusson. Here the marks did not have the function of identifying the masters or of certifying quality, but merely of identifying the origin. Even if the Wardens of Paris had the right to inspect carpets brought from Aubusson, the Regulation is silent as to their authority to mark them with a quality seal.

Decision of the King's State Council, which approves Forty-Four Articles of the Regulation for the Body & Community of Masters & Merchant Carpet Makers of this City of Paris.

February 13, 1719

Extract from the Records of the State Council

> XIV. The Merchants, Hawkers, Workers of the City of Aubusson, when selling tapestries in Paris, according to the Letters Patent granted to them in July one thousand six hundred and sixty, registered in Parliament on August thirteenth one thousand six hundred and sixty-five, shall not sell tapestries other than those that are new and coming from their factories, and they shall, in accordance with the said Letters Patent, mark the said tapestries of their manufacture, with a piece of lead, on one side of which the King's Arms will be imprinted, and on the other, those of the said City of Aubusson; they also shall mark at the bottom of the said tapestries, in characters made of wool, these words: *Manufacture d'Aubusson*. The said Hawkers and Workers of Aubusson are prohibited from selling any tapestries, whether new or old, other than those from their factories, or even those from their

31. The designation of "halliers" concerns those merchants who sold shoes they had not made themselves.

factories when they are old; as well as renting any old or new tapestries, including those from their factories, all on the penalty of confiscation and a fine of three hundred pounds; and the said Workers of Aubusson shall accept the inspections that will be made in their workshops, stores and warehouses, by the said Master and Sworn Juror Carpet Makers, and shall treat them with honor and respect during said inspections, on the penalty of exemplary punishment.

§ 1.57 LILLE ADOPTS A REGULATION ON THE MANUFACTURE OF CLOTHS AND *PINCHINAS*[32]—1732

The French Revolution, with its ideals of individual freedom, was approaching, but authorities in the middle of the eighteenth century continued imposing rules on business identifiers (marks of certification, cities' seals) to ensure compliance with mandatory technical standards. In this example, it is interesting to see a special reference to the obligation to keep the mark in the cloth even after its having been cut.

Regulation for the Perfection of the Manufacture of Cloths (of Lille)

June 14, 1732

We, etc. Being informed that the Manufacture of Cloths and *Pinchinas*, which we have strived for a long time to establish in this City, could not be sustainable in the absence of the exact observation of a general and uniform Regulation, We have, upon the opinion of the Chamber of Commerce, ordered and order the following Points and Articles. ...

II. We order all said Manufacturers, to affix their marks and numbers on each piece of their factory, on the penalty of a fine of fifteen *florins*, which pieces thus marked and numbered, on the same penalty, they shall bring to the office of inspection as soon as they have been taken out of the loom by the Workers who have woven them, for being examined, seen, inspected, and, if that is the case, receiving the seal of approval, which will be marked with the letter B. to signify well worked, and otherwise, a seal marked M. will be affixed, which will signify poorly worked, and the Worker sentenced to pay such fine as appropriate, in proportion with the nature of the offense. ...

X. But when the said Cloths and *Pinchinas* are found to be well conditioned, a piece of lead of good manufacture will be affixed to each piece, bearing on one side the lily flower, and on the other the letters B.F. to signify good manufacture, as it is the practice. ...

XVIII. To avoid the abuses that are committed by the Cloth makers who sell wholesale or in detail, who pass the Cloths of Lille for those of Elboeuf, Louviers and others made in France, the Manufacturers of Lille shall affix their names and signs to one of the ends of the pieces of Cloth, in the middle, without the said Sellers being allowed to cut them until the end of the piece; but they will be required to leave the seals so as the factory be recognized, on penalty of a fine of six *florins* for each offense. ...

32. *Pinchina*: sort of woollen cloth, made of thick, non-crossed thread.

§ 1.58 IN THE EIGHTEENTH CENTURY, IN ENGLAND, EXCLUSIVITY IN A TRADEMARK WAS NOT UNCONDITIONAL—1742

In the eighteenth century, with the Industrial Revolution gaining strength and speed, an environment of increasing competition and slow, but firm, lifting of corporatist controls, put emphasis on the use of business identifiers as elements of differentiation and acquisition or maintenance of competitive advantages. This naturally led to an increase in disputes involving the protection and enforcement of trademarks. As a consequence, a body of jurisprudence started being built on the definitions and scope of rights.

In 1742, an English court issued a decision that would not stand the test of time: Lord Hardwick refused to issue an injunction to protect the exclusivity in the right of using a trademark in the absence of fraudulent intent.

In this particular aspect, French common law (if we can say so, in the absence of a written, general, and abstract statute) had moved further already, in the sense that it had already formulated a general understanding of the exclusivity of trademarks and shop signs based on the principle first in time, first in right *(see § 1.50).*

Blanchard v. Hill

December 18, 1742. Lord Hardwicke, C. 2 Alk. 484; R. Cox, 633

> Motion for injunction, to restrain the use of the Great Mogul stamp on cards, refused.
>
> Every particular trader has some particular mark or stamp; but I do not know of any instance of granting an injunction here to restrain one trader from using the same mark with another, and I think it would be of mischievous consequence to do it. Mr. Attorney General has mentioned a case where an action at law was brought by a clothworker against another of the same trade for using the same mark, and a judgment was given that the action would lie. But it was not the single act of making use of the mark that was sufficient to maintain the action, but doing it with a fraudulent design, to put off bad clothes by this means, or to draw away customers from the other clothier; and there is no difference between a tradesman's putting up the same sign, and making use of the same mark, with another of the same trade. An objection has been made that the defendant, in using this mark, prejudices the plaintiff by taking away his customers. But there is no more weight in this than there would be in an objection to one innkeeper setting up the same sign with another.

§ 1.59 ENGLAND ESTABLISHES RULES OF ORIGIN FOR PREVENTING THE EXPORTATION OF FOREIGN LINENS UNDER ENGLISH OR IRISH MARKS AND SEALS—1744

This text, although presenting some aspects that in the half of the eighteenth century could be deemed anachronistic, such as condemning an offender standing on the pillory—a typical medieval punishment—has surprisingly modern aspects. Indeed, this text is about rules of origin, one of the core pillars on which the GATT (General Agreement of Trade and Tariffs) was established in 1947. In this case, the focus of the rules was not on certifying the true origin of goods for the purpose of setting tariffs, but on certifying that origin for securing prestige and reputation linked to the renowned quality of British cloths. Business identifiers here played the role of geographical indications, with a straightforward differentiating function.

An Act for effectually preventing the Exportation of Foreign Linens under the Denomination of British or Irish Linens.

> Whereas by reason of the bounty or allowances granted on the exportation of British and Irish linens, evil-minded persons may fraudulently endeavour to export linens of foreign fabric and manufacture and to receive the said bounties or allowances for the same, as if the same were of the manufacture of Great Britain and Ireland: And whereas certain stamps are required by law to put upon linens made in that part of Great Britain called Scotland, or of Ireland: For remedy whereof, be it enacted by the King's most excellent Majesty, by and with the advice and consent of the lords spiritual and temporal, and commons, in this present Parliament assembled, and by the authority of the same, that from and after the twenty ninth day of September one thousand seven hundred and forty-five no stamp master or lapper in Scotland or Ireland shall any way mark, stamp, or seal any linens whatsoever until such stamp master or lapper shall have taken an oath for the true and faithful execution of his office before one or more justice or justices of the peace in Scotland and Ireland respectively (which oath the said justice or justices is and are hereby authorized and required to administer), nor until after the owner or manufacturer of any linen brought to be marked or stamped shall, before the stamp master of the place next adjoining to the place of abode of the owner or maker of such linen, take an oath (which oath the said stamp masters, severally and respectively, are hereby authorized to administer) that such linens desired to be marked or stamped, and every part thereof, is and are really and truly of the manufacture of Scotland or Ireland, and of no other place.
>
> [II.] And be it further enacted by the authority aforesaid, that no bounty shall be paid or allowed on the exportation of any British or Irish linens but on such only at both ends of every piece whereof the name and place of abode of the manufacturer or maker thereof, together with the year of our Lord wherein the said piece was manufactured or made, and also a number denoting the order in which such piece was so manufactured or made in such year, beginning with N° I. and proceeding progressively according to the number of pieces made by such manufacturer or maker in each year, and also the name and place of abode of the exporter or seller thereof for exportation, shall be severally marked or stamped in plain, distinct, and legible letters, figures, and words at length; and unless at the ends of every piece of such linen there shall be marked or stamped in plain, distinct, and legible letters, words, and figures the month and year when, and the name of the port at which such linens shall be entered for exportation, claiming the bounty; and unless (except in the instance herein after mentioned) the ends of every such piece of linen near which such marks shall be made shall be whole and entire, as the same were when it was cut or taken out of the loom, any law or statute to the contrary thereof in any wise notwithstanding; all which marks or stamps shall be marked or stamped with lamb-black and burnt oil, in a plain, legible and durable manner.
>
> [III.] And whereas it is a frequent practice in Scotland to cut a piece of linen after it is taken out of the loom into two or more pieces for the purpose of bleaching or whitening the same, whereby one or more of such pieces may not have the maker's or manufacturer's name made or set thereon as in herein before directed: For remedy thereof, be it enacted by the authority aforesaid, that every piece of

cloth intended to be cut for the purpose of bleaching or whitening shall so be cut in the presence of the stamp master of the place next adjoining to the place of abode of the owner of such cloth, and each piece cut off not having the manufacturer's or maker's name and place of abode stamped thereon shall be stamped with the name and place of abode of the manufacturer and maker thereof, together with the year of our Lord wherein the same was so bleached or whitened, which the stamp master is hereby empowered and directed to stamp thereon … . And if any person or persons shall, from and after the twenty fourth day of June one thousand seven hundred and forty five, stamp or mark any linens, or cause or procure any linens to be stamped or marked, contrary to all or any of the directions of this Act, or shall mark or stamp, or cause or procure the same to be marked or stamped, with a mark or stamp expressing the name or place of abode of any person or persons other than that of the real and true manufacturer of maker thereof, or expressing an untrue description of the real and true manufacturer's or maker's place of abode, or of the year of our Lord in which such linen was manufactured, or of the order in which the same was manufactured or made, or shall wilfully mark or set on any such linens any false or counterfeit stamp in imitation of the mark or stamp used by any manufacturer or maker of British or Irish linens, or shall wilfully or maliciously cut off, obliterate, wash, take out, or destroy, or cause or procure to be cut off, obliterated, washed, or taken out or destroyed, any stamp or mark marked or stamped on linen, such person or persons shall forfeit the sum of five pounds for every piece of linen so stamped as aforesaid, to be sued for and recovered by bill, plaint, or information in any of his Majesty's courts of record at Westminster, the Court of Session, Court of Justiciary, or Court of Exchequer in Scotland, or in any of his Majesty's courts of record in Dublin respectively, wherein no essoin, privilege, wager of law, or more than one imparlance shall be allowed; and one moiety of the said penalties shall be to the use of the King's Majesty, his heirs and successors, and the other moiety to such person or persons as will sue or prosecute the same.

[IV.] And be it further enacted by the authority aforesaid, that if any person shall make or affix, or cause or procure to be made or affixed, on any linens of foreign manufacture or fabric imported into Great Britain or Ireland any of the marks or stamps required by law to be put on linens of the manufacture of Scotland or Ireland, or shall make or affix, or cause or procure to be made or affixed, on any such foreign linens any of the marks or stamps hereby required to be marked or stamped upon linens of the manufacture of Great Britain or Ireland, or shall make or affix, or cause or procure to be made or affixed, on any such foreign linens any mark or stamp, marks or stamps, in imitation of any of the said marks or stamps hereby or by any other law or laws now in force required to be marked or stamped on British or Irish linens, such person so offending, and being thereof convicted, shall stand on the pillory during the space of one hour in the forenoon, and also be punished by fine not exceeding fifty pounds or by imprisonment for any time not exceeding twelve months, at the discretion of the court before whom such offender shall be convicted: And if any person shall, after the said twenty fourth day of June one thousand seven hundred and forty five, sell, or expose to sale, or pack up for sale, or enter for exportation any foreign linens marked or stamped with all or any of the marks or stamps hereby or by any other law now in force required to be marked or stamped upon linens of the manufacture of Great Britain or Ireland, knowing such linen to be foreign, every person so offending, and being thereof convicted, shall forfeit the said linens and the sum of five pounds for each piece thereof so sold, exposed to sale, or packed up for sale, or entered for exportation as aforesaid, to be sued for and recovered by bill, plaint, or information in any of his Majesty's courts of record at Westminster, the Court of Session, Court of

Justiciary, or Court of Exchequer in Scotland, or in any of his Majesty's courts of record in Dublin respectively, wherein no essoin, privilege, wager of law, or more than one imparlance shall be allowed; and one moiety of the said penalties shall be to the use of the King's Majesty, his heirs and successors, and the other moiety to such person or persons as will sue or prosecute for the same; and in case it shall be made a question, whether such linens are of any foreign country, in such case the *onus probandi* thereof shall lie upon the claimer of such linen or the defendant in such action or suit.

[V.] Provided, always, and it is hereby declared, that nothing herein contained shall extend to vary or alter the method of stamping of linens of the manufacture of Ireland and Scotland by virtue of any law or laws now in force relating thereto, but that, besides the marks or stamps hereinbefore mentioned, all such linens shall be marked and stamped in the same manner as the same ought to have been if this Act had not been made.

Figure 17 The pillory, a medieval instrument of punishment, often used to penalize cloth counterfeiters. Earthenware tile painted in manganese over a tin glaze. Manufactured in London, 1680. © The Trustees of the British Museum.

§ 1.60 TWO DISPUTES BETWEEN THE COMMUNITY OF SHOEMAKERS OF PARIS AND "PRIVILEGED" SHOEMAKERS—1749, 1758

The first of the following texts concerns a dispute between the widow of a master shoemaker and her son, on the one hand, and the community of shoemakers of Paris, on the other. The former were "privileged" shoemakers, in the sense that was explained above: they were not members of the guild but had received the privilege of engaging in the trade of shoes because they had inherited it from the late husband and father, who was a shoemaker in the King's court. Nevertheless, the privilege was not absolute: not having passed the master examination, they were not allowed to have a trademark of their own, which they could imprint on the shoes. In other words, their inherited privilege did not extend to the making of shoes, but only to their selling. They needed therefore to have their shoes marked (hence, inspected) by a master.

The second text involves a similar issue, with the difference that the defendant's privilege included the possibility of making shoes. By contrast with the widow of the previous case, he was entitled to have his own mark. This text is an excerpt from a long and complex opinion, full of procedural details, concerning a dispute involving the seizure of shoes between the community of shoemakers of Paris and Nicolas Noel, a "privileged" shoemaker. Within certain limits, and because he was at the King's service, Noel was authorized to hire assistants and have his own trademark, which he had previously registered with the Community's office. From an intellectual property perspective, it is interesting to note that the Community of shoemakers of Paris, like other guilds, was in charge of "registering" the trademarks of its members. Actually, this is not a nonsense measure. Trademarks are used as tokens of commercial rivalry, even when they assume the nature of certification marks, and no one could be better placed to deal with the matters of registration, including distinctiveness, than the community.

§ 1.60.1 Decision of the Grand Council Against the Widow of a Privileged Shoemaker—1749

Decision of the Grand Council in favor of the Mayor and Jurors of the Community of Master Shoemakers of the City and Suburbs of Paris, against the Privileged Shoemakers following the Court and the Royal Houses. Which declares the seizure made upon the Widow Mozac and her Son, Privileged shoemakers, good and valid

June 22, 1749

> Louis [XV], by the grace of God, King of France and Navarre, to all those who see these Present Letters; Greetings. We make known, as per the Judgment held today in our Grand Council, between our beloved Mayor and Jurors of the Community of Master Shoemakers of the City and Suburbs of Paris, Appellants of a Sentence of the Provost of the City Hall, of February 21, last, following the Request from our Council and act of summons of March 4 and 5, 1749, and requesting that the Appeal and the matter of the appeal be nullified, and that their purposes and conclusions of the main cause[33] be amended and corrected, reversing in their favor with costs, on the one hand. And Marie-Jeanne Lhomme, widow of Mr. Alexandre Mozac, Shoemaker of our Wardrobe, and Alexandre Mozac her son, Respondents, on the other hand. ...
>
> In doing so, to declare the seizure made on the said widow Mozac by procedure of October 25, 1748, good and valid; to order that the seized Goods will

33. Here the term "main cause" means the decision rendered by the lower court.

> be and will remain confiscated for the benefit of the Community of Master Shoemakers of Paris; additionally, to prohibit the said widow Mozac, in the future, from keeping the Shop open, from selling or buying on the day of Saint Crispin and Saint Crispinian[34] any goods belonging to the profession of Shoemaker, as well as from buying and selling them if they are not marked with the first two letters of the name of the Master Shoemaker who has made them, or of another person having permission to work in the said profession, on the penalties and rigors of the law, and for having done it, that the said widow Mozac will be condemned to the damages and interest of Plaintiffs, and in all costs, both of the main cause and of the appeal. ...

§ 1.60.2 Decision of the Grand Council Against a Privileged Shoemaker—1758

Decision of the King's Grand Council, which prohibits a Privileged shoemaker from offending the By-laws of the Master Shoemakers

> Louis [XV], by the grace of God, King of France and Navarre: To all those who will see these present Letters; Greetings. We make known that, by Judgment held today in our Grand Council, between the Mayor and Jurors in charge of the Community of Master Shoemakers of Paris, Appellants of a Sentence of the Provost of the City Hall, of June 22, 1757 ..., on the one hand; and Nicolas Noel, Privileged Shoemaker, Defendant, on the other hand; ... and taking into consideration that the matter involves our service ... the said Noel remains authorized to employ in the works which will be ordered from him, for our service, a sufficient number of Workers, both in his workshop and outside, being the said Noel, according to his own proposal, obliged (i) not to employ outside his workshop any Companions or Workers, whose names and addresses he has not previously indicated to the Office of the Community of Master Shoemakers, and that he will only have them finishing Boots, (ii) to continue having them cut in his workshop; and (iii) to mark his name beneath the foot, and the same mark of which he left the imprint at the Office of the Master Shoemakers; ... .

§ 1.61 FRENCH AUTHORITIES PROHIBIT COMPETITION AMONG MASTER TAILORS, INCLUDING THEIR ADVERTISING OF LOW PRICES—1760, 1761, 1782

The period preceding the French Revolution knew many constraints to competition—a sort of revival of Medieval rules. The following texts contain prohibitions against competition within the textile industry, including the offering of low prices, on the argument that such competition was based on greed and that low prices necessarily led to low quality.

The first text concerns a judgment of the Court of Parliament of Paris and is addressed to the Master Tailors. The second text concerns a directive issued by the Municipality of Paris, under the regulations of the community of hat makers, which were introduced in

34. Saints Crispin and Crispinian were the saint patrons of cobblers and shoemakers.

1578, through a patent letter signed by Henry III, and several times amended. The third text is a continuation of the second one and consists of the denunciation of an official of the Community of hat makers who did not abide by the rules and advertised his prices on his shop's signboard. The fourth text is the advice of a French jurist, Prost de Royer, on the legality of the merchants' practice of advertising their names, addresses, and articles' prices through trade cards. This advice was motivated by the seizure of address cards and defective cloths made by a tailor. Reporting the case, de Royer suggests that the seizure was justified by the defective cloths, not by the fact that Tissot had advertised his business through those cards.

§ 1.61.1 A Judgment of the Court of Parliament Prohibits Tailors from Announcing Their Articles at Low Prices—1760

Judgments of the Court of Parliament in favor of the Community of Master Tailors and Dealers of garments. Which approves a deliberation of the said community of May 29, 1760, against several Masters who distribute Cards announcing garments to the Public at mediocre prices

December 10, 1760

Louis by the grace of God, King of France and Navarre; to the first bailiff of our court of Parliament or our bailiff or sergeant, to this appointed.

We make known that, our said Court having seen the Request presented by the jurors and communities of the Master Merchant Tailors of Garments of Paris, that for the causes contained therein it has pleased our court, in view of the opinion of Lord Lieutenant General de Police and of our deputy Attorney General, we have ordered that the deliberation made by the supplicants in their office on the twenty-ninth of May last, will be homologated, to be executed according to its form and content, both by them and by the masters of said community, and that for this purpose the judgment in question will be registered in the registry of their community and read, printed, published and posted where it will be necessary; ...

Having regard to the documents attached to the said Request. Signed Morise Prosecutor.

The content of said Deliberation follows.

Today, May 29, one thousand seven hundred and sixty, in the Assembly of the Jurors in charge, the Dean and former jurors of the community of Masters and merchant Tailors of the City and Suburbs of Paris, convened by Notices in the usual manner, in their Office, at the Quai de la Régisserie, it was stated by the jurors that various abuses had been introduced into the community that should be repressed, and that consist in the fact that several Masters who compose [the community] distribute printed cards by which they advertise to the public garments and clothes of all fashions at very mediocre prices, with a view to attracting a greater number of sales to the detriment of their colleagues and the public, since it is true that those who act in this way always deceive the public, under the appearance of a pretended cheapness, which they never employ to make the articles that they advertise and sell, as well as cloths of a very inferior or even completely defective quality and in which the sufficient quantity of those goods are never used because often the pieces that form their final product are cut against the grain, and consequently in offense of the by-laws and regulations of the community; that, for obtaining the proof of all these facts, the jurors have gone to the stores of the named Goffroy and Broussin, two of the Masters of the Community, who announced to the Public *redingotes*[35] at twenty seven pounds each piece, whereas they found new *redingotes* whose parts or extremities were all against the grain, and moreover very narrow and so small, that as little as they are wet by the rain during the use, it will be impossible to use them; for that reason the judges have had them seized and brought to the Office for the purpose of ruling on the said offenses and punishing the authors in order to repress them, and preventing by this means the Public from being deceived; and as it is quite impossible, whatever precaution the jurors have taken, to generally stop these kinds of offenses without a public regulation; they convened the assembly of the Company to inform it of the above and to request it as needed to require and to give its opinion on the matter stated.

The matter having been submitted to deliberation, the assembled community, with a unanimous voice, by common agreement has decided under the good pleasure of the Magistrates, that in the future the masters of the Community cannot distribute to the Public Cards either printed or handwritten, other than those that purely and simply contain their names, qualities and addresses, without adding or offering any price for the garments or other clothes that they will announce for sale to the Public, on the penalty of a fine of three hundred pounds for the first offense, applicable in alms to the poor Masters, Widows of the Community, and in case of recidivism, the prohibition and loss of the Mastership.

§ 1.61.2 Ordinance Prohibiting Cloth Merchants from Competing with Each Other, Including Announcing Their Articles at Low Prices—1761

Ordinance of Police, Which makes iterative and express prohibitions to all Wholesale and Retail Merchants of this City and Suburbs of Paris from competing with each other, for the sale of their Goods, forbids them in particular to distribute or otherwise distribute any Cards to announce the sale and under any pretext whatsoever, all on the penalty of a fine of 300 pounds for the first time, and the closing of the Store in the event of recidivism

April 10, 1761

Upon what has been stated to us by the Public Prosecutor, that in spite of the rules of the Police that very expressly prohibits all the Merchants from competing with each other for the distribution of their Goods, and from using any trick to surprise buyers and to deal with them to the detriment of freedom of commerce, some Merchants of this City, nevertheless, have for some time engaged in distributing cards in their name to the public, advertising the sale of their Cloths and other Goods, at a price that they announce to be lower than that usually charged by the other Merchants: That such an offense, which is almost always the last resource of an unfair merchant, with the purpose of selling his Cloths promptly, cannot be too severely repressed, otherwise it would mean giving rise to all the frauds that interest and greed can inspire, from which it would result a great prejudice even for the public, and this because, under the pretext of selling the Goods at a low price,

35. *Redingote*, from the English "riding coat," was an overcoat used for horse riding.

often only defective ones would be sold; for these reasons, it has been requested that we provided thereupon.

We order that the old Police Regulations will be executed according to their form and content, and consequently, make iterative and express prohibitions to all Wholesale and Retail Merchants of this City and Fauxbourgs of Paris, from competing with each other for the distribution of their Goods, and we forbid them in particular to spread or otherwise distribute any cards announcing the sale, and this, under any pretext whatsoever; all on the penalty of a fine of 300 pounds for the first offense, and of closing their Store in the event of recidivism. ...

§ 1.61.3 The Provost of the Community of Clothmakers Is Denounced for Infringing the Ordinance and Inserting on His Signboard Indications of Articles' Prices—1761

Made in our Office on the eighteenth day of May. The General Assembly convened, it was ordered to communicate the above Ordinance to all the Masters, which Ordinance was read to them, and to represent to the Magistrates that Mr. Provost, against his Ordinance, puts the indications of the prices of merchandise on his signboard, and that he does not take out any hat case from his store without these indications being affixed to it.

§ 1.61.4 A French Jurist Defends the Practice of Distributing Cards Advertising the Name and Address of Merchants—1782

Judgment of the Parliament of Paris of May 11, 1782. ... The facts. Tailor Tissot had distributed to the public printed addresses, bearing the indication of his name, his profession, his domicile and the price of his works. The community of tailors believed that the interest of its members and that of the public required a drastic approach that might, on the one hand, take away from Tissot the goods he had offered from his address, and on the other, prevent the public from being victim to the preference it would give [Tissot], resulting from poor quality supplies. The jurors therefore went to Tissot's store, seized a large quantity of his printed addresses and several clothes made with pieces cut across and against the grain, in violation of the regulations of the community. Sentence of the lieutenant of police who declares the seizure valid and condemns Tissot to a fine of 50 pounds. The court confirms, and yet, gracefully, reduces the fine to 10 pounds.

But, if the seized goods had not been defective, would there have been a condemnation to the payment of the fine? The judgment does not prohibit the distribution of these addresses; we see them every day, we see them in all public newspapers. So it seems that these addresses are for the merchant the same as the sign that is put over the shop, and for the entrepreneur the same as the circular letter circulating throughout the entire commerce of Europe. This is also the notice given in private newspapers of their change of domicile, and of public establishments of matters of their interest. From all these points of view, the address made, printed and distributed honestly does not seem to be reprehensible.

Figure 18 Trade cards ("cartes d'addresse") of two tailors of the eighteenth century. Since the seventeenth century, trade cards were abundantly used by artisans and merchants for advertising. At some point, in the eighteenth century, their use was so intensive that it gave rise to two problems: the scarcity of paper caused them to be very expensive; and the postal service was accused of overpricing their distribution. On top, the card of Edeler, a German tailor, who, in the second half of the eighteenth century, moved his business to Paris. This particular card informs potential customers of the technical and artistic qualities of the tailor and gives examples of some of his works through illustrations on the sides. He announces he holds a secret of cleaning four-colored velvet cloths. And he sells everything for fair prices. Below, the trade card of Navarre, Master, and Merchant Tailor. The card says that Navarre makes all sorts of garments for men and women, in the last fashion. He delivers in the interior and abroad, provided body measurements are sent to him.

§ 1.62 FASHION LAW'S BIRTH CERTIFICATE?—1728, 1779

The following texts, and in particular, as far as intellectual property is concerned, the second one, can be seen as a true watershed.

The first text is an excerpt from a decree issued by the Intendant of Flanders settling several disputes between the woollen clothmakers of Roubaix and those of Lille. The latter claimed exclusivity in the making of certain fabrics and in the use of certain special equipment for that purpose. The Intendant agreed with them, except as regards the making of new cloths by the clothmakers of Roubaix, who were authorized to make new cloths according to whatever taste and design they deem convenient and following the fashions.

The second text is, from a legal perspective, the recognition of fashion law. For the first time, the King of France (Louis XVI) admits a compromise between marks certifying compliance with technical standards and marks distinguishing new fabrics and fashions. This suggests a shift in the legal regime of business identifiers in the textile industry and the acknowledgment that fashion was already imposing a new approach to existing standards of intellectual property protection. Although most aspects of the old corporatist regime were preserved (see Article 15)—the rupture with corporatism would occur ten years later, with the advent of the Revolution—these Patent letters admitted freedom in inventing new fabrics and new designs, and submitted those new materials to self-regulation; they also expressed concern with free competition as regards the use of the term "manufacture royale," which implied official approval and quality standards; and all this under the overall concern with the circumstances that arose from the fleeting nature of taste and fashion ("the succession of fashions and the diversity of tastes").

This regulation brought also two other trademark-related breakthroughs: first, it admitted that, as far as new cloths and garments were concerned, trademarks had the main, if not only, function of making it clear for consumers that "they have no other guarantee of the manufacture that their own scrutiny and the trust that the manufacturer or the dealer to whom they turn may deserve." This is twenty-first-century trademark law, undoubtedly.

And, second, for the first time, the notion of well-known trademarks has been acknowledged (see clause 13).

§ 1.62.1 The Sayetteurs of Lille Are Authorized to Make New Cloths According to Whatever Taste and Design They Deem Convenient and Following the Fashions—1728

Decision of the Intendant of Flanders on various matters concerning the *sayetteurs*

July 3, 1732

Jean Louis Bidé, knight, lord of Grandville, etc. ... The different requests that are submitted to the council's decision consist:

... of the request presented by the prince of Rohan in the sense that the seizure of March 15, 1728 by the *bourgeteurs* of the city, of several pieces of *calleman-dilles* [a sort of light woolen cloth] at the shops of some manufacturers of Roubaix be declared void and that they be allowed to continue making them as well as all other cloths in their factories according to whatever taste and design they deem convenient and following the fashions.

... For all these reasons we decide that it is opportune that, dismissing the opposition by the sayeteurs and bourgeteurs of the city of Lille ... the seizure of May 15, 1728 be declared good and valid ... except that the said manufacturers may diversify the cloths that they are permitted to make following the fashions and as they deem convenient ...

§ 1.62.2 Louis XVI Acknowledges the Incompatibility of Existing Rules on Textiles with the Fleeting Nature of Fashion and for the First Time Admits a Duplicity of Legal Regimes for Trademarks Certifying Cloths' Quality and Origin—1779

Patent letters providing for the regulation of manufactures

Tuesday, May 5, 1779. Registered in Parliament on May 19.

Louis [XVI], etc. Attentive to making all the resources of the State more fruitful, and to preparing new means of expanding, on the return of peace, its commerce and its industry, we have had to look carefully at the situation of manufactures. We know that it is by their prosperity that agriculture is fostered, that population grows and that wealth accumulates; we have noticed that the systems adopted for a fairly large number of years have varied so much that efforts have been made to subject the manufacture to a code of regulations which has become, by its complication and its age, of difficult execution; ...

We have also been informed that because the stamp that is applied to cloths manufactured according to the rules, being at the same time the distinctive sign of national manufacture, cannot apply to cloths of a new invention, and which consequently cannot be provided with the regulatory seal, those [cloths of a new invention] are necessarily deprived of the only mark that can attest that they are manufactured in France; which exposes them to seizures as they circulate in the kingdom; and the industry is thus blocked and thwarted by the very authority of the laws.

Finally, considering this question in its depth, we have noticed that, while regulations are useful in serving as a brake to unwarranted greed, and in ensuring public confidence, these same institutions should not extend to the point of defeating the imagination and the genius of an industrious man, and even less so far as to resist the succession of fashions and the diversity of tastes; and, as we have found that these different views could not be accommodated by too rigid a subjugation to regulations, nor by their destruction and the establishment of an indefinite freedom, we have had to seek whether it was not by some intermediary regime that could be used to maintain the main advantages of the two systems. We have thought, moreover, that the laws of commerce should change over time, and that when new businesses opened up and new competitors arose, it was necessarily required to slightly deviate from the rules and institutions that had been adopted in other circumstances. ...

To distinguish these cloths and to prove the examination by the jurors-wardens, they will have a particular stamp and distinctive marks inherent to the fabric. At the same time, however, that we are taking these precautions, we have deemed it just and useful for the State to grant to all manufacturers the absolute freedom of making such new or different cloths as they see fit, provided they do never put in them the name or the marks of a known and regulated cloth, so that the buyers are then informed at a glance that, for that [new] kind of cloth, they have no other guarantee of the manufacture that their own scrutiny and the trust that the manufacturer or the dealer to whom they turn may deserve; and yet so that these same cloths may circulate freely in the kingdom, they will also be marked with a piece of lead, but distinct from that assigned to the regulated fabrics. ...

We have also believed it necessary to grant an honorable distinction to those among the manufacturers who, linked to their profession by the spirit of wisdom, would have perpetuated in their family an old establishment and a good reputation; that is why we want that those among the manufacturers whose names have been known for sixty years in the same factory, may, by engraving it on their cloths, be exempted from submitting them to the examination of the jurors-wardens; so that the name of an old and famous manufactory becomes a sufficient seal of the regularity of the manufacture; on the condition, however, of losing this advantage, if such a distinguished trust is ever abused.

At the same time, having noticed that the title of royal manufacture had often been granted by simple favor, and could still be granted by similar motives; that even several new manufacturers have solicited it, in order to obtain over their competitors an advantage of opinion which should only be the fruit of real works and successes, we considered it advisable to order that this title should be granted only to unique manufactures of their kind; which could then harm no one; and as for the manufactures which currently enjoy this title, wishing well, for the sake of their possession, not to deprive them suddenly of it, we propose, according to the report that will be submitted to us, to determine the time when all these privileges will have to end. ...

1. It will henceforth be free for all makers and manufacturers, either to follow in the manufacture of their cloths such dimensions or combinations which they deem appropriate, or to subject themselves to the execution of the regulations.

2. New manufacturing regulations will soon be drafted; to the effect of which, the communities of manufacturers, in the principal places of manufacture, will be required to promptly send us memoirs in which they will indicate the manner in which the cloths must be manufactured, according to their specification, or their different qualities under the same specification; so that, once the aforesaid memoirs have been seen and examined, the matter will be ruled as appropriate. ...

5. The carpets, serges and any woolen fabric without distinction, which will be manufactured according to the prescribed rules, will continue to be provided with the selvages determined by the old regulations; and they will also bear, on the two heads, the letter R,[36] woven at the loom, as well as the denomination of the cloth, the name of the manufacturer and that of the place of manufacture; said cloths will be brought in canvas, upon leaving the loom, to the office of manufacture, to receive there, if they are recognized as being of good workmanship, a provisional mark, in oil and in black carbon, which will be replaced, after their being finished, if this finishing has been made in accordance with the prescribed

36. Article 7 of this statute explains that the letter "R" stands for "réglée" ("regulated," meaning the cloths made in accordance with the regulation).

rules, a seal bearing on one side the word *réglée* and the year, and on the other, the name of the inspection office; and with regard to the cloths of the same nature that will be manufactured according to arbitrary combinations,[37] their selvages will be striped with a thousand stripes, in such colors as the manufacturers deem suitable to adopt; provided, however, that there is alternately a larger black or blue thread, and several threads of any color whatsoever, thinner in between. The aforementioned free cloths will not be presented to the inspection office until after the finishing, to receive there, once the inspection of their selvages is made, a piece of lead of a different shape than that intended for the regulated fabrics, and which will bear on one side the indication of the inspection office, and on the other, the year only. ...

(Several provisions that apply to other sorts of cloths follow; in their essence, they are very similar to Article 5, and thus it is not worth repeating: those cloths that followed previously adopted standards were subject to the old system of inspection and certification; but the branding and the appearance of new cloths and new designs were left to the decision of manufacturers).

12. From now on, no title of royal manufacture will be granted, except for establishments that are unique in their kind; and with regard to the aforementioned titles granted, we wish that the entrepreneurs who have obtained them be required to inform our council, within three months, the decisions by virtue of which they enjoy them, so that the time at which the said privilege must cease be determined by us; and, for those who fail to comply with the provisions of this article, within the term prescribed above, we have from now on declared the said title of royal manufacture extinguished and suppressed.

13. Manufacturers who have operated from father to son for sixty years, and with a sustained reputation, the same manufacture, may themselves affix the prescribed seals to their cloths, and will be exempted from presenting them to the inspection offices, after having been authorized by us; and the said authorization shall be revoked in the event of abuse. ...

15. Nor do we mean, under the pretext of the freedom granted by art. 1 of the present [letters], to add anything new to the provisions of our edicts concerning the communities of arts and crafts; we want the said edicts to be executed according to their form and content. ...

§ 1.63 PATENT LETTERS CONFIRMING THE PREVIOUS TEXT IN CONNECTION WITH LINEN CLOTHS—1780

The following patent letters confirm the previous text, in the specific context of linen cloths or canvases. Cloths made outside rigid regulatory standards (cloths "of arbitrary combination") still needed to be inspected after their being whitened and laundered, and these special certification seals were known as "marks of freedom" (as opposed to "regulated trademarks"). On the eve of the French Revolution, the French textile industry was craving freedom in responding to consumers' demands. Gradually, law was responding to that social pressure, but a few years later, freedom would come abruptly and uncontained, with the advent of the French Revolution, in 1789.

37. These are the cloths whose fabric is of new invention, new method of making, or of new design.

Patent letters concerning the manufacture of linen cloths

Versailles, June 28, 1780. Registered in Parliament on July 25.

Louis [XVI], etc. The reasons that have led us to give, by our letters patent of June 4, 1780, a general regulation for the manufacture of woolen cloths, request the same attention from us for the manufacture of linen cloths, which also form an important object of commerce, both in the interior of our kingdom and abroad. ...

5. We order the manufacturers, weavers and workers to leave at both ends of each piece of canvas manufactured in accordance with the regulations, a strip of one-sixth of an ell in excess of the prescribed length. Said strip will be separated from the piece of cloth by the transverse bars prescribed by art. 4 of the letters patent of May 5, 1779; and the marks mentioned below will be affixed to them. ...

6. All manufacturers or merchants who place orders for the making of cloths, will each have a token or mark, on which the first letter of their name will be engraved, and their unabbreviated surname, as well as the place of their residence. We order them to affix to the head and end of each piece of canvas that they will make and cause to be made according to the rules prescribed by the production tables, an imprint of the said mark with oil and carbon black; as well as a mark indicative of the length of said linen cloths; and this before presenting them for the inspection. We also order them to leave an imprint of their token or mark in the offices where usually they have their cloths marked. And with regard to those who want to make, or have made linen cloths under arbitrary combinations, we do not intend to deprive them of the faculty of affixing on the said canvases the imprint of their name and surname, and of the place of their residence, as well as the one that will indicate the lengths of the cloths. ...

7. All the cloths marked as provided by the preceding article, will, before laundering, be brought to the mark office to be inspected there. If they are manufactured in accordance with the rules prescribed by the production tables, they will be provided with a mark or imprint, whose form and engraving will be determined by the said tables. And in the event that they do not conform to them, they will be seized, and a legal procedure will be established, for the judgment by the judges of the manufactures to whom this matter will concern. With regard to the linen cloths made according to arbitrary combinations, the imprint or mark that will be affixed on them, will be of an octagon form, and will contain only the year and the name of the office in which it will have been affixed. ...

12. The whiteners or launderers shall not receive any pieces of linen cloth if they are not marked with the mark intended for the regulated fabrics, or that of freedom. ...

14. The said whiteners or launderers shall have a token, or mark, bearing their name, surname, and the name of the place of their residence. They shall apply the imprint with oil or carbon black to both ends of each piece which they have bleached, and shall be required to deposit a similar imprint with the office of the jurisdiction of the manufactures. The said whiteners and launderers will also be required to affix to each of the said pieces of cloth, a mark indicative of their dimension after the laundering. ...

§ 1.64 TWO FRENCH CITIES DISPUTE THE OWNERSHIP AND USE OF COLORED SELVAGES—1782

Louis XVI, in 1782, settled a dispute between the manufacturers of cloth of Louviers and Elbeuf concerning the misguiding use of a colored pattern (the selvage or border of cloths). Today this would correspond to a figurative trademark, something like the well-known trademark of National Geographic (a yellow rectangle following the edges of its magazine cover).

Interestingly, when the Industrial Revolution was already in full swing in England, France, whose industry's competitiveness was left behind and was about to engage in its own (political) Revolution, the industries were still using the city's seals and trademarks, in the old medieval way. This does not reveal, however, tardiness in the evolution of trademark law, but rather the strictness of French law in protecting geographical indications as differentiating signs of quality and certification. In parallel, as we have seen in the previous texts, France was already engaging in legal changes dictated by the social pressures of aesthetical tastes and fashion.

Judgment of the council concerning the yellow border of the cloths of Louviers, and the red border of the cloths of Elbeuf

Versailles, December 5, 1782.

> On what has been represented to the king, being in his council, by the manufacturers of Louviers and those of Elbeuf, that under Article 6 of the letters patent of March 1, 1781, regulating the manufacture of woolen cloths in Rouen, it would have been allowed to all manufacturers to make all kinds of woolen cloths, yarn and wool or floss silk, included in the boards of manufacture that would be prepared for the other manufactories of the kingdom, complying with what would be prescribed by the said boards; that the same provision is found in the letters patent that have been issued to regulate the manufacture of woolen cloths of the other places; that this faculty, granted indiscriminately to all manufacturers of cloths wherever their manufactures may be situated, would doubtless have had for main object the greatest perfection in the manufacture, but that it would become disastrous to the manufacturers of Louviers and Elbeuf, which have always distinguished themselves by the delicacy of their cloths, by their beauty and by the manner in which they are made, if [other] factories that employ only inferior wools, or whose production is less perfect, had the liberty of circulating, trading, and exporting their cloths abroad as if they had been made at Louviers or at Elbeuf, placing on them the characteristic marks assigned to these two manufactories; that it would be easy, by hiding the true place of manufacture, to mislead the merchant, and still more the consumer; that there were already several examples of this abuse; that finally, the selvages assigned to the main manufactories of the kingdom form in some way their patrimony, and are guarantors towards the public of the kind, the nature, and the quality of the cloths or fabrics. And H. M. being informed that difficulties would have arisen between the said manufacturers of Louviers and Elbeuf, as to the color of the selvages that must distinguish the fine cloths of these two manufactories; that at all times, and even since the new regulations, the manufacturers of Elbeuf would have claimed that the red selvage should belong to their manufactory, as being the oldest; that, on the other hand, the manufacturers of Louviers contested this claim, and maintained that they were in possession of [the right] of finishing their cloths with the said red selvage; that, moreover, this color was attributed to their manufactory by the board of manufacture annexed to the letters patent of March 1, 1781; that, however, in order to put an end to these difficulties, they were determined to abandon the said red selvage to the Elbeuf factory, and to adopt for theirs the yellow selvage, provided that the said Elbeuf factory could not, in any case, use the yellow selvage, and that it would not begin

until two years later to attach the red selvage to its cloths, so as to give the manufacturers of Louviers the time to dispose of the stock of cloths made with a red color selvage. ...

The king, being in his council, has ordered and orders that in the future the cloths of Louviers will be finished with a yellow selvage, having four or six blue threads, either inside the cloth's selvage, or outside the said selvage, at the choice of the manufacturers of the said manufactory, according to the color of those cloths; and that with regard to the fine cloths that will be made at Elbeuf, they will be finished with a red selvage; derogating, in favor of the said manufactories, from the provision of Article 6 of the Letters Patent of March 1, 1781: as a result, H. M. makes very express prohibitions and inhibitions to all manufacturers of the other cloth factories of the kingdom to finish their cloths with the mentioned selvages, on penalty of seizure and confiscation of said cloths, and yet, to give to the cloths of Louviers that are already manufactured and that will be made with red selvages until the day of the publication of the present judgment, the time necessary to be sold by the merchants who will buy them, H. M. orders that the manufacturers of Elbeuf will not start to put the red selvage in their cloths before one year from the day of publication of that judgment. Moreover, it is the wish of H. M. that the said letters patent of March 1, 1781 be fully and entirely executed, in what it has not been derogated from by the present judgment, concerning which all necessary letters patent will be issued.

§ 1.65 DECISION OF LOUIS XVI'S COUNCIL CONCERNING THE MARKS OF WOOLLEN CLOTHS—1783

In spite of the gradually increasing liberalization in the trade of cloths, many entrepreneurs still felt compelled to counterfeit certification marks that applied to "regulated" articles. The following text is the response of the King's Council to such counterfeiting.

Decision of the Council concerning the mark of cloths, serges, and other woolen fabrics indistinctly

Versailles, February 15, 1783

Seen in the King's Council the letters patent of May 5, 1779, by Article 3 of which it is, among other things, ordered that cloths, serges, and all woolen fabrics indistinctly, bear in their heads the designation of the cloth, the name of the manufacturer and that of the place of manufacture, woven at the loom: and H.M. being informed that in several places of manufacture the manufacturers allow themselves to deviate from this provision, and only print the said inscription in gold letters, after the finishing, from which results the possibility of removing the middle or end of the pieces, and then cover them with names and inscriptions that may be the most advantageous for the sale of said articles. Wishing to remedy this: heard, etc., the King, being in his council, has ordered and orders that, in accordance with art. 3 of the letters patent of May 5, 1779, the designation of the cloth, the name of the manufacturer and that of the place of manufacture, will be woven at both ends of each piece at the loom: H.M. makes consequently very express prohibitions and inhibitions to all manufacturers to print, under any pretext whatsoever, the said inscription on their cloths, in gold letters and with a varnish or otherwise, and this, on the penalty of seizure of the offending cloths, and a fine of 300 pounds: H.M. nevertheless authorizes the said manufacturers to do the weaving above ordered with such material as they see fit, provided however that, during the finishing, it can be integrated with that which will have been used in the manufacture of the cloth.

§ 1.66 NEW REGULATION OF THE MARKS OF LINEN CLOTHS (CANVASES)—FRANCE, 1785

The growth of the trade of printed and painted linen clothes in the eighteenth century has led to the adoption of a new regulation, consolidating various existing laws, which had become dated and inconsistent. Showing a change in times, as well as in the way the function of marks was seen by authorities, the new regulation has given special attention to individual trademarks.

Decision of the Council establishing a new regulation on the mark of canvases painted and printed in the Kingdom.

Fontainebleau, November 10, 1785

> The king having had submitted to him, in his council, the decisions of September 5 and October 28, 1759, laying down regulations for the canvases painted and printed in the kingdom, H.M. has recognized that these laws, which were intended to promote the establishment of a new branch of industry and trade, were insufficient today, given that the manufactories of painted and printed canvases have greatly multiplied, and that it would be interesting to unite in a single law all the provisions relating to this kind of manufacture, and to prescribe fixed and invariable rules, so as to make the entrepreneurs of these manufactories enjoy the opportunities that other entrepreneurs and manufacturers have of distributing their cloths, as well as to assure to these cloths the reputation they have acquired. Wishing to rule on that, heard the report, etc.
>
> 1. Every printer or manufacturer of painted or printed canvases shall, within one month after the publication of these regulations, enroll himself by name, surname and residence, in a register that will be filed with the clerk of the jurisdiction of manufactures, in the jurisdiction of his domicile; and an extract of said registration on unsealed paper will be issued to him by the clerk of the jurisdiction; who may not request more than ten *sous* as fees and shipping costs.
>
> 2. All printers shall leave at the head and tail of each piece of canvas they print a white strip three-fingers wide, on the printed side of which they will place the first letter of their name, and their surname without abbreviation, as well as the place of their residence, with these words, *large or small dyeing*, according to the quality of the dyeing of each printed piece. ...

§ 1.67 DECISION OF THE LOUIS XVI'S COUNCIL ON THE TRADEMARKS OF CANVASES—1787

The following text illustrates a new step towards modern trademark law—manufacturers of canvases were authorized to change their trademarks anytime they so wished, provided they brought their new trademarks to the public register. Another interesting aspect was the reference to the protection of consumers against deception.

Decision of the council on the mark of canvases

Versailles, January 19, 1787

Taking into consideration the report submitted to the king, being in his council, stating that in several places of manufacture in the kingdom the merchants have abusively used to put on the cloths they have in their shops and stores a mark bearing their name, [and] their place of residence with the letters F A B; and that under this vague indication, which does not mean either the manufactory or the manufacturer, articles of an inferior quality are traded as if they came from a well-reputed factory; H.M. thought it was necessary to take measures appropriate to ensure to each article the reputation it has acquired, and to prevent the consumer from being deceived. Wishing to solve this matter; heard the report, etc.; the king being in his council, has ordered and orders the following:

1. The letters patent of May 5, 1779 and June 28, 1780 will be executed according to their form and content; consequently all the manufacturers shall apply to the cloths made by them a mark bearing their names, their surnames, and that of the place of their residence, in distinct and legible characters, without any abbreviation, on the penalty of a fine of 50 pounds. H.M. forbids all merchants or traders to put on the said canvases any marks of any kind whatsoever, and in particular the words *fabrique* or *fabricant* in short or in full, on the penalty of seizure and confiscation of the canvases, and the fine of 100 pounds.
2. Every manufacturer shall, within three months from the date of this decision, communicate to the wardens, jurors or officials in charge of the service of the office where he is in the habit of having the canvases of his factory marked, the mark that he applies thereon, so that, by the said wardens, jurors or officials, an imprint of the said mark be taken in a register [kept] for this purpose, and to have recourse to it if necessary; however, the said manufacturers may change their mark every time and as frequently as they deem appropriate, by entering in the register of the inspection office an imprint of their new mark.
3. H. M. commands Messrs. intendants and commissioners spread throughout the kingdom, the judges of the manufactures, inspectors and sub-inspectors, wardens, jurors or officials, to ensure, within their competences, the execution of this decision, which will be printed, read, published, and posted wherever needed, and concerning which all necessary letters patent will be issued.

§ 1.68 *BURBERRYS V. RAPER AND PULLEYN*: WHEN MISBRANDING DECEIVES THE CUSTOMER—1906

Between the previous text and this one, there is a gap of more than one hundred years. The reason is that between the end of the eighteenth century and the beginning of the twentieth century, nothing significant took place as regards business identifiers in the textile industry. In that period, many countries adopted encompassing trademark statutes, most of which revealed features that correspond to modern trademark law. But those statutes were not specific to textiles. This industry, still of great importance, had lost relevance by comparison with other industries that emerged from the Industrial Revolution. There was no longer reason for treating the trademarks of textiles in a particular and dedicated manner. By contrast, that was the period in which fashion, as an industry in its own right, emerged and the debates on how to appropriate designs and associated reputations started. We will see that in the next chapter.

Discussions on the branding of fashion in particular would emerge after the middle of the twentieth century when the industry reached such a significant dimension that it led to the arising of specific problems in securing prestige and reputation. The blending of ideas and brands—brands that are expression of ideas and expression of ideas that become brands—in the spirit of fashion designers and consumers has given rise to specific problems as to finding the right legal mechanism of protection. We will see more about this in the second chapter.

One of the legal issues that are specific to fashion concerns the identification of the boundaries of trademarks and how far their owners may go in pushing their limits so as to fight competitors' parasitism and consumers' deception. This court opinion, from which a few excerpts follow, acknowledges that the defendant was not branding the overcoats of their manufacture with the well-known Burberry's trademark. But the references to the inventor of that type of overcoat that the defendant made in its advertisements were confusing—up to the point that a customer ordered from the defendant a "Burberry's coat." It was the customer, after all, who was misbranding the article, but it was the defendant who gave cause to that mistake.

In the High Court of Justice.—Chancery Division.

Before Mr. Justice Warrington.

February 2, 1906.

Burberrys v. Raper and Pulleyn

The Plaintiffs, *Burberrys*, a firm trading in the Haymarket London, and elsewhere, had for many years made a specialty of waterproof garments, and under the name "Burberry," the fancy name of "Slip-on," which they attached to their garments in 1895, and also the term "Burberry Slip-on" they had made large sales of goods of their manufacture. They alleged that the names were of great value to them owing to their wide circulation, and that when used in connection with garments they meant and meant only weather and waterproof garments of their manufacture or merchandise.

In December 1905 the Defendant's firm *Raper and Pulleyn*, carrying business in York as makers of and dealers in waterproof articles, advertised as follows in certain issues of the "Yorkshire Evening Press" and the "Yorkshire Herald":—

BURBERRY'S SLIP-ON COATS.

RAPER AND PULLEYN have now added this Manufacture to their Macintosh Department. In appearance the Coats are identical with *Burberry's*, and the cloth is equal to theirs in every way, being treble proofed. The Firm's reputation for Macintoshes is itself a guarantee to purchasers. The Price is Two Guineas.

... On the 21st of December 1905 the Plaintiffs commenced an action against the Defendants for an injunction to restrain Passing off, and for the usual consequential relief. They filed evidence by London merchants and outfitters to the effect that "Burberry" and "Slip-on" signified their goods.

The Defendants filed evidence by themselves and by two clothiers doing business in York to the effect that the public had come to use the terms "Burberry Coat" and "Slip-on Coat" to denote coats by any maker which were of the shape and material of the waterproof coats by any maker which were of the shape and material of the waterproof coats originally introduced by the Plaintiffs; one of the clothiers stating that when a customer asked to see a "Burberry Coat" he inquired, "Do you particularly want one made by *Burberrys*?" ...

Warrington *J.*—In my opinion the defendants in this case have actually passed off a coat not of the Plaintiffs' manufacture as and for a coat of the Plaintiffs' manufacture. I have not, therefore, merely to consider whether their advertisement and trade description are calculated to deceive: I have a case of actual deception. The Plaintiffs, Messrs. *Burberrys*, are well-known manufacturers of waterproof coats of a particular description, and they have largely advertised their coats, and have obtained a wide reputation for them. The Defendants are wholesale and retail dealers and manufacturers of clothes.

They inserted two advertisements, one in the "Yorkshire Press," and one in another paper: and I have the one in the "Yorkshire Press" before me. It is headed in large letters, larger than any others in the advertisement, "Burberry's Slip-on Coats." Then there is a line, and then in smaller type "*Raper and Pulleyn*," and then in still smaller type "have now added this manufacture to their Macintosh Department." If the advertisement went no further than that I should have concluded that they had added to their Macintosh Department coats of this manufacture—that is *Burberrys*; but the advertisement goes on to qualify that: "In appearance the coats are identical with *Burberry's*, and the cloth is equal to theirs in every way, being trebled proofed." Then it begins again in a way which is certainly ambiguous, to say the least: "The firm's reputation for macintoshes" (that might well be either *Burberrys*' or *Raper and Pulleyn*'s) "is itself a guarantee to purchasers"; and then "the price is Two Guineas."

Now if I had to say whether that advertisement was calculated to deceive, as at present advised, seeing the form in which it is put, and the contrast between the types in various parts of the advertisement, and knowing something of the way in which people look at advertisements like that, I should myself come to the conclusion that it was calculated to deceive. But I have not got to do that, for what happened was that a farmer named *Beresford*, seeing the advertisement, sent an order for "one of your Burberry coats." ...

Putting all these things together I think there is ample ground for an interlocutory injunction; and I shall therefore grant an injunction to restrain the Defendants from selling, advertising for sale, or otherwise dealing with weather and waterproof coats not being the Plaintiffs' manufacture or merchandise under the description of "Burberry," "Burberry Slip-on" or "Slip-on," or from in any other way passing off goods not of the Plaintiffs' manufacture or merchandise as and for the goods of the Plaintiffs' manufacture.

The parties subsequently agreed to treat the hearing of the Motion as the trial of the action, and the injunction awarded was made perpetual.

§ 1.69 *SOCIÉTÉ ANONYME VALISÈRE V. TINET-CLAVERIE AND F. CLAVERIE*: THE PROTECTION OF PRESTIGE AND REPUTATION AGAINST UNFAIR COMPETITION—1935

The importance of this opinion is that the reputation of the underwear made by Valisère was not only associated with design and style but also, as the manufacturer itself highlighted in advertisements, with the special, high-quality fabric with which they were made. Trademark law therefore would not cover the whole issue, only a broad claim of unfair competition would.

Commercial Court of Lyon, December 30, 1935

Société anonyme Valisère v. Tinet-Claverie and F. Claverie

> The fact that a traveling salesman sells in a marketplace underwear described by him as "Valisère type" is sufficiently proven by a bailiff's report whose value is generally accepted in case law and, moreover, by the confession of the person against whom it was requested. Thus, there is no doubt that, presenting his merchandise in this form, all the more likely to mislead a clientele less informed than other buyers, he was abusing their credulity by letting them suppose that those were genuine products of the renowned trademark "Valisère," thereby committing an act of unfair competition, which on principle must lead to his condemnation to damages and the publication of the opinion determining his conviction.

Figure 19 On top, brief text publicizing the opinion of the Court of Lyon in favor of the Société Anonyme Valisère (as ordered by the court). La Dépêche, May 10, 1936. Below, a piece of advertisement of underwear Valisère in the same newspaper, of November 3, 1937. The advertisement highlights three aspects. First, the designs of the 15 new underwear models: "Latest models very 'lingerie', conceived by the greatest creators of fashion. The most beautiful designs, the most elegant fashion." Second, the technical quality of the fabric employed in the underwear: "Hurry! Go today to the Big Stores or to the reseller 'Valisère' in your neighborhood and buy the quality 'Valisère.' Thanks to the 'Valisère' process, these fabrics are practically immune to wearing out. They return from each washing more beautiful and always as resistant. ... The underwear and lingerie 'Valisère' are warm in winter and cool in summer. They allow the body to breathe—finally!—freely. Their cut is fit and because they adjust ideally to the body, the dresses fit much better." Third, the ad highlights the two trademarks, nominative and figurative: "The trademark of DURATION. The trademark of COMFORT. The trademark of ELEGANCE. If there is no three-leaf clover, it is not 'Valisère'." Source: < gallica.BnF.fr >.

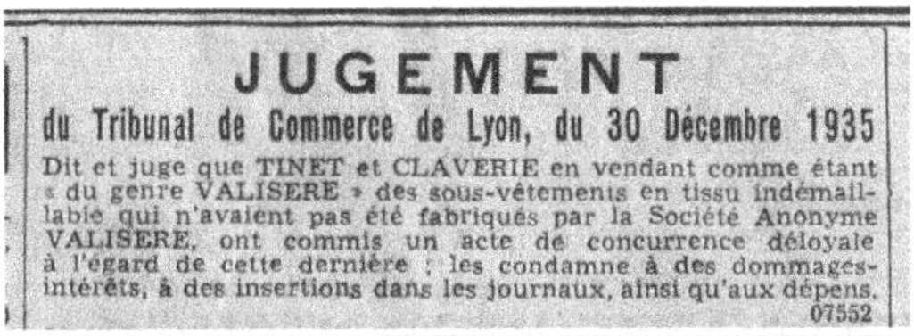

JUGEMENT

du Tribunal de Commerce de Lyon, du 30 Décembre 1935

Dit et juge que TINET et CLAVERIE en vendant comme étant « du genre VALISERE » des sous-vêtements en tissu indémaillable qui n'avaient pas été fabriqués par la Société Anonyme VALISERE, ont commis un acte de concurrence déloyale à l'égard de cette dernière ; les condamne à des dommages-intérêts, à des insertions dans les journaux, ainsi qu'aux dépens.

07552

§ 1.70 MARK FOY'S LTD V. DAVIES COOP & CO LTD ("TUB HAPPY CASE"): AN AUSTRALIAN COURT DEFINES THE ESSENCE OF TRADEMARKS—ESTABLISHING EMPATHY BETWEEN THE CONSUMER AND THE ARTICLE (OR SERVICE) THEY DESIGNATE—1956

The importance of Mark Foy's opinion lies in two elements: the careful analysis of the distinctive effect of words that are part of the common vocabulary; and the conclusion that trademarks do not need to transmit a defined idea. It is enough that they create in consumers a pleasant feeling that leads them to take the decision of purchasing, i.e., that they originate in consumers' empathy towards the product (or service) they designate. In other words, it is consumers who make the trademarks, not the merchants. This corresponds to the concept of the social construction of marks, which also applies in the field of patents—for the commercial success of an invention, it does not matter that it be covered by a patent, what matters is that society approves and uses it (see § 2.40).

The idea behind this opinion is not specific to textiles or fashion, but it was enunciated in their context. That is why it is here partly reproduced. Moreover, the nature of fashion increases the importance of the pleasant feeling produced by certain brands (and products). A great deal of purchases of fashion articles is dictated by impulse, and in that context, the pleasing factor may be controlling.

Mark Foy's Ltd v. Davies Coop & Co Ltd ("Tub Happy case")

[1956] HCA 41; (1956) 95 CLR 190

August 9, 1956

High Court of Australia

1. Dixon C.J. I have had the advantage of reading the judgment prepared by considerations which Kitto J. has marshalled with so much force against the view that the words "tub happy" are words having no direct reference to the character or quality of the goods within the meaning of par. (d) of s. 16 (1) of the Trade Marks Act 1905-1948. But nevertheless I am unable to adopt the conclusion that these words are disqualified from forming a registrable trade mark under s. 16 (1) (d) because they directly refer to the character or quality of the goods.

2. It is, I think, a mistake first to assume that words like "Tub Happy" do convey a meaning either to people in general or to a particular class of persons and then on that assumption to inquire what exactly the meaning is. Indeed to institute a search for a meaning almost necessarily implies that in ordinary English speech the words do not possess a connotation sufficiently definite to amount to a direct reference to the character or quality of the goods. And that is true even when to standard English usage is added all the figurative idiomatic and slang phraseology that may be currently in use. Once, however, the question is asked what do the words mean and there is started a search for a meaning, a process of analysis and of reasoning by exclusion of alternatives is begun. No doubt such a search may, without any sacrifice of logic, end in construing the words as meaning that the garments will emerge happily from the washtub. But if they are so interpreted, the interpretation is chiefly the consequence of failure to find another meaning. I venture to think, however, that a man, or for that matter a woman, hearing for the first time the words used in combination and in connection with cotton garments,

would not so understand the words at once. Certainly such a person would not so understand them intuitively and without stopping to reflect and ask himself or herself what meaning the words could really possess.

3. The fallacy of asking what is the meaning of the phrase lies in the basal assumption that the words are intended to convey some definite meaning and perhaps the further assumption that the meaning has reference to the garments or the cottons. The assumption is fallacious because it overlooks the fact that language is not always used to convey an idea. Many uses of words are purely emotive. A word or words are often employed for no purpose but to evoke in the reader or hearer some feeling, some mood, some mental attitude. This is true of much advertising, which common experience shows to be full of meaningless but emotive expressions supposedly capable of inducing a generally favourable inclination in the almost subconscious thought of the passing auditor or hasty reader. Words put forward as trademarks are very likely indeed to be chosen in the same way.

4. Though Mr. Holmes for the respondent did of course put forward the claim that "tub happy" means washable, it was a meaning it was necessary to suggest. It was not a meaning that had sprung unaided to the mind and it was not one which he was able to establish by reference to instances of known usage. ...

7. I cannot think that the words now in question go further than, if as far as, suggesting in a vague and indefinable way a gladsome carelessness a propos of the tub. They may have an emotive tendency, but they do not appear to me to convey any meaning or idea sufficiently tangible to amount to a direct reference to the character or quality of the goods.

8. I agree in the judgment of Williams J. and I have added the foregoing only in an endeavour to make clear why I remain unconvinced by the judgment of Kitto J.

1. Williams J. This is an appeal by the plaintiff company from a decree of the Supreme Court of New South Wales in Equity (McLelland J.) dismissing with costs a suit brought by the plaintiff appellant against the defendants-respondents to restrain the alleged infringement by the defendants of its registered trade mark No. 103308. This trade mark was registered under the provisions of the Trade Marks Act 1905-1948 on July 25, 1950 in class 38 in respect of articles of clothing and consists of the words "tub happy." The plaintiff owns a large retail store at 143-147 Liverpool Street, Sydney where it has for more than forty years carried on an extensive retail business. This business consists principally of retailing clothing for men, women and children, materials for such clothing and draper's manchester and household requisites. The plaintiff also owns and operates in the vicinity woollen mills, a knitting mill and shirt factory and a clothing factory. Since the date of registration the plaintiff has used and advertised the trade mark extensively upon and in connection with articles of clothing, particularly cotton frocks of various designs and good quality, manufactured by itself for which there is a ready sale. Each frock has attached to it by sewing a label bearing in bright colours the words "Tub Happy Cottons by Mark Foy's Limited, Sydney." The plaintiff has also extensively advertised its cotton frocks under the trade mark in newspapers published in Sydney and has, in each summer since 1950, exclusively displayed "Tub Happy" frocks in one of its largest show windows and has used show cards in such windows and in its departments carrying these words in large type.

2. The defendant Davies Coop (N.S.W.) Pty. Ltd., a New South Wales company which carries on business at Marrickville, is a subsidiary of the defendant Davies Coop & Co. Ltd., a Victorian company which carries on business at Swanston Street, Melbourne. In August or September 1953 the plaintiff received a letter from the Victorian company advising it of a projected 1954 sales promotion

campaign of "Exacto Cotton Garments—Tub Happy Cotton Fresh Budget Wise" manufactured by this defendant. The circular stated that the weight of advertising would tell the public the story of "Exacto Cotton Garments—Tub Happy Cotton Fresh Budget Wise" and would ensure an immediate demand for Exacto products. One suggested advertisement was "Buy Tub Happy Windcheaters Skimps etc." The plaintiff immediately drew this defendant's attention to the existence of its trade mark "Tub Happy" and claimed that any use by the defendant or any of its traders of these words in connection with any line of clothing would be an infringement. But the defendants through their patent attorney replied that they were not using the words "Tub Happy" as a trade mark and that the words "Tub Happy Cotton Fresh and Budget Wise" were being used "in a modern descriptive sense," whatever this may mean, and that these words when used in relation to Exacto garments referred to their good washing properties, freshness and economy. The defendants pointed out that their garments were in every instance prominently branded as Exacto goods, that this was their trade mark, and that it was this mark that was distinctive of their goods. Considerable correspondence followed, the plaintiff being desirous of avoiding litigation in the trade and hoping that the defendants would abandon the use of the controversial words. But they refused to do so, continuing to claim that the words "tub happy" were merely descriptive of a quality of their cotton goods and finally, in October 1954, the plaintiff commenced this suit. ...

4. The plaintiff filed a statement of claim and moved for an interlocutory injunction and by consent the motion was turned into a motion for a decree. His Honour dismissed the suit on the ground that the words were being used by the defendant as a bona fide description of the character or quality of the goods within the meaning of s. 53A of the Trade Marks Act. He said: "In my opinion, the facts in this case bring the defendants within s. 53A, assuming otherwise a valid trade mark and facts showing an infringement. I have examined all the advertisements very carefully, but, in my opinion, each must be read as a whole, even bearing in mind the various elements to which Mr. Hardie directed my attention, and all must be read, I think, in the light of the evidence of Mr. Furphey, which I accept. Reading the advertisements in the manner I have indicated, I am of opinion that the use up to this point of time by the defendants of the words "Tub Happy" has been a use by the defendants of a bona fide description of the character or quality of the goods of the defendants." We were informed by counsel for the defendants that his Honour said that he was prepared to dismiss the motion either on this ground or on the ground that the defendants had not used the words "tub happy" as a trade mark, that it was only if they were so doing that the plaintiff's rights in the trade mark would be infringed, and that his Honour only adopted the former ground after he had given counsel for the plaintiff the option to choose between them. ...

6. The first question is whether the words "tub happy" are registrable as a trade mark under s. 16 (1) (d) of the Trade Marks Act. To qualify they must be words having no direct reference to the character or quality of articles of clothing. In his speech in *Eastman Photographic Materials Co. Ltd. v. Comptroller-General of Patents*, Designs and Trade Marks ("Solio" Case) (1898) AC 571 Lord Herschell explained the meaning of this qualification. He said: "any word in the English language may serve as a trade-mark—the commonest word in the language might be employed. In these circumstances it would obviously have been out of the question to permit a person by registering a trade-mark in respect of a particular class of goods to obtain a monopoly of the use of a word having reference to the character or quality of those goods. The vocabulary of the English language is common property: it belongs alike to all; and no one ought to be permitted to

prevent the other members of the community from using for purposes of description a word which has reference to the character or quality of goods" (1898) AC, at p 580. ... Any reference that the words "Tub Happy" have to the character or quality of articles of clothing is very remote. They are in the nature of a coined phrase. Inanimate objects including articles of clothing cannot have the character or quality of happiness whether they are in a tub or not. But the defendants' case is that the common metaphorical use of the adjective would convey to prospective buyers of the fabrics that the cotton emerged from the wash tub more attractive than ever in appearance with fibres and colours as good if not better than ever. Therefore, so it is said, the words are a description of the character or quality of the goods and moreover are not entitled to registration. This claim gives far too specific a meaning to the vague figurative use of the word "happy" in connection with "tub." Like so many expressions used in advertisements no definite or actual meaning seems to belong to the combination "Tub Happy." There is a cloudy suggestion only about it that all will be well in a wash tub but that is all. The attitude of mind of those who glance at such advertisements may be affected favourably by some sort of vague association of ideas but it falls a long way short of conveying any meaning to them. To say that articles of clothing are tub happy is in the ordinary use of English meaningless. The words contain at most a "covert and skillful allusion" to the quality of washability which is characteristic of articles of clothing made of some kinds of material including cotton. At most they create an impression that this is what they are intended to convey. They do not trespass upon the rights of other traders to use any ordinary English words or phrases referring to the washable qualities of their goods. They do not attempt to "enclose and appropriate as private property certain little strips of the great open common of the English language." No doubt the words are intended to "contain a meaning—a meaning is wrapped up in them if you can only find it out." ... And it may not be hard to find out that meaning but the words do not refer in any ordinary sense, laudatory or otherwise, to any character or quality of articles of clothing, still less do they do so directly.

7. The conclusion that the words "Tub Happy" are registrable under s. 16 (1) (d) of the Trade Marks Act because they have no direct reference to the character or quality of articles of clothing goes a long way towards deciding the ground on which his Honour ruled against the defendants. There is nothing in the registration of these words to prevent the defendants from describing their cotton goods as having the qualities of washability, freshness and cheapness, and in particular the first of these qualities. The whole English language is open to them, even the most up to date English, if the defendants wish to refer to these qualities "in a modern descriptive sense." In *J. B. Stone & Co. Ltd. v. Steelace Manufacturing Co. Ltd.* (1929) 46 RPC 406 Lawrence L.J. said: "In my opinion the object of s. 44" (of the English Trade Marks Act 1905 which corresponds to s. 53A of the Commonwealth Act) "was to safeguard traders in cases where the registered trade mark consisted of more or less descriptive words forming part of the ordinary English language, without the use of which other traders would find some difficulty in describing certain qualities of their goods; but was never intended and does not operate to enable a trader to make use of a rival trader's registered trade mark consisting of a fancy word having no reference to the character and quality of the goods in order more readily to sell his own goods" (1929) 46 RPC, at p 417. ... Section 53A of the Trade Marks Act protects the use by any person of any bona fide description of the character or quality of his goods. But that means a description and not a mere suggestion in fanciful language. It does not protect an attempt by the defendants to usurp a metaphorical phrase like "Tub Happy" however magnetic the force of its public appeal may be. ...

§ 1.71 THE *YKK* CASE: A BRAZILIAN COURT DEFINES THE ESSENCE OF INTELLECTUAL PROPERTY'S ROLE—TO SERVE HONESTY IN TRADE—1982

The text that follows, although it speaks to trademark law only, states the essence of intellectual property: all merchants and manufacturers aim at differentiating themselves and their products or services from competitors' but society is not served when they do so through dishonest practices.

This opinion gains more relevance when one realizes that Brazil is not a common law country. And yet, for the sake of the preservation of the fundamental value of fairness in competition, this court has not hesitated to put aside a written norm of administrative law (the presumption of validity of a certificate of registration issued by the Trademark Office) and has given predominance to that value. In this manner, this court acted like an equity court.

As in the previous text, the principle on which this opinion was constructed is not specific to fashion or even textiles, but because it was delivered in the context of an apparel's accessory—slide fasteners—it is partly reproduced here. Almost eighty years before, in a case involving the fraudulent advertisement of a medicine, a Scottish court had enunciated the same principle:

> *No man is entitled to obtain the aid of the law to protect him in carrying on a fraudulent trade, but the cases quoted at the debate by the Lord Ordinary establish, as I think, very clearly that the Courts have in the past given effect to the principle which allows nothing to the man who comes before the seat of justice with a* turpis causa.
>
> *Lord Justice Clerk in* Bile Bean Manufacturing Company v. Davidson; *In the Court of Session of Scotland, Inner House.—Second Session, 1905, 1906.*[38]

Brazil—Court of Criminal Appeals of São Paulo (5th Chamber)

HC 114.846 ("YKK Case")

Judgment on June 29, 1982

Opinion delivered by Appellate Judge Adauto Suannes.

1. Attorney José Antonio Ivo Galli applies for a habeas corpus order, aiming at the dismissal of the criminal action moved by Metalúrgica Brasileira Ultra against Iwao Kamiichi, Yutaka Ikegami and Norio Miyaguchi, to whom the crime of Article 175 I, II and IV, (a), of Decree-Law 7.903/45 is attributed, arguing in brief that the crime of the defendants consisted of using the trademark YKK for the zippers they manufacture, trademark which had regularly been registered by the plaintiff. It happens, however, that the trademark YKK is registered in about 116 countries by its legitimate owner, the company Yoshida Kabushiki Kaisha, which exported those devices to Brazil for many years. On December 29, 1967, the

38. This opinion is partly reproduced in FROM ANTIQUITY TO THE COVID-19 PANDEMIC, *supra* note 2, at 94-97.

defendants filed with the National Institute of Industrial Property an application for the registration of the said mark, which, once granted, led to registration nr. 837,584. Because of a mistaken translation, the term *slide fasteners*, which refers to zippers and similar products, was registered in class 8, which concerns *photo slides*. Having noticed the mistake, the defendants are currently engaged in correcting it administratively. However, in the meantime the plaintiff, surreptitiously, registered, on May 16, 1969, under nr. 884,377, the same trademark YKK for designating *slide fasteners*. Alleging the lack of fair ground for the criminal action, given the doubt surrounding the right of the plaintiff, the defendants expect its dismissal.

Opinion by the Prosecutor. In a nutshell, it says that: (a) the allegation of lack of fair ground is unacceptable because [that is] a matter of civil law, given that the plaintiff is still the owner of the trademark; ...

This is the report in synthesis.

2. In the analysis of this case, one must bear in mind two superior principles: a) The Law does not exist to reward malice; b) mistakes do not give rise to rights.

...

It happened that Yoshida Brasileira Indústria e Comércio, of which the defendants are partners, in attempting to register the trademark YKK for zippers, by an obvious mistake of the firm in charge of that, obtained the registration as if it concerned photographic material.

Hence registration 837,584, of 19.11.74 (filed on December 29, 1967). It refers to metal, cardboard and plastic frames for photo slides, an area of business to which YKK is absolutely strange.

But on May 16, 1969, Metalúrgica Brasileira Ultra S/A, with the obvious and ineludible purpose of appropriating the fame that the products that bear that mark certainly enjoy, and having knowledge of the blatant mistake in the classification of the product, decided to apply for the global trademark YKK as if it were its own. And it got the registration, exactly because of the mentioned mistake.

One might even wonder how Ultra was informed of that mistake and who would have promised it the possibility of incorporating into its equity the reputation of a product it has never manufactured.

It is certain, however, that it will never be understood how a company with that name decides to have as a trademark that term formed by two letters that do not exist in the Portuguese alphabet. What relation could there be between Metalúrgica Brasileira Ultra S/A and YKK?

Obviously, none.

Therefore, the registration obtained by the plaintiff was animated by a completely immoral purpose, because a manufacturer of zippers could not ignore the existence of a worldwide known company, as Yoshida Kabushiki Kaisha is, or simply YKK.

To the surprise of Law lovers, however, to the dock of defendants does not come the company that, without any scruple, benefitted from another's mistake, waving as its own a worldwide known trademark, created so many decades ago. On the contrary, going further in its unfortunate adventure, under the cover of a stillborn acquired right, it brings a criminal action against no less than the representatives in Brazil of the legitimate YKK.

And it expects the support of the Judiciary for such an adventure.

For the solution of the present request of habeas corpus eventual considerations of a civil nature concerning the good or bad repercussions of the glaring and absolutely unacceptable malice of the plaintiff do not matter.

Here the issue is that it is more than evident that the defendants have not committed any crime whatsoever. The fault is on the side of the managers of

Metalúrgica Ultra who, without any scruple, are imposing on consumers, with the usual blessing of our powerless authorities, a product to whose name they have not contributed anything that could justify its use.

That the plaintiff would not respect its competitor, one can understand. That it would not respect consumers, it would be blameful. But that it does not respect the Judiciary, inducing it to condone with an act of piracy is quite appalling.

If the minimum one expects from a criminal charge is that it is provided of *fumus boni juris*, how could we accept that a criminal action born from such a procedure, which is supported by Law only formally, can embarrass anyone?

It would lack what illustrious Luis Recaséns Siches called *logos del razonable* ... And Justice Carlos Maximiliano recalled Cicero's praise to jurist Caius Aquilius Gallus, because he "always interpreted laws in a way so that reprehensible maneuvers and flaws would never benefit their authors." ...

3. In view of the above, defendants not having practiced any crime, the requested order is granted, so as to dismiss, definitively, the criminal action moved against them by Metalúrgica Brasileira Ultra S/A ...

§ 1.72 WHERE DOES PARODY STOP AND INFRINGEMENT START (OR VICE-VERSA)? *LOUIS VUITTON MALLETIER S.A. V. HAUTE DIGGITY DOG, LLC AND OTHERS*—2007

Because fashion is very much about prestige (prestige for those who make fashion, and prestige for those who buy and wear it), reputed fashion brands are particularly vulnerable to dilution. In 2006, the United States Trademark Dilution Revision Act (TDRA) was enacted, and a new type of dilution was included as an unlawful use of another's trademark: dilution by blurring and tarnishment. One might expect that this amendment would bring relief to major fashion houses because any sort of unauthorized use of trademarks that contribute to the reduction of their prestige might be deemed as a sort of blurring or tarnishment. Indeed, to some extent, the amendment helps fashion houses because the massive infringement of branded garments by knock-off companies leads to a loss in prestige and reputation. The amendment to the Act may have put it in restrictive terms, but the loss of prestige can be understood as a form of loss of the capacity to distinguish.

And yet, as the following opinion shows, famous brands are still vulnerable to a special sort of dilution: that caused by parody. The text that follows concerns a case that involved a complaint by Louis Vuitton Malletier against a retailer of objects for dogs, which imitated LVM's trademark.

A very lenient treatment of parody makes LVM's business identifiers (including designs) as well as all other well-known fashion business identifiers highly vulnerable to imitation. But it seems that US courts are inclined to treat that sort of undeniable commercial parasitism with sympathy. In another case, Louis Vuitton lost an infringement lawsuit against a US company, My Other Bag, Inc. (Louis Vuitton Malletier, S.A. v. My Other Bag, Inc., 674 F. App'x 16 (2d Cir. 2016)) (summary order). The Court of Appeals agreed with the District Court, which concluded that the imitation of LVM's designs and trademarks in My Other Bag's tote bags were a parody. Denying My Other

Bag's motion for attorney's fees (in an amount of about $ 800,000), the District Judge said:

> *As this Court's decision granting summary judgment to MOB made clear, Louis Vuitton certainly needs to learn how to take a joke. ... ("In some cases ... it is better to accept the implied compliment in a parody and to smile or laugh than it is to sue. This ... is such a case." (citations, brackets, and internal quotation marks omitted)). Its lack of a refined sense of humor, however, is not a reason to pile on further by awarding MOB—however sympathetic its cause may be—attorney's fees and costs. Accordingly, and for the reasons stated above, MOB's motion for attorney's fees is denied. (14-CV-3419 (JMF), United States District Court for the Southern District of New York), decided on January 8, 2018. Order confirmed by the Court of Appeals in 2019.*

The problem lies in the concept of parody. While a trademark parody necessarily copies enough of the original design with the purpose of bringing the original design to consumers' minds, a successful parody also distinguishes itself and, because of the implicit message communicated by the parody, allows the consumer to appreciate it. However, the Court of Appeals for the Fourth Circuit did not explain what message it could see in the use of LVM's trademark by the defendant. But where the court saw an "implicit message" (whatever that message is), an attentive observant might see simply a matter of parasitism. After all the defendant is not in the business of making jokes with a brand that gives rise to intensive conspicuous consumption but of making money out of selling objects used by dogs.[39] *In the parody, it might have been argued, it is the intention that counts. The fact that the alleged parody does not give rise to confusion (one of the mentioned Pizzaria Uno factors invoked by the Court) should be irrelevant. After all the defendant is making money out of associating his products with those of LVM. This seems to be parasitism in our view, and an act of unfair trade, which the currently prevailing construction of the 2006 amendment to the United States Trademark Dilution Act allows. The Court said:* "And because the famous mark is particularly strong and distinctive, it becomes more likely that a parody will not impair the distinctiveness of the mark." *But the whole issue should not be that of keeping the distinctiveness of the original mark, but that of avoiding parasitism, dishonest opportunism. Otherwise, any company will obtain access to famous brands and sell whatever its products are, provided it imitates those brands in the way of a parody. Parody is associated with art and culture. Actually, art and culture may have a commercial impact (books are sold; films are licensed; etc.), but the commercial aspect must be subsidiary to the parody, not the opposite. So, the use of a well-known trademark by parody should be tolerated (for the purposes of being used as a defense of trademark infringement) when it acquires the nature of a commercial product. But a product that primarily has a*

39. Discussing the limits of a parody trademark defense, two commentators have written: "But when a product is purely commercial in nature, a defendant's use of the plaintiff's mark may need to be more than just funny—the humorous use of a similar mark merely to increase sales without meaningful commentary is more likely to be deemed an infringing use." Sandra Edelman and Kaleb McNeely, January 6, 2016, at thetmca.com. The point suggested here is that no parody defense should be accepted in the case of a "purely commercial use," or when the use departs significantly from art and culture.

commercial impact and only incidentally has the nature of a parody should not be tolerated. The fundamental legal principle behind intellectual property accepts a parody that acquires the dimension of a commercial venture—a book, a film—but does not accept a commercial venture that disguises itself as a parody. Here we can apply the same standard as Section 107(1) of the US Copyright Act (USC Title 17) sets for fair use, to the extent that the commercial nature of the use "for nonprofit educational purposes" has to be taken into account.

Actually, the nucleus of the problem is that the imitation of Louis Vuitton's patterns on canvas should not be treated as trademark infringement. Instead, such imitation, of a purely commercial nature, should be dealt with as an act of parasitism on LVM's designs that have acquired a secondary meaning.

Due to the length of the opinion, the following text reproduces the parts discussing the parody and dilution topics, only.

United States Court of Appeals, Fourth Circuit.

Louis Vuitton Malletier S.A. v. Haute Diggity Dog, LLC and others

November 13, 2007

Louis Vuitton Malletier S.A., a French corporation located in Paris, that manufactures luxury luggage, handbags, and accessories, commenced this action against Haute Diggity Dog, LLC, a Nevada corporation that manufactures and sells pet products nationally, alleging trademark infringement under 15 U.S.C. § 1114(1)(a), trademark dilution under 15 U.S.C. § 1125(c), copyright infringement under 17 U.S.C. § 501, and related statutory and common law violations.

Haute Diggity Dog manufactures, among other things, plush toys on which dogs can chew, which, it claims, parody famous trademarks on luxury products, including those of Louis Vuitton Malletier. The particular Haute Diggity Dog chew toys in question here are small imitations of handbags that are labeled "Chewy Vuiton" and that mimic Louis Vuitton Malletier's LOUIS VUITTON handbags.

On cross-motions for summary judgment, the district court concluded that Haute Diggity Dog's "Chewy Vuiton" dog toys were successful parodies of Louis Vuitton Malletier's trademarks, designs, and products, and on that basis, entered judgment in favor of Haute Diggity Dog on all of Louis Vuitton Malletier's claims.

On appeal, we agree with the district court that Haute Diggity Dog's products are not likely to cause confusion with those of Louis Vuitton Malletier and that Louis Vuitton Malletier's copyright was not infringed. On the trademark dilution claim, however, we reject the district court's reasoning but reach the same conclusion through a different analysis. Accordingly, we affirm.

I. Louis Vuitton Malletier S.A. ("LVM") is a well-known manufacturer of luxury luggage, leather goods, handbags, and accessories, which it markets and sells worldwide. In connection with the sale of its products, LVM has adopted trademarks and trade dress that are well recognized and have become famous and distinct. Indeed, in 2006, BusinessWeek ranked LOUIS VUITTON as the 17th "best brand" of all corporations in the world and the first "best brand" for any fashion business.

LVM has registered trademarks for "LOUIS VUITTON," in connection with luggage and ladies' handbags (the "LOUIS VUITTON mark"); for a stylized monogram of "LV," in connection with traveling bags and other goods (the "LV mark"); and for a monogram canvas design consisting of a canvas with repetitions of the LV mark along with four-pointed stars, four-pointed stars inset in curved diamonds, and four-pointed flowers inset in circles, in connection with traveling bags and other products (the "Monogram Canvas mark"). In 2002, LVM adopted a brightly-colored version of the Monogram Canvas mark in which the LV mark and the designs were of various colors and the background was white (the "Multicolor design"), created in collaboration with Japanese artist Takashi Murakami. For the Multicolor design, LVM obtained a copyright in 2004. In 2005, LVM adopted another design consisting of a canvas with repetitions of the LV mark and smiling cherries on a brown background (the "Cherry design").

As LVM points out, the Multicolor design and the Cherry design attracted immediate and extraordinary media attention and publicity in magazines such as Vogue, W, Elle, Harper's Bazaar, Us Weekly, Life and Style, Travel & Leisure, People, In Style, and Jane. The press published photographs showing celebrities carrying these handbags, including Jennifer Lopez, Madonna, Eve, Elizabeth Hurley, Carmen Electra, and Anna Kournikova, among others. When the Multicolor design first appeared in 2003, the magazines typically reported, "The Murakami designs for Louis Vuitton, which were the hit of the summer, came with hefty price tags and a long waiting list." People Magazine said, "the wait list is in the thousands." The handbags retailed in the range of $ 995 for a medium handbag to $ 4,500 for a large travel bag. The medium size handbag that appears to be the model for the "Chewy Vuiton" dog toy retailed for $ 1,190. The Cherry design appeared in 2005, and the handbags including that design were priced similarly in the range of $ 995-$ 2,740. LVM does not currently market products using the Cherry design.

The original LOUIS VUITTON, LV, and Monogram Canvas marks, however, have been used as identifiers of LVM products continuously since 1896.

During the period 2003-2005, LVM spent more than $ 48 million advertising products using its marks and designs, including more than $ 4 million for the Multicolor design. It sells its products exclusively in LVM stores and in its own in-store boutiques that are contained within department stores such as Saks Fifth Avenue, Bloomingdale's, Neiman Marcus, and Macy's.

LVM also advertises its products on the Internet through the specific websites < www.louisvuitton.com > and < www.eluxury.com >.

Although better known for its handbags and luggage, LVM also markets a limited selection of luxury pet accessories-collars, leashes, and dog carriers-which bear the Monogram Canvas mark and the Multicolor design. These items range in price from approximately $ 200-$ 1, 600. LVM does not make dog toys.

Haute Diggity Dog, LLC, which is a relatively small and relatively new business located in Nevada, manufactures and sells nationally-primarily through pet stores-a line of pet chew toys and beds whose names parody elegant high-end brands of products such as perfume, cars, shoes, sparkling wine, and handbags. These include in addition to Chewy Vuiton (LOUIS VUITTON), Chewnel No. 5 (Chanel No. 5), Furcedes (Mercedes), Jimmy Chew (Jimmy Choo), Dog Perignonn (Dom Perignon), Sniffany & Co. (Tiffany & Co.), and Dogior (Dior). The chew toys and pet beds are plush, made of polyester, and have a shape and design that loosely imitate the signature product of the targeted brand. They are mostly distributed and sold through pet stores, although one or two Macy's stores carries Haute Diggity Dog's products. The dog toys are generally sold for less than $ 20, although larger versions of some of Haute Diggity Dog's plush dog beds sell for more than $ 100.

Haute Diggity Dog's "Chewy Vuiton" dog toys, in particular, loosely resemble miniature handbags and undisputedly evoke LVM handbags of similar shape, design, and color. In lieu of the LOUIS VUITTON mark, the dog toy uses "Chewy Vuiton"; in lieu of the LV mark, it uses "CV"; and the other symbols and colors employed are imitations, but not exact ones, of those used in the LVM Multicolor and Cherry designs.

In 2002, LVM commenced this action, naming as defendants Haute Diggity Dog; Victoria D.N. Dauernheim, the principal owner of Haute Diggity Dog; and Woofies, LLC, a retailer of Haute Diggity Dog's products, located in Ashburn, Virginia, for trademark, trade dress, and copyright infringement. Its complaint includes counts for trademark counterfeiting, under 15 U.S.C. § 1114(1)(a); trademark infringement, under 15 U.S.C. § 1114(1)(a); trade dress infringement, under 15 U.S.C. § 1125(a)(1); unfair competition, under 15 U.S.C. § 1125(a)(1); trademark dilution, under 15 U.S.C. § 1125(c); trademark infringement, under Virginia common law; trade dress infringement, under Virginia common law; unfair competition, under Virginia common law; copyright infringement of the Multicolor design, under 17 U.S.C. § 501; and violation of the Virginia Consumer Protection Act, under Virginia Code § 59.1-200. On cross-motions for summary judgment, the district court granted Haute Diggity Dog's motion and denied LVM's motion, entering judgment in favor of Haute Diggity Dog on all of the claims. It rested its analysis on each count principally on the conclusion that Haute Diggity Dog's products amounted to a successful parody of LVM's marks, trade dress, and copyright. *See Louis Vuitton Malletier S.A. v. Haute Diggity Dog, LLC*, 464 F.Supp.2d 495 (E.D.Va.2006).

LVM appealed and now challenges, as a matter of law, virtually every ruling made by the district court. ...

To prove trademark infringement, LVM must show (1) that it owns a valid and protectable mark; (2) that Haute Diggity Dog uses a "re-production, counter-feit, copy, or colorable imitation" of that mark in commerce and without LVM's consent; and (3) that Haute Diggity Dog's use is likely to cause confusion. 15 U.S.C. § 1114(1)(a); CareFirst, 434 F.3d at 267. The validity and protectability of LVM's marks are not at issue in this case, nor is the fact that Haute Diggity Dog uses a colorable imitation of LVM's mark. Therefore, we give the first two elements no further attention. To determine whether the "Chewy Vuiton" product line creates a likelihood of confusion, we have identified several nonexclusive factors to consider: (1) the strength or distinctiveness of the plaintiff's mark; (2) the similarity of the two marks; (3) the similarity of the goods or services the marks identify; (4) the similarity of the facilities the two parties use in their businesses; (5) the similarity of the advertising used by the two parties; (6) the defendant's intent; and (7) actual confusion. *See Pizzeria Uno Corp. v. Temple*, 747 F.2d 1522, 1527 (4th Cir.1984). These *Pizzeria Uno* factors are not always weighted equally, and not all factors are relevant in every case. ... Because Haute Diggity Dog's arguments with respect to the *Pizzeria Uno* factors depend to a great extent on whether its products and marks are successful parodies, we consider first whether Haute Diggity Dog's products, marks, and trade dress are indeed successful parodies of LVM's marks and trade dress.

For trademark purposes, "[a] 'parody' is defined as a simple form of entertainment conveyed by juxtaposing the irreverent representation of the trade-mark with the idealized image created by the mark's owner." ... "A parody must convey two simultaneous—and contradictory—messages: that it is the original, but also that it is not the original and is instead a parody." ... This second message must not only differentiate the alleged parody from the original but must also communicate some articulable element of satire, ridicule, joking, or amusement. Thus, "[a] parody relies upon a difference from the original mark, presumably a humorous difference, in order to produce its desired effect." ... (finding the use of

"Lardashe" jeans for larger women to be a successful and permissible parody of "Jordache" jeans).

When applying the PETA criteria to the facts of this case, we agree with the district court that the "Chewy Vuiton" dog toys are successful parodies of LVM handbags and the LVM marks and trade dress used in connection with the marketing and sale of those handbags. First, the pet chew toy is obviously an irreverent, and indeed intentional, representation of an LVM handbag, albeit much smaller and coarser. The dog toy is shaped roughly like a handbag; its name "Chewy Vuiton" sounds like and rhymes with LOUIS VUITTON; its monogram CV mimics LVM's LV mark; the repetitious design clearly imitates the design on the LVM handbag; and the coloring is similar. In short, the dog toy is a small, plush imitation of an LVM handbag carried by women, which invokes the marks and design of the handbag, albeit irreverently and incompletely. No one can doubt that LVM handbags are the target of the imitation by Haute Diggity Dog's "Chewy Vuiton" dog toys.

At the same time, no one can doubt also that the "Chewy Vuiton" dog toy is not the "idealized image" of the mark created by LVM. The differences are immediate, beginning with the fact that the "Chewy Vuiton" product is a dog toy, not an expensive, luxury LOUIS VUITTON handbag. The toy is smaller, it is plush, and virtually all of its designs differ. Thus, "Chewy Vuiton" is not LOUIS VUITTON ("Chewy" is not "LOUIS" and "Vuiton" is not "VUITTON," with its two Ts); CV is not LV; the designs on the dog toy are simplified and crude, not detailed and distinguished. The toys are inexpensive; the handbags are expensive and marketed to be expensive. And, of course, as a dog toy, one must buy it with pet supplies and cannot buy it at an exclusive LVM store or boutique within a department store. In short, the Haute Diggity Dog "Chewy Vuiton" dog toy undoubtedly and deliberately conjures up the famous LVM marks and trade dress, but at the same time, it communicates that it is not the LVM product.

Finally, the juxtaposition of the similar and dissimilar—the irreverent representation and the idealized image of an LVM handbag—immediately conveys a joking and amusing parody. The furry little "Chewy Vuiton" imitation, as something to be chewed by a dog, pokes fun at the elegance and expensiveness of a LOUIS VUITTON handbag, which must not be chewed by a dog. The LVM handbag is provided for the most elegant and well-to-do celebrity, to proudly display to the public and the press, whereas the imitation "Chewy Vuiton" "handbag" is designed to mock the celebrity and be used by a dog. The dog toy irreverently presents haute couture as an object for casual canine destruction. The satire is unmistakable. The dog toy is a comment on the rich and famous, on the LOUIS VUITTON name and related marks, and on conspicuous consumption in general. This parody is enhanced by the fact that "Chewy Vuiton" dog toys are sold with similar parodies of other famous and expensive brands—"Chewnel No. 5" targeting "Chanel No. 5"; "Dog Perignonn" targeting "Dom Perignon"; and "Sniffany & Co." targeting "Tiffany & Co."

We conclude that the PETA criteria are amply satisfied in this case and that the "Chewy Vuiton" dog toys convey "just enough of the original design to allow the consumer to appreciate the point of parody," but stop well short of appropriating the entire marks that LVM claims. ...

Finding that Haute Diggity Dog's parody is successful, however, does not end the inquiry into whether Haute Diggity Dog's "Chewy Vuiton" products create a likelihood of confusion. *See* 6 J. Thomas McCarthy, Trademarks and Unfair Competition § 31:153, at 262 (4th ed. 2007) ("There are confusing parodies and non-confusing parodies. All they have in common is an attempt at humor through the use of someone else's trademark"). The finding of a successful parody only influences the way in which the *Pizzeria Uno* factors are applied. ... Indeed, it becomes apparent that an effective parody will actually diminish the likelihood of confusion, while an ineffective parody does not. We now turn to the *Pizzeria Uno* factors.

A. As to the first *Pizzeria Uno* factor, the parties agree that LVM's marks are strong and widely recognized. They do not agree, however, as to the consequences of this fact. LVM maintains that a strong, famous mark is entitled, as a matter of law, to broad protection. While it is true that finding a mark to be strong and famous usually favors the plaintiff in a trademark infringement case, the opposite may be true when a legitimate claim of parody is involved. As the district court observed, "In cases of parody, a strong mark's fame and popularity is precisely the mechanism by which likelihood of confusion is avoided." ... "An intent to parody is not an intent to confuse the public." ... We agree with the district court. It is a matter of common sense that the strength of a famous mark allows consumers immediately to perceive the target of the parody, while simultaneously allowing them to recognize the changes to the mark that make the parody funny or biting. ... In this case, precisely because LOUIS VUITTON is so strong a mark and so well recognized as a luxury handbag brand from LVM, consumers readily recognize that when they see a "Chewy Vuiton" pet toy, they see a parody. Thus, the strength of LVM's marks in this case does not help LVM establish a likelihood of confusion.

B. With respect to the second *Pizzeria Uno* factor, the similarities between the marks, the usage by Haute Diggity Dog again converts what might be a problem for Haute Diggity Dog into a disfavored conclusion for LVM.

Haute Diggity Dog concedes that its marks are and were designed to be somewhat similar to LVM's marks. But that is the essence of a parody-the invocation of a famous mark in the consumer's mind, so long as the distinction between the marks is also readily recognized. While a trademark parody necessarily copies enough of the original design to bring it to mind as a target, a successful parody also distinguishes itself and, because of the implicit message communicated by the parody, allows the consumer to appreciate it. ... In concluding that Haute Diggity Dog has a successful parody, we have impliedly concluded that Haute Diggity Dog appropriately mimicked a part of the LVM marks, but at the same time sufficiently distinguished its own product to communicate the satire. The differences are sufficiently obvious and the parody sufficiently blatant that a consumer encountering a "Chewy Vuiton" dog toy would not mistake its source or sponsorship on the basis of mark similarity.

This conclusion is reinforced when we consider how the parties actually use their marks in the marketplace. ... The record amply supports Haute Diggity Dog's contention that its "Chewy Vuiton" toys for dogs are generally sold alongside other pet products, as well as toys that parody other luxury brands, whereas LVM markets its handbags as a top-end luxury item to be purchased only in its own stores or in its own boutiques within department stores. These marketing channels further emphasize that "Chewy Vuiton" dog toys are not, in fact, LOUIS VUITTON products.

C. Nor does LVM find support from the third *Pizzeria Uno* factor, the similarity of the products themselves. It is obvious that a "Chewy Vuiton" plush imitation handbag, which does not open and is manufactured as a dog toy, is not a LOUIS VUITTON handbag sold by LVM. Even LVM's most proximate products-dog collars, leashes, and pet carriers-are fashion accessories, not dog toys. As Haute Diggity Dog points out, LVM does not make pet chew toys and likely does not intend to do so in the future. Even if LVM were to make dog toys in the future, the fact remains that the products at issue are not similar in any relevant respect, and this factor does not favor LVM. ...

E. The sixth factor, relating to Haute Diggity Dog's intent, again is neutralized by the fact that Haute Diggity Dog markets a parody of LVM products. As other courts have recognized, "An intent to parody is not an intent to confuse the public." ... Despite Haute Diggity Dog's obvious intent to profit from its use of parodies, this action does not amount to a bad faith intent to create consumer confusion. To the contrary, the intent is to do just the opposite-to evoke a humorous, satirical association that distinguishes the products. This factor does not favor LVM. ...

III. ... We begin by noting that parody is not automatically a complete defense to a claim of dilution by blurring where the defendant uses the parody as its own designation of source, i.e., as a trademark. Although the TDRA does provide that fair use is a complete defense and allows that a parody can be considered fair use, it does not extend the fair use defense to parodies used as a trademark. As the statute provides:

"The following shall not be actionable as dilution by blurring or dilution by tarnishment under this subsection:

(A) Any fair use *other than as a designation of source for the person's own goods or services, including use in connection with* parodying."

15 U.S.C.A. § 1125(c)(3)(A)(ii) (emphasis added). Under the statute's plain language, parodying a famous mark is protected by the fair use defense only if the parody is not "a designation of source for the person's own goods or services."

The TDRA, however, does not require a court to ignore the existence of a parody that is used as a trademark, and it does not preclude a court from considering parody as part of the circumstances to be considered for determining whether the plaintiff has made out a claim for dilution by blurring. Indeed, the statute permits a court to consider "all relevant factors," including the six factors supplied in § 1125(c)(2)(B).

Thus, it would appear that a defendant's use of a mark as a parody is relevant to the overall question of whether the defendant's use is likely to impair the famous mark's distinctiveness. Moreover, the fact that the defendant uses its marks as a parody is specifically relevant to several of the listed factors. For example, factor (v) (whether the defendant intended to create an association with the famous mark) and factor (vi) (whether there exists an actual association between the defendant's mark and the famous mark) directly invite inquiries into the defendant's intent in using the parody, the defendant's actual use of the parody, and the effect that its use has on the famous mark. While a parody intentionally creates an association with the famous mark in order to be a parody, it also intentionally communicates, if it is successful, that it is not the famous mark, but rather a satire of the famous mark. ... That the defendant is using its mark as a parody is therefore relevant in the consideration of these statutory factors.

Similarly, factors (i), (ii), and (iv)—the degree of similarity between the two marks, the degree of distinctiveness of the famous mark, and its recognizability—are directly implicated by consideration of the fact that the defendant's mark is a successful parody. Indeed, by making the famous mark an object of the parody, a successful parody might actually enhance the famous mark's distinctiveness by making it an icon. The brunt of the joke becomes yet more famous. ...

In sum, while a defendant's use of a parody as a mark does not support a "fair use" defense, it may be considered in determining whether the plaintiff-owner of a famous mark has proved its claim that the defendant's use of a parody mark is likely to impair the distinctiveness of the famous mark.

In the case before us, when considering factors (ii), (iii), and (iv), it is readily apparent, indeed conceded by Haute Diggity Dog, that LVM's marks are distinctive, famous, and strong. The LOUIS VUITTON mark is well known and is commonly identified as a brand of the great Parisian fashion house, Louis Vuitton Malletier. So too are its other marks and designs, which are invariably used with the LOUIS VUITTON mark. It may not be too strong to refer to these famous marks as icons of high fashion.

While the establishment of these facts satisfies essential elements of LVM's dilution claim, see 15 U.S.C.A. § 1125(c)(1), the facts impose on LVM an increased burden to demonstrate that the distinctiveness of its famous marks is likely to be impaired by a successful parody. Even as Haute Diggity Dog's parody mimics the famous mark, it communicates simultaneously that it is not the famous mark, but is only satirizing it. ... And because the famous mark is particularly strong and distinctive, it becomes more likely that a parody will not impair the distinctiveness of the mark. In short, as Haute Diggity Dog's "Chewy Vuiton" marks are a successful parody, we conclude that they will not blur the distinctiveness of the famous mark as a unique identifier of its source. ...

The judgment of the district court is

Affirmed.

Figure 20 On top, Louis Vuitton's easily recognizable multicolor monogram Speedy. The product has been discontinued, but the pattern is still an undeniable element of LVM's identification. Below, left: White Chewy Vuiton Bowls & Mat, sold by Haute Diggity Dog (originally in various colors: pink, yellow, black, and white). Below, right: Tote bag London/Multi, sold by a Mexican company claiming to represent My Other Bag, Inc. in that country.

§ 1.73 WHERE DOES A FASHION DESIGN STOP AND A TRADEMARK START (OR VICE-VERSA)? THE OPPOSING VIEWS OF THE EUROPEAN UNION GENERAL COURT AND OF THE UNITED STATES COURT OF APPEALS FOR THE NINTH CIRCUIT

The insertion of trademarks in fashion articles—fabrics, garments, accessories—has become frequent as a measure to increase the level of protection of the designs behind those articles. Louis Vuitton's monogram, Versace's medusa, Bimba Y Lola's full name, and many other trademarks are often printed on the very products they distinguish, not only as elements of pure identification and differentiation but also as elements of decoration.

This is a strategy that is used exclusively by the fashion industry and is explained by its essentially visual nature. But for those symbols to be accepted as trademarks they must be clearly distinguishable from the background on which they are inserted.

The two texts that follow concern trademarks for apparel that were intended to follow an opposite path: to be inserted as a decorative element and at the same time to be acknowledged as a trademark.

In the first example, the problem with that intended combination of trademark and ornament was that, as an ornament, i.e., as part of the design, it was not sufficiently original—hence, it was not susceptible of being recognized by consumers as a trademark (in the absence, as a matter of course, of secondary meaning—which no new trademark can ever show). Indeed, it appears that the criteria used by the OHIM as well as by the EU General Court for assessing the registrability of the mark in question were more related to its nature as a design than as a mark. When both instances referred to elements such as "common features of goods," "eye-catching features," and "visual stimulus," they seemed to have in mind the factors for the registrability/protection of industrial designs. After all, as far as trademarks are concerned, the presence or absence of "distinctive character" is analyzed, among other factors, as regards the nature of the goods (e.g., the drawing of an apple does not serve as a trademark for selling fruit; the drawing of a TV set does not serve as a trademark for electronic appliances, including TV sets; etc.), but not as regards arbitrary visual elements of those goods.

The second example is about a successful trademark that plays an important ornamental role: the famous Arcuate, Levi Strauss's trademark composed of two lines of stitches that are sewn on the back pockets of Levi's jeans. The text brought here does not discuss the registrability of such a design as a trademark. Instead, it discusses the correct interpretation of the Trademark Dilution Revision Act (TDRA) of 2006, in the sense that for a junior trademark to dilute a senior one there is no need for absolute identity between the two signs, provided other two factors are present (i.e., that the trademark in question is distinctive and well-known). If these two factors are found, similarity is enough. One could say that the Ninth Circuit did not need to discuss the registrability of Levi Strauss's Arcuate trademark because it has taken it for granted.

Anyway, the sources included here serve as illustrations that what in the view of a European Union court is not sufficiently distinctive to become a trademark, in the United States is.

§ 1.73.1 *Rosenruist—Gestão e serviços, Lda v. Office for Harmonisation in the Internal Market (Trade Marks and Designs) (OHIM)*—In Case T-388/09—2010

General Court (First Chamber), European Union

September 28, 2010

(Community trade mark—Application for Community figurative mark representing two curves on a pocket—Absolute ground for refusal—Lack of distinctive character—Article 7(1)(b) of Regulation (EC) No. 207/2009).

Action brought against the decision of the Second Board of Appeal of OHIM of June 18, 2009 (Case R 237/2009-2) concerning an application for registration as a Community trade mark of a figurative sign representing two curves on a pocket,

Judgment:

Background to the dispute

1. On May 9, 2008 the applicant, Rosenruist—Gestão e serviços, Lda, filed an application for registration of a Community trade mark with the Office for Harmonisation in the Internal Market (Trade Marks and Designs) (OHIM) pursuant to Council Regulation (EC) No. 40/94 of December 20, 1993 on the Community trade mark (OJ 1994 L 11, p. 1), as amended (replaced by Council Regulation (EC) No. 207/2009 of February 26, 2009 on the Community trade mark (OJ 2009 L 78, p. 1)).

2. The trade mark in respect of which registration was sought is the figurative sign reproduced below:

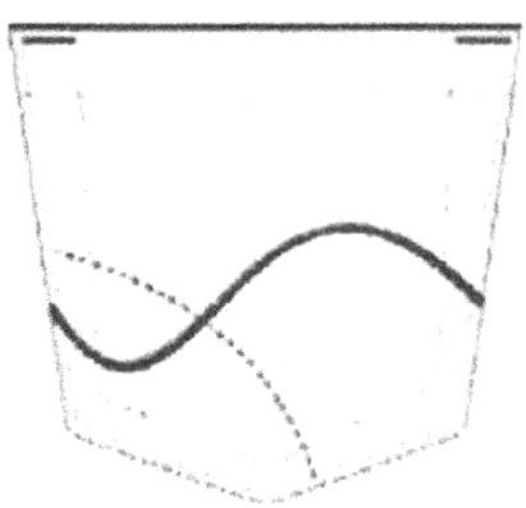

3. The description of the mark given in the application for registration reads: "Two Curves Crossed in One Point Design inserted in a Pocket; the mark consists of a decorative stitching made of Two Curves Crossed in One Point Design Inserted in a Pocket; one of the curves is characterised by an arched form, dr[a]wn with a fine stroke, while the second one is characterised by a sinusoidal form, dr[a]wn with a thick stroke; the unevenly broken lines represent the perimeter of the pocket to which applicant makes no claim and which serves only to indicate the position of the mark on the pocket."

4. The goods for which registration was sought are in Classes 18 and 25 of the Nice Agreement Concerning the International Classification of Goods and Services for the Purposes of the Registration of Marks of June 15, 1957, as revised and amended, and correspond, for each of those classes, to the following description:

- Class 18: "Bags, pouches, purses, wallets, valises, trunks, make-up bags and empty vanity cases, document holders, umbrellas, handbags."
- Class 25: "Dresses, skirts, trousers, shirts, jackets, overcoats, raincoats, coats and pullovers, jerkins, hats, scarves, foulards, hosiery (clothing), neckerchieves, gloves (clothing), belts for clothing, shoes, boots, sandals, clogs, slippers."

5. By decision of December 17, 2008, the examiner refused registration for all the goods on the ground that the mark in question was devoid of any distinctive character within the meaning of Article 7(1)(b) of Regulation No. 40/94 (now Article 7(1)(b) of Regulation No. 207/2009).

6. On February 13, 2009 the applicant filed a notice of appeal before OHIM against that decision, pursuant to Articles 57 to 62 of Regulation No. 40/94 (now Articles 58 to 64 of Regulation No. 207/2009).

7. By decision of June 18, 2009 ("the contested decision"), the Second Board of Appeal of OHIM dismissed the appeal. The Board of Appeal held that, since the goods in question were goods which either covered or protected the human body or which were fashion accessory or travel goods that met basic fashion needs, the relevant public was composed of average consumers in the European Union who were reasonably well informed and reasonably observant and circumspect. Taking into account the description of the trade mark applied for, the Board of Appeal considered that that mark was a "position mark" consisting of a stitched pattern that had a specific position on a pocket. It considered the stitched pattern to be a mere variation of a common feature of goods covered by the mark in question that would not enable the average consumer to recognise the origin of those goods. It concluded that the trade mark applied for was devoid of any distinctive character within the meaning of Article 7(1)(b) of Regulation No. 207/2009. ...

Law

10. In support of its action, the applicant submits a single plea in law alleging infringement of Article 7(1)(b) of Regulation No. 207/2009. The applicant, unlike the Board of Appeal, considers that the sign in question will not be perceived by the relevant public as an exclusively decorative element or a mere variation of a common feature of the goods in question, but as an original sign which has the minimum degree of distinctive character sufficient to function as a trade mark.

11. OHIM disputes the applicant's arguments.

12. According to Article 7(1)(b) of Regulation No. 207/2009, trade marks which are devoid of any distinctive character are not to be registered. According to settled case-law, the marks referred to in Article 7(1)(b) of Regulation No. 207/2009 are those which are regarded as incapable of performing the essential function of a trade mark, namely that of identifying the commercial origin of the goods or services at issue, thus enabling the consumer who acquired the goods or services covered by the mark to repeat the experience if it proves to be positive, or to avoid it if it proves to be negative, on the occasion of a subsequent acquisition ... .

13. The distinctive character of a mark must be assessed, first, by reference to the goods or services in respect of which registration or the protection of the mark has been applied for and, second, by reference to the perception of the relevant public, which consists of average consumers of those goods or services ... .

14. A minimum degree of distinctive character is, however, sufficient to render the absolute ground for refusal set out in Article 7(1)(b) of Regulation No. 207/2009 inapplicable ... .

15. In the present case, the applicant does not dispute the assessment of the Board of Appeal according to which, since the goods in question are goods in Classes 18 and 25 which either cover or protect the human body or which are fashion accessories or travel goods that meet basic fashion needs, the relevant public is composed of average consumers throughout the European Union who are reasonably well informed and reasonably observant and circumspect.

16. By contrast, the applicant disputes the Board of Appeal's assessment regarding the distinctive character of the mark in question.

17. It is apparent from the description of the mark in question given in paragraph 3 above that it consists of two crossed curves which are stitched (topstitched) on a pocket in a precise position. The Board of Appeal therefore rightly considered, without being contradicted by the applicant, that the mark in question was a "position mark" consisting of a stitched pattern that had a specific position on a pocket.

18. The Board of Appeal took the view that a stitched pocket was a usual and commonplace feature of many fashion goods, in particular those in Classes 18 and 25. The average consumer would perceive the stitching merely to be decorative features rather than an indication of the origin of the goods. The Board of Appeal stated that the stitched pattern covered by the application for registration was a mere variation of a common feature found on pockets of clothing and on the other fashion goods covered by the trade mark in question. It added that even if it were correct that it was unusual to see a pocket on some of the goods in question, the consumer would pay scant attention to the stitched pattern on the pocket when purchasing such goods. The Board of Appeal considered that the mark in question would not trigger a "visual stimulus" enabling the average consumer to recognise the origin of those goods "unless he or she [had] been previously educated to do so through intensive use."

19. That analysis by the Board of Appeal must be endorsed. It should be noted that in the fashion sector patterns stitched on pockets are commonplace. Topstitched lines are typical decoration for pockets in general and in particular for pockets of clothing in Class 25. Furthermore, a number of fashion goods in Class 18 also usually have pockets with decorative stitching. Consumers are therefore used to seeing patterns stitched on pockets of clothing or fashion goods. They will therefore perceive them as a decorative element and not as an indication of the commercial origin of those goods.

20. Since the mark in question represents two crossed curves stitched on a pocket, one of which is a fine, arched form while the other is a thicker, sinusoid form, it constitutes a simple pattern, as the applicant accepts. The mark does not contain any element that is eye-catching and will attract the attention of consumers. As OHIM states, the description of the mark in question specifically refers to "decorative stitching."

21. Since the applicant itself gives a number of examples of stitched patterns on pockets that may be described as curved lines that cross each other, it must be concluded that the mark in question does not have any unique, original or unusual character.

22. It is true that it could be maintained that whether or not a mark may serve a decorative or ornamental purpose is irrelevant for the purposes of assessing its distinctive character. A sign which fulfils functions other than that of a trade mark in the traditional sense of the term is only distinctive for the purposes of Article 7(1)(b) of Regulation No. 207/209, however, if it may be perceived immediately as an indication of the commercial origin of the goods or services in question, so as to enable the relevant public to distinguish, without any possibility of confusion,

the goods or services of the owner of the mark from those of a different commercial origin ... .

23. Moreover, a finding that a mark has distinctive character within the meaning of Article 7(1)(b) of Regulation No. 207/2009 is not subject to a finding of a specific level of creativity on the part of the applicant for the trade mark. None the less the trade mark should enable the relevant public to identify the origin of the goods or services it covers and to distinguish them from those of other undertakings ... .

24. It is always necessary therefore for the sign in question, even if it may serve a decorative purpose and need not meet a specific level of creativity, to have a minimum degree of distinctive character.

25. In order to have the minimum degree of distinctiveness required under Article 7(1)(b) of Regulation No. 207/2009, the mark concerned must simply appear prima facie capable of enabling the relevant public to identify the origin of the goods or services covered by the Community trade mark application and to distinguish them, without any possibility of confusion, from those of a different origin ... .

26. That is not, however, the position in the present case. The mark in question does not have any characteristic element, nor any memorable or eye-catching features likely to confer a minimum degree of distinctive character and enabling the consumer to perceive it otherwise than as a typical decoration of a pocket for goods in Classes 18 and 25. As OHIM points out, it does not depart significantly from the standard presentation of pockets and will therefore be perceived simply as decoration. The Board of Appeal was therefore right to consider that the mark in question constituted a mere variation of topstitching commonly found on pockets of clothing and other fashion goods covered by the trade mark in question.

27. The mark in question must accordingly be considered to be a simple, commonplace pattern with an exclusively decorative function, which has no aspect that would enable the relevant public to identify the commercial origin of the goods described in the trade mark application or to distinguish them from others with a different origin.

28. That conclusion is not affected by the arguments put forward by the applicant. ...

30. Second, it is necessary to reject the applicant's argument that the mark in question has a specific appearance and cannot be considered to be altogether banal, since the sign in question is entirely arbitrary and, although simple, it is elegant and eye-catching and hence capable of attracting the attention of consumers and impressing itself on their consciousness; it sufficiently diverges from any common symmetrical lines or geometric pattern and conveys the idea of movement. In fact, such elements only make a mark distinctive in so far as it is immediately perceived by the relevant public as an indication of the commercial origin of the applicant's goods, thus enabling the relevant public to distinguish, without any possibility of confusion, the applicant's goods from those of a different commercial origin ... . The fact that the mark in question may be perceived as elegant or may convey the idea of movement, and hence be memorable, nevertheless does not mean that it is distinctive.

31. Equally unconvincing is, third, the applicant's argument that the relevant public would not perceive a stitched pattern on a pocket as mere decoration, since, in the fashion sector, it is accustomed to distinguishing the origin of different goods not only by word marks but also by "position marks" and it is particularly sensitive to graphical signs and stylised elements, such as stitch devices, which are frequently used as trade marks in the fashion world.

32. Assessment of the distinctive character of the mark in question consists in ascertaining whether it is, per se, capable of being perceived, by the relevant public as an indication which makes it possible for it to identify the commercial origin of the goods in question without any possibility of confusion with those of a different origin. Accordingly, the mere fact that other marks, although equally simple, have been regarded as being so capable and, therefore, as not being devoid of any distinctive character, is not conclusive for the purpose of establishing whether the mark at issue also has the minimum degree of distinctive character necessary for registration … .

33. Moreover, the argument that the consumer is used to recognising stitch devices as an indication of the commercial origin of goods is also irrelevant, since the fact that such signs are recognised as marks by consumers does not necessarily mean that they have intrinsic distinctive character. It is in fact possible for a mark to acquire distinctive character through use over time.

34. Fourth, as regards the applicant's argument that the fact that there are on the market simple and stylised logos on the pockets of clothing is not an obstacle to registration of this kind of mark, it should be noted that the Board of Appeal considered the stitched pattern covered by the application for registration to be a mere variation of a common feature found on pockets of clothing and on other fashion goods covered by the trade mark in question. Contrary to what the applicant maintains, the Board of Appeal did not consider that the mere fact that there are on the market stitched patterns on the pockets of clothing constitutes an obstacle to registration of the mark in question. The Board of Appeal found that, since the mark in question had no originality as compared with stitching usually present on the goods in question, that mark would not particularly catch the attention of consumers, who would perceive it as mere decoration. The Board of Appeal did not therefore refrain from examining whether the mark in question possessed a minimum degree of distinctive character.

35. It follows that the applicant is wrong in maintaining that the Board of Appeal did not analyze why the mark in question was devoid of any distinctive character and, without any real assessment of the actual circumstances of the case, merely made general assumptions. It is thus necessary to reject also the applicant's argument that the contested decision does not refer to the mark in question, but more generally to the lack of distinctive character of any kind of "stitching signs."

36. Fifth, it is necessary to reject the applicant's argument that the Board of Appeal, in stating that the mark in question would not trigger a "visual stimulus" enabling the average consumer to recognise the origin of the goods in question "unless he or she has been previously educated to do so through intensive use," applied more stringent criteria for assessing distinctive character to figurative marks than to other marks. That argument stems in fact from a misreading of the contested decision, since the Board of Appeal did not infer that the mark in question lacked distinctive character from lack of use. It is apparent from the contested decision that, having examined the mark in question, the Board of Appeal found that that mark had no intrinsic distinctive character. It then stated that the mark in question would not therefore enable the average consumer to recognise the origin of those goods unless it could be shown that the existence of distinctive character had been acquired through use.

37. Sixth, as regards the argument that the burden of proof with respect to lack of distinctiveness was borne by OHIM, which did not produce a single example of use of the sign in question or of a similar sign on the marketplace, on the one hand, it must be pointed out that if an applicant claims that a trade mark applied for is distinctive, despite OHIM's analysis, it is for that applicant to provide specific and substantiated information to show that the trade mark applied for has

an intrinsic distinctive character … . On the other hand, although the fact that a mark is capable of being commonly used in trade for the presentation of the goods or services in question is a relevant criterion in relation to Article 7(1)(c) of Regulation No. 207/2009, that criterion is not the yardstick by which Article 7(1)(b) of that regulation must be applied … . It follows that, in order to find that the mark in question was devoid of any distinctive character within the meaning of Article 7(1)(b) of Regulation No. 207/2009, the Board of Appeal did not in any event have to refer to such examples. … .

42. It follows from all the above that the Board of Appeal was correct in holding that the mark in question was devoid of a minimum degree of distinctive character and that it could not be registered to designate the goods in question, pursuant to Article 7(1)(b) of Regulation No. 207/2009.

43. Accordingly, the single plea in law, alleging infringement of Article 7(1)(b) of Regulation No. 207/2009, must be dismissed as unfounded, as must the action in its entirety. …

§ 1.73.2 *Levi Strauss & Company v. Abercrombie & Fitch Trading Company*—2011

Court of Appeals for the Ninth Circuit

February 8, 2011

Opinion by Ripple, Senior Circuit Judge:

Levi Strauss & Co. ("Levi Strauss") seeks review of a district court judgment that Abercrombie & Fitch Trading Co. ("Abercrombie") did not dilute Levi Strauss's trademarked

"Arcuate" design in violation of the Trademark Dilution Revision Act of 2006 ("TDRA"), 15 U.S.C. § 1125(c). Levi Strauss maintains that the district court applied an incorrect legal standard in evaluating its dilution claim, namely that the junior mark be "identical or nearly identical" to the senior one. We agree with Levi Strauss that the "identical or nearly identical" standard did not survive Congress's enactment of the TDRA and that the district court's use of the incorrect standard was not harmless error. Accordingly, we reverse the judgment of the district court and remand the case for further proceedings consistent with this opinion.

Background

A. The Stitched Designs

Levi Strauss created, and began selling, blue jeans in the 1870s. Since 1873, the company has stitched the back pocket of its jeans with two connecting arches that meet in the center of the pocket; Levi Strauss holds a federally registered trademark on this "Arcuate" design. Sales of garments bearing the Arcuate mark have accounted for more than 95% of Levi Strauss's revenue over the past thirty years, totaling roughly fifty billion dollars. Levi Strauss actively monitors use of competing stitching designs and enforces its trademark rights against perceived infringers.

In 2006, Abercrombie began using a stitching design on the back pockets of its jeans that, according to Levi Strauss, "incorporates the distinctive arcing elements of the Arcuate trademark." Abercrombie's "Ruehl" design consists of two

> less-pronounced arches that are connected by a "dipsy doodle," which resembles the mathematical sign for infinity. The design on the Abercrombie jeans sits lower on the pocket than Levi Strauss's Arcuate design.
>
> 
>
> These designs appear in the Appendix to the Ninth Circuit's opinion. Left: Levi Strauss's Arcuate design (and trademark); right: Abercrombie's "Ruehl" design.
>
> B. District Court Proceedings
>
> In 2007, Levi Strauss brought an action against Abercrombie for trademark infringement, unfair competition and trademark dilution under both federal and California state law. Before trial, Levi Strauss dropped its state-law trademark dilution claim, and it withdrew its claim for monetary relief on its federal dilution claim. Consequently, Levi Strauss's federal trademark dilution claim, for which it sought only injunctive relief, was tried before the court with advisory rulings from the jury. ...

Turning to its conclusions of law, the court first reviewed the elements of a claim under the TDRA, 15 U.S.C. § 1125(c). The court stated:

> To prevail on its dilution claim, [Levi Strauss] has the burden of proving by a preponderance of evidence the following elements: (a) that [Levi Strauss] is the owner of a trademark that is famous; (b) that the famous mark is distinctive, either inherently or through acquired distinctiveness; (c) that [Abercrombie] is making or has made use in commerce of an *identical or nearly identical* trademark, in this case the Ruehl design; (d) that [Abercrombie]'s use of its Ruehl design began after [Levi Strauss]'s Arcuate mark became famous; and (e) that [Abercrombie]'s use of its Ruehl design is likely to cause dilution by blurring of [Levi Strauss]'s Arcuate mark. ...

The district court noted that the advisory jury had not found that the Ruehl design and the Arcuate mark were "*identical or nearly identical,*" a standard that required that "the two marks ... be similar enough that a significant segment of the target group of customers sees the two marks as *essentially the same.*" *Id.* (emphasis added). After setting forth this standard for similarity, a standard which "is more stringent than in the infringement context," ... the court observed that, although the evidence showed that Levi Strauss had "expended significant amounts of money advertising the Arcuate mark," this was not "a case where the two marks at issue involve only minor differences," *id.* The district court then reviewed aspects of the Arcuate mark and the Ruehl design and observed that "[t]his evidence demonstrates that a significant segment of the target group of customers would not view the marks as *essentially the same.*" ... It concluded that, consistent with the advisory jury's finding, Levi Strauss "has not established that [Abercrombie] is making commercial use of a mark that *is identical or nearly identical* to the Arcuate mark." ... The court then concluded:

> As noted, the test for similarity of the marks is more stringent in the dilution context than for likelihood of confusion purposes, and the two marks must be "*essentially the same mark.*" For the reasons set forth above, the Court finds that the Ruehl design and the Arcuate mark are not visually similar. Furthermore, as set forth above, the Court does not find the results of Dr. Sood's survey to be entitled to any great weight. Thus, [Levi Strauss] has not put forth persuasive evidence of actual association between the Arcuate mark and the Ruehl design. Therefore, these factors weigh in [Abercrombie]'s favor and against a finding of likelihood of dilution. ...
>
> Having considered all of the evidence, even if the degree of inherent or acquired distinctiveness of the Arcuate mark and the degree of recognition of the mark weigh in [Levi Strauss]'s favor, the Court finds that those factors do not outweigh the factors that weigh in [Abercrombie]'s favor. Accordingly, the Court concludes, consistent with the advisory jury's finding, that [Levi Strauss] has not met its burden to establish by a preponderance of the evidence that the Ruehl design is likely to cause dilution by blurring of the Arcuate mark. ...

In summary, the court stated: "[T]he Court concludes, consistent with the advisory jury's finding, that [Levi Strauss] has not established that [Abercrombie] is making commercial use of a mark that is identical or nearly identical to the Arcuate mark." Use of the "identical or nearly identical" standard permeated the court's analysis and provided the basis upon which the court evaluated the evidence. This standard also played a pivotal role in the court's determination that the Ruehl design was not likely to dilute the Arcuate mark. With respect to the similarity of the marks, the court observed that the two marks must be essentially the same and that, "[f]or the reasons set forth above, the Court finds that the Ruehl design and the Arcuate mark are not visually similar." In other words, the court equated similarity with sameness and employed the latter, more stringent definition when entering its findings of fact.

[9] Finally, our review of the district court's balancing of the relevant factors convinces us that application of the incorrect standard affected its dilution determination. According to the district court, degree of similarity was only one of three factors that weighed in Abercrombie's favor. The district court assumed, without deciding, that Levi Strauss also had two factors—acquired distinctiveness and degree of recognition—that weighed in its favor. Thus, application of the correct, less-demanding standard could have tipped the balance in favor of Levi Strauss. The degree of similarity between the Ruehl and Arcuate marks may be insufficient to support a likelihood of dilution, but that conclusion can come only after consideration of the

degree of similarity in light of all other relevant factors and cannot be determined conclusively by application of an "essentially the same" threshold.

[10] Given the relative balance of the parties' positions, we cannot say, with any confidence, that the district court would have reached the same result absent the legal error. ... We therefore must reverse the judgment of the district court with respect to Levi Strauss's claim under the TDRA.

Reversed and remanded.

Figure 21 Two trademarks in a single registration. Left: Levi's USA registration nr. 2791156, of December 9, 2003 (renewed). The mark is thus described: "The mark consists of the combination of a double arcuate and tab design shown on the shape of a pocket, as indicated by a solid line. The lining and shading shown in the drawing are features of the mark and not intended to indicate color." The mention of the tab refers to the famous red tab (but which appears in other colors as well), a position trademark that Levi Strauss advertises as a brand in its own right (and which is the subject matter of separate registrations by itself). The trademark has even been enforced against rivals who have attempted to use the same tab but with other sayings or with no sayings at all. See, e.g., Levi Strauss & Co. v. Shah and Another, in the High Court of Justice, Chancery Division, before Mr. Justice Whitford, May 2, 1985 [1985 R.P.C. No. 16 371]. Right: the Arcuate and the (red) tab trademarks. On the tab, only the ® symbol appears.

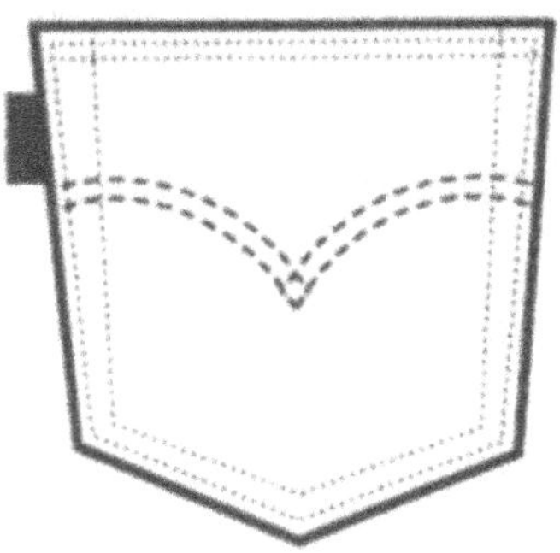

§ 1.74 A LEGAL DRAMA IN VARIOUS EPISODES: LOUBOUTIN'S TRADEMARK: THE RED SOLE OF WOMEN'S SHOES—2012, 2017, 2018, 2020

The following texts reproduce excerpts from the opinions of four courts from different jurisdictions, discussing different angles of and expressing different views on exactly the same matter (the registrability of Louboutin's red sole), thus leaving the same trademark protected in two jurisdictions—the United States and the European Union (with its 27 members)—but not in the third, Switzerland. Worth noticing is the different inclination of the Swiss Court (which, in a dictum, said that the sole to which Louboutin's red color is affixed is generally of the same shape, which contributes to the lack of distinctiveness of the trademark) and that of the EU Court of Justice (which held that the shapes of shoes' soles can vary, thus reinforcing the independence of Louboutin's red color from the sole's shape).

This divergence in itself substantiates the importance of Austria's proposal, during the Uruguay Round negotiations of the TRIPS Agreement, in the sense that the fashion industry needs to be protected by a new legal regime—a sui generis *regime (see § 2.73). Such a regime would bring a minimum level of harmonization, of crucial importance for an industry that became global many years ago.*

§ 1.74.1 Christian Louboutin Obtains Protection for His Red Shoes' Sole Trademark in the United States—2012

Christian Louboutin S.A. v. Yves Saint Laurent Am. Holding, Inc.

United States Court of Appeals for the Second Circuit

Decided: September 5, 2012

José A. Cabranes, *Circuit Judge*:

> The question presented is whether a single color may serve as a legally protected trademark in the fashion industry and, in particular, as the mark for a particular style of high fashion women's footwear. Christian Louboutin, a designer of high-fashion women's footwear and accessories, has since 1992 painted the "outsoles" of his women's high-heeled shoes with a high-gloss red lacquer. In 2008, he registered the red lacquered outsole as a trademark with the United States Patent and Trade Office ("PTO"). [note omitted] We are asked to decide whether that mark is protectable under federal trademark law.
>
> Louboutin, Christian Louboutin S.A., and Christian Louboutin, L.L.C. (jointly, "Louboutin"), bring this interlocutory appeal from an August 10, 2011 order of the United States District Court for the Southern District of New York (Victor Marrero, *Judge*) denying a motion for a preliminary injunction against alleged trademark infringement by Yves Saint Laurent America Holding, Inc., Yves Saint Laurent S.A.S., and Yves Saint Laurent America, Inc. (jointly, "YSL"). The District Court, in addressing a difficult and novel issue of trademark law, held that, because a single color can never be protected by trademark in the fashion industry, Louboutin's trademark was likely not enforceable. It therefore declined to enter a preliminary injunction to restrain YSL's alleged use of the mark.
>
> We conclude that the District Court's holding that a single color can never serve as a trademark in the fashion industry ... is inconsistent with the Supreme Court's decision in *Qualitex Co. v. Jacobson Products Co.*, 514 U.S. 159, 162 (1995) ("*Qualitex*"), and that the District Court therefore erred by resting its denial of Louboutin's preliminary injunction motion on that ground. We further conclude that Louboutin's trademark, which covers the red, lacquered outsole of a woman's high fashion shoe, has acquired limited "secondary meaning" as a distinctive symbol that identifies the Louboutin brand. As explained below, pursuant to Section 37 of the Lanham Act, 15 U.S.C. § 1119, we limit the trademark to uses in which the red outsole contrasts with the remainder of the shoe (known as the "upper"). We conclude that the trademark, as thus modified, is entitled to trademark protection. Finally, we conclude that, because the monochrome design employed by YSL is not a use of Louboutin's modified trademark, we need not, and

indeed should not, address whether YSL's use of a red outsole risks consumer confusion or whether the Louboutin mark, as modified, is "functional."

We therefore (1) affirm in part the order of the District Court, insofar as it declined to enjoin the use of all red lacquered outsoles; (2) reverse in part the order of the District Court insofar as it purported to deny trademark protection to Louboutin's use of *contrasting* red lacquered outsoles; and (3) enter judgment accordingly. We remand for further proceedings with regard to YSL's counter-claims.

Background

This appeal arises out of an action for injunctive relief and enforcement of a trademark brought by Louboutin, together with the corporate entities that constitute his eponymous French fashion house, against YSL, a venerable French fashion institution. Louboutin is best known for his emphasis upon the otherwise-largely-ignored outsole of the shoe. Since their development in 1992, Louboutin's shoes have been characterized by their most striking feature: a bright, lacquered red outsole, which nearly always contrasts sharply with the color of the rest of the shoe.

Christian Louboutin introduced his signature footwear to the fashion market in 1992. Since then, his shoes have grown in popularity, appearing regularly on various celebrities and fashion icons.

The District Court concluded, and YSL does not dispute, that "Louboutin [had] invested substantial amounts of capital building a reputation and good will, as well as promoting and protecting Louboutin's claim to exclusive ownership of the mark as its signature in women's high fashion footwear." ... The District Court further found that Louboutin had succeeded in promoting his shoes "to the point where, in the high-stakes commercial markets and social circles in which these things matter a great deal, the red outsole became closely associated with Louboutin. Leading designers have said it, including YSL, however begrudgingly." ... As a result of Louboutin's marketing efforts, the District Court found, the "flash of a red sole" is today "instantly" recognizable, to "those in the know," as Louboutin's handiwork. *Id.*, at 448.

On the strength of the fashion world's asserted recognition of the red sole, Louboutin on March 27, 2007 filed an application with the PTO to protect his mark (the "Red Sole Mark" or the "Mark"). The trademark was granted in January 2008, and stated: "The color(s) red is/are claimed as a feature of the mark. The mark consists of a lacquered red sole on footwear." ... The written description was accompanied by a diagram indicating the placement of the color:

In 2011, YSL prepared to market a line of "monochrome" shoes in purple, green, yellow, and red. YSL shoes in the monochrome style feature the same color on the entire shoe, so that the red version is all red, including a red insole, heel, upper, and outsole. This was not the first time that YSL had designed a monochrome footwear line, or even a line of footwear with red soles; indeed, YSL maintains that since the 1970s it had sold such shoes in red and other colors.

In January 2011, Louboutin avers, his fashion house learned that YSL was marketing and selling a monochrome red shoe with a red sole. Louboutin requested the removal of the allegedly infringing shoes from the market, and Louboutin and YSL briefly entered into negotiations in order to avert litigation.

The negotiations having failed, Louboutin filed this action on April 7, 2011, asserting claims under the Lanham Act, 15 U.S.C. §§ 1051 et seq., for (1) trademark infringement and counterfeiting, (2) false designation of origin and unfair competition, and (3) trademark dilution, as well as state law claims for (4) trademark infringement, (5) trademark dilution, (6) unfair competition, and (7) unlawful deceptive acts and practices. Louboutin also sought a preliminary injunction preventing YSL from marketing, during the pendency of the action, any shoes, including red monochrome shoes, bearing outsoles in a shade of red identical to the Red Sole Mark, or in any shade which so resembles the Red Sole Mark as to cause confusion among consumers.

In response, YSL asserted two counterclaims: (1) seeking cancellation of the Red Sole Mark on the grounds that (a) it is not "distinctive," [note omitted] but instead merely "ornamental,"[40] (b) it is "functional,"[41] and (c) it was secured by fraud on the PTO; and (2) seeking damages for (a) tortious interference with business relations and (b) unfair competition. On July 22, 2011, after a limited and expedited discovery process, the parties argued the preliminary injunction motion. ...

On August 10, 2011, the District Court issued a Decision and Order denying the injunction and holding that the Louboutin fashion house had not shown a likelihood of success on the merits of its claims. As the District Court saw it, the "narrow question" presented by the case was "whether the Lanham Act extends protection to a trademark composed of a single color used as an expressive and defining quality of an article of wear produced in the fashion industry"—that is, "whether there is something unique about the fashion world that militates against extending trademark protection to a single color." ...

Interpreting the Supreme Court's holding in *Qualitex*, the District Court explained that color is protectable as a trademark only if it "acts as a symbol that distinguishes a firm's goods and identifies their source, *without serving any other significant function*." ... The District Court further observed, albeit without citation to authority, that "whatever commercial purposes may support extending trademark protection to a single color for industrial goods do not easily fit the unique characteristics and needs—the creativity, aesthetics, taste, and seasonal change—that define production of articles of fashion." ... For that reason, the District Court held that, in the fashion industry, single-color marks are inherently "functional" and that any such registered trademark would likely be held invalid. ... The Court therefore held that Louboutin was unlikely to be able to prove that

---

40. [Note in the original]. An ornamental feature is one that "do[es] not serve a purpose" in the design of a product. ... *See TrafFix Devices, Inc. v. Marketing Displays, Inc.*, 532 U.S. 23, 35 (2001); *see also Wallace Int'l Silversmiths, Inc. v. Godinger Silver Art Co., Inc.*, 916 F.2d 76, 80 (2d Cir. 1990) (holding that "the features at issue are strictly ornamental because they neither affect the use of the [product] nor contribute to its efficient manufacture").
41. [Note in the original] "'[I]n general terms, a product feature is functional,' and cannot serve as a trademark, 'if it is essential to the use or purpose of the article or if it affects the cost or quality of the article,' that is, if exclusive use of the feature would put competitors at a significant non-reputation-related disadvantage." ...

the Red Sole Mark was eligible for trademark protection, and denied Louboutin's motion for a preliminary injunction. [note omitted] This appeal followed.

On appeal, Louboutin argues that the District Court erred in (1) holding, based on the doctrine of "aesthetic functionality," that the Red Sole Mark was not entitled to legal protection; (2) applying the doctrine of aesthetic functionality to hold that a single color on a fashion item could not act as a trademark; (3) failing to give weight to the statutory presumption of validity deriving from the Red Sole Mark's registration; (4) applying an improper analysis of trademark infringement and dilution; (5) ignoring allegedly undisputed proof of likelihood of confusion and irreparable harm; and (6) announcing a per se rule of functionality in a manner that violated Federal Rule of Civil Procedure 52. [note omitted]

Discussion

I. Standard of Review

... We address the District Court's order in three parts. We first consider whether a single color is protectable as a trademark, both generally and in the specific context of the fashion industry. We then address the doctrine of "aesthetic functionality" and consider whether, as the District Court held, a single-color mark is necessarily "functional" in the context of the fashion industry—with the result that no such mark could ever be trademarked in that industry. Finally, we determine whether the Red Sole Mark is a valid trademark entitled to the protection of the Lanham Act. ...

iii. Aesthetic Functionality in the Fashion Industry

We now turn to the per se rule of functionality for color marks in the fashion industry adopted by the District Court—a rule that would effectively deny trademark protection to any deployment of a single color in an item of apparel. As noted above, the *Qualitex* Court expressly held that "sometimes ... a color will meet ordinary legal trademark requirements, [a]nd, when it does so, no special legal rule prevents color alone from serving as a trademark." .... In other words, the Supreme Court specifically forbade the implementation of a per se rule that would deny protection for the use of a single color as a trademark in a particular industrial context. *Qualitex* requires an individualized, fact-based inquiry into the nature of the trademark, and cannot be read to sanction an industry-based per se rule. The District Court created just such a rule, on the theory that "there is something unique about the fashion world that militates against extending trademark protection to a single color." ...

Even if *Qualitex* could be read to permit an industry-specific per se rule of functionality (a reading we think doubtful), such a rule would be neither necessary nor appropriate here. We readily acknowledge that the fashion industry, like other industries, has special concerns in the operation of trademark law; it has been argued forcefully that United States law does not protect fashion design adequately.19[42] Indeed, the case on appeal is particularly

42. [Note in the original] The intellectual property protection of fashion design has been for years a subject of controversy among commentators. Some have proposed working within the confines of the current intellectual property system, while others have advocated that fashion design may be an appropriate area for sui generis statutory protection. *See generally* C. Scott Hemphill & Jeannie Suk, *The Law, Culture, and Economics of Fashion*, 61 Stan. L. Rev. 1147 (2009); *see also id.*, at 1184–1190. (Indeed, suggested legislation creating such protection has been considered several times by Congress, although not adopted. *See*, e.g., Design Piracy Prohibition Act, H.R. 2033, 110th Cong. § 2(c) (2007); Design Piracy Prohibition Act, S. 1957, 110th Cong. § 2(c)

difficult precisely because, as the District Court well noted, in the fashion industry, color can serve as a tool in the palette of a designer, rather than as mere ornamentation. ...

Nevertheless, the functionality defense does not guarantee a competitor "the greatest range for [his] creative outlet," ... but only the ability to fairly compete within a given market.[43] *See Wallace Int'l Silversmiths, Inc.*, 916 F.2d at 81 ("It is a first principle of trademark law that an owner may not use the mark as a means of *excluding* competitors from a ... market." (emphasis added)). The purpose of the functionality defense "is to prevent advances in functional design from being *monopolized* by the owner of [the mark] ... in order to encourage competition and the broadest dissemination of useful design features." *Fabrication Enters., Inc.*, 64 F.3d at 58 (internal quotation marks omitted) (emphasis added).

In short, "[b]y focusing upon hindrances to legitimate competition, the [aesthetic] functionality test, carefully applied, can accommodate consumers' somewhat conflicting interests in being assured enough product differentiation to avoid confusion as to source and in being afforded the benefits of competition among producers." *Stormy Clime*, 809 F.2d at 978–79.

IV. The Red Sole Mark

Having determined that no per se rule governs the protection of single-color marks in the fashion industry, any more than it can do so in any other industry, we turn our attention to the Red Sole Mark. As we have explained ... we analyze a trademark infringement claim in two stages, asking first whether the mark

---

(2007).) Still other commentators have suggested that intellectual property protection of fashion design would be damaging to the industry and should be avoided. *See* Kal Raustiala & Christopher Sprigman, *The Piracy Paradox: Innovation and Intellectual Property in Fashion Design*, 92 Va. L. Rev. 1687, 1775–1777 (2006).

It is arguable that, in the particular circumstances of this case, the more appropriate vehicle for the protection of the Red Sole Mark would have been copyright rather than trademark. *See generally Kieselstein-Cord v. Accessories by Pearl, Inc.*, 632 F.2d 989, 993–994 (2d Cir. 1980) (addressing the broad issue of aesthetically functional copyrights and holding that decorative belt buckles that were used principally for ornamentation could be copyrighted because the primary ornamental aspect of the buckles was conceptually separate from their subsidiary utilitarian function); Laura A. Heymann, *The Trademark/Copyright Divide*, 60 SMU L. Rev. 55 (2007). However, because Louboutin has chosen to rely on the law of trademarks to protect his intellectual property, we necessarily limit our review to that body of law and do not further address the broad and complex issue of fashion design protection.

43. [Note in the original] The trademark system, in this way, stands in sharp contrast to the copyright system. Copyright, unlike trademark, rewards creativity and originality even if they interfere with the rights of an existing copyright holder. In the copyright system there is a defense to infringement known as "independent creation": if a writer or musician, through the creative process, independently arrives at an arrangement of words or notes that is the subject of a copyright, he may market the result of his creativity despite the existing copyright. *See Feist Publ'ns, Inc. v. Rural Tel. Serv. Co.*, 499 U.S. 340, 346 (1991) (requesting that the reader "assume that two poets, each ignorant of the other, compose identical poems. Neither work is novel, yet both are original and, hence, copyrightable"); *Procter & Gamble Co. v. Colgate-Palmolive Co.*, 199 F.3d 74, 77–78 (2d Cir. 1999). The trademark system, unlike the copyright system, aims to prevent consumer confusion even at the expense of a manufacturer's creativity: in trademark, if a branding specialist produces a mark that is identical to one already trademarked by another individual or corporation, he must "go back to the drawing board." *See Blendco, Inc. v. Conagra Foods, Inc.*, 132 F. App'x 520, 523 (5th Cir. 2005) (although defendant's allegedly independent creation of infringing mark tended to show that infringement was not willful, defendant remained liable for damages); *Tuccillo v. Geisha NYC, LLC*, 635 F. Supp. 2d 227 (E.D.N.Y. 2009) (same).

"merits protection" and, second, whether the allegedly infringing use of the mark (or a similar mark) is "likely to cause consumer confusion." ... The functionality defense (including the tripartite aesthetic functionality test) is an affirmative defense that we consider at the second stage of this analysis. ...

We have stated the basic rule that "[a] certificate of registration with the PTO is prima facie evidence that the mark is registered and valid (*i.e.*, protect[a]ble), that the registrant owns the mark, and that the registrant has the exclusive right to use the mark in commerce." ... As the District Court correctly noted, "Louboutin's certificate of registration of the Red Sole Mark gives rise to a statutory presumption that the mark is valid." [notes omitted] ... But the District Court found, in effect, that YSL had rebutted that presumption by showing that the Red Sole Mark is ineligible for protection because a single color can never achieve trademark protection in the fashion industry. As explained above, that holding was error.

Although, as set forth below, we determine that the Mark as it currently stands is ineligible for protection insofar as it would preclude competitors' use of red outsoles in *all* situations, including the monochromatic use now before us, we conclude that the Mark has acquired secondary meaning—and thus the requisite "distinctness" to merit protection—when used as a red outsole *contrasting* with the remainder of the shoe. Because in this case we determine that the Red Sole Mark merits protection only as modified, and because YSL's use of a red outsole on monochromatic red shoes does not infringe on the Mark as modified, we need not, and do not, reach the issues of customer confusion and functionality at the second stage of the trademark infringement analysis described above.

A. Distinctiveness

We first address whether the Red Sole Mark "merits protection" as a distinctive mark. As discussed above, distinctiveness may be shown either by proof that the mark is itself inherently distinctive, or by showing that the mark has acquired, through use, secondary meaning in the public eye. *See Wal-Mart Stores, Inc. v. Samara Bros., Inc.*, 529 U.S. 205, 210–11 (2000); *Inwood Labs.*, 456 U.S. at 851 n.11 ("[S]econdary meaning" is acquired when "in the minds of the public, the primary significance of a product feature ... is to identify the source of the product rather than the product itself"). For the reasons that follow, we hold that the Red Sole Mark has acquired limited secondary meaning as a distinctive symbol that identifies the Louboutin brand, and that it is therefore a valid and protectable mark as modified below. ...

Although a single color, standing alone, can almost never be inherently distinctive because it does not "almost automatically tell a customer that [it] refer[s] to a brand" ... a color as used here is certainly capable of acquiring secondary meaning. As the *Qualitex* Court put it, over time, customers may come to treat a particular color on a product or its packaging (say, *a color that in context seems unusual*, such as pink on a firm's insulating material or red on the head of a large industrial bolt) as signifying a brand. And, if so, that color would have come to identify and distinguish the goods—*i.e.*, "to indicate" their "source"—much in the way that descriptive words on a product ... can come to indicate a product's origin. ... In the case of a single-color mark, therefore, distinctiveness must generally be proved by demonstrating that the mark has acquired secondary meaning. ...

We see no reason why a single-color mark in the specific context of the fashion industry could not acquire secondary meaning—and therefore serve as a brand or source identifier—if it is used so consistently and prominently by a particular designer that it becomes a symbol, "the primary significance" of which is "to identify the source of the product rather than the product itself." *Inwood Labs.*, 456 U.S. at 851 n.11; *see also Mana Prods., Inc.*, 65 F.3d at 1071 ("In light of the Supreme Court's decision in *Qualitex*, color is today capable of obtaining trademark status in the same manner that a descriptive mark satisfies the statutory definition of a trademark, by acting as a symbol and attaining secondary meaning.").

"The crucial question in a case involving secondary meaning always is whether the public is moved in any degree to buy an article because of its source."[note omitted] *Genesee Brewing Co.*, 124 F.3d at 143 n.4. "Factors that are relevant in determining secondary meaning include '(1) advertising expenditures, (2) consumer studies linking the mark to a source, (3) unsolicited media coverage of the product, (4) sales success, (5) attempts to plagiarize the mark, and, (6) length and exclusivity of the mark's use.'" ... Whether a mark has acquired distinctiveness is "an inherently factual inquiry." ... Where, as here, the record contains sufficient undisputed facts to resolve the question of distinctiveness—not to speak of facts found by the District Court that are based upon evidence of record and not clearly erroneous—we may do so as a matter of law. ...

The record before the District Court included extensive evidence of Louboutin's advertising expenditures, media coverage, and sales success, demonstrating both that Louboutin has created a "symbol" within the meaning of *Qualitex* ... and that the symbol has gained secondary meaning that causes it to be "uniquely" associated with the Louboutin brand ... There is no dispute that Louboutin originated this particular commercial use of the lacquered red color over twenty years ago. As the District Court determined, in findings of fact that are supported by the record and not clearly erroneous, "Louboutin invested substantial amounts of capital building a reputation and good will, as well as promoting and protecting Louboutin's claim to exclusive ownership of the mark as its signature in women's high fashion footwear." ... And there is no dispute that Louboutin's efforts were successful "to the point where, in the high-stakes commercial markets and social circles in which these things matter a great deal, the red outsole became closely associated with Louboutin" ... and where unsolicited media attention to that red sole became rampant. Indeed, the Chief Executive Officer of YSL's parent corporation, François-Henri Pinault, himself acknowledged that, "[i]n the fashion or luxury world, it is absolutely clear that we recognize the notoriety of the distinctive signature constituted by the red sole of Louboutin models in contrast with the general presentation of the model, particularly its upper, and so for all shades of red." [note omitted] ...

In light of the evidence in the record, including extensive consumer surveys submitted by both parties during the preliminary injunction proceedings, and of the factual findings of the District Court, we think it plain that Louboutin's marketing efforts have created what the able district judge described as "a ... brand with worldwide recognition" ... By placing the color red "in [a] context [that] seems unusual" ... and deliberately tying that color to his product, Louboutin has created an identifying mark firmly associated with his brand which, "to those in the know," "instantly" denotes his shoes' source ... These findings of fact by the District Court in addressing a motion for a preliminary injunction are not clearly erroneous. We hold that the lacquered red outsole, as applied to a shoe with an "upper" [note omitted] of a different color, has "come to identify and distinguish" the Louboutin brand ... and is therefore a distinctive symbol that qualifies for trademark protection.

We further hold that the record fails to demonstrate that the secondary meaning of the Red Sole Mark extends to uses in which the sole *does not* contrast with the upper—in other words, when a red sole is used on a monochromatic red shoe. As the District Court observed, "[w]hen Hollywood starlets cross red carpets and high fashion models strut down runways, and heads turn and eyes drop to the celebrities' feet, lacquered red outsoles on *high-heeled, black shoes* flaunt a glamorous statement that *pops out* at once." ... As clearly suggested by the District Court, it is the *contrast* between the sole and the upper that causes the sole to "pop," and to distinguish its creator.

The evidentiary record further demonstrates that the Louboutin mark is closely associated with contrast. For example, Pinault, the chief executive of YSL's parent company, wrote that the "distinctive signature" of the Mark is in its "contrast with the general presentation of the [shoe], particularly its upper." ... Of the hundreds of pictures of Louboutin shoes submitted to the District Court, only *four* were monochrome red. ... And Louboutin's own consumer surveys show that when consumers were shown the YSL monochrome red shoe, of those consumers who misidentified the pictured shoes as Louboutin-made, nearly every one cited the red *sole* of the shoe, rather than its general red color. We conclude, based upon the record before us, that Louboutin has not established secondary meaning in an application of a red sole to a red shoe, but *only* where the red sole contrasts with the "upper" of the shoe. The use of a red lacquer on the outsole of a red shoe of the same color is not a use of the Red Sole Mark.

Because we conclude that the secondary meaning of the mark held by Louboutin extends only to the use of a lacquered red outsole that contrasts with the adjoining portion of the shoe, we modify the Red Sole Mark, pursuant to Section 37 of the Lanham Act, 15 U.S.C. § 1119,26 insofar as it is sought to be applied to any shoe bearing the same color "upper" as the outsole. We therefore instruct the Director of the Patent and Trade Office to limit the registration of the Red Sole Mark to only those situations in which the red lacquered outsole contrasts in color with the adjoining "upper" of the shoe.

In sum, we hold that the Red Sole Mark is valid and enforceable as modified. This holding disposes of the Lanham Act claims brought by both Louboutin and YSL because the red sole on YSL's monochrome shoes is neither a use of, nor confusingly similar to, the Red Sole Mark. We therefore affirm the denial of the preliminary injunction insofar as Louboutin could not have shown a likelihood of success on the merits in the absence of an infringing use of the Red Sole Mark by YSL.

B. Likelihood of Confusion and Functionality

Having limited the Red Sole Mark as described above, and having established that the red sole used by YSL is not a use of the Red Sole Mark, it is axiomatic that we need not—and should not—address either the likelihood of consumer confusion or whether the modified Mark is functional.

Conclusion

To summarize:

We hold that the District Court's conclusion that a single color can never serve as a trademark in the fashion industry was based on an incorrect understanding of the doctrine of aesthetic functionality and was therefore error. We further hold that the District Court's holding, that Louboutin's trademark has developed "secondary meaning" in the public eye, was firmly rooted in the evidence of record and was not clearly erroneous, and that the Red Sole Mark is therefore a valid and enforceable trademark. We limit the Red Sole Mark pursuant to Section 37 of the Lanham Act, 15 U.S.C. § 1119, to a red lacquered outsole that contrasts with the color of the adjoining "upper."

Accordingly, we (1) affirm in part the order of the District Court, insofar as it declined to enjoin the use of a red lacquered outsole as applied to a monochrome red shoe; (2) reverse in part the order of the District Court insofar as it purported to deny trademark protection to Louboutin's use of *contrasting* red lacquered outsoles; and (3) enter judgment accordingly.

We remand for further proceedings with regard to YSL's counterclaims. In the interest of judicial economy, either party may restore jurisdiction to this Court to consider whatever arguments remain or arise relating to this case by sending a letter to the Clerk of this Court within 14 days of the District Court's final judgment. Any such proceedings will be assigned to this panel.

The Clerk of the Court is hereby directed to notify the Director of the United States Patent and Trade Office of this Judgment, which concerns U.S. Trademark Registration No. 3,361,597 held by Christian Louboutin and dated January 1, 2008.

§ 1.74.2 The Switzerland Federal Supreme Court Refuses to Acknowledge Louboutin's Red Sole as a Trademark—2017

Federal Supreme Court (Switzerland)

C. Louboutin v. Federal Institute for Intellectual Property

February 7, 2017

Position mark. Analysis of the original distinctive character of a trademark.

Christian Louboutin, Paris, France, (applicant, complainant) is the owner of the International registration No. 1'031'242 "red (Pantone No. 18.1663TP) women's shoe sole (Position mark)," with a basic registration in the United Kingdom. On March 25, 2010 the World Intellectual Property Organization (WIPO) notified this Registration for the purpose of extending its protection to the territory of Switzerland. The list of goods includes "high-heel women's shoes" (class 25). The position mark looks like this:

The Federal Institute of Intellectual Property (Defendant) has issued a refusal of the extension of protection with the justification that the red color on the shoe sole constitutes per se banal presentation of goods and is therefore perceived as a decorative element. The sign thus lacks specific distinctive character and it is part of the public domain.

(C. Louboutin has unsuccessfully complained against this order to the Federal Administrative Court. The following text is a summary of the Supreme Federal Court's opinion that, on appeal, maintained the lower court's holding).

The lower court considered that for the question of distinctiveness the specific type of mark in question was irrelevant. The legal question to be clarified was basically the same as that raised by a common trademark—and that question consisted of the elements to be taken into account in the perception of a trademark by consumers.

Position marks, such as the one claimed, are marks whose subject matter is additionally derived from the specific positioning of one or more two- or three-dimensional components of the sign on the articles or on a part of the articles. The distinctive character of a position mark is therefore the result of an overall consideration of the claimed position and of the mark's figurative elements. The position element is important for generating distinctive character when its location in the articles or their packaging appears unusual or conspicuous. Obviously functional positions should not be registered. The position of one graphic element on a product is often banal and only has a decorative effect. Decorative or banal elements inherently cannot be distinctive.

With regard to the relevant public for the purposes of assessing distinctiveness, the lower court found that high-heel shoes did not entail particularly higher production costs than other shoes and could therefore be offered in all price segments. Therefore it cannot be assumed that high-heel shoes are exclusively or mainly purchased by a better-off class of consumers. Regarding the age of customers, high-heel women's shoes, besides some physical restrictions against their use, are purchased by women of all ages. Accordingly, the age of the relevant public ranges from fairly young to quite aged. It can also be assumed that shoes are first tried on before the purchase, which means that women are mainly to be counted among the relevant public. It should also be noted that high-heel shoes are chiefly worn on festive or more formal occasions, where the fashionable appearance is of decisive importance; thus, the public would consist of people with at least a slightly increased fashion consciousness.

The sign under discussion claims trademark protection for the color red (Pantone No. 18.1663TP), affixed to the entire underside of the sole of high-heel women's shoes. The color is clearly determined by the Pantone scale. The sign's size results from the contours of the bottom of the shoe. This is probably not exactly the same size for every women's shoe. The bottom of the sole shown in the figure as a position claim does not need interpretation, as shoes can only be worn in one way and thus the underside is undisputedly to be fixed. The bottom sole is slightly curved and wide as shown in the illustration. The part shown in dashed lines in the figure is not claimed; it is only used for illustration and a better understanding of what is claimed. In principle, the underside of a women's shoe sole is not a position where a brand can be attached as unusual or noticeable, since for aesthetic reasons almost only the inner and outsoles of high-heel women's shoes are used for affixing trademarks.

At far as the claimed color red (Pantone No. 18.1663TP) is concerned, as applied to the outsole's surface, that is not a question of a contourless color, which could become protectable only through use. However, the contours of a shoe sole in connection with the claimed goods (high-heel women's shoes) are banal and descriptive. In addition, the red color belongs—even in a slightly brighter tone, like Pantone No. 18.1663TP—to the category of basic colors and is often used as a decorative element, especially for articles of the fashion industry.

The evidence presented by the Defendant has shown that high-heel women's shoes with colored outsoles are offered by various shoe sellers. Those shoes do not just appear sporadically in the Swiss market. A colored (including a red) outsole does not deviate from the usual or current standard design of the product segment in the case of women's shoes. On the basis of an overall assessment, it can be assumed that the relevant public circles (primarily female customers with a slightly increased fashion consciousness) perceive red-colored soles in high-heel women's shoes primarily as a decorative element and not as a brand. The disputed sign therefore lacks distinctive character, which is why it cannot be protected as a trademark.

The Plaintiff essentially submitted that the lower court's examination of the distinctive character of the sign in question is not based on the overall impression, but on the details only. His position mark, a bright red outsole, was completely unusual when he first marked his high-heel women's shoes and it has remained so to this day. If one takes a step back and looks at the trademark from an objective point of view, one cannot avoid finding that it is a position mark, particularly if compared to the usual way of marking shoes. Actually, the Plaintiff's trademark is one of the most innovative and unique shoe brands that have been created over the past 25 years. The glowing red outsole deviates significantly from the usual practice and represents an unexpected and original way of branding high heel women's shoes. That is why average consumers perceived the red outsole as a trademark when they first used it and still perceive it as a brand today. For these reasons, the Plaintiff's position mark is originally distinctive and should enter the Swiss trademark register.

Under Article 6*quinquies* lit. B of the Paris Convention for the Protection of Industrial Property, revised in Stockholm on July 14, 1967, trademarks may be denied registration when they are devoid of any distinctive character and/or are regarded as pertaining to public domain.

A sign can be protected as inherently distinctive if it has a minimal distinctive character that enables it to individualize goods and services, thereby enabling the consumer to use them for recognizing those goods and services against the other goods and services on the market. When checking whether this protection requirement is met, the sign is to be viewed as it was filed by the applicant. Other signs that have already been used or will be used in the future and may affect the perception of the relevant consumers' circles must be disregarded. The sign must be self-sufficient and independent as regards its capability to distinguish the goods and services of the trademark owner from those of competitors. As a matter of law, the Federal Supreme Court examines freely how the relevant target group for the required goods or services are to be delimited and, for goods of general use, how potential consumers perceive the sign based on their expectations.

For the purposes of the definition of trademark, under the Trademark Statute, position marks are not deemed as a separate category. Every sign that is capable of distinguishing the articles and services of one company from those of another company can be protected as a trademark. A position mark is characterized by consisting of an element that is always affixed to the same precisely designated position on the article it distinguishes. As far as such sort of trademark is concerned, the special way of affixing or arranging a two or three-dimensional drawing element on a product is relevant for determining its distinctive character.

However, the main object of the position mark is not that position alone or the isolated element itself, but the combination of the element with its specific position. The protection area is based on the connection of the graphic or combined sign element with its position on the article. In addition to the distinctive character of the sign, the strength of the position is also important to consider. Not every positioned character is distinctive; the position can only contribute to this if, in the perception of the relevant public, it represents a sufficiently characteristic element and is therefore strong enough to transform the element into a distinctive one. Just like a colour or graphic design cannot by itself make a sign to become distinctive, the simple position cannot have that result either. The position must actually convey an understanding as an indication of commercial origin; the positioned character in contrast to a non-positioned one has to pose a riddle that cannot be solved other than by assigning it the meaning of an designation of commercial origin.

Whether the relevant public understands a figurative element in a particular position of the article as a trademark, and not as a technical element or mere ornament, is to be determined in the context of the examination of the distinctiveness in the specific individual case. The perception of the relevant public can, however, be influenced by the type of sign—in particular when the signs consist in the appearance of the goods themselves.

The registered basic symbol exists regardless of its position. The contour of the chosen color (Pantone No. 18.1663TP) is determined as the entire area of the shoe sole. Such shape for the claimed women's shoes with high heels is not originally distinctive. This is an extremely weak part of the character, particularly if one takes into consideration the fact that the alleged trademark does not present any specific design which could be perceived as a designation of commercial origin. As the lower instance correctly has explained, it is true that the absence of a special contour for the claimed color was not at stake; however, the outlines of shoe soles are banal because they consist in the appearance of part of the articles themselves. So, this is not a matter of one word or one image that is positioned on the shoe sole, which, with subsequent use, it would be possible for consumers to learn to recognize. Rather, the sign consists of a monochrome representation of the underside of a high heel women's shoe, making it compatible with the appearance of the article itself, with which it merges.

But signs that consist in the appearance of the articles are usually not used as an indication of their commercial origin—they are at most perceived as special designs. As it happens with the notion of original distinctive character, it may not be sufficient that a sign acquires distinctiveness only because of its pleasant design. On the contrary, such sign must stand out from what exists in the same product segment at the time the application for registration is filed. The difference must be sufficiently conspicuous so that potential consumers may perceive the sign as an indication of commercial origin.

The peculiarity of Plaintiff's claimed trademark consists neither in a characteristic form nor in a in itself eye-catching design, but is limited to the choice of a specific color for a functionally indispensable and area-wise significant part of the corresponding articles. The argument that such color contrasts with the black, brown or beige outsoles commonly present in the market for women's high-heel shoes is not enough to accord to the sign a distinctive character.

As it can be seen from the lower court findings, there are also high-heel women's shoes with an outsole in green, yellow, blue, purple or pink. The fact that the outsoles of women's shoes are colored cannot therefore be regarded as so exceptional that it stands out from the usual designs and conclude that its eye-catching peculiarity should be considered as a designation of commercial origin. High-heel women's shoes are in high demand in the fashion industry, which has generated a large variety of designs. Creative developments are therefore almost expected, and this explains that the mere coloring of part of the product surface in the form of the outsole is acknowledged by potential consumers but not as a designation of commercial origin. To them, the red coloring (Pantone No. 18.1663TP) on the underside of the sole represents an aesthetic style element, which—even if viewed separately from the previous use or disregarding any familiarity with the shoes designed and sold by the Plaintiff—does not deviate from the standard fashionable designs of high-heel women's shoes. This is true also taking into account those considered to be the potential consumers of Plaintiff's shoes—for wealthy women between 20 and 65 years of age those shoes do not stand out in such a way that the claimed red color acquires the sense of an indication of commercial origin. In this context, we do not need to reexamine whether the lower court has defined the relevant public too broadly. ...

§ 1.74.3 The EU Court of Justice Holds That Louboutin's Red Sole Is Independent of the Shape of the Sole—2018

EU Court of Justice (Grand Chamber)

In Case C-163/16

Christian Louboutin and Christian Louboutin SAS v. Van Haren Shoenen BV

June 12, 2018

Reference for a preliminary ruling—Trade marks—Absolute grounds for refusal or invalidity—Sign consisting exclusively of the shape of the product—Concept of "shape"—Colour—Position on a part of the product—Directive 2008/95/EC—Article 2—Article 3(1)(e)(iii).[44]

Request for a preliminary ruling under Article 267 TFEU from the Rechtbank Den Haag (District Court, The Hague, Netherlands), made by decision of March 9, 2016, received at the Court on March 21, 2016.

Christian Louboutin, Christian Louboutin SAS v. Van Haren Schoenen BV

Judgment

1. This request for a preliminary ruling concerns the interpretation of Article 3(1)(e)(iii) of Directive 2008/95/EC of the European Parliament and of the Council of 22 October 2008 to approximate the laws of the Member States relating to trade marks (OJ 2008 L 299, p. 25).

2. The request has been made in the course of infringement proceedings between, on the one hand, Mr Christian Louboutin and Christian Louboutin SAS (together, "Louboutin") and, on the other, Van Haren Schoenen BV ("Van Haren") concerning the sale, by Van Haren, of shoes which allegedly infringe the trade mark owned by Mr Louboutin.

44. This Directive is no longer in force. It was superseded in 2019 by Directive (EU) 2015/2436, of December 16, 2015.

Legal context

EU law

3. Article 2 of Directive 2008/95, entitled "Signs of which a trade mark may consist," provides:

> A trade mark may consist of any signs capable of being represented graphically, particularly words, including personal names, designs, letters, numerals, the shape of goods or of their packaging, provided that such signs are capable of distinguishing the goods or services of one undertaking from those of other undertakings.

4. Article 3 of that directive, entitled "Grounds for refusal or invalidity," provides:

> 1. The following shall not be registered or, if registered, shall be liable to be declared invalid: ...
>   (e) signs which consist exclusively of:
>   (i) the shape which results from the nature of the goods themselves;
>   (ii) the shape of goods which is necessary to obtain a technical result;
>   (iii) the shape which gives substantial value to the goods; ...

Benelux Convention on Intellectual Property (Trade Marks and Designs)

5. Article 2.1, entitled "Signs that may constitute a Benelux trade mark," of the Benelux Convention on Intellectual Property (Trade Marks and Designs), signed in The Hague on 25 February 2005 by the Kingdom of Belgium, the Grand Duchy of Luxembourg and the Kingdom of the Netherlands, states:

> 1. The names, drawings, imprints, stamps, letters, numerals, shapes of goods or packaging and all other signs that can be represented graphically and that serve to distinguish the goods or services of an undertaking shall be considered as being individual trade marks.
> 2. However, signs consisting solely of a shape which results from the nature of the goods, which gives a substantial value to the goods or which is necessary to obtain a technical result, cannot be considered as being trade marks. ...

The dispute in the main proceedings and the question referred for a preliminary ruling

6. Christian Louboutin designs and produces shoes.

7. On 28 December 2009, Mr Louboutin filed an application for registration of a Benelux trade mark with the Benelux Office for Intellectual Property, leading to the registration, on 6 January 2010, under number 0874489, of a trade mark for goods in Class 25 of the Nice Agreement concerning the International Classification of Goods and Services for the Purposes of the Registration of Marks of 15 June 1957, as revised and amended, and corresponding to the following description: "Footwear (other than orthopaedic footwear)" ("the mark at issue").

8. That mark is reproduced below:

[The illustration is the same that appears in the Swiss case, see the preceding text].

9. In the application for registration, the mark at issue is described as follows: "The mark consists of the colour red (Pantone 18-1663TP) applied to the sole of a shoe as shown (the contour of the shoe is not part of the trade mark but is intended to show the positioning of the mark)."

10. On April 10, 2013, the registration was amended in such a way as to limit the goods covered to "High-heeled shoes (other than orthopaedic shoes)."

11. In the course of 2012, Van Haren, which operates shoe retail outlets in the Netherlands, sold high-heeled women's shoes with red soles.

12. On 27 May 2013, Christian Louboutin initiated proceedings before the Rechtbank Den Haag (District Court, The Hague, Netherlands), claiming that Van Haren had infringed the mark at issue. On 17 July 2013, that court delivered a default judgment upholding in part the claims of Christian Louboutin.

13. Van Haren challenged that judgment before the referring court, the Rechtbank Den Haag (District Court, The Hague), claiming that the mark at issue was invalid on the basis of Article 2.1(2) of the Benelux Convention. Van Haren maintains that that mark is a two-dimensional figurative mark that consists of a red coloured surface.

14. The Rechtbank Den Haag (District Court, The Hague) considers, first, having regard to the graphic representation and the description of the mark at issue, that the colour red is inextricably linked to the shoe sole and therefore that mark cannot be regarded merely as a two-dimensional figurative mark. In the view of the referring court, that assessment is not undermined by the fact that the description of that mark states that "the contour of the shoe does not form part of the mark." The referring court states that, on the contrary, that assessment is confirmed by that specification, in particular since, according to the description, the shape of the shoe, as illustrated in the graphic representation of the mark at issue, is not intended to reduce the sign to a two-dimensional mark, but is intended rather to show the positioning of that mark.

15. The referring court also considers that, in autumn 2012, "a significant proportion of consumers of women's high-heeled shoes in the Benelux States was able to identify [Christian Louboutin] shoes as goods originating from that producer and was thus able to distinguish them from women's high-heeled shoes [from] other undertakings." Therefore, at that time, the mark at issue was perceived as a trade mark in relation to those goods.

16. Furthermore, in the view of the referring court, the red sole gives substantial value to the shoes marketed by Christian Louboutin since that colour forms part of the appearance of those shoes and plays an important role in a consumer's decision to purchase them. In that regard, the referring court notes that Christian Louboutin first used red colouring on soles for aesthetic reasons and only later started regarding it as an identifier of origin and using it as a trade mark.

17. Lastly, the referring court states that, since the mark at issue consists of a colour which is applied to the sole of a shoe and is thus also an element of the product, the question arises as to whether the exception set out in Article 3(1)(e)(iii) of Directive 2008/95 applies to that mark. In that regard, it is unsure whether the concept of "shape," within the meaning of that provision, is limited solely to three-dimensional properties of a product, such as its contours, measurements and volume, or whether that concept also covers properties that are not three-dimensional.

18. In those circumstances, the Rechtbank Den Haag (District Court, The Hague) decided to stay the proceedings and to refer the following question to the Court of Justice for a preliminary ruling:

> Is the notion of "shape," within the meaning of Article 3(1)(e)(iii) of [Directive 2008/95] (respectively referred to in the German-, [Dutch-] and French-language versions of [that directive] as "Form," "vorm" and "forme"), limited to the three-dimensional properties of the goods, such as their contours, measurements and volume (expressed three-dimensionally), or does it include other (non-three-dimensional) properties of the goods, such as their colour?

Consideration of the question referred

19. By its question, the referring court asks, in essence, whether Article 3(1)(e)(iii) of Directive 2008/95 must be interpreted as meaning that a sign consisting of a colour applied to the sole of a high-heeled shoe, such as that at issue in the main proceedings, consists exclusively of a "shape," within the meaning of that provision.

20. Given that Directive 2008/95 provides no definition of the concept of "shape," the meaning and scope of that concept must, as the Court has consistently held, be determined by considering its usual meaning in everyday language, while also taking into account the context in which it occurs and the purposes of the rules of which it is part ... .

21. As noted by the European Commission, in the context of trade mark law, the concept of "shape" is usually understood as a set of lines or contours that outline the product concerned.

22. It does not follow from Directive 2008/95, the case-law of the Court, or the usual meaning of that concept, that a colour per se, without an outline, may constitute a "shape."

23. Nevertheless, the question arises as to whether the fact that a particular colour is applied to a specific part of the product concerned results in the sign at issue consisting of a shape within the meaning of Article 3(1)(e)(iii) of Directive 2008/95.

24. In that regard, it must be noted that, while it is true that the shape of the product or of a part of the product plays a role in creating an outline for the colour, it cannot, however, be held that a sign consists of that shape in the case where the registration of the mark did not seek to protect that shape but sought solely to protect the application of a colour to a specific part of that product.

25. As has been observed by the German, French and United Kingdom Governments, as well as by the Commission, the mark at issue does not relate to a specific shape of sole for high-heeled shoes since the description of that mark explicitly states that the contour of the shoe does not form part of the mark and is intended purely to show the positioning of the red colour covered by the registration.

26. In any event, a sign, such as that at issue in the main proceedings, cannot be regarded as consisting "exclusively" of a shape, where, as in the present instance, the main element of that sign is a specific colour designated by an internationally recognised identification code.

27. In the light of the foregoing considerations, the answer to the question referred is that Article 3(1)(e)(iii) of Directive 2008/95 must be interpreted as meaning that a sign consisting of a colour applied to the sole of a high-heeled shoe, such as that at issue in the main proceedings, does not consist exclusively of a "shape," within the meaning of that provision. ...

On those grounds, the Court (Grand Chamber) hereby rules:

Article 3(1)(e)(iii) of Directive 2008/95/EC of the European Parliament and of the Council of 22 October 2008 to approximate the laws of the Member States relating to trade marks must be interpreted as meaning that a sign consisting of a colour applied to the sole of a high-heeled shoe, such as that at issue in the main proceedings, does not consist exclusively of a "shape," within the meaning of that provision.

§ 1.74.4 The Court of Milan Takes Louboutin's Red Sole European Trademark for Granted and Enforces Exclusive Rights in It—2020

Court of Milano, Section XIV, Civil, Specialized in corporative matters

Christian Louboutin S.A.S. and Baseroma S.R.L. v. RWD S.R.L., Farfetch UK Ltd. and Made S.R.L.

July 17, 2020

1. In a complaint filed on May 24, 2019 Christian Louboutin s.a.s. (hereinafter Louboutin) stated it is a famous women's shoe manufacturing house. Baseroma s.r.l. was a company of the Group that carried out marketing activities in Italy of *Maison*'s products.

RWD s.r.l. had marketed some shoes under the *Gianni Rienzi* brand that constituted the slavish imitation of two [Louboutin's] well-known models called, respectively, *Kaleikita* and *Guerilla*. ...

A pair of pumps that reproduced the famous *red sole*, protected by Louboutin with the registration of the EU trademark nr. 8845539, was also found and purchased on *farfetch.com*, owned by Farfetch UK limited. ...

Such conduct constituted counterfeiting of the designated models and of the aforementioned trademark, as well as unfair competition for servile imitation, appropriation of prestige and parasitism.[45]

[The plaintiff] concluded by asking for access to all the imitative products, the related advertising material and the accounting records, with the subsequent injunction throughout the EU of the illegal conduct, the establishment of a penalty, the advertisement of the decision as well as the seizure and the order to withdraw the counterfeit products from trade. ...

[RWD] alleged the exception of lack of novelty of EU registration nr. 8845539. RWD had started using the red sole in 2005, hence long before the filing date of the aforementioned trademark (January 29, 2010). It also invoked that the prior use did not have not purely local notoriety. ...

[The lower Court] instead found RWD's conduct to be parasitic as well as counterfeit of the *red sole* trademark, having issued an injunction against the copies of the *Guerilla, Pigalle Follies, Chasse à clou* and *Roller-boat* models, as well as of its red sole affixed to the models photographed on page 15 of the appeal, with the seizure and the order to withdraw the products counterfeiting the aforementioned brand from the market, the publication of the decision on the website of RWD and the establishment of a penalty. ...

[RWD] opposed that the sign used on its shoes was not identical to that registered by Louboutin, since its red was of a different pantone expressly indicated in the certificate. ...

[Louboutin and Baseroma] noted the lack of proof of the prior use invoked by RWD and reiterated that there was counterfeit by identity of the signs and that,

45. Parasitic competition, or simply parasitism, is a modality of unfair competition that is not based on the specific infringement of intangible assets, such as unregistered brands, trade secrets, or trade dress, but rather on a multitude of elements developed or acquired by a company in organizing its business so as to reach commercial success. These elements are many, and parasitic activities can target some of them only, such as the way in which that company communicates with its clients, the line of products offered for sale, their prices, the sorts of guarantees offered, as well as rebates and commercial promotions.

in the alternative, there was still counterfeiting because the red sole used by RWD, Made and Farfetch was a distinctive sign very similar and susceptible of creating a risk of confusion among final consumers. ...

7. Moving on to the merits and starting with the controversial aspects concerning the protection of the *red sole* trademark owned by Louboutin, the Court firstly observes that in the file there is no proof of the prior use of a similar sign invoked by RWD, with consequent rejection of the exception of lack of novelty raised on the basis of the combined provisions of Articles 8, EU regulation nr. 1001/2017, and 12 of the CIP [Code of Industrial Property]. ...

Louboutin's registration claims a precise red color tone, unequivocally identified with a pantone number, applied evenly across the entire surface of a shoe's sole.

In the file there is no certain proof of the actual correspondence of the red color present on the soles of the disputed products. It is well known that the perception of the different shades and tonalities of the colors is highly subjective and is considerably conditioned also by the sorts of presentation and reproduction of the colors themselves (surface, light, etc.). It therefore does not seem possible to entrust the appreciation of this alleged identity to a purely empirical judgment. ...

In fact, a simple visual examination allows to find a remarkable chromatic similarity between the *red sole* trademark and the color affixed to the sole of the product purchased on the Farfetch website.

At the same time the risk of confusion is evident, especially after sale, because consumers can easily see the red sole when the shoes are worn, with the possibility of taking the shoes for the original Louboutin ones.

The presence of additional elements in the sole of the RWD shoe, in particular the initials of the designer *GR*, is not suitable to exclude this effect and indeed introduces a risk of association between signs, as consumers may think of the existence of a different product line, eventually at a lower price, or an association between signs, in the form of a partnership between the manufacturers.

9. Louboutin has requested an augmentation of the injunction against use of the trademark, referring it to every possible form of use of the *red sole* protected by registration, even if affixed to shoes different from the only model with these characteristics that appears to have been marketed by the defendants.

The Court notes a complete correspondence between the scope of the preliminary injunction and Louboutin's original complaint, circumscribed to the counterfeiting use of the *red sole* on a well-identified model of shoe ... .

In the file, therefore, the conditions do not seem to exist for an augmentation of the injunction in the terms requested in the complaint. ...

12. The reassessment of the matter of unfair competition in the terms just clarified leads the Court to also revoke the order for the publication of the contested injunction, which found its main justification in the deemed existence of the parasitic conduct charged to RWD. The mere infringement of the red sole trademark, limited to a single model of shoes brings it to a much more limited dimension, and thus it does not make it essential to publish the provision as a matter of urgency.

Figure 22 Detail of Christian Louboutin's Guerilla model (discontinued), showing the red soles, Louboutin's trademark that the court of Milan deemed infringed by RWD.

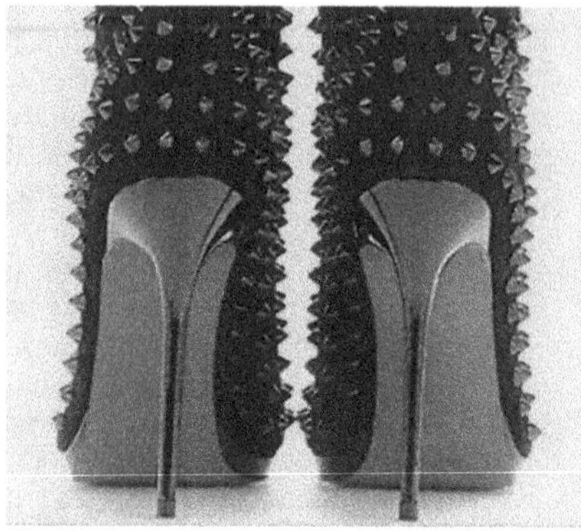

§ 1.75 THE PROBLEM OF CONVERTING DESIGNS AND PATTERNS INTO TRADEMARKS

The different functions of designs and trademarks and the different requisites for their protection create serious difficulties for the interchangeable use of those legal titles: brands as ornaments, and ornaments as brands. This is perhaps the most serious problem that the fashion industry faces today in order to obtain a full protection for the intangible assets on which it so significantly depends.

The first problem is found in registering a formerly registered design as a trademark. The Lego doctrine, as set by the European Court of Justice, gives a precise indication of that problem. The migration from an industrial design to a trademark may conceal the purpose of perpetuating ownership in a practical idea that is supposed to fall into the public domain so that others can benefit from its functionality.

The second problem—but here could also lie the solution—is calling for the protection under the frame of repression of unfair competition of designs whose registration—hence exclusivity—has expired. But evidence of unfair competition practices is found on a case-by-case basis only, which leaves fashion houses insecure about the success of using that approach. Of course, once several courts agree to outlaw the unauthorized reproduction or imitation of designs as acts of unfair competition, fashion designers might find themselves protected by case law, which in many jurisdictions represent effective law.

Another solution is to admit that designs, whether originally associated with the shape of the product they ornament or not, can acquire secondary meaning, *hence distinctive character, and be indefinitely protected (as long as consumers keep that impression). This would be an interesting legal avenue for many fashion houses that develop certain patterns and shapes that consumers learn to identify and recognize as indications of who manufactures and/or sells those products: Missoni's wavy lines and patterns, in different colors (registered as industrial designs[46]), Louis Vuitton's checkerboards (in various colors), Kenzo's flowery fabric pattern and its well-known bottle of perfume, Versace's fabric patterns with golden wild animals, etc.*

Close to the idea of secondary meaning, *a third approach is to see in a copied design an infringed trademark by means of passing off, as we will find in the next Chapter (see § 2.79).*

It is interesting to note that a quick search through the WIPO Global Design Database has revealed that LVM has registered their Damier Ébène Canvas pattern as an International Trademark (Registration No. 1479417, of May 22, 2019, class 18),[47] with no less than eighty-two country designations, including a large proportion of European Union Member States. This means that in these EU Member States, LVM has been able to circumvent OHIM's and General Court's refusal to recognize such pattern as a trademark.

The first of the following texts is an excerpt that corresponds to the Court's analysis on the merits—the distinctive nature of LVM's design and the possibility (or impossibility) of having it protected as a trademark. The two procedural matters that the Court discussed are omitted.

In the second case, involving Birkenstock's shoe sole pattern, the European Union General Court confirms its absolute lack of sympathy for attempts to convert patterns into trademarks. Nevertheless, and contrary to EUIPO's understanding, the Court admits that a pattern may be registrable as a trademark. However, such a pattern must have a particularly strong distinctive character in order to become a trademark. And, second, once the pattern has been registered as a design, how could the trademark owner be assured that the Court will not be inclined to apply the LEGO doctrine?—"damned if you do; damned if you don't."

46. The WIPO Global Design Database shows several registrations for Missoni's wavy patterns in various combinations of colours and shapes, including in the United States, in the European Union and under the Hague international system. Some of those registrations have expired, others are about to expire. Would Missoni be able to transform those designs into trademarks? Would they be accepted by the EUIPO and the European Court as having sufficiently distinctive character? After all, wavy patterns are common ornaments, even if those of Missoni seem to present a certain uniqueness, which indisputably makes of them a branding element. See *infra* the introductory comments to *Freddy Spa v. Hugz Clothing Ltd. and others*, November 19, 2020 (§ 2.79).
47. The WIPO Global Design Database shows the registration, on the same date, of another LVM's checkerboard pattern, in grey and black.

§ 1.75.1 *Louis Vuitton Malletier v. OHIM*—2015

General Court (Second Chamber)

April 21, 2015

(Community trade mark—Invalidity proceedings—Community figurative mark representing a brown and beige chequerboard pattern—Absolute ground for refusal—No distinctive character—No distinctive character acquired through use—Article 7(1)(b) and Article 7(3) of Regulation (EC) No. 207/2009—Article 52(1) and (2) of Regulation No. 207/2009)

Louis Vuitton Malletier v. Office for Harmonisation in the Internal Market (Trade Marks and Designs) (OHIM)—Case T-359/12

The General Court (Second Chamber), gives the following Judgment.

Background to the dispute

1. On 18 September 1996, the applicant, Louis Vuitton Malletier, filed a Community trade mark application at the Office for Harmonisation in the Internal Market (Trade Marks and Designs) (OHIM), pursuant to Council Regulation (EC) No. 40/94 of 20 December 1993 on the Community trade mark (OJ 1994 L 11, p. 1), as amended (replaced by Council Regulation (EC) No. 207/2009 of February 26, 2009 on the Community trade mark (OJ 2009 L 78, p. 1)).

2. The trade mark in respect of which registration was sought is the figurative sign below:[48]

3. The goods in respect of which registration was sought are in Class 18 of the Nice Agreement concerning the International Classification of Goods and Services for the Purposes of the Registration of Marks of 15 June 1957, as revised and amended, and correspond to the following description: "Goods made of leather or imitations of leather not included in other classes in particular boxes of leather or of leatherboard, envelopes of leather for packaging; trunks, valises, travelling bags, travelling sets, garment bags for travel, vanity-cases, rucksacks,

48. The squares in the original illustration are beige and dark brown.

handbags, beach bags, shopping bags, shoulder bags, attaché-cases, briefcases, pouches, fine leather goods namely pocket wallets, purses, key-holders, card holders, checkbook holders; umbrellas, parasols, ombrelles, canes, walking-stick seats."

4. The application was published in *Community Trade Marks Bulletin* No. 19/1998 of 16 March 1998.

5. On 27 August 1998, the applicant was granted registration of the above-mentioned Community figurative mark under number 370445.

6. On 28 September 2009, the intervener, *Nanu-Nana Handelsgesellschaft mbH für Geschenkartikel & Co.KG,* filed an application for a declaration of invalidity relating to all of the goods protected by the registration of the Community trade mark, in accordance with Article 52(1)(a) and Article 7(1)(b), (c), (d),(e)(iii) and (f) of Regulation No. 207/2009. That application was based on the fact that the contested trademark was descriptive and devoid of any distinctive character, that it had become customary in the current language or in the bona fide and established practices of the trade, that it consisted exclusively of the shape which gives substantial value to the goods and that it was contrary to public policy or to accepted principles of morality. The intervener also claimed that the applicant had acted in bad faith when filing the application for the trade mark, within the meaning of Article 52(1)(b) of Regulation No. 207/2009.

7. By decision of 11 July 2011, the Cancellation Division upheld the application for a declaration of invalidity on the basis of Article 7(1)(b) of Regulation No. 207/2009, read in conjunction with Article 52(1)(a) of that regulation, and Article 7(3) of that regulation, read in conjunction with Article 52(2) of that regulation. The Cancellation Division, first, held that the Community trade mark consisted of a chequerboard pattern with a weft and warp structure intended to be applied to the surface of the goods in question. It went on to hold that that pattern was one of the most basic patterns used as a decorative element, and as such the relevant public would see it as merely a decorative feature and not as a sign indicating the origin of the goods in question and that, in any event, the contested trade mark did not depart significantly from the norms or customs of the sector. It considered, lastly, that the documents submitted by the proprietor of the Community trade mark did not prove that, at the date of filing or after its registration, the Community trade mark had acquired distinctive character through the use which had been made of it in at least a substantial part of the European Union, namely Denmark, Portugal, Finland and Sweden.

8. On 9 September 2011, the applicant filed a notice of appeal against the decision of the Cancellation Division.

9. By decision of 4 May 2012 ("the contested decision"), the First Board of Appeal of OHIM upheld the decision of the Cancellation Division and therefore dismissed the appeal.

10. The Board of Appeal stated, in essence, first, in paragraph 37 of the contested decision, that the chequerboard pattern, as represented in the contested trade mark, was a basic and banal feature composed of very simple elements and that it was well-known that that feature had been commonly used with a decorative purpose in relation to various goods, including those falling within Class 18. The Board of Appeal went on to hold, in paragraphs 41 and 42 of the contested decision, that the contested trade mark, in the absence of features capable of distinguishing it from other representations of chequerboards, was not capable of fulfilling the essential "identification" or "origin" function of a trade mark. Furthermore, in paragraphs 43 and 47 of that decision, the Board of Appeal considered that the weft and warp structure of the contested trade mark did not constitute a substantial feature of that trade mark and did not give it a distinctive

character. Moreover, according to paragraph 46 of the contested decision, the fact that the weft and warp structure of that trade mark had been copied does not demonstrate that it acted as an indication of commercial origin for the relevant public. The same was true, according to paragraph 48 of the contested decision, of the specific combination of colours, namely brown and beige. The Board of Appeal therefore found, in paragraph 49 of the contested decision, that the contested trade mark was very simple and contained no element capable of individualising it in such a way that it would not appear as a common and basic chequerboard pattern. It added, in paragraph 50 of the contested decision, that signs such as the contested trade mark were typically used as supplementary signs which coexisted beside the manufacturer's house mark and, therefore, the Board of Appeal concluded, in paragraph 51 of the contested decision, that that trade mark was devoid of any distinctive character. The Board of Appeal also took the view, in paragraph 55 of the contested decision, that the documents produced by the proprietor of the contested trade mark did not demonstrate that the relevant public would be in the habit of making an assumption on the commercial origin of the goods at hand based on patterns. Lastly, the Board of Appeal considered, in paragraphs 73 to 75 of the contested decision, that, on the basis of the evidence provided by the applicant, it had not been established that the contested trade mark had acquired distinctive character through the use which had been made of it in a substantial part of the relevant territory, namely in Denmark, Portugal, Finland and Sweden, either at its filing date or after its registration. ...

Law

14. In support of its action, the applicant raises two pleas in law, alleging infringement, first, of Article 7(1)(b) and of Article 52(1) of Regulation No. 207/2009 and, second, of Article 7(3) and Article 52(2) of that regulation.

The first plea in law, alleging infringement of Article 7(1)(b) and Article 52(1) of Regulation No. 207/2009

15. It should be noted that the first plea, alleging a breach of Article 7(1)(b) and Article 52(1) of Regulation No. 207/2009, is divided into two limbs. By the first limb, the applicant, in essence, complains that the Board of Appeal did not confine itself to assessing whether the contested trade mark had a minimum degree of distinctive character, but also assessed whether that trade mark had other features which could attract the attention of the relevant consumer, thus requiring that trade mark to reach a higher threshold of distinctive character. ...

The inherent distinctive character of the contested mark

16. It should be recalled that, under Article 52(l)(a) of Regulation No. 207/2009, a Community trade mark is to be declared invalid on application to OHIM where that mark has been registered contrary to the provisions of Article 7 of that regulation.

17. According to the case-law, an absolute ground for refusal must be interpreted in the light of the general interest underlying it. As regards Article 7(1)(b) of Regulation No. 207/2009, the underlying notion of general interest is, manifestly, indissociable from the essential function of a trade mark, which is to guarantee the identity of the origin of the marked product or service to the consumer or end-user by enabling him, without any possibility of confusion, to distinguish the product or service from others which have another origin. ...

18. For a trade mark to possess distinctive character for the purposes of Article 7(1)(b) of Regulation No. 207/2009, it must serve to identify the product in respect of which registration has been applied for as originating from a particular undertaking, and thus to distinguish that product from those of other undertakings. ...

19. That distinctive character must be assessed, first, by reference to the products or services in respect of which registration has been applied for and, second, by reference to the perception of the relevant public, which consists of average consumers of the products or services in question, who are reasonably well informed and reasonably observant and circumspect. ... The level of attention of the average consumer, who is deemed to be reasonably well informed and reasonably observant and circumspect, varies according to the category of the products and services in question. ...

20. According to equally established case-law, the criteria for assessing the distinctive character of three-dimensional marks consisting of the appearance of the product itself are no different from those applicable to other categories of trade mark. ...

21. However, it should be borne in mind that, for the purpose of applying those criteria, the relevant public's perception is not necessarily the same in the case of a three-dimensional mark, which consists of the appearance of the product itself, as it is in the case of a word or figurative mark, which consists of a sign unrelated to the appearance of the products it denotes. ...

22. Average consumers are not in the habit of making assumptions about the origin of products on the basis of their shape or the shape of their packaging in the absence of any graphic or word element and it could therefore prove more difficult to establish distinctiveness in relation to such a three-dimensional mark than in relation to a word or figurative mark. ...

23. Furthermore, in accordance with the case-law, the more closely the shape in respect of which registration as a trade mark is applied for resembles the shape most likely to be taken by the product in question, the greater the likelihood of the shape being devoid of any distinctive character for the purposes of Article 7(1)(b) of Regulation No. 207/2009. In those circumstances, only a mark which departs significantly from the norm or customs of the sector and thereby fulfils its essential function of indicating origin is not devoid of any distinctive character for the purposes of Article 7(1)(b) of Regulation No. 207/2009. ...

24. That case-law, which was developed in relation to three-dimensional trade marks consisting of the appearance of the product itself, also applies where the contested mark is a figurative mark consisting of the two-dimensional representation of that product. In such a case, the mark likewise does not consist of a sign unrelated to the appearance of the products it covers. ...

25. That is also the case for a figurative mark consisting of a part of the shape of the product that it represents, inasmuch as the relevant public will immediately and without further thought perceive it as a representation of a particularly interesting or attractive detail of the product in question, rather than as an indication of its commercial origin. ...

26. It is in the light of those considerations that the applicant's arguments challenging the legality of the contested decision must be examined.

27. In the first place, it must be noted that, in the present case, the parties do not dispute the Board of Appeal's assessment, in paragraph 29 of the contested decision, that the goods covered by the contested mark are for everyday use, so that the relevant public is made up of the average consumer in the European Union, taken to be reasonably well informed and reasonably observant and circumspect. Furthermore, as the Board of Appeal correctly points out, it is not

apparent from the description of the goods in question that they are luxury goods or goods that are so sophisticated or expensive that the relevant public would be likely to be particularly attentive with regard to them.

28. In the second place, it must be held that, having regard to the goods in question, the contested mark is presented in the form of a pattern intended either to be placed on part of the goods or to cover the whole of their surface area, as the applicant expressly admitted at the hearing in response to a question by the Court.

29. Thus, with regard to the goods in question, namely leather and imitation leather goods, various bags, wallets, umbrellas and sunshades which may contain fabric parts, the pattern at issue may to a greater or lesser extent cover their surface and thus correspond to the outward appearance of the goods. ...

30. It follows that the Board of Appeal was correct to hold, in paragraph 33 of the contested decision, that the determinative factor for the contested mark was the fact that it coincided with the appearance of the product in question.

31. Consequently, contrary to the applicant's submission that the Board of Appeal required it, wrongly, to demonstrate that the contested mark had reached a higher threshold of distinctive character, the Board of Appeal was, on the contrary, fully entitled to base its assessment of the distinctive character of the contested mark on the principles applicable to three-dimensional marks. The considerations set out in paragraphs 24 and 25 above justify the application of the case-law developed in respect of three-dimensional marks, cited in paragraphs 20 to 23 above, also to figurative marks consisting in the shape of the product concerned or a part of the shape of the product concerned, since such marks are also not unrelated to the appearance of the product that they designate. ...

32. In the third place, it is necessary to examine the applicant's argument that a practice exists whereby figurative marks of this kind are used for the purposes of commercial identification in the marketing of goods to which the contested mark relates, with the result that the public is accustomed to perceiving as trade marks signs other than word marks, and in particular patterns covering the entire surface of leather articles of various kinds. It follows, according to the applicant, that it suffices that the mark at issue has a minimum degree of distinctive character to retain the registration granted.

33. In that regard, it should be recalled that the Court of Justice has already rejected ... the argument that goods, in respect of which the consumer is accustomed to the shape of certain components of the whole product serving to indicate the product's origin, are excluded from the application of the case-law referred to in paragraph 23 above. The Court found, on the contrary, that it follows from that case-law that, if the appearance of goods in a given sector, or that of a component of those goods, serves to indicate the manufacturer, that is only because the appearance of a sufficient number of those goods or of their components differs significantly from the norm or customs of that sector. ...

34. It follows that, in any event, the applicant's argument that consumers are accustomed to perceiving a pattern as an indication of the commercial origin of goods is irrelevant because the fact that such signs are recognised as marks by consumers does not necessarily mean that they have an inherent distinctive character. It is in fact possible for a mark to acquire distinctive character through use over time. ...

35. In the fourth place, it must be examined whether the pattern at issue differs significantly from the norm or customs of the sector and, accordingly, allows consumers to identify the pattern corresponding with the contested form of presentation as originating from a particular company and therefore to distinguish it from patterns originating from other companies.

36. In the present case, the contested mark consists, as the Board of Appeal correctly held in paragraph 30 of the contested decision, of a regular pattern of squares in two alternating colours, namely brown and beige, which is reminiscent of a chequerboard pattern. A weft and warp structure, which constitutes, as the applicant points out, a pattern within a pattern, also appears on the inside of the squares in the manner of a weaving method shown by two interlacing threads.

37. On the one hand, the chequerboard pattern is a basic and commonplace figurative pattern, since it is composed of a regular succession of squares of the same size which are differentiated by alternating different colours, in this case brown and beige. The pattern thus does not contain any notable variation in relation to the conventional representation of chequerboards and is the same as the traditional form of such a pattern. Even applied to goods such as those falling within Class 18, the pattern in question does not differ from the norm or customs of the sector inasmuch as such goods are generally covered with fabrics of different kinds, and the chequerboard pattern, due to its great simplicity, might constitute precisely one of those patterns.

38. In that regard, as the Board of Appeal correctly stated in paragraph 37 of the contested decision, without being challenged on this point by the applicant, the chequerboard pattern is one that has always existed and has been used in decorative arts. The latter, notwithstanding the applicant's denials, have an indisputable link with the goods in Class 18. In that regard and in any event, it is clear from information contained in OHIM's case-file that such a pattern has been commonly used in the decorative sector (in particular, clothes and floor tiles) and also appears in the Bayeux tapestry.

39. On the other hand, the weft and warp pattern that appears on the inside of each of the chequerboard squares corresponds with the desired visual effect of interlacing two different fabrics, of whatever type they may be (wool, silk, leather, etc.), which is thus customary as regards goods such as those within Class18.

40. Applied to the goods within Class 18 at issue in the present case, the presentation of a chequerboard in the alternating colours of brown and beige and the impression of interlacing threads do not, from a graphic point of view, contain any notable variation in relation to the conventional presentation of such goods, so that the relevant public will in fact perceive only a commonplace and everyday pattern.

41. It should be noted that the juxtaposition of two elements that are not in themselves distinctive cannot alter the perception of the relevant public as to the absence of distinctive character, *ab initio*, of the contested mark. The juxtaposition of a chequerboard and of a weft and warp pattern does not give rise to any element that diverges from the norm or customs of the sector concerned; accordingly, the applicant's submission that the contested mark is complex, particular and original cannot succeed. ...

42. The applicant is also incorrect in its submission that the Board of Appeal has wrongly assessed the contested mark in that it reduced it to a chequerboard rather than examining it taking account of all of its features (namely, the chequerboard device, the weft and warp structure and the brown and beige colours).

43. In addition to the fact—noted moreover by the applicant—that the Board of Appeal correctly described, in paragraph 30 of the contested decision, the contested mark as being composed of a chequerboard pattern with alternating colours of brown and beige and presenting a weft and warp structure, it is apparent from subsequent parts of the contested decision that the Board of Appeal examined in turn, first, in paragraphs 37 to 42 of the contested decision, the chequerboard pattern, next, in paragraphs 43 to 47 of the decision, the weft and warp structure

and, finally, in paragraph 48 of that decision, the combination of colours used, namely brown and beige, in order to reach the conclusion, in paragraphs 49 to 51 of the contested decision, in the context of an analysis of the overall impression created by that juxtaposition of elements, that the contested mark was devoid of any distinctive character.

44. While it is true that the Board of Appeal examined the pattern formed by the weft and warp structure after concluding that the chequerboard pattern was devoid of any distinctive character, it must be recalled that, for the purposes of assessing the distinctive character of a trade mark made up of several components (a composite mark), it is necessary to consider it as a whole. However, that is not incompatible with an examination of each of the mark's individual components in turn. ...

45. Thus, the Board of Appeal, in, on the one hand, examining the various components of the contested mark in turn, and, on the other hand, carrying out an assessment of the contested mark as a whole, did not infringe Article 7(1)(b) of Regulation No. 207/2009. ...

Figure 23 LVM's well-known "Neverfull" bag, made of "damier ebène" ("ebony checkers board," in beige and dark brown colors), one of the many LVM products displaying this pattern. LVM's checkerboard is a class 18 registered trademark in a vast quantity of countries all over the world, including in a significant number of European Union Member States (through the designation of its international trademark nr. WO 1479417, of June 22, 2019, for class 18), in spite of EUIPO's (formerly OHIM) decision to strike it from the EU register (as confirmed by the General Court).

§ 1.75.2 *Birkenstock Sales GmbH v. European Union Intellectual Property Office (EUIPO)*—2016

European Union's General Court (Fifth Chamber)

November 9, 2016

Birkenstock Sales GmbH v. European Union Intellectual Property Office (EUIPO)

Case T-579/14

Action brought against the decision of the First Board of Appeal of EUIPO of May 15, 2014, concerning the international registration designating the European Union of the figurative mark representing a pattern of wavy, crisscrossing lines

Background to the dispute

1. The applicant, Birkenstock Sales GmbH, is the successor to Birkenstock Orthopädie GmbH & Co. KG, which on June 27, 2012 obtained international registration from the World Intellectual Property Organization (WIPO) on the basis of a German trade mark designating *inter alia* the European Union[49] for the following figurative mark:

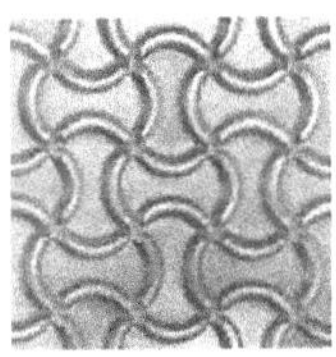

2. On 25 October 2012, the European Union Intellectual Property Office (EUIPO) received notification of the international registration of the sign at issue.

3. The goods in respect of which the Community trade mark was registered are in Classes 10, 18 and 25 of the Nice Agreement concerning the International Classification of Goods and Services for the Purposes of the Registration of Marks of 15 June 1957, as revised and amended, and correspond, for each of those classes, to the following description:

- Class 10: ...[50]
- Class 18: "Leather and imitations of leather, and goods made of these materials and included in this class; animal skins, hides; trunks and travelling bags; umbrellas, parasols and walking sticks; whips, harness and saddlery; change

49. The WIPO Global Trademark Database shows that besides the European Union (EM), Austria, Spain, France, Italy, Turkey and Brunei have also been designated in the registration of Birkenstock's figurative trademark (No. 1132742, of June 27, 2012, classes 10, 18 and 25).
50. The list is long and has been omitted. It covers surgical materials and orthopaedic articles—the latter of certain interest to Birkenstock, which originally was specialized in making orthopaedic footwear (this explains the particular shape of the inside of its shoes). Anyway, this opinion dedicates a good deal of space finding that the Birkenstock's wavy pattern is distinctive as far as surgical materials are concerned—a finding that, I believe, does not raise any interest for the company.

purses; bags; handbags; document cases; waist pouches; garment bags for travel; key cases (leatherwear); beauty cases; toilet bags, vanity cases; travelling bags; rucksacks";

- Class 25: "Clothing, headgear, footwear, including comfort footwear and footwear for work, leisure, health and sports, including sandals, gymnastic sandals ...; belts; shawls; neckerchiefs."

4. On November 21, 2012, the examiner issued the applicant with an ex officio provisional total refusal of protection of the international mark in the European Union. The ground relied on in support of that refusal was the lack of distinctive character of the sign at issue within the meaning of Article 7(1)(b) of Council Regulation No. 207/2009 of 26 February 2009 on the Community trade mark (OJ 2009 L 78, p. 1) in respect of all the goods concerned.

5. By decision of 29 August 2013, after the applicant had responded to the objections set out in the notification of provisional refusal, the Examination Division upheld, on the same ground as that previously given, the total refusal of protection of the international mark in the European Union.

6. On 4 October 2013, the applicant filed a notice of appeal with EUIPO against that decision pursuant to Articles 58 to 60 of Regulation No. 207/2009.

7. By decision of 15 May 2014 ("the contested decision"), the First Board of Appeal of EUIPO dismissed the appeal on the ground that the trade mark applied for was descriptive and devoid of any distinctive character in respect of the products at issue.

8. The Board of Appeal found *inter alia* that the sign at issue presented wavy lines crisscrossing at right angles in a repetitive sequence that could extend in all four directions of the square and therefore be used on any two- or three-dimensional surface. The sign at issue would thus be perceived immediately as representing a surface pattern.[51]

9. The Board of Appeal also observed that it was well known that the surfaces of goods or their packaging are decorated with patterns for a variety of reasons, including enhancing their aesthetic appearance and/or for technical reasons.

10. It observed that, according to the case-law, as the average consumers do not usually presume the commercial origin of goods on the basis of the signs that are indissociable from the goods themselves, those signs will have distinctive character within the meaning of Article 7(1)(b) of Regulation No. 207/2009 only if they depart significantly from the sectoral standards or usual practices. It considered that case-law to be applicable in the present case, as the sign at issue was indissociable from the appearance of the goods in question.

11. The Board of Appeal considered that the overall impression produced by the sign at issue was banal and that that surface pattern could be found on all of the goods in question, for which it could fulfil an aesthetic and/or technical function. It took the view that the overall impression produced by the sign at issue did not depart significantly—or even at all—from the usual practices of the sectors concerned.

12. The Board of Appeal concluded that the relevant public would in all likelihood perceive the sign as a simple surface pattern, not as an indication of any particular commercial origin. ...

51. Birkenstock actually uses the pattern in the sole of some of its models (*see* Figure 21).

Law

15. In support of its action, the applicant raises a single plea in law, alleging infringement of Article 7(1)(b) of Regulation No. 207/2009.

16. The applicant argues *inter alia* that the Board of Appeal applied criteria not included in Article 7(1)(b) of Regulation No. 207/2009. The Board of Appeal did not base itself on the international mark in its registered form, being an image with a clearly delimited surface that is not indissociable from the shape of the goods, but unjustifiedly expanded the mark by affirming that it could be reproduced and continued.

17. The international registration claims protection for a square-shaped figurative mark with an abstract pattern, whose appearance is in itself complete, singular and unusual.

18. EUIPO considers that the Board of Appeal found, correctly, that the sign at issue represented a surface pattern and that it was devoid of distinctive character for the goods in question.

General points

19. Under Article 154(1) of Regulation No. 207/2009, any international registration designating the EU is subject to examination as to absolute grounds for refusal in the same way as applications for EU trademarks.

20. Under Article 7(1)(b) of Regulation No. 207/2009, trade marks which are devoid of any distinctive character are not to be registered.

21. For a trade mark to possess distinctive character for the purposes of Article 7(1)(b) of Regulation No. 40/94 it must serve to identify the goods in respect of which registration is sought as originating from a particular undertaking, and thus to distinguish those goods from those of other undertakings. ...

22. Furthermore, it is apparent from settled case-law that the distinctive character of a trade mark must be assessed, first, by reference to the goods or services in respect of which registration has been applied for and, second, by reference to the perception of them on the part of the relevant public, which is made up of the average consumers of those goods or services. ... The level of attention of the average consumer, who is reasonably well informed and reasonably observant and circumspect, is likely to vary according to the category of goods or services in question. ...

23. According to equally consistent case-law, the criteria for assessing the distinctive character of three-dimensional marks consisting of the appearance of the product itself are no different from those applicable to other categories of trade mark. Nonetheless, for the purpose of applying those criteria, the average consumer's perception is not necessarily the same in the case of a three-dimensional mark consisting of the appearance of the product itself as it is in the case of a word or figurative mark consisting of a sign which is independent of the appearance of the products it denotes. Average consumers are not in the habit of making assumptions about the origin of products on the basis of their shape or the shape of their packaging in the absence of any graphic or word element, and it could therefore prove more difficult to establish distinctiveness in relation to such a three-dimensional mark than in relation to a word or figurative mark. ...

24. It is apparent from those considerations that only a three-dimensional mark, consisting in the appearance of the product itself, only a mark which departs significantly from the standards or usual practices of the sector and thereby fulfils its essential function of indicating origin is not devoid of any distinctive character for the purposes of Article 7(1)(b) of Regulation No. 207/2009. ...

25. The case-law referred to in paragraphs 23 and 24 above, which evolved in relation to three-dimensional trade marks consisting of the appearance of the product designated, also applies where the trade mark in question is a figurative mark consisting of the shape of that product. In such a case, the mark does not consist of a sign that bears no relation to the appearance of the products it identifies. ...

26. That case-law is also applicable in the case of a sign composed of a design applied to the surface of goods. ...

27. That is also the case for a figurative mark consisting of a part of the shape of the product that it represents, inasmuch as the relevant public will immediately and without further thought perceive it as a representation of a particularly interesting or attractive detail of the product in question, rather than as an indication of its commercial origin. ...

28. As observed by the Board of Appeal in paragraph 27 of the contested decision, the decisive element for the applicability of that case-law is not the categorisation of the sign in question as a figurative sign, be it three-dimensional or otherwise, but rather the fact that it is indissociable from the appearance of the product designated.

The relevant public

29. The Board of Appeal observed that the goods in Class 10 concerned essentially orthopaedic shoes and parts therefor. It also found that those products could be purchased by consumers in general as part of the general public or by health professionals and that they are chosen with care.

30. The Board of Appeal also observed that the goods "surgical, medical, dental and veterinary apparatus and instruments; artificial limbs, eyes and teeth; orthopaedic articles; suture materials; suture materials for operations" were intended essentially for health professionals displaying an average level of attention when choosing them.

31. Lastly, it found that the goods in Classes 18 and 25 were intended for the general public displaying an average level of attention at the time of purchase.

32. Those considerations—which are not disputed by the applicant—must be endorsed, except as regards the goods "leather and imitations of leather" and "animal skins, hides," in Class 18. Those goods are intended principally for a professional public that uses those goods to make other goods.

The applicability in the present case of the case-law relating to marks that are indissociable from the appearance of the goods

33. It is appropriate to turn now to the question of whether the Board of Appeal was correct in applying in the present case the case-law relating to signs that are indissociable from the appearance of the products.

34. To that end, it is appropriate to begin by examining the characteristics of the sign at issue.

35. The sign at issue is made up of a square graphic representation with crisscrossing wavy lines so that the pattern is the same vertically and horizontally. The representation has no contours.

36. As observed by the Board of Appeal, the repetitive sequence can extend infinitely in all four directions of the square and therefore be applied to any two- or three-dimensional surface.

37. It is therefore a sign composed of a series of components that repeat themselves regularly and lends itself particularly well to being used as a surface pattern.

38. As the applicant stated, EUIPO must, in its examination of the distinctive character of a sign, refer to the reproduction of the mark sought attached to the registration application and the description included in that application, where there is one. ...

39. It should be noted, however, that, in finding that the repetitive sequence could extend infinitely in all four directions of the square and therefore be applied to any two- or three-dimensional surface, EUIPO based itself on the intrinsic characteristics of the sign at issue, as apparent from the reproduction of the international mark. It cannot therefore be criticised for having based its assessment on aspects which are not apparent from the reproduction of the sign at issue.

40. The applicant submits that if the reasoning in the contested decision were to be taken literally, no figurative mark could be registered, because any figurative mark could, in principle, be extended infinitely and be used as a pattern on a surface of goods.

41. It is true that a figurative sign representing a "classic" logo may be reproduced infinitely and be used as a surface pattern. If the Board of Appeal were to base itself on a possible infinite duplication of such a sign in order to find that it was indissociable from the appearance of the goods, then that approach would be purely speculative.

42. However, where a sign in itself is made up of a repetitive sequence of elements, EUIPO may take into account the intrinsic characteristics of that sign in order to examine its nature, including the question whether it is a sign that is indissociable from the appearance of the goods covered. In the present case, the Board of Appeal based its reasoning on an analysis of the intrinsic characteristics of the sign at issue. That approach cannot be criticised.

43. It is also apparent from the case-law that the fact that a sign has been designated as a figurative mark does not prevent the Board of Appeal from finding, on the basis of the practical experience generally acquired from the marketing of the goods covered by the registration application, that there is a surface pattern. ...

44. In the judgment of September 19, 2012, *Tartan pattern in dark grey, light grey, black, beige, dark red and light red* (T-50/11, not published, EU:T:2012:442, paragraphs 46 and 47), the Court rejected the argument to the effect that EUIPO had distorted the purpose of the registration application in finding that a mark for which registration as a figurative mark had been sought was a pattern on fabric.

45. The Court observed that the abstract pattern presented in the image that made up the mark sought could constitute the pattern on a fabric. ... The Court noted that the products at issue in that case were fabrics or goods made up of fabrics which "could" have surfaces of fabric. ...

46. It should be noted that, in that case, in accordance with the case-law to the effect that the distinctive character of a sign must be examined by reference to the goods in respect of which registration has been applied for (*see* paragraph 22 above), the Court did not therefore restrict itself to finding that the image making up the mark sought could be a pattern on fabric, but also examined, in the light of the goods covered by the trade mark application, whether they could have fabric surfaces.

47. It should be noted that the goods at issue in that case were fabrics or fashion items in the broad sense of the term, which obviously often have surface patterns.

48. It should be noted that, in the present case, some of the goods covered by the international mark are goods that often have surface patterns, such as fashion

items in the broad sense of the term, whilst others will not obviously lend themselves often to having surface patterns.

49. The question then arises as to which criterion is the relevant one for determining whether a figurative sign that is made up of a series of regularly repetitive elements and therefore lends itself particularly well to being used as a surface pattern, may in fact be regarded as being a surface pattern for a given good.

The relevant criterion for regarding a figurative mark, made up of a series of regularly repetitive elements, as being a surface pattern for a given good

50. In the contested decision, the Board of Appeal observed, in essence, that all of the products at issue, or their packaging, could have a surface pattern, either for decorative purposes or for technical reasons, in order to enhance their grip. It implicitly considered that the possibility of applying a surface pattern on the products at issue or their packaging was sufficient for the case-law relating to signs that are indissociable from the appearance of the products to be applicable.

51. When questioned on this point at the hearing, EUIPO confirmed that, in its submission, in order for the case-law relating to marks that are indissociable from the appearance of the goods to be applicable in the present case, it was sufficient that the use of the sign at issue as a surface pattern on the products at issue or on their packaging was possible and that it was not necessary that it be the most likely use of the sign.

52. The applicant stated at the hearing that the assessment criterion should be much stricter and that the mere possibility that the sign at issue might be used as a surface pattern on the products at issue or on their packaging was not sufficient.

53. It is necessary, first of all, to identify the relevant criterion for determining whether the case-law relating to signs that are indissociable from the appearance of the products is applicable in the case of possible use of a sign, made up of a series of regularly repetitive elements and designated as a figurative mark, as a surface pattern on the products at issue themselves (*see* paragraphs 54 to 57 below). Next, an assessment will have to be made of the specific case of possible use of such a sign as a surface pattern not on the products at issue themselves, but on the packaging (*see* paragraphs 58 to 68 below).

54. In order to determine the relevant criterion, it must be remembered that a sign that is made up of a series of regularly repetitive elements lends itself particularly well to being used as a surface pattern. There is therefore, in principle, a probability, inherent in that sign, that it will be used as a surface pattern, irrespective of its designation by the trade mark applicant as a figurative mark, a three-dimensional mark, a surface pattern or other type of mark.

55. In those circumstances, it is only when the use of a surface pattern is unlikely in the light of the nature of the products at issue that such a sign cannot be considered a surface pattern in respect of the products at issue. Otherwise, the sign at issue, bearing the typical characteristics of a surface pattern owing to the repetitive sequence of its elements, may in fact be held to constitute a surface pattern.

56. As regards the judgment of April 13, 2011, *Deichmann v. OHIM (Representation of a curved band with dotted lines)* (T-202/09, not published, EU:T:2011:168), relied on by EUIPO, the Court found, in paragraph 47 of that judgment, that the Board of Appeal was free to base its examination of the mark at issue on the "the most likely" use of it.

57. That judgment did not concern the registration of a sign made up of a repetitive sequence of element. Given that factor, the Court held that the decorative or strengthening use of the sign on the products at issue was "the most likely." When a sign is made up of a repetitive sequence of elements and, owing to its intrinsic characteristics, lends itself particularly well to being used as a surface pattern, there is, in principle, a probability, inherent in that sign, that it will be used as a surface pattern. For that reason, there are valid grounds for holding that it is only when the use of a surface pattern is unlikely in the light of the nature of the products at issue that such a sign cannot be considered a surface pattern in respect of the products at issue (*see* paragraphs 54 and 55 above). That is an objective criterion that is not contingent on the commercial intentions of the undertaking concerned.[52] ... [a few paragraphs discussing the use of a surface pattern on the packaging of products follow; they have been omitted].

The applicability of the case-law relating to signs that are indissociable from the appearance of the goods in respect of the products at issue

70. It is not unusual for the products "footwear, including comfort footwear and footwear for work, leisure, health and sports, including sandals, gymnastic sandals, flip-flops, slippers, clogs, including with footbeds, in particular with anatomically moulded deep footbeds, foot supports and foot and shoe inserts, protective inserts" in Class 25 to have a surface pattern. Footwear are fashion items and may therefore have a surface pattern for aesthetic purposes. A surface pattern may also be applied to their outsoles for technical reasons. Outsoles are often profiled as serving to improve the footwear-to-surface grip, as observed by the Board of Appeal in paragraph 33 of the contested decision.

71. The applicant submits in that regard that the sign at issue is not suitable for fulfilling a technical function, since a figurative mark, by its very nature, has two dimensions.

72. However, the wavy lines making up the sign at issue produce a shade effect, giving a three-dimensional aspect to the sign. In fact, the edge of those lines is darker than the part in the middle of those lines. Although it is true, as the applicant states, that the international mark was applied for as a two-dimensional figurative mark, and the application does not contain any description showing that it has raised or recessed elements, the Board of Appeal was correct to base itself on the characteristics of the sign at issue, including the shade effect produced by the wavy lines, to find that the sign could also be applied in raised format.

73. Moreover, it should be noted that, according to the case-law, there is nothing precluding the Board of Appeal from taking into account, as part of a registration application for a sign designated as a figurative mark, a possible use of that sign as a three-dimensional shape. ...

74. Regarding the applicant's argument to the effect that the contested decision is self-contradictory because a mark cannot simultaneously be both a two-dimensional surface pattern and a three-dimensional overlay, the following remarks are apposite.

75. There is nothing precluding two-dimensional or three-dimensional use of a sign from being taken into consideration. For example, in the judgment of

52. As noted above, Birkenstock indeed uses the crisscrossed waves as a pattern for the outsole of some of its shoes. This fact is mentioned in paragraph 76 of the opinion. Eventually, the shoemaker might have preferred to avoid this clarification because of the consequent application of the high standard of distinctiveness that has been required from patterns being applied for registration as trademarks, as in the Louis Vuitton checkerboard case.

September 10, 2015, *Representation of white dots on an ivory background* (T-144/14, not published, EU:T:2015:615, paragraphs 40 and 43), the Court took into account a possible use of a figurative sign representing white dots on an ivory background on printed matter and internet sites (two-dimensional use) and use in the form of small protuberant points serving to make the surface of a product less slippery. Therefore, contrary to the applicant's assertions, the contested decision is not self-contradictory on this point.

76. Moreover, the applicant stated, in the course of the administrative procedure and in its pleadings before the Court, that it had been using the sign at issue for over 40 years. When questioned about that use at the hearing, the applicant acknowledged that that use consisted in an application of the sign at issue on outsoles of footwear and that the pattern covered the entire sole. Use such as that corresponds to a use of the sign as a raised surface pattern.

77. As the applicant observed, it is true that, when the distinctive intrinsic character of a sign is being examined, the assessment must be based on the characteristics of the sign at issue, independently of any use that might have been made of the sign.

78. It must nevertheless be observed that the applicant's line of argument is inconsistent in that it states, on the one hand, that the international mark is a "common" two-dimensional figurative mark and not a surface pattern, whilst on the other affirms that use on the outsoles of footwear as a raised surface pattern also constitutes a use of the mark.

79. Moreover, the only example of use of the sign at issue provided by the applicant in the course of the administrative procedure consists of one photograph of a signboard displaying the pattern at issue and serving as a background for shoe racks, reproduced in paragraph 6 of the contested decision. Such use corresponds to a use of the sign at issue in two-dimensional form. It should be noted that, in being used as a background for shoe racks, the sign at issue has not been used in square form but has been extended on all sides in order to cover the entire background of the shoe rack, and thus has been used as a two-dimensional surface pattern.

80. In affirming both the use as a background for shoe racks and a use on the outsoles of footwear constitutes a use of the international mark, the applicant implicitly concedes that the sign at issue may also be used in both two-dimensional and three-dimensional form.

81. As regards the applicant's argument, put forward at the hearing, to the effect that it plans to use the international mark in the future in the shape of a square to be applied on parts of its products where, in its view, the relevant public expects to find marks, the following remarks are apposite. As the applicant itself observed, EUIPO must assess the distinctive character of a sign by reference to the reproduction of the mark sought attached to the registration application and to the description included in that application, where there is one (*see* paragraph 38 above). The business intentions of the trade mark applicant, which may vary in time and according to its wishes, are not relevant.

82. Moreover, when the applicant of a mark representing a pattern made up of a repetitive sequence of elements plans to use that sign in a particular manner and considers that the sign at issue has distinctive intrinsic character when used in that specific manner (e.g., applied in square form to a specific place on the products at issue), it may, for example, apply for registration of a position mark, in order to ensure that EUIPO takes into account, in the assessment of distinctive character, the use of the pattern in the particular form envisaged. As observed by EUIPO at the hearing, however, it cannot base its decision on the registration of a

mark, or on the protection of an international trade mark in the EU, on mere promises made by an applicant to use the mark in a certain manner.

83. It follows from the foregoing that it is unlikely that footwear will have a surface pattern, either for aesthetic purposes or for technical purposes. The Board of Appeal was therefore correct in applying the case-law relating to signs that are indissociable from the appearance of the goods to "footwear, including comfort footwear and footwear for work, leisure, health and sports, including sandals, gymnastic sandals, flip-flops, slippers, clogs, including with footbeds, in particular with anatomically moulded deep footbeds, foot supports and foot and shoe inserts, protective inserts" in Class 25.

84. Next, as regards "parts and fittings for the aforesaid footwear, namely footwear uppers, heel pieces, outsoles, inner soles, shoe bottom parts, including footbeds, foot supports," in Class 25, the following should be borne in mind.

85. It is not unlikely that the parts and fittings for footwear will have a surface pattern. For "outsoles," a raised surface pattern, may serve to improve the grip between the footwear and the surface. The same considerations apply for "heel pieces," whilst a surface pattern may be applied for decorative purposes to "footwear uppers."

86. A surface pattern on the upper part for decorative purposes may be found on "inner soles, shoe bottom parts, including footbeds, foot supports." Although inner soles are not visible when footwear is worn, they are parts that are visible for the footwear user when he puts them on or takes them off. The applicant in fact acknowledged in its reply that the inner soles of footwear may show patterns such as flowers or animal prints. Therefore, the mere fact that the inner sole of the footwear is not visible when the footwear is worn does not prevent the decorative patterns from being applied to them; such use is not unlikely.

87. Inner soles may also include a raised surface pattern on their lower part for technical purposes, in order to prevent the sole from sliding inside the footwear; nor is this type of use unlikely.

88. The considerations set out in paragraphs 86 to 87 above also hold true for "foot and shoe inserts, in particular with anatomically moulded deep footbeds, in particular of natural cork, thermal cork, plastic, latex or foamed plastic materials, including of elastic compounds of cork latex mixtures or plastic cork mixtures" and "inner soles," in Class 25.

89. Moreover, the considerations set out in paragraphs 70, 83 and 85 to 87 above also apply to "footwear, namely shoes and sandals, boots, and parts and fittings for all the aforesaid goods, included in this class," in Class 25.

90. The Board of Appeal was therefore correct in applying the case-law relating to signs that are indissociable from the appearance of the goods to the following products, in Class 25: ...

91. The considerations relating to footwear and their parts and fittings, set out in paragraphs 70, 83 and 85 to 87 above, also apply to footwear in Class 10. Orthopaedic shoes in Class 10 may, like footwear in Class25, show a surface pattern for decorative purposes on footwear uppers or for technical purposes on the outsole. The considerations set out in paragraphs 84 to 87 above apply to parts and fittings for orthopaedic shoes. ...

93. Next, it is appropriate to consider whether the Board of Appeal was correct in applying the case-law relating to signs that are indissociable from the appearance of the goods for the other products in Class 10 covered by the international mark.

94. As regards "surgical, medical, dental and veterinary apparatus and instruments," the Board of Appeal observed, correctly, that they may have a raised

surface pattern applied to a handle, and thus part of their surface, for technical reasons, namely to enable a more sure and precise grip; such use is not unlikely.

95. The "orthopaedic articles" listed in Class 10 comprise a vast category of products, some of which are likely to have a raised surface pattern for technical purposes, namely to improve their grip.

96. The Board of Appeal was therefore correct in applying the case-law relating to signs that are indissociable from the appearance of the products to "surgical, medical, dental and veterinary apparatus and instruments" and "orthopaedic articles," in Class 10. ...

113. Next, "clothing, headgear" and "belts," "shawls" and "neckerchiefs," in Class 25 are fashion items. They often have surface patterns for decorative purposes. The applicant's statement that belts, as a rule, do not have any pattern, except on the buckle, cannot be upheld. It is well known that belts often have surface patterns for decorative purposes. In any event, it is not unlikely that they will have a surface pattern.

114. The Board of Appeal was therefore correct in applying the case-law relating to signs that are indissociable from the appearance of the products at issue to the following goods in Class 25: "clothing, headgear," "belts," "shawls" and "neckerchiefs."

115. Next, the following should be borne in mind with respect to the goods covered by the international mark in Class 18.

116. The goods "trunks and travelling bags" and "change purses; bags; handbags; document cases; waist pouches; garment bags for travel; key cases (leatherwear); beauty cases; toilet bags, vanity cases; travelling bags; rucksacks' are items which may fulfil, in addition to their primary function, a common aesthetic function by contributing to the outward image of the consumer concerned. ... (*see*, to that effect, judgment of November 6, 2014, *Vans v. OHIM (Representation of a wavy line)*, T-53/13, EU:T:2014:932, paragraph 54 (not published)).[53]

117. As the Court has already held, the various leatherware and luggage goods in Class 18 may be regarded as part of the fashion sector in the broad sense of the term. ...

121. It is therefore not unlikely that those goods will have surface patterns for decorative purposes. ...

128. It follows from the foregoing that the contested decision must be annulled in so far as concerns the following goods: "artificial limbs, eyes and teeth," "suture materials; suture materials for operations" and "animal skins, hides." For those goods, the Board of Appeal was incorrect in applying the case-law relating to signs that are indissociable from the appearance of the products, with the result that it based itself on incorrect assessment criteria.

The alleged significant departure of the sign at issue from the standards and usual practices of the sectors concerned

129. It must now be examined whether the Board of Appeal was correct in finding that the sign at issue departed significantly from the standards or usual practices of

53. In this case, VANS, INC., a US manufacturer and seller of apparel and accessories, attempted (unsuccessfully) to overturn the decision by the OHIM to refuse registration of its figurative trademark that consists of a wavy line that appears in many of its shoes. The registration was refused on grounds of its lack of a distinctive character. Unfortunately the decision (Case T-53/13) has not been published as far as the debate on distinctiveness is concerned.

the sectors concerned with respect to the other goods covered by the international mark.

130. As observed by the Board of Appeal, the sign at issue is made up of crisscrossing horizontal and vertical wavy lines having the same shape.

131. It is a simple pattern, made up of a simple combination of wavy lines, crisscrossing repeatedly. As observed by the Board of Appeal, the overall impression produced by the sign remains banal and merely represents the sum of the components making up the sign.

132. The applicant's assertion that the shapes making up the sign are already unusual taken in isolation, and that, in the overall impression produced by it, the pattern is original and unusual, cannot be upheld. The applicant merely makes a general statement, without providing evidence liable to establish what could be considered "original" and "unusual" in the simple combination of wavy lines.

133. Moreover, as observed by the Board of Appeal, general experience shows that patterns applied to surfaces are characterised by infinite different designs. It also observed, correctly, that the elements of patterns applied to surfaces were often simple geometrical shapes such as spots, circles, rectangles or lines, which could be straight or go up and down in a zigzag or wavy pattern.

134. The Board of Appeal considered that the overall impression produced by the sign examined did not depart significantly—or even at all—from the usual practices of the sectors concerned and that the relevant public would therefore perceive the sign at issue as a simple surface pattern and not as an indication of any particular commercial origin.

135. The applicant submits in that regard that the Board of Appeal provides no evidence in support of its statement that the sign at issue does not depart significantly from other surface patterns used in trade for the goods in question. In its submission, the sign at issue or similar signs are not used for the goods in question, stating that, contrary to the Board of Appeal's findings, it cannot be presumed that the sign at issue or a similar sign is usually employed for decorative or technical purposes on the products at issue.

136. It must be remembered in that regard that, if an applicant claims that a trade mark applied for is distinctive, despite EUIPO's analysis, it is for that applicant to provide specific and substantiated information to show that the trade mark applied for has either an intrinsic distinctive character or a distinctive character acquired by usage ... since it is much better placed to do so, given its thorough knowledge of the market. ...

141. In the present case, the applicant has not provided evidence liable to cast doubt on the Board of Appeal's finding that, in essence, given the banality of the sign at issue and the infinite number of different designs used as surface patterns, there is no significant departure by the overall impression produced by the sign at issue from the standards or usual practices of the sectors concerned. ...

149. It is, moreover, clear from the case-law that, although the appearance of the goods in a given sector, or a component of those goods, serves to indicate the manufacturer, that is only because the appearance of a sufficient number of those goods departs significantly from the standards or usual practices of the sector. That does not in any way mean that the appearance of a good or a component of a good of the same sector that, in regards to it, does not depart significantly from that standard is liable to indicate the origin of that good in the mind of the relevant public. ...

150. Moreover, the fact that certain signs are recognised as trade marks by consumers does not necessarily mean that they are devoid of intrinsic distinctive character. It is in fact possible for a mark to acquire distinctive character through use over time. ...

151. The considerations set out in paragraphs 149 and 150 above also hold true for the applicant's argument to the effect that, for shoes, consumers are accustomed to manufacturers' always designing their goods with the same mark affixed to certain places.

152. Lastly, regarding the applicant's argument, put forward at the hearing, to the effect that it is entitled to register the mark when it has distinctive character, it should be noted that that fact does not mean that the examination conducted at the time of the application for trade mark registration or at the time of assessment of an application for extension of the protection of an international trade mark for the EU, must not be strict and complete in order to avoid marks being unduly registered or protected in the European Union. ...

153. In the present case, the conclusion is that, given the banality of the sign at issue and the infinite number of different designs used for surface patterns, the Board of Appeal was correct in finding that there was not a significant departure by the sign at issue and from the standards and usual practices of the sectors concerned. It was therefore correct in finding that the relevant public would perceive the sign as a simple surface pattern, applied for decorative or technical purposes, and not as an indication of any particular commercial origin.

154. It follows from all the foregoing that the contested decision must be annulled in respect of the following goods: "artificial limbs, eyes and teeth," "suture materials; suture materials for operations" (Class 10) and "animal skins, hides" (Class 18) (*see* paragraph 128 above).

155. As regards the other goods covered by the international mark, however, the single plea in law put forward by the applicant must be dismissed, as must therefore the action in its entirety. ...

Source: < curia.europa.eu > .

Figure 24 Birkenstock's slippers, with its original innersole (in brown).

§ 1.76 THE DISPUTE OVER THE NEW YORK FASHION WEEK TRADEMARK: ANOTHER CASE OF *TURPIS CAUSA*?—2016

The following text concerns the (ongoing at the time of this writing) dispute over the trademark New York Fashion Week. Like the YKK case (see § 1.72), it seems that the dispute over NYFW is a case of "turpis causa." Actually, the frequency in which fashion-related disputes grounded on "turpis causa" are brought to courts reveals the tensions behind the fashion industry, whose success is strongly based on prestige. This is a value that naturally is very fragile, as it may disappear along with rapidly changing tastes. Prestige calls for admiration but it also calls for rivals' envy, and envy is behind some of the most abject forms of violation of intellectual property, namely the parasitic reliance on the prestige built by the creativity and efforts of genuine artists—or, in the case of the NYFW, creative entrepreneurs.

Fashion Week, Inc. v. Council of Fashion Designers of America, Inc., CFDA Foundation Inc., and WME IMG LLC

United States District Court, Southern District of New York

New York, August 12, 2012

Memorandum Opinion and Order

This case is about the ownership and use of "NEW YORK FASHION WEEK" and its acronym "NYFW," and "NYFW THE RUNWAY SHOWS." The plaintiff, Fashion Week Inc. ("FWI"), brings this action against the Council of Fashion Designers of America, Inc. and the CFDA Foundation, Inc., (together "CFDA") and WME IMG LLC ("WME-IMG") (collectively referred to as the "defendants") alleging trademark dilution, unfair competition and false designation of origin, and trademark infringement in violation of the Lanham Act, 15 U.S.C. § 1051 et seq., as well as claims for violations of New York State law.

On June 28, 2016, FWI sought a temporary restraining order ("TRO") and a preliminary injunction barring CFDA and WME-IMG from using FWI's asserted trademarks, NEW YORK FASHION WEEK, NYFW, and NYFW THE RUNWAY SHOWS, and terms infringing on those marks in connection with live semi-annual events in New York during which fashion designers launch new clothing lines. On June 29, 2016, the Court held a hearing on the request for a TRO and denied the request concluding that the plaintiff had not made the requisite showing of irreparable harm. ... The request for a preliminary injunction is denied.

I. The following facts are based on the parties' submissions in connection with the TRO [temporary restraining order] and the preliminary injunction.

CFDA, with its principal places of business in New York, is a non-profit trade association whose membership includes more than 4,500 members, all from America's foremost womenswear, menswear, jewelry, and accessory designers. WME-IMG, also based in New York, is a management and production company. CFDA schedules and coordinates and WME-IMG produces fashion events in New York City comprised of a series of fashion shows featuring the works of prominent designers for members of the fashion industry.

These shows feature the work of famous designers and give designers the opportunity to showcase their designs to prospective retailers and promote them to the media.* These events date back to 1943 when "Press Week" was launched, an event dedicated to promoting American designers of women's fashion.

Since its founding in 1962, CFDA has organized semi-annual womenswear fashion events, in addition to other related events focusing on different areas of the fashion industry. The week-long events consist of multiple presentations and installations featuring the works of CFDA members and other fashion industry professionals, which annually draw over 230,000 attendees and generate close to $ 900 million. CFDA oversees the scheduling and organization logistics for all the week's events as a whole, and WME-IMG is responsible for the official fashion week venue, where the majority of designer runway shows occur. Taken together, the semi-annual week-long events in New York are recognized as one of the four major fashion weeks in the world. The New York City government also works with CFDA to schedule and promote the event.

From 1993 to 2015, the CFDA/WME-IMG events were formally named after their location or sponsor. Such names included "Olympus Fashion Week" and "Mercedes-Benz Fashion Week." In the press and the fashion industry, the events were widely referred to as "New York Fashion Week" from at least 1993 onwards. After Mercedes-Benz ceased sponsoring the CFDA/WME events in July 2015, WME and CFDA announced they would be featuring "New York Fashion Week," "NYFW," and in the case of WME-IBM specifically, "NYFW The Shows," in their promotion and production of the fashion events. In April 2015, WME-IMG also announced that it would be using a new domain name, NYFW.com, as the address for the events and began using NYFW on social media platforms.

The plaintiff, FWI, is a corporation organized under New York law and is in the business of producing fashion shows and selling tickets to consumers and fashion aficionados. Intended to attract a consumer audience, FWI fashion shows position themselves as publicly accessible alternatives to CFDA and WME-IMG fashion events which are restricted to members of the fashion industry and media only. FWI shows are scheduled to coincide with the defendants' semi-annual schedule. FWI only puts on a one-day show during the defendants' week of activities.

FWI was founded in November 2013 by Trisha Paravas. Prior to incorporating FWI, Paravas produced "consumer fashion shows" under a company named "Roche Inc." ("Roche"). In December 2012, Roche successfully applied for and obtained a trademark for the term NEW YORK FASHION SHOWS. From December 2012 to September 2013, Roche produced three fashion shows in total, all under the name "New York Fashion Shows." In November 2013, Paravas renamed Roche "Fashion Week Inc.," and incorporated it under the same name.

On November 14, 2013, FWI applied to trademark the term NEW YORK FASHION WEEK on the Supplemental Register, and the application was granted on July 29, 2014. The trademark is for online entertainment ticket agency services. According to FWI, FWI produced a show under the NEW YORK FASHION WEEK mark in September 2014. In total, FWI produced and sold tickets to two fashion shows under the NEW YORK FASHION WEEK mark—a show in September 2014 and a show in September 2015. While the shows organized under Roche earned no profit, 500 tickets were sold to the September 2014 FWI show and FWI earned a $ 25,000 profit, while the September 2015 show earned $ 30,000, also selling 500 tickets.

In January 2015, CFDA filed a petition to cancel FWI's July 2014 registration for NEW YORK FASHION WEEK. Paravas spoke to CFDA's counsel about collaborating with CFDA shortly after the petition to cancel was filed. FWI subsequently moved to dismiss CFDA's cancellation petition on the grounds that CFDA had failed to prosecute the petition, and the Trademark Trial and Appeal Board granted the motion on February 2, 2016.

In May 2015, after WME-IMG had announced its intention to use NYFW online to promote the CFDA/WME-IMG fashion events, FWI applied for the NYFW mark for its online ticket sales for entertainment and fashion shows. The mark was granted and registered on the Principal Register on December 15, 2015. In August 2015, WME-IMG sent FWI a letter requesting that FWI cease promoting its fashion shows online in a manner that might mislead consumers into thinking they were purchasing tickets to the CFDA/WME-IMG events. In discussions between Paravas and WME-IMG representatives, Paravas offered to transfer FWI's trademarks and sponsors to WME-IMG and threatened litigation, delay, and bad press. WME-IMG declined. FWI subsequently filed trademark applications for the marks NEW YORK FASHION WEEK THE RUNWAY SHOWS, NYFW THE RUNWAY SHOWS, NYFW and NEW YORK FASHION WEEK for organization of fashion shows for entertainment purposes. Applications to register the marks for the organization of fashion shows have not been granted. After CFDA and WME-IMG announced their intention in April 2015, to use NYFW in promoting their events, and after the defendants announced their intention to use "New York Fashion Week" in July 2015, CFDA and WME-IMG organized and produced the September 2015 and February 2016 fashion events. On April 19, 2016 and June 13, 2016, FWI sent cease and desist letters to WME-IMG demanding it cease using the trademarks.

FWI filed this lawsuit on June 28, 2016. At the hearing for the preliminary injunction, CFDA and WME-IMG represented that their next fashion events were scheduled to begin on September 8, 2016. FWI represented that it did not have any fashion shows presently scheduled and that plans to hold an event in February 2017 had been put on indefinite hold after FWI's anticipated sponsors severed ties with FWI. ...

III. ... In this case, FWI's delay in filing suit and in seeking injunctive relief argues strongly against granting the preliminary injunction. The evidence shows that FWI should have been aware of the defendants' competing claim to NEW YORK FASHION WEEK and NYFW long before FWI sought a preliminary injunction in late June 2016. In January 2015, CFDA filed a petition to cancel the NEW YORK FASHION WEEK mark, and the petition included CFDA's representation that *it* had made continuous use of the trademark since at least 1994. In April 2015, WME-IMG announced that it would be using NYFW as part of its domain name and on social media platforms. Moreover, in August 2015, the plaintiff was on notice that WME-IMG and CFDA would be unveiling a new logo for their events using "New York Fashion Week" and NYFW. In fact, in its papers in support of its motion for a TRO, the plaintiff included a news article from January 2015, reporting that the defendants' event in September 2015 would be called "New York Fashion Week."

FWI claims that it did not sue the defendants because it was investigating possible infringement. Beginning in August 2015 and through September 2015, WME-IMG and FWI engaged in discussions over FWI's ticket sales and the possibility of consumers making a false association between FWI and WME-IMG's products. According to Paravas, she was waiting to see what WME-IMG would do in the fall of 2015 and in early 2016.

To the extent that the plaintiff argues that its delay in requesting a preliminary injunction was caused by the fact FWI was engaging in settlement discussions with WME-IMG about WME-IMG's branding, the plaintiff has not adduced any evidence that WME-IMG suggested it would revert back to a sponsor-based title for its events. In light of the very public announcement of WME-IMG's use of "New York Fashion Week," at least by August 2015, the plaintiff's belief that WME-IMG would reverse course was unreasonable. The plaintiff certainly knew after the shows in September 2015 and February 2016 that CFDA and WME-IMG were using the marks it claimed a right to use, but FWI continued to do nothing.

The plaintiff argues that settlement discussions with WME-IMG continued through January 2016, but FWI has not provided any credible factual evidence to support this assertion. Moreover, even taking as true the plaintiff's story that settlement discussions only ended in January 2016, the alleged lapse between settlement discussions ending in January 2016 and the filing of the preliminary injunction in late June 2016 is completely unexplained. This six-month delay is wholly unaccounted for and further counsels against a finding of irreparable injury. ...

FWI argues that although it was aware that the defendants were using "New York Fashion Week" and NYFW for their September 2015 events, FWI was unaffected by this branding until after August 2015 and that the time for FWI to address the defendants' infringement ripened in April 2016. The plaintiff relies on the doctrine of progressive encroachment which "focuses the court's attention on the question of whether defendant, after beginning its use of the mark, redirected its business so that it more squarely competed with plaintiff and thereby increased the likelihood of public confusion of the marks." ... As CFDA points out however, FWI cites no cases extending the doctrine of progressive encroachment to justify a preliminary injunction.

Because FWI unduly delayed seeking relief for at least twelve months, and for as many as eighteen months, after becoming aware that the defendants were using the major marks FWI claims, the urgency necessary to enter a preliminary injunction pending a decision on FWI's claims does not exist. ...

Moreover, FWI has also failed to show actual irreparable harm. "Irreparable harm exists in a trademark case when the party seeking the injunction shows that it will lose control over the reputation of its trademark ... because loss of control over one's reputation is neither calculable nor precisely compensable." ... FWI argues that it has and will continue to suffer the loss of good will. But FWI has not provided sufficient evidence of its goodwill in the industry. According to FWI, it produced two fashion shows in 2014 and 2015 after registering the NEW YORK FASHION WEEK mark in July 2014. FWI only presented evidence it used the mark in connection with the September 2015 fashion show. FWI used a different name for the September 2014 fashion show. FWI also did not submit evidence of brand loyalty or recognition in the industry. ...

Moreover, FWI's motion for a preliminary injunction should be denied because FWI has not demonstrated either a likelihood of success on the merits of its claim or sufficiently serious questions going to the merits of its claims plus a balance of hardships tipping in its favor.

FWI asserts several federal claims. Count One alleges federal trademark dilution in violation of the Trademark Dilution Act, 15 U.S.C. § 1125(c); Count Two alleges unfair competition and false advertising in violation of Section 43(a) of the Lanham Act, 15 U.S.C. § 1125(a)(1)(A) and (B); Count Three alleges trademark infringement under Section 32(1) of the Lanham Act, 15 U.S.C. § 1114(1). FWI also asserts three claims under New York law that overlap with its federal claims.

The Trademark Dilution Act provides that "the owner of a famous mark shall be entitled ... to an injunction against another person's commercial use in commerce of a mark or trade name, if such use begins after the mark has become famous and causes dilution of the distinctive quality of the mark." 15 U.S.C. § 1125(c)(1). Section 43(a) protects both registered and unregistered marks against the use of any symbol or mark that "is likely to cause confusion, or to cause mistake, or to deceive as to the affiliation, connection, or association of such person with another person, or as to the origin, sponsorship, or approval of his or her goods, services, or commercial activities by another person. ..." 15 U.S.C. § 1125(a)(1)(A). Section 32(1) provides protection against the "reproduction, counterfeit, copy, or colorable imitation of a registered mark" where "such use is likely to cause confusion, or to cause mistake, or to deceive. ..." 15 U.S.C. § 1114(1)(a).

Essential to all its claims, FWI bears the burden of showing that it has an exclusive right to the marks and that its marks are entitled to protection. ...

A certificate of registration of a trade or service mark issued by the United States Patent and Trademark Office is "prima facie evidence of the validity of the registered mark and of the registration of the mark, of the registrant's ownership of the mark, and of registrant's exclusive right to use the registered mark in commerce on or in connection with the goods or services specified in the certificate. ..." 15 U.S.C. § 1057(b).

In this case, FWI registered NEW YORK FASHION WEEK on the Supplemental Register and the registration is limited to online entertainment ticket agency services. Like the registration for NEW YORK FASHION WEEK, the registration for NYFW THE RUNWAY SHOWS, approved in May 2016, appears only on the Supplemental Register and is limited to online entertainment ticket agency services. A registration on the Supplemental Register does not enjoy the advantages of 15 U.S.C. § 1057(b). *See* 15 U.S.C. § 1094. For a registration on the Supplemental Register, there is no prima facie evidence of the validity of the registered mark, the registrant's ownership of that mark, and exclusive right to use that mark. The "very presence [of the mark] on the Supplemental Register indicates a preliminary determination that the mark is not distinctive of the applicant's goods." 3 McCarthy on Trademarks and Unfair Competition § 19:36 (4th ed.).

With respect to FWI's other mark, NYFW, FWI argues that because the NYFW mark is registered on the Principal Register, it does enjoy a presumption of validity under § 1057(b). However, the presumption of an exclusive right to use the NYFW mark extends only to the goods noted in that registration certification. ... NYFW may have a presumption of validity with respect to online entertainment ticket agency sales ("for on-line entertainment ticket agency sales"), but NYFW does not enjoy a presumption of validity for use as a mark for the organization of fashion shows.

Because FWI does not have marks registered on the Principal Register for the organization of fashion shows—the area in which FWI seeks to preclude the defendants' use of the marks—FWI must show that NEW YORK FASHION WEEK, NYFW, and NYFW THE RUNWAY SHOWS are either inherently distinctive or have acquired distinctiveness through secondary meaning. ...

The marks at issue in this case are not inherently distinctive because FWI does not contend that the terms NEW YORK FASHION WEEK, NYFW, and NYFW THE RUNWAY SHOWS are suggestive, fanciful, or arbitrary. Indeed the parties appear to agree that the terms are descriptive. Accordingly, FWI's marks are only protectable trademarks if they acquired secondary meaning before the defendants commenced their use of the allegedly infringing marks no later than August 2015.

A mark has acquired secondary meaning if "the primary significance of the term in the minds of the consuming public is not the product but the producer." ... "[S]omeone seeking to establish secondary meaning must show that the purchasing public associates goods designated by a particular mark with but a single—although anonymous—source." ... The following factors help determine whether a mark has acquired secondary meaning "(1) advertising expenditures, (2) consumer studies linking the mark to a source, (3) unsolicited media coverage of the product, (4) sales success, (5) attempts to plagiarize the mark, and, (6) length and exclusivity of the mark's use." *See id.*, at 1222.

FWI has not adduced any evidence showing the typical indicia of secondary meaning, such as consumer surveys, unsolicited media coverage, or advertising expenditures, and can only point to two shows with 500 attendees at each show. The short length of FWI's use of marks also cuts against a finding of secondary meaning. The use of "branding" in the form of place cards, VIP tickets, banners, and giveaway bags, do not show that the minds of the consuming public associated NEW YORK FASHION WEEK, NYFW, or NYFW THE RUNWAY SHOWS with the plaintiff's business. Moreover, FWI cannot rely on past shows and the expenditures associated with past shows under a different mark to make a showing of secondary meaning. ...

With respect to exclusivity of use, FWI concedes that "New York Fashion Week" has "been used as a general descriptor of multiple fashion events taking place bi-annually in New York City" but argues that the defendants' alternative branding campaigns only began in August 2015.

FWI argues that consumer confusion shows that FWI's marks had achieved secondary meaning in the marketplace. FWI argues that people emailed FWI, asking to purchase tickets to the CFDA/WME-IMG events, and that this confusion shows that FWI is prejudiced by CFDA/WME-IMG's alleged infringing use of FWI's marks. This evidence undercuts FWI's attempts to show secondary meaning. Based on the evidence on the record before this Court, it is the defendants, not the plaintiff, who are likely to show that when faced with an advertisement for tickets to "New York Fashion Week" consumers associated that term with the defendants.

The defendants contend that FWI did not make exclusive use of the mark, and that in fact, CFDA and WME-IMG, and their predecessors made prior use of the asserted marks in connection with their promotion and organization of fashion events over the last two decades. Although it is clear that the formal name given to CFDA/WME-IMG's fashion events varied from year to year based on the sponsor associated with a given year's event, the evidence of the defendants' prior use and identification with "New York Fashion Week" undercuts FWI's claim to the NEW YORK FASHION WEEK mark. Indeed there is no persuasive evidence that the purchasing public associates the plaintiff, which runs one consumer-oriented fashion show on one day during the series of events that constitute New York Fashion Week, with the organizer of New York Fashion Week or with the organization that actually puts on the shows that make up New York Fashion Week.

Moreover, the use of sponsorship branding does not negate the defendants' right to use "New York Fashion Week" and the claim to protectable rights arising from that use. ... The defendants make a persuasive argument that the terms "New York Fashion Week" and NYFW have been associated with them and not with the plaintiff who has attempted to cash in on the decades of publicity for New York Fashion Week that the plaintiff had nothing to do with.

The timeline of FWI's trademark applications and registrations is also significant. The registration for NEW YORK FASHION WEEK in July 2014 was only on the Supplemental Register and came long after the term was generally associated with the defendants. FWI filed its application for the NYFW trademark *after* WME-IMG announced it would be using NYFW on its website and invited readers to the new NYFW.com website. Similarly, FWI filed an application for NYFW THE RUNWAY SHOWS after WME-IMG used the mark NYFW: THE SHOWS.

FWI cannot show secondary meaning based solely on trademark registrations for limited use, particularly in light of the defendants' apparent superior rights to the marks.

Based on the extensive evidence in the form of affidavits of industry professionals, media coverage, and the plaintiff's own evidence of alleged confusion in the marketplace showing the strong association between the marks and the defendants, it is clear that the public strongly associates "New York Fashion Week" with the events organized by CFDA and produced by WME-IMG.

At this stage in the litigation, it is FWI's burden to show it has protectable trademark rights in NEW YORK FASHION WEEK, NYFW, and NYFW THE RUNWAY SHOWS. Based on the available evidence, the plaintiff has failed to satisfy its burden to show that the consuming public and the fashion industry associate the marks in this case with FWI. Accordingly, FWI has failed to make the requisite showing necessary to prove that FWI has a protectable trademark, making it impossible to conclude that FWI has a likelihood of success on its trademark infringement and dilution claims. FWI argues that its marks have acquired high levels of consumer recognition and are strong signifiers of FWI and its consumer-oriented fashion shows. But the evidence shows that FWI produced at most two shows while using the trademark NEW YORK FASHION WEEK, and has produced no shows since registering NYFW in December 2015. FWI appears to have some trademark rights—limited ones—in online entertainment tickets sales, but seeks to enforce those rights to preclude the use of the trademarks in the broad ambit of organizing and producing fashion shows.

The balance of the equities and the public interest also argue against granting a preliminary injunction in this case. The equities tip in favor of the defendants who would be seriously impacted if they were enjoined from using terms that in the fashion industry, are synonymous with the events and activities CFDA and WME-IMG expend so many resources to organize and promote. Moreover, the public interest argues against an injunction because the defendants' New York Fashion Week is an important asset to the New York economy, employs many people, useful for the promotion of New York's fashion industry and a bar on using them would present a serious disruption to the defendants' upcoming events.

Accordingly, FWI's motion for a preliminary injunction is denied.

Figure 25 A snapshot of one of the fashion shows organized by IMG in the course of the NYFW.

CHAPTER 2

Appropriation of Knowledge and Creativity in Textiles and Fashion

§ 2.01 THE CITY OF BORDEAUX GRANTS AN INDUSTRIAL PRIVILEGE TO A CLOTHMAKER—1236

In 1236, Henry III, of England, confirmed an industrial privilege that the city of Bordeaux had granted two years earlier to Bonafusus de Sancta Columba. Like all privileges of that kind that were granted between the thirteenth and the eighteenth centuries, this one was basically an administrative license for Bonafusus to carry out his manufacture and trade. By contrast with modern patents, which provide primarily for a right to exclude—and never a right to use, because this right results from today's laws on economic freedom—industrial privileges were essentially the grant of a right to use. This explains the specific language of the privilege, which consisted of "a licence by Galcelinus' Columb', the mayor, and the jurats of the commune of Bordeaux, for the said Bonafusus."

Moreover, this early industrial privilege corresponds to what later would become an administrative practice among those countries and territories that sought to expand their economy by importing skilled workers who could contribute to the establishment of new industries. Those early privileges, unlike modern patents, were granted in respect of general knowledge of a certain technological field, rather than in respect of a specific invention or improvement. There were exceptions to this rule, but those were very rare. Only in the fifteenth century would European governments start targeting specific technical advancements through industrial privileges.

Those readers who are familiar with today's patent system will be surprised with one of the main features of industrial privileges, such as Bonafusus's: they did not describe the technology of which the beneficiaries claimed to be in possession. Actually, until the modern patent system emerged in the eighteenth century when British courts imposed new legal patentability requirements (such as disclosure, which was deemed a component of the social contract between inventors and society), industrial privileges were not supposed to convey technical knowledge. Indeed, many privileges were even granted for trade secrets. The reason was that, in that period, technology transfer occurred through personal contact (or, eventually, through emulation, when technology was visible and did not need to be supplemented with the communication of know-how—it seems this has taken place with fundamental inventions, such as the windmill, the knowledge of which has migrated from Persia to Europe, and the stirrup, of which the Europeans have learned from the Arabs). Until the Scientific Revolution of the seventeenth century, inventors would not even be capable of describing their ideas in writing. Today, although the practice does not always correspond to the theory, patents realize the transfer of technology by themselves, through the enabling disclosure mechanism.

Apparently, Bonafusus and his family have made good use of this privilege, his name having climbed from the status of an artisan to that of city counselor and magistrate. Indeed, the name of Bonafusus de Sancta Columba (probably referring to a son or grandson of the patentee) appears as a "jurat" (magistrate) of the city of Bordeaux in a document reflecting the oath of loyalty to the French king Philippe the Beau, on May 22, 1293.

March 2, 1236

Inspeximus and confirmation to Bonafusus de Sancta Columba, citizen of Bordeaux, of letters patent to him, sealed with the common seal of Bordeaux, dated 1234, 2 Kal.

April by P. Calhu, the mayor, and the jurats of the commune of Bordeaux, being a ridimus of a licence by Galcelinus' Columb', the mayor, and the jurats of the commune of Bordeaux, for the said Bonafusus, granted in the presence of the said mayor and jurats, and of the consuls of that city; to make cloths of Bordeaux, for fifteen years, to wit, for him and such of his fellows as he shall see fit to join with him on the following conditions:—it shall be lawful for him and his fellows to be (*evenire*) weavers, engage fullers, dyers and other workers of woollen cloths, and make cloths of divers colours after the manner of the Flemings, the French or the English, and for him only and his fellows. Any women, however, may spin and prepare wool in any other way without requiring licence from them. Grant also that wool or dye or any apparatus necessary for making colours of cloth or cloths, borne to Bordeaux within the said term, shall be bought by him and his fellows only, so that no one may buy the same unless he be of them or obtain their licence. Grant especially to him and his fellows, that they may use any plates, stone courtyards (*atriis litiis*), enclosure within the walls and other common pastures (*paduentiis*) of the city of Bordeaux freely and quietly, for making, drying, stretching or in other ways preparing cloth, on condition, however, that houses, roofs or other lasting impediments be not made in the above mentioned places, nor water kept back from its course or diverted, except by the will of the mayor and jurats and only with respect to the pastures and waters of the town of Bordeaux or within the banlieu. At the expiration of the term of fifteen years, anyone is to be at liberty to make any and as many clothes as they please, and the said Bonafusus and his fellows are to have no advantage in any of the above particulars.

Figure 26 Map of Bordeaux in 1229, by Gustave Chariol, engraver. 1862.

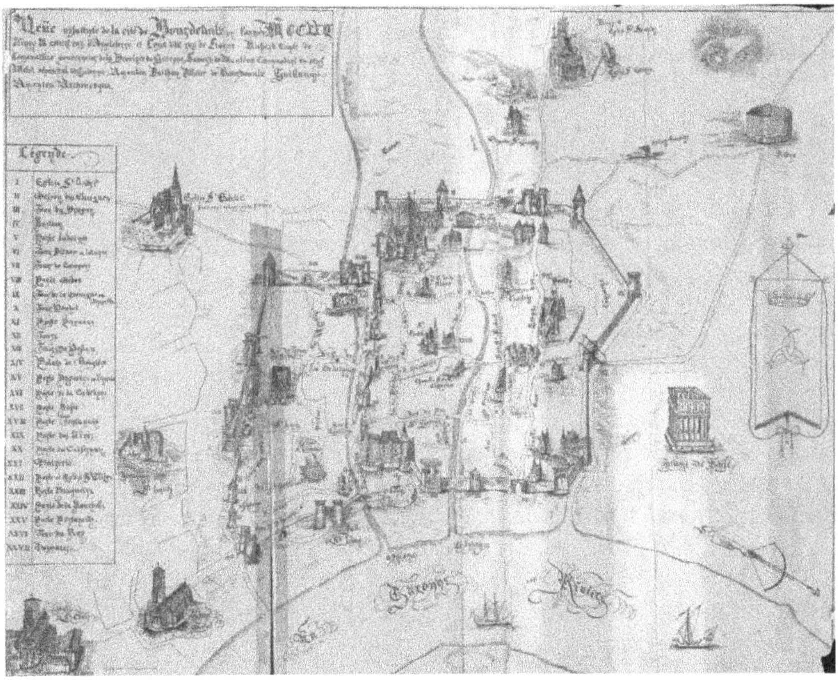

§ 2.02 ENGLAND INAUGURATES A SYSTEM OF INDUSTRIAL PRIVILEGES TO LURE FOREIGN CLOTHMAKERS—1331

The Commercial Revolution, in the eleventh and twelfth centuries, benefited some regions of Europe more than others—Italy and Flanders being the first winners. The economic imbalances that resulted from the different speeds of countries' economic growth have persuaded a number of national leaders to introduce measures so as to lure foreign skilled artisans to their realms in order to open new fronts of industrial production, thus expanding national tax bases. In the fourteenth century, England took the first measures aiming at establishing manufactures of wool cloth, which would allow the country to exploit the raw materials it had in abundance and that it exported to Continental Europe. The text that follows is the first industrial privilege with a broad application (it was granted to John Kempe, but it promises equal favors to other artisans) that encouraged the immigration of skilled foreign artisans.

The king to all bailiffs, etc., to whom these letters may come, greeting. Know that, whereas John Kempe, of Flanders, weaver of woollen cloths, has come to dwell within our realm of England for the sake of exercising his craft therein and of instructing and informing those who wish to learn the same, and has brought with him certain men and servants and apprentices of that craft:

We take this John, his men, servants, and apprentices aforesaid, together with all their goods and chattels, into our protection, and we promise to other men of that craft, as well as to dyers and fullers, wishing to come from across the sea to dwell within our kingdom for the same cause, that similar letters shall be granted.

Witness the king, at Lincoln, the 28th day of July 1331.

§ 2.03 THE CLOTH ACT—1337

In 1331, England had already granted an industrial privilege to a foreign artisan with the general purpose of importing a new industry to the country—that of wool cloth manufacturing. That privilege (see § 2.02) included a promise of similar privileges to all artisans in the same circumstances. Six years later Edward III moved that promise further and included it in a statute, The Cloth Act (11 Edw. 3, c. 2), thus overcoming the resistance that London-based clothmakers had offered against the 1331 privilege.

The Cloth Act also included sumptuary rules, i.e., rules prohibiting the use of some garments by certain social classes. As explained in the Introduction, to the extent that the sumptuary laws corresponded to a pre-established pattern of dressing, they can be seen as one of the factors that contributed to the resistance against the lower classes' adhering to fashionable trends. So, if the Cloth Act was an important instrument in the promotion of the English textile industry, it was at the same time a tool against the early rising of fashion. This phenomenon existed, of course, as it has always existed, but it was strictly circumscribed to the highest social classes.

Item, It is accorded, That all the Cloth-works of strange Lands, of whatsoever country they be, which will come into England, Ireland, Wales and Scotland, within the King's Power, shall come safely and surely, and shall be in the King's protection and safe Conduct, to dwell in the same Lands, choosing where they will; and to the Intent the said Cloth-workers shall have the greater Will to come and dwell here, our Sovereign Lord the King will grant them Franchises, as many and such as may suffice them.

§ 2.04 EDWARD III GRANTS ANOTHER PRIVILEGE TO A FLEMISH CLOTHMAKER—1343

Making good his word given in the Cloth Act, Edward III granted several privileges to foreign clothmakers, mainly to those from Flanders, whose knowledge and skills in the making of woollen cloths was had in great consideration.

August 20, 1343

Protection during pleasure, out of consideration for the king's lieges of Flanders, for John de Bruyn, burgess of Ghent, now making stay in Abydon, making woollen cloth there and trading in other ways within the realm, and his men and servants.

§ 2.05 THE STRUGGLE BETWEEN GUILDS' STRICT STANDARDS AND INNOVATIONS DICTATED BY FASHION—1398

One of the reasons that caused fashion to evolve so slowly in the Middle Ages was the resistance of corporations against accepting innovations both as regards technical methods and as designs. The reason for that resistance was not only the imposition of uniform standards for the sake of ensuring quality but also an issue of competition. The masters of corporations tended to stand against novelty because otherwise they would be obliged to change their own methods and designs.

The following text illustrates a significant moment when tradition in the design of socks was confronted with innovation. Responding to popular demand, some masters of the corporation of manufacturers of socks of Paris had introduced changes in the way of fastening socks, thereby infringing the rules of the community. Upon the prohibition of those changes by older masters, some of those innovative craftsmen appealed to the king, who expressed his agreement to an exception to the old rules but made the final verdict depend on the decision of the Prosecutor at the Châtelet (where court and public notarial services were located). The Prosecutor in ex parte proceedings found for the Plaintiffs, and they were allowed to make socks in accordance with the new fashion.

Letters that authorize the sock makers of Paris to sell socks with *Aiguillettes* or *Lanières*[54]

October 23, 1398

To all those who will see these Letters, Jehan Lord of Folville, Knight, Counselor to the King our Lord and Warden of the Provosts of Paris: Greetings. We make known that we have received the Letters from the King our Lord, obtained and requested on behalf of Girart Megret, Jehan Hardou, Geuffrin Hervieu, Olivier Fouques, Estienne le Goux, Eliot Burgevin, and several other Sock makers of the City of Paris, their Co-applicants in this matter, holders and requesting their endorsement of these, whose content is as follows.

Charles [VI] by the grace of God King of France and Navarre. To the Provost of Paris or to his deputy: Greetings. Girart Megret, Jehan Hardou, Geuffrin Hervieu, Olivier Fouques, Estienne le Goux, Eliot Burgevin, all Sock makers, and several other Sock makers of the City of Paris, co-applicants in this matter, have informed and requested us that, as in the present day and since a short time, several members of the population have become accustomed to garnish Socks by attaching *Aiguillettes* or *Lanières* to them, and to wear those regularly, which in the past was not common; but the usage was to make Socks without any addition, and thus they were fastened with a knot in the front; and because today it is convenient that the said Sock makers, for the comfort of the people, make and sell them with additions ready to fasten, as it is customary today; because if this was not the case, those who would like to buy Socks would need to wait for a long time for the Socks to be garnished; nevertheless, at the instigation of some old workers selling Socks in the said City of Paris, you have forbidden all Sock makers from selling garnished Socks, under the argument that, as said, such [authorization] is

54. *Aiguillettes* or *Lanières* were strips that were sewn to the socks with the double purpose of ornamenting and permitting to fasten them to the doublet. *See* Figure 27.

not contained in the old Registers; and because it may well be that at present this has become the pleasure of the people and of common use, it is expedient that it be done, and each [artisan] who knows it and knows better than other people how to do it, and it is not repelled by the ancient custom, because it was not used, as said; and people who can assess whether there is falsehood, as in Cloths, may order [garnished Socks], as the supplicants affirm, requesting our provision on this; That is why, these things considered, and wishing that everyone earns his living lawfully, We instruct and order that this matter be submitted to our Prosecutor at the Châtelet of Paris, and to others who for this may be called, and if it appears to you that it is in the profit of the public interest that the said Socks be sold thus garnished, as said, you the Applicants and each one of you may make, permit and let make and sell the said Socks fully garnished and other Socks in our said city of Paris; and in the event of challenge or opposition among the Parties, hereby heard, good and brief delivery of Justice [be done], and in such a way that the applicants do not have cause for returning as plaintiffs before Us in our Court. Because it pleases Us that it be done; and We have granted and grant them, by special grace, the present letters; notwithstanding any Ordinances enacted or to be enacted contrary to this. Given in Paris, the xxiiith day of October, the year of grace thousand CCC IIII^{xx} and eighteen, and of our Reign the XIXth. Thus signed. By the King.

Seen these Royal letters above reproduced, for the causes and considerations contained and declared therein, and in the presence of the Prosecutor of the King our Lord, at the Châtelet of Paris, for this present in Judgment before Us, who had advice and deliberation on the content of the said letters, to the Attorneys of the King our Lord, at the Châtelet, will not contradict or prevent the endorsement of the said Letters; and moreover after the reading of these Letters has been done in the Court and Audience of the said Châtelet, in the presence of several Lawyers and Prosecutors, and other assistants in the Court of Châtelet, by their opinion, we have said and say that these Letters will be executed; and in ratifying them, we have ordered and order that the above named Sock makers and their co-applicants, experts and practitioners of said trade, for the present time and until otherwise ordered, may make and sell Socks fully garnished and others, in the City of Paris, according to what the King our Lord has granted by the said Letters; notwithstanding the old Ordinances to the contrary. In testimony of which We had caused the Seal of the Provost of Paris to be put on these Letters. This was done in Judgment at the said Châtelet, in the presence of the said Prosecutor on the one hand, and the above-named Sock makers on the other hand, on Tuesday vth day of November, the year of grace one thousand ccc iiii^{xx} and eighteen.

Figure 27 Portrait of a nobleman wearing socks garnished with aiguillettes. Painting on canvas, 1598.

§ 2.06 SIENA GRANTS AN INDUSTRIAL PRIVILEGE TO A FLEMISH CLOTHMAKER—1438, 1439

Interested in promoting the establishment of the tapestry industry, the Italian city of Siena has taken the same approach as England and granted a number of industrial privileges to foreign skilled clothmakers who accepted to migrate to and reside in the city. The texts that follow concern an industrial privilege granted to Flemish carpet maker Rinaldo di Gualtieri. Besides setting and operating the looms, Rinaldo took the commitment of teaching his craft to whoever was interested in learning it. The privilege was granted in 1438, for a two-year term. One year later, the master asked for a ten-year extension (but got a six-year extension only).

Several other Italian cities resorted to the granting of similar privileges, with the same purpose. Soon, Italian cities would be in competition with each other in the making of tapestries with wool and silk, and fine cloths.

§ 2.06.1 Rinaldo Di Gualtieri Obtains a Privilege for Two Years—1438

November 19, 1438.

Petition of Rinaldo di Gualtieri, Flemish, master of tapestry

Before you, magnificent and powerful lords and Priors and Leaders of the People of the city of Siena, he exposes with all due reverence.

Rinaldo di Gualtieri of the Low Lands, master of tapestry, who happens to be in this city of yours, and who left his home for the bad times he passed there, would gladly settle in your city and work in the said trade and teach the profession to those who wanted to learn And because he is poor, this could not be done without the subsidy and help of Y[our] N[oble] L[ordship], with what he can sustain his life. For that reason he asks Y.N.L. that you please to solemnly provide and order, on your opportune advice, that some provision be granted to him as Y.N.L. pleases and for the period that also may please Your N.L.: and he accepts the obligation to teach the said mystery to two or more apprentices, who may wish to learn it, and as it will be determined by Y.N.L. And anything that will be provided and decided will be held as the very unique grace of Y.L., whom the Almighty deign to preserve in perpetuity.

[In Latin] Year of the Lord MCCCCXXXVIII, on the second day of November. The petition having been read—and the favor must be granted, on the advice of Chamberlain Bicherne, Senator—with twenty looms—for the two coming years—and [the obligation] to teach his art to three or four apprentices.

§ 2.06.2 Gualtieri's Privilege Is Extended for an Additional Six-Year Term—1339

Petition of Rinaldo di Gualtieri, Flemish, master of tapestry.

Before you, magnificent and powerful lord Governors of the Commune and Leaders of the People of the magnificent city of Siena.

The poor, mean, and miserable, and devoted servant of Y.N.L., Rinaldo di Gualtieri of the Low Lands, master of the Low Lands, master of upholstery and tapestry, humbly says to Y.N.L. that he has been in your city for about two years, and thus he has become indebted for the reason that in this magnificent city of yours there has been no person other than him who has done similar articles, who has already done several upholsteries and tapestries, and is at present doing beautiful works and is even more requested by several citizens. And those cloths that beforehand were imported now are made in Siena for this short period; so that your magnificent city may be seen to be endowed with such a beautiful and honored mystery. Which mystery I want to oblige myself to teach to any person, be him a child or an adult; that I have already been requested by several people, to teach them. And because I realize that teaching for six months, or one year, is the same as nothing; because this mystery cannot be learned in such a short time; and I can follow the art and teach every person who wants to learn it to perfection; I supplicate Y.N.L. that for the honor of Y.N. city you deign, on your opportune advice, to provide and order, for the sake of God and for great charity you will provide me for ten years, as it pleases Y.N.L.: whatever you decide to give me, I accept it as great charity, receiving and acknowledging in grace what by Y.N.L. and your council will be decided; praying to God that He keeps you happy, in accordance with your wishes.

> [In Latin] Read and approved the said petition—and decided to submit it to the General Council with limitations—and Rinaldo shall have from the Municipality of Siena twenty gold pieces per season, for six years—and he shall maintain over that time at least two citizens to whom he will teach the craft—and he will teach the art to all the other citizens who want to learn it, without any [additional] salary.

§ 2.07 SIENA OFFERS PRIVILEGES TO ALL SILK WORKERS WILLING TO SETTLE IN THE CITY AND INVEST IN THE INDUSTRY—1439

Following a policy that was very common to the States that wished to introduce a new or expand an existing industry without having to wait for their own artisans to learn the techniques and assume the risks of investing, the city of Siena—as England had made one century earlier, as regards the wool industry, as seen above (§ 2.03)—passed a statute promising privileges to all foreign craftsmen who were willing to immigrate to the city and set new looms for the manufacture of silk cloth. The promises did not include exclusivity in the making of the techniques, because the statute did not concern new inventions, but it provided for two of the main components of medieval industrial privileges: a permission to use the techniques in question and financial subsidies to encourage the investment.

Privileges granted to everyone who works in the silk industry in Siena

September 25, 1439

> First, taking into consideration the fact that the industry of silk is an honorable thing, and brings great convenience and utility in the cities where it has grown (and this can be seen by experience from the little that has been done in our city until now), and it seems an honorable thing and very useful to support, that the said industry of silk may grow and expand; in order to induce and encourage to that effect, it is determined and ordered that it be, for any person of any degree or condition, lawful and permitted to work and practice freely in the city of Siena, without any opposition, the said industry of silk, enjoying all the benefits and privileges that are granted to those who work in the silk trade; it is declared that those who presently work in that industry and invest in it, shall obtain from the Municipality such provision in the manner that today applies to those who exercise the silk trade; which, although at no expense for the Municipality, it is understood that the benefit that follows is so significant that each citizen is required to put every thought into giving practical execution to the things that are ordered for such purpose.

§ 2.08 ON INDUSTRIAL ESPIONAGE, SABOTAGE, AND DUMPING BY FLORENCE, AGAINST THE SILK INDUSTRY OF SIENA—1440

In the Middle Ages and Renaissance, competition among States as regards the establishment and growth of textile industries could be fierce—industrial privileges with the purpose of luring foreign skilled workers being just one of the instruments used in that competition. The following text is an example of Florence's resorting to sabotage and dumping in order to disrupt the then Siena's growing silk industry. The clothmakers of Siena complained against the attempts by Florence's guild of silk makers and merchants to destroy their business and asked the Priori del Comune (the magistrates of the municipality) to intervene more rigorously to protect it. The main protective measure they requested was the imposition of heavy taxes against cheap (subsidized) imported cloths that competed with those made in Siena. Today, this would be designated as countervailing duties.

Memory presented to the Priors of the Municipality against the Florentines who were trying to divert the art of silk from Siena

October 27, 1440

Before you, magnificent and powerful lords, Lord Priors and Leaders of the People of the city of Siena.

On behalf of your loyal servants Giovanni di Savino and Nello di Francescho and companions of the silk [corporation], it is exposed that since they have begun recently to weave and make silk cloths in Siena, the Florentines have continually engaged in creating obstacles and spoiling this art in your city, as well as luring the workers and masters who work here; and if this were not enough, they have sent [persons] here twice and more to bribe our weavers and other workers; and of this we have been informed by or most faithful friends in Florence, of the instructions [of those persons], as well as of their names and surnames and of their businesses. And when they came, we appealed to your Council, and by order of the Council, they were caught by the hands of the Captain of the Justice, and without any torture or torment confessed that two of them had spoken with our weavers and other workers, and that they had persuaded them under promises of money to, during one night, break and burn all our looms and other buildings, and then flee away, as it can clearly be seen by from the questioning done by the said Captain; and by the said Captain they were sentenced to the payment of money and to imprisonment, but subsequently, as a result of several letters written by the Florentines to your Council, your Council has graciously released and freed them; and then not happy with this, the *Arte de Porta Sancte Marie da Fiorenza*[55] decided to deliver velvet cloths to Siena every six months for fifteen hundred florins maximum, and to accept the corresponding losses, so as to destroy our jobs, and to lead us to mistakenly abandon this profession; and this was told to us by Grassellino, who came from Siena sometime ago, [to whom we paid] six hundred or more florins; and as we interrogated him, he did not deny, and asked us that we did not denounce him to the Council, but we did; and as he heard this, he immediately mounted his horse and went away. And afterwards, seeing that nothing had been done, and unhappy with the aforementioned things, we requested that something be done to save us, because we do not wish to accept to sell all of our silk in whatever looms they are made, and our building and looms, which we use to our great advantage. And still not happy with what has been said, they have done it again, that is, our main loom operator as well as our dyer have gone away together; and it can be said that the profession has lost its head, and for that we are all shocked, and we have great fear that said profession will remain without dignity and with great shame to your Municipality, which by God may cease. And all the aforementioned things can be certified to anyone who wishes, even to show them the safe-conducts issued to the said Florentines, and the

55. The guild of silk makers and merchants in Florence.

promises made to our workers, and which twice have been found under examination by the said Captain, and those safe-conducts sealed with the seal of the mentioned *Arte de Porta de S. Maria de la Seta di Fiorenza.*

Therefore, our magnificent Lords, if these practices aimed at destroying our profession continue, we do not feel able to resist their subtleties; and that is why we humbly appeal to your humanity and wisdom, [and beg] that you please to have your Council providing, because such harm and shame to your Municipality we do not need to stand; reminding with respect your magnificent Lordship, that in order to encourage any person willing to enter this profession, it may please to you that it would be convenient to set on three bridges places for taxing any velvet or cloth [similar to velvet and cloths] made in Siena; that is, any pieces of foreign velvet and cloth entering the city should pay four large coins per measure; certifying that by doing this, it will be the reason that in a few weeks in Siena there will be more than four workshops of the said profession, and to remove the many practices that are continuously carried out by the aforementioned Florentine; and this being provided, it will be also reason for us to hire new masters, and we will not abandon you, praying to God that now and always He will conduct your good deliberations.

§ 2.09 THE MUNICIPALITY OF SIENA LURES ANOTHER FLEMISH TAPESTRY MAKER AND ORDERS THREE CARPETS FROM HIM—1442, 1447

The first of the following texts concerns another industrial privilege granted by the city of Siena to a Flemish carpet maker, Master Giachetto.

The second text concerns a contract that a few years later the municipality of Siena and Master Giachetto signed, under which the latter took the charge of making and weaving three designs into carpets. The agreement provided that only Master Giachetto, and no other, would make the designs. Significantly (in an intellectual property context), after the work was finished, the three designs should remain in the palace—apparently, with the purpose of avoiding their being copied. If this interpretation is correct, this seems to be a very early measure aiming at the protection of original designs against copy.

The three designs may have been based on the fresco by Ambrogio Lorenzetti, a Sienese painter of the fourteenth century, who painted on the walls of a room of the Palazzo Publico of Siena several frescos representing the allegory of the Prince's Good Government (1338-1339). The carpets have been lost.

§ 2.09.1 Agreement Between Master Giachetto di Benedetto and the Municipality of Siena—1442

October 27, 1442

Item; having seen how honorable and useful it would be that the noble exercise of making tapestry be established in our city and that our citizens learned it; and at the present one of the most famous masters of this art, called maestro Giachetto de Arazzo, is here: I provide and order that it be attributed to the magnificent Lords, Captain of the People and Head Masters [of the guilds] the incumbency of accepting and leading the said master Giachetto, for the period of ten years, or less, as they wish, to begin in the calendar of next January; obliging him to hold a workshop, and at least two large looms, and obliging himself to teach how he does the said art to anyone who wants to learn; it being allowed to provide the aforementioned master Giachetto with a salary they will consider reasonable to pay him, not passing the sum of fifty florins for each year, four lire per florin, free of taxes.

Present the said master Giachetto, and voluntarily accepting the obligation to proceed in the manner above described, with the conditions, fees, formalities, and costs above described.

Registered in the Council, City Hall—Johanne Guccii de Bichis and Johanne Angeli Andree, notary of Siena, witnesses.

I Franciscus—Stefani Vannini de Senis—notary—have written it.

§ 2.09.2 The Municipality of Siena Orders Three Carpets from Master Giachetto—1447

September 25, 1447

Excellent Lords and Captain of the People ... together with the masters summoned to the Council, in accordance with the law ... they brought Master Giachetto de Arazzo, and hired him, at the present and for the future, his heirs and successors, for the production and the making, for our Municipality, of three carpets of the quality and perfection according to the terms stated below, as follows:

First, that the said carpets be made by the said Master Giachetto, beautiful, honorable and well ornamented, because the honor of the palace requires that an excellent thing be made, and as such a noble fantasy deserves.

Item, that the three citizens below indicated, citizens of Siena, known as makers and merchants of carpets and cloths, and are knowledgeable about the manner and the form of the design of those carpets, and the beautiful form in which they will be made; that first the design of the middle be made, which is *of the prince's good governance*, and that the prince come in the middle of the carpet; afterwards, that *della pace* be made; and afterwards, *della guerra*. ...

Item that it be understood that Master Giaccheto shall make the histories and the figures from start to finish, like the other works.

Item that all drawings of the figures of those carpets shall be made by the hands of Master Giaccheto, and not of others.

Item that before the designs are woven into the fabric, they shall be approved by the three citizens; and that those designs afterwards remain in the palace.

§ 2.10 PEDRO OF PORTUGAL, REGENT, GRANTS AN INDUSTRIAL PRIVILEGE TO PRINCE HENRY, THE NAVIGATOR, FOR ESTABLISHING A FACTORY OF PASTEL DYE—1445

Besides a visionary who was behind the beginning of the adventure of the Portuguese discoveries, Prince Henry, the Navigator, was also a very successful entrepreneur. This text concerns an industrial privilege that on behalf of his uncle, King Afonso V, the Regent Pedro of Portugal, duke of Coimbra, granted him for his introduction of the devices that permitted the preparation of the pastel dye, a very common dye used in the Middle Ages.

This privilege had two interesting aspects: (i) it was granted for the life of Henry; (ii) it granted Henry the right to charge any fees (or royalties, as we would say today) he wished for permitting the use of his mills, provided, however, he did not charge abusive prices ("and taking the benefit that he wishes, provided it is good, and not otherwise").

August 28, 1445

> We, Dom Afonso, to all who see this letter, make known that Prince Henrique, my very dear and beloved uncle, has told us that seeing that in our kingdom nobody used pastel dye, he had worked in the way of acquiring the device so as to be able to build and use it, asking us to give him our permission for him to facilitate its use for dyeing by whoever he ordered. Having seen his request and wishing to give him grace and mercy, deeming such thing to be of our service and to the benefit of our land, we please and wish and order that he may cause the said pastel dye to be made through all our kingdoms, in whatever cities, and towns, and places he wishes, without any further obstacle or challenge. Verifying how he first has sought this device and also the labor and fatigue that he has endured so as to acquire it, it pleases us that in all days of his life no one can either make or order the said pastel dye, except whoever he wants or commands in any way and condition that he sees fit, and taking the benefit that he wishes, provided it is good, and not otherwise, on penalty that whoever does the contrary and use the said pastel dye without his authorization shall lose the device he makes and the building in which it is found and everything in it. And we order all our agents, judges, justices, officers and people that will see this [letter] in any way whatsoever, that they permit him to do all this, as it is said, and make this letter to be observed and kept without putting any obstacle or challenge to it, and that those who are against it be sure that they will be punished according to what we think they deserve. Given in the city of Coimbra on the 28th day of August, by the authority of Lord Prince Dom Pedro, Regent, and Gonçalo Anes made it in the year of our Lord Jesus Christ, one thousand four hundred and forty-five.

§ 2.11 EDWARD IV AUTHORIZES TWO BRITISH MERCHANTS TO HIRE TWENTY FOREIGN CLOTHIERS KNOWLEDGEABLE IN THE ART OF MAKING CLOTHS NOT KNOWN IN THE COUNTRY—1483

The interesting aspect of this privilege is that it was a very open document in the sense that it did not specify those masters who would receive the king's protection. Supposedly, the two merchants who received the privilege would gain from the introduction of the making and selling of the new cloths. As we will see in the next texts, France would also grant special favors to foreign workers who would bring new manners of making cloths, as an encouragement for the importation of technology.

February 27, 1483

> Grant to John de Salvo and Anthony Spynule, denizens, and their attorneys of licence to bring into the realm from any part of the world masters to the number of twenty or thereabouts to make and dye cloths of another fashion to those now

made in the realm, so that the king's subjects may be able to learn the art; and grant to the masters of protection.

§ 2.12 INDUSTRIAL PRIVILEGES CONCERNING THE TEXTILE INDUSTRY GRANTED BY THE SENATE OF VENICE, UNDER THE STATUTE OF 1474—1497 ONWARDS

On January 19, 1474, the Senate of Venice introduced a statute ("Parte") establishing a mechanism for the granting of industrial privileges.[56] *The statute corresponded to the particular economic circumstances that Venice experienced at that time when its industry had great success and businesses were treated with relative liberalism. The statute was enacted with the purpose of inviting local and foreign inventors to contribute to the expansion of the city's industrial basis. Venice had already granted industrial privileges before the adoption of the statute, but after 1474, a regular flow of new inventions was communicated to the Senate with the aim of obtaining privileges. Two important works analyze and summarily describe the privileges granted to inventors under the* Parte *of 1474: Giulio Mandich,* Venetian Patents (1450-1550), *30 Journal of the Pat. Off. Soc'y 166 (1948), and Roberto Berveglieri,* INVENTORI STRANIERI A VENEZIA *(1474-1788)—*IMPORTAZIONE DI TECNOLOGIA E CIRCOLAZIONE DI TECNICI ARTIGIANI INVENTORI *(IVSLA, 1995).*

The following texts reproduce several privileges granted by the Senate of Venice, under the 1474 statute, for inventions related to textiles. Most of those privileges concerned processes and devices of carding wool, which could be qualified as low-level technology. Indeed, Venice's textile industry, which had thriven in the thirteenth and fourteenth centuries, due to the immigration of skilled Flemish and French artisans, went through a significant decline in the fifteenth and sixteenth centuries. According to historians, the main reason for such decline was the competition with the British industry for export markets combined with some neglect in pursuing innovation. The small number of privileges granted in the field of textiles seems to confirm this.

Of particular significance is the privilege granted in 1627 to three French inventors, who claimed that the fabric they had invented, besides its impermeability against rain, could "also be useful to several women who will have optimal appearance." This was, undoubtedly, about fashion.

> 1497, December 18 (*S[enato] T[erra]* r. 13 p. 26). Frances di Uberti and sons, from Verona want a patent for 10 years for a "new thing" to be used in cloth fulling; acquired from "a certain person from Verona." Granted. ...
>
> 1519, March 1 (*S. T.* reg. 21, p. 6). ... Giovanni Vitturi, a Venetian clothier, lists new types of textiles ("As made in Valencia or Berne; felted and woven cloth of wool in mixed colors like brown, roan or tan, etc.; for all kinds of clothing, notably hat material of French wool, skullcaps for monks, and dark roan materials for fishermen"). He wants a patent for 25 years throughout the territory. Imitation of foreign materials seems to be involved since the employment of foreigners as

56. *See* FROM BABYLON TO THE SILICON VALLEY, *supra* note 1, at 15.

workmen is mentioned. Granted by the Senate but only for 10 years; test required within 1 year. The *Provveditori* certify to the successful test. ...

1531, May 6 (*S. T.* r. 26 p. 131 r.) and July 22 (*ibid.* p. 153 r.). Master Arcangelo Romitan from Vicenza seeks a patent throughout the territory for his "secret for carding cloth of all kinds." Granted by the Senate for 20 years and for Venice only. Later Romitan complaints of the restriction and the patent is extended to the entire territory. ...

1610, April 17 (*S. T.* r. 80 p. 56v-57). Isaac Cohem, Hebrew, merchant from Constantinople, applied to the Doge for a privilege concerning the introduction of the manufacture of *zambelotti* (thick fabric made of wool from the Angora goat) and *mochagiari* (fabric of camel or goat hair, mixed with silk) in Venice, with the same perfection as those made in Angiari (a municipality on the province of Verona). As an exception to the rule that prohibited the Jews from making cloths in Venice, the privilege was granted for a thirty-year term, for the exclusive making and selling of the new fabrics. Offenders would be penalized with imprisonment for three months. The privilege contained a caveat: the license or assignment of the privilege could only be granted in favor of Christians.

1627, January 15 (*S. T.* r. 98, p. 392). Esdras Gallasino, Francesco Noel and Giovanni Budet, French, apply to the Doge for a privilege for a new invention of a type of *baracco* (fabric of wool mixed with other threads, very resistant) made of wool and thread, "which, although light, resists heavy rain and can also be useful to several women who will have optimal appearance." After examining the invention, the Senate granted the privilege for fifteen years. This privilege was later renewed and extended to new fabrics and manners of making certain cloths.

§ 2.13 THE FIRST STATUTE PROVIDING FOR THE PROTECTION OF DESIGNS AGAINST COPYING? BY-LAWS OF THE GUILD OF TAPESTRY WEAVERS OF BRUSSELS—1525

The following text is an excerpt from the by-laws of the guild of carpet makers of Brussels, as approved by the city authorities in 1525. One of its provisions is of great importance from an intellectual property standing: it prohibits workers and apprentices from copying the designs that masters give them to weave into the fabrics. Also interestingly, even when the carpets were made on request—as most of them were, because of their very high price—the purchaser was not allowed to keep a blueprint or copy of the figurative ornaments woven into the carpets; these had to remain with the master who designed them.

By-laws of the guild of tapestry weavers of Brussels

April 24, 1525

It is ordered and provided that from today when new patterns and designs of woollen tapestries, on historical or other motives, are given by the masters to workers and apprentices, for their better understanding of the patterns, those patterns and designs shall not be counterfeited or copied, or punctured, or smeared with coal, and even if the master who has made the first pattern makes a copy, the purchaser has to pay for it but cannot keep the pattern, which shall be returned to that master, and in the case of counterfeit, the counterfeiter shall pay the penalty of fourteen Rhine guilds, one third to the lord, one third to the municipality, and one third to the guild's jurors.

Figure 28 Carpet from Brussels, sixteenth century, made of wool and silk. Metropolitan Museum of Art

§ 2.14 FRANÇOIS I, OF FRANCE, EXTENDS THE PERIOD OF APPRENTICESHIP OF CLOTHMAKING FROM TWO TO THREE YEARS—1531

The introduction of new articles in the line of production of the textile industry increased the technical complexity of the work and required an extended period of apprenticeship. This was in the sixteenth century, when the resistance against novelty was already in recession, as we have seen in the First Chapter. Thus, the following text—an excerpt from the by-laws of the guild of shearers of Paris—reveals that, imperceptibly perhaps, but firmly, consumers' preferences had already started putting pressure on the making and on the designs of cloths. This was still very far from today's fashion, but it was a beginning of a change in the regulation of industry and of work.

Patent letters of François I confirming the by-laws of the cloth shearers and increasing the period of apprenticeship

September 1531

François, by the grace of God, King of France ... because under the aforesaid by-laws and ordinances the apprentices must remain in apprenticeship two years or more, and that presently they are engaged in weaving in the said city fine *estamets, crezés, cadits, cordillats,*[57] fine cloths of England, Carcassonne, Perpignan, fine serges, drapery from Milan, Venice and other cities, and that it is impossible to make apprentices learn about that profession in such a short time of two years, which could result in scandal and reduction of the good prestige, and

57. *Estamets, crezés, cadits, cordillats*: types of small woollen cloths.

fame, and esteem of the said trade, We have been asked, for the sake of the profit and utility of the public good, and taking the new inventions required by the said trade in consideration, to order the aforementioned apprenticeship of two years to be set and ordered to three years ... we order that those who henceforth want to reach the franchise and mastership of the said trade of shearer will be apprentices by the time and space of three years before acquiring the said mastership. Given at Nantouillet, in the month of September, the year of grace one thousand five hundred and thirty one and of our reign the seventeenth.

§ 2.15 A CONTRACT OF APPRENTICESHIP CONTAINING A SECRECY CLAUSE—1535

Apprenticeship was a serious matter under corporations' legal regime. The ultimate value of the organization of medieval labor was providing consumers with articles with good and stable quality. So, the possession of technical skills was a must in such an environment. Generally, the by-laws of the guilds contained detailed provisions on the relations between masters and their apprentices, but private contracts would go into further detail, dealing with the obligations of masters towards the apprentices, namely of feeding them appropriately, dressing them, treating them well, and paying them a salary (frequently that salary would be paid, in the form of a lump sum, to the apprentice's parents), as well as the obligations of the apprentices towards their masters. Eventually, apprenticeship agreements would contain a clause of secrecy, under which the apprentice was obliged not to reveal the technical and financial secrets of his master. This clause, truth be said, was not common, because the guild regime did not encourage commercial or technical rivalry between masters—on the contrary, strict technical standards called for uniformity of methods and products, which did not favor masters' keeping trade secrets from other masters. Anyway, as said, eventually clauses on secrecy might be included in apprenticeship agreements, perhaps motivated by a certain amount of freedom accorded to the masters of a specific guild. This seems to be the case in the following text.

June 8, 1535

In the name of God, it be done, Amen. To all be manifest that, in the year one thousand five hundred and thirty five and on the eighth day of June, in front of me, undersigned notary public and the witnesses hereunder named, existing and personally constituted Symon de Despit, alias Guilhomet, son of honest man Pierre of Despit, the elder, of the jurisdiction of Rochefort, who, in his good, pure and frank will, on behalf of himself and his heirs and any successors, under the license and authority of the mentioned Pierre the Elder, his father, servant, to master Pierre Gobert, cloth maker of the city of Romans, here present on behalf of himself and of his heirs and any successors, stipulating and accepting and Symond as apprentice for learning and practicing the art and craft of cloth making, which the mentioned Gobert uses and that is by the term and period of three continuous years next already begun on the first day of May last and passed, during which, for three years, Symond de Despit, apprentice, will be held liable, up to his power and possibility, for duly and faithfully serving and obeying the master Pierre Gobert, his master, and his family in all lawful and honest things, and not revealing his secrets, escaping and avoiding his injury, treating his profile and honor, and

> Gobert similarly will be required to duly and honestly nourish and treat Symond, apprentice, and, up to his power and faculty, show and teach him the art and craft of cloth making, ... and thus promised and swore the masters Pierre Gobert, Pierre and Symond de Despit, Symond, under license of Peter, his father, and promises, by means of their oaths by them and each of them, touching the scriptures on the holy gospels of God made and ready and under obligation ... and were made and publicly recited the things above said in the city of Romans and in my shop, notary, present Glaude Burel, master Glaude Bonardel, potter of the city of Romans, Glaude Falonnet of Saint John d'Alteveon, Sabastin Julhian of the place of Tein, residents, called as witnesses.
>
> And I, Jehan de Aqua, notary, under the apostolic and public authorities of the city of Romans, on behalf of Master Pierre Gobert undersigned. De Aqua.

§ 2.16 TWO PRIVILEGES GRANTED BY THE MUNICIPALITY OF AMIENS, FRANCE, FOR INVENTIONS IN THE TEXTILE INDUSTRY—1539, 1543

The textile industry being one of the two main economic engines of growth in the Middle Ages—the other being food—naturally, the techniques involving its production excited the ingenuity of industrialists and inventors. Although the invention was not greatly appreciated within the corporations, where the competition of any sorts—including that arising from technical differentiation—was discouraged, in the sixteenth century the textile industry started, as we have seen, to free itself from such sort of constraints. These were privileges different from those that were granted with a certain frequency to lure foreign artisans and bring new industries to the city. These were privileges for genuine inventions (absolutely or relatively new) and their main purpose was raising the competitive standing of the granting cities. Amiens, a city whose prosperity in the Middle Ages heavily depended on the success of its textile industry, granted several privileges in that sense.

The following texts reproduce minutes of meetings of the aldermen of Amiens, in which they decided to grant privileges for inventions. The first privilege did not give rise to exclusivity but provided for a financial reward. Interestingly, the privilege contained a clause that prohibited the inventor from refusing to license his invention (but granting him the right to charge a reasonable fee or royalty).

The second text corresponds to a genuine patent because it grants the exclusive use of a method of calendering satin, claimed by the inventor.

§ 2.16.1 Privilege Granted by the City of Amiens to the Inventor of a Furnace That Could Be Used for Dyeing Cloths and Making Beer—1539

At the meeting of the aldermen of Thursday, April 18, 1539, Hector de Palet or Palot, after having undertaken to produce saltpeter for the city, offers to make furnaces for the brewers and the dyers. It is agreed to give ten *écus* of reward, if this kind of furnace is found to be useful. If the dyers and the brewers want to order the making of similar ones, Hector will be obliged to have those made for them, being reasonably satisfied for the labor.

§ 2.16.2 Privilege Granted by the City of Amiens to the Inventors of a Machine That Reduced the Costs of Satin Calendering—1543

Thursday, March 27 1543.—Pierre Gestin and Robert de la Roche, residing in Amiens, having invented and found the manner of calendering satin without the help and expenses of horses, but with the assistance of one or two men only, request the exclusive privilege of making those machines during four years. The privilege is granted to them for three, and it is permitted that they use four counterweighs that belong to the city so as to load their calendar.

§ 2.17 THE MUNICIPALITY OF LILLE PASSES AN ORDINANCE SETTLING A DISPUTE BETWEEN TWO CATEGORIES OF CLOTHMAKERS—1544

In the context of one of those disputes that were so frequent between different corporations, whose members would fall in the temptation of trespassing into in the areas of work that were exclusively reserved to another corporation, the magistrates of Lille, settling a conflict between the sayeteurs[58] *and the* bourgeteurs[59]*—both categories of wool clothmakers, but with different specialties—enacted an ordinance that, among other provisions, provided for the right to use any new inventions introduced in their industry, depending on their being approved by the council. This provision confirms what was noted above: in the fifteenth and sixteenth centuries, the textile industry became gradually receptive to the introduction of new techniques in the making of cloths. This, of course, placed the corporatist regime into question but corresponded to the new spirit of competition and rivalry that was emerging in the Renaissance and the early Modern Age, with the expansion of trade and industry dictated by the maritime expansion of Europe.*

In 1610 this holding would be clarified and partly modified, because the disputes between the two categories of workers did not cease, given that the bourgeteurs *insisted that they should be entitled to exclusivity in the exploitation of certain inventions concerning the making of cloths (see § 2.26).*

58. *See, supra,* the introductory note to § 1.21.
59. Term exclusive to Lille, which meant workers in the wool industry. It seems that this particular term is explained by the fact that the wool industry was introduced in Lille by artisans who migrated from Bourges, France.

Ordinance settling the dispute between the *sayeteurs* and the *bourgeteurs*, concerning the cloths that each of the two bodies may manufacture

October 14, 1544

> The aldermen and the council of this city have met to put an end to the questions and the disputes described and brought to us, among the masters of the trades of the *sayeteurs* and *bourgeteurs* of this city, concerning the pieces of fabric in the manner of *chambgeans*[60] of a single color of pure *sayette*, which are now made in this city, which each of the said two professions has claimed to have the right to make and that it be prohibited to the other; and also touching the stripes of velvet of pure *sayes* that the said *sayeteurs* claimed were prohibited to the said *bourgeteurs*; and pieces of *chambgeans* with the protuberances or mixtures of gold or silver thread that the said *bourgeteurs* maintained that they should not be made or woven by the said *sayeteurs*. We, upon mature deliberation of the Council, and having the public good of this city into account ... by these present [letters], order and rule by provision and until decided otherwise, and in the manner of a policy, the points and articles that follow: ...
>
> And as to the *chambgeans* of various colors and other cloths woven in the form of *chambgeans* of a single color of pure *sayette*, except the white and the blue, which will remain [exclusive] to the said *sayeteurs*, as stated, and all other works above not specified, as well as those mentioned in particular by the by-laws of the two trades, invented at present or to be invented hereinafter by anyone, will be made by each of the two trades that will see a profit in it, and the *sayeteurs* shall carry their cloths to the office of the *vingtaine*,[61] and the *bourgeteurs*, to the office of the wardens, so that they are inspected there, approved or rejected according to the rules of the offices to which they will be brought; except that if the aforesaid trades or one of them invents any new works of pure *sayette* of one color, after the test made of one piece, it will not be allowed to continue [making them] without first bringing them to the market hall, before us or our legal successors, so that we give authorization to the concerned trades, as it will be decided by the council; prohibiting the said trades and each of them from interfering with each other in the future, on the penalty to those who transgress this ordinance, for each piece and each time that they do the opposite, of a fine of ten gold *carolus* to be applied, a third to the profit of the common fund of the poor of this city, another third to the profit of the office that will order the punishment and correction, and the surplus to the profit of the accuser.

§ 2.18 SEVERAL INDUSTRIAL PRIVILEGES GRANTED BY ELIZABETH I—1561 ONWARDS

Although the name of Elizabeth I, in patent-related literature, is often associated with her refusal to grant a privilege to William Lee, the inventor of the knitting machine (see infra § 2.29), the Queen was a great supporter of the introduction of new technologies to foster the development of the textile industry of England, whose economic and social importance was then growing by the day. Elizabeth I would grant privileges of three sorts: industrial privileges for new inventions, either invented by the grantee or simply

60. Fabric made of pure wool. This is another term from Lille.
61. *See supra* note 14.

imported (the same approach that would later be crystalized by the Statute of Monopolies, of 1623); commercial privileges for the importation and trade of certain cloths, in spite of existing rules contrariwise; and exceptions to various statutes on apprenticeship, permitting certain artisans to engage in the making and selling of certain cloths, in certain places, in spite of their not having exercised the trade for seven years or been apprenticed.

The following texts are just a few examples of the many industrial privileges of the first sort pertaining to the textile industry and their raw materials and ingredients. In most of those privileges, the concern with ensuring that imported technology be taught to local artisans is noteworthy.

§ 2.18.1 Privileged Granted to Several Dutch Clothmakers—1561

December 24, 1561

Licence for Francis Boll, Garret Matte, Peter Aell, John Hussucke, William de Husseer and Francis de Rade and such others to the number in all of 25 Dutchmen, aliens born, not denizens, belonging to the Dutch church of aliens in London, as shall be signified by the archbishop of Canterbury, diocesan of Sandwich, the bishop of London and the warden of the Cinque Ports under their seals to the mayor, jurats and commonalty of Sandwich, co. Kent, to settle in the town and port of Sandwich, in the following terms,—licence for the mayor, jurats and commonalty to permit the said Dutchmen to reside there with their servants and families, Dutch or English, to lease tenements there to them for seven years or less as to the queen's subjects born in England, and, if any of the Dutchmen shall die or leave the town, to admit such others in their place as shall be signified as above by the said archbishop, bishop and warden; licence for the said Dutchmen with their servants not exceeding the number of twelve in each family and not exceeding the number of 25 households in all at any one time to live in Sandwich for the exercising only of the trades of making says, bay and such other cloth or tapestry as has not been accustomed to be made in England or sea fishing; notwithstanding stat. 1 Rich. Ill or stat. 32 Hen. VIII; the licence to continue until revoked by another patent directed to the mayor, jurats and commonalty. For the help, repair and amendment of the said town and port by planting in the same men of knowledge in sundry handicrafts and for the relief and convenient placing of the said Dutchmen being very skilful there.

§ 2.18.2 Privilege Granted to the Inventors of a Method of Obtaining Oil to Be Used in the Cloth Industry, Including the Right to Plant and Sow Plants Used in the Making of Such Oil—1565

January 29, 1565. Licence for thirty years for Armigill Wade and William Herlle to make sulphur and oil in the manner discovered by them and to enjoy the whole benefit thereof; from Pentecost next; no others to use the said art now invented or introduced by them without licence of the licensees under pain of imprisonment for a year without bail or mainprise and forfeiture of 20*l*. for each offence (one moiety to go to the Crown and the other to the licensees); power to dig, search, plant or sow on any ground throughout the Queen's dominions for this purpose, provided that they first compound with the occupiers thereof; where controversy arises it shall be decided according to the custom of the country and the law of the realm by three Justices of the Peace of the district, and, if they cannot decide, the cause of contention shall be referred to the Council. Wade and Herlle have by their great industry and no small expense discovered a way of making sulphur in the Queen's dominions and of planting or sowing certain plants in suitable places from which oil may be pressed very necessary for the cloth and wool of the realm.

§ 2.18.3 Privilege Promised to All Persons, Either Foreigners or British, to Be Appointed by the Municipality of Coventry, for the Making of Certain Cloths of *Great Estimation in Foreign Realms* and Unavailable in England—1568

March 22, 1568. Licence during pleasure for the Mayor, Bailiffs and Commonalty of the City of Coventry, and all persons, strangers as well as Englishmen and denizens, which shall be appointed thereto by the Mayor with the assent of a majority of the Aldermen of Coventry, to make cloths like those made in Armentyers, whereof one sort is called "ulterfynes" and the other "cromple lystes," made in pieces about 22 1/2 yards long and 1 5/8 yards wide (so varying in length and otherwise from the cloths usually made in England), in the said City and the liberties thereof, to work, dress and dye them there, and to sell them throughout England. Also—that the cloths may be perfectly made and thereby grow to be of greater estimation in foreign realms—power for the Mayor, with the assent of a majority of the Aldermen, to make and enforce ordinances for the making of the cloths and the government of those concerned therein; so that it be not to the prejudice of the royal prerogative or the damage of the Crown or of the City or realm. Also licence for the Mayor, Bailiffs and Commonalty and known merchants born in the Queen's obedience, and their servants, factors and attorneys likewise born in the Queen's obedience, to export, in ships of English ownership, from the Ports from which other cloths are usually shipped, to any parts to which other cloths might heretofore lawfully be shipped, the said cloths made, wrought, dressed and dyed in the said City and the liberties thereof and fulled there or within 15 miles of the City, paying only 4*s.* 8*d.* on every cloth; also for every 19 cloths wrought, dressed and dyed and so exported, to export one cloth of the same sort wrought and dressed but not dyed. No others to make such cloths until the Queen shall by patent signify her pleasure to the contrary, on pain of imprisonment and fine.

The said cloths are, chiefly for the perfect and true making thereof, greatly esteemed in foreign countries to the great benefit of Armentyers and Flanders, and the Queen is persuaded that there can be no remedy more natural for the relief of Coventry, fallen of late with other towns of England to great decay, than some specially profitable trade of cloth making.

§ 2.18.4 Privilege Granted to a Spanish for an Imported Method of Dyeing Cloths—1568

November 10, 1568. Licence for seven years for Peter de la Croce, born at Lysle in Flanders, Spanish subject, to exercise the art of making a stuff, mixture or composition called "cendre de Namours" and to sell the same; from the present date; provided that the dyers of London be served with as much as they shall require and at prices less than they paid for the stuff when imported from Flanders, and the remainder to be sold to other dyers, subjects of the Queen, at prices fixed by the Privy Council; no others to exercise the art of sell the stuff without consent of the licensee, on pain of forfeiture of 100*l.* for every offence and the stuff so made or sold (one moiety to be to the use of the Crown and the other to the use of the licensee), besides the danger of the Queen's further displeasure. He has offered to make "cendre de Namours" with stuff grown in the realm or otherwise to make it in the realm; it is useful for setting woad, whereby the woad when used for dying cloth will make a better and surer colour and at less cost than usual, and it will be as good as any imported from Flanders; he offers to sell it to the dyers of London and others better and cheaper than they can obtain elsewhere.

§ 2.18.5 Privilege Granted to the Introducer of a Method of Making Certain Cloths in the Manner of Holland—1569

May 26, 1569. Licence for 21 years for John Hastinges, the Queen's Servant, to make in any of the Queen's dominions and sell woollen cloth called "frezead-owes," as made in Harlem, Leyde, Rotterdam, Amsterdam or Dirgowd in Holland or elsewhere overseas; from the present date; duties to be paid; power to make ordinances for making the cloth and for the government of aliens and others making it, so that they tend not to the prejudice of the Queen's prerogative or to her loss; no others without his licence to make it under pain of forfeiture of the cloth made and 100*l.* (one half to go to the Crown and the other to the licensee), besides such punishment as the Queen or Privy Council shall think fit. Hastinges has introduced the making of the said cloth, which contains in length, the double piece, 24 yards and, the single piece, 12 yards and in breadth 1 3/4 yards.

§ 2.18.6 Privilege for the Introduction of Imported Techniques Concerning the Making of Cloths and Earthenware—1570

June 16, 1570. Licence for 21 years for Richard Bartye of Grymsthorpe, co. Lincoln, Thomas Cecill of Burghley, co. Northampton, Edmund Hall of Gretford, co. Lincoln, and Francis Harrington to exercise in the counties of Lincoln and Northampton and in the "nasse" of Peterborough, co. Northampton, the arts of (1) making, dressing, dyeing and perfecting woollen cloths or kerseys usually made in Amersfort, Naerden, Hoirne, Weerdt, Oysterwicke, Malines, Breda and Delft and all sorts of cloths made overseas which any person is authorised by patent to make in the Queen's dominions but the making of which has been discontinued, (2) planting and dressing madder after the manner of Almayne and Netherland, (3) baking earthen vessels and other earthen works with colours or "purtraictes" after the manner of Turkey, Italy, Spain and Netherland and (4) dressing leather after the manner of Spain and Netherlande both for shoes and other garments and uses; also to buy all necessary materials, and to sell the finished goods to their best profit; saving to the Crown any customs etc. due; power to make rules for the making thereof and for the government of the workmen whether brought from overseas or the Queen's subjects; so that such rules be not prejudicial to the royal prerogative, the Crown or the law; no other persons to exercise the arts under pain of forfeiture of the goods made and £100 (one moiety of such forfeitures to go to the Crown and the other to the licensees) and other punishment at the discretion of the Queen or Privy Council; the patent not to prejudice any former patents of licence to exercise any of the said arts if they be still in force. The art of making cloths for hosing and other garments has lately greatly enriched Amersfert and the other said towns overseas to the decay of the sale of cloth made in the Queen's dominions, and Bartye, Cecill, Hall and Harrington have been attempting at great expense to establish the said art in the Queen's dominions, and have been procuring stranger workmen skilful in this and the other arts aforesaid.

§ 2.19 AN INDIRECT METHOD OF APPROPRIATION OF TECHNOLOGY: A SPANISH TAILOR WRITES ABOUT CERTAIN TAILORING TECHNIQUES AND OBTAINS A PRIVILEGE FOR THE EXCLUSIVE PRINTING OF HIS BOOK—1589

Historically, not always those in possession of technical knowledge have been keen or able to appropriate it through patents or similar legal mechanisms, such as industrial privileges, or through trade secrets. Sometimes the person did not have access to the official channels that might grant him/her the coveted privilege. Other times the knowledge in question was not of the adequate type to fit those regimes, mainly because it was not unique and unknown. Eventually, what separates the possessor from his rivals is his capacity to organize the knowledge, thus making it easier to be communicated to and absorbed by others. Or, simply, in the impossibility of obtaining a patent, the possessor wishes to extract prestige and reputation, which keeping it as a trade secret could not give him/her, at least in the short run. So, the possessor of such knowledge would write about it, in the expectation of extracting revenue from the rights obtained in the printing, rather than in the knowledge itself. That is, nevertheless, an indirect way of asserting exclusivity in that knowledge.

After the reinvention of the movable printing characters by Johannes Gutenberg, many artisans and inventors resorted to publishing their knowledge, thereby acquiring industrial privileges—the legal mechanism used at that time to protect printed works, in the absence of copyright, which would be introduced later in Venice, in 1544, and in England, in 1710.[62]

The following text is an example of a tailor's indirect appropriation of his technical expertise, through a printing privilege. Juan de Alcega, a master tailor of Madrid, had obtained from the king of Spain, Felipe II, a ten-year privilege for publishing his book with instructions on how to cut and sew a number of garments commonly used at that time by the nobility, the clergy, and common people. Following the legal standard of that time, the privilege meant not only exclusivity but also an administrative permission to publish the book, and a certification that the manuscript had been checked for conformity with political and religious values as well as text quality, and had the price fixed.

The original privilege has been extended for a further term of six years. The following text reproduces the additional grant.

Prior to its publication, the book in question was examined by two tailors—Hernan Gutierrez, tailor of the Princess of Portugal, and Juan Lopez de Burgette, tailor of the Duke of Alba—who "after having seen and examined the book on geometry, design, and

62. *See* From Babylon to the Silicon Valley, *supra* note 1, at 221 and 233.

practice, and after having discussed and conferred in great detail, found that Juan de Alcega had everything well studied and worked." In particular, the two judges deemed that the book "was right and truthful as to the quantity of cloth and silk, in the form and manner that are stated in the mentioned book." The book, therefore, "was very good, useful, and fruitful for the whole of the Republic."

The King,

Because on your behalf, Juan de Alcega, Master of the profession of tailor, it has been reported to us that we had gracefully granted you the privilege for printing a book concerning the said trade, and that the term of ten years is about to expire, begging us to extend the said privilege for another ten years, or whatever as per our mercy. Which has been seen by those of our Council, as well as the said privilege, above mentioned, and it has been agreed that we should grant this letter of ours for that reason, and we have deemed it good. Therefore we extend the privilege that we have given you, so that no one can print and sell the aforementioned book, but you, or the person named by you, for six more years: which will run and be counted from the end and expiry of said term. And we give you license and faculty, so that you, or the person authorized by you, and not anyone else, can cause to print and sell the aforementioned book in all these Kingdoms of Castile, for the time and space of the said next six years; On the penalty that the person or persons who, without having your authorization to do so, print or sell it, or cause it to be printed or sold, lose the printings that they have made, with the corresponding molds and equipment; and moreover on the penalty [of a fine] of fifty thousand *maravedís* each time it is done otherwise. Which penalty, be the third part for the person who accuses him, and the other third part for the judge who convicts him, and the other third part for our chamber and Treasury; Provided that, every time you want to cause the book to be printed, during the said term of six years, you bring it to our Council together with the original [manuscript] in which it has been seen, of which each plan is initialed, and signed at the end by Juan Gallo de Andrada, our chamber man, one of the members of our Council, so that it can be seen if said printing is in accordance with it. And you shall have faith in public form, given that the corrector appointed by us has seen and corrected each one of those books that were printed, and he has fixed the price that you will receive for each volume: on the penalty of incurring the penalties contained in the laws and pragmatics our Kingdoms. And we order those of our Council, and all other magistrates, to keep, and observe, and execute this letter of ours, and everything contained in it. Done in Madrid, on the ninth days of the month of February, one thousand five hundred and eighty-nine years.

I, the King.

By order of the King, our lord, Juan Vazquez.

Figure 29 Left: Cover of the second edition of Libro de Geometria, Pratica, y Traça, el qual trata de lo tocante al oficio de sastre *[Book on Geometry, Practice, and Design, concerning the tailor's profession], printed by Guillermo Douy in Madrid, in 1589. The cover shows Acelga's portrait. Right: one of the more than eighty plates included in the Book on Geometry, with detailed explanations on the materials used and how to cut and sew them. This particular plate concerns a cape made of cloth.*

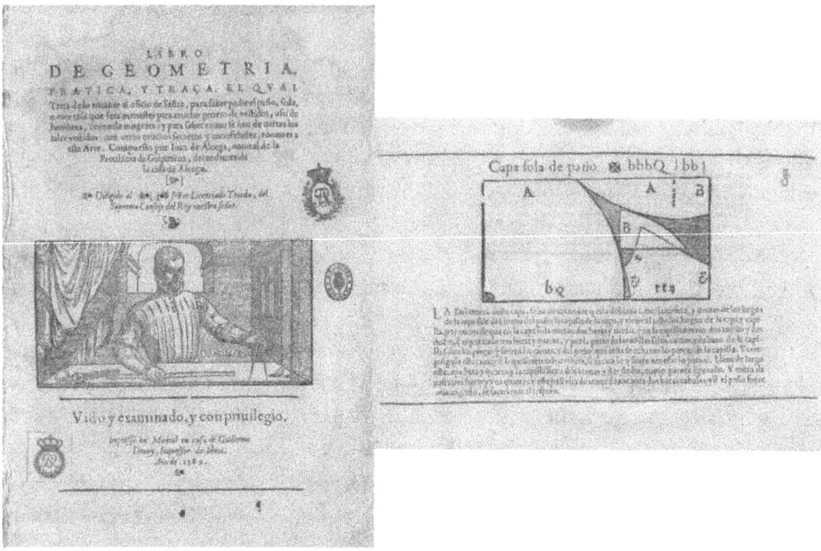

§ 2.20 THE GENERAL REGULATION OF THE FACTORIES OF FRANCE PROMISES A NUMBER OF PRIVILEGES TO FOREIGN SKILLED CLOTH WORKERS, IN PARTICULAR TO THOSE WHO BRING NEW INVENTIONS—1601

The following text is an extract from the general regulation of manufacture approved by King Henry IV, of France, in 1601. One of its provisions offers citizenship to foreign workers with skills and expertise in the making of cloths in the manner of foreign countries—hence, not made in France. Of special interest is the additional privilege promised to those masters who brought "new inventions of cloths and works of any kind." These masters were entitled to the automatic grant of citizenship (i.e., without having to spend a three-year period in France working in their profession), provided their products were previously examined and approved.

By comparison to the manifestations of resistance against technological change between the thirteenth and the fifteenth centuries, in the early seventeenth century the scenario of the textile industry had completely changed: now authorities were eager to receive new inventions, and obstacles to their introduction on the market were very few.

April 13, 1601

XXII. Foreign workers will be naturalized.

To all foreign workers working on cloths in the manner of the serges of Florence, *raz* of Milan, and serges from Ascot, Ypres, *camelots*, *moncayarts*,[63] foreign cloths, and other works of new inventions, we say and declare that within two years from the day of the publication of this edict, that all those who will come and bring all kinds of works, take residence in France and will work there for three full and continuous years, to the satisfaction of people knowledgeable in this matter, in cities and places that they will choose for living, where their work will be judged, and the said workers having worked during the said period, will be on their request, presented to and countersigned by the controller general or particular to the trade, before our local judges, appointed for this purpose and our prosecutor heard, declared naturalized French, to enjoy all the rights and privileges of the bourgeoisie in this kingdom, as our natural subjects do, without their needing to have recourse to us for obtaining other letters of naturalization, thus the declaration which will be sent to them by the said judges will suffice, without further verification by our chamber of accounts. And as for the master workers who from now on will bring new inventions of cloths and works of any kind, will be by us immediately and without delay received as true French [citizens], and as such by us declared, held and reputed on the attestation which will be made to us by the master jurors of their profession, or people knowledgeable about this in the case of absence of expert masters, and provided the aforementioned general or particular prosecutor is called, who will countersign the attestation made of the test of the work done by the said masters, and of the quality and beauty of their works.

§ 2.21 HENRY IV SETS A FACTORY OF FINE CLOTHS IN PARIS—1603

Since the revocation of sumptuary laws, in the sixteenth century, the inclination for luxurious consumption by the wealthy French has become a powerful engine for the devising and using of mechanisms for the appropriation and protection of differentiating assets.

The following text reproduces excerpts from an edict approved by Henry IV, of France, establishing a manufacture of fine cloths in Paris (silk cloths, and cloths with gold and silver threads embroidered),[64] *in the manner of those from Milan.*

In order to expand the manufacture of fine cloths in France, the king granted some privileges to a number of merchants who committed themselves to erect such manufacture: nobility, exclusivity, and money. Besides, the workers were excluded from some constraints specific to the guilds such as the obligation to present a masterpiece as a condition for being promoted from apprentice to companion.

63. *Raz*, *camelots*, and *moncayarts* were types of woollen cloths.
64. In 1602, the king granted a privilege to a certain Turrato, goldsmith from Milan, who promised to bring to France the technique of working gold and silver and make threads that could be used in the making of fine cloths, in the manner of Milan.

Edict of establishment of a manufacture of cloths and fabrics of gold, silver, and silk in Paris.

Saint-Germain-en-Laye, August 1603. Registered in the parliament, April 9, 1604.

Henry, etc. ...

One of the main solutions for this purpose[65] is the establishment of arts and manufactures, both because of the hope that they bring to enrich and embellish this kingdom and no longer have recourse to our neighbors, as [if we were] beggars and poor in inventions, and seek far away what we have within our country, and also because it is an easy and sweet remedy to purge our kingdom of so many vices that idleness produces, and the only way to avoid transporting gold and silver out of the kingdom to enrich our neighbors, only the introduction of manufactures is left, which until now have been disdained and seem to be peculiar to some of our neighbors, be it because of the material, the industry or the perfection of the work, especially those of gold, silver and silk, which have been lacking to us only through negligence and (*illegible in the original*) the establishment of which we would have previously ordered commissioners, who would have drawn up and shown our council the memoirs and articles by which we have recognized how easy it was to remedy this fault; ...

(i) For these causes, and several other considerations, we have, by these present [edict], charged, instructed and appointed them[66] to set the establishment and enterprise in our good city of Paris of manufactures of gold, silver and silk, in respect of mills for silk, and foundries of gold and silver for melting, cutting (into threads), and spinning them, in the manner of Milan ... and to shape and work all kinds of silk cloths, both plain and ornamented, and mixed with gold and silver, according to the regulations and the order that afterwards we will issue. ...

(3) We have declared the aforesaid Moisset, Sainctot, Limagne, Camus, Parfait, and Collebert servants and commensals at our house, decorating them, moreover, as well as their posterity born and to be born, in loyal marriage, with the title of nobility, so that they enjoy it as the other nobles of our kingdom do, provided, however, that they will continue and maintain the said manufactures for the period of twelve years. and they shall not be imputed, nor their posterity, because of the trade they do and will do of goods during the said twelve years, in addition to the said erection of the manufactures, as acts derogating from nobility, and of which, if need be, we have relieved and dispensed, relieve and dispense them, by the present [edict] for the mentioned period, during which no one other than them will be allowed, in this said city, suburbs and outskirts of Paris, erect or cause to be erected silk mills, looms, and open workshops to work at the said manufactures of silk, both plain and ornamented by all kinds, except by their permission and consent. ...

(5) And for this purpose the said entrepreneurs are authorized, from the first year, to work enough (*erased in the original*) and gold and silver spun in the manner of Milan (*erased in the original*) as much as is necessary for the use of our

65. The Edict's main purpose was to provide for remedies aimed at overcoming the dire economic situation of the king's subjects caused by war. In the end of the sixteenth century, France came out from a three-year long war against Spain, and, in the beginning of the seventeenth century, from a one-year long war against the Savoyards (the house of Savoya).

66. The Edict here refers to Jehan de Moissct, comptroller of artillery and affairs of king's chamber, and P. Sainctot, J. A. Limaigne, N. Camus, C. Parfait, and Odard Collebert, merchants.

said kingdom; we wish and it pleases us that during the said period of twelve years, both in our said good city of Paris and in our kingdom, no one else than them can keep a workshop or work in any way whatsoever the said gold and silver in the manner and fashion of Milan, without their authorization and consent, with the exception of Devieux, our valet and ordinary perfumer, Vexin, Laforêt and Taltot, to whom we have permitted to set up one workshop only and work jointly in it, prohibiting them from associating other people with them, or assigning this right to anyone; and as regards the privileges [granted] both to them and their workers, they shall enjoy such and similar privileges as those that we grant to the said entrepreneurs, only as far as the said gold and silver is concerned, and on condition that they shall acquire the silk from the entrepreneurs, provided that the latter sell it as good and at the same price as it can be found elsewhere, on the condition, moreover, that after the work they will cause to be done is done and countermarked with their mark, they shall, before selling it, have it marked with the general mark that we have placed for this purpose in the hands of said Sainctot and Parfait, both for the said factory and for the other silk fabrics.

(6) And from now, within three months from the present [edict], everyone of whatever quality and condition is prohibited from bringing into this kingdom, and all persons from selling, distributing or applying in any cloths whatsoever the said gold and silver in the said manner and fashion of Milan, except the one who will have been made in France by the said entrepreneurs and the said Devieux, Vexin, Laforêt and Taltot, countermarked by the mark that will be given by us to the above said Sainctot et Parfait, as provided, on the penalty of confiscation and of fine, [to be applied] half to us and the other half to said entrepreneurs; and to avoid abuses from occurring, the cloths shall be countermarked by the said entrepreneurs within the said three months.

(7) And to facilitate the sale of everything that the entrepreneurs will produce, both said gold and silver thread in the manner and fashion of Milan, as well as gold, silver and silk cloths, both plain and ornamented, and to encourage foreigners to buy it and take them; we want that, once our mark is affixed by them, they can be sold and distributed freely without any taxation both within the country and at the border of our kingdom, from which we have exempted them. ...

(11) And in order to assist somehow to the large advances that it is convenient to make for this establishment, we have granted and grant to the said entrepreneurs a loan in the sum of 130,000 pounds, which will be deducted from our savings, so that they receive them immediately, without any delay, which sum will remain in their hands for the time and space of twelve years without any profit and interest, and at the end of said time those entrepreneurs shall return and pay back to us the sum of 100,000 pounds only, and as regards the remaining thirty thousand pounds, we have made and make a donation to them henceforth, in consideration of the extraordinary costs and expenses that we have recognized necessary and which are appropriate for them to cover the loss and damage to the said establishment.

Hereby we order, etc.

§ 2.22 INDUSTRIAL PRIVILEGE GRANTED TO OLIVIER DE SERRES ON A METHOD OF EXTRACTING FIBERS FROM THE WHITE MULBERRY TREE FOR THE MAKING OF CANVASES AND CLOTHS—1603

The following text concerns an industrial privilege granted to Olivier de Serres, a celebrated expert in agriculture, author of a famous book—Le Théatre de l'Agriculture et Ménage des Champs—which, between its publication, in 1600, and its last edition, in 1675, was reprinted more than seventy times. This is an industrial privilege for a genuine invention, not for the introduction of a foreign technique. It is very probable, indeed, that de Serres was not aware that the technique of producing fabric and paper from the fibers of the white mulberry tree had been known and used since long in the Pacific region. Anyway, the industrial privilege does not contain the requirement that the inventor teaches his technique to local apprentices and manufacturers. Eventually, this is explained by the fact that de Serres submitted a technical memory describing his invention to the king's council. That memory was published in the form of a booklet in 1603, under the title La seconde richesse du Mûrier blanc, qui se trouve en son écorce pour faire des Toiles, non moins utile que la Soie, qui se tire de ses feuilles [The second richness of white mulberry, which is found in its bark to make Cloth, no less useful than Silk, which is extracted from its leaves] (see Figure 30). It seems that this privilege has never been put to practice. In de Serres's personal diary only one mention is made to the bark extracted from the white mulberry: "In the month of March 1607, the moon being old, I had several mulberry trees near the vineyard pruned, so as to extract the bark from the branches; in one of those trees the bark was green." Henri Vachalde, Olivier de Serres, Seigneur du Pradel—Sa Vie et ses Travaux, at 111 (E. Plon, Nourrit et Cie., 1886). Source: <gallica.BnF.fr>. It does not seem that such a small quantity of bark could have had an industrial use.

Tuesday, September 2, 1603, chancellery's room.

Notice concerning the cloths made of the fibers of the white mulberry tree.

> The commissioners appointed by the King [Henry IV] for the general trade of France, who saw the request presented by Olivier de Serres, lord of Pradel, that he be authorized to establish the manufactures of canvases and other fabrics and works that can be made from the bark of white mulberry trees, according to the invention he has found, and set up workshops in any city of this kingdom as he sees fit, and hire workers there, and all other things necessary for said establishment, to sell and trade in said canvases and works without paying any duties or taxes, either in France or abroad, for the time and space of twenty years, with similar privileges for himself, his children and servants and each of those who will be appointed by him to keep and lead the offices and various workshops that it will be necessary to establish in several cities of this kingdom, to those enjoyed by the officers commensals and king's servants, and prohibition to all persons to undertake and interfere with said manufactures, in any way or manner whatsoever, without his leave and permission, on penalty of confiscation and fine applicable to his benefit; [who also saw] the printed memoirs of the new manufacture of said mulberry bark cloths under the name of said de Serres; and this having been heard by the said Commissioners, both on the content of the said memoirs and on the

manner in which he said and affirmed to have extracted from the bark of the said white mulberry trees the thread that he presented and maintained that he could easily spin and manufacture other similar fabrics, as it is easy to conjecture, and all considered:

They are of the opinion, under the good pleasure of the King and of our lords of his council, that in order to introduce and facilitate the establishment of the said new manufactures of the fabrics and other works that can be made and extract from the bark of the white mulberry trees by the invention and industry of said de Serres, that he may be allowed to erect and cause to be erected looms in such city and places of this kingdom that he will find the most convenient, hire workers and introduce all other things necessary for said establishment, sell and cause to sell the aforesaid canvases and works without paying any duties or taxes, either in France or abroad, by the time and space of twenty years, and that such privilege and exemption similar to that enjoyed by the commensal officers and servants of the King can be granted to him, for him to enjoy during his life only, counting from the day on which he will have demonstrated the said manufactures in the presence of the said commissioners or other persons appointed, with exemption from fees, public charges and other taxes and subsidies, enjoyed by the exempt and privileged of this kingdom, for its main clerks, limited to twelve, from the day they are employed in the establishment of the said new manufactures, and as long as they continue at it, and effectively serve for the said twenty years, and after their expiry, they will enjoy [the exemption] for the rest of their lives; with the prohibition to all persons to undertake or interfere in the said factories without the permission from de Serres, during the said time, on penalty of confiscation and a fine of three hundred pounds, half of which shall belong to him and the other to the King.

Figure 30 Cover page of the technical memoir that Olivier de Serres submitted to the King's trade commission in support of his application for an industrial privilege: "The Second Wealth of the White Mulberry Tree."

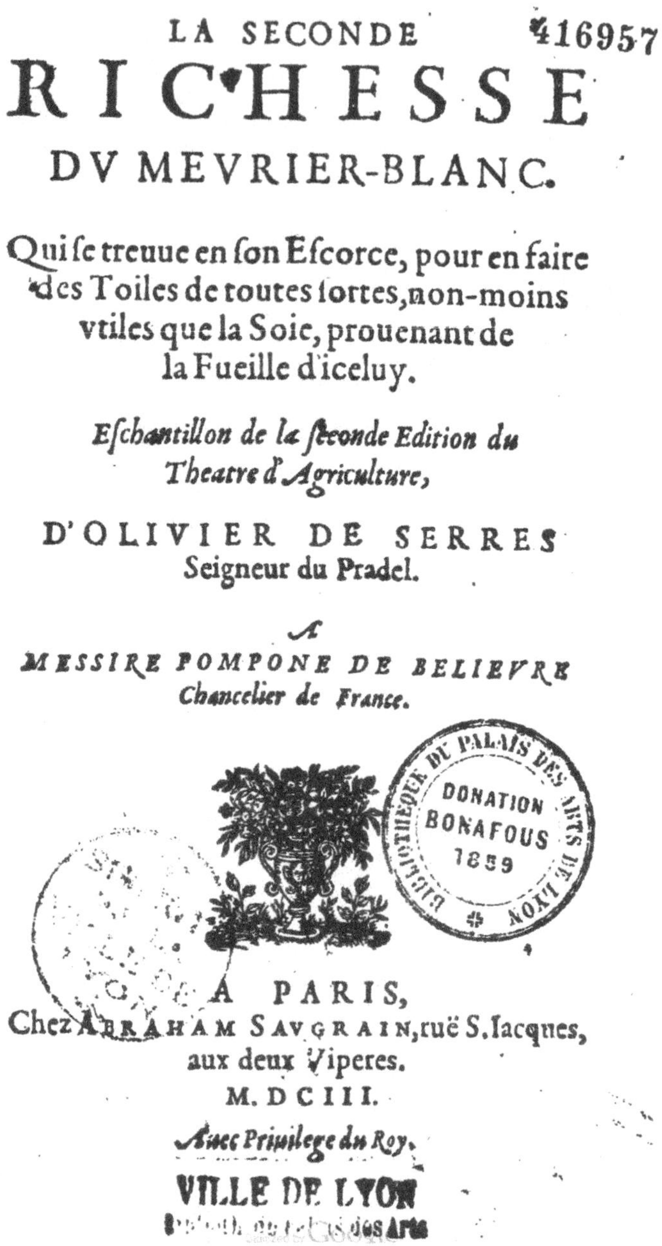

LA SECONDE 416957

RICHESSE

DV MEVRIER-BLANC.

Qui se treuue en son Escorce, pour en faire des Toiles de toutes sortes, non-moins vtiles que la Soie, prouenant de la Fueille d'iceluy.

Eschantillon de la seconde Edition du Theatre d'Agriculture,

D'OLIVIER DE SERRES Seigneur du Pradel.

A

MESSIRE POMPONE DE BELIEVRE Chancelier de France.

A PARIS,
Chez ABRAHAM SAVGRAIN, ruë S. Iacques, aux deux Viperes.
M. D C I I I.

Auec Priuilege du Roy.

§ 2.23 A CARPET MAKER AND UPHOLSTERER RECEIVES AN INDUSTRIAL PRIVILEGE FOR THE INTRODUCTION IN FRANCE OF A NEW TECHNIQUE OF MAKING CARPETS IN THE MANNER OF SPAIN—1604

The following text corresponds to excerpts from an industrial privilege granted to a carpet maker and upholsterer for his introduction in France of a technique of making gilded leather rugs and cloths in the same manner and of the same quality as those made in Spain. The privilege is divided into two parts—one concerning a technique unknown in France, which the recipient of the privilege claimed to have invented, the other concerning the manufacture of carpets that were already made in France. The rights conferred were different—exclusivity was accorded to the making of the first kind of carpets only. Because the purpose of the privilege was to terminate with imports of carpets from Spain, it came with a requirement: Rozan had to manufacture the quantity of carpets that were in demand in France, otherwise, he would be deprived of the privilege. This is the exploitation requirement, which today is a common feature in patent laws. Although such a requirement was not mentioned in the Statute of Monopolies, of 1623, a few years later, several patents granted under the Statute were cancelled for lack of use.

An interesting component of this privilege is the prohibition of débauchage.[67] *Avoiding the débauchage of employees and apprentices by competitors has always been a concern of artisans and entrepreneurs. But in this case, the applicant had an added interest in making the prohibition explicit in the text of the privilege—an uncommon feature—arising from the secret nature of his knowledge. It was the possession of the trade secret that gave him the competitive advantage and justified the privilege.*

Friday, April 9, 1604, chancellery's room.

> The commissioners appointed by the King [Henry IV] for the trade and reestablishment of the manufactories of France, who have seen the request presented to H. M. and to the gentlemen of his council by Scipion Rozan, that, in order to give him the means to establish in this kingdom the manufacture of gilded leather tapestries, with the same perfection as it is made in Spain and other foreign countries, the privilege be granted to him that only him would make it for ten years, with the prohibition to all persons from making or selling it without his permission, on the penalty of confiscation, under the charges and conditions set forth in the articles and memoirs attached to the said request, the decision of the council taken on the xxvith February last, referring the same request to the said commissioners for them to give an opinion on the content thereof, the works and manufactures made by said Rozan concerning the said materials and tapestries of gilded leather, draped both with the new invention and in the common way, heard on this matter several expert merchants, knowledgeable on the making and trading of said tapestries, and also the said Rozan on the experiences by him made and explanations concerning the said art:

67. *See, supra* note 22 and accompanying text.

They are of the opinion, under the good pleasure of the King and the aforesaid gentlemen of his council, whereas the use of the said tapestries of gilded leather, draped and not draped, is useful and has become very common in France, as much for their beauty and convenience as their modesty of price, that it would be expedient and profitable to the public, so as to prevent the transport of gold and silver outside France for the purchase of these, to establish their manufacture in this kingdom, and that to this end letters patent may be granted to Rozan, by which it will be permitted to him, and to those with whom he wishes to associate, to make tapestries of draped gilded leather and to set up the looms and workshops in all the cities and other places of France as he sees fit, with prohibitions for all people from making or selling it, if it does not have its trademark and is not made in his manner or his associates', without his permission, for the time and space of ten years, on penalty of confiscation and a fine of three hundred pounds, applicable half to the King and the other half to Rozan.

And as far as the other tapestries of gilded leather in the common manner are concerned, such permission may be granted to him with the same penalties and defenses that apply in the jurisdiction of the parliaments of Paris and Rouen, and for the time and space of five years only, except as regards the merchants who would be established in the cities of Paris, Lyon, Rouen and others engaging in similar manufacture of gilded leather tapestry, either draped or in the common manner, at the time of the publication of the privileges of said Rozan, who, to avoid surprise and collusion, will be required to bring or send to the said commissioners certificates from the ordinary judges of the places where they will be established, within three months from the day that Rozan will have given notice to them of his privilege, attesting to the time they will have started the establishment of the manufacture and trade of the said tapestries in the aforesaid manner: and failing to do so in the said time, and the past, will be forfeited from the continuation of their business and subject to the privileges of said Rozan. ...

[Rozan] shall supply France with sufficient tapestries of gilded leather and draped, and the said merchants of Paris and Rouen with those made in the common manner, as good and fine and in such perfection as that made in Spain and other foreign countries, on the penalty of being deprived of his privilege;. ...

That prohibition would be made to all master carpet makers and others to lure [*débaucher*] or receive in their workshops the apprentices or companions that the said Rozan will have, either French or foreign, without his express written consent, as far as the apprentices are concerned, during the period of four years of their apprenticeship, and as far as the companions are concerned, during the time they will be hired and obligated, on the penalty of a fine of three hundred pounds fine against the masters and twenty-five pounds against the companions, for the first time, and greater penalty for the other times, even of corporal punishment if it applies, the aforesaid fines to be applied half to the King and half to the said Rozan, as above.

That said Rozan, for so long as he will continue to establish the said tapestries of gilded leather, draped and common, under the above conditions, may qualify himself as the King's carpet maker of those sorts of tapestries, and in this capacity stay in the lodges of the domestic officers of the King's household, to enjoy the same privileges; ...

That he and his associates may also buy and finish in their workshops the tanned leathers and other fabrics necessary for the manufacture of the said tapestries only, and he shall not sell or trade them to apply to another use, and his manufactures where the said tapestries are made shall not be subject to any inspection or search by any master or trade whatsoever, nor for what will be sold or traded elsewhere in France, marked with their marks, except if an abuse or defect is found, to file complaints to and obtain protection from the ordinary and police judges of the places where the said defects and abuses would be committed and found.

And that His Majesty will be begged to grant said Rozan his residence in a small dwelling which is behind the garden of the hotel de la Reine, or in some other place of Pont-Neuf sur l'île, or of his buildings and public houses of that city or suburbs of Paris, both to aid in the public convenience and in the decoration of the said city.

§ 2.24 THE TRADE COUNCIL OF HENRY IV, OF FRANCE, APPROVES THE GRANTING OF A PRIVILEGE FOR THE MAKING OF TURKEY-STYLE CARPETS—1604

The following text corresponds to another industrial privilege that Henry IV granted for the making of carpets—this time for carpets made in the manner of Turkey, by a certain Jehan Fortier. In 1607, Fortier petitioned for and obtained the recognition of his invention of a technique of making carpets in the manner of Turkey. This reveals that this patent letter was different from the industrial privileges that Henri IV granted with frequency, which were aimed at encouraging the importation of foreign techniques. Those privileges, as seen above, consisted basically of providing permission for the introduction of such foreign techniques and for assuring the exclusivity in using them for a certain term. But the case of Fortier was different: he was not merely importing the technique, he had actually invented it (so he claimed). The patent did not refer explicitly to the exclusivity in the making of all sorts of carpets in the manner of Turkey, Egypt, and Persia. Probably he did not need it because allegedly his invention was new and he had kept it secret. But, in 1608, just four years after Fortier obtained the privilege and one year after he was acknowledged as the inventor of the technique of making carpets in the manner of Turkey "à fond d'or, soie et laine," Henri IV signed a patent letter authorizing another carpet maker, Pierre Dupont, "tapissier ordinaire en tapis de Turquie et façons de Levant," to establish himself in the gallery of the Palace of the Louvre and produce the same general sort of carpets. The language of Fortier's privilege indicates that what he pursued—and obtained—was the exclusivity in making carpets by his own technique as well as all carpets "embélis de diverses figures d'animaux et personnages jusques ici inconnues," which he created. Therefore, we may have here the first episode in France of exclusive protection—albeit indirect—of designs applied to textiles.

Fortier's privilege contained a few legal features that were well advanced. First, Fortier had kept the method for making carpets whose invention he claimed as a trade secret, and thus one of the explicit effects of the privilege was that potential competitors could not make any attempts to acquire that knowledge through espionage.

Second, Fortier was liable for the quality of his teaching. Apprentices were expected to have fully learned Fortier's techniques after a period of three years. Similar clauses appear frequently in today's contracts of technology transfer.

Moreover, after that three-year period expired—hence, after the apprentices were supposed to be in possession of Fortier's techniques—they had to observe a two-year period during which they could not compete with him. This is another feature of modern labor contracts, which, when sensitive jobs and functions are at stake, usually contain clauses of time-limited noncompetition.

Finally, from an institutional point of view, Fortier's privilege was very distant from the by-laws of medieval guilds that, exceptionally, admitted the introduction of fabrics of new invention and design under the condition that they be previously approved by the wardens or jurors. By contrast, Fortier was authorized to use any techniques "in the manner and as he deemed to be required to use these manufactures." This clause confirms the suggestion that, in the seventeenth century, freedom of invention in the textile industry was already an accepted idea. Behind it was the pressure of a rising fashion industry.

Friday, June 4, 1604, chancellery's room.

> *Carpets from Turkey.* A man named Jehan de Fortier, master worker in Turkish-style tapestry, who has submitted some samples of his work, and who has been asked if he wanted to reside in France and train carpet makers of his art and manufactures, and what he wanted for such purpose, on which he required and requested time to draw up a few memoirs and articles of what would be necessary for him to make his business successful.

Friday, July 23, 1604, chancellery's room.

> *Notice about the carpets from Turkey.* On the proposal made by Jehan Fortier to the commissioners appointed by the King for the matters of trade, to establish in this city of Paris and others of this kingdom the manufacture of the carpets of Turkey, Querins [*Cairins*, from Cairo, in Egypt], Persians, and others of new invention, embellished with various figures of animals and characters hitherto unknown, on which, before the said establishment being approved, would have been ordered by the said commissioners that he would give proof of his art and experience: seen the said proofs and patterns made by him of the said carpets, both in the ordinary way and in that of the new invention, submitted to H. M., who has pleased with them, jointly with the articles containing his proposals and offers, with the conditions that he wishes to be granted to him as a reward for said inventions and establishment, after the whole has been heard:
>
> The said commissioners (having regard to the utility that France may receive from this industry, both in saving money that is transported to foreign countries for the purchase of carpets of this kind and sort, and in the occupation of the people who may be employed there) are of the opinion, under the good pleasure of His Majesty and the gentlemen of his council, that it is expedient to admit and retain the said Fortier to establish in this city of Turkey the said manufacture of Turkish carpets, Quérins et Persians, in addition to those others of new invention and until now unknown to the peoples and workers of the Levant; in order to be able to make them with perfection by the necessary finishing of the fabrics, to allow him to cause the dyeing, spinning and shearing wools and silks in the manner and as he deems to be required to use these manufactures.
>
> To promote his industry and give him the means to establish it, H. M. will be begged to give him the sum of three thousand pounds or such other sum as he pleases, to buy the materials, to build and install the necessary looms, and to allow him to obtain clean and convenient lodgings for the said manufacture free of

charge for the term of six years, or until H. M. decides to lodge him with the other workers of the most exquisite manufactures, at the place which H. M. has allocated to them, on whose behalf he will order, if it pleases him, that he [Fortier] be immediately received under the name and quality of ordinary carpet maker of H. M. in Turkish carpets and Levantine style, concerning which letters shall be granted to him, bearing permission in the said capacity to make and finish the said carpets; the master carpet makers of this city or others, or workers of any profession or condition whatsoever shall not search him, disturb or visit his work and finishing of his fabrics under the pretext that he could find anything that would pertain to their arts and crafts; the whole on the condition that, for the conservation of the aforesaid industry in this kingdom, the aforesaid Fortier shall take French apprentices and not foreigners, up to such a number and for a such price that will be considered reasonable by the aforesaid commissioners, or other than it will please H. M.; within three years from the day that the apprentices have been allocated to him, he shall make them capable of working in his art, to set up looms in workshops in this city or others, according to his offers, provided however that they shall not work in whatever industry they may have acquired, within two years of their apprenticeship, without the consent of the said Fortier; they shall, if he deems it convenient, serve him during the said two years as companions, at reasonable prices and conditions, before becoming masters, or to keep shops, which they may do once the said two years expire; and to preserve the said new manufacture in its quality and loyalty, that it cannot be put for sale on penalty of confiscation without having first been visited by the said Fortier, and sealed with the seal that for this purpose will be given to it, until by H. M. more detailed provisions regulating the said manufacture are enacted; of whose invention and establishment, so that France may receive some obvious utility, the said Fortier shall charge reasonable prices for his products, and shall not sell them for more than [the prices of those] that come from foreign countries and are sold at the entry of the kingdom in the same beauty and quality. And if within six years it happens that the said Fortier comes to die, in this case his widow and children continuing the said manufacture will enjoy the [same] benefit of the privilege as if the said Fortier were alive.

[*In the margin of the text of this privilege's public record, the following note has been added:*

As per the request made by the said Fortier, the Gentlemen have ordered that to the said opinion his names as the first and inventor of the art of making Turkish-style carpets with a background of gold, silk and wool, in this kingdom, and the first who came to establish the art of carpets, as provided in the article of August 17, 1607, fol. 18 of the 3rd register, will be added.].

§ 2.25 THE MUNICIPALITY OF LILLE SETTLES A DISPUTE CONCERNING THE EXCLUSIVITY OF MAKING CERTAIN CLOTHS BETWEEN THE SAYETEURS AND THE BOURGETEURS—1610

The two major categories of woollen clothmakers of Lille—the sayeteurs *and the* bourgeteurs*—disputed the exclusive right of making certain types of fabrics, whose differences consisted in the colors and methods used. It seems that the antagonism of the parties had worsened because of divergent court opinions. The dispute was settled by the authorities of the municipality, upon an appeal by both contenders.*

From an intellectual property standing, it is interesting that the claim of the bourgeteurs *was based on the allegation that they had invented a particular technique of making cloths.*

Ordinance regulating the exclusivity in the making of certain cloths by the *sayeteurs* and the *bourgeteurs*

December 18, 1610

> As the masters and wardens of the trade of *bourgeterie*[68] of this city of Lille have submitted to us by request that by the letters of their trade, in particular article LXXIX, and other ordinance in the form of a notice of the xiiiith of October, fifteen hundred and forty-four, it had been accorded to them the authorization of making new works of new invention, and the permission to make all ornamented works either of *sayette* and pure silk or mixed, and that some franchisees of that trade had invented certain work of plain *sayette* on the high loom and made of silk,[69] designed in the manner of England and according to what they have begged us, that this be taken into account, notably that the said new invention had come from their side, and that the said works, if wrinkled, will be damaged, we should declare such works to depend on and to belong to the said *bourgeterie* and not at all to the profession of *sayeterie*, the opposite having been maintained by the officers of the *vingtaine*[70] in favour of the trade of *sayeterie*, who decided that these works made of plain *sayeterie* woven in the manner of *chambgeans*[71] will depend, once wrinkled and ornamented, on the profession of *sayeterie*, and thus the white and the blue must remain with them, excluding all the others, and the works in all other colors shall remain free to both professions, which caused a great dispute and controversy that erupted between the two parties, wishing to maintain both trades in their rights and settle all disputes between them, for the sake of the public good, after having communicated everything to the lords president and people of the accounts of their serene highnesses in Lille, we have, by dismissing all procedures pending, in the manner of a policy, ordered and order that said works, either spotted or wrinkled, made of plain sayette in white and in blue, will belong to the trade of *sayeterie*, those of *bourgeterie* being excluded therefrom, and as for the others of various colors, they may be made by each one of the two trades as they believe they profit from it, provided however that if the works are white and blue, and have no other colors, and are not made of silk, in this case their making will belong to those of the *bourgeterie* alone.
>
> Published at the *bretesque*[72] of this city of Lille, the XVIIIth of December, one thousand six hundred ten, by Mathieu Haze.

68. *See supra* note 28.
69. *Étoffes faites à la tire,* in ancient French, means cloths made in the manner of Tyr, thus designating a sort of cloth containing silk.
70. *See supra* note 15.
71. *See supra* note 60.
72. *Bretesque*: balcony of the city hall, from where the laws and public notices were shouted out.

§ 2.26 PRIVILEGES GRANTED BY THE MUNICIPALITY OF TOURNAI, BELGIUM, TO INVENTIONS IN THE TAPESTRY INDUSTRY—1615, 1684

We saw above that after the sixteenth century, the textile industry started to free itself from the constraints generated by the strict and mandatory obedience to technical standards. This movement has led to an increase in the competitiveness between cities and motivated those cities to encourage the introduction of new techniques and new products. We have seen already several examples. Now we will see references to a few privileges for inventions related to the tapestry industry, granted by the city of Tournai, Belgium (which has been mentioned in Chapter 1; see §§ 1.08 and 1.14). The two following references have been extracted from the work a historian, Eugène Soil, has written about the tapestry industry of that city.

§ 2.26.1 Privilege for Simon Bedoret—1615

> In 1615 Simon Bedoret, carpet maker, makes "new works from the high loom that he has invented and which is called *tapis sandré*"; the following year the city grants him a reward of one hundred florins for his new invention of "carpets in the manner and fashion of tapestry."

§ 2.26.2 Privilege for Jean Duquesne—1684

> In 1684, Jean Duquesne, carpet maker, invents "a sort of tapestry ... in which enters a diversity of figures" by using a certain dye and requests a patent of invention from the magistrates.
>
> Is this the same Jean Duquesne who in 1694 proposed to the magistrates of Gand the establishment in the city of a "laundry and a manufacture of carpets of an entirely new sort"?
>
> André Duquesne, the young, another carpet maker made "works of carpets, moucade, Hungary's stitch," which he declares a new invention, and which seem to us to be the first attempts of foot mats, made at Tournai."

§ 2.27 ORDINANCES OF THE ART OF SILK OF TOLEDO—1616

We have already seen several examples of how the seventeenth century was accepting the introduction of new techniques and designs without great resistance (or, in some cases, without any resistance). The following text is another example. In 1616, the master makers of silk cloths of Toledo received explicit permission to seek new methods and designs. They were however required to obtain the previous approval of those changes before they sent their articles to the market.

Ordinances that the Masters of the Art of Silk of the Imperial City of Toledo have confirmed by the Royal Council of His Majesty [Felipe III, of Spain]. [excerpt]

August 12, 1616

> ... *Item* that if other new methods of weaving silks are invented from here on, that they [the master makers of silk cloths] show them to the high inspectors so that the latter can see how much such clothes are convenient, and if this is not the case, that they decide as they see that it is best, and not otherwise, on penalty of loss [of the cloths] and the fourth part [to be applied] to the chamber of his Majesty. ...

§ 2.28 JUDGMENT SETTLING THE DISPUTE BETWEEN THE CARPET MAKERS AND THE TURNERS OF PARIS ON THE EXCLUSIVITY OF MAKING PARASOLS—1638

The administrative regulations of corporations did not only set specific, detailed standards concerning the quality of the articles produced and rules on labor, such as working hours and the number of apprentices but also provided for exclusivity of manufacture. Only those artisans who had followed an apprenticeship period and had submitted a masterpiece could engage in the manufacture of the articles described in the by-laws (except if those artisans were the sons or daughters of masters, in which case they could be exempted from apprenticeship). This type of exclusivity represented a significant privilege for the members of corporations, and they would enforce it very strictly. This has led to an abundance of disputes (including physical fights, as already noted) among artisans of different specialties, many of which were solved in courts.

The following text is an excerpt from an opinion delivered on appeal, settling a dispute between carpet makers and turners, and involved the alleged infringement by a maker of parasols of the by-laws of the former's corporation. At that time parasols used the same sort of fabric that was used in some carpets. Carpet makers, therefore, wished to enforce what they believed was their exclusive right.

The dispute involved the seizure of a number of parasols that were in possession of François le Mosnier, Master of the turners' guild. The king's prosecutor at the Châtelet found in favor of the turners. It is significant that François alleged that he was the "inventor" of that particular sort of parasols, having brought the knowledge from Lyon to Paris, where they were unknown.

Judgment *inter partes* with the Community of Master Turners, concerning the Parasols

September 25, 1638

> To all those who will see these present Letters, Louis Seguier, Knight, Lord Baron of Saint Brisson, Lord of Ruaux and of Saint Firmin, Counselor to the King our Lord, Ordinary Gentleman of his Chamber, and Guard of the Provosts and Vice-county of Paris: Greetings. We make known that having seen the procedure, pending judgment, moved before Us at the Châtelet of Paris, between the Juror Carpet Makers of this City of Paris, Plaintiffs in execution of the opinion delivered

in the Chamber of the King's Prosecutor at the said Châtelet, of the twentieth May one thousand six hundred and thirty-five; opponents to the release [of the seized articles], on the one hand; François le Mosnier, Master Turner, in this said City, Defendant, and applicant of the outright release of the Parasols seized on him, and the other Master Juror Turners, in the said City, interveners with the said Le Mosnier, on the other hand; because of the aforesaid complaints, and defenses, Requests, purposes and conclusions of the said Juror Carpet Makers, who pleaded that, by our Sentence and final judgment, it should be said that the opinion and judgment rendered by the King's Prosecutor, in their favor, and against the said Mosnier, on the twentieth day of May one thousand six hundred and thirty-five, should be confirmed; and according to this, the twenty-two Parasols seized, at their Request, on said Defendant, should be confiscated; ... moreover condemned in twelve pounds sixteen *sols Parisis* of fine, with prohibitions against his selling and trading in the future any merchandise concerning the profession of carpet making, on a greater penalty, and this notwithstanding the arguments proposed, alleged, maintained to the contrary, by the said Mosnier, Defendant, of which he would be dismissed, and ordered to pay the costs of the proceedings; all as a consequence of the Statutes and Ordinances of the said Carpet Makers, and Regulations obtained by them against the Juror Turners of this City, on the twenty-second of May last: and of the arguments, pleas, causes, reasons, and means, made and proposed in the opposite sense, by Mosnier, which would have told us and proved that he is confident that among all the Arts and Crafts of Paris, each one is based on Statutes and Ordinances, according to which they must work, so that one does not interfere in other's work, and indeed that each one can carry its profession. Le Mosnier has made this particular invention; for eleven years he alone has made Parasols of all manners in Paris, more properly and with more industry than any other, being true that beforehand none was made in Paris; previously, those were made and brought from the City of Lyon, where the invention had been found; the said Mosnier having for some years also worked with the aforesaid Parasols, he has become so experienced that he has continually made those that the King uses, when he goes hunting, and also the Princes and Lords of the Court and other qualified people have used them since said time, and none other than him having the invention, or the experience; but the aforesaid Jurors, and others of several other bodies and trades, recognizing Mosnier's success, have become envious, all the more that some individuals, either Artisans, or others of this City, having no Statutes or Ordinances that give and attribute to them the right to make the said Parasols, other than the Turners, the said Mosnier in his defense would have researched in all the Bodies and Arts and found that only to the said Turners belonged [the right] to make the said Parasols, and he would have been advised to enter the Mastership of the said trade of Turner, for which purpose he would have obtained Letters from His Majesty, by virtue of which he was received in the said Mastership eight years ago, more or less; so, given that by means of this Mastership, the said Mosnier has the freedom and the right to make Parasols of all manners, as provided by article twenty-two of the Statutes and Ordinances of the same trade of Turner, how come the Juror Carpet Makers of Paris would decide again to seize on the said Mosnier, once a dozen Parasols of barracan, and another time ten Parasols, as contained in the Reports of Moris and Thiersault, bailiffs at the Châtelet? ... [*a long and detailed report of the many procedural steps that preceded the judgment follows this introduction; that report has been omitted*]

Heard the report, and everything seen and considered; We, heard the King's Prosecutor in his conclusions, and without having regard to the opinion given by one of his Deputies on the fifth of May, one thousand six hundred and thirty-five, against the said Mosnier, and concerning the seizures of Parasols in question made against him, which we have released and are releasing outright, have permitted and permit that the said Mosnier and other Turners make and offer for sale Parasols, ornamented in all manners, and prohibit the said Juror Carpet Makers from giving them disturbance or impediment in that freedom, notwithstanding the things by them said and proposed to the contrary, which are rejected; and they are condemned to the costs to be levied in the accustomed manner, by our Sentence and final judgment by law: In witness of what We have caused the seal of the Provosts to be put on these present letters. These [letters] were made and pronounced at the Châtelet of Paris, in the presence of Master Claude Bretonneau, Attorney for the said Mosnier, and of the said Jurors intervening with him, and in the absence of Master Hubert de Saint Amoury, Attorney for the said Juror Carpet Makers, on Saturday, the twenty-fifth day of September, one thousand six hundred and thirty-eight.

§ 2.29 THE INVENTION OF THE KNITTING MACHINE: JEAN HINDRET OBTAINS IN FRANCE THE PATENT THAT WAS DENIED TO WILLIAM LEE IN ENGLAND; DISRUPTIVE TECHNOLOGIES AND THE PROVERB "ONE MAN'S LOSS IS ANOTHER MAN'S GAIN"—1656

The intellectual property of textiles does not generate the same social and political concerns as those that surround the intellectual property of medicines. In the latter case, the main concern lies in the private appropriation of techniques that may be essential for preserving human lives.[73] *In the case of textiles, the concerns that may arise are not generally linked to the legal aspect of appropriation, but to the nature of the technology, which may be disruptive, this meaning that a certain invention may bring significant changes to methods of production and cause massive unemployment among those who work in the soon-to-become outdated factories. This book shows two conspicuous examples of disruptive textile-related technologies, and how immediate, emotional collective reactions have led to the loss by one man—the inventor—and the subsequent and consequent gain by another (actually by many others: another inventor, or a copier, and those many women and men who were hired to work in the new industries that were born from the disruptive invention).*

The first example is that of William Lee, a British clergyman (so it is said, even if the biographical facts around his life are somewhat nebulous), who in 1589, after a few years of essays and experiments, invented the knitting machine.[74] *Elizabeth I had popularized in England the fashion of using socks, and the industry of knitting had quickly spread through the kingdom. Knitting was a manual operation—and Lee's proposition was to mechanize it. The story goes that the Queen, when asked for a patent by Lee, refused to grant it, because of her fear of the vast unemployment and misery that the mechanization of knitting would cause among hand knitters.*

73. Many of the debates generated by this topic are referred to in From Antiquity to the COVID-19 Pandemic, *supra* note 2.
74. The second example regards the invention of the sewing machine, by Barthelémy Thimonnier (*see* § 2.49).

This matter is linked to the old notion of industrial privileges, which, as noted above, were essentially administrative permissions for a certain technique to be exploited (as an exception to the general rule that only corporation members could engage in manufacturing and selling industrial goods). In other words, in denying the privilege, Elizabeth I was actually denying permission for the setting of the looms and the making of socks mechanically.

Frustrated by the Queen's denial, the inventor succumbed to the lure offered to him by Henry IV of France, a proactive promoter of domestic industry, and migrated to Rouen, France, where he intended to open a factory with the king's financial assistance. However, the death of the French king interrupted Lee's efforts. Having lost the royal protection, he felt ignored and harassed because of his protestant beliefs. He died poor in France. His invention was recovered by William Lee's brother, who returned to England with a number of Lee's employees, and—this time without resistance—put the invention to work.

Colbert, the Prime Minister and close advisor to Louis XIV, has sent a man to England, Jean Hindret, who somehow succeeded in having access to one of Lee's knitting machines, and memorized its technical details, thereby acquiring what was then a trade secret. Back in France, Jean Hindret and a partner applied for and, as the first of following texts shows, obtained a privilege for the exploitation of Lee's invention. In 1664 this privilege was significantly expanded by another patent letter, giving Hindret and his partner the right to bring skilled workers from England to the Madrid Palace, in Paris, where they had set several looms. After five years of working and teaching the apprentices, those British workers were granted French citizenship.

The second text is the product of historical irony: about forty years after Lee's having seen refused a patent for his invention, William III of England prohibited the export of knitting machines or their parts to other countries. The reason was that the use of knitting machines and the success of the industry in other countries—namely in France—was causing "the Impoverishment of many Families [in England] who have been thereby maintained." The irony was that the initial refusal of the patent was exactly motivated by the fear that the introduction of the knitting machine would cause the impoverishment of those hand-workers that made socks and other knitted apparel.

Lee's loss was Hindret's gain. England's loss was France's gain.

§ 2.29.1 Patent Granted to Jean Hindret and Léonard Blaise for Lee's Invention of the Knitting Machine—1656

Letters patent of July 1656 allowing Messrs. Jean Hindret and Léonard Blaise to establish in Paris or another place of the Kingdom a manufacture to make on looms all kinds of camisoles, boxers, socks, canons,[75] slippers and all other works of silk, thread, wool, cotton and other threads, with privilege for 15 years.

> Louis, by the grace of God, King of France and of Navarre, to all those present and to come, greetings. Our dear and beloved Jean Hindret and Léonard Blaise have had stated and exposed to us that, for the sake of the public utility, and the good of France, they had the intention of establishing, in our good city, or suburb of Paris or other places of our kingdom, a factory to make on looms, all kinds of camisoles, callesons, boxers, *canons*, slippers and all other works of silk, thread, wool, cotton and other threads, suitable for use at the loom in the same manner as they are made in foreign countries, but because they have the need to incur in many expenses for the said establishment, they fear that some others, out of envy, jealousy, or otherwise, frustrate them of the profit they wished to make there, on the wholesale only, and would establish similar ones, which would cause a great loss, and the entire ruin of the aforesaid applicants, if they did not have on this our necessary letters; for these reasons, wishing the good and the utility of our subjects, and to gratify and favorably treat Hindret and Blaise, with our special grace, full power and royal authority, we have permitted, granted and accorded, permit, grant and accord by these present [letters], signed by our hand, the establishment of the said manufacture, for making on the said looms all kinds of camisoles, callesons, boxers, *canons*, slippers and all other works of silk, thread, wool, cotton and other threads, suitable for use on said looms, in our good town of Paris or other places of our Kingdom that they will deem more convenient, with prohibitions to all our subjects, of whatever state, quality or conditions they may be, from erecting or assembling any similar loom, and causing the aforesaid works above mentioned to be made in the whole extent of our Kingdom, except with the consent of the said Hindret and Blaise or of their successors, on the penalty of a fine of thirty thousand pounds, applicable one third to us, one third to the Hôtel-Dieu of Paris, and the other third to the said applicants, confiscation of the said looms and all the works that would be made there and all costs, damages and interest, provided, however, that the said privilege by us thus granted and accorded to Hindret and Blaise shall not in any way hinder the freedom of merchants or traders in our Kingdom from going to buy, bring and sell, said works made in England, and in the foreign countries as they see fit, as well as all subjects from making the said knitting works, as they have been accustomed, but they shall not make them at the looms as it is above stated without the authorization and consent of said Hindret and Blaise, or others succeeding or empowered by them, thus we order our beloved and lord counselors holding our court of parliament of Paris that they register these present [letters], and ensure that the aforesaid Hindret and Blaise and their successors enjoy and use plainly and peacefully their contents, not admitting that any trouble or obstacle be made, raised or given contrary to this, and if it is made, raised or given, they shall make it cease immediately and without delay; we order our first bailiff or sergeant concerned to take all restricting seizures and other measures required and necessary, for the

75. *Canon*: garment made of linen, with lace and thread ornaments, which was fixed under the knee. According to the Wiktionnaire, it was very popular in the time of Louis XIV.

execution of the present [letters], without the need for other permissions; and because these present [letters] may produce effects in several places, we wish that the copies checked by one of our beloved counselors and secretaries, be copied as herein in original and that they be printed, published and posted as necessary, because this is our pleasure, notwithstanding any objections or appeals, *clameur de Haro, Charte Normande,*[76] and other letters to this contrary, and in order that it be firm and stable for ever, we have had our seal put to these present [letters], given in Paris in the month of July, the year of grace of one thousand six hundred and fifty six and of our reign the thirteenth; signed Louis, ...

§ 2.29.2 William III Prohibits the Export of Knitting Machines from England—1696

And whereas a very useful and profitable Invention or Mystery has been lately found out for the better and more speedy making and knitting of Worsted and Silk Stockings, Waistcoats, Gloves and other wearing Necessaries whereby great Quantities are wrought off in a little time His Majesties Dominions abundantly supplied and great Quantities exported into Foreign Nations to the Increase of His Majesties Customs and the Improvement of Trade and Commerce. And whereas several of the Frames or Engines for the making and knitting of such Stockings and other wearing Necessaries have been of late exported out of this Kingdom whereby the said Commodities have been made in Foreign Parts which were heretofore made in this Kingdom only to the great Discouragement of the Woollen Trade in general and the great detriment of the said Mystery and the Impoverishment of many Families who have been thereby maintained For the Prevention of which Inconveniencies for the future be it enacted by the Authority aforesaid That from and after the First Day of May One thousand six hundred ninety six no Person or Persons whatsoever shall load or put on board any Ship or Vessel any such Frame or Frames or any Part or Parcel thereof in order to bee exported beyond the Seas upon payne that the Person or Persons offending herein shall not only forfeit or loose such Frame and Frames Parts or Parcels of Frames which shall be so loaded and put on board in order to be exported beyond the Seas as aforesaid but also the Sum of Forty Pounds of lawful Money of England for such Frame or Part or Parcel thereof the one Moiety thereof to His Majesty His Heirs and Successors the other Moiety thereof to the Person or Persons who shall inform and sue for the same to be recovered by Action of Debt Bill Plaint or Information in any of His Majesties Courts of Record wherein no Essoigne Protection or Wager of Law shall be allowed or more than one Imparlance.

76. This was a sort of complaint, with suspensive effects, that anyone could submit to a court against any measure that might violate his/her rights. This procedure was specific to Normandy. In common law, there is a similar measure called *writ of mandamus*.

Figure 31 William Lee's knitting machine, invented in 1589. Initially a very rustic machine, the invention was successively improved and, according to the Britannica Encyclopedia (< www.britannica.com >), stood as the standard knitting machine for several centuries, when it was confronted with the competition of other inventions, such as the flatbed machine and Jacquard's loom.

§ 2.30 THE DEMANDS OF NEW FASHIONS HAVE LED THE GUILD OF HAT MAKERS OF PARIS TO APPLY TO THE KING FOR HIS APPROVAL OF NEW BY-LAWS—1658

The following text is particularly important in that it shows that, in France, in the middle of the seventeenth century, the constraints of the corporatist regime were losing strength, and the necessity of serving consumers new demands, imposed by new fashions, had already an impact on how the textile industry worked. The new by-laws of the guild of hat makers, approved by Louis XIV, including their right to add one new master into membership, are justified by the fact that "the conjuncture of modern times has given rise to entirely new fashions in the subject of their manufactures."

By-laws of the hat makers in 38 articles and patent letters of Louis XIV, confirming [excerpt]

March 1658

Louis, by the grace of God, King of France and Navarre, to all those present and to come, greetings. Our dear and beloved wardens, jurors, elders, bachelors and masters of the community of hat makers of our good city, suburbs, outskirts, and vice-county of Paris, have very humbly shown Us that they have discovered the excellence of their art to the point that all nations seek to associate with their commerce all the more useful to our said city, and to all extension of our kingdom, so that the greater part of our people find there the principal means of making their families to subsist happily, but that the conjuncture of modern times has given rise to entirely new fashions in the subject of their manufactures, no less advantageous than they are necessary, and that the common usage [of those fashions] has caused the exercise of the old ways to be lost and that the delicacy of their inventions destroys all the manners their predecessors taught them, so that the by-laws that the late King Henry III gratified them with .... cannot at present give them security in their trade nor maintain the trust that We wished, and that it would be necessary that We wished to grant them those [by-laws] that they have drafted in accordance with what is practiced for the good of our subjects, begging Us very humbly in that sense. For these reasons, given the payment of the sum of four thousand pounds that the applicants paid on February 3, 1644, concerning the right of confirmation that they owe Us, because of our accession to the crown; another payment of a similar sum of four thousand pounds to enjoy the benefit of the dispensation of and exemption from receiving henceforth any master of their art on [patent] letters that were customarily granted, in consideration of the accessions of the kings. ... Given in Paris, in the month of March, the year of grace one thousand six hundred and fifty-eight and our reign the fifteenth.

§ 2.31 FRANCE DETERMINES, FOR THE FIRST TIME, THE EXCLUSIVITY OF INDUSTRIAL DESIGNS APPLIED TO TAPESTRY—1664

One of the first legal acts determining the protection of industrial designs was a decree signed by Louis XIV, in the context of permission for the establishment of a carpet factory in Beauvais. It is probable that the idea for the temporary exclusivity in designs has been inspired by Colbert—the same politician who, in 1699, had the idea of putting the Royal Academy of Sciences in charge of examining patent applications as to their novelty and utility.[77]

Decree for the establishment of a tapestry factory in Beauvais (excerpt)

Vincennes, August 1664.

As one of the most important works of peace that God has pleased to give us, is that of restoring all kinds of commerce in this kingdom, and of putting it in a condition to dispense with the recourse to foreigners for things necessary for the use and convenience of our subjects: so we have hitherto forgotten nothing that would be able to procure this advantage, by all the means that we have judged to be

77. *See* FROM BABYLON TO THE SILICON VALLEY, *supra* note 1, at 29.

adequate for the success of this grand design: among which means is that of the re-establishment of the manufactory of tapestries, in the manner of those of Flanders, whose making had been introduced before in our good city of Paris and others of this kingdom, by the care of the late King Henri-le-Grand, our very honored ancestor, appearing with reason of a very great consequence; and our dear and well-loved Sieur Colbert, our counselor in all our councils, superintendent and general organizer of our buildings, arts and manufactures of France, having made known to us that the restoration of this factory and manufacture of said tapestries could not be better entrusted to no one more capable of leading him to a happy end than Louis Hinard, a merchant upholsterer and bourgeois of Paris, recognized as one of the most skillful in the industry, not only in the said manufacture, but also in the commerce of that kind of merchandise, if it pleased us to grant him permission to establish the manufactory in our city of Beauvais, or any other of our province of Picardy, whichever he sees fit, which he will judge the most convenient to enjoy by him, his heirs and successors in title, during the time and in accordance with the provisions dictated by the conditions and articles he has us for this purpose presented.

For these reasons ... we have allowed Hinard to establish the said manufactory and making of all kinds of tapestries of *verdures* and characters of high and low level. We wish that the said Hinard, his heirs and successors in title enjoy the said permission and establishment for 30 years: and this to the exclusion of and privately from all others, under the penalty of a fine of 10,000 pounds, confiscation of their goods, and all costs, damages and interest, all applicable to the benefit of said Hinard. ... And because it is necessary for such establishment that the mentioned Hinard and his associates can easily maintain in the premises of said establishment all the workers and other people who will be employed by them, we allow them to take and establish in such places such number as they see fit of painters, dyers, beer brewers, bakers, masters or companions; who will enjoy the same privileges and exemptions as the so-called upholsterers. We wish that the wool and dyeing substances that will be purchased by the said Hinard and associates and their agents, within the kingdom, ... be and may be by them brought and transported to the place of the said establishment without being subject to the payment of any fees. To which effect we allow those mentioned to put and carry a blanket of our colors and coat of arms on their carts, boats and other things used for the transportation, both said wools and dyeing substances as well as the tapestries that will be manufactured by them: which will be marked by them by working and weaving the said tapestries with the mark given to them by the said superintendent, and without all others being prohibited from using the said mark for other tapestries, or copying the designs on which they will be made, under the penalty of a fine of 10,000 pounds, and of confiscation.

Figure 32 Tapestry of wool and silk, from Beauvais, Psyche at the Basketmakers, after a design by François Boucher (1703–1770), woven under the direction of André Charlemagne Charron, possibly 1756–1757 (but probably 1767–1771).

§ 2.32 LOUIS XIV GRANTS AN INDUSTRIAL PRIVILEGE FOR A NEW INVENTION CONCERNING THE TANNING OF LEATHER—1666

The texts that follow concern an industrial privilege for a trade secret (a method for tanning and currying leather) and its subsequent interpretation that resulted in its expansion.

Indeed, it seems that the initial privilege did not satisfy the inventor entirely, for it covered the process of tanning only. Under the regime of corporatism then still in force, and because the process of finishing leather and hides was the monopoly of curriers, the inventor feared that the privilege would not exempt him from sending his leathers and hides to the curriers. Thus, he asked the King for an extension of the privilege, in a way that it would also cover the acts of currying. Because, as mentioned before, medieval industrial privileges were primarily permissions to use, the required extension would imply permission for the inventor to engage in that additional activity.

The first text states the intention of the French government of fostering inventions. Such intention corresponded to the general policy then formulated by Colbert, which resulted in the creation of the Royal Academy of Sciences (in 1666) and, later, in attributing it the task of examining patent applications (in 1699).

The first text makes a reference to a petition submitted by three persons, apparently opposing the grant of the privilege. Indeed, such events of opposition and challenge by competitors of the applicants were not unusual in France. And in certain cases, the oppositions would not be flatly dismissed. On the contrary, they would be submitted to a thorough examination by a commission designated by the king himself or another authority. One example of such an event can be seen elsewhere.[78]

§ 2.32.1 Patent Granted to Ellie Bonnet—1666

Letters-Patent [based] on a Decision of the Council, of December 31, 1664, granting to the named Elie Bonnet, Bourgeois of Paris, the exclusive privilege of establishing, for the term of twelve years, in the cities and places of the kingdom he sees fit, Tanneries of a new invention.

November 6, 1666; Registered in Parliament, January 4, 1667, with amendments.

Louis, by the grace of God, King of France and Navarre: To all those who will see these present [letters], Greetings. We have always taken particular satisfaction, when the opportunity arose, to hand over our graces, gifts, permissions and privileges, to all those who, through their studies, travels, long works and experiments, have acquired considerable knowledge, secrets and inventions, so that those who apply themselves to the study of beautiful things, be encouraged to engage in them with more affection, in order to achieve those high perfections that make men illustrious and commendable; and well informed of the ability, knowledge and experience that our beloved Elie Bonnet, bourgeois of our good city of Paris, has acquired in the art and manufacture of tanning and preparing all kinds of leathers and hides, of a completely new invention and not yet used in our Kingdom, more prompt, and with significantly less costs than those used today, the hides incomparably more beautiful and more perfect, be it for the grain, color, strength and duration, We have favorably received the petition that he has caused to be presented to Us, so that We should grant him the permission and special privilege to establish, in our Kingdom, workshops and factories for the tannery and preparation of the aforesaid leathers, of the aforesaid new invention, with the right to show the composition of waters, drugs, liquors and mixtures thereof to those who wish to learn, and to prevent all persons, of whatever condition they may be, from using or practicing said new invention, and the composition of said waters, on the penalty of a fine of 3,000 pounds, damages and interests; and following the advice given by the Lieutenant-Civil and our Prosecutor at the Châtelet de Paris, subsequently to the said petition having been sent to them, by the Decision of our Council of October 8, 1663, after having previously seen and inspected some of the said leathers of the new making and preparation, and thereupon informed of the convenience or inconvenience, by notable people, merchants, former Consuls and Aldermen of our good city of Paris, and Master juror tanners, We have granted said Bonnet, preferably to all others, said permission, power, and right to establish said workshops and tanneries in our Kingdom, by another Decision of our Council of the last December 1664, in accordance with which said applicant very humbly has

78. *See* From Babylon to the Silicon Valley, *supra* note 1, at 21, reporting on a dispute on the patentability of a claimed invention that took place in 1610, under Henry IV.

begged us to grant him our Letters for this necessary. For these reasons, wishing favorably to support the good intentions of the said applicant, and to facilitate to him the means of giving the public said kind of leather tannery, and of recovering the costs in which he has already incurred, and those in which it is appropriate for him to incur to achieve the perfection of his works, as per our Council's advice, and our certain science, special grace, full power and royal authority, We have, following the Decree of our Council of the last December, attached hereto under our counterseal, and ignoring the petition presented by the named Auguerre, Vrancy and Lubray, as well as the process made in consequence, ordered and order by these Present [letters], signed by our hand, We wish and are pleased that, in accordance with the opinion of the Lieutenant-civil and our Prosecutor at the Châtelet of Paris, the aforesaid Bonnet enjoys, exclusively to all other persons, the permission, grant and privilege to practice alone, in the extent of our Kingdom and lands of our obedience, the new invention proposed by him, to tan hides and leathers of all kinds, and for this purpose to establish all workshops and tanneries of the said new invention, in such cities and places of our Kingdom that he sees fit, during the time of twelve years; the freedom nevertheless remaining to our other subjects, to bring from foreign countries, leathers of the said manufacture, as has been done until now, and the said Bonnet and his successors may not claim any rights of inspection on the Tanners, Curriers and other people who finish the leathers, except, in the event that they infringe the present privilege, granted to the said Bonnet, of being entitled to denounce the fact to the Judges of the places, to receive justice by them as reasonable. Therefore, we mandate our beloved Counselors, the persons holding our Court of Parliament in Metz, Bailiffs, Seneschals, their Deputies, and other our Magistrates and Officers to whom it will concern, that they facilitate the said Bonnet and his successors the enjoyment of the content of the said Judgment and of these present Letters of permission and grant, fully and peacefully, ceasing and making cease all contrary troubles and impediments, with prohibition to all Tanners and Curriers and other persons, of whatever quality and condition they may be, to disturb them in the effect and execution of the Present [Letters], under any pretext whatsoever, and to establish tanneries and leather currieries of the invention of said applicant, or use all or part of the drugs, waters, liquors and preparations used therein, without his consent, or his associates', in our Kingdom, during the said time, on penalty of disobedience, a fine of three thousand pounds, costs, damages, and interests, and for this purpose, accept and obey, constrain all those concerned: For such is our pleasure. In witness whereof, We have had our seal put on these said Presents. Given at Saint Germain-en-Laye, on the sixth day of November, the year of grace one thousand six hundred and sixty-six, and of our reign on the twenty-fourth. Signed Louis.

§ 2.32.2 Patent Letter Interpreting the Privilege Granted to Ellie Bonnet—1667

Patent Letters, interpreting those granted to Elie Bonnet, November 6, 1666

Registered, in Parliament, on January 4, 1667; with modifications

Louis [XIV], by the grace of God, King of France and of Navarra:

To our beloved and senior Councilors, the People holding our Court of Parliament in Metz, greetings. Having considered how much the manufacture of leather, and the preparation of all kinds of hides, is useful and necessary to our subjects, and having made our Council to examine the proposal of Elie Bonnet, a citizen of our good city of Paris, on tanning and preparing all kinds of leathers and hides of a new invention, and not yet used in our kingdom, more promptly and making the hides more beautiful and more perfect, because of their grain, color, strength and duration, We have, by our Patent Letters, addressed to you, of the November 6, 1666, upon the advice of the Lieutenant-Civil and Deputy to our Solicitor-General at the Châtelet of Paris, following the return to them on behalf of the said Bonnet, granted him the enjoyment, with the exclusion of all other persons, of the permission, grant, and privilege of practicing alone, in the extent of our Kingdom and the lands of our obedience, the mentioned new invention, by him proposed, to tan the hides and leathers of all kinds, and for this purpose, to establish the works and tanneries of the said invention in such cities and places of our Kingdom that he will see fit, during the time of twelve years.

But because the secret of the mentioned Bonnet is for the complete perfection of the leathers and hides, which consists in currying as well as in tanning, and that, under the pretext that in our said letters the said privilege is not sufficiently extensive, it mentioning nothing else than tanning and preparing the leathers and hides, the Curriers might pretend to oblige the said Bonnet to pass through their hands, to have the leather and skins of his new factory curried, which would be of great consequence to him, and all the more so that, by this means, the secret of the said Bonnet would be imperfect, and said Curriers could alter and spoil the said leathers, to discredit the said factory and new invention, whereupon the said Bonnet would have required us to grant him our Letters to this necessary.

For these reasons, wishing that such a beautiful secret, so advantageous to our subjects, be given to the public, and not wanting it to remain without effect, under the pretext of the injuries that be made to the said Bonnet, we have declared and declare our intention to have been in granting, by our mentioned Letters of November 6, 1666, the privilege of the said Bonnet, to tan and prepare all kinds of leathers and hides, to grant him likewise, as We grant him by these Present [letters], signed by our hand, the faculty and the privilege of currying or having curried, as well as tanning, all sorts of leathers and hides of his new manufactory and invention; and moreover we have discharged and exempted [him] from bringing to the leather markets those he will have manufactured, which he may sell in his shops and workbenches, provided he makes the necessary declarations at the offices of the control of the Revenue, and paying the corresponding fees.

And to prevent that frauds be committed and the new factory be counterfeited, we allow the mentioned Bonnet to affix his mark to the leathers and hides that he will have worked, and even to hold a clerk, if he thinks fit, at his own expense, in the mentioned leather markets, to prevent such abuses, and in the event of contravention, to order their seizure; to the charge by the said Bonnet to have apprentices, to make his secret public, after the expiry of the twelve years of his privilege, which apprentices will be received and admitted to the masterships of Tanners and Curriers, in the ordinary forms, in all the Cities of our Kingdom.

We order to all our Bailiffs, Seneschals, their Deputies and other officials to whom it may concern, that they shall ensure that the said Bonnet and his representatives enjoy and use [the rights described] in our Letters of the 6th of November, 1666, the judgment of our Council of the last December 1664, and these Present [Letters], fully and peacefully, ceasing and making to cease all disturbances and impediments to the contrary. We forbid all Tanners, Curriers and other persons, of whatever quality and condition they may be, to disturb them as to the effect and execution of the Present [Letters], under any pretext whatsoever, and to establish tanneries and curriers' shops of leathers and hides of the invention of the said Bonnet, to use totally or partly of the drugs, waters, liqueurs and preparations used in them, without his consent or of his associates, during the said time, under the penalty of disobedience, a fine of three thousand pounds, expenses, damages and interest; and to do this, to suffer, to obey and to compel all those to whom it may concern: for such is our pleasure. ...

§ 2.33 SOME INVENTORS FROM POITIERS ASK FOR A PRIVILEGE, CONCERNING A LOOM FOR THE MAKING OF BRAID AND RIBBON—1666

Revealing that the inventive spirit was well awakened in the second half of the seventeenth century and that French authorities—and Colbert, minister of Louis XIV, in particular—were receptive to proposals for supporting inventors, the following text reveals excerpts from a letter sent by the Intendant of Poitiers to Colbert, informing him of an application for an industrial privilege from several inventors of that city who claimed to have devised a method of increasing ten-fold (at least) the productivity of braid and ribbon makers, by allowing one single man, even if handicapped or blind, to operate several looms at the same time.

Barentin, Intendent, to Colbert.

Poitiers, May 8, 1666.

... I am sending you a memoir of a machine that some individuals of this city have invented, which contains the whole truth, having seen the effect myself, I believe, Sir, that if you please to propose to the king the privilege that its authors request, H. M. will have no problem in granting it to them, in order to facilitate its establishment, this machine being capable of making the helpless and even the blind to work, which will be of very great use.

I will wait for the grace of your reply to let them know the intention of H. M. and yours.

Proposal of a machine for making ribbon, so that a single man will make as much and even more than ten.

There are people in Poitiers who have invented a machine by which, with the work of one man only, they promise to operate 10 looms for making braid and ribbon. These inventors very humbly beg the king that he please to allow them to enjoy the benefit of their invention and the fruit of their labor, by granting them for twenty years the privilege of establishing themselves and their associates, and of making their machines work in all parts of the kingdom that they find appropriate, and the right to license and assign their privilege, and to sell their machines, with the prohibition to all persons, of whatever quality they may be, to use their invention during the time of their privilege, on the penalty of confiscation and a fine of 5,000 pounds in their favor. After which period the inventors want to give their machine to the public.

This machine is of admirable invention and very great utility, considering the quantity of ribbon that is used in the kingdom; besides, it must be considered that a thousand looms will occupy only a hundred men, and, in other words, only a hundred hands; for the silks being well arranged on each loom, a man of mediocre strength only needs one arm to make 10 work; so it is possible to make idle crippled people work, as long as they still have one arm.

It is even easy to make a blind man work there. So a master who has 10 boys in his workshop will only need one: he will save a lot, and these will be 9 people who can be employed elsewhere. It is true that the 10 looms carried out by one single man may not make as much ribbon or braid as 10 common looms operated by 10 men; but that depends on the accuracy and proportion of the movements that are employed in the said machine; for if we make them entirely equal and uniform, which is very easy, they will work almost as quickly as the others; besides that, the inventors assure that a single man will work well 12 [looms], and that even it is not difficult to reach the number of 20.

§ 2.34 PRIVILEGES GRANTED TO FOREIGN CLOTHMAKERS WHO BROUGHT SECRET KNOWLEDGE TO LYON AND WERE WILLING TO COMMUNICATE IT TO THE GUILD AUTHORITIES—1667

The following texts speak to the initiatives aiming at importing human skills into the manufacture of fine cloths of Lyon. In this case, the privileges had the purpose of persuading foreign artisans to bring "the secret of some new Cloth" to Lyon. The first text offered privileges to any foreign skilled worker but promised additional benefits to those in possession of trade secrets. The second text, on the request of local Masters, with the purpose of protecting jobs for local workers, reduced the offer to the latter.

§ 2.34.1 By-Laws Concerning the Manufacture of Fine Cloths of Lyon—1667

Regulations and By-laws concerning the Commerce, Art and Manufacture of gold, silver, and silk Cloths, and other mixed cloths that are made in the City and Suburbs of Lyon, and in all the region of the Lyonnais.

May 13, 1667

XXXV. The Master Traveling Salesmen and Foreigners, Companions, sons of Masters, also Traveling Salesmen and Foreigners arriving in this City, after working five years without interruption at the workshop of one of its Masters, will acquire the right to become Masters: And in the event that they bring the secret of some new Cloth, they will be exempted from the said five-year service, by an assembly of twenty of the most considerable Masters of the Community, who will be chosen by the Provost of the Merchants and Aldermen, and by the Elders who will have passed through the charges, and the Wardens in charge, by a plurality of votes: after which the said Traveling Salesmen or Foreigners will be received into the said Body, paying a fee of twenty pounds to the affairs of the Community, and twenty *sols* for the act of their reception. And as a consequence of their reception, at the good pleasure of the King, these foreign Workers will be declared Natural and Citizens of the Kingdom, and exempt from the right of *Aubaine*;[79] they shall not be required to take other Letters of Naturality than these present letters, or pay any fee for that; they and their successors and heirs will enjoy the goods and possessions they have acquired and will acquire hereafter in this Kingdom, like the

79. *Droit d'aubaine*: A feudal right that accorded to the local lord the goods of foreigners who resided in the lands of his/her dominion.

> other Subjects of His Majesty, by working in the said Manufactories: And in the event they leave the Kingdom and go to reside in foreign countries, all their property will belong to His Majesty. However, no one can in the future be received Master of the said profession to remain in the said City, Suburbs and Municipality of the Lyonnais, if he does not make profession of the Catholic, Apostolic and Roman Religion.

§ 2.34.2 Amendment to the By-Laws Concerning the Manufacture of Fine Cloths of Lyon—1700, 1702

Decisions establishing the Regulation of the Community of the Merchants and Master Workers in gold, silver, and silk Cloths of the City of Lyon

November 2, 1700 and December 26, 1702

Extracted from the Records of the State Council.

> Seen at the King's State Council the Request presented to it by Silk Master Workers with a seven-year tenure, part of the Community of Merchant-Master-Workers in gold, silver and silk of the City of Lyon, asking that it pleased His Majesty to receive them as opponents to the execution of the Decision of May 13, 1667, approving the By-laws and Regulations adopted in the same year of 1667 by some of the Merchant-Masters of the said Community; ...
>
> That in the future, given the almost infinite number of poor Masters who are in the City of Lyon, who for lack of work are reduced to the last poverty, foreigners should not be allowed to work in Lyon for more than six months, and that they can only be received as Masters after having completed their apprenticeship and worked for five years as Companions in the City of Lyon, if they have brought some advantageous secret to the trade and to the manufacture of silk Cloths; which secret they shall communicate and disclose to the Masters and Wardens in exercise: That prohibitions will be made to all Masters, Merchants and Manufacturers of the City of Lyon, to cause the Cloths that can be made in Lyon to be manufactured in Avignon, and other foreign countries. ...

§ 2.35 LOUIS XVI GRANTS A PRINTING PRIVILEGE FOR THE PUBLICATION OF THE SINCERE TAILOR—1670

As we have seen above, certain tailors resorted to the strategy of publishing their technical memoirs and have them protected by printing privileges rather than by applying for privileges targeting their knowledge directly. Here we have a second example.

The complete title of LE TAILLEUR SINCÈRE *reads:*

> *The Sincere Tailor—Containing the means to properly practice all kinds of work-pieces for men's clothes, and the quantity of cloth that must enter each type; i.e., from the age of fifteen to the greatest height and obesity that men can have, and in all kinds of fabric, not only for common clothes, but also for those of the Holy Father the Pope, and of the Cardinals, Bishops, and for all kinds of Ecclesiastics: As well as for the Ceremonies of the Kings, Princes, Lords and Officers, both of the Parliaments, and Magistrates of the Cities: The robes and clothes of the Grand Turk, Hungarians,*

Spaniards and Italians: With a collection of all the main pieces that are not very common, and the instruction of what has to be observed to cut and assemble them well and return them in their perfections, all with an explanation very easy to understand—Enriched with several Engraved Plates, in which the aulnages and measurements of each fabric are imprinted.

King's Privilege.

Louis by the grace of God, King of France and Navarre: To our beloved Counselors, Persons holding our courts of parliament, Masters of the Ordinary Requesters of our Hall, Bailiffs, Seneschals, Provosts, their Deputies, and all other our Officers concerned, Greetings. Benoist Boullay, Master Tailor of clothes at the Faubourg Saint Germain, of our good city of Paris, has caused to be shown to Us that for the sake of the public satisfaction, the economy of both general and individual families, the relief of those of his profession, and the instruction of Merchants, after several years of study, he has arrived to know in detail the fabrics, both of silk and wool, which are used in each garment of a man of whatever quality, age and profession he may be, the means of cutting said fabrics, and how to reduce them by the application and distribution of the pieces, for the perfect composition of the said clothes with a considerable management, [which knowledge] has not yet appeared to the public, and that for this purpose he has caused a number of Plates to be engraved on which the aulnages and measurements of each fabric are imprinted, as well as the quantity of what must be used in each garment, in proportion to the sizes of men and the places where the pieces must be taken and put the pieces marked by alphabetical letters, with instructions at the bottom of each of the Plates, of which he wished to compose a Book entitled *Le Tailleur Sincère* [The Sincere Tailor], containing the means and instructions for using the fabrics in all kinds of men's clothes and the quantity that must be used in them, which he cannot do without our Letters. For these reasons, wishing to treat the applicant favorably, We have allowed and granted him, allow and grant him by these Present letters to have printed by such Printers by us reserved, to whom he will communicate the aforementioned Book, and to sell and to trade in all the places of our obedience, for seven years, starting from the day on which its printing will be finished, during which we very expressly make prohibitions to all other Printers and Booksellers from printing, selling or distributing it, under pretext of increase or change of character in any way whatsoever, without the consent of the applicant, or of those who will be authorized by him, on the penalty of confiscation of the copies that will be counterfeited, and of a fine of one thousand pounds, applicable one third to Us, one third to the General Hospital of our good City of Paris, and the other third to the applicant, provided that two copies of the said Book will be placed in our public Library, one in that of our Office of the Louvre, and one in that of our very dear, and loyal Mr. Seguier Chevalier, and whose content We instruct you to facilitate the enjoyment by the applicant without any hindrance, and that by putting at the beginning, or at the end of each of said Book, an extract from the Present letters, and that only those copies duly checked by one of our beloved Counselors, and secretaries, be held valid; and faith be added to it as in this original. We order our first Bailiff or Sergeant, as requested, to take all measures necessary to the execution of the Present Letters, without the need for further permission. Because such is our pleasure, notwithstanding *Clameur de Haro, Charte Normande,*[80] and other letters to this contrary. Given in Paris on the fourteenth of June, the year of grace one thousand six hundred and

80. *See supra* note 76.

seventy: And of our reign the twenty-eighth. Signed, By the King in his Council, Renouard. And sealed with the big yellow seal, on a single tail. Registered in the Book of the Community of Printers and Booksellers of this City, according to the Decision of Parliament of April 8, 1653, with the charges, clauses and conditions set forth in these Letters: And in addition that he will cause it to be sold and traded by one of the Referenced printers. Made on the twenty-second of October 1670.

Figure 33 Cover page of LE TAILLEUR SINCÈRE, *by Benoist Boullay, and a few drawings illustrating some techniques described in the book.*

LE

TAILLEVR

SINCERE.

CONTENANT LES MOYENS POUR BIEN pratiquer toutes sortes de pieces d'ouvrage pour les habits d'hommes, & la quantité des estoffes qu'il y doit entrer en chaque espece ; Sçavoir depuis l'âge de quinze ans jusqu'à la plus grande hauteur & grosseur que les hommes puissent avoir, & en toutes sortes d'estoffe, non seulement pour les habits du commun ; Mais aussi pour ceux du S. Pere le Pape, & des Cardinaux, Evesques, & pour toute sortes d'Ecclesiastiques : Comme aussi pour les Ceremonies des Roys, Princes, Seigneurs & Officiers, tant des Parlements, que Magistrats des Villes : Les robes & habits du Grand Turc, des Hongrois, Espagnols & Italiens: Avec un receuil de toutes les principalles pieces qui ne sont pas bien communes, & l'instruction de ce qu'il faut observer pour les bien couper & assembler & les rendre dans leurs perfections, le tout avec une intelligence tres facille à comprendre.

Enrichis de plusieurs Planches Gravées, dans lesquelles sont emprimées les aulnages & mesurages de chaques estoffes.

Composez par B. BOULLAY.

A PARIS,

M. DC. LXXI.

AVEC PRIVILEGE DV ROY.

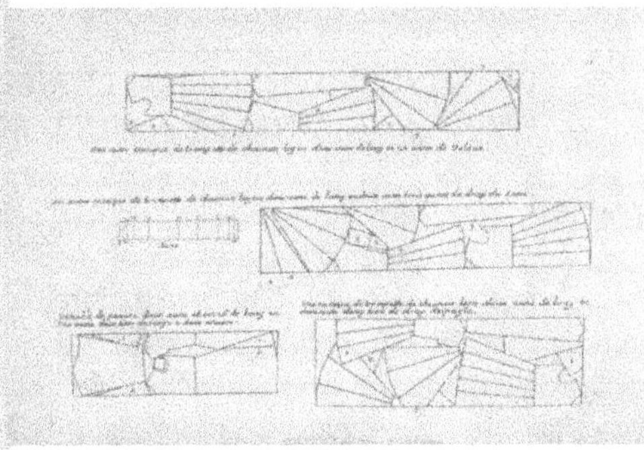

§ 2.36 ACTS AND ORDINANCES CONCERNING THE TAILORS' TRADE OF ABERDEEN—1678

It has been said above that clothmakers' guilds were not particularly concerned in regulating the management of trade secrets because of the generally low level of commercial rivalry among masters within the same city. However, that rule might not apply to commercial secrets, as opposed to technical secrets. The text that follows confirms this: new entrants in the guild of tailors of Aberdeen were prohibited from disclosing secrets concerning "the composition or other expenses and disbursements."

Acts and Ordinances of the Tailor Trade of Aberdeen, ordained by John Forbes, deacon of the Trade

February 18, 1678

Anent [Concerning] Keeping the Secrets of the Craft.

February 18, 1678. In presence of Alexander Milne, deacon, it is strictly statute and ordained unanimously be the hail trade that whatever entering freeman of the craft, or any other freeman thereof, shall anyways reveal or divulge to the Magistrates or any Burgess of Guild, directly or indirectly, any of the craft's secrets, especially anent their procedure when entering freemen of the trade, anent the composition or other expenses and disbursements, that the person or persons so doing (being made out) shall never carry public charge amongst the said trade as deacon, master, or box master, until they give to the trade all satisfaction anent the said misdemeanor.

§ 2.37 PRINTING PRIVILEGE FOR LE MERCURE GALANT, THE FIRST FASHION JOURNAL PUBLISHED IN FRANCE—1678

Le Mercure Galant may be considered the first fashion journal in France and probably in the world. It was a periodical gazette published in France between 1672 and 1724 (with some interruptions), founded by French writer Ecuyer de Vizé. It contained news about literature, theater, and social events (there was a lot of gossiping on its pages), and, frequently, notes on the latest fashions. Some of its editions included figures depicting apparel accompanied with their description. The newspaper publisher and editor received a privilege, granting him exclusivity in the text and illustrations of each edition of the magazine for a period of six years. Subsequently, the author transferred his privilege to the printer—a measure that was common practice when the privileges were directly granted to the authors, and not to the printers and/or booksellers.

The text (and the figure) that follow have been extracted from a supplement to the gazette, which was published with certain regularity for a few years.

Extract of the King's Privilege

By Grace and Privilege of the King, Given at S. Germain en Laye on December 31, 1677. Signed by the King in his Council, Junquieres. It is permitted for J. D. Ecuyer, Lord of Vizé, to have printed a book entitled MERCURE GALANT, presented to My Lord the Dauphin, and all in respect of said Mercury, for the time and space of six years, from the day on which each of said Volumes will finish to be printed for the first time: As well as prohibitions are made to all Booksellers, Printers, Engravers and others, from printing, engraving and trading the said Book without the consent of the Applicant, and extracting from it excerpts, or Plates serving to the ornament of the said Book, including selling separately, and giving the said Book to read, the whole on the penalty of a fine of six thousand pounds, and confiscation of the counterfeit copies, as it is further provided for in the said Privilege. Registered in the Community Book [of Printers and Booksellers] on January 5, 1678. Signed, E. Couterot, Trustee.

And said D. Ecuyer, Lord of Vizé, has assigned and transferred his right of Privilege to C. Blagenat, Printer-Bookseller, to enjoy the agreement made between them.

(*Finished printing for the first time on July 20, 1678*).

Figure 34 Plate from EXTRAORDINAIRE DU MERCURE GALANT. *The comment on this illustration was as follows (excerpt): "The latest fashion is what we call the Invisible. They are of several colors, but the one that reigns the most is the color of Prince. A fabric has also been used that from a two-step distance appears to have been cut out of plush. There are hardly any Ladies who have not had Garments made in all these different ways. They are wearing skirts of Point de France, and the new ones are of Point d'Angleterre, plain, sometimes with a lace, the same skirt being folded at the bottom. They are also made of white linen or striped muslin, with a beaded lace at the bottom of the skirt. Skirts of the same fabric as the coats continue being used; but when the Coats or Skirts are of Gauze, another Taffeta Skirt should be put under that of Gauze, and that it be of a browner or a lighter color. Thus the Gauze Skirt is brown in color, the Underskirt must be a lighter color; like also the one [in the picture below], being lighter; a darker color for the Underskirt should be chosen. ... Please examine the following Figure. It represents the way of dressing that is presently the most in use among the Ladies."* EXTRAORDINAIRE DU MERCURE GALANT, *Quartier d'Avril 1678, vol. 2, at 288-290 (1678).*

§ 2.38 THE ALDERMEN OF LILLE DECIDE IN FAVOR OF PRESERVING THE TRADE SECRETS OF THREE CLOTHMAKERS—1692

As a testimony to the growth of commercial freedom and rivalry within the textile industry at the end of the seventeenth century, which was the consequence of the lifting (albeit partial) of strict technical controls, the following text shows that finally trade secrets began occupying an important place in the constellation of intellectual property rights that clothmakers used to protect their competitive advantages. In a decision settling a dispute involving three manufacturers of woollen cloth (sayeteurs) *of Lille, who disagreed with the procedures and costs involved in the inspection and sealing of their products, which was attributed to the master* sayeteurs, *the magistrates of the municipal council acknowledged the manufacturers' worry with the possibility that the requirement to submit their products to such inspection would entail the disclosure of their secret methods of manufacture to those masters—who, after all, were their direct competitors. Thus, the magistrates granted them that the inspection should be carried by someone else with independence vis-à-vis their trade—and without a conflict of interests.*

The clothmakers' request and the aldermen's decision was something unthinkable under the old corporatist regime.

> ... which having been seen and all considered, we have ordered and order the said Anselme Carpentier and Rose, father and son, manufacturers of cloths in the fashion of London serges, to conform themselves to the obligation of apposing the seal of their trade in the manner they are applied to the serges made by the master *sayeteurs* of this city and for which no more than one *patar* shall be payed for each piece, on penalty in case of offense that the said Carpentier and Rose will incur the fine imposed by the ordinances of the said body and trade of *sayeterie*, in which fine they will also incur in the event of refusal of opening their workshops to the masters of the said *sayeterie*, so that they inspect their workshops and working places. Made in the assembly of aldermen this twenty-fifth of June 1692, signed G. Tesson. ...
>
> On request presented by Anselme Carpentier, Jean-Baptiste and Jean-François Rose, so that it pleased us to appoint others who are not *sayeteurs* for applying the seal to their manufactures, in execution of the above ordinance, given that the *sayeteurs*, in applying the aforesaid seals, could discover the secret of manufacture of the aforesaid Carpentier and Rose, which would be detrimental to them, this matter having been put under deliberation and all considered, we have ordered and order the inspectors of the office of *sayeterie* to go to the workshops of the said Carpentier and Rose to apply the seals to their articles in accordance with the ordinance above, to receive the *deniers* that will result from that and pass it into the hands of the collector of the office, who will report it, as he has done in respect of the other *deniers* of his revenue concerning the seal of the looms, to which effect copies of the ordinance above and of the present one will be delivered to said inspectors and collector, for their compliance. Made in assembly, this July 5, 1692. Signed B. Herreng.

§ 2.39 THE SOCIAL CONSTRUCTION OF INVENTIONS: JEAN MARIUS, INVENTOR OF THE FOLDING PARASOL/UMBRELLA, OBTAINS AN INDUSTRIAL PRIVILEGE, BUT SOCIAL PRESSURE CREATES RESISTANCE TO ITS USE—1710 AND ONWARDS

The historian Fernand Braudel, referring to the pace of invention in the historical period that followed the Middle Ages, wrote:

> *... [I]f the textile industry showed little development from the fifteenth to the middle of the eighteenth century, it was because its economic and social organization, the elaborate division of operations and the low wages of workers enabled it to face the exigencies of the market without any change. There were so many obstacles that we can agree with James Watt when he confided to his friend Snell (26 July 1769) "that in life there is nothing more foolish than inventing." The successful inventor had to have society on his side.*
>
> *Nine times out of ten the patents of inventions, serious or not, recorded on the pages of registers and dossiers in the Venetian Senate corresponded to the particular problems of the city: they sought to make the waterways converging on the lagoon navigable; dig canals; raise water; drain swampy land; turn mills without resorting to hydraulic power (unobtainable in this world of stagnant waters); work saws, millstones, hammers to powder the tannin or raw materials used to produce glass. Social considerations were uppermost."[81] Fernand Braudel, CIVILIZATION AND CAPITALISM—15TH-18TH CENTURY, VOL. I, THE STRUCTURES OF EVERYDAY LIFE—THE LIMITS OF THE POSSIBLE, 433-5 (translation and revision Siân Reynolds, Univ. of California Press, Berkeley, 1992).*

Somewhere else I designated the social phenomenon Braudel referred to in this excerpt as "the social construction of inventions," this meaning that:

> *It is society that attributes a certain value to an invention, not the inventor. The inventor makes the invention, but it is society that determines whether it will be used or not. In other words, the invention is not only the result of individual construction, which stems from the inventor's creative mind, but also (and mainly) from the interests that society has in its making. This social construction [of inventions] is not dictated only by considerations of an economic nature. It is also composed by relevant aspects of social sensitiveness, from mere idiosyncrasies to deeply embedded values that are related to beliefs, religions, and so on. See Nuno Pires de Carvalho, September 2010,* The Theorem of the Social Value of Inventions and The Happiness Machine Patent Syndrome, *available at <works.bepress.com/nuno_carvalho/1>.*

The following texts are a clear illustration that the value of inventions is determined by society, regardless of (and sometimes against) inventors' expectations and wishes.

In 1705 Jean Marius submitted to the French Royal Academy of Sciences his invention of the folding parasol/umbrella. In 1710, upon the Academy's favorable advice, Louis XIV granted him an industrial privilege for five years. For a couple of years, Marius—a

81. Even though this translation is not inaccurate, Braudel's original expression is much more expressive: *La société commande.* Literally, it means: "society commands."

prolific inventor, according to the records of the Academy—kept improving the parasol/umbrella. In spite of the high marks his invention received in the press, namely the Mercure Galant, *it seems that the inventor failed in obtaining commercial success. The reason was that only those who could not afford a carriage would carry a parasol/umbrella. Thus, using or displaying an umbrella was giving public proof of poverty—which most people tended to avoid. Besides, because at that time French cities kept much of their medieval configuration, with very narrow, winding streets, where buildings would lean on those standing across, there was not much of a need for carrying parasols/umbrellas. This fact, in combination with the high price of umbrellas, explains the privilege granted in 1769 to a company authorizing it to set a business of renting parasols/umbrellas for those who crossed the Pont Neuf, in Paris. Subsequently, the privilege was extended to other bridges, avenues, and squares of Paris.*

The business has had so great a success that it has given rise to a new profession: some individuals rented umbrellas and offered passers-by, against a price, the service of accompanying them while they crossed the bridge, thus protecting them against the rain. It seems that those individuals, known as gagne-deniers *("penny earners," in literal translation) would frequently harass passers-by, thus creating a problem of public security. This has led the municipality of Paris to regulate the practice of renting umbrellas.*

The exclusive privilege to rent umbrellas was revoked by a Decree of the Revolutionary Parliament, in 1792. But this does not mean that the business of renting umbrellas has come to an end. Through the nineteenth century the business expanded through France, England, and Germany—but now under a system of competition—given that the price of folding umbrellas remained high. This explains why umbrellas and parasols from the eighteenth century onwards became a fashion item. Being expensive, they were exclusive to those who could afford them. Conspicuous consumption would encourage certain members of the upper classes to acquire and display them, as an integral component of their dressing.

In other words, the use of umbrellas, which in the beginning was a motive of shame, because it meant poverty, became later an item of fashion.

*Polyester had not been invented yet. Thus the coverage offered by parasols and umbrellas would be obtained by the treatment of certain fabrics, such as linen and taffetas. Because the makers and merchants of umbrellas were not incorporated into a guild, in the second half of the eighteenth century several disputes concerning the exclusive right in making parasols and umbrellas erupted between the community of purse makers (*boursiers*) and that of workers in wood (*boisseliers*). The latter has been granted the right to manufacture parasols and umbrellas with waxed cloth, and the former, the right to make those same articles using taffeta and any other sorts of fabrics. See* Statuts de la Communauté des Maîtres et Marchands Boursiers de la Ville et Fauxbourgs de Paris *(Valade, 1774). Source: <gallica.BnF.fr>.*

Although Marius' invention represented a major advance in parasols and umbrellas, those were still heavy and cumbersome. Fifty years later, a certain Navarre improved *them, by making them much lighter and more portable. His invention consisted basically of replacing the tube to which the ribs were fixed with a movable one. According to the Royal Academy of Sciences, even if the insertion of folding umbrellas into a cane was already a known matter, Navarre's invention made the umbrella (or parasol) much more convenient and susceptible of having its size and weight greatly reduced. (*HISTOIRE DE L'ACADÉMIE ROYALE DES SCIENCES*, year of 1759, at 243-244 (Imprimerie Royale, 1765); Source: <gallica.BnF.fr>).*

The reduced weight and the possibility of using them as canes reinforced the use of parasols/umbrellas as accessories to fashion.

§ 2.39.1 Industrial Privilege Granted to Jean Marius for the Invention of the Folding Parasol/Umbrella—1710

> Louis, by the grace of God King of France and Navarre, to our beloved gentlemen holding our courts of Parliament, Grand Council, ordinary requests from of our hall and our palace, provost of Paris or his deputy, bailiffs, seneschals, their deputies and other officers magistrates concerned, Greetings. Our beloved Jean Marius has shown us that he has invented a new kind of parasol or umbrella, which, being open, is as large, firm and even more solid than those that are in use, and opens and closes with the same speed, and which however being folded up can be placed in a case about an inch and a half in diameter and seven to eight inches long, and can be made so light by the different shapes or ways that he will give them and by the different materials of which they will be composed, that there will be some that will weigh only five to six ounces, everything included, without diminishing anything in their amplitude: therefore this new umbrella will become, by its lightness and the smallness of its volume, a pocket object that one can always have with oneself to use it as needed, which will give opportunity to men and most women, who could not get used to the use of ordinary umbrellas, both because it is not suitable for everyone to carry them under the arm, and because of their weight and their awkward volume, of using those of the applicant, and to all the public to enjoy an invention so useful and so reduced in its volume and weight, which can be reduced to a twelfth or fifteenth of those which are in use. But, fearing that after having made a great deal of expense to cause several umbrellas of this new sort to be made, the workers might try to imitate them, counterfeit and trade them, which would cause him great harm and prevent him from profiting from the fruit of his work and his invention, he very humbly has begged us to grant him our letters of privilege, to this necessary.
>
> Wishing to treat the applicant favorably and to facilitate to him the means to profit from this invention: after having seen the testimonies that our Royal Academy of Sciences has given to the novelty and usefulness of this invention by its certificates attached under the counterseal of our chancellery, we have allowed and granted, allow and grant the said Marius, by these present letters, signed by our hand, [the privilege] to make or have made alone, by such workers as he sees fit, to sell or have sold or distributed in all the cities and places throughout the extension of our kingdom, for the time of five consecutive years, folding parasols or umbrellas susceptible of being carried in the pocket, according to the descriptions and models he left in our said academy, and to have a particular mark put on them so as to resort to them during the inspections, in the event they are counterfeited.

Establishing very express inhibitions and prohibitions to all workers and to all other persons, of whatever quality and condition they may be, from imitating or counterfeiting them, under any pretext whatsoever, and from selling or distributing similar ones without his or his successors' consent; on the penalty of confiscation of the counterfeited parasols or umbrellas, and a fine of one thousand pounds, applicable one third to us, one third to the Hôtel-Dieu of Paris and the other third to the applicant, and all costs, damages and interest.

Therefore we instruct that you have these present letters registered, and that they be enjoyed and used by the applicant, fully and peacefully, ceasing and making to cease all troubles and obstacles. We wish that to the copies of the present letters, confirmed by one of our beloved Counselors, be accorded faith as in the original. We order our first bailiff or sergeant, upon request, to take all measures necessary for the execution of the present letters, without [the need for] asking for other permission.

Because this is our pleasure.

Given at Versailles on the 1st of January, the year of grace of 1710, and of our reign the seventeenth.

Figure 35 Drawing of Marius' original invention of the folding parasol/umbrella, as submitted to (and approved by) the French Royal Academy of Sciences in 1705 and patented in 1710.

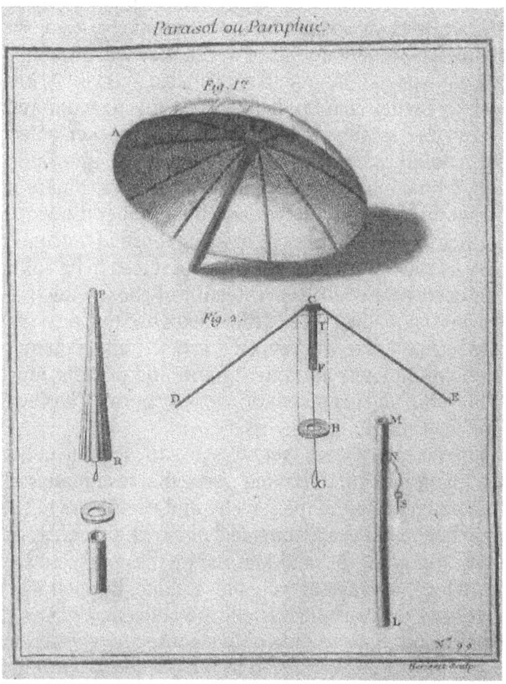

§ 2.39.2 Le Mercure Galant Praises (And Advertises) Marius' Invention—1711

Newly invented umbrellas and parasols that can be carried in the pocket. This new invention reminds me of a soldier who during a terrible storm quietly followed his path despite the rain that falls on him. I shouted at him from a house I was in for him to come in and take cover. "You don't know," he shouted, "that a good Soldier always has in his pocket enough to protect himself from the harms of the weather"—and saying this, he drew out a long tin bottle which he finished emptying, asking me for something with which he could fill it. So presently we can say very seriously, I have in my pocket enough to protect myself from the harms of the weather, because these new Umbrellas, which we can use, do not take more place than the Soldier's bottle. I would give here its exact description, but it would be long; you just have to buy them: it is the shortest way. They are sold near the St. Honoré barrier [door]. The one who invented them was Mr. Marius to whom we owe those broken Clavessins that one could almost also call Pocket Clavessins. [82] I do not despair that his ingenuity will manage to give us, for our Armies, pocket Tents, or at least Pocket Barracks.

§ 2.39.3 The Folding Parasol/Umbrella Becomes a Fashion Item and, at the Same Time, a Sign of Social Division—1768

We must believe that the umbrella thus modified [by Navarre] ended up winning all the votes, because the Oratorian[83] Caraccioli depicts the Parisian citizen of 1768 [as being] inseparable from his umbrella, which he carried around with him for half the year: "The custom, he wrote, has been for some time to never go out without an umbrella and bother to carry it under the arm for six months to use it perhaps six times. Those who don't want to be confused with the vulgar like better to run the risk of getting wet than to be looked at their promenades as if they were people going on foot."

82. Here the author refers to the fact that Marius was a manufacturer of musical instruments. In 1716, he submitted to the Academy an invention concerning the small pieces that give tension to clavessins' strings.
83. Member of an Oratory, a Catholic society.

Figure 36 At the end of the eighteenth century, umbrellas/parasols had already become a fashion item. Women and men would use them as canes. Part of the caption of this illustration reads: "La femme, pour plus de maintien, porte, de la main droite, une canne en parasol." ("The woman, for more support, carries, with her right hand, a cane as a parasol.")

§ 2.39.4 In 1769 a New Business Model Was Born in Paris: The Commercial Rental of Umbrellas at the Entry and Exit Points of the Pont Neuf

> When you take a coach because of bad weather, you propose yourself two things: to put your head under cover and to avoid getting mud on your shoes. This is wonderful for those who can devote twenty-four cents to this double convenience; but human conditions consist of more half-prosperities than whole prosperities, and it is in favor of the former that a business worthy of mention has just been formed. A company has obtained the exclusive privilege of renting umbrellas at the extremities of Pont Neuf, so that the ladies, the small gentlemen, the voluptuous can cross this bridge without danger of getting wet or being inconvenienced by the sun. By paying two *liards* up front, an attendant provides you with the useful device, which you drop across the river into the hands of another attendant, who stands there to give or receive the umbrella. Small offices are established at both ends of the bridge; there the payment and the deposit of the protective devices

are made. The service has run very busy for the past eight or ten days; already a good number of passers-by have tried to forget to hand over the umbrella at the office after using it; but a tireless surveillance watches over forgetful or absent-minded memories. There is talk of expanding the business to other bridges, to main streets, to main squares. This is not a philosophical innovation; it seems rather sybaritic to me: that's why I believe in its success.

Figure 37 The rental of umbrellas on Pont Neuf. Drawing by Janet-Lange, CHRONIQUES DE L'OEIL DE BOEUF, *at 240.*

Loueurs de parapluies sur le pont Neuf.

§ 2.39.5 Regulation on the Business of Renting Umbrellas at the Bridges and Main Streets of Paris—1769

Public notice

On behalf of the King and the Lieutenant General of Police

Public umbrellas

Our objective in establishing public [rental of] umbrellas for the night as well as for the day is to provide the residents with an additional convenience and the penny-earners a manner of earning a living.

But because it is important for public safety that there are no prowlers during the night in the streets and neighborhoods, the lieutenant general of police orders:

1. That the penny-earners who will carry umbrellas during the night, shall get them from the office of the Directorate, where they will be registered by description, names and addresses, as well as from Mr. Heancre, Inspector of Police, and from the office of Security.
2. That these penny-earners carry a small lantern, on the door of which the same number of the umbrella will be cut, not to serve as a lamp, the lamp posts being more than sufficient, but to serve to recognize the bearer of the umbrella, and to receive his payment.
3. These umbrellas, commonly referred to as parasols, are of green taffeta, solid, packaged blue, and numbered. Their distribution to the penny-earners will begin on Saturday, September 16, 1769, at the Directorate's office, Saint-Denis Street, near that of Grand-Heurleur, at the Magasin d'Italie.
4. Because the season no longer requires umbrellas for the Pont Neuf, the Directorate will stop this public service on the 17th, only to resume when the fine weather returns, both for this bridge and for that of La Tournelle, the Royal bridge, the Carrousel, the square of Louis-Quinze and other places where it will be understood that this convenience can be useful.

Impression and posting authorized, on September 14, 1769. Desartine.

§ 2.40 IN ANOTHER INITIATIVE LINKED TO THE TAPESTRY INDUSTRY (AUBUSSON), FRANCE REAFFIRMED THE EXCLUSIVITY OF INDUSTRIAL DESIGNS—1730

Apparently, the tapestry industry appreciated the first experiment (in France) of protecting the exclusivity of designs in Beauvais (§ 2.32). Several decades later, through a patent letter, the same protection was granted to the designs created for the tapestries of Aubusson. And a few years later a similar patent letter would be issued in connection with the manufacture of tapestries of Feuilletin, which competed with those of Aubusson. Such competition was not always fair: in 1736 the King's Council issued a judgment ordering the two factories to stop copying each other's trademarks.

By that time it had already become clear that the beauty and quality of the designs woven into the tapestries, if protected, constituted competitive advantages and were a significant factor of industries' success.

Decision providing a regulation for the Tapestries of Aubusson

December 12, 1730

Extracted from the Records of the King's Council

The King, having had shown to him the statutes and regulations made in 1665 for the merchants, master manufacturers and workers of the manufactory of tapestry in the city and suburbs of Aubusson, burgh of the Court, authorized by letters patent given in July 1665, by which the late King, to preserve this factory's old reputation and give it the means to improve its works, would have granted it a painter and a dyer who would be maintained at his expense: And His Majesty being informed that, because this provision has not been followed, the manufacturers are working on very imperfect designs, and that it is necessary to restore the good order and rule in this manufacture, to prevent it from falling into total weakness; wishing to address this, and provide this manufacture with singular marks of his protection. ...

XXVI. His Majesty prohibits all painters, merchants, master manufacturers and workers of tapestries, from copying or causing to be copied the designs which will have been made at the expense of merchants or master manufacturers, on penalty of a fine of five hundred pounds against each offender. ...

XXVIII. His Majesty wishes that, in accordance with the letters patent of July 1665, a painter be immediately sent to and maintained at His Majesty's expense in the town of Aubusson, to make the designs of the tapestries that will be made there, to train students and to inspect the workers of the said factory, as regards the beauty and the regularity of the shades of the tapestries.[84]

Figure 38 Armchairs with upholstery from Aubusson, Paris, 1760. Gulbenkian Museum, Lisbon, Portugal.

§ 2.41 REGULATION OF THE INDUSTRY OF WOOLLEN CLOTHS OF LILLE—1732

We have already seen several examples of this trend: in the eighteenth century, when the Industrial Revolution was gaining speed, the pressure of consumers on novelty started becoming uncontrollable. The strictness of the legal structures that prohibited cloth

84. Five years later, an identical provision was included in the regulations concerning the manufacture of carpets of Feuilletin (Patent Letters Establishing the Regulation for the Manufacture of the Tapestries of Fueilletin, January 29, 1737, Article xxiv; SUPPLÉMENT DU RECUEIL, at 513, 521).

manufacturers from deviating from predetermined standards was abated, and lawmakers started admitting the introduction of new fabrics and new designs. However, a certain level of reluctance and control of change continued. In France, it disappeared with the Revolution, in 1789.

Decision providing a regulation on the widths and lengths of the cloths of Sayeterie, Bourgeterie[85] and others, made in the city and jurisdiction of Lille

April 19, 1732

Extracted from the records of the State Council

> LXXIX. As far as the cloths of new invention are concerned, the making of which is not regulated by this decision, His Majesty orders that the Master *Sayeteurs* and *Bougeteurs*, before making them, shall present themselves to the offices of *sayeterie* and *bourgeterie*, to hear the decision from the mayors and authorities of those offices.

§ 2.42 LOUIS XV, OF FRANCE, CANCELS AN INDUSTRIAL PRIVILEGE ON GROUNDS THAT IT HARMS IMPORTS—1736

Industrial privileges have often been used with the main, if not only, purpose of import substitution. For that reason, many privileges were granted to foreign skilled artisans willing to immigrate, bringing techniques not known in the receiving country.

Interestingly, the following text operates in the opposite direction. But only to a certain extent. The text shows a decision of Louis XV's State Council canceling a privilege granted to the inventor of a method of making fabrics in imitation of furs. The privilege was canceled because it harmed the interests of French furriers who imported furs from Canada. However, the State Council's decision should not be seen as a pure matter of support to free trade, because in 1736 Quebec and Acadia were still French territories and their main source of revenue was exactly the export of furs. So, in canceling the privilege, the Council was actually protecting French merchants on both ends of the trade.

This decision is a clear illustration of two aspects of the system of industrial privileges that preceded the current regime of patents. First, their grant and canceling were based on an idea of public interest or convenience. What qualified a product or a process for a privilege was not its inventive character, but the convenience in promoting its commercialization. And, second, the privilege was primarily a permission to use the invention—exclusivity was a secondary feature. So, when the privilege in question was granted, permission to use the method of making imitations of furs was inherently granted. Canceling the privilege meant, therefore, canceling that permission.

85. *See supra* note 28.

At the end of the day, there is no lesson to extract from this example, other than it serves as an illustration of how governments struggle to give effective use to the patent system for the sake of pursuing fleeting industrial and commercial policies.

Decision that prohibits the brothers Mouchot from Lyon and all manufacturers, from making cloths that imitate furs

May 19, 1736

Extracted from the Records of the State Council

> Seen at the King's State Council, His Majesty being there, the ordinance established by the Provost of the Merchants and Aldermen of Lyon, on December 29 last, by which, on the consent given by the masters and wardens of the community of merchants and master manufacturers of the said city, the said provost of the merchants and aldermen would have declared the Mouchot brothers, merchants and manufacturers of this city, the first inventors of a kind of fabric made with raw dyed silk, mixed with goat hair, and finished in the manner of imitating the furs of different animals; and consequently they would have granted to the said Mouchots, under the good pleasure of His Majesty, an exclusive privilege for the manufacture of the said fabrics for six years, with prohibitions to all persons to imitate or counterfeit them, on the penalty of confiscation and a fine of five hundred pounds; [seen] the memoir presented on this subject by the said Mouchot brothers. Seen also the allegations made by the wardens of the community of furriers of Paris, and by the Chamber of Commerce of La Rochelle, on the damage that this factory could receive from the trade in furs that come from Canada, jointly with the opinion of the deputies at the trade office; the report of Mr. Orry, Counselor of State, and member of the Royal Council, General Comptroller of Finances, The King being in his Council, dismissing the ordinance of the provosts of the merchants and aldermen of the city of Lyon, of December 29 last, which will remain null and void, has made and makes very express inhibitions and prohibitions to the Mouchot brothers and to all other manufacturers to make the fabrics in question, which imitate furs, on the penalty of confiscation and a fine of five pounds, and moreover of forfeiture of the mastership. [The King] Commands the Intendant and Commissioner appointed to the province of Lyon, to ensure the execution of this decision, which will be read, published and posted wherever necessary. Done at the King's State Council, His Majesty being there, held at Versailles on May nineteen, one thousand seven hundred and thirty-six. Signed Chauvelin.

§ 2.43 THE PROTECTION OF INDUSTRIAL DESIGNS IS CONFIRMED AND STRENGTHENED IN RESPECT OF THE FINE CLOTH INDUSTRY OF LYON AND LATER EXTENDED TO OTHER CITIES—1744 ONWARDS

In 1744, Louis XV, of France, approved the regulations of the silk industry, in Lyon, confirming a number of by-laws previously approved by the magistrates of that city, which prohibited the unauthorized copy of designs. Four decades later, those rules were extended, with more details, to other French cities. This new regulation included detailed provisions on the process of registering designs.

These provisions and their effective enforcement reveal that French authorities at that time had already realized that exclusivity in ideas and their expressions was a significant factor that contributed to the progress of a competitive industry. This policy was clearly expressed in the 1787 regulations.

§ 2.43.1 Regulation of the Industry of Fine Cloths of Lyon—1744

Statutes and Regulations for the Community of Master Merchants, and Master Workers in fabrics made of gold, silver and silk, and other mixed of silk, wool, fur, yarn and cotton, of the city and suburbs of Lyon; and for the manufacture of the said fabrics (excerpt)

Title IX

XII. Similar prohibitions are imposed to the said master workers from selling, giving or lending, for whatever cause and under any pretext whatsoever, the designs entrusted to them for manufacturing, under the penalty of a fine of one hundred pounds and the forfeiture of the mastership, and even of corporal punishment; for the payment of which fine the said master workers shall be subject to imprisonment [*contraint par corps*], by virtue of the Consulate's judgment that will have condemned them to it.

XIII. Similar prohibitions are made to all designers and other persons whomever, from removing and copying, causing the removal and copy directly or indirectly, and in any way whatsoever, any design on fabrics, both old and new, or on design sketches of the said fabrics; under the penalty of a fine of one thousand pounds against the designer who would have removed or copied the said designs, and of the same fine against the person who had caused them to be removed or copied, and in addition to the seizure of the fabrics which were made upon the removed or copied designs; the said seizure applicable half in favor of the said community, and half in favor of the master whose designs would have been removed or copied.

§ 2.43.2 A Lawsuit Involving the Infringement of Industrial Designs in Lyon—1749

Judgment of the King's State Council which confirms, with fine and costs, a judgment of the Judges of the Consulate of Lyon, which condemns Mr. Ribier, Merchant Manufacturer of Silk Cloths in Lyon, with the penalties provided by Articles XIII and XIV of the Regulations of 1744, concerning the Manufacture of Silk Cloths of Lyon, for having removed one design from Mr. Duperet & Company, also Merchant Manufacturers in Lyon, and having had made Silk Cloths with the same design

April 29, 1749

Extracted from the Records of the State Council

Between Aymé Ribier, Merchant Manufacturer in Cloths of Gold, Silver and Silk of the City of Lyon, Appellant of a Judgment of the Consulate of the City of Lyon of June 13, 1747, according to the Requests by him presented to the State Council on

January 9, 1748 and January 22, 1749, on one side; and Jean-Baptiste Duperet & Company, also Merchants Manufacturers in Gold, Silver and Silk Cloths of the said city of Lyon, Respondents and Defendants, on the other side. ...

The definitive and *inter partes* judgment of the Consulate of Lyon, of June 13, 1747, rendered after having heard the advice of the Masters and Guards, who said that as a result of the clarifications and observations found in the Minutes above mentioned, they believed that the said Duperet & Company are the first Inventors and first Manufacturers of the Design and Druggets in question; by which Judgment, deciding on the merits of the dispute of the Parties, reserved by the said inter partes judgment of the previous 31st of May, that the said Duperet & Company are declared inventors of the Design in question, and the first makers of the Druggets upon the said Design; and consequently, given the infringement committed by the said Ribier by having it copied and having worked upon it, against the provisions of Articles XIII and XIV of the Regulations for the Manufacture of Silk Cloths of Lyon, the said Ribier is condemned to the penalties and fines against him pronounced by the Judgment of the 24th of the said month of May, which would be executed for that purpose, and, moreover, ordered to pay the costs. ... The King in His Council, ruling on the whole, without regard to the appeal filed by the said Aymé Ribier of the said Judgment of the Consulate of Lyon of June 13, 1747, or to all his requests, in which His Majesty has declared it non receivable and ill-founded, and which He has dismissed, has ordered and orders that the said Judgment shall be executed in accordance with its form and content: Condemns the said Ribier to the fine of 75 pounds and to the costs ... Made at the King's State Council, held at Versailles on the twenty-ninth of April, one thousand seven hundred and forty-nine. ...

§ 2.43.3 Decision of the King's Council Extending the Protection of Industrial Designs to the Fine Cloth Industry of France—1787

Decision of the council providing for regulations for the new designs that the manufacturers of silk and gilding fabrics of the kingdom will have composed or caused to be composed

Versailles, July 14, 1787

The King having had submitted to him, in his council, the requests and memoirs of the bodies and communities of the manufacturers of Tours and Lyon on the attacks brought to their properties and the general interest of the factories concerning the copying and counterfeiting of designs, H. M. would have recognized that the superiority that the silk factories of his kingdom have acquired is principally due to the invention, the correctness and the good taste of the designs; that the emulation that animates the manufacturers and designers would be annihilated if they were not assured of reaping the fruits of their labors; that this certainty, in accordance with the rights of property, has maintained until now this kind of manufacture, and has caused it to deserve the preference in foreign countries, He would therefore have deemed it necessary, in order to retain all its advantages, to extend to the other silk factories of his kingdom the regulations made in 1737 and 1744 for that of Lyon, on the copying and counterfeiting of the designs, and by giving to the true inventors the right of enforcing in the future their property in a sure and invariable way, and to further excite their talents by an exclusive enjoyment, proportionate in its duration to the costs and the merits of the invention. Wishing to solve this: seen the advice of the trade deputies, heard the report, etc. The King, being in his council, has ordered and ordered the following:

1. The manufacturers who will have composed or caused to be composed new designs, will have alone, exclusively to all others, the right to have them executed in silk cloths, silk and gilding, or mixed with silk; the duration of this privilege will be fifteen years for fabrics intended for church furnishings and ornaments, and six for those stitched and finished for apparel or other use, all from the day on which they have completed the formalities hereinafter prescribed.
2. H. M. prohibits all workers from selling, giving or lending, for any reason and under any pretext whatsoever, the designs that will have been entrusted to them to manufacture, on the penalty of a fine of one hundred pounds, of forfeiture of mastership, if appropriate, and even of corporal punishment; to the payment of which fine they will be corporally constrained, by virtue of the decision of the judges to which the police and the knowledge of the causes of the manufactures is attributed by the regulations.
3. H. M. also forbids to all designers and other persons, whoever they are, to extract and copy, to cause the extraction and the copy, directly or indirectly, and in any way whatsoever, of any design on fabrics, both old and new, on the cards of the designs of the said fabrics, on the penalty of 1,000 pounds against the designer who would have extracted or copied the aforementioned designs, and the same against the one who would have caused him to extract or copy them, and additionally the confiscation of the fabrics manufactured on the extracted or copied drawings, the said confiscation to be applied, half in favor of the community of which the manufacturer whose design has been extracted or copied will be a member, and half to the profit of said manufacturer or merchant. ...
5. The manufacturers who have invented or caused a design to be made, and who wish to keep for themselves its execution, shall, as regards the new designs to be made, from the date of publication of this decision, submit the original sketch, or a sample, as they wish, to the office of their community, of which a report of description will be prepared, free of charge, by the acting jurors-wardens, in a register kept for this purpose and initialed by them or by the trustee and custodian, which report will contain the name, trade name and address of the master and merchant manufacturer, who will, as author and inventor of the said designs or fabric, have his property recorded, the date of the year, month and day on which he will have submitted his design or sample. All the reports will be continuous, without blanks; the number will be placed in the margin of the document which will be elaborated on the register, the stamp of the community and that of the owner will be affixed at the time of writing on the design sketch or on the sample, which will remain between the owner's hands, and on this square the report and its number will be mentioned by extract, certified by the trustee so that there may be recourse to it if necessary. The master and merchant manufacturer may obtain a copy of the entire report, paying 2 pounds for all rights.
6. In the case the manufacturers fail to have completed the formalities prescribed by the preceding article, before the sale of the fabrics manufactured according to new designs, they will be and will remain forfeited of all claims.
7. The manufacturers who have completed the formalities prescribed by Article 5, will be considered sole owners of the designs that they have submitted to the office of their community, and consequently they may sue before the judges of the police of arts and crafts of the domicile of the offenders, both those who would extract, copy or imitate the same designs as those which they

would have executed, to request against them the pronunciation of the penalties imposed by Articles 2, 3, and 4 above, and the confiscation of the fabrics, both against the manufacturer who would have it executed, and against any merchant who would offer them for sale, except the merchants' appeal as regards the value of the goods, and damages, and interests, which could be owed to them against the manufacturer who would have sold the fabrics made on designs extracted, copied or imitated.

8. H. M. forbids any manufacturer to execute in silk cloth, in silk cloth and gilding, or in cloth mixed with silk, any design executed in painted paper or otherwise, without having verified whether the design executed in paper has not already been so in cloth; consequently, the manufacturer who executes in fabric a design of paper already imitated from the fabric, will be in breach of Article 3, and will incur the penalties there established.
9. H. M. orders the lieutenant of police of the city of Paris, the intendants and commissioners designated in the various provinces, as well as the provost of the merchants and aldermen of the city of Lyon, lieutenant of police, judges of the factories of Tours and others, the wardens, trustees and assistants of the communities, and to all to whom this will concern, to ensure, within their attributions, the execution of the present decision, on which all the necessary letters will be issued, and which will be printed, read, published and posted wherever needed.

§ 2.43.4 A Formal System of Registration of Fashion Designs Is Established in Lyon—1806

March 18, 1806

Law of March 18, 1806 establishing a council of prud'hommes in Lyon (excerpts)

Title II

...

Section III

On the conservation of the property of the designs

Art. 14.—The council of prud'hommes is charged with the conservative measures of the property of the designs.

Art. 15.—Any manufacturer, who wants to be able to claim, subsequently, before the commercial court, the property of a design of his invention, will be required to deposit in the archives of the council of prud'hommes a specimen under envelope, bearing its stamps and signature, on which will also be affixed the stamp of the council of prud'hommes. ...

Art. 17.—In case of dispute between two or more manufacturers on the property of a design, the council of prud'hommes shall open the envelopes deposited by the parties; it will provide a certificate indicating the name of the manufacturer who will have the priority of the date.

Art. 18.—In depositing his sample, the manufacturer shall declare whether he intends to reserve the exclusive ownership for one, three or five years, or for perpetuity; this statement shall be noted. On the expiry of the period of time indicated by the said declaration, if the reservation is temporary, any packet of samples deposited under seal in the archives of this council must be sent to the registry of arts of the city of Lyon, and the samples contained therein be added to the collection of the registry. ...

§ 2.44 GREAT BRITAIN AWAKENS FOR THE IMPORTANCE OF PROTECTING INDUSTRIAL DESIGNS FOR CLOTHS—1787

In the middle of the eighteenth century, copyright in artistic designs, such as engravings and etchings, was already recognized in England, through a number of statutes passed by the Parliament. But their use as aesthetic patterns or molds for consumer goods had still to wait several years. Great Britain was confident in the power of its manufacture for winning the trade wars against other European powers and the United States. The first British Act granting protection for designs was passed in 1787. It was a very limited Act, however. It would apply to certain fabrics only, and it would not extend to articles of manufacture. Moreover, the term of protection was very short, which would make this Act ineffective as far as certain textiles were concerned. Interestingly, it provided for the exhaustion of rights. In 1839 the registration requirement was introduced.

An Act for the encouragement of the arts of designing and printing linens, cottons, calicoes, and muslins, by vesting the properties thereof in the designers, printers, and proprietors, for a limited time

June 1, 1787

Whereas it may be expedient, for the encouragement of the arts of designing original patterns for printing linens, calicoes, cottons, and muslins, to vest the property thereof in the designers, printers, or proprietors, for a limited time; for which purpose may it please your Majesty that it may be enacted; and be it enacted by the King's most excellent majesty, by and with the advice and consent of the Lords spiritual and temporal, and commons, in this present parliament assembled, and by the authority of the same. That, from and after the first day of June one thousand seven hundred and eighty-seven, every person who shall invent, design, and print, or cause to be invented, designed, and printed, and become the proprietor of any new and original pattern or patterns for printing linens, cottons, calicoes, or muslins, shall have the right and liberty of printing and reprinting the same for the term of two months, to commence from the day of the first publishing thereof, which shall be truly printed with the name of the printer or proprietors at each end of every such piece of linen, cotton, calico, or other person whatsoever, from and after the fifth day of June one thousand seven hundred eighty-seven, within the time limited by this act, shall print, work, or copy, such original patter or patterns, or cause to be printed, worked, or copied, such original pattern or patterns, or shall print or reprint, or cause to be printed or reprinted, any such pattern or patterns, and shall publish, sell, or expose to sale, or in any other manner dispose of, or cause to be published, sold, or exposed to sale, or in any other manner disposed of, any linen, cotton, calico, or muslin, so printed without the consent of the proprietor or proprietors thereof, first had and obtained in writing, signed by him or them respectively in the presence of two or more witnesses, knowing the same to be so printed or reprinted without the consent of the proprietor or proprietors of such pattern, then every such proprietor or proprietors shall and may: if the offence be committed in England, by and in a special action upon the case, to be brought against the person or persons so offending, recover such damages as a jury on the trial of such action, ...; and if the offence be committed in Scotland, every such proprietor or proprietors shall and may, ... provided nevertheless, that it shall and may be lawful for any person or persons who shall hereafter purchase any plate or plates, block or blocks, for printing, from the original proprietors thereof, to print, reprint, and expose for sale, or cause to be printed, reprinted, and exposed for sale, from the said plates or blocks, without being liable for any action on that account. ...

§ 2.45 THE INVENTION OF THE COTTON GIN AND THE AFFLICTION OF ITS INVENTOR, ELI WHITNEY—1794 ONWARDS

Eli Whitney was the inventor of the cotton gin, a machine that separates cotton fibers from the seeds, thus mechanizing and speeding the process of preparing the material for yarning. That was a fantastic, albeit technically simple, invention, for it has considerably increased productivity. The invention had significant social repercussions because it permitted the cotton business to remain afloat in the wake of the end of slavery in the Southern States of the United States, to the extent it significantly reduced the pressing need for human labor.

And yet Eli Whitney's sowing the financial fruits of his invention was not without serious tribulations. As evidence of the "syndrome of the happiness patent machine,"[86] *Whitney's patent was attacked from all sides—by opponents who claimed lack of patentability; by users, who abundantly infringed the patent (in Savannah, Georgia, alone, Eli Whitney and his partner filed no less than sixty infringement lawsuits); and by political authorities, such as the Governor of the State of Georgia, who, in a message to Georgia Legislature, asserted that Whitney's patent was "an extortion" to cotton producers.*

And yet Eli Whitney and his capitalist partner, Phineas Miller, could consider themselves lucky because, at the end of the day, they were able to reap significant gains not only from verdicts obtained against infringers but also from payments from the assignment of patent rights they made to the three Southern States—South Carolina, North Carolina, and Tennessee—in the amount of $90,000, which was a fortune at that time.

The following texts reflect just a tiny part of Whitney's main problem—that of having invented an invention with a huge social value. Whitney's invention was significantly improved by Hodgson Holmes, who just two years later (in 1796) obtained a patent for

86. "The higher the social value of inventions the lower is the proportion of revenue that inventors are able to capture from their exploitation. This formulation is a hypothesis that stems from the observation of facts: most patents covering highly valuable inventions are subject to attacks that are difficult to explain. Those attacks have social causes, such as the monopoly stigma, the urge for penance and the idea of just price. Together they form the happiness machine patent syndrome. There is no evidence making a definitive case for the theorem above, and yet observation of the difficulties that have insistently haunted the exploitation of a number of fundamental patents suggests that it may be more than a mere hypothesis." *See* the introductory note to § 2.40.

a similar gin that operated with the assistance of saws. Nevertheless, Whiney's invention has survived as the fundamental idea.

The partial reproduction of the specification has not been extracted from the original document, which was lost in the fire that in 1836 destroyed the archives of the United States Patent Office. The source is an official copy that was filed by Whitney with the Court of Savannah, Georgia, in support of one of his infringement lawsuits.

§ 2.45.1 Eli Whitney's Cotton Gin Patent Specification

United States of America

To all to whom these Letters Patent shall come

Whereas, Eli Whitney, a citizen of the United States, hath alleged that he has invented a new and useful improvement in the mode of spinning cotton, which improvement he states has not been known or used before his application; hath made oath that he does verily believe that he is the true inventor or discoverer of the said improvement; hath paid into the Treasury of the United States the sum of thirty dollars, delivered a receipt for the same, and presented a petition to the Secretary of State, signifying a desire of obtaining an exclusive property in the said improvement, and praying that a patent may be granted: These are therefore to grant, according to law, to the said Eli Whitney, his heirs, administrators or assigns, for the term of fourteen years from the sixth day of November last, the full and exclusive right and liberty of making, constructing, using, vending to others to be used, the said improvements; a description whereof its given in the words of the said Eli Whitney, himself, in the schedule hereto annexed, and is made a part of these presents.

In testimony whereof I have caused these Letters to be made Patent, and the Seal of the United States to be hereunto affixed.

Given under my hand, at the City of Philadelphia, this fourteenth day of March, in the year of our Lord one thousand, seven hundred and ninety-four, and of the Independence of the United States of America the eighteenth.

(Seal.) G. Washington. Edm. Randolph, Secretary of State.

§ 2.45.2 Message from the Governor of Georgia, James Jackson, Attacking Whitney's Patent—1800

Extract from a message relating to the Gin Monopoly by Governor James Jackson to Legislature of Georgia, November 3, 1800

And here I request your attention to the patent gin monopoly under the law of the United States, entitled, "An act to extend the privilege of obtaining patents for useful discoveries and inventions to certain persons therein mentioned and to enlarge and define the penalties for violating the rights of patents."

The operation of this law is the prevention and cramping of genius as it respects cotton machines, a manifest injury to the community and in many respects a cruel extortion on the gin holders. The two important States of Georgia and South Carolina where this article appears to be becoming the principal staple are made tributary to two persons who have obtained the patents and who demand, as I am informed $ 500.00 for the mere liberty of using a ginning machine, in the erection of which the patentees do not expend one farthing and which sum, as they now think their right secured, it is in their power in future licenses to raise to treble that amount from the information given me by a respectable merchant of this town (Louisville, Ga.) ... Monopolies are odious in all countries, but more particularly so in a government like ours. The great law meteor, Coke, declared them contrary to the common and fundamental law of England, their tendency certainly to raise the price of the article from the exclusive privilege—to render the machine or article worse from the prevention of competition and improvement—and to impoverish poor artificers and planters who are forbidden from making, vending or using it without license from the patentees, or in case of doing so, are made liable to penalties in a court of law.

The Federal Court docket, it is said, is filled with these actions. I do not doubt the power of Congress to grant these exclusive privileges for the constitution has vested them with it, but in all cases where they become injurious to the community, they ought to be suppressed, or the parties be paid a moderate compensation for the discoveries from the government granting the patent. The celebrated Dr. Adam Smith observed that monopolies are supported by cruel and oppressive laws, such as is the operation at present of the law on the subject—its weight lays on the poor industrious mechanic and planter. Congress, however, did not intend it so, for when the first law on its head was passed in February 1793, a few individuals only cultivated cotton, and it was not dreamt of as about to become the great staple of the two Southern States ... .

§ 2.45.3 Eli Whitney and Phineas Miller Respond to Governor of Georgia's Letter—1800

(Copied from "The Columbian Museum and Savannah Advertizer," Dec. 23, 1800).

To Governor Jackson

I have read with sensations peculiar to the occasion your official attack upon our private property, acquired under the patent law of the United States, but we have long doubted whether it were proper to communicate these sensations to the public.

It has always appeared to us that the private pursuits of individual industry are entitled to the most sacred and inviolable protection of the laws, and that a good cause where private right alone was concerned might suffer trivial injuries without acquiring the claim to be presented before the solemn tribunal of public opinion. But when the title to our property is slandered and political persecution openly commenced against us under pretence of official duty by our chief magistrate, silence on our part might be supposed to sanction the abuse. ...

In the first place, your Excellency will permit us to remove the deception which is palmed on the public to our disadvantage in the opprobrious term "monopoly." The respectable authors whose names were brought forward to sanction your opinion on this subject speak of the exclusive right to carry on a trade or manufacture as a "monopoly," and not of the protection which government chooses to give to the arts. The principle of the patent law, your Excellency will please to observe, consists of a fair compromise between the government and the author of the invention. There can be no doubt but what an invention in the arts must remain the exclusive right of the inventor under the most oppressive laws, while the secret is confined to him, and many instances have occurred of the preservation of the secret for years and even of its final loss to the public to the death of its inventor.

To remedy which evil and to stimulate ingenious men to vie with each other, governments, by enacting patent laws, substantially agree that they will afford to the author of the invention the most ample protection in the use of the discovery for a certain term of years on condition that after that period it shall become public property. And in carrying into effect of all such discoveries, it is well-known that every inventor must incur the whole expense and take on himself the entire risk of the success of his invention, in which if he fails, his loss of time and money does not always constitute his greatest mortification, and if he succeeds, the public advantage must of necessity go hand in hand with his acquirements, since the inventor cannot expect his invention to be employed or paid for unless it exceeds all others in point of utility. In the present case, we believe the utility of our invention well known and candidly admitted by all rational men. At the time it was brought forward, there were millions of pounds of cotton in the seed, which awaited the event of some improvement in the mode of ginning, and wealth, honor and gratitude were promised to the fortunate exertions of genius which would insure the culture of green seed cotton to the up-country.

Under such flattering auspices and the protection of the law, the invention was perfected, and at great expense in money, which has never been repaid, and of time and labor, which is unrewarded, and now your excellency would direct your influence to blast the harvest so hardly earned, and which for many years has waived in distant view and buoyed up our hopes under the existence of adversity and oppression, which would have better suited the perpetrators of vice than the industrious and successful improvers of so useful an art. ...

The alternative which your excellency suggests of paying a moderate compensation to the patentees, or suppressing the patent, appears to us to be injudiciously chosen, for in the first of these cases, if the bargain is to be all on one side and the persons who would defraud us of our right are to be the sole judges of the compensation to be made the oppression would be too manifest; and the proposition of suppressing the patent is so bold a thing that we forbear giving it comment. ...

§ 2.45.4 Confronted with Rampant Infringement, Whitney and Miller Advertise Their Intention to Sue All Infringers and Offer Settlement

A Caution.

The subscribers having, by the industry and attention of Eli Whitney, and at a heavy expense on the part of Phineas Miller, invented, perfected, and brought into use, a newly constructed machine for ginning cotton, had flattered themselves that the Planters would have been satisfied with the moderate terms proposed for cleaning out their crops, and that a property, acquired in a manner so advantageous to the general interest of the public, would have been protected from injury, without the intervention of the laws. But since this is not likely to be the case, the best information having been received that several attempts have been made, under the pretext of improvements on their machine, to trespass on their rights, and to wrest from them their hard-earned privileges, they are induced to give the following public notice: That the said Eli Whitney did, on the 14th day of March, 1794, obtain a patent, executed in due form, under the great seal of the United States, granting to him the full and exclusive right and liberty of making, using, and vending the others to be used, his new and useful improvement in the mode of ginning cotton, for the term of 14 years, beginning from the 6th day of November, 1793, as will appear on record in the office of the Secretary of State to the United States: That, on the 21st day of June, 1794; the said Eli Whitney, by deed of transfer on record at said office, made conveyance of one half of his interest in said patent to the said Phineas Miller. That the principle of the Improvement on which said patent is founded consists in picking the cotton from the seed with teeth, from which it is afterwards removed with a brush. This improvement being perfectly different from any method heretofore practiced for ginning cotton is the more clearly and explicitly secured by the laws of the United States made for the encouragement of the arts. And since the property acquired by the patentees in this invention is placed under the same protection as any real estate belonging to their fellow citizens, they will view in the same light every trespass or injury to which it may be exposed, and will certainly make use of the means which the laws of their country have placed in their hands to obtain ample redress. As they will be forced, however, with great reluctance, to this necessity, they now offer to those who have hitherto been ignorant of their patent, and who have constructed the machines upon principles, the use of which is thereby exclusively secured to the patentees, that if they will immediately desist from all further trespasses, and deliver up the machines so constructed, they shall not be prosecuted for the heavy penalty they have forfeited by the laws, but meet with every reasonable indulgence from Miller and Whitney. Savannah, May 1, 1795.

Miller & Whitney. "A Caution." *Georgia Gazette.* May 7, 1795.

§ 2.45.5 Denison Olmsted, One of Whitney's Attorneys, Speaks of His Determination in Enforcing His Patent Rights

... More than sixty suits had been instituted in Georgia before a single decision on the *merits* of his claim was obtained, and at the period of this decision, thirteen years of his patent had expired. In prosecution of this troublesome business, Mr. Whitney had made six different journeys to Georgia, several of which were accomplished by land, at a time when, compared with the present, the difficulties of such journeys were exceedingly great, and exposed him to excessive fatigues and privations, which at time seriously affected his health, and even jeopardized his life. A gentleman [Hon. S. M. Hopkins] of much experience in the profession of law, who was well acquainted with Mr. Whitney's affairs in the South, and sometimes acted as his legal adviser, observes, in a letter obligingly communicated to the writer of this memoir, that "in all his experience in thorny profession of the law, he has never seen such a case of perseverance, under such persecution; nor (he adds) do I believe that I ever knew other man who would have met them with equal coolness and firmness, or who would finally have obtained even the partial success which he had. He always called on me in New York, on his way South, when going to attend his endless trials, and to meet the mischievous contrivances of men who seemed inexhaustible in their resources of evil. Even now, after thirty years, my head aches to recollect his narratives of new trials, fresh disappointments and accumulated wrongs."

Figure 39 Eli Whitney's cotton gin, patented in the United States in 1794.

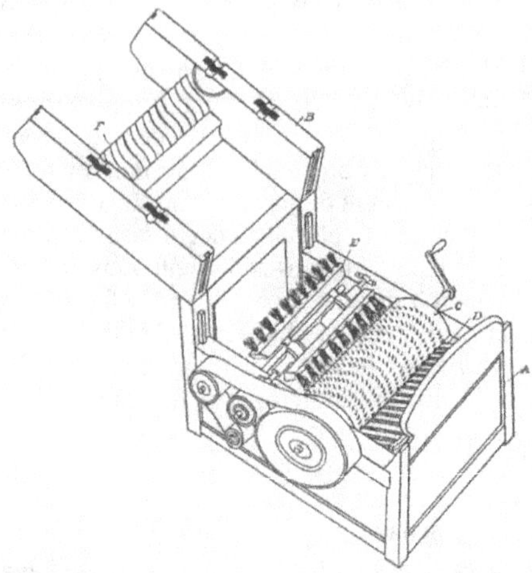

§ 2.46 IN A CASE INVOLVING A TEXTILE-RELATED INVENTION, THE BRITISH COURT OF CHANCERY HOLDS THAT THE INVENTION DISCLOSURE REQUIREMENT IS EMBEDDED IN THE RATIONALE OF THE PATENT SYSTEM—1816

The subject matter of the following text is not specific to the textile industry. It deals with the mandatory disclosure of inventions, which is a requirement that pertains to the patent system and cuts across all technologies, except those that are covered by national security concerns. However, this particular opinion is of importance to a book that deals with the evolution of intellectual property in the textile and fashion industries because the main argument raised by the English inventor of a machine for the making of lace for keeping his invention secret was the fear that his French competitors would soon find its details and copy it.

This speaks to the high level of bitter rivalry between the cloth industries of France and England concerning export markets.

In part, the design of the patent system at the end of the eighteenth and nineteenth centuries was influenced by that rivalry, when the two economies were immersed in the Industrial Revolution. In their eagerness to gain competitive advantages, they developed efforts to acquire each other's trade secrets and triggered initiatives to counter those efforts. We have seen an example of those counter initiatives in § 2.30.2. The following text involves the same topic.

The French patent act of 1791 admitted that some inventions could be patented without the need for their disclosure. This rule was in part explained by the intent of the French to use the patent system to their advantage in the dispute they had with England for industrial and technological supremacy. By contrast, English common law was much stricter in requiring that inventions' specifications be disclosed.

The text that follows is a report of a judgment holding that disclosure of British patented inventions was too important for being dispensed with, even if it gave some advantage to the French industry.

In Re Lacy's Patent

In the Court of Chancery—July 25, 1816

> Mr. Bell stated, that this was an application to the Court, praying that his Lordship would not put the great seal to a patent which Mr. Lay, of Nottingham, had sought to obtain for making lace by a machine, to be worked by a steam-engine. The ground objection to the patent was, that Mr. Lacy wanted to keep his specification secret for the space of fifteen months, which was contrary to the policy of the law, and great injustice to the king's subjects in general. ...
>
> The Lord Chancellor Eldon said, that he could not put the great seal to a patent which gave the party fifteen months to make out his specification. In the present reign thousands of patents had been granted, and this indulgence was extended only in two or three of them. Where the letters patent were for an invention to be used in England, Scotland, and Ireland, the usual period for the specification was six months; but where they were confined to England only, two months was the given time. Mr. Lee's case was a very peculiar one; it was for securing to the State, in a time of war, the benefit of a most important discovery. If Mr. Lacy could make out that the State was to be benefitted by his invention in any peculiar way, as in the case of preparing hemp and flax, it might be doubtful whether he might not have a secret specification. His Lordship was of opinion, however, that the Legislature would pause a long time before they passed such an Act in future; and he thought he might venture to say, that if Mr. Lacy were to apply for such an Act he would not procure it. The gentleman had said, that if this specification was not kept secret the French might copy it; but his Lordship could not establish a new principle merely to prevent the French from smuggling; neither could he put the great seal to a patent without seeing the specification, for it might turn out not to be worth a farthing, and then public genius would be discouraged merely for the benefit of the patentee. Many cases of this nature had occurred. The patent could not pass without the responsibility of the great seal; and if his Lordship could bring himself to pass it, he might be called upon to give an account in Parliament why he had extended this particular privilege to this individual. It was certainly contrary to the general policy of the law, and he could not in justice to the King's subjects affix the great seal to it merely because it was a manufacture which other countries had in common with this.

§ 2.47 A BRITISH COURT ENFORCES A NON-COMPETING COVENANT AND A TRADE SECRET IN DYEING—1822

In the course of the nineteenth century, English courts developed the fundamentals of trade secret law. The majority of the cases that led to such development concerned secret medicinal formulae. But the following text concerns the textile industry. Significantly, the High Court of Chancery not only stated its support to the enforceability of rights in a trade secret but also acknowledged the validity of a clause of non-competing.

Bryson v. Whitehead

High Court of Chancery

1822

This was a Bill for the specific Performance of an Agreement, for the sale of the Goodwill of a Trade, and of a Secret in Dying.

The Plaintiff had for many years carried on the trade of a Dyer in Spitalfields and had a particular mode of dying Bombazeens and Stuffs. None but himself and his Son-in-law, one Portlock, knew the secret of dying Stuffs in that mode; and this secret was esteemed of great value. In December 1820, Bryson being about to retire from Business, agreed to sell the Good-will of his trade, together with the Plant and Fixtures, to the Defendant for 1,500 /., and the exclusive benefit of the Secret for 1,000/. Heads of the Agreement in writing were signed by both Parties, and were expressed as follows: "Heads of Agreement between Mr. Bryson, of, &c. and Mr. John Whitehead, of, &c. Mr. Bryson possesses a Secret in the art of dying Bombazeens, Princes Stuffs, and other Goods, which is known to himself and Son-in-law, Samuel Portlock, only: Mr. Bryson is about to retire from his Business, and therefore he has agreed with Mr. Whitehead as follows: Mr. Whitehead is to pay him, for himself and Son, 1,000/. for the Secret, and 1,500/. for the Plant and Fixtures upon his Premises, and for the Goodwill of the Trade, and to have the Premises leased or assigned at the following Rents: [then followed a description of the Buildings, and the amount of the Rent]. Mr. Bryson to make the Secret known to Mr. Whitehead, and instruct him in the Art, and to make over the Trade and Goodwill, and use his endeavours to secure it to Mr. Whitehead, by circular Letters, and other usual means; and he is not himself to engage in the business of a Dyer for Twenty-years; and he is to engage that his Son-in-law will not divulge the Secret, or engage in the business of a Dyer for the same term as Mr. Bryson; and that neither of them shall do anything to prejudice Mr. Whitehead in the Trade of Mr. Bryson, and in securing and continuing the Business of the connections of Mr. Bryson; and he is to procure his Son-in-law to enter into an Engagement to the same effect to Mr. Whitehead: An Inventory of the Plant to be delivered, &c. Possession to be delivered to Mr. Whitehead on payment of the 1,000/., and a Circular immediately issued, so that the Trade may be continued in the usual manner, under the direction of Mr. W., with the assistance of Mr. Bryson, who is to divulge the Secret, and instruct Mr. W. there in immediately after the payment of the 1,000 /. ...

Whitehead forthwith paid the 1,000/. and was put into Possession of the Trade, and had the Secret communicated to him.

Bryson and his Son-in-law soon afterwards executed a Bond to Whitehead in the common form, with a Penalty of 2,000/. reciting the Agreement, and with the condition, that they or either of them would not, for Twenty years, in any manner exercise the trade of Dyers within the distance of Fifty miles from Spitalfields, and would not, at any time, disclose the Secret.

Whitehead, however, thought that this Bond (which was prepared by Bryson's Solicitor) was not sufficiently restrictive, and that Bryson and his Son might, at any time, without incurring any Penalty, resume their trade at any place beyond the distance of Fifty miles from London; as at Kidderminster, Norwich, or in York shire, where Bombazeens and Stuffs are principally manufactured. For this reason he insisted on a Deed of Covenant more restrictive in its terms, and with Clauses for liquidated Damages in case of breach of the Agreement.

Disputes arose in consequence, as to the terms of the Deeds to be executed under the Agreement, ... Mr. Heald, and Mr. Whitmarsh, for the Plaintiff.

Mr. Bell and Mr. Theobald, for the Defendant, submitted it to the judgment of the Court, whether the Agreement was of such a kind as could be carried into execution. It was the essence of the Agreement that neither Bryson nor his Son-in-law should, for Twenty years, carry on the Trade of Dyers. If, however, the Agreement was to be acted on so as to confine the Restriction on exercising the Trade to places within Fifty miles from London, then the Defendant would not have that Benefit which he had stipulated for by the Agreement; because the Plaintiff, or his Son-in-law, by removing to Norwich, or any other convenient Situation beyond the distance of Fifty miles, would come into direct competition with him. If considered as an Agreement not to exercise the trade of a Dyer anywhere for Twenty years, it was void by the policy of Law, *Mitchell v. Reynolds*. If, on the other hand, it was to be acted on so as to limit the Restraint on carrying on the trade to the distance of Fifty miles from London, the Defendant would lose the benefit for which he had contracted.

The Vice-Chancellor:—

> Although the policy of the Law will not permit a general restraint of trade, yet a Trader may sell a Secret of Business, and restrain himself generally from using that Secret. Let the Master, in settling the Deed which is to give effect to this Agreement, introduce a general Covenant to restrain the use of the Secret for Twenty years, and a limited Covenant, in point of locality, as to carrying on the ordinary business of a Dyer, both Parties being willing that the Agreement should be so modified.

The Decree therefore referred it to the Master to settle a proper Deed.

§ 2.48 THE SEWING MACHINE: A DISRUPTIVE INVENTION THAT HAS GIVEN RISE TO THE EMERGING OF THE FASHION INDUSTRY—1830

As noted in the Introduction, the industry of fashion was born in the nineteenth century as the product of the combination of three factors: the invention of the sewing machine, in France; the increase of consumerism in the middle class, as a by-product of the Industrial Revolution; and the emergence of the ready-to-wear ("prêt-à-porter") in the United States.

The sewing machine was particularly important in that it mechanized an activity that until then was carried out by hand—that of sewing—thus speeding the process of apparel making, and permitting the setting of manufactories where tens or hundreds of workers could align behind machines and sew previously cut garments.

However, the sewing machine, when it appeared, was a seriously disruptive technology, to the extent that it threatened to put every tailor and seamstress, whose work until then was purely manual, out of work. It followed that Barthélemy Thimonnier, the inventor of the sewing machine, like William Lee (see § 2.19), would not receive a fair share of the social value his invention generated. But, unlike Lee, Thimonnier was able to secure patent rights (in France, England, and the United States). His first patent was granted in France on July 17, 1830, for a "Métier propre à la confection des coutures dites à points de chainettes." The Catalogue des Brevets mentions the name of a co-grantee, Ferrand, but Thimonnier's biography does not explain what role that person has played in making the invention. Eventually, he might have been a partner in Thimonnier's first efforts to complete the invention. As it was a common practice at that time, the inventor—a tailor by profession, who spent four years and his scarce savings in making the invention—may have secured the support of a capitalist and entrepreneur, Beaunier, to help him set a business.[87] *To some extent, Thimonnier's luck was even worse than Lee's: at his first attempt to set a factory for clothmaking, in Paris, with eighty of his devices installed, he was physically attacked and his establishment destroyed by fire and vandalism. Later Thimonnier associated with another capitalist, J. A. Magnin, who helped him improve the machine, and secured patent protection for the improvement under the name of Couso-Brodeur (literally, "Sewer-Embroiderer"). Following a route inverse to that of Lee, Thimonnier at a certain point went to England, where he assigned his patent to a Manchester-based company. After a brief (and, businesswise, unsuccessful) stay, Thimonnier returned to France.*

In the following years, a number of patents for improvements on the sewing machine were obtained by several distinguished inventors, such as Elias Howe, in various countries. No less than seventeen patents were granted in France, England, and the United States, between 1830 and 1857, covering improvements to Thimonnier's fundamental invention.

Thimonnier died in dire poverty, leaving an old, frail, and sick widow, who survived by gaining a few cents spinning cotton in a factory based at Amplepuis (near Lyon, France), his late husband's hometown. In response to the initiative of an association of manufacturers of Lyon, the Minister of Agriculture, Commerce, and Public Works, of France, in 1866, granted a sum of 600 francs to Thimonnier's widow. This story is told in detail by a French historian and partly reproduced in one of the following texts. (J. Meyssin, HISTOIRE DE LA MACHINE À COUDRE—PORTRAIT ET BIOGRAPHIE DE L'INVENTEUR, BARTHELEMY THIMONNIER (Rey et Sézanne, 1867)).

§ 2.48.1 Specification of the Patent Obtained in England by Thimonnier and Magnin for an Improved Sewing Machine—1848

February 9, 1848—Patent No. 12,060

> Magnin, Jean Marie.—(*Partly a communication from Barthelemy Thimonnier.*)—Machine for sewing, embroidering, and making cords or plats by the employment of a needle or hook, a nipple, and a rotatory thread carrier in combination. The thread carrier is situated beneath the table whereon the fabrics to be sewed or embroidered are placed. The needle has a descending and ascending movement, so as to cause its hooked end to pass through the fabrics down to the thread carrier, and then to ascend therefrom. The nipple surrounds the stem of the needle, and descends on to the fabric at stated intervals. When the hooked end of the needle descends through the fabrics, the nipple, which then ascends, carrying the loop of thread through the fabrics, and through the loop previously made; after which the nipple rises, the fabrics are moved onward a

87. At the end of the nineteenth century, the number of this sort of partnerships decreased because inventions started being made systematically under the supervision of capitalists, who hired inventors to join large firms' research departments. Inventors have, thus, become employees.

distance equal to the length of stitch required, and the above-described movements are repeated.

If the above mechanism is put in operation without placing and fabrics on the table, a looped cord is produced.

PATENTS FOR INVENTIONS—ABRIDGEMENTS OF SPECIFICATIONS RELATING TO SEWING AND EMBROIDERING, 1755-1866, at 13 (2nd ed., George E. Eyre and William Spottiswoode, 1871). Source: < archive org >.

Figure 40 The original model of Thimonnier's sewing machine—a very rude one, made of wood.

§ 2.48.2 Patent Obtained by One of Thimonnier's Assignees in the United States—1850

United States Patent Office

Barthelemy Thimonnier, Aîné, of Amplepuis, France, Assignor to Philip May, of London, England

Improvement in Sewing Machines.

Specification forming part of Letters Patent No. 7,622, dated September 3, 1850

To all whom it may concern:

Be it known that I, Barthelemy Thimonnier, Aîné, of Amplepuis, Department Du Rhône, in the Republic of France, a citizen of the Republic of France, have invented or discovered new and useful Improvements in Machinery for Forming Stitches in Fabrics for Plain and Ornamental Purposes; and I, the said Barthelemy Thimonnier, Aîné, do hereby declare that the nature of my said invention and the manner in which the same is to be performed are fully described and ascertained in and by the following statement hereunto annexed, and to the figures and letters marked thereon—that is to say: ...

Having thus described the invention, I wish it to be understood that I do not claim the mechanical details of which the machine is composed; but

What I claim is—

The hook *z*, the surface *a*, the tube or holder *s*, and thread-carrier *e*, working substantially as above described.

Thimonnier, Aîné.

Figure 41 Drawing annexed to the patent granted in the United States, in 1750, for an improvement to Thimonnier's invention.

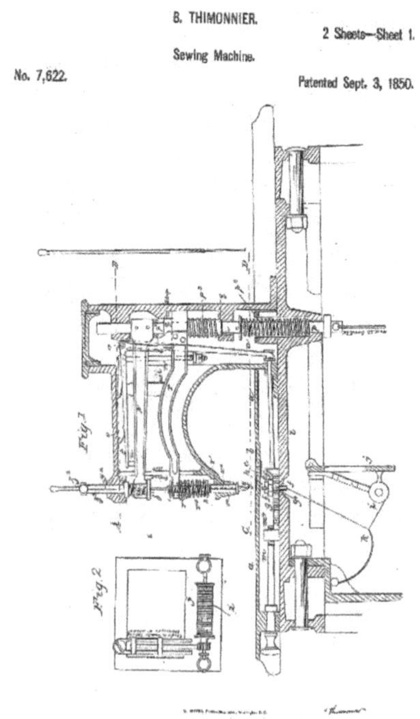

§ 2.48.3 Public Charity Comes to the Rescue of Thimonnier's Widow

By publishing in its Records the two preceding reports and the design of the machine donated to its collections by the Thimonnier family, the *Société des Sciences Industrielles de Lyon* has established, unquestionably, the priority rights of the poor and modest inventor.

Its right of initiative was limited to that; but there was something else to do: it was necessary to call the benevolent attention of the authority on Barthélemy

Thimonnier's widow and family. For this purpose, the Members of the association sent, on May 2, 1886, to the Senator, Prefect of Rhône, the following petition:

To the Senator, Prefect of Rhône.

Sir,

The undersigned claim your contribution and support. This is about their claim, on behalf of our country, of the honor of one of the greatest modern inventions: the sewing machine. ...

That a large part in the history of the sewing machine be attributed to those who successively brought it to a present stage of perfection, that is a matter of justice; but only on this condition it will be recognized and proclaimed that our compatriot, Barthélemy Thimonnier, is the first who has mechanically sewed fabrics using a machine of his invention, with needle and continuous thread.

The job of inventors is a tough one. Too often for them the ancient legend of Prometheus becomes a fatal law. Thimonnier has suffered it.

The work we are putting before your eyes tells of the long and painful adventures, the endless struggles of his entire life; he died miserable, on August 5, 1857.

His children are now workers in various professions; his widow, aged, crippled and destitute, earns 30 cents a day by reeling cotton in Amplepuis.

In claiming Thimonnier's industrial heritage, we have never had the thought of repudiating its charges; today we would ask you for the authorization to make an appeal on behalf of his unfortunate widow to our fellow citizens; a consideration stops us; others before us and above us have the right to provide for it: it is the country, the department, the city. ...

In our opinion, in claiming for Lyon an invention that honors us, the duty to help the widow of the unfortunate inventor arises—two good deeds that, once pointed out to you, have their success ensured.

We are, Mr. Senator, your respectful and devoted subjects. (Signatures follow)

The response has been swift. On the proposal of the Senator, Prefect of Rhône, on June 8, 1866, the Minister of Agriculture, Trade and Public Works, taking into consideration the services rendered by Barthélemy Thimonnier to the industry, granted his widow a relief of six one hundred francs. The public opinion has applauded this act of benevolent justice; it hopes to see it completed, and recommends the widow of Thimonnier to the solicitude of His Majesty the Emperor, so that her last days may be protected from misery, the only inheritance left to her by her husband.

Figure 42 Poster of 1855 advertising the sewing machine improved by Magnin. The poster includes the announcement of an award (Medal of 1st Class) granted to the invention at the Universal Exhibition of Paris, 1855. The term (on top, right corner) "Breveté s.g.d.g." means "Patented without the government's guarantee." The reason is that under the patent statute of 1791, French patents were granted without prior substantive examination.

§ 2.49 IN A CASE INVOLVING TRADE SECRETS CONCERNING THE JAPANNING OF LEATHER, A SCOTTISH COURT CONDEMNS THE UNDUE INTERFERENCE IN A LABOR CONTRACT—1836

In the nineteenth century, businesses had already definitely got rid of the encumbrances of the corporatist regime and embraced open, unrestricted competition. This involved the recourse to the whole panoply of intellectual property rights to ensure competitive advantages and the differentiation that results therefrom. In reality, not all those rights were already available, in particular as far as the fashion industry was concerned. Entrepreneurs in that industry would still have to wait several decades for the discussions on the effective protection of fashion designs to emerge—and longer than that for French courts to reach a conclusion.

Anyway, in the nineteenth century, trade secrets were already an intangible asset to which the textile industry resorted routinely, with the associated risks of inviting dishonest competitors to do whatever they could to acquire the knowledge of those secrets. We have seen above one example (§ 2.48). Now we have here another.

The text that follows is one of the earliest cases dealing with trade secrets under common law in Scotland. The issue involved is interference in a labor contract, with the intention of luring a competitors' employee who was in possession of certain secrets of the trade (the so-called "débauchage").

John Rutherford v. William Boak

Jury Cause.—Second Division.—(J.D.M.) Scotland

March 19, 1836

Master and Servant—Seduction of Workman–Action of damages for seduction of a workman—verdict for defender.

The pursuer of this action was a leather japanner in Edinburgh, and the defender a tanner, and also leather japanner. The issues were as follows:

Whether one Charles Bryan was engaged by the pursuer for a year from 5th April 1834 until the 5th April 1835, to assist the pursuer in his trade as a leather japanner; and whether, on or about the month of May 1834, the defender, being in the knowledge of the said engagement, by himself or another, or others, wrongfully seduced the said Charles Bryan from his said service, and caused him to desert the same, whereby the pursuer was deprived of the service of the said Charles Bryan, from the 26th day of May 1834, until the 11th day of September 1834, or during any part of the said period, to the loss, injury, and damage of the pursuer. Damages laid at £1000.

In defence, the seduction of Bryan was denied, or that he had been bribed, as alleged by the pursuer, to reveal any secrets of his trade; and though Bryan might have conversed with one of the defender's work men about his method of operation, Bryan was under no obligation to conceal any particular secret, and he was therefore not guilty of breach of contract or good faith.

Mr. Graham Bell stated the case for the pursuer. If a workman deserts his service, his master is entitled to have him brought before a magistrate and imprisoned until he finds caution to complete his engagement. This step the pursuer had adopted, and it had been rendered necessary by the defender's conduct, and that of one of his workmen named Nisbet. It was not incumbent on the pursuer to aver that any express secret had been revealed, as he held no patent, nor had applied for any in regard to the preparation or composition of the materials employed in his trade, or that Bryan had contracted to conceal such. Damages were not therefore craved for injury, through a specific secret revealed, but upon the general issue here taken, the pursuer was entitled to the consequential damages arising from the loss of the services of his workman.

The pursuer was then about to refer to certain English cases, as showing the amount of damages awarded in similar cases, when it was objected by the defender that this was incompetent.

The evidence adduced established that the defender had not instructed his workman, Nisbet, to entice Bryan from his engagement, but that Nisbet and Bryan had been formerly acquainted, and Nisbet had prevailed on Bryan to show him the preparation of the materials. That Bryan had been absent a whole day from the pursuer's work, and on that occasion was drunk, and that during that day he had been seen in the defender's premises looking over the preparation of the materials there. That Bryan was after this detained in prison for four months at the pursuer's instance. That he was a valuable workman to the pursuer, who, during this time, had several large orders to execute for japanning certain articles, of which he was considered the most skillful manufacturer in Scotland.

Rutherford, for the defender, declined leading evidence, but contended that the proof of enticing had failed, and that the loss of Bryan's services had been caused by the pursuer's own act.

The Lord Justice-Clerk summed up the evidence. Statements had been made of alleged secrets in the preparation of this japanning composition, yet the pursuer had taken no issue as to any engagement to keep any specific secret of trade, or that such had been learned from Bryan by any improper means on the defender's part. Before a verdict could be returned for the pursuer, the jury must be satisfied that this person had been induced to desert his service by the defender, or through the agency of others on his account. His Lordship did not think the issue had been proved, but if the jury thought otherwise, and that there was here seduction of the workman, then they would consider the amount of damages to be awarded. From the issue it might be supposed that Bryan's seduction had been the act of the defender throughout, but it appeared that the pursuer himself had thrown him into jail for four months; and even if it had been proved that Bryan had been seduced for a short period, damages for that period was all that could be found due.

The jury found a verdict for the defender.

Lord Justice-Clerk, Boyle.

§ 2.50 COMPETITION FOR FOREIGN MARKETS WITH OTHER TRADE POWERS SPURS GREAT BRITAIN TO INCREASE PROTECTION FOR INDUSTRIAL DESIGNS—1839 ONWARDS

In the first half of the nineteenth century, a movement led by the calico manufacturers (soon embraced by other sectors of the British industry) got the attention of Parliament. Their major concerns were that insufficient intellectual property protection for fashion designs and patterns facilitated piracy and counterfeiting; and that such situation favored the French industry, which, albeit less productive, had developed art and taste in consumer goods, and had the preference of consumers—and, moreover, was already, to some extent, under the protection of fashion law.

As a result of that pressure, the British Parliament in 1839 passed a statute extending the protection of designs to all industrial articles, increasing its term, and requiring registration. A few years later, amendments would be introduced to further improve the system. However, England kept for several decades a dual system of protection, based on the distinction between designs for ornamental purposes and designs for the shape and configuration of useful articles. Only in 1883 would the Parliament reunite the two notions under one single concept—that of designs "applicable to any article of manufacture, or to any substance artificial or natural, or partly artificial and partly natural" (see § 2.58).

The texts that follow are excerpts from a treatise on copyright in designs authored by James Emerson Tennent (1804-1869), chair of the Committee of the House of Commons on the Copyright of Designs, and who, sensitive to the plea of the industry, sponsored and successfully promoted the legislative changes.

> To the Honourable The Commons of the United Kingdom of Great Britain and Ireland, in Parliament Assembled,
>
> The humble Petition of the undersigned Printers of Calicoes and other woven Fabrics, Merchants, Manufacturers, Engravers, and others, carrying on business in and near Manchester, in the County of Lancaster.
>
> Sheweth,
>
> That your Petitioners have learnt with the greatest satisfaction the introduction of a bill into your honourable house for extending the protection given to original designs, or patterns, printed upon woven fabrics, from the term of three months to twelve, thereby giving to the original inventor, or proprietor of such designs, a right of property for a reasonable time in the produce of his skill, or capital, of which he has hitherto been unjustly deprived.
>
> That your Petitioners are all deeply interested in, and many of them wholly dependent on the welfare and prosperity of the print trade, which is one of the great staple manufactures of the country, and they most respectfully and earnestly submit to the consideration of your honourable house, that whilst the various fabrics themselves enjoy that natural protection which the law affords to property, yet, by a strange anomaly, the original designs or patterns which give to these fabrics a great portion of their value, and which are equally the produce of labour, skill, and capital, are left almost wholly unprotected, the inventors or proprietors of such designs having no proprietary interest in them beyond a few weeks, when they become the common property of the trade. ...
>
> Four years ago, a Select Committee of your honourable house investigated the subject of arts and manufactures, and in an interesting Report, accompanied by most important evidence disclosing this humiliating fact, that however much the manufacturers of this country surpass their continental rivals in the goodness and cheapness of their productions, they are immeasurably below them in the taste and elegance of their designs. The fact is incontestable, and your Petitioners ascribe it mainly to the want of adequate protection, for no one will devote much time, attention, and money, to an object of which, if unsuccessful, he must bear the loss, and of which, if it succeeds, he must share the profit with the public.
>
> Without protection, Schools of Design, your Petitioners venture to predict, will accomplish nothing; protection, without schools, may do much, but both united would give a stimulus to this deficient branch of our national industry, which would soon place the productions of this country on a level with those of the most distinguished nations. ...
>
> Wherefore your Petitioners humbly pray that the Bill now before your Honourable House may be passed into a Law,
>
> And your Petitioners will ever pray. ...
>
> That the present limited term of three months is utterly inoperative as any protection to the trade, I have already exhibited proofs, not merely in the complaints of the sufferer whose property has been wrested from him, but in the confessions of those who have made the pirated copies, and the declaration of the merchants who have purchased them as a systematic trade. Mr. Brookes, who has accumulated wealth as a calico printer, avows, that down to a very late period his business consisted of an indiscriminate appropriation of the designs of others, notwithstanding the law of copyright, which he boldly set at defiance.
>
> And Mr. Lucas, with all the unreserve of a man speaking of an ordinary line of business, admits that his extensive trade in printed calicoes is carried on with pirates alone; that so ordinary a matter is it to disregard the law, that it never enters

into his head when he wants a lot of goods copied, to ask the question whether the designs be pirated property or not; and that he never meets the slightest difficulty in obtaining any quantity he requires, provided he finds the price to suit him, and that as to the present term of three months, "he never felt it to be any protection to the printer at all."

The present term of three months is stated, by those printers and designers who have petitioned the House of Commons for its extension, to be utterly inadequate for their protection, either in the home market or the foreign, or in that in which goods are suited conjointly for both, and that it fails to afford them that remunerative property in their inventions which the law designed and professes to confer. ...

The improvement of the art of design by increased protection will, at the same time, augment the consumption both at home and abroad; abroad, because the Americans and others now buy French goods, under the feeling that they are superior in style to ours, whilst taste, if improved, added to our existing facilities for cheaper production, would ensure us the preference; and at home, because dresses would be more frequently changed and bought by the upper classes, on the same principle which leads to the purchase of a painting, to gratify taste and fancy, "as a dress, after all, is not a mere covering, else we should have no printed dresses at all"; and those whose trade now is to copy patterns, being compelled, as they will be, to produce originals, "the trade generally will be increased, from the circumstance of there being a greater number of producers than at present"; and Mr. Ross declares that "parties always buy a large quantity where there is a large assortment and variety." ...

But, independently of pecuniary advantage to be gained by the suppression of copying, strong objections have been made to its continuance, on the moral ground of its dishonesty and injustice, as well as on the temptation which it holds out to servants and others, to purloin the designs entrusted to them by their masters, for sale to other houses, a practice of which serious complaints were made by various witnesses examined before the committee, cases having occurred in which, from this circumstance, copies of printed goods have been published by a rival house, almost simultaneously with the appearance of the original.

Those printers who think humility of price is the sole and only introduction to public favour, are opposed to the alteration of a law that in general gives an unjust advantage to the pilferer over the honest producer. Those who see taste and superior elegance opening the door to French manufactures in every quarter of the globe, perceive their own inferiority, and whilst they are conscious of their powers and capabilities, pray only for protection and encouragement to develop them.

The petitioners for copyright are those who, though they produce in the aggregate the smallest number of pieces because their works are the most elaborately beautiful, are nevertheless those who, in proportion to their production, give the greatest amount of employment. On the other hand, the opponents of extension are those who produce the coarsest and most ordinary articles those mountains of cloth, whose superficies is counted by "miles" instead of yards, but which are produced by little labour, affording but scanty employment, and the whole value of the article, cloth, printing, and profit inclusive, falls short of the mere wages of labour of printing alone, of most styles of the former class.

§ 2.51 AN ACT REGULATING LABOR AND COMMERCIAL MATTERS IN THE ENGLISH TEXTILE INDUSTRY—1843

The following text reflects the gradual maturation of intellectual property as applied to the textile industry through the nineteenth century. The text is an excerpt from a British statute regulating several topics related to the English textile industry, namely labor and commercial matters. Importantly, as far as intellectual property is concerned, the Act contained a provision that, while acknowledging the right of inspection of those who ordered the finishing of garments and other pieces of cloth from textile manufacturers, excluded that same right when the industrial premises to be visited contained machinery, devices, and tools comprising trade secrets ("any new invention or improvement not disclosed to the public").

Above (§ 2.39) we have seen a similar measure concerning three manufacturers of woollen cloth of Lille, who expressed the fear that the inspection and sealing of their products by the master sayeteurs*—their competitors—would cause the unwarranted disclosure of trade secrets. The council of municipal magistrates has agreed and has given instructions that the inspection should be carried out by other persons. This was in 1692.*

An Act to amend the Laws for the Prevention of Frauds and Abuses by Persons employed in the Woollen, Worsted, Linen, Cotton, Flax, Mohair and Silk Hosiery Manufactures; and for the further securing the Property of the Manufactures; and for the further securing the Property of the Manufacturers and the Wages of the Workmen engaged therein

August 1, 1843

... Be it therefore enacted, That from and after the commencement of this Act so much of the said recited Acts or any of them as relates to the woollen, linen, cotton, flax, mohair, and silk manufactures, or any of them, or any manufactures whatsoever made of wool, cotton, flax, mohair, or silk materials, whether the same be or be not mixed with each other or with any other materials, shall so fas as respects the manufactures, trades, occupations, and employments hereinafter mentioned, be and the same are hereby repealed, save and except so far as the same may have repealed any former Acts or enactments. ...

13. That it shall be lawful for the owner of any such materials as aforesaid, or any other person duly authorized by him, or other the person who shall have so intrusted such materials, from time to time, as occasion shall require, to demand leave of entrance and enter at all reasonable hours in the daytime into the shops or outhouses of any person employed to work up or manufacture, either by himself or by any other person under him, any of the said materials, or other place or places where the work shall be carried on, and there to inspect the state and condition of such materials; and in case of refusal or neglect by any such person or persons so employed to permit such entrance or inspection, such person shall, for so refusing to permit such entrance or inspection, forfeit any sum not exceeding twenty shillings, as the justices before whom he shall appear or be brought shall think proper, to be applied in the same manner as is hereinafter directed for the disposal of any other penalty under this Act: Provided always, that nothing herein contained shall authorise any such owner or other person as aforesaid to inspect

any frame, tools, or apparatus wherewith such materials are worked up, in case such frame, tools, or apparatus comprise any new invention or improvement not disclosed to the public.

§ 2.52 THE DEBATE ON HOW TO BEST PROTECT FASHION DESIGNS STARTS IN FRENCH COURTS—1857, 1860

It was in the nineteenth century that French courts started building a body of jurisprudence dealing with the protection of fashion designs against copy and imitation. The understanding that first emerged was that industrial designs were the adequate mechanism for achieving such results. Actually, the courts, in adopting this view, were merely following the same approach as lawmakers, for the laws already enacted for protecting industrial designs had the textile industry as their original and main targets—first the tapestry industry, and later the fine cloth industry.

The following texts reproduce two opinions of French courts that discussed whether the manner of combining materials used in the making of hats was sufficient in terms of creativity to trigger industrial design protection for their makers. Importantly, in the first text, the Court has taken into consideration that the products as designed by their creators "have their own character, which allows their origin to be assessed, and carry in themselves a special distinction of novelty that constitutes an individuality." It is this factor that brings designs into the realm of business identifiers and enormously broadens the scope of their protection.

§ 2.52.1 *Lafont et Davasse v. Durst, Wild et Cie.*—1857

Commercial court of Seine.—June 12, 1857

Industrial designs (*Dessins de fabrique*).—Straw Hats.—Assembly of known materials.—Filing.—Property.—Counterfeiting.

The assembly of known materials, but combined in such a way as to produce a new effect, can constitute an industrial design susceptible to filing and private property.

Messrs. Lafont and Davasse, manufacturers of straw hats, have applied various designs and embroideries in velvet to straw fabrics, and thus have obtained a novelty that they have filed with the Council of prud'hommes.—Messrs. Durst, Wild et Cie. have manufactured and sold this same article. Summoned for this fact before the Commercial Court, they maintained that the plaintiffs' products did not constitute an industrial design and that in any case there was no novelty.

The Court, chaired by Mr. Fossin ... delivered at the hearing of June 12, 1857, the following judgment:

The court:

- Whereas on April 22, by virtue of an order from the President of the Civil Court of Seine, Lafont and Davasse had various articles seized from Durst, Wild et Cie. that they claim have been made in infringement of those of which they wanted to reserve the exclusive property, through the filing, on December 20, with the Council of prud'hommes, in accordance with the law;

- That Durst, Wild et Cie. maintain that the alleged designs of which Lafont and Davasse claim ownership are produced only by a mixture of various materials known for a long time in the trade, and whose combination can in no way constitute in their favor a private and privileged right under the terms of the law of March 18, 1808;
- Whereas the triple assembly of fabrics already known, but combined in such a way as to produce a new effect, may in the spirit of the law constitute a design susceptible of private property;
- That it appears from the documents of the case and of the comparison made of the articles in question with their analogues, that the products filed by Lafont and Davasse have their own character, which allows their origin to be assessed, and carry in themselves a special distinction of novelty that constitutes an individuality, and consequently establishes a right of property in their favor;
- Whereas it is not denied that the flapper hats seized from Durst, Wild et Cie., at the request of Lafont and Davasse, are the servile imitation of the article deposited by the latter with the Council of prud'hommes;
- That Durst, Wild et Cie. have done nothing else than taking hold of the result of the work of others; that consequently this imitation constitutes counterfeiting;
- On damages:
- Whereas, by the infringement of which they are accused, Durst, Wild et Cie. have caused Lafont and Davasse damage for which they owe compensation, and which the Court fixes at 1,500 francs;
- For these reasons, declares the articles seized at the premises of Durst, Wild et Cie., at the request of Lafont and Davasse, to be counterfeited;
- Condemns Durst, Wild et Cie. to pay to Lafont and Davasse, by all legal channels and by body, the sum of 1,300 francs for damages, and all costs.

§ 2.52.2 *Erhardt v. Durst-Will et autres.*—1860

Criminal Court of Seine.—May 16, 1860.

Industrial designs and models.—Straw hats.—New forces.—Ornaments. The law of 1806, which allows ownership of an industrial design to be reserved through the filing with the Council of prud'hommes, does not apply to a shape, even a new one, given to hats made from ordinary straw fabrics.

Mrs. Erhardt, manufacturer of straw hats, in Paris, filed with the office of the Council of Prud'hommes, in the course of 1859, various models and designs of straw hats of which she intended to keep the exclusive property. The novelty of her product lay, she said, both in the very shape of some of her hats and in certain accessory ornaments. Based on this filing, she believed she could have seizures made at the shops of Durst-Will and Co., Chaumonot et Cie., widow Stoffel, Gallot, Delattre and Thibaut, and sued them before the Criminal Court of Seine, under the charge of infringement, in [asked for] 5,000 francs in damages, with publication of the judgment in five newspapers. Let us add, for the sake of understanding the lawsuit, that among the articles alleged to be counterfeit was a straw hat with turned-up edges, and another having three knots of straw attached by a loop on the front.

Master Cresson, attorney for the plaintiff, after explaining the question of the identity of the samples and drawings existing at the Council of prud'hommes with the hats seized, argued in law that the shapes invented by Mrs. Erhardt constituted genuine industrial designs, protected by the law of March 18, 1806—a special statute, it is true, in its origin, specific to fabrics from Lyon, but extended by jurisprudence to all kinds of designs, whatever the material, to which these designs were applied. The attorney invoked in support the judgment of the Commercial Court of June 12, 1857, and relating specifically to straw hats woven with velvet.

Masters Delorme and Binoche, attorneys for the defendants, denied to all accessory ornaments of hats, placed by hand, the character of industrial designs, which suppose an application by means of weaving or printing or any other industrial process; ... They added that the very large industry of straw hats would become impossible if the law recognized and protected by the penalties of counterfeiting the alleged property of those thousands of ornaments and varieties of forms that every year the vicissitudes of fashion bring in the ladies' hats, ephemeral novelties of which no one is the inventor, and which could not belong to the person who would file them against the uses of this industry. ... The Tribunal (7th Ch.), under the chairmanship of Master Bonnefoi des Aulnais, rendered, at the hearing of May 16, 1860, the following judgment, which acquired the authority of res judicata.

The Court:

- Whereas the law of March 18, 1806 only applies to designs that are reproduced on fabrics by printing, weaving and stitching; that if, in certain circumstances, this privilege has been extended to designs on all materials, it does not follow that it must be applied to all objects composed of various elements and shapes;
- Whereas it results from the debates that the hats filed by lady Erhardt are made only with fabrics of ordinary straw; that they do not reproduce any designs, but that they only take a form that belongs to [existing] fashion; that consequently they are not included in the category indicated by the law of 1806, from where it follows that lady Erhardt cannot claim their property and sustain the conclusion that their reproduction is an infringement;
- For these reasons, acquits Gallot, Chaumonot, Durst-Wild et Cie., Thibaut and widow Stoffel of the complaint without costs; ...

J. Pataille, A. Huguet, and Ed. Calmels, ANNALES DE LA PROPRIÉTÉ INDUSTRIELLE, ARTISTIQUE ET LITTÉRAIRE, vol. 6, 1860, at 425-427 (Bureau des Annales, 1860). Source: <gallica.BnF.fr>.

§ 2.53 BRITISH PATENTS FOR FASHION DESIGNS—1857 ONWARDS

As in France, in the absence of adequate design protection, English fashion and accessory designers sought protection for their creations under patent law. Those were not many cases, because the definition of the subject matter of patent protection under British statutory law (the Statute of Monopolies, of 1623, as amended by the Act of 1852) was narrower than under French law to the extent it provided that invention meant "any manner of new manufacture" (Section LV). Prima facie, *therefore, ornamental designs did not deserve patent protection. This explains the language of the specifications of the few British patents covering designs, which attempted to link them to modes of manufacturing or assembling garments and their accessories. Anyway, patents for designs, as the following texts imply, required a very low standard of inventiveness.*

March 5, 1857.—No. 642

Bardin, Jean Louis Frédéric.—"A new mode of ornamentation." The patentee applies "the thin elastic skin, pellicle, or cuticle of natural feathers or quills" to the manufacture of ornamental head dresses or other attire for women, of artificial flowers, of hatters' articles, &c.

The pellicles are stript off either by hand or by machinery, and the removal will be easier if the quills are soaked in water or softened in any manner. The pellicles obtained from either the stalk or the barrel of the quill "are very flexible, and offer at the same time a brilliant glossy appearance"; they may be divided into threads, be coloured in any manner, and be used alone or in combination with other threads, or with tapes, wires, &c.

August 24, 1858.—No. 1925

Biggs, John.—"Improvements in the manufacture of caps resembling in form the Turkish fez." The cap is knitted by machinery or hand, or partly by machinery and partly by hand, to the required shape. The yarn used is of wool or of other fibre containing "sufficient felting fibre to cause it to felt or mat when milled after being knitted." The cap when knitted is "milled, as is well understood," and by this means "a seamless cap is formed resembling the Turkish fez."

August 5, 1862.—No. 2195

Simon, Siegfried.—(*Provisional protection only.*)—"An improvement in ornamenting ladies' and children's slippers." Any ornamental design is cut or stamped out of the front of the uppers, and a piece of differently coloured leather is gummed on and then stitched to the back of the uppers so as to show through the perforations. It is preferred that the back piece should be the complementary colour of the upper, and the stitching is to follow the outline of the design. The colour of the binding should harmonize with that of the upper. The inside lining covers the back piece.

August 6, 1862.—No. 2207

Nauheim, Ferdinand.—(*Provisional protection only*).—"An improvement in the ornamenting of boots, shoes, and goloshes," which are made of enamelled leather. The ornament may consist of "any appropriate devices"; the effect is obtained by removing the glossy surface being left "to form the background." This dulling of the surface may be effected in various ways; the inventor prefers to place a stencil plate cut to the form of the device on the enamelled leather and to destroy the exposed glossy surface by friction with pumice stone or other suitable material.

§ 2.54 FRENCH PATENTS FOR INDUSTRIAL DESIGNS—1864

As in England, in France, fashion designers also resorted to the patent act to seek protection for their creations. But, as mentioned in the preceding note, there was a major difference between the two statutes: whereas the English statute (of 1852) referred to "manners of manufacture" as the subject matter of patents, the French statute (of 1844) mentioned "invention of new industrial products"—a more imprecise language that permitted a more liberal, comprehensive interpretation. Despite the emerging of industrial design law, the fine line that distinguished the mode of manufacture (patents) from the shape of a manufactured product (designs) led French clothmakers and designers to hesitate between the two systems. It is noteworthy that, by contrast with the several examples of English patents cited above, the abstracts of several of the following examples of French patents for designs show that the patent applicants did not even bother to make reference to the industrial processes of making cloths.

Bulletin of Laws No. 1201

No. 12,258—Imperial Decree proclaiming 1379 Patents of Invention and Certificates of Addition. Napoleon, by the grace of God and the national will, Emperor of the French, to all those present and to come, greetings. Considering Article 14 of the law of July 5, 1844. We decreed and decree the following:

Art. 1. The following are proclaimed: ...

187. The fifteen-year patent for invention, the application for which was filed on August 20, 1862, with the secretariat of the prefecture of the department of Seine, by Mr. Traversier (Étienne), merchant, represented by Mr. Lavialle, in Paris, boulevard Saint-Martin, 29, for a kind of corsets, belts, brassieres, etc.

302. The fifteen-year patent for invention, the application for which was filed on September 5, 1862, with the secretariat of the prefecture of the department of Haute-Garonne, by Sieur Maraval (Auguste), hat maker, rue du Pont, 9, in Toulouse, for a felt hat mounted on cork.

347. The fifteen-year patent for invention, the application for which was filed on August 2, 1862, with the secretariat of the prefecture of the department of Seine, by Messrs. Voisin and company, manufacturers of fabrics, represented by Mr. Amouroux, at Paris, rue Saint-Martin, 333, for the application of various textile materials to the weaving of seamless corsets, as well as for their method of manufacture.

431. The fifteen-year patent for invention, the application for which was filed on September 8, 1862, with the secretariat of the prefecture of the department of Seine, by Messrs. Mantin brothers, shoe manufacturers, represented by Mr. Lavalle, in Paris, boulevard Saint-Martin, 29, for a kind of ornamentation of certain fabrics for shoes.

439. The fifteen-year patent for invention, the application for which was filed on September 30, 1862, with the secretariat of the prefecture of the department of Seine, by Mr. Belingard (Jean-François-Isidore), manufacturer of ribbons, rue de Saint-Louis, 19, in Saint-Étienne, for the application of stitches or stitched fabrics on all kinds of fabrics and particularly on tulle and other light fabrics, after their manufacture.

538. The fifteen-year patent for invention, the application for which was filed on September 25, 1862, with the secretariat of the prefecture of the department of Rhône, by Mr. Gataz (Michel), rue Imbert-Colomès, 5, in Lyon, for curling, pricking out and reproducing weaving patterns.

630. The fifteen-year patent for invention, the application for which was filed on October 2, 1862, with the secretariat of the prefecture of the department of Seine, by Mr. Colette (Jean-Jacques-Victor) and his wife, née Fontaine (Célestine-Adrienne), lace makers, represented by Sieur Courrouve, in Paris, rue Feydeau, 28, for a kind of lace called *Colette lace.*

707. The fifteen-year patent for invention, the application for which was filed on October 10, 1862, with the secretariat of the prefecture of the Vosges department, by Messrs. Parizot (Michel-Joseph-Ernest), manufacturer of lace, and

Streiff (Charles-Joseph), lace designer, in Mirecourt, for a kind of lace known as *pot-kilma lace.*

849. The fifteen-year patent for invention, the application for which was filed on October 18, 1862, with the secretariat of the prefecture of the department of Seine, by Mr. Chevallier (Eugène), blouse manufacturer, represented by Mr. Lavalle, at Paris, boulevard Saint-Martin, 29, for a kind of shirt bibs.

1048. The certificate of addition the application for which was filed on June 19, 1862, with the secretariat of the prefecture of the department of Seine, and associated with the fifteen-year patent for invention taken on January 23, 1862, for a type of clothes.

Done at the Palace of Tuileries, January 27, 1864.

Signed Napoléon.

§ 2.55 THE SUPREME COURT OF MASSACHUSETTS PROTECTS A TRADE SECRET CONCERNING A PROCESS OF MAKING CLOTH—1868

The right to keep information, of vital importance for a cloth manufacturing company, under secrecy was confirmed—and enforced—by the Supreme Court of Massachusetts. The following text is an expression of the prohibition of the practice of "débauchage," a millenary legal canon.[88]

Peabody v. Norfolk.

January 1868. Mass. Sup. Ct.: Gray, J. 98 Mass. (2 Browne) 452.

The plaintiff having invented a secret process of manufacture of cloth, and the defendant Norfolk having, on entering into the plaintiff's service, undertaken not to give information in regard to the process to any one, the defendant Norfolk left the plaintiff's employ, and entered into an arrangement with other persons, by which they were to build another factory for the purpose of manufacturing there according to the plaintiff's secret process, which the defendant Norfolk was to communicate to them.

Injunction granted to restrain the defendant Norfolk from carrying out such arrangement and making such communication, and also to restrain the defendant Cook, who was one of the persons with whom the arrangement had been made, and who was fully aware of the circumstances, from acting in execution of such arrangement.

§ 2.56 FROM FUNCTION TO ORNAMENT: LEVI STRAUSS' JEANS RIVETED POCKETS—1873

In 1873, Jacob W. Davies and Levi Strauss & Co. obtained a patent for the use of rivets to strengthen the resistance of pockets in working pants. At that time Levi Strauss manufactured garments to be used in working environments. Hence the utility in introducing an element that increased the resistance of those garments against the ripping of seams. It was only in the twentieth century, under the influence of far-west

88. *See supra* note 22 and accompanying text.

movies, that Levi's jeans became fashion items and their use generalized outside working classes. The rivets were, originally, a functional item—an invention, actually, that was transported from shoes to pants, as the inventor explained in the patent specifications. But, with the generalization of the use of jeans, Levi Strauss made of those rivets, in combination with designed stitches, an element of ornamentation of the garments it produced.

However, because of the inherent impossibility of appropriating patented inventions, once the patent expires, as elements of product designation, Levi Strauss & Co. could never have registered the position of the rivets as trademarks. Otherwise, Levi Strauss would obtain the equivalent for a patent with an indefinite term. At most, the company could have—and as it did, actually—registered the two-dimensional figurative element of the rivet, with the saying Levi Strauss & Co.—SF—CAL—around its center. A number of these registrations appear in WIPO Global Brand Database.

United States Patent Office.

Jacob W. Davis, of Reno, Nevada, Assignor to Himself and Levi Strauss & Company, of San Francisco, California.

Improvement in Fastening Pocket-Openings.

Specification forming part of Letters Patent No. 139, 121, dated May 20, 1873; application file August 9, 1872.

> ... My invention relates to a fastening for pocket-openings, whereby the sewed seams are prevented from ripping or starting from frequent pressure or strain thereon; and it consists in the employment of a metal rivet or eyelet at each edge of the pocket opening, to prevent the ripping of the seam at those points. The rivet or eyelet is so fastened in the seam as to bind the two parts of cloth which the seam unites together, so that it shall prevent the strain or pressure from coming upon the thread with which the seam is sewed. ...
>
> I am aware that rivets have been used for securing seams in shoes, as shown in the patents to Geo. Houghton, No. 64,015, April 23, 1867, and to L. K. Wasburn, No. 123,313, January 30, 1872; and hence I do not claim, broadly, fastening of seams by means of rivets.
>
> Having thus described my invention, what I claim as new, and desire to secure by Letters Patent, is—
>
> As a new article of manufacture, a pair of pantaloons having the pocket-openings secured at each edge by means of rivets, substantially in the manner described and shown, whereby the seams at the points named are prevented from ripping, as set forth.
>
> In witness whereof I hereunto set my hand and seal.
>
> Jacob W. Davis.

Figure 43 Drawing accompanying the specifications of the 1873 US patent letter for the application of rivets to the seams of pockets in pantaloons.

§ 2.57 THE UNITED STATES SUPREME COURT RAISES THE BAR FOR THE NOTION OF INVENTIVENESS AND REFUSES PATENTABILITY TO NEW USES OF KNOWN LOOMS AND TEXTILE MATERIALS—1875

The Smith *opinion opens a consistent line of opinions that express the United States Supreme Court's view that new uses of known machines and materials are not patentable. This opinion has very important competition policy implications. The assumption is that, with the first patent, the inventor has already received the right to oppose any uses whatsoever, even those that he does not about at the time of inventing and filing the application for the patent. But this only during the life of the patent. After the patent expires, the invention is free to be used.*

It is significant that this opinion was delivered in the context of a textile-related patent, because of the very high level of intensity that competition and rivalry within that industry reached in the nineteenth century.

Smith v. Nichols, 88 U.S. 112 (1875) (excerpts)

Supreme Court of the United States

Mr. Justice Swayne delivered the opinion of the court.

The bill is founded upon a patent, and was filed by the appellant. It charges infringement. Its object and prayer are to have the defendant enjoined from infringing further, and required to account for the profits he has wrongfully made. ...

In the specification the loom and process for weaving corded elastic india-rubber fabrics are described, and the excellence of such fabrics so woven, and the points in which they are superior to fabrics not so woven, are pointed out and insisted upon. ...

The substance of the specification as limited by the disclaimers may be thus summarized: The elastic cords are placed side by side, equidistant from each other. They are stretched several times their normal length. In the spaces between the cords warp threads are placed parallel with the cords, and of less size. The cords remain stationary. The warp threads are thrown open by the machinery of the loom. Every alternate thread is thrown upwards and the intermediate one downwards. What is termed a "shed" is thus formed above the cords and one under them. Through each of these sheds a weft thread is passed by means of a shuttle. One of the shuttles is thus passed above and the other below all the rubber cords. After both the weft threads have been driven home by the lathe, the position of the warp threads is inverted by the treadle. Sheds are thus formed on the opposite sides of the cords. Weft threads are then again passed across the fabric. This process is continued until the weaving is completed.

The weft threads form the only covering on the upper and under side of the cords. When their tension ceases after the weaving is done the cords contract in length and increase proportionately in thickness. The weft threads are necessarily brought into proximity with each other. They partially imbed themselves in the cords, holds them firmly, and prevent them from slipping back, if cut anywhere, while at the tension which subsisted when the weaving took place. So the weft threads cling tightly to the rubber cords in every degree of tension to which they may be subjected. Each of the former grasps firmly each of the latter half round.

The points with respect to this litigation, which the complainant claims as covered by his patent, we understand, are that fewer warp threads are used, that the tightness of the weaving is greater, that the rubber cords in all stages of tension are more firmly and effectually held in his fabric than in any which preceded it—and especially, the manner in which the weft threads, one above and the other below, grasp each of the rubber cords half round. ...

The defense mainly relied upon is want of novelty; in other words, the prior public use of the things patented.

The counsel for the appellant admits expressly that an elastic fabric with silk on one side and cotton on the other, one woven with two shuttles, one woven with stationary elastic cords, and one with elastic cords covered above and below solely by weft threads, were known and in public use by themselves separately before the alleged invention of the complainant. It is also admitted that suspended webbing of different kinds, some provided with elastic cords having strips of cloth interwoven between them, and another class without the strips of cloth and similar to the complainant's, "except that the weft threads in pairs were not made to grasp the elastic cords in the manner described in the complainant's specification," also in like manner preceded his invention. The proof to the same effect, less the exception named, is voluminous and conclusive. It is unnecessary particularly to refer to it. The testimony is equally full as to webbing for shoe gores. That, made in the same way as the suspender webbing, also came into public use and was largely sold at as early a period.

The testimony of Hotchkiss [*Hotchkiss v. Greenwood*, 52 U.S. 248 (1850)] establishes conclusively that—also prior to the defendant's invention—he made and sold suspender webbing with what were called binding warps between the rubber warps, with weft threads which "went over all the rubber warps, and under all the rubber warps," and that the fabric was woven while the rubber cords were in a state of tension. He says further, that he had never known suspender webbing made by American manufacturers in any other way. There is a large mass of other testimony relative to the case in this aspect, but it is deemed unnecessary to pursue the subject further.

The evidence before us leaves to the complainant none of the particulars claimed as of his invention, except perhaps greater tightness of the weaving, a firmer grasping of the elastic cords by the weft threads half round, above and below, and greater beauty and value of the fabric. The entire ground of the controversy between the parties is reduced to this narrow isthmus, and the question presented for our determination is one rather of law than of fact.

A patentable invention is a mental result. It must be new and shown to be of practical utility. Everything within the domain of the conception belongs to him who conceived it. The machine, process, or product is but its material reflex and embodiment. A new idea may be engrafted upon an old invention, be distinct from the conception which preceded it, and be an improvement. In such case it is patentable. The prior patentee cannot use it without the consent of the improver, and the latter cannot use the original invention without the consent of the former. But a mere carrying forward or new or more extended application of the original thought, a change only in form, proportions, or degree, the substitution of equivalents, doing substantially the same thing in the same way by substantially the same means with better results, is not such invention as ill sustain a patent. These rules apply alike, whether what preceded was covered by a patent or rested only in public knowledge and use. In neither case can there be an invasion of such domain and an appropriation of anything found there. In one case everything belongs to the prior patentee, in the other, to the public at large.

The question before us must be considered in the light of these rules. All the particulars claimed by the complainant, if conceded to be his, are within the category of degree. Many textile fabrics, especially those of cotton and wool, are constantly improved. Sometimes the improvement is due to the skill of the workmen, and sometimes to the perfection of the machinery employed. The results are higher finish, greater beauty of surface, and increased commercial value. A patent for the better fabric in such cases would, we apprehend, be unprecedented. The patent in the present case rests upon no other or better foundation. ...

§ 2.58 ENGLAND UNIFIES THE PROTECTION OF DESIGNS FOR ORNAMENTAL PURPOSES WITH THOSE FOR THE SHAPE AND CONFIGURATION OF USEFUL ARTICLES—1883

Today the protection of copyright is based on the dichotomy expression v. idea—copyright covers the expression; industrial property, the idea. The practical consequence of this dichotomy is that copyrights are enforceable against the unauthorized copy or reproduction of the protected subject matter, whereas industrial property rights are enforceable against the use of the protected idea in the making of an article.

We will see, however, that as far as fashion designs are concerned, this dichotomy has not always been—and is not still—clear. On the one hand, common law countries tend to designate as copyright the exclusive right of designers in making and selling articles embodying the designs of their creation. In that case, according to the language of the British statute of 1883, the exclusive right was granted "to apply such design, or any fraudulent or obvious imitation thereof, in the class or classes of goods in which such design is registered, for purposes of sale, to any article of manufacture." Actually, the finding of a counterfeit in the application of the idea expressed in the design for the making of a piece of cloth constitutes a blend of the idea with the expression. On the other hand, such a definition of copyright in designs excludes their reproduction in magazines or journals from exclusivity, unless such reproduction is aimed at giving instructions on how to counterfeit.

This second issue was a matter of lively debate in France in the last quarter of the nineteenth century and the first quarter of the twentieth century because fashion designers were greatly harmed by the unauthorized reproduction of their creations in magazines and journals. The reason was that, at that time, newspapers and magazines were the main sources of information for counterfeiters—small boutiques that made cloths for sale. Today this concern makes no sense. Counterfeiting occurs beyond national borders and is carried out by large factories, aiming at international markets.

August 25, 1883

An Act to amend and consolidate the Law relating to Patents for Inventions, Registration of Designs and of Trade Marks.

> Be it enacted by the Queen's most Excellent Majesty, by and with the advice and consent of the Lords Spiritual and Temporal, and Commons, in this present Parliament assembled, and by authority of the same, as follows: ...
>
> Part III.
>
> Designs.
>
> Registration of Designs.
>
> 47.(1.) The comptroller may, on application by or on behalf of any person claiming to be the proprietor of any new or original designed not previously published in the United Kingdom, register the design under this part of the Act.

48.(1.) On application for registration of a design the applicant shall furnish to the comptroller the prescribed number of copies of drawings, photographs or tracings of the design sufficient, in the opinion of the comptroller, for enabling him to identify the design; or the applicant may, instead of such copies, furnish exact representations or specimens of the design. ...

50. (1.) When a design is registered, the registered proprietor of the design shall, subject to the provisions of this Act, have copyright in the design during five years from the date of registration. ...

58. During the existence of copyright in any design—

(a) It shall not be lawful for any person without the licence or written consent of the registered proprietor to apply such design, or any fraudulent or obvious imitation thereof, in the class or classes of goods in which such design is registered, for purposes of sale, to any article of manufacture, or to any substance, artificial or natural, or partly artificial and partly natural; and

(b) It shall not be lawful for any person to publish or expose for sale any article of manufacture or any substance to which such design, or any fraudulent or obvious imitation thereof, shall have been so applied, knowing that the same has been so applied without the consent of the registered proprietor.

60. In and for the purposes of this Act—

"Design" means any design applicable to any article of manufacture, or to any substance artificial or natural, or partly artificial and partly natural, whether the design is applicable for the pattern, or for the shape or configuration, or for the ornament thereof, or for any two or more of such purposes, and by whatever means it is applicable, whether by printing, painting, embroidering, weaving, sewing, modelling, casting, embossing, engraving, staining, or any other means whatever, manual, mechanical, or chemical, separate or combined, not ebbing a design for a sculpture, or other thing within the protection of the Sculpture Copyright Act of the year 1814 (54 George III. c. 56).

"Copyright" means the exclusive right to apply a design to any article of manufacture, or to any such substance as aforesaid, in the class or classes in which the design is registered.

§ 2.59 A FRENCH COURT DENIES PROTECTION TO FASHION DESIGNS UNDER THE ACT ON INDUSTRIAL DESIGNS DUE TO THEIR EPHEMERAL NATURE—1895

The following text is a very important opinion from a French court, not because of its conclusion but because of the two topics it discussed.

First, the court refused protection for a design that modified an existing article (a corset) only as far as its dimensions were concerned. The plaintiff alleged that his corset had more grace and was more elegant than the others. But to the court what mattered was that the change was very minor, therefore there was not enough creativity involved. In other words, the court applied a very strict standard of creativity, ignoring the possibility that minor changes can lead to an impressively new visual impact.

Second, the court held that the industrial design law, "despite its broad scope of application, does not protect fashion articles, whose models are ephemeral like the fantasy that created them."

These two topics are revealing of the inadequacy of traditional forms of intellectual property when applied to fashion because the success of fashionable garments is frequently based on very subtle changes—just think of the mini skirt, which commanded a true revolution in the fashion of apparel for women. One may wonder whether this same court, in 1895, would refuse design protection for the first mini skirt, because as its name says, its creation was solely based on a reduction in the garment's length.

But if the mini skirt has become an icon of fashion—one of those moments that change the course of events—fashion is composed of a myriad of designs and actions that are fleeting, which do not last more than a few months, or even weeks. This court would not approve of the law of industrial designs being applied to so short-lived ideas.

Anyway, this second view would be changed two years later (see § 2.61), but, as we will see, the inadequacy of a legal system of protection of designs that is based on clearly identifiable elements of differentiation, such as novelty and originality, remains inadequate for the treatment of situations in the fashion industry that may involve subtle, and yet perceivable, changes in shapes, patterns, and colors.

Court of Appeals of Paris

Monin v. Lanclair

April 25, 1895

Lack of originality. A belt which is nothing else than the corset with ribbons, already known, only reduced in length from the top, is not an original model, differing from previous models enough to be protected by the law of March 18, 1806.

The 11th Chamber of the Criminal Court of Seine had, on December 18, 1894, rendered the following judgment:

The Court,

Whereas according to the terms of the pleadings, Monin accuses the couple Lanclair of manufacturing and selling a corset entirely identical to that of which he would have the property by virtue of a filing regularly made on August 19, 1892;

Whereas the law of March 18, 1806 recognizes to the manufacturers a right of property, an exclusive right in the designs of their invention filed with the secretariat of the Council of prud'hommes;

Whereas firm case law extends the application of this law to industrial models;

Whereas on April 19, 1892, Monin filed, under number 14,881, a model of corsets with ribbons of his invention, of which he intends to keep the exclusive property for five years and to prosecute any infringer;

Whereas the ribbons corset which had been the subject of a patent in 1867 fell for many years in the public domain; that it appears in particular in the catalogs of department stores published in 1890; that it has become commonplace, as Monin acknowledges, moreover, who does not claim to be its inventor;

But considering that Monin limits himself to maintaining that he created a corset with ribbons called corset-belt, having more grace and elegance than the others;

Whereas a more elegant or more graceful form is not always sufficient to give the object a distinctive and original character, and could not constitute, in this case, a new creation;

Whereas Monin did not give his model a particular appearance, a real stamp of individuality;

Whereas it is the individuality given to the design that, by making of it a new work, creates the right of property;

Whereas it clearly emerges from the debates and documents of the case that the corset as claimed by Monin is not a novelty; that it existed on the market very prior to the filing of April 19, 1892;

Whereas, on the other hand, under the case law, the law of March 18, 1806, despite its broad scope of application, does not protect fashion articles, whose models are ephemeral like the fantasy that created them;

That if the corset is not strictly speaking a fashion article, it is true to say that it follows the variations and the whims of fashion;

Whereas it first results from the documents produced and the depositions of the witnesses heard that the corset manufactured and sold by the couple Lanclair is in no way made according to the Monin model and cannot be considered as a copy or reproduction;

Whereas there is no offense of counterfeiting in this case;

For these reasons, remands ...

Confirmatory judgment of April 25, 1895 by the 7th chamber of the Court of Paris, acting as an appellate court, under the chairmanship of Master Caze, Master Taillefer, rapporteur, ...

The Court,

Considering that from the depositions of the witnesses heard in the 1st instance and from the certificates and documents produced, it follows that the corset with ribbons was invented more than 25 years ago and fell into the public domain before the filing, by Monin, with the Council of Prud'hommes, of a model which he claims to have been counterfeited by Lady Lanclair;

That this corset with ribbons is made freely in any length, top or bottom, according to the will of the buyers;

That the model of the corset, belt with ribbons, which Monin has filed and which he calls the *Roman belt* or *fascia mamillares*, is, in reality, only a corset with ribbons, reduced in length, from the top, i.e., to use the expression of a witness, a low corset; Considering that by shortening the corset with ribbons in the public domain so as to reduce it to the size of a belt, Monin has not invented anything new and has not created an original model that stood out from those known and used before him and which might be protected by the decree-law of 1806; Adopting in addition the reasons of the first judges in that they have nothing contrary to those of the present judgment; For these reasons, confirms ...

§ 2.60 THE ENGLISH HIGH COURT OF JUSTICE REFERS TO THE BASIC ELEMENT OF CLOTH-RELATED INDUSTRIAL DESIGN PROTECTION: THE APPEAL TO THE EYE—1897

In a case involving the counterfeiting of registered dust cloths, the English High Court of Justice touches upon the essence of the legal protection of fashion: the determinant factor is the appeal to the eye. According to the Court, "the ultimate test [of counterfeiting] was by the eye," and even when there are considerable differences between the first article and its knock off, similarity between the articles may still exist in the face of a "resemblance in the general effect." Moreover, the court resorted to the common law notion of passing off, applied not exclusively to trademarks, but also involving the relative—but significant—similarity of the designs. In this understanding, as we will see, may lie a solution for the still-unsolved problem of adequately protecting fashion designs that are without industrial design registration.

The following is just the summary of a very long opinion, but it gives a clear idea of the legal rationale behind the holding.

In the High Court of Justice—Chancery Division, Manchester District

Jones v. Hallworth

Before Mr. Justice Kekewich—January 21 and 22, 1897

Passing off.—Action to restrain.—"Get ut."—"Selvyt," name of dusters.—Deception (probability of).—Injunction granted.

The Plaintiffs manufactured and sold polishing cloths or dusters known as "Selvyt." The dusters were made in special sizes, and as sold were packed in cardboard boxes of the colour of the dusters, and the dusters were folded in a special manner. "Selvyt" was a velveteen cloth, yellowish brown in colour, the self-colour of the material. On two edges of the duster there was printed "Registered Selvyt Trade Mark," on another edge "Superior to chamois leather," and on the remaining edge "A polishing cloth." The centre of the duster was surrounded by a square, in one corner of which was the duster "Registered," and in the other "Patented." The duster had a broad border. The Plaintiffs alleged that "Selvyt" had become well known, and that as that Plaintiffs were the only manufacturers of such dusters, it had become known as the Plaintiffs' manufacture, and that the Defendants had put similar dusters on the market so as to unfairly reap the benefit of the Plaintiffs' reputation and expenditure, and they brought this action for an injunction to restrain the defendants from making and selling dusters so nearly resembling the Plaintiffs' dusters as to be calculated to deceive, and from passing off any dusters not the Plaintiffs' as or for the goods of the Plaintiffs. The Defendants' dusters were of a similar colour to the Plaintiffs'; the printing was not quite the same depth of brown, but a little darker; "Vellutina" was substituted for "Selvyt," and there was also printed "The best polishing cloth" and "Better than chamois leather." The border of the Defendants' was of the same colour as the Plaintiffs', but it was a zig-zag, and there was an additional centre-piece in the Defendants' dusters. The Defendants adopted the sizes of the Plaintiffs.

Held that the question to be decided was whether the Defendants' dusters were so like the Plaintiffs' dusters that the ordinary purchaser intending to buy the Plaintiffs' dusters might be induced to buy, or by inadvertence buy, the defendants'; that the ultimate test was by the eye, and that in this case, although there were considerable differences, the resemblance in the general effect was calculated to deceive the unwary purchaser; and, further, that the Defendants had intended to pass off their goods on the public as those of the Plaintiffs. An injunction was granted.

§ 2.61 A FRENCH COURT CHANGES COURSE, AND TAKES THE FIRST STEP TOWARDS MODERN FASHION DESIGN LAW—1899

Only two years after the Criminal Court of Seine held that the law of industrial designs was not adequate for the protection of fashion designs because of the fleeting nature of fashion (see § 2.59), the Commercial Court of the same department changed course and held quite the contrary. The previous argument of the fleeting nature of fashion—as opposed to an implicit stability of industrial designs for other sectors of industry—is not even mentioned in this opinion.

Commercial Court of Seine

Vimont v. Yung

November 11, 1897

Industrial models.—Shirt for cyclist. The model, duly filed, of a shirt for a cyclist, where the shirt presents a new, distinct appearance, and that it causes by its shape, its kind and its making, a special impressive effect [*cachet*], constitutes an industrial model, the exclusive property of which is acquired by the manufacturer.

The Court, [under the chairmanship of Master Gateclout]

Whereas by judgment, dated August 5, 1897, this Court ordered, before deciding, the opening of the box containing, according to Vimont, the model of a shirt for cyclist, in flannel, with knitted collar and cuffs, the bottom of the shirt in madapollam calico, with opening on the left shoulder fastened with buttons, the said model filed, in accordance with the law, with the secretariat of the Council of Prud'hommes of Seine for the cloth industry, on 15 December 1896, under nr. 18,150;

That it appears from the extract from the records of the secretariat of the Council of Prud'hommes of Seine for the cloth industry, exhibited during the debates, that on October 1, 1897, that the said box was opened in the presence of the parties in cause and that the model contained therein conformed in all its details to the aforecited declarations of Vimont;

Whereas, moreover, Yung does not dispute at all that the shirt manufactured by him is identically similar to that manufactured by Vimont and, consequently, conforms to the filed one;

That he limits himself to maintaining that a shirt, whatever it is, cannot be considered as a new object capable, by its filing, of creating an exclusive property right;

But given that it results from the debates, from the documents submitted and in particular from very many declarations of buyers of the said shirt, that never, until the day of its manufacture by Vimont, no shirt for bicyclist offering some analogy to this one had been put on sale;

That it is established that the shirt manufactured by Vimont presents a new, distinct appearance, and that it causes by its shape, its kind and its making, a special impressive effect;

That, under these conditions, the filing done by Vimont on December 15, 1896 is valid and constitutes an industrial model whose property is attributed to him;

That it is, therefore, on good legal grounds that Vimont asks the Court to say that he is the owner of this model and to prohibit Vung from manufacturing shirts of this model in the future and this, on the penalty of a constraint on grounds of proved counterfeiting;

And whereas it is common ground that the competition made in the past by Yung to Vimont caused the latter damage for which compensation is due to him;

That, consequently, the compensation of 1 franc by him claimed under this heading must be granted;

That it is therefore appropriate to grant the above measure according to Vimont's request;

For these reasons, [the Court] Finds that Vimont is the owner of the model of shirt for cyclist by him filed on December 15, 1896;

Finds that he alone has the right to make shirts after this model;[89]

Finds that in the future, Yung will have to stop making or selling shirts made according to this model, other than those made by Vimont and this on the penalty of 100 francs per violation found;

Orders Yung to pay Vimont the sum of 1 franc as damages;

And orders him, moreover, to pay the costs.

§ 2.62 AN ENGLISH COURT DISCUSSES THE TENSION BETWEEN THE DESIGN OF FASHION AND THE MODE OF MANUFACTURE—1906

The following text is an important opinion on the tension between the design of a product and the mode of its manufacture, i.e., between arbitrariness and functionality. At the time this opinion was delivered fashion designers were already struggling for the best mechanism to protect their original designs—patents v. designs; designs v. copyright; designs v. trademarks; trademarks v. unfair competition. In this case, the design's owner, Charles Bayer & Co., was a corset manufacturer that established himself in Bath (UK), in the nineteenth century, and set a very successful business through the middle of the twentieth century.

89. Based on a law of 1806, defining the attributions of the Council of Prud'Hommes as regards the filing and registration of industrial designs, in 1905 the Court of Seine confirmed this understanding:

> Whereas the purpose of the Decree of March 18, 1806 is to ensure the ownership of the designs to the manufacturers who invented them; that the general terms of the law include designs of apparel, costumes, coiffures, etc. ... as well as all the others; that the forms and fantasies of fashion are expressed through the designs that manufacturers keep inventing, and after which models are executed; that it is proved that the Paquin Company has invented several designs of this kind and regularly filed them that their novelty is not disputed; ...

Georges Maillard et al., ANNALES DE LA PROPRIÉTÉ INDUSTRIELLE, ARTISTIQUE ET LITTÉRAIRE, vol. 52, at 7 et seq. (Arthur Rousseau, 1906). Source: gallica.BnF.fr.

In the Court of Appeal

Before Lords Justices Vaughan Williams, Fletcher Moulton, and Buckley

November 28, 29, 30, and December 3, 1906

In the Matter of Bayer's Design (No. 454,848)

This was a Motion by *R. and W.H. Symington & Col. Ltd.* for the rectification of the Register of Designs by the removal therefrom of the Design numbered 454,848. This Design was for a corset, and was registered in Class 10 by *Charles Bayer* (who trade as *Charles Bayer & Co.*) on the 19th of April 1905. The Application for registration contained the following passage:—"Statement of nature of design, shape or configuration of corset. The novelty consists in a corset having the gores or gussets cut horizontally and from the front of the busk towards the back of the corset, as shown in the representations." A representation of the Design is shown below.

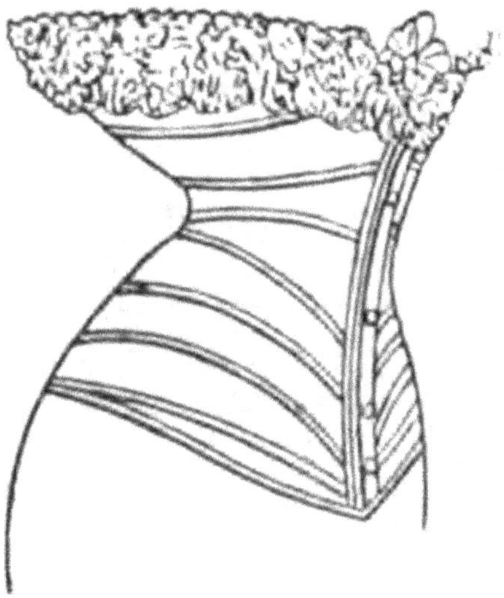

The grounds on which the Applicants relied were as follows:—"1. That the Respondent's claim in his registered Design to a corset having the gores or gussets cut horizontally and from the front of the busk towards the back of the corset, as shown in the representations lodged, is for a method or mode of manufacture, and it is not the subject-matter for a Design. 2. Want of novelty. 3. (a) Prior publication in the following Specifications of patented inventions: ... (b) by the manufacture and sale or offering for sale of corsets constructed according to the said Design, as claimed, ... 4. That the alleged Design as claimed was not subject-matter for a valid Design considering the prior publications (mentioned above) and the common knowledge of the trade regarding the construction of corsets. That the Respondents had been guilty of misrepresentation in their use of the said alleged Design in the wording and illustrations of certain advertisements, and in the marking of the corresponding corsets. ...

On the 29th of September 1905, the Respondent wrote to a certain firm in the following terms:—"Our attention has been called to the imitation by you of our registered design No. 454,848 in respect of 'tailor-made' corsets which you are selling. We, of course, lay no claim to the exclusive use of these descriptive words, but we must ask you to immediately discontinue the imitation of our registered system of making corsets, and shall be glad to receive a letter from you stating that you agree to do so forthwith." ...

The Motion came on for hearing on June the 18th before Mr. Justice Warrington. The learned Judge held that the Design as registered was for a particular form of straight-fronted corsets made with horizontal gussets; that the fact that the Design incidentally described a mode of manufacture did not make it any less a Design; that there was subject-matter and that the Design was novel; and that it was not shown that the pictures of the Design in the advertisements were not covered by the Design; and that a statement made after registration by the owner of the Design as to the extent of his protection ought not to affect the construction of the Application or the validity of the registration. The Motion was dismissed with costs. ...

Williams *L.J.*—Mode of manufacture is one thing and form of manufacture another. A form of manufacture may be the subject of a Design. There is no question about infringement here; the Applicants have made exact copies of the Design. A Design is to be distinguished from an invention. A Design is the representation of an idea. The idea may be new or old, but the representation of it must be new. A Patent is granted for the embodiment of an idea, and it is the invention and not its mere representation that is protected. The invention claimed in a Patent Specification is claimed in words, and also in some cases by Drawings, but the grant for a Design is measured only by section 58, which forbids fraudulent or obvious imitations. A Design, therefore, is a representation and nothing else; for registration it must be novel, and the infringement of the copyright in the Design must be a colourable or obvious imitation. There are no conditions regulating the registration of Designs corresponding to the sufficiency or utility in the case of a Patent. A Design can be taken off the register only if it does not come within the definition in the Act. Novelty and originality are the conditions required. Utility has a bearing on the question of novelty, because an apparently inconspicuous variation in a combination may, by reason of its utility, appear to the instructed eye of a person in the trade as a striking and material alteration ... .

Vaughan Williams *L.J.*—I have had some hesitation as to the conclusion we should arrive at in this case. It is a case in which I cannot help thinking that the registration has been unfortunate in form. I have before me the Application, which is addressed to the Comptroller, and he is requested "to register the accompanying Design in Class 10"—that is the millinery and wearing apparel class—"in the name of Charles Bayer," and then it goes on say:—"Statement of nature of Design: Shape or Configuration of Corset. The novelty consists in a corset having the gores or gussets cut horizontally, and from the front of the busk towards the back of the corset, as shown in the Representation." The Representations consist of three copies of this photograph, which had to be deposited under the Rules. ...

It is said that a Design, in order to be a Design, must be something which can be drawn, and thus represented on paper; it must be something which, when it is applied to any article of manufacture, shall appeal to the eye. It is said that in judging whether a particular thing is a Design, or not, you have not to trouble yourself with any question of utility, or any question of that sort at all. It is clear from the *Hecla Foundry* cases that, if a Design is a Design, when tested by the eye, it will not cease to be a Design, or the less be a Design, because when you use this piece of ornamentation by applying it you will attain a mechanical result which could be subject matter of Letters Patent. I myself have not got to judge whether this particular Design could have been protected by obtaining Letters Patent, but I am by no means disposed to say it could not have been so protected. I am only saying that under the decision in the *Hecla Foundry* case the fact that it could be so protected in no way prevents, in my judgment, the Design being a Design which can be registered under the Act. The question here, applying the eye test, is:—Is, or is not, this a Design? It is, I think, perfectly clear law, that if that which you propose to register is a mere mode of manufacture you cannot register that mode of manufacture. ... It is said here that which is sought to be registered is a mere mode of manufacture. It is an effective system for the manufacture of these straight-fronted corsets, and I feel that there is great force in that contention. It must, I think, be obvious to everyone, at all events to everyone who has heard the arguments in the present case, that the line between "shape," "pattern," and "configuration," on the one hand, and mode of manufacture on the other hand, is not a very plain line, and not one which is easy to express in words. I think it is extremely difficult to do so; and the more so because under this Act of Parliament relating to Designs you may, as I have already said, register a Design, even though the effect of the Design is, when applied, to bring about an enormous improvement in the mode of manufacture. That makes the line very difficult to draw. ...

Under these circumstances I think that this appeal ought to be allowed; but I come to the conclusion with some considerable reluctance, because, taking the whole of the evidence together, I have no doubt myself that a corset made like this exhibits very considerable novelty and is of great usefulness, which had not been attained before. It may be that the improvement is such that it cannot be protected by registration of a Design, however worded. I do not know whether this invention of this shape of corset, with the seams and gussets relatively of this size and this position, could or could not be protected under Letters Patent. On the whole I have come to the conclusion that Mr. Justice Warrington was not justified in the conclusion that he came to—that this was a Design capable of registration.

Fletcher Moulton *L.J.*—I have come to the same conclusion. ...

Now ..., I want to say a word or two with regard to what a Design is. The distinction between a Design and an invention, the subject of a Letters Patent, is very wide. If you want to realise how wide it is, it is well to keep in mind that in all these cases the basis of the legislation is that persons who do anything original either in the way of designing or making an invention are allowed a monopoly for a time, but only on terms that they so publish to the public their original work that at the end of the time the public may have the full benefit of it. That applies as well to Designs as it does to Letters Patent. In the case of Letters Patent you have precisely to define what it is you claim, and you have to give the public full instructions as to how to use it in order that when it becomes *publici juris* they may be able to reap the benefit of it. You do not find any such obligations with regard to Designs. Why is that? It is because Designs apply to nothing but that which the eye can tell entirely. Nothing in my opinion is a good Design but that of which full knowledge is given when you have once shown to the eye what your Design is. It may be shape or configuration; that is given by a specimen or by a proper drawing, and the eye can see it, and the eye can recognise whether it has been imitated. It may be by a pattern, to which the same applies. It may be by an ornament, to which the same applies. But in my opinion nothing beyond that can rightly be called a Design within the meaning of this Statute. ...

One remark further, until this case came into Court I can find no trade of any limitation of the Design to a particular description of corset. It is perfectly true that the representation shows a straight-fronted corset. That was the fashionable corset of the day, and I should think, if one may trust to one's knowledge of these matters from cases which I have been in Court, probably the one which is most largely manufactured at the present time. But if you are only going to put one representation of a corset it must be a corset of some particular kind; it cannot be both one with a curved busk and one with a straight busk; and the consequence is that you must take your choice how you represent it. But because you represent it with one, it does not exclude the other unless that is excluded by words. No doubt if a person wanted to show a pattern of a shoe, the shoe shown would be either a gentleman's shoe or a lady's shoe; but because you only show one shoe, and it was one or the other, it would be a most unfair principle of construction to say that a claim for a particular pattern of shoe excluded shoes made for the other sex. So I can see nothing here which in any way restricts the claim to a particular class of content, namely, straight-fronted. ...

Buckley *L.J.*—I also am of opinion that this appeal ought to be allowed. After the judgments which have been delivered I should content myself with that bare statement but for the fact that we are differing from the learned judge below, and I therefore owe to him that I should give my reasons in my own way. ...

The application before the Court is one to rectify the Register by striking out this Design. The question to be examined is whether the Design was one which was capable of being registered under the Act of Parliament. Now the thing which may be registered is by Section 47 defined as being "any new or original Design." Then passing on to inquire what a Design is for the purposes of the Act, I find it established by authority that the Design must be something which must be altogether expressed to the eye or, as has been said, appeals to the eye. The person who registers it is not bound to give, beyond compliance with the Rules, which I will refer to presently, any statement of the ambit of that which he claims, but he has to produce a pictorial illustration of the idea or suggestion which he has to establish as new or original.

That therefore is the first quality of a Design, it must appeal to the eye. Secondly, I think it must possess this feature, that the pictorial representation must not be a mere representation of a single article, but must be a suggestion of something which, on account of the language of Section 60, is capable of being applied to an article of manufacture or to a substance. That may be expressed by saying that the Design must be a thing which exists apart from its expression. There must be a suggestion capable of being applied and in general, certainly I think in this case as regards a corset, capable of being applied under varying circumstances. It must suggest something to a person which is new and original, and is capable of being applied to an article of manufacture or to a substance. ...

Let me assume that Mr. Bayer is right in saying that his claim is to a straight-fronted corset. What has he done in any way to show that the Design—meaning by that the width of the different pieces, the position of the seams and the like—will produce that effect at all. I apprehend that he has done nothing for that purpose. What really was wanted in order to explain that was to show that you must so expose the bottom of the busk to strains as to compel the body to assume that form. If you take the Design, meaning by it a corset of that shape made up of pieces of that shape, that corset will only fit one particular body and will fit none other at all, and it is quite plain that that is not the least what he meant to do; because if you look at his own evidence what he says is this: He is asked "Having ascertained your Design is it a difficult matter or not to adapt that Design to different figures of women?" Then he answers, "Not when you know how to go about it. To a stranger it would be." That is to say, when you know that the secret lies in getting your lengths right and that you must adjust your lengths as to compel the straight front, then you can adapt what he is pleased to call "my Design." Of course he is abandoning the meaning of the word "Design" as used in the Act of Parliament: and that means not a corset of particular measurement as

> shown in my picture, but the mode of manufacture of a corset by establishing a particular length and the like, by which you would insure that lateral tension at the bottom of the busk which will give you the straight front. I conclude therefore that in this case the Design is either bad altogether as having nothing new or original in it, or it is bad because it merely shows a picture of a single isolated article, and contains no Design at all in the sense of suggestion or something which may be used to produce a particular form of corset, namely a straight-fronted corset. If you read it as meaning that, then it appears to me plain to be a mode of manufacture and not a Design. For these reasons I think that this Appeal ought to be allowed.[90]

§ 2.63 THE FRENCH PARLIAMENT ENACTS A STATUTE ON INDUSTRIAL DESIGNS WITH EXPRESS COVERAGE OF APPAREL AND ACCESSORIES—1909

In France, all possible doubts about the coverage of fashion designs by industrial design law ceased in 1909 when the Parliament passed a statute on designs (and models, in French terminology, which distinguished—conceptually but not in terms of protection—two-dimensional designs from three-dimensional ones) with a very comprehensive language defining its scope.

The following text is an excerpt from the work by a French jurist, Hermine Valabrègue, who, in a booklet on fashion law, stated that the statute's legislative history was unequivocal in that it covered fashion designs.

A first point seems indisputably established: that the protection of the law of July 14, 1909 is acquired for creations of the Arts of Fashion. We have indeed indicated, in the Section relating to the law, the extremely broad definition of the scope of this statute:

> This law is applicable to any new design, to any new plastic form, to any industrial object that differs from its similars, either by a distinct and recognizable configuration giving it a character of novelty, or by one or more external effects giving it a clean and new appearance. (Article 2.)

In addition, and to avoid any misunderstanding, rapporteur Prache has clarified to the Chamber of Deputies that the protection of the law of 1909:

> was extended ... to all forms foreign to the rules of industrial sculpture, for example to new models of coiffures, hats, corsets, etc. ...

and moreover he specified:

> So that the benefit of protection cannot be refused to any creation, whatever it is, for example to articles of fashion, of embroidery, of clothing, etc. ... the project takes the precaution of adding that the law applies to any industrial object.
>
> No doubt can therefore remain: fashion articles are undoubtedly protected by the law of July 14, 1909. ...

---

90. It seems that Judge Buckley would deny protection to apparel designs that apply to *slim fit* or *skinny fit* models, which are adapted to specific measures of the human body.

§ 2.64 THE BUILDING OF CASE LAW IN FRANCE INVOLVING THE PROTECTION OF FASHION DESIGNS—1911-1913

The following texts concern five opinions that show how French courts started to establish the foundations of fashion law as far as the protection of designs is concerned.

The first two texts are related to a lawsuit that opposed a then famous Paris fashion house—Bechoff, David et Cie.—to Galeries Lafayette—one of the first French store departments and, in that period, an insistent counterfeiter of luxury fashion. The first text—a few excerpts from the oral arguments of Maurice Bernard, an attorney who represented the plaintiffs—is particularly interesting insofar as it explains the method Galeries Lafayette, one of the first fast-fashion outlets created for catering to the middle-class market, used at that time to systematically counterfeit the designs created by high fashion houses. It is noteworthy that reference is made to other fast fashion brands of that time—Louvre, Printemps, Bon Marché—which, like today's Zara, Mango, and H&M, had their own designers and created fashion specifically targeting their own clientele and therefore would not engage in systematic counterfeiting.

Another important topic in these arguments is the allegation that the infringement of high fashion designs had a financial impact on the houses that created them by causing deterioration in their brands' value, hence leading to a loss of earnings. This argument is often used to deny the occurrence of damages in the knock-off of luxury articles, such as Louis Vuitton's bags. However, the Court, in this case, has accepted it.

Given the gravity of Galeries Lafayette's unfair competition practices, the court ordered the publication of the opinion in three newspapers. This order, which would become customary, and is adopted by today's courts in some sorts of cases, namely those involving unfair competition, is not very different in nature and in purpose from the old provisions of medieval by-laws and statutes that imposed on counterfeiters the penalty of the pillory or the stocks. Excluded the physical suffering that those old punishments implied, there was in them the same purpose of publicly shaming the offenders.

The third text concerns another lawsuit against Galeries Lafayette. Its relevance lies in the careful analysis of novelty and originality in fashion designs.

The fourth and the sixth texts concern two disputes between fashion houses and specialized fashion journals. The contention was about the scope of the exclusivity in industrial designs—does the exclusivity in designs extend to their reproduction by the specialized press or is it limited to the making of the products embodying the protected designs? Is the protection granted to designs a combination of industrial property (exclusivity in the making or using the idea) and copyright (exclusivity in reproducing the expression of the idea)? These same questions were behind the opposition that for some time fashion journals raised against the protection of fashion designs in the United States (see § 2.65). Importantly, it seems that the fact that the designs in the magazines were accompanied by detailed captions has had weight in the courts' holdings. The combination of the designs and the captions were decisive in assisting the competitors of the designers in manufacturing the fashion apparel in question. So, at the end of the day, the matter was not only of infringing proprietary designs by publishing them without permission, but also of contributing to infringement by designers' rivals.

The fifth text brings an important opinion concerning the exclusive protection accorded to designs under an unfair competition approach. This case deals with an aspect of great importance for fashion houses: the protection granted to original designs printed or woven into fabrics that are used in the making of garments. Of particular importance is the acknowledgment by the Court that certain designs show an "individual spirit," from which consumers identify the origin of the fabrics or cloths. This amounts to recognizing a distinctive role in certain designs, beyond their purely ornamental purpose. In this sense, the functions those designs perform are not different from that of trademarks. Such an understanding may lead to the acceptance of the notions of secondary meaning and dilution as applied to designs.

This opinion was confirmed by the Cour de Cassation (Court of Appeals) on June 18, 1913 (Bulletin Mensuel de la Cour de Cassation)

§ 2.64.1 *Béchoff, David et Cie v. Galeries Lafayette:* Oral Arguments of Master Maurice Bernard, for the Plaintiff—The Fashion Wars in Paris, in the Early 1900s

Civil Court of Seine (3rd Chamber)

Béchoff, David et Cie v. Galeries Lafayette

March 24, 1911

Oral arguments of Master Maurice Bernard (excerpts)

Gentlemen.

Today's trial, you will see in a moment, goes far beyond the scope of a difficulty between Maison Béchoff-David and Galeries Lafayette.

All the great Parisian couture and fashion houses are currently struggling against plagiarists and looters of novelty. Paris, which is and will remain—your judgment, moreover, will help us with regard to the part that my clients take in it—the homeland of art and beauty, must suffer the burden and the price of its supremacy and its kingship. Wherever there is the maximum of beauty, there is the maximum of imitation; wherever there is art, there is imitation; wherever there is beauty, there is also the false chic and the fake. ...

Great dressmakers and designers are inspired by the general idea that is in the air ... I say it is in the air because have you wondered where it comes from? It is easy to tell the Court that the great dressmakers meet in a tavern, in a cafe, in a restaurant at night, so that they are not seen and that they decree then what will be the fashion.

That is a mistake. If you knew them better ... you would know that the great dressmakers hide from each other, fight over the models they are going to create and that the designers of each house carefully seek the most jealous of the models that will come out of their imagination. Twice a year, on February 15 and August 15, they see what the models for the following summer will be, then in August they see the models that will be worn during the winter.

The great dressmakers thus have designers whom they pay dearly, much more dearly than the seamstresses who afterwards manufacture them or than the saleswomen and the mannequins. Indeed, it is those who have brought the idea, who have imagined the more or less happy combination of models, the real fathers and creators of these models. Fashion has nothing to do with it. It is like a river whose flow no one can stop. ...

When fashion has said that this year the hobble skirt will be worn, it is understood that an intelligent and wise dressmaker is not going to have fun—he would waste his time and it would be useless—in swimming upstream and make voluminous or puffed skirts. But it is this order of ideas that indicates to him—I was going to say that fashion imposes on him, and which the dressmaker seeks to adopt—following the general model that, in the eyes of all Parisian women constitutes fashion, the special model which will be that of his invention. This, Gentlemen, is the difference whose sight should not be lost.

How do these houses operate? It is very simple. Although the models for each season that come out on February 15 are jealously guarded until then, there are always leaks and indiscretions, in these special houses where everybody watches, spies and elbows each other. It is a little seamstress who will be given alms so that she will commit a small indiscretion on such and such a model; it is a higher-ranking employee who, for one night, will lend a model or a drawing that will be photographed. Finally, there is the known process used by the Galeries Lafayette and with which, thus far, they have had infallible success to plunder the models launched by the houses of the great dressmakers.

There is a lady who works as a seamstress in Monte-Carlo and her name is Madame Ernestine. When the models are launched, she comes to the Paquin house, or rather she came there, because today she is known, but there are others; she came, I said, to the Paquin house and there she asked to buy three, four, five or six models of dresses for the following season, using the following language: "Do not be afraid, I am a seamstress, it is true, but not in Paris, I am a seamstress in Monte-Carlo." I will inform the Court, if it does not know it already, that the models are sold abroad to agents who carry the renown of Parisian and French couture abroad. The models are sold to Parisian customers for direct sale and abroad by agents who come to look for the models as soon as they appear. ...

Let us return to Madame Ernestine, seamstress in Monte-Carlo. She comes to rue de la Paix when the models are launched; she then goes to the Place de l'Opéra to pick up those from the Drecoll house. She has all of this sent to Monte-Carlo. The models make the trip, they arrive in Monte-Carlo, but they are not even unpacked. Madame Ernestine, who is nothing more than a Galeries Lafayette beater, immediately makes them turn around as soon as the box arrives in the Principality of Monaco. Then, the models are copied at Galeries Lafayette. There lies one of the secrets of the prosperity of this house, which amazes all of Paris. They are made to be copied by unfortunate seamstresses who are paid the most derisory, the smallest, and the most shameful wages. There are so many mouths in Paris to feed and so many unfortunate little seamstresses who do not know how to use their time, who agree to work in these conditions day and even at night; malnourished, they often get tuberculosis! As for the work, we know what a dozen pants or a dozen shirts are worth at Galeries Lafayette! ...

Thus, having on the one hand the models and on the other the means of reproducing them very cheaply with less expensive cloths and fabrics, and of less value, we get a trompe l'oeil that has chic, allure, which permits that the clientele I was talking about earlier [middle-class women] and even a few elegant women, at nightfall, after having had the Galeries Lafayette label removed, can walk around with a model that is supposed to come from Paquin or Béchoff-David and which they could afford for 150 or 200 francs [instead of 1,000 francs]. Here is how the trick works.

The consequence is that the agents who supply foreign customers come to the Béchoff-David house to say for example: "But the models that you send me as being the emanation of the couture of the rue de la Paix, we find them at Galeries Lafayette! How do you expect me to sell them to the very wealthy American or English women, or to the opulent German women, these models that they can find at Galeries Lafayette at the price of 150 francs?"

And the Parisian clientele? You see, Gentlemen, what my kind of prejudice is. It may be snobbery and for my part I will never fall into this trap, but the elegant women who agree to pay 500, 600, 800 francs or 900 francs for a dress with a special impressive effect, just because it comes out from a great house ... the model is known; it is known that such dress worn by such great lady in such ceremony or by such actress in such premiere, is a model of the house. The day the model is worn by the humble, it immediately finds itself depreciated, discredited. Gentlemen, if you want to take a look at the books of the Béchoff-David house, you will see that the figures concerning the orders increase for the models that have remained exclusive until they can be found at Galeries Lafayette, then from that moment onwards you see the curve falling, because the fever of the vogue decreases and because the elegant women who go to Béchoff-David no longer want a depreciated model. ...

In a word, and this will decisively persuade you that the Galeries Lafayette cannot be admitted to speak of their good faith, because what they have done vis-à-vis the Béchoff-David house, they have repeated it four times in succession by the most detestable and dishonest methods; they have carried the same acts out towards all the other fashion houses as well.

It is not by chance that Galeries Lafayette is the only victim of what their honorable lawyer qualified some moments ago as an unfortunate accident, as a sort of involuntary similarity. Come on, are you alone in Paris, and aren't there any houses other than you? Have the Printemps, the Louvre, the Bon Marché ever had difficulties and troubles of this nature? I have questioned the records, I have questioned the rumours of the Courthouse. Well, know this, the great dressmakers have never had a complaint about Louvre, Bon Marché or Printemps. They have all affirmed, and the Chamber of Commerce attests it, that these correct establishments, not addressing a clientele of supreme elegance like that of rue de la Paix, but having a good clientele only in the best sense of the word, I will call it the bourgeoise clientele, the old, solid and loyal French bourgeoisie, that these establishments, I say, consequently pay their employees, their designers, to make models appropriate to the taste of their clientele.

This, Gentlemen, is what it was necessary to tell you from a general point of view. ...

§ 2.64.2 *Béchoff, David et Cie v. Galeries Lafayette.* The Opinion of the Civil Court of Seine, 3rd Chamber—1911

Model of coat called "Good Hope."—Borrowed from old fashions.—New combination. Lack of good faith based on the declaration of a saleswoman and the reproduction of characteristic signs.—Counterfeit.—Losses. Loss of earnings. Damages.—Unfair competition.

The Bechoff David house owns a model of coat, with Japanese-shaped sleeves, which it has called "Good Hope" and filed as an industrial model. It has sued Galeries Lafayette for infringement of this model: this house claimed that it was in good faith, the coats it has sold having been made from a sketch taken by a cutter seeing such a coat on the shoulders of a Galeries Lafayette client. The court ... under the chairmanship of Master More has delivered the following judgment.

The Court:

Whereas Béchoff-David et Cie, dressmakers in Paris, on March 23, 1907, had obtained the report on the appraisal of a coat, with Japanese-shaped sleeves, at the Galeries Lafayette Stores, which they claim to be the counterfeit of a coat called "Good Hope" by them filed under nr. 2,975, as an industrial model, at the Secretariat of the Council of Prud'hommes on January 17, 1907;

Whereas the Société des Galeries Lafayette does not dispute that the law of March 18, 1806, assures the ownership of the designs to the manufacturers who sell them after having filed them, but, to evade the charge formulated against it, it claims that the model of Béchoff-David et Cie would have been borrowed from fashions of the fourteenth, fifteenth, sixteenth, and seventeenth centuries, and that, moreover, far from being the servile copy of "Good Hope," the cloth coat whose purchase was made during the preparation of the report of appraisal, had been made according to the sketch taken by one of the cutters of Galeries Lafayette, who would have seen it on the shoulders of a customer of these stores.

Whereas, with regard to the alleged lack of novelty, none of the illustrations submitted by the defendant has, from a general point of view, the appearance of the filed model. There is no need to find out whether some of its features have been borrowed from old fashions. It is the judiciously chosen combination of the various elements that compose it, which gives it an indisputable originality and fantasy, and which makes it susceptible of private property.

Whereas with regard to the alleged good faith, if it is true that in matters of infringement of designs, it is possible to plead good faith, since the filing made is under seal, the explanations provided by the defendant are far from satisfactory.

Whereas it is enough to refer to the report of March 23, 1907 to allow the affirmation that the coat sold by Galeries Lafayette could not be seen in March during the afternoon, on the shoulders of a client. Indeed, the saleswoman to whom the person accompanying the bailiff spoke said "it was a theatrical coat, and they were often used on the winter beaches as well."

Whereas, moreover, that if a doubt were still possible, it would disappear in the face of the observation that, whatever the skill of the employee of the Galeries Lafayette in making sketches, he could not have realized that on the small inner sleeve, which in the filed model is concealed by a small piece of Scottish silk, an S was drawn, particularly characteristic, since one of its ends is sharp and the other is round.

Whereas the counterfeiting is most flagrant; everything, in the Galeries Lafayette model, recalls the model of Bechoff, David et Cie., the sewing, the shaped cut, the metal buttons trim, the inside of the sleeve, the tie with threaded edges; if there is a difference in the size of some of the metal buttons, this difference does not modify the particular appearance of one of the models compared to the other.

Whereas there is not only infringement, but unfair competition; it actually follows from the statements of the saleswoman that Galeries Lafayette have sold a large quantity of these coats, of all shades, green, chamois, pastel, beige, etc., at a price of 150 francs, much lower than the price established by the plaintiffs. There is therefore a loss of earnings by the Béchoff-David house, and in addition, the filed model is inevitably greatly depreciated in the eyes of the elegant clientele.

Whereas the shameful practices which have just been noted against the Galeries Lafayette company are not isolated; that it is therefore appropriate, not only to award part of the damages claimed, but to order also the publication of this judgment in the press.

For these reasons:

[The Court] Holds that the Company "Les Galeries Lafayette" is guilty, in prejudice of Bechoff, David et Cie, of counterfeiting a model of a "Good Hope" coat filed with the secretariat of the Council of Prud'hommes under number 2,975.

It holds further that said company is guilty of unfair competition.

It orders the company "Les Galeries Lafayette" to pay the plaintiffs the sum of 4,000 fr., as damages.

It also orders, as a complement to the damages, the insertion of this judgment in three newspapers in Paris, at the expense of the said company, the cost of each insertion not exceeding the sum of 150 fr.

And finally it condemns [the defendant] to all costs.

Figure 44 Left: Mrs. Emma Montbryon, a French actress, wears a coat designed and made by Béchoff-David. Within their vast and successful collections of apparel and accessories, Béchoff-David's coats were particularly appreciated and sought by Parisian wealthy women. Photo by Émile-Paul Reutlinger, a famous French fashion photographer (1863-1937). Right: The Galeries Lafayette at the beginning of the twentieth century. The ad informs readers that the house has the best prices in all of Paris.

§ 2.64.3 *Rodier frères v. Galeries Lafayette*—1911

Commercial Court of Seine

Rodier frères v. Galeries Lafayette

December 4, 1911

Messrs. brothers Rodier have submitted to the Council of prud'hommes a model of fabrics for kimono-shaped blouses. They have claimed that in violation of their rights, Galeries Lafayette copied, offered for sale and advertised in their catalog an identical blouse, thus making themselves guilty of counterfeiting and unfair competition. The Seine Commercial Court, chaired by Mr. Petit ... has delivered the following judgment:

The Court:

Whereas the lawsuit on which the Court is called upon to rule had origin in the dispute that has arisen between the brothers Rodier and the Society of Great Department Stores "Aux Galeries Lafayette" concerning a model of fabrics intended for making blouses for women's apparel, blouses whose creation the brothers Rodier claim, and which they accuse Galeries Lafayette (the Company at trial to be so designated here for simplicity) of having copied and put up for sale; the brothers Rodier have argued that their creation was characterized by a particular combination of lines producing a special effect that gave it a proper and new appearance; this model was filed with the secretariat of the Council of prud'hommes of Seine, section of cloths, on August 2, 1910, under number 287 of the second part of register nr. 7; it was made public on February 10, 1911; however, they would have noticed that in the catalog distributed by Galeries Lafayette for their exhibition, announced for Monday, February 13, 1911, there was an insert relating to special occasions, and that in this insert appeared, under number 314,050, a half-made blouse similar to the one created by them; moreover, on the day of the exhibition, a model of blouse a little different from that marked in the catalog, but also imitating the creation of the brothers Rodier, was offered to the public and sold; these actions would have constituted counterfeiting established by the law of July 14, 1909, and an act of unfair competition with regard to them, and this would have caused them clear damage for which they intend to obtain compensation; consequently, they sue the Society of Galeries Lafayette with the purpose: that it be held and decided that the aforementioned actions constitute an infringement of the model filed by them, and an act of unfair competition in their regard; that the immediate prohibition of the distribution of the catalog and the sale of the offending articles be ordered; that the defendant be condemned to pay damages to be fixed by liquidation, and by provision of a sum of 20,000 francs; ...

On the main cause of action: Whereas the Galeries Lafayette, opposing the accusation of which they are the object, are pleading: that not only there would not have been on their part the slightest intention to copy the model of the brothers Rodier, but that in the present case, there would not even be a matter of plagiarism; that one could add that there would not even be grounds for filing designs for this sort of apparel; that in truth, the model of a half-made blouse announced in the February 1911 catalog would not have distinguished itself as a new type; that the general idea of printing on a square of fabric a design whose cutting followed four transverse bands arranged in a cross, resulting in a corsage derived from the Japanese shape called *kimono*, would have been very old, and would have been used many times in various periods of women's fashion; that everyone could have made the blouse offered in the catalog under number 314,050 in the simplest way possible; that any blouse intended for the same use should inevitably have resembled either that of the brothers Rodier, or that of Galeries Lafayette, or any other put on sale by a department store; that the brothers Rodier could not seriously maintain that the fashion for kimono-shaped blouses has arisen from their creativity; that they say that the filing of their design was made only in August 1910; that then for a long time women had already worn blouses of this kind; that it should be noted that the brothers Rodier explained in their initial briefing that the model of blouse sold by Galeries Lafayette was a little different from that marked in the catalog, that this difference occurred because the model appearing in the catalog came from Jarrasson, Bornet et Cie, while the one for sale came from the Lowensohn house; that it should be therefore concluded that these two houses, which worked independently, with their own designers and their different processes, would have copied each other and would both have plagiarized the brothers Rodier; that the material impossibility of such facts would suffice to demonstrate the futility of the complaints formulated by the brothers Rodier; that in reality, the brothers Rodier would be unable to prove that the design of their blouse caused in itself an impressive effect of novelty and originality so special that any professional designer would have been obliged to copy it in order to make a blouse in the shape of a kimono; that such a proof would moreover be impossible to make, given the considerable quantity of designs that each new fashion gives rise to; that it would be obvious that, the vogue of a fashion having arisen, the designers would all be obliged to enclose themselves in a necessary framework, and that it would be in the details alone that their originality would emerge; that it would have been so for the blouse in dispute; that its general shape, its frame if you will, could not have varied appreciably from one model to another; that it would always have been necessary to provide a gap for the neckline and cross lines for the location of the sleeves, front and back; that this compulsory general layout would have nothing new; that consequently, the brothers Rodier should not have the pretension of attributing the invention to themselves; that, as regards the drawings of detail or filling, always composed of lines, dots, garlands, flowers whose kind, their arrangement varying ad infinitum, it would be childish to maintain that they could constitute a property, especially when they are only accessory, as in the current case; that finally, the claim of the brothers Rodier could not go so far as to maintain that the Galeries Lafayette have themselves manufactured the criticized model; that they have proved in the proceedings that it was only in December of 1910, about two months before their exhibition, that the Jarrasson, Bornet et Cie. house would have submitted offers for the said model, which they would not have not known until then; ...

Whereas the Galeries Lafayette also plead: that the law of July 14, 1909, which ensured the ownership of industrial designs, stipulated that, when the incriminated facts would be subsequent to the filing but prior to its publication, they could not give rise to an action unless the injured party establishes the bad faith of the accused; that the case currently submitted to the Court falling into this category, it would belong to the brothers Rodier to demonstrate that the Galeries Lafayette acted in bad faith; that they would not provide this proof; that, on the contrary, good faith would appear most clearly; that in fact, while the exhibition opened on Monday, February 13, Galeries Lafayette, learning of the publicity of brothers Rodier's drawings made on February 10, and made aware of their complaints, deleted from their catalogs, as of the previous Thursday, the page on which the offending design was placed; that this suppression was notified to Rodier by letter of February 14; that the lawsuit of the brothers Rodier having been launched that same day, Galeries Lafayette notified them, by letter of February 18, that they had removed from their sale the blouse designated in the said lawsuit;

that the brothers Rodier not denying the existence of these letters, nor the materiality of the deletions made, it would appear that at no time did the Galeries Lafayette have thought of engaging in unfair competition with the brothers Rodier, so that their good faith would not be challengeable, and that the action brought by the brothers Rodier would be groundless and should be dismissed.

But whereas, first of all, the brothers Rodier sue Galeries Lafayette because of a quasi-offense resulting from acts that were purely personal to them, in the sense that it was in their stores and under their sole responsibility that they were performed; the Court must therefore restrict the dispute between the brothers Rodier and Galeries Lafayette to the single point of knowing whether the brothers Rodier's complaints are or are not well-founded vis-à-vis their adversary, without having to examine by whom and how Galeries Lafayette could have been incited to commit the quasi-offense;

And whereas if blouses with the kimono shape have been on the market for a long time, it is no less possible for men skilled in the art to find combinations of lines whose general harmony, technical effort and spirit of invention will be such that the blouse that will come out of their hands will immediately be distinguished from those already existing; it is obvious that, in the whole of the design, the composer whoever he is, will have to consider the use of the garment that he establishes and that any model of feminine bodice will have to provide a gap for the neckline and a location for the sleeves; in this regard, Galeries Lafayette are right to say that such is an obligatory and necessary layout, without anything new; if brothers Rodier' complaints concerned the use of such layout only, their complaints would be frivolous and childish;

But whereas Galeries Lafayette in no way destroy the presumption of novelty that is attached to the blouse design created by the brothers Rodier, and characterized mainly by the use of a division into four segments separated by a wide cross-shaped band serving support for the entire composition; in this regard, the Court does not have to investigate whether similar layouts may have existed in old fashions and what is the importance of the borrowings which may have been made from them; it is the judiciously chosen combination of the various elements that make up the new design, which gives it an indisputable originality and fancy character, and which makes it susceptible of private property; whatever the resources that nature or previous works put at the artist's disposal and however infinite the possibilities of combinations, it is certain that invention has its full value when it produces a work that has not yet been seen or used and which, by that very fact, is likely to attract the attention of those interested; it is after such work that the creator can have the legitimate claim of making the best use of his invention for himself alone and of preventing a third party from depriving him of it, by seizing his idea; in the present case, it should be recognized that the blouse design, imagined by the brothers Rodier, had all the characteristics necessary to produce a special effect, giving it a proper and new appearance according to the very terms of the law of July 14, 1909; the brothers Rodier were therefore justified in securing ownership of it, as they did by filing it regularly;

And whereas it emerges from an examination of the blouses catalogued and put on sale by Galeries Lafayette, that they offer the most striking and least questionable points of resemblance with those created by the brothers Rodier; the arrangement in segments and in cross are found there; for one of these blouses, the servility of the copy is so great that if one superimposes it flatly on brothers Rodier's model, one concludes that all the main lines are thus modeled on each other, and that hardly the copier has taken care to modify somewhat the ornaments used by the brothers Rodier;

Whereas it is inadmissible that this identity is the result of pure chance: it is necessary, on the contrary, to decide that it only occurred because of the firm desire to offer the public a blouse capable of immediately compete with that of the brothers Rodier, whose arrival was then imminent; the latter's complaint is therefore well founded;

And whereas, as far as the good faith alleged by Galeries Lafayette is concerned, it does not result in any way from the facts invoked to demonstrate it; it results on the contrary from the elements of proof produced by the brothers Rodier, that if the filing of their designs was not published until February 10, 1911, it was made on August 12, 1910; in reality, the models intended for the future fashion season are, from their creation by the cloth manufacturers, shown to the representatives, agents and buyers, either to prepare their orders or with a view to exporting; this communication, done in complete trust, must not result in those models being placed in the public domain; if employees, using the information thus collected, make known to their employers the ideas of third parties, it is up to these employers to rigorously refuse to make use of them, so as not to deserve the reproach of counterfeiting or of unfair competition;

Whereas the facts detailed above demonstrate that Galeries Layafette, either by themselves or through third parties too willing to flatter their desires to always be ahead of their competitors, were aware, before their exhibition, on February 1911, of the models created by the brothers Rodier; undoubtedly appreciating them, they were wrong in either having them copied, or, what amounts to the same thing, in ordering similar ones without personally ensuring that no one would have to complain about that; if they maintain that the orders would have been made a little hastily and a few days before the exhibition, it is to be noted that it took them quite a long time, however, to prepare their catalog, to have the pictures taken of the design of the blouse in question and all the others, and to receive these catalogs from the printer in good time to send them to their customers; this amount of time was more than sufficient to obtain all the necessary information, and to act with the necessary caution;

Whereas in these conditions, bad faith in the legal sense of the term is peremptory, and the Court has no doubt about it; it occurred before the publication of the filing; the lawsuit of the brothers Rodier, is therefore admissible; it matters little, except from the point of view of the importance of the damage, to investigate whether Galeries Lafayette subsequently did the necessary to mitigate their fault to a certain extent; this fault exists, and by its very nature there is not only counterfeiting, but above all unfair competition; it is therefore on valid grounds that the brothers Rodier ask the Court to rule in this sense; therefore their request must be accepted, under the sanctions that the Tribunal will determine below;

And whereas the actions of Galeries Lafayette have resulted in causing the brothers Rodier a certain damage for which compensation is due to them; this Court has the elements of assessment that are necessary for it to decide, as of now and without resorting to arbitration, that the allowance to the brothers Rodier of a lump sum of 5,000 francs, by way of damages, will be the sufficient compensation to which they are entitled; ...

For these reasons:

[The Court] holds that the actions of the Société des Galeries Lafayette constitute, with regard to the brothers Rodier, an act of unfair competition and also an infringement of the model filed by them; orders, consequently, the immediate cessation of the distribution of the catalog and the sale of the offending articles; and in compensation for the damage caused, orders the Société des Galeries Lafayette to pay the brothers Rodier, definitively, the sum of 5,000 francs, as damages; ...

§ 2.64.4 The Protection of Industrial Designs Extends to the Unauthorized Publication in Fashion Journals: *Callot soeurs v. Finkelstein et Gruenwald*—1911

Civil Court of Seine, Third Chamber

December 14, 1911

The Callot Sisters house, claiming to be the owner of various models of dresses filed with the Council of prud'hommes, has sued Messrs. Finkelstein and Gruenwald, publisher and manager of the Journal le Grand Chic Paris, for their having published in certain issues of this newspaper designs that would constitute a counterfeit of its models. The Third Chamber of the Tribunal chaired by Mr. Petit ... has rendered the following judgment:

The Court:

Whereas ... the sisters Callot, claiming to be owners of the various models filed with the Secretariat of the Council of Prud'hommes of Seine, have sued Finkelstein, editor-owner of Le Grand Chic Paris, and Gruenwald, manager of the said Journal, for having, in the issues of October 1908, in the special issue of September 1908, and in the issues of January, February, April, May and June 1909, published designs that they claim to be an infringement of their models and ask that the defendants be declared infringers and condemned to pay damages, the details of which are indicated in each of the briefs;

Whereas the sisters Callot have well proved having done the filings on the dates indicated in their submission;

Whereas in their oral explanations the defendants alleged that the publication made in the incriminated issues could not take the character of a counterfeit because it would not have been made in violation of authors' rights, as provided in the laws of July 19-24, March 11, 1902 and March 18, 1806;

Whereas models of dresses and coats can be the subject of a valid filing and an exclusive property when they cause by themselves a special impressive effect of novelty, which accord to them a proper appearance and a real character of originality;

That the law of March 18, 1806 intended to ensure its protection to the creators of models, use terms that by their generality include dresses and coats in the same way as all the other productions of the industry, the fruit of a real spirit of invention;

That it matters little that this protection is only ephemeral and is exercised only during the very short period of time assigned to it by the incessant variations of fashion; that the law itself, in its Article 18, has admitted in fact that the term of protection could be reduced and even limited to one year;

Whereas these models, which, because of their dimensions and their intrinsic value, do not lend themselves easily to a filing in kind, can be validly protected by a figurative filing, which, by including simultaneously photographs, muslins, and samples of each of the elements of the garment, gives the exact and complete representation of the dresses and garments claimed by the sisters Callot:

Whereas the defendants maintain that it is true that the infringement would not result from the publication of designs in a fashion newspaper, even if they were (which they dispute in fact) the exact copy of the models of the Callot house; that there would be illegal reproduction only if the filed object would have been materially reproduced, but that a simple design that represents it without replacing it in any way could not be held as an infringement;

But given that the purpose of the law of March 10, 1806 is to protect the creator of a model against any usurpation likely to harm him/her;

That the publication of engravings and designs, especially when these are accompanied by technical explanations and patterns, makes it possible to easily reconstitute the garments represented not only in their broad outlines, but often even down to their details, and therefore deprive the filer of the legitimate profit that he/she was entitled to expect from the sale of his/her model patterns;

That to require in matters of industrial property for there to be illegal publishing, i.e., counterfeiting, that the reproduction can serve the purpose for which the infringing object was intended, would be to arbitrarily add a condition to the requirements of the law;

Whereas this disclosure by the Journal of fashions that reproduce the models, disseminates among the public and in fact makes their reproduction possible, constitutes the punishable edition provided for by Article 425 of the Penal Code;

Whereas the defendants object that from the moment when they would have been presented to the agents and the representatives of the fashion houses, the models would have fallen into the public domain and could have been freely reproduced;

That in any case they would not have committed any counterfeiting by publishing in their newspaper dresses and garments after having had them photographed or drawn at the races, at the theater and in all other public places;

But whereas one cannot consider as constituting a true publicity susceptible of jeopardizing the rights of the filers the fact that the sisters Callot have shown the new models to the agents and representatives, themselves during a time interested in avoiding publicity that could lead to their disclosure; that moreover the defendants do not prove that this restricted publicity would have preceded the filings through which the Callot soeurs house asserted its right of exclusive property;

Whereas, therefore, fashion newspapers cannot be allowed to publish, unless expressly authorized, designs or engravings reproducing, with a commercial purpose, the models that they have been able to have photographed in public places and to undermine property recognized by law;

That even the difficulty they might sometimes experience in locating the owners and creators of these models does not authorize them to disregard the necessity of obtaining authorization;

Whereas this does not in any way endanger the existence of fashion journals, which limit themselves to drawing inspiration from the models of the great fashion houses for the making of the designs presented to their readers; but the fashion journals, which, without creating models, limit themselves to reproduce those that the fashion houses establish at great expense, can only engage in such publishing at their own risk and peril and only in the case where the owners of these models do not believe they should stand in their way;

Whereas by the filing that was regularly done with the Council of prud'hommes, the models claimed by the house Callot are entirely and completely protected against every usurpation that could affect them; therefore it becomes irrelevant to investigate whether these models can in fact also benefit from the special protection provided to works of art by the law of March 11, 1902, which extended the benefit of the law of July 19 and 24, 1793,[91] to ornamental designers, whatever the merit and destination of the work;

91. These statutes dealt with copyright.

Whereas the defendants dispute that the incriminated designs are a reproduction of the models filed by the Callot house and oppose that moreover the latter did not have any novelty and originality;

That the Court, absent any evidence on this question of fact, is required to have recourse to the guidance of experts;

For these reasons:

Before deciding on the merits, if the parties do not settle within eight days from the summons,

[The Court] Instructs Bonnaire, Director of Maison Laferrière, 28, rue Taitboul; Poron, 32, avenue Carnot et Broquelet, artist engraver, 40, rue d'Hauteville; experts, who have been sworn beforehand before the Chair of this Chamber, to hear the parties and, obtaining all useful information, examine and describe the models covered by the pleadings and the filings with the Conseil des Prud'hommes, to investigate whether, on the date they were done, these filings showed a character of novelty and originality; to compare them with the designs and engravings published in the incriminated fashion journals and albums; to indicate the similarities and dissimilarities they present; to say finally if the publications made in the fashion journals and albums could or not enable the material reproduction of the models of the house Callot; ...

Figure 45 Fashion designs published by the journal Le Grand Chic Paris, in 1908. In the bottom, right, the designs are signed "Ateliers Finkelstein." The models are numbered, making reference to captions with detailed explanations of the designs, thus facilitating their use by makers of fashion apparel. Actually, these were the main target public of similar fashion journals.

§ 2.64.5 A Court Acknowledges That Certain Designs Serve as Identifiers of Origin—*Chamussy et Cie. v. Favier et Beurrier*—1911

The Court of Lyon rendered on December 22, 1911 … the following judgment, confirming by adoption of reasons the judgment of the Commercial Court of Roanne, of January 18, 1911:

The court,

Whereas following an official report drawn up by the bailiff Salomon, of Roanne, dated October 6, 1910, registered, Chamussy et Cie., by investigation of the same bailiff dated October 17, 1910, has summoned Favier and Beurrier, merchants in Roanne, before this court for the purposes of: holding that Messrs. Favier and Beurrier are prohibited from manufacturing or having manufactured and sold articles reproducing the industrial designs that are the exclusive property of the Chamussy et Cie. house; ...

Whereas Favier and Beurrier resist the demand and oppose:

That they have never committed the acts of unfair competition of which they are accused, adding that the request is inadmissible, the invoked facts falling according to them within the scope of the laws relating to the infringement of the trademarks affixed on products;

And they argue that they are used to building a personal collection not by creating their designs, but by assembling designs belonging to the collections of different manufacturers, notably Chamussy et Cie.; that they have the right to have these designs reproduced by whomever they please;

On what the court [held],

Whereas it is opportune first of all to find out whether Favier and Beurrier have manufactured, caused to be manufactured and put up for sale designs that are the property of Chamussy et Cie.;

Whereas it results from the file and from the examination of the respective samples submitted to the Court, that Favier and Beurrier have delivered to their customers pieces of fabric slavishly reproducing the designs that had been entrusted to them by the Maison Chamussy et Cie., that there can be no doubt about that on this point, and that therefore the appointment of an expert seems unnecessary;

Whereas it results from the discussions that Favier and Beurrier delivered to Veuve Prat, of Moulins, merchandise that does not come from the house of Chamussy et Cie., but that this merchandise is inspired by the designs chosen by Favier et Beurrier from the collections of Chamussy et Cie., in view of the current season, and that they have reproduced them in a photographic way;

Whereas each of the collections of the different cotton cloth manufacturers has designs with an individual spirit, from which the buyer easily recognizes the origin of the fabrics;

Whereas Veuve Prat, to whom Favier and Beurrier had sent Chamussy et Cie.'s designs, despite the designation of CK, under which they had offered him the articles, expected all the more to receive Chamussy articles, as she was familiar with Chamussy's designs and that she had been able to recognize their provenance in the reference she had received from Favier and Beurrier;

That Veuve Prat's expectation would have been all the more admissible since she had asked Favier et Beurrier for Destre-Cherpin or Chamussy et Cie. articles;

Whereas Favier and Beurrier have created confusion from which they have taken advantage;

Whereas, indeed, at the start of each season Chamussy et Cie., like all cotton fabric manufacturers in Roanne, organize their collections of designs and samples for submission to their buyers;

Due to the need in each season to submit to customers designs different from those of the previous season, the organization of a collection of new designs is, for manufacturers such as Chamussy et Cie., a capital thing, because it is mainly on its success that the good functioning of their factories depends for a whole season;

Because of this major importance, the manufacturers of cotton fabrics, Chamussy et Cie. in this case, incur the expenses of designers, samplers, of those who put the designs on paper, etc., considerable expenses that can be estimated approximately to the tenth of the total expenses and amount, in certain weavings, to twenty thousand francs, thirty thousand francs and even forty thousand francs per year;

Therefore, the initiative of Favier and Beurrier to build up a personal collection with samples entrusted to them by different manufacturers and to have them manufactured where they please is inadmissible;

This would allow them to appropriate the fruits of the work and expenses of others;

Whereas Favier and Beurrier, not being the creators, cannot therefore own the designs that they submit to their customers;

Their role is limited to the condition in which they place themselves, to that of an intermediary, i.e., that it consists in selling to their customers, by taking the profit that pleases them, fabrics to be worked upon those that the manufacturers have entrusted to them;

They implicitly have contracted vis-à-vis the latter, and in particular in this case Chamussy et Cie., the formal obligation to transmit to each of them, in order to manufacture them, all the orders that they would accept from their customers on their respective designs, which is in conformity with the most common practice and the most basic commercial loyalty;

Whereas Favier and Beurrier, by fraudulently reproducing designs that they knew to be the exclusive property of Chamussy et Cie., have diverted from this house orders that were due to it and thus have caused damage to it;

Whereas on the other hand Favier and Beurrier have made an unjustified profit by copying and using Chamussy's collection;

That by saving the considerable costs [associated with a collection] to the manufacturer to whom they gave to copy Chamussy's designs, they were able themselves to benefit from prices lower than those that the house Chamussy et Cie. could make them for its merchandise, which was encumbered with sampling facts;

Whereas if the merchandise that Favier and Beurrier delivered to Veuve Prat [based] on the designs of Chamussy et Cie. has the same filling and the same selvage as that of Chamussy et Cie., the identity of quality of these two articles is only apparent;

The merchandise delivered by Favier et Beurrier is made of more ordinary threads, its appearance is less flattering, the coarser touch gives the impression of a merchandise of a quality lower than that of Chamussy et Cie.;

Therefore, if Veuve Prat could, according to the designs, believe that she was receiving merchandise from Chamussy et Cie., she could have noticed nonetheless that this merchandise was less beautiful than usual;

The confusion created by Favier and Beurrier by depreciating the manufacture of Chamussy et Cie. has therefore caused the latter undeniable harm;

Whereas advertisements are necessary to destroy in the customers of Chamussy et Cie. the consequences produced by the actions of Favier and Beurrier;

Whereas nothing could mitigate the fault of the latter, whose bad faith is obvious;

Whereas in the present case, it is a question of the creation of a deliberate and detrimental confusion in the manufacture and the designs entrusted by the plaintiffs to the defendants and belonging to Chamussy et Cie.;

That this intentional confusion and the consequences it entails cannot escape the application of Article 1382 of the Civil Code; [92]

92. Article 39 of the Civil Code then in force reads:

> Any fact whatsoever of man, which causes damage to others, obliges that who has caused the fault, to repair it.

That a merchant has no right ... through a trick to throw uncertainty at the public as to the true origin of the products he sells and to lead people to believe that they are the product of a known manufacturer; ...

For these reasons,

The Court, judging publicly, contradictorily and at first instance: ... Orders the defendants to pay Chamussy et Cie., in compensation for the damage caused, the sum of 1,000 francs; ...

§ 2.64.6 *Bachwitz et autres v. Société Paquin limitée*—1913

Court of Appeals, Civil Chamber

July 29, 1913

Chairmanship of Master Baudoin, first chair

Bachwitz et autres v. Société Paquin limitée

Messrs. Bachwitz and others have appealed against a judgment of the Court of Paris, of March 11, 1909, delivered in favor of Société Paquin.

Opinion.

The Court,

On the first issue of the appeal:

Whereas from the judgment under appeal it follows that the Société Paquin, claiming that it had reserved to itself, by filings done with the secretariat of the Council of prud'hommes of Paris, the exclusive property of various models of garments, brought an action for damages against the fashion newspapers *Le Chic* and *Le Chic Parisien*, for having published designs and engravings, which would constitute an infringement of the models filed by it;

Whereas the law of March 18, 1806, applicable to the case, granted any manufacturer the ability to ensure, by fulfilling the formalities prescribed by art. 15, the property of the designs of his/her invention;

Whereas the said law governed not only the designs, but also the industrial models that result from those; that both were entitled to legal protection, once it was established that they carried in themselves a proper and special character, which made it possible to appreciate its origin and to know its individuality;

Whereas it mattered little that the designs might have borrowed their essential elements, their lines, and their colors from the public domain, if they differed from their similar ones by particular provisions or combinations, or by any other external effect giving them a new appearance;

Whereas the judgment under appeal has made an exact application of these rules to the designs according to which the models of apparel and garments are manufactured, by declaring that they were eligible for a valid filing, under the condition of being new;

Whereas the appeal objects in vain that these productions are essentially ephemeral and intended to quickly lose any value by a prompt abandonment;

But whereas, on the one hand, art 18 of the aforementioned law provides that by filing a sample, the manufacturer must declare whether he intends to reserve the property for one, three or five years or in perpetuity, and thus authorizes him/her to limit his right, depending on the useful life that he/she believes he/she must attribute to his/her creation;

Whereas, on the other hand, the confidential communication of a design or model of this kind, made before the filing to agents or to heads of fashion houses, cannot be considered, by itself only, as having publicized this design;

On the second issue:

Whereas the filing done with the archives of the Council of prud'hommes confers on the manufacturer the right to claim, subsequently, the exclusive property of the design or model; that this right implies, as a necessary consequence, the right to oppose any imitation or reproduction of such a nature that might cause damage to the filer;

Whereas the appealed judgment rightly decides that the counterfeiting of a garment may result not only from the imitation made by a couturier, but also from any other form of reproduction, and, in particular, from the publication of designs or engravings permitting to reconstruct the original models;

Whereas, in the circumstances of the case, it is not necessary to consider whether this prohibition could extend to all the newspapers illustrated, without distinction; it suffices to retain the findings of the judgment establishing that Bachwitz and others have published the designs of the Société Paquin in two special fashion journals, the engravings of which have an industrial character and purpose, and are accompanied by patterns and technical explanations, which allow to easily manufacture the works they represent;

On the third issue:

Whereas the appeal claims that the filing of the dress models, done in the form of photographs showing neither the outline nor the fabric, and not even having any captions, would be void;

Whereas in this regard, the judgment under appeal declares that due to the price and volume of the garments, the filing can be done by means of an equivalent; it adds with reason that the photograph without caption protects them only insofar as it has the means of representing them, but that, if it reduces the effectiveness of the filing, it does not destroy its validity; and without judging anything, for the moment, it does not go beyond appointing experts with the mission of examining the models covered by the pleadings, the photographs filed with the Council of prud'hommes, as well as the designs and engravings accused of infringement, to indicate their similarities or their dissimilarities, and to say if these designs or engravings made it possible to reconstitute models and, if so, to what extent, all rights of the parties reserved;

Whereas by deciding in this manner the judgment under appeal has not violated the legal provisions invoked by the appeal;

Rejects … .

§ 2.65 IN THE UNITED STATES, FASHION JOURNALS OPPOSE THE ENACTMENT OF A LAW ON INDUSTRIAL DESIGNS—1916

In 1916, a bill aiming at setting a system of registration and protection of designs was introduced in US Congress. In the end, the bill was not voted. The records of the respective hearings provide useful insights on why there were disputes between fashion designers and fashion journals, which strongly opposed the bills. The reason is that fashion journals of that time, differently from today's fashion magazines, did not target fashion consumers in general, but specifically small dress makers and in particular those who made dresses at home. Fashion journals, therefore, were an important vehicle for the dissemination of unauthorized reproductions of designs owned by fashion houses, and that led to their counterfeiting. In that sense, fashion journals in the first quarter of the twentieth century, as opposed to today's magazines, inflicted direct financial losses on fashion houses.

The statements of the publishers of two United States fashion journals—Le Bon Ton and Elite Styles—made this point very clear. Before the Patent Commission of the House of Representatives, they joined the repair industry (worried with the prices of original designs for spare parts) in opposing the bills. These, indeed, provided for some elements that catered directly to the fashion industry, such as the possibility of registering a series of designs under one single filing, and the short term of protection. Those who benefited from using fashion designs were naturally concerned with the possible approval of such a statute.

§ 2.65.1 H.R. 6,458, on the Registration and Protection of Designs—1916

Registration of Designs

Committee on Patents,

House of Representatives,

Washington, D.C., March 22, 1916

The committee met at 10.30 o'clock a.m.

Present: Representatives Oglesby (presiding), Alexander, Smith, Crosser, McClintic, Nolan, Carter, Watson, Glynn, Venable, and Charles.

The committee thereupon proceeded to the consideration of H.R. 6,458, which is as follows:

A Bill providing for the registration of designs.

Be it enacted by the Senate and House of Representatives of the United States of America in Congress assembled, That authors or inventors of designs for manufactured products being recognized as promoters of the progress and science and the useful arts, the following law is established for the protection thereof:

The author of any design, new and original, as embodied in or applied to any manufactured product of an art or trade, or his assignee, may have copyright therein by registering such design in the United States Patent Office and obtaining from the Commissioner of Patents a certificate of such registration, which shall be prima facie evidence of the exclusive right of the registrant and his legal representatives and assigns to reproduce, sell, and use said design embodied in or applied to said manufactured product within the United States: ...

Sec. 10. That registration hereunder may be granted and certificates issued for different terms and fees as follows:

A term of three years for a fee of $1.

A term of ten years for a fee of $10.

A term of twenty years for a fee of $30. ...

Designs may be registered in series of not less than ten and not more than one hundred under a single certificate where all designs relate to the same class of manufactured product and are included in a single application for a period of one year and a fee of $1. ... Copies of designs included in such series will not be furnished by the Commissioner of Patents except when required as evidence in cases in litigation or for court records, or on other due showing of reasons in his judgment sufficient. ...

§ 2.65.2 Statement of Mr. B. von Witzleben, Representing S. T. Taylor Co., Publishers of *Le Bon Ton*, a Fashion Journal, New York City

Mr. von Witzleben. Mr. Chairman, I am only objecting to one classification of this bill, which is No. 14, entitled "Apparel." We publish a fashion journal, of which I have a copy here, which is published in the interest of dressmakers and is bought by women and dressmakers who make their own clothes. A large classification of women's clothes is made in two ways: One where a design is made hundreds and thousands of times over. That is the class that we do not cater to. The class that we do cater to each makes their own dresses, their individual dresses, or one of the dressmakers makes them for them.

I am not authorized to speak for them, but I think the manufacturers of dress would not be interested in this bill because of the fact that the fashions change so quickly and there would be so much chance for copyists to take their designs, which they have used and which they are selling, and copy them in time to get them into the season's business. The season would change, and there would be [a new] style by that time. ...

Mr. von Witzleben. ... I think [fashion houses] manufacture and their sales would be over for the season before their designs could be copied, so that you would never think of their being particularly interested. I don't know who, if anybody, is interested in this one classification. I do not know that anybody is.

The people that we are afraid of are the people that go over to Paris and get assignments of designs over there and then register them here more or less wholesale. We would not then solely copy their things. We would copy the trend of their style.

We do as much to originate it as anybody else does, but we are bound to copy. We can not help copying, and unconsciously, but we copy the trend of the style they put out in Paris, because of the great reputation Paris has as the great leader and creator of fashions. Then our designs and those of all other American designers, in many instances, would be substantial violations of their registered designs. That is the specific thing that we are afraid would happen.

Mr. Oglesby. Don't let us take Paris. Let us find out the designers in New York, for instance, who, at a great deal of expense, design very attractive costumes and want to register them. And, of course, if they do they should be entitled to do so.

Mr. von Witzleben. If it were new and original, to meet the requirements of this act, they might, but the whole question of fashion enters here. A fashion is only what is substantially imitation anyway. If one person alone wore a thing you could not call it a fashion. To make it a fashion it has to be communicated through some journal like ours, so that a great many people get to wearing it. I think that this raises the objection to this registration. ...

Mr. Oglesby. Let me ask you this: A publication like Le Bon Ton employs a great many designers to design new fashions in dresses, etc., and you select such of those as you think would be attractive?

Mr. von Witzleben. Yes.

Mr. Oglesby. And you insert them in your publication?

Mr. von Witzleben. Yes.

Mr. Oglesby. Now, is it not a fact that ninety-nine out of a hundred of those designs that are made by these people employed by Le Bon Ton are made by your young women going around to the different dressmaking establishments and stores here and there and either copying something out of the windows or surreptitiously copying something they saw in the dressmaking establishments, making an outline sketch of it and then going back to the office and filling out the details, coloring them, and touching them up?

Mr. von Witzleben. There is some of that. We try to get our things as original as we can, but our design reporters have to get their information from somebody else. ...

Mr. Oglesby. I don't know that it is pertinent; but, as a matter of fact, where you copy a design outright do you give credit for it?

Mr. von Witzleben. Yes, sir; where the design is copied outright and where we know the designer. It is very hard usually to tell who the designers are, and for that reason we do not want to give false credit or blame the design on someone who did not originate it. We do not do it very often, excepting we buy the design from the designer ourselves, and then we buy the right to call it our own.

Mr. Oglesby. But designs taken from show windows you regard rather as public property?

Mr. von Witzleben. Yes, sir; we do. ...

Mr. Oglesby. The difficulty that these fashion papers would be under is that they might be restricted to a very limited number of styles and make their publications of styles practically useless. They would be afraid to publish designs which might bring them into litigation, whether it was registered or not, and they could not go ahead and investigate everything.

[USPTO] Commissioner Ewing. I think it raises a very broad question of grave importance, because of the large number of people who make their own clothes, or the small dressmakers in the different towns.

Mr. Oglesby. The small dressmakers throughout the country get their styles very largely from these fashion publications?

Mr. von Witzleben. Yes, sir; I think almost entirely.

Mr. Oglesby. They go to town about once a year and go around and see the fashions and styles themselves; that is, a good many of them do, but I apprehend that the large majority of them really depend entirely on publications and the ideas that they get from these fashion publications?

Mr. von Witzleben. They do; they depend almost entirely upon them. The larger ones may come to New York and other places twice a year, but not more than that except in exceptional cases, and the others depend upon mediums like this paper for their designs. ...

Statement of Mr. Philip Gotthelf, Publisher of Elite Styles, New York City, N.Y.

Mr. Oglesby. State your business, Mr. Gotthelf.

Mr. Gotthelf. I am the publisher of this magazine, called Elite Styles, and I believe it is used by 100,000 women scattered all over the country, who are subscribers or who buy the magazine at the news stands.

This magazine is bought in open competition with every other thing of this kind, and when bought is carried into from 10 to 20 homes in the course of a month, and there marked and where the designs from it are copied. So we really furnish pictorial designs for the women of this country to that extent. A million homes are reached every month all over the country by this publication.

Mr. Oglesby. A million homes?

Mr. Gotthelf. A million homes; yes, sir.

Mr. Oglesby. That is a pretty good advertisement.

Mr. Gotthelf. I am not saying this to advertise it. I am trying to bring out that each copy is sold to a dressmaker and it reaches all the families that the dressmaker serves in a day in her regular course of business. Of course, we have to bring out enough designs to attract her and make her want the magazine. ...

Mr. Gotthelf. Surreptitiously, or anywhere without due regard to the original author, if he can be identified. But so far as we are able to see there is no ultimate author any more than there is an ultimate consumer. Everybody is a producer, and everybody copies from everybody else, and that is why we call it "fashion"—imitation on a desire to please the eye, to look the best, to dress like the best-dressed people dress. Anyone who copies has a right to do so.

Mr. Oglesby. Do you, as a matter of fact, ever give credit to the designer of a costume, where you are sure who the designer is?

Mr. Gotthelf. We have never located one.

Mr. McClintic. Do the manufacturers in your city furnish you with designs to be published in your periodical?

Mr. Gotthelf. No, sir; not at all. We furnish them with designs that they can use freely, and make the most of. They buy our book, and buy patterns of these designs, and are well served. ...

Mr. McClintic. Do the designs carried in your paper represent the styles across the water?

Mr. Gotthelf. Very largely; yes, sir.

Mr. McClintic. Do you get them by copying?

Mr. Gotthelf. By purchase from people in this country who have the information sent to them, and who trade in these photographs and sketches that you can buy for a dollar up. And they are often brought over here by people who, while going around, see the things and have the wit and ability to record these impressions on paper, making pencil sketches or otherwise, sometimes accompanied by pieces of the materials from which they are made. That, we believe, would be interfered with by the enactment of this law largely on the score of section 14, but we believe that all design registration is unfair.

Mr. Oglesby. The success of your publication depends upon your ability to please the public?

Mr. Gotthelf. To please the public.

Mr. Oglesby. Without fear of prosecution?

Mr. Gotthelf: Quite so.

Mr. Oglesby. To publish without fear of prosecution any styles which you may find?

Mr. Gotthelf. Which we discover—yes, sir; or which we make. ...

Mr. Oglesby. The secret registration, I am frank to say, does not appeal to me. I have so expressed myself to the gentleman interested in the bill. However, I think you are not giving proper credit to our American designers. I know a couple of young ladies who sell hundreds of dozens of dresses and negligee dresses of different kinds that are advertised as being imported direct from Paris. Neither of them have ever been across the water, but their dresses give just as much satisfaction as if they did come from Paris.

Mr. Gotthelf. That is right, but they are all as nearly stolen as these are, because everybody steals from everybody else, and you [can] not get away from it. That is what constitutes fashion. Le [me be] frank about it.

Mr. Oglesby. You mean copy.

Mr. Gotthelf: Yes, sir: copy, remodel and reshape and introduce new features and new designs in laces. All these lace and fancy silk designs would not have a market if we did not create an appetite for them by these publications. We are the silent salesman. ...

§ 2.66 MADELEINE VIONNET'S RELENTLESS AND INFLUENTIAL STRUGGLE IN FAVOR OF THE PROTECTION OF FASHION DESIGNS—1934

Madeleine Vionnet was one of the most successful fashion designers and entrepreneurs during the period between the two Great Wars in Paris. But she did not confine herself to designing and selling apparel and accessories to the wealthy; she also has taken a firm stance in the protection of her creations against the myriad of counterfeiters who did not cease to copy and reselling them as knock-offs. As the following texts show, her lobbying and her lawsuits had a significant impact on the setting of standards of protection of fashion intellectual property law in France.

The first text is a piece of advertisement published in the press warning potential customers of the measures taken by the Société Vionnet towards ensuring the genuineness of her models.

The second text is another ad, offering a reward to those seamstresses who could denounce those persons who had stolen some figurines from Vionnet's workshop. This particular piece is significant because it speaks to the most common method that unfair rivals used to obtain the knowledge of the new collections being prepared by the main fashion houses: espionage, through the bribery of workers. In fact, although industrial design (and soon, copyright) protection was available for designs, fashion's main trump card is anticipation, i.e., being first on the market. That is why fashion houses, in Madeleine Vionnet's time—and today, as well—would keep the preparation of the new collections under strict secrecy. We have already seen a reference to this strategy, in the pleadings of Master Maurice Bernard, attorney for another prestigious Paris fashion house (see § 2.64.1). Interestingly, this particular piece of Vionnet's advertisement was published in the official newspaper of France's Communist Party. The reason may very well have been either because Vionnet knew that the culprits of the stealing of her mannequins were little seamstresses in her workshop, or she supposed that seamstresses working in other workshops would identify the stolen mannequins. The best way to communicate with members of the working class was undoubtedly through that vehicle. Anyway, Vionnet claimed that protecting the genuine fashion industry of Paris was, indirectly, the interest of those who worked in it. In this respect, Vionnet, in the advertisement that appears in Figure 46, claimed that those living from the luxury industry and who, therefore, catered for the well-off, had a social responsibility "of assuring the comfort of the humble."

The third text contains excerpts from an article published in Vogue magazine, congratulating the fashion industry for the victory obtained by Madeleine Vionnet in court, when for the first time it was held that fashion designs were copyrightable. The importance of that holding was not only of a conceptual value, insofar as the value of fashion designs as artistic works was acknowledged, but also and mainly because enforcing rights became easier, given the informality of copyright protection.

The same judgment, given its importance for the fashion industry—an important sector in France's economy—did not go unnoticed to other newspapers of a more general nature, as the fourth text shows.

The fifth text shows another, perhaps unexpected, facet of Madeleine Vionnet's strategy in defense of her creations: patents. Indeed, Madeleine Vionnet was not only a fashion designer but also a proficuous inventor. One of her inventions—probably the one that the advertisement contained in the fifth text refers to, given its impact on the visual appearance of fabrics (hence a matter of interest to potential buyers of the apparel she designed)—was mentioned in an international patent application filed by two Spanish inventors, in 2006, for a "Method for the manufacture of a fabric with threads configuring a rhombus or rhomboid and the obtained fabric." Opening the description of the prior art, the application reads:

> *Different patents are known in the state of the art that describe various procedures for the manufacture of fabrics, based on the oblique arrangement of their cut to increase their adaptability. In fact, the most important couturiers and dressmakers of all ages, among which Mrs. Madeleine Vionnet should be mentioned, made of the obliquely or reverse fabric cutting an art, to increase the adaptability of the fabric and make it impeccable in the user's body. A technique related to said cut was even developed, which came to be called the "bias technique." (International patent application WO PCT / IB2006 / 055067. Source: Google Patents).*

It is interesting to note that Madeleine Vionnet understood her patent not only as a legal way to secure the result of her inventive work but also as a tool of prestige and reputation, which could serve to lure clientele. The same advertisement was published in other newspapers.

The sixth text—a newspaper editorial—reveals that Madeleine Vionnet's success in persuading the courts to extend copyright protection to fashion designs could not count with unanimous approval. It seems that the easing of obtaining protection had led to abuses in enforcement. Thus, instead of promoting creativity, the enforcement of rights in fashion designs might be causing exactly the opposite result.

The last two texts reproduce excerpts from court opinions that express the status of fashion intellectual property law in the 1930s. The seventh text is about industrial espionage and the corruption of a Madeleine Vionnet's employee with the purpose of obtaining precise information on new designs (before, of course, they reached the market). This was—and is—a practice not uncommon in the fashion industry. The main competitive advantage of fashion houses as regards new collections does not result from intellectual property—even if this legal branch provides for some effective enforcement mechanisms—but, as said above, from anticipation, the head start, the advantage that results from being the first on the market. Fashion houses are aware that certain designs will be counterfeited anyway, so for them, it is vital to cause them to be delayed. The best way of achieving it is to keep new designs, new fabrics, and new styles, under strict secrecy until the day they are shown on the catwalks of fashion shows.

The second opinion (on a case of counterfeiting, which has also involved the indiscretion of a fashion house employee) confirmed the copyrightability of fashion designs and the resulting access of their creators to stronger and swifter mechanisms of enforcement.

§ 2.66.1 Under an Ironic Heading, Madeleine Vionnet Advertises in the Press the Measures Taken by Her House for the Sake of Ensuring Authenticity of the Garments She Designed and Sold—1921

New Year's gifts for the counterfeiters

From January 1, 1922, all of Madeleine Vionnet's creations will bear a double signature.

Each dress leaving the workshops of Madeleine Vionnet will carry inside:

(1) Her autograph.
(2) A special order number.
(3) *A fingerprint of Madeleine Vionnet.*

Anyone all over the world will therefore be able to easily verify the authenticity of the dresses that will be sold to them as being Madeleine Vionnet creations. If any doubt arises on this subject, it will be easy to unsew the label, to send it to Madeleine Vionnet, 220-222, rue de Rivoli, Paris, mentioning:

(1) The name and address of the client.
(2) The name and address of the seller.
(3) The date of purchase.

The identification will be made immediately and the answer given by mail.

Reproductions authorized by Madelene Vionnet and manufactured in the Evai Boex workshops, 14, rue Castiglione, in Paris, sold at least in three copies of each model, will bear:

(1) The autograph of Eva Boex.
(2) A special order number.
(3) The mention "License Madeleine Vionnet."
(4) *A fingerprint of Madeleine Vionnet.*

The identification of Eva Boex reproductions will be done under the same conditions and with the same speed. In this way, our customers will always be able to ensure that their dresses are indeed authentic creations of Madeleine Vionnet.

Figure 46 Advertisement of Madeleine Vionnet's fashion house published in the VOGUE Magazine of June 1, 1924. At the center, the ad reads: "Madeleine Vionnet sells neither to agents nor to dressmakers. The dressmaker's models are filed and published in France. Madeleine Vionnet also fulfils in other countries the requirements provided by the laws of each state and by the international treaties. She will prosecute every counterfeiting and every copying, even if partial, done in violation of her rights. The creations of Madeleine Vionnet bear her signature and her fingerprint." Below, left, it reads: "All of us owe our tribute to human progress—the luxury of wealth must assure the comfort of the humble—the workshop of Madeleine Vionnet meets all exigencies."

§ 2.66.2 Madeleine Vionnet Offers a Reward to Who Provides Information on a Stolen Mannequin

Counterfeiting prosecuted

During the course of the last season, Madeleine Vionnet, continuing her work of purgation, was able to catch in the act of counterfeiting a certain number of "Copiers" who derived most of their profit from the trade in counterfeit models.

These art parasites will have to answer for their counterfeiting before the criminal court and their accomplices will also be prosecuted.

To sediment the results already obtained and to reach more quickly the "Copiers" who still hold the mannequin, Madeleine Vionnet asks anyone with knowledge of these looting acts to kindly report them in a spirit of fairness and in the interest of all workers. It is imperative that such acts cease. They lead to the lowering of the level of art in fashion, they diminish the good reputation of Paris abroad and consequently, indirectly affect the interests of the personnel working in the fashion houses.

Madeleine Vionnet will reward the efforts of the people who will help her to flush out the plundering copiers.

Madeleine Vionnet et Cie., dresses, coats, furs, 220-222, rue de Rivoli, Paris.

§ 2.66.3 Vogue, a Fashion Magazine Publishes a Long Article Celebrating the Landmark Court Opinion (In an Action in Which Madeleine Vionnet Was the Plaintiff) That for the First Time Held That Fashion Designs Were Protected under Copyright

The defense of haute couture

The law that protects pictorial or literary works of art also protects the works of art of Parisian couturiers.

The other day Lady Couture went to Thémis to ask her for protection and it was a pretty audience that attended the lawsuit brought by Miss Madeleine Vionnet against the counterfeiters of her models. The audience was more feminine than masculine: fashion creators and saleswomen abounded in the room, escorted by a few mannequins, with their strawberry mouths and sharp fingers, all ready to appear in front of the courtroom, sheathed in the traditional black sheath, to put on the litigation robes and win hands down the opinion of the judges. President du Bousquet de Florian chaired. He didn't seem to mind having to enter the realm of cloths. He watched with interest this unusual audience of elegant women and young female lawyers, who were doubly interested in this affair since it involved their two passions: law and apparel. The main witness, Mr. Jacques Worth, underlined the importance of the trial by testifying to the effort necessary to bring to light a new and beautiful model. An artist came after who declared that the couturier can take rank among painters and sculptors and that a dress by Madeleine Vionnet is worth from an artistic point of view the statue of Gambetta that threatens the Tuileries; after beautiful debates and rich oratorical games, Justice ruled and Miss Madeleine Vionnet obtained the conviction of the counterfeiters of her models.

We consider this judgment to be most interesting. It opens up a jurisprudence that is dear to us and that is why we would like to highlight it in *Vogue* and to devote this column, generally occupied with lighter subjects, to a legal question.

A double lesson emerges from the court ruling. It first pays tribute to the artistic effort that it is necessary to spend to design a new dress. Personally we have been given the opportunity of watching the preparatory work of a Doeuillet, a Poiret, a Chanel, and we have realized how much culture, how much taste, were necessary for such work. We followed for hours the ceaseless hunt of a brain applying itself to modify folds and lines, uniting fabrics, kneading velvets or silks, coupling lace and taffeta, throwing, with the verve of a painter who lavishes cadmium and cinnabars, rich colors against each other. On this living canvas that the mannequin is, the couturier posed, attached, fixed with pins, a pattern, a theme of elegance, and all of a sudden, the dress appeared and the black chrysalis became a little magical fairy, suitable to bewitch all heads. ...

From a second point of view this trial interests us. The campaign opened by Miss Madeleine Vionnet is not new. It is enough to go back to the year of 1914 to remember that, moved by the way in which their models were copied and their trademark counterfeited, a group of great Parisian couturiers founded, on the advice and with the active collaboration of the man who is now the director of this newspaper [Philippe Ortiz], a French haute couture defense union. The aim of this union was to fight against any counterfeiting, to protect the interests of the houses of Paris. Shortly after its foundation, war broke out. During the years 1915 and 1916, he tried to fight, but his concerns were very small compared to the formidable events that agitated Europe. The defense of haute couture in France disappeared in the defense of the country. In America, on the contrary, far from the battlefields, it asserted itself through a vigorous campaign waged against the counterfeiters of Parisian brands, a campaign whose success was such that this miserable practice disappeared for some time in the United States.[93]

In France, however, it was only a temporary sleep. The judgment that has just done justice to Miss Madeleine Vionnet revives the hopes of those who conceived this defense organization. *Vogue* wishes to mark this day with a white stone. It emphatically underlines this trial; it calls on all French couturiers to come together and once again ensure the protection of the masterpieces of Parisian genius. The presence of Mr. Jacques Worth at the hearing is the sign of a professional solidarity of good omen that allows us to hope that in a short time the reconstruction of the old group will no longer be simply a dream but a reality and that the French haute couture defense union will rise from its ashes.

Many of our readers will be astonished at the importance we attach to this debate, but it is because they do not know, even the most elegant, that there is not one great Paris couture house that has not suffered and still does not suffer on a daily basis from the usual copying and imitation of his most personal models by houses without honor and shamelessness. The law that protects works of art and condemns plagiarism until now seemed to apply only to writers or painters. It took the determined tenacity of a fashion house for this law to finally be intelligently interpreted and applied effectively.

It is to the honor of the president of Bousquet de Florian for having rendered such a judgment and for having formulated a rule of law, which will forever protect the creators of Parisian elegance, those who hold the torch of this charming art, where we are unmatched without a doubt.

93. The column here refers to the campaign for the adoption in the United States of a statute providing for the protection of industrial designs, including those relating to fashion. The initiative was a failure (*see* § 2.66).

§ 2.66.4 Illustrating Its Importance, the Same Judgment Was Reported in Other Newspapers of a More General Nature

Echoes

The models of the couturiers are works of art

It emerges from a judgment rendered yesterday, by the 12th appellate chamber chaired by Mr. du Bousquet de Florian, that the creations of the couturiers, models of dresses, garments and coats, must be considered as works of art, and are, as such, protected by the laws on counterfeiting.

The judgment says in particular that these models are the result of personal experience and work and most often add to their elegance an undeniably aesthetic impression of originality that individualizes them; that it has also become common practice to classify fashion creations in trade fairs and exhibitions under the heading: "Applied arts, in the same way as works of glassware, goldsmith or furniture manufacturer."

And on the complaint of Mme Madeleine Vionnet, who accused them of having counterfeited some of her models, three seamstresses, Mrs. Millet elder, Mrs. Millet young and Mrs. Veuve Boudreau, were condemned yesterday by the 12th chamber, the first two to 1,000 Fr. of fine each, and 16,000 fr. in damages, and the third to 1,000 fr. of fine, and 12,000 fr. in damages.

§ 2.66.5 Madeleine Vionnet Advertises a Patent She Obtained for a Secret Invention, *Jalousement Gardé (Jealously Kept)*—1923

Patented S.G.D.G.[94]

Madame Madeleine Vionnet, the delicate artist of Parisian elegance, has just patented in France and abroad a novelty of which she is the inventor.

The secret, jealously guarded until now, will be revealed to the ladies who are already clients of Madeleine Vionnet, on Thursday, September 20 at 2 p.m., 20-30 Avenue Montaigne.

The full presentation of Madeleine Vionnet's creations and her patented invention will continue every day of the week at the same hour.

§ 2.66.6 A Fashion Magazine Claims That Enforcement of Copyright in Fashion Designs Has Led to Excesses and Abuses—1933

Small echoes from Paris and elsewhere

On some exaggerations

Of course, it is still true that "to copy is to steal," according to the lapidary formula invented by Madeleine Vionnet's attorney. And since a dress can rightly be considered a work of art, it is right and natural to prosecute counterfeiters with perseverance. But there have been exaggerations. However, until 1909, the plastic arts were protected by a law on designs and models. This law required the person

94. *See* the caption to Figure 42.

who was victim of counterfeiting to submit a request to the Court, a long procedure, waste of time, possible indiscretions.

After a judgment of 1922, it suffices for a couturier to claim to have been wronged to get a police commissioner to act and, assisted by ten or fifteen people, to carry out a real search in the building occupied by the infringer or allegedly such, during which some piece in fraud can be slipped, or subtracted ... even personal letters, which has already happened.

Who cannot see the drawbacks and exaggerations of such a system? While usually a search is only authorized when the Public Prosecutor or the Trial Court has issued a warrant, in the case of couturiers, their creations are assimilated to original works ... even if for an imitated dress there can only be a question of copying or plagiarism and not of the work of art itself. ...

Clumsy, untimely searches have done more harm to French couture than counterfeiting itself. They have been sometimes a means of discouraging bold young houses envied by established couturiers. ... They ended up discrediting both the prosecutors and the prosecuted. So, to remedy a state of affairs so harmful to such an important industry and commerce, it is opportune that new measures be introduced.

§ 2.66.7 *Dames Segall et Dodu v. Société Vionnet*—1934

Designs and models. Counterfeiting, a) Filed dress model. Couturier. Fraudulent reproduction of "patterns" and "canvases." b) Good faith claimed. Burden of proof.—Corruption of labourer or employee. Job traffic. Active corruption and passive corruption of employee. Elements of the offenses. Employee of couture.

Cour of appeals (Criminal chamber)

May 15, 1934

1. The sole fact of having fraudulently reproduced the "patterns and canvases" necessary for the making of a model of dress, filed, when these patterns and canvases are identical to the original patterns and canvases or at least present their essential features of originality, constitutes, by itself, an offense of counterfeiting.

2. When the offense of counterfeiting is characterized in its materiality, the accused, who disputes the intentional element in it, has the burden of proving his/her good faith.

3. The judgment has established all the elements constituting the offenses of employment trafficking, active corruption and passive corruption of an employee, provided for and punished by Articles 117 and 179 of the Penal Code, modified by the law of February 16, 1919, the judgment that finds, on the one hand, that the corrupting defendant, by donations, promises, offers, gifts, commissions, discounts or bonuses, has led a salaried employee of a competing firm to provide him/her, in violation of the duties that his/her job required of him/her, with information on the models newly created by this house and, on the other hand, that this salaried employee, without the knowledge and the consent of his/her boss, has agreed to receive these gifts, offers or promises and delivered this information in violation of his/her professional obligations.

Mses. Segall, couturier, and Dodu, employee of couture, appealed against a judgment rendered on April 28, 1933 by the Paris Court of Appeal, which had condemned them: Mrs. Segall to a fine of 3,000 francs for infringement and corruption of employee, as well as 10,000 francs in damages, for the offense of counterfeiting, and 1,000 francs in damages for the offense of corruption, in favor of Société Vionnet, couturier, civil party, and Mrs. Dodu, to 100 francs of fine for corruption of employee and, jointly with Mrs. Segall, to 1,000 francs in damages in favor of Société Vionnet.—Judgment:

The court: ...

With regard to Mrs. Segall's appeal: On the first plea, alleging violation of the law of July 19-24, 1793, amended by the law of March 16, 1902, of Article 425 Penal Code and of Article 7 of the law of April 20, 1810, lack of and contradiction of reasons, lack of legal basis, in that the judgment under appeal declared Mrs. Segall guilty of the offense of counterfeiting of a model of the house Vionnet, because there were similarities between the pieces of canvas and Chinese crêpe seized in Mrs. Segall store and dress nr. 3,850 of the Vionnet house, whereas, on the one hand, the existence of the offense of counterfeiting can only be found by establishing the absolute identity of the original work with its reproduction, which in no way results from the judgment, on the other hand, in that the challenged decision does not establish the bad faith of the defendant, an essential element of the offense of infringement:

Whereas, both by its own grounds and by those of the opinion, which it adopted on this point, the judgment under appeal notes that on February 15, 1929, at the request of Société Vionnet, couturier in Paris, four pieces of canvas and two pieces of printed Chinese crêpe were seized in the workshops of Mrs. Segall, couturier at the same place, "all based on the designs of model 3,850 from the Vionnet house"; whereas the judgment specifies that the canvases and pieces seized "reproduce exactly all the originalities of the cut indicated in this model 3,850" and that the Chinese crêpe used is of the same cut, the same fabric and the same design as those of the counterfeited model;

Whereas these findings, based at the same time on the conclusions of the expertise and the judges' considerations on the merits, do not present any contradiction between them; whereas they are sovereign and establish, in their materiality, all the constituent elements of the offense of counterfeiting;

Whereas, on the other hand, by declaring the defendant "guilty," the challenged decision held the existence of the intentional element of the offense; whereas the judgment did not need to explain itself otherwise on the bad faith of the accused, given that, once established in its materiality, the crime of counterfeiting implies, except proof to the contrary, that this offense has been committed knowingly; that, consequently, in its two parts, this first plea must be rejected;

On the second plea, based on the violation of articles 177 and 179 of the Penal Code, of Article 7 of the law of April 20, 1810, of lack of grounds and of legal basis, in that the judgment under appeal declared Mrs. Segall guilty of the offense of corruption of employee, without establishing that the remunerations paid by Mrs. Segall to Mrs. Dodu had as a precise objective the communication of a specific model of the Vionnet house, whereas especially the judgment notes, on the other hand, that Mrs. Dodu did not work in the workshop where the disputed model had been created and that she worked for Mrs. Segall on a regular basis;

Whereas the judgment under appeal states that, although since then, Mrs. Dodu has retracted, nothing has come to destroy the scope of the declaration that she made and signed at the start of the investigation and by which she formally confessed "that, harassed by Mrs. Segall, as soon as she entered Madeleine Vionnet's firm, she has provided the former with information, in particular on the latest models in progress, which enabled her to make canvases"; whereas the judgment adds that Mrs. Dodu had to admit that, in the Vionnet house, she worked "in a room next to the one where the disputed model, which she had seen, had been created"; that "in the evening," she came "to work" for Mrs. Segall who, on various occasions, gave her sums of money and who assured her food; finally, the judgment declares that it has been established that Mrs. Segall, by harassing Mrs. Dodu with her solicitations, by providing her with food and by remitting to her the various sums of money that she acknowledges having received, did not have another goal than to get Mrs. Dodu to provide her, in violation of the duties imposed by her job, with information on the models newly created by Société Vionnet;

Whereas these finds, which are sovereign, suffice to establish, both in fact and in law, the offense of corruption of employee;

For these reasons, and given that the judgment under appeal is formally regular ... rejects Mrs. Segall's appeal. ...

Figure 47 Dress designed by Madeleine Vionnet, taffeta blue marine with white peas. Under the photo, the caption reads: "Modèle déposé P. A. I. S.—Repr. interdicte" ["Model filed—Reproduction prohibited"]. Extracted from Les Modes *nr. 374, July 1935, at 11.*

Studio Dorvyne   Modèle déposé P. A. I. S. — Repr. interdit

Mlle SIMONA

§ 2.66.8 *Société Madeleine Vionnet et Demoiselle Chanel v. Dame Laniel*—1934

Court of Appeals (Criminal Chamber)

December 8, 1934

The 9th Criminal Chamber of the Paris Court of Appeals had, under the presidency of Master Laroque, on December 17, 1931, delivered the following judgment:

The Court:

Whereas Mrs. Laniel criticizes unsuccessfully the first judges for having condemned her to a fine of 2,000 francs and to the publication of the verdict for infringement of models created by Société Madeleine Vionnet, when in fact, she was not guilty of this offense, and anyways, as a matter of law, the law of July 19, 1793, on which the prosecution is based, would not apply to the case, and, in consequence, the seizures made by the police commissioner, were null and illegal, would cause the invalidation of the proceedings against her;

Whereas it results, in fact, from the seizures carried out on June 14, 1927 and October 11, 1927, by the police commissioner, on the requisitions of Société Madeleine Vionnet et Cie., owner of various models of dresses and coats filed with the Council of prud'hommes of Paris (cloths) under various numbers and names, together with the subsequent expertise, that Mrs. Laniel, with the complicity of the Ms. Graftiaux, in 1927, in Paris, made, put on sale and sold 27 counterfeit dresses and coats, which, apart from a few slight differences in detail, are nothing else than their slavish copy;

Whereas when questioned by the police commissioner on June 14, 1927, Mrs. Laniel declared: "I admit having copied the models of the houses of Madeleine Vionnet, Patou, Chanel, Molyneux, etc. ... I have been indulging in these counterfeits for about four months; I did it knowingly ... I usually sell these dresses for 1,500 to 1,800 francs, I know they are worth 3 to 6,000 francs"—and Ms. Graftiaux: "After staying for five years in the Madeleine Vionnet house, I left in August 1926, when I was leader in the workshop, to enter the Laniel house ...; I recognize that the house copied the Madeleine Vionnet, Patou and Chanel models, and also the considerable damage done to these houses"; ...

Whereas, moreover, in legal terms, the law of July 19-24, 1793, modified by the law of March 11, 1902, protects not only the authors of writings of all kinds, composers of music, architects and statute makers, but also sculptors, ornamental designers, whatever the merit and destination of their work, i.e., all designs and sculptures in the purely technical sense of these words;

Whereas article 1 of the law of July 14, 1909 on designs and models expressly accorded their authors the right to avail themselves of the provisions of other laws which may protect them, in particular that of 1793, as amended in 1902, and to combine their benefits with that of the protection set by the new law;

Whereas, therefore, there is nothing that prevents the law of 1793, amended in 1902, from applying to models created by the great fashion houses, such as Société Madeleine Vionnet, when, as in the present case, these models, the result of personal experience and work, are the realization and translation of elaborate designs [sold] at high prices, conceptions of lines and colors, combinations and assemblies of fabrics capable of producing a new effect, and that they add to their elegance a special impression of originality that individualizes them; ...

On appeal from Mrs. Laniel, the Criminal Chamber of the Court of Appeals, under the chairmanship of Master Scerdlin, on December 8, 1934, rendered the following judgment of rejection:

The Court:

On the argument concerning the violation of the laws of July 19-24, 1793 [on copyright], of March 11, 1902 [on copyright, extending the application of the 1793 statute to certain works of art, such as drawings and sculptures], of 14 July 1909 [on the registration and protection of designs and models] ... [that the first judgment] would be groundless and baseless, in that the judgment under appeal wrongly declared that the special legislation relating to the protection of authors and artists was applicable to the creations of dresses and coats, and moreover, it does not at all follow from the statements of the judgment that the models that would have been counterfeited were of an artistic character, hence authorizing their assimilation to the artistic productions covered by this special legislation;

Whereas Mrs. Laniel, seamstress, was prosecuted for infringement; according to the findings of the judgment under appeal, she has admitted having been involved for some time, knowingly, in the counterfeiting of models established by various fashion houses, and in particular by the houses of Chanel and Madeleine Vionnet, civil parties; because of these facts, she was sentenced to fines and the payment of damages under the law of July 19-24, 1793, amended by that of March 11, 1902;

Whereas it results from the same findings that the models of dresses and coats created by the aforementioned houses and counterfeited by Mrs. Laniel, are the result of a personal experience and work, they constitute the realization and the translation of elaborate designs [sold] at high prices and also the result of a design of lines and colors, of combinations and assemblies of fabrics capable of producing a new effect, and they add to their elegance a special impression of originality that individualizes them;

Whereas, from these findings, the Court of Appeal has been able to conclude that these models were protected against reproductions and imitations made for speculative purposes, not only by the law of July 14, 1909 on industrial property, but also by that of March 11, 1902, which broadened the scope of the law of July 19-24, 1793, and decided that the exclusive right granted by it would henceforth belong to designers of ornaments, whatever the merit and destination of the work; whereas, moreover, the aforementioned law of 1909 contains an express reservation with regard to the rights resulting from that of 1793; ...

And whereas the judgment under appeal is formally regular;

Rejects.

Figure 48 Left: Madeleine Vionnet in her workshop using a doll as a model for sketching one of her creations. The photo illustrates an article "La Vie et le Secret de Madeleine Vionnet" [The life and the secret of Madeleine Vionnet], published in a fashion magazine of 1937. Right: The salon of Madeleine Vionnet's fashion house at Rue de Montaigne, Paris, which was used as a sort of catwalk, where her collections were presented to prospective clients. Madeleine Vionnet moved to this new house in 1923. She herself participated in the design and decoration of the salon.

§ 2.67 THE UNITED STATES COURT OF APPEALS FOR THE SECOND CIRCUIT ACKNOWLEDGES THAT FASHION DESIGNS ARE UNPROTECTED—1929

Judge Learned Hand, in this opinion, acknowledges that in 1929 in the United States fashion designs were unprotected. This, naturally, facilitated the uncontrolled copying of fashion in that country. French designers were the main victims, but, as this opinion, shows, so were US designers. It results from the opinion that Judge Hand sympathized with the designer's claims, but his role was not that of replacing Congress.

US Court of Appeals for the Second Circuit 35 F.2d 279 (2d Cir. 1929)

Cheney Bros. v. Doris Silk Corporation

October 21, 1929

L. Hand, Circuit Judge.

The plaintiff, a corporation, is a manufacturer of silks, which puts out each season many new patterns, designed to attract purchasers by their novelty and beauty. Most of these fail in that purpose, so that not much more than a fifth catch the public fancy. Moreover, they have only a short life, for the most part no more than a single season of eight or nine months. It is in practice impossible, and it would be very onerous if it were not, to secure design patents upon all of these; it would also be impossible to know in advance which would sell well, and patent only those. Besides, it is probable that for the most part they have no such originality as would support a design patent. Again, it is impossible to copyright them under the Copyright Act (17 USCA § 1 et seq.), or at least so the authorities of the Copyright Office hold. So it is easy for any one to copy such as prove successful, and the plaintiff, which has put too much ingenuity and expense in fabricating them, finds itself without protection of any sort for its pains.

Taking advantage of this situation, the defendant copied one of the popular designs in the season beginning in October 1928, and undercut the plaintiff's price. This is the injury of which it complains. The defendant, though it duplicated the design in question, denies that it knew it to be the plaintiff's, and there thus arises an issue which might be an answer to the motion. However, the parties wish a decision upon the equity of the bill, and, since it is within our power to dismiss it, we shall accept its allegation, and charge the defendant with knowledge.

The plaintiff asks for protection only during the season, and needs no more, for the designs are all ephemeral. It seeks in this way to disguise the extent of the proposed innovation, and to persuade us that, if we interfere only a little, the solecism, if there be one, may be pardonable. But the reasoning which would justify any interposition at all demands that it covers the whole extent of the injury. A man whose designs come to harvest in two years, or in five, has prima facie as good right to protection as one who deals only in annuals. Nor could we consistently stop at designs; processes, machines, and secrets have an equal claim. The upshot must be that, whenever any one has contrived any of these, others may be forbidden to copy it. That is not the law. In the absence of some recognized right at common law, or under the statutes and the plaintiff claims neither a man's property is limited to the chattels which embody his invention. Others may imitate these at their pleasure. ...

This is confirmed by the doctrine of "non-functional" features, under which it is held that to imitate these is to impute to the copy the same authorship as the original. ... These decisions imply that, except as to these elements, any one may copy the original at will. Unless, therefore, there has been some controlling authority to the contrary, the bill at bar stands upon no legal right and must fail.

Of the cases on which the plaintiff relies, the chief is *International News Service v. Associated Press*, 248 U.S. 215. Although that concerned another subject-matter—printed news, dispatches—we agree that, if it meant to lay down a general doctrine, it would cover this case; at least, the language of the majority opinion goes so far. We do not believe that it did. While it is of course true that law ordinarily speaks in general terms, there are cases where the occasion is at once the justification for, and the limit of, what is decided. This appears to us such an instance; we think that no more was covered than situations substantially similar to those then at bar. The difficulties of understanding it otherwise are insuperable. We are to suppose that the court meant to create a sort of common-law patent or copyright for reasons of justice. Either would flagrantly conflict with the scheme which Congress has for more than a century devised to cover the subject-matter.

Qua patent, we should at least have to decide, as tabula rasa, whether the design or machine was new and required invention; further, we must ignore the Patent Office whose action has always been a condition upon the creation of this kind of property. *Qua* copyright, although it would be simpler to decide upon the merits, we should equally be obliged to dispense with the conditions imposed upon the creation of the right. Nor, if we went so far, should we know whether the property so recognized should be limited to the periods prescribed in the statutes, or should extend as long as the author's grievance. It appears to us incredible that the Supreme Court should have had in mind any such consequences. To exclude others from the enjoyment of a chattel is one thing; to prevent any imitation of it, to set up a monopoly in the plan of its structure, gives the author a power over his fellows vastly greater, a power which the Constitution allows only Congress to create. ...

True, it would seem as though the plaintiff had suffered a grievance for which there should be a remedy, perhaps by an amendment of the Copyright Law, assuming that this does not already cover the case, which is not urged here. It seems a lame answer in such a case to turn the injured party out of court, but there are larger issues at stake than his redress. Judges have only a limited power to amend the law; when the subject has been confined to a Legislature, they must stand aside, even though there be a hiatus in completed justice. An omission in such cases must be taken to have been as deliberate as though it were express, certainly after longstanding action on the subject-matter. Indeed, we are not in any position to pass upon the questions involved, as Brandeis, J., observed in *International News Service v. Associated Press*. We must judge upon records prepared by litigants, which do not contain all that may be relevant to the issues, for they cannot disclose the conditions of this industry, or of the others which may be involved. Congress might see its way to create some sort of temporary right, or it might not. Its decision would certainly be preceded by some examination of the result upon the other interests affected. Whether these would prove paramount we have no means of saying; it is not for us to decide. Our vision is inevitably contracted, and the whole horizon may contain much which will compose a very different picture.

The order is affirmed, and, as the bill cannot in any event succeed, it may be dismissed, if the defendant so desires.

§ 2.68 THE PROTECTION OF FASHION DESIGNS BY FRENCH COURTS REACHES MATURITY: *DEMOISELLE JACQUET V. CAROLINE ROUX, ROSE DESCAT ET AUTRES*—1934

The following text concerns the condemnation of the counterfeiter of two designs of hats to the payment of compensation. The argument of the Defendant (and Appellant), Demoiselle Jacquet, was that the designs had not been registered, and thus they were not protectable. The discussion, therefore, was about whether industrial designs could be protected under copyright law, which did not require any formality. Both courts answered yes.

This opinion is particularly important not only because it clearly confirmed the right accorded to fashion designers to pursue the legal avenue that better protected their interests—copyright vis-à-vis industrial property—but also engaged in a deep, clear, concise, and significant discussion on the creative nature of fashion designs, regardless of or beyond the necessary appropriation of existing patterns and standards of other designs previously existing on the market.

Paris Court, 9th Chamber of Appeals

Demoiselle Jacquet v. Caroline Roux, Rose Descat et autres

July 18, 1934

The Court of Paris, at its hearing of July 18, 1934, under the chairmanship of Master Rossel ... rendered the following judgment:

The Court,

After having deliberated in conformity with law,

Whereas criticizing the judgment of the Court of Seine dated February 9, 1933, which, for the counterfeiting of hats created by Maison Rose Descat, condemned her to a fine of 100 francs, 2,000 francs in damages and to the confiscation of the counterfeited models, this penalty to be combined with that of 300 francs pronounced the same day against her, Ms. Jacquet maintains that the law of July 19-24, 1793, modified by that of March 11, 1902, on which the prosecution is based and whose sole purpose is to protect the works of writers, composers, painters, designers, statue makers, architects, sculptors and designers of ornaments—an eminently restrictive law—does not protect industrial models; that only the law of July 14, 1909 could be invoked in this case, the prescriptions of which have not been observed, the complainant not having filed the model or design claimed by her; ...

But whereas if it is true that article 9 of the law of July 14, 1909, in its paragraph 3, provides that "those objects protected by the new law that constitute designs or sculptures, in the technical sense of these words, can also be protected by the law of July 19-24, 1793, modified by the law of March 11, 1902," it does not follow that the hats that do not constitute either sculptures or designs "in the technical sense of the word," escape the protection of this last text;

This expression must, as it results from the legislative history of the law of 1909, and more especially from the report of the Chamber, by Mr. Pranche, be understood in the sense that, in the designs or in the sculptures, as far as their protection is concerned, there is no need to consider either the artistic or aesthetic value;

After having recalled, in fact, that thanks to the law of March 11, 1902, there was no longer the right to inquire about the merit or purpose of protected works, and [after having] clarified that given that the law of 1793 protected the authors of designs and sculptures of all kinds—as it protects authors of writings, also of all kinds, even without any literary value, such as prospectuses, doctrine and jurisprudence—in order to respect the law of 1902, that said Law of 1793 applied to designs without aesthetic character, the rapporteur added: "one should repeat this interpretation, the only one in conformity with the intention of the lawmaker, that, in paragraph 3 of article 9, your Commission will suggest that you recall, incidentally but formally, that the law of 1793 modified by that of 1902 guarantees the exclusive right to reproduce all the designs and all the sculptures, in the purely technical sense of these words";

Very far, therefore, from opposing the law of 1793 to that of July 14, 1909, which, in its Article 1, specifies: "any creator of a design or model has the right to exploit it without prejudice to the rights that it would receive from the other laws, in particular from the law of July 19-24, 1793 [the first French copyright statute] modified by that of March 11, 1902," the lawmaker has understood, by establishing a simple parallel between their respective provisions, that the creator could, at his/her will, invoke the benefit of one or the other;

Whereas, therefore, in the fullness of their right, the plaintiffs have placed themselves under the protection of the law of 1793, to the exclusion of any other, and that cannot be held against them;

Whereas the protection is not limited to the works of architects, statue makers, painters, designers, sculptors and designers of ornaments, but also, and as specified without restriction in Article 7 of this law, "to any production of the spirit or the creativity that belongs to the fine arts," i.e., to anything that proceeds from the art, in the broadest sense of the word, whatever the merit and the destination of the work, subject to an intelligent and personal effort, generating a creation, in which the originality is inscribed;

Whereas it would be disregarding these principles to divest fashion houses from the right to avail themselves of the provisions of the law of 1793;

That we cannot deny, in fact, that the hats they make come from the science of forms, volumes, lines, values, colors, elements that are the basis of painting and sculpture, when, thanks to the ingenious combination of fabrics, straws, feathers, even furs, chosen with care, their workers materialize the designs they conceive, which take shape and life as their skillful fingers, obeying their thought, modify the aspects and the contours successively imagined, to finally reveal, in its final aspect, a work never yet realized, true creation and production of the object;

If it can be rightly maintained that, obliged to be inspired by Fashion, i.e., the taste of the moment, in the need to obey, therefore, to a fleeting conception of lines, shapes or even colors, hats, like all the other objects of women's dressing, a relatively small number of types present in each season, as to their general aspect, and if one can claim that the simple interpretation and even, in its broad lines, the imitation of a model does not constitute an infringement in the true sense of the word, the secondary details being only reproduced to let the author's work subsist and appear, it cannot however be disputed that certain hats made with a deeper science, a more sure taste, a choice and an assembly still unsuspected of the raw materials that compose them or serve as ornaments to them, thus affirming by a succession of original and personal notes, much more than by a perfection which does not have to be envisaged, and thus the creative talent of the house that launches them escapes the public domain and must be classified among the number of the objects whose reproduction, when it results in the slavish or quasi-slavish copy of the essential specificities and details from which their personality derives, constitutes an infringement as understood by the law, which justly punishes it; ...

With regard to the damage, it cannot be discussed;

It suffices to note that while the plaintiffs are obliged to incur in considerable expenses to ensure the development of collections whose development requires not only long months of research and combinations, [and] the collaboration of a large staff, but also and above all renowned makers of outfits, the counterfeiters, without high general costs, without any merit of invention, resort not to the creative brain but to the copying hand, spread both in Paris and in the interior of the country, but even more abroad, from where they are overwhelmed with orders, [which provides] superabundant proof of the originality of French creations in terms of fashions, the works that they have systematically plagiarized;

Whereas, in fact, and these principles being established, during the seizure carried out on January 27, 1931 in the premises occupied by the Denise house of which Ms. Jacquet is the owner, 20 rue de Montaigne in Paris, two hats were found claimed by Maison Rose Descat, which gives proof of its ownership, one in black skin, a copy, according to the plaintiff, of its model nr. 155, the other in blue velvet, copy, according to the same plaintiff, of its model nr. 164;

Whereas the characteristics of the 155 model consist, according to the expert, of the particular cut of three parts that make up the hat, that of the headband covering the top of the head simulating small shells covering the ears, the one indicating a small heart-shaped cut, their assembly giving the hat its original note;

Whereas, apart from a few unnoticeable differences in detail, says the expert, the cut of the three main parts, their arrangement and their organization are found in the offending hat; he concludes that the black antelope hat seized from the defendant is an almost slavish copy of the claimed model; ...

Whereas with regard to the alleged precedencies, in particular a model of the couturier Lucien Lelong, which appears on page 13 of the issue of *Fémina* dated

April 1930, and which, according to Ms. Jacquet, would have presented analogies with the disputed hat, the expert, after analyzing and comparing the particularities likely to be noted in the two hats, has declared that the precedency invoked was not justified and again concluded that was a slavish copy of the Rose Descat model;

Whereas the second hat seized on the same date from Ms. Jacquet, also claimed by Rose Descat, offers as special characteristics, according to the expert, the particular interpretation of the small overlocked velvet bands, decreasing on each side towards the ears, as well as the arrangement of the patterns formed of overlocked small rolls; that it is specified by the expert that, despite its simplicity, this touch represents a new idea that must be considered personal to Maison Rose Descat and that the model established by Ms. Jacquet is an almost slavish copy; ...

For these reasons,

And for those of the first agreeing judges;

Confirms the judgment made on the principle of guilt; ...

Figure 49 Left, a woman wears a hat designed by Lucien Lelong, as published on page 13 of the April 1930 issue of Fémina, a specialized fashion magazine. The defendant alleged that this particular design preceded Rose Descat's hat and thus destroyed its novelty and originality—an argument that the court rejected.

§ 2.69 FRENCH CASE LAW ASSUMES THAT THE MERE POSSESSION OF UNAUTHORIZED SKETCHES IS COUNTERFEITING—1937

Pushing further the construction of copyright law in the direction of strong protection of fashion designers, the Paris Court of Appeals, mentioning well-settled case law, has held that counterfeiting was not limited to the actual making of new apparel without the creator's permission, but that it extended actually to the simple making or knowingly possession of unauthorized sketches. In this case, the damages caused to the copyright holder were undoubtedly smaller, but they existed nevertheless.

Of course, this a legal reasoning that makes sense in connection with artistic designs, which are not aimed to be translated into functional objects or devices. In that case, the copying of the designs exhausts the full scope of the right. But when it comes to fashion designs, unless the perspective in question be that of a free-lancer designer, who makes the sketches to sell them to the fashion houses, they have no economic meaning in themselves. At most, the possession of unauthorized designs by a rival couturier could constitute attempted counterfeiting.

The same Paris Court delivered five additional opinions against a United States citizen whose job was to travel to Paris and acquire sketches of new fashion models and bring them to his country—where, naturally, they would feed the thriving industry of imitation of Parisian fashion.

Interestingly, the opinions partially transcribed below do not mention how all those sketches were obtained, but one can wonder that espionage, bribery, and stealing were the techniques used by the counterfeiters against creative fashion houses.

Paris Court (13th Chamber)

Heuzé et dame Heuzé v. Bruyère et Syndicat La Protection artistique des industries saisonnières.

March 5, 1937

> The Paris Court (13th Chamber), functioning as an appellate court, on March 9, 1937, under the chairmanship of Master Vergelot, on the conclusions of Master Gavalda, general attorney ... rendered the following judgments:
>
> The Court: ...
>
> On the facts:
>
> Whereas at the opening of the sealed [register] by the expert, one dress, one piece of coat fabric, one piece of dress fabric, and two sketches, have been found; ...
>
> Whereas in support of her appeal, Mrs. Heuzé maintains by conclusions that the mere possession of the incriminated sketch cannot constitute the offense of counterfeiting, whereas she has never exhibited, nor put up for sale, nor sold the said sketch, that she only kept it in her shop for information and to keep abreast of fashion and that it is not proved or even alleged that this sketch has been used to make dresses;
>
> Whereas it is correct to maintain that the infringement being the violation of a property right, those who, without diminishing the exclusive enjoyment of the author, are satisfied to learn about the works of this author, either by purchasing

from him/her a model of the work, in this case a dress, or by obtaining a lawfully established drawing of the dress, are not infringers;

But whereas this is not what the accused is charged of; the proof established against her shows that she had made or caused to be made, either by herself, or by designers, without the author's authorization, in the form of sketches, reproductions of models of dresses exclusively belonging to the plaintiff;

Whereas there is no need to investigate, in order to prove the existence of the offense, whether the sketch, reproduction of the model of women's clothing, was subsequently used or not to have the same garment manufactured, which would constitute, in a different way, another reproduction and, in the form itself in this case, of the model; that these other facts could only be considered for the assessment of the damage caused to the owner of the model;

Whereas the application, as set by jurisprudence, to the couturiers, for their models of dresses, of the decree-law of July 19-24, 1793, on the protection of authors' property rights, entails the consequence that such protection cannot be limited to the reproduction in an identical materialization of the protected work; that the protection extends to any form taken by the reproduction, regardless of the material means employed; therefore the appellant cannot, with good reason, maintain that by reproducing a robe, an original model, in the form of a sketch or a design only, she did not make a copy, any more than the couturier who would have reproduced, in the form of a dress, the sketch of a designer or the fabric of a couturier;

Whereas, therefore, the examination of the argument, namely that the mere possession of sketches representing fashion models do not constitute the offense of counterfeiting, amounts to asking whether such possession is lawful or not, exactly as it should be so in the case of possession of a copy, in the form of a dress itself, of a fashion model;

Whereas, in fact, it is jurisprudence that the texts invoked by the complaint protect the creators of models of dresses by protecting their work of spirit, their original idea;

Whereas this idea, which is their intellectual work, is a dress; whereas, for externalizing this idea, the couturiers can do so either through the dress itself (a chosen fabric) or the pattern, or the model (a canvas), or the design (a sketch);

Whereas copying the idea of the dress in any of these forms is reproducing this idea and therefore counterfeiting it, if all the elements of the offense are there, because this idea, once conceived and manifested by a creation, if it is undoubtedly allowed to all to appropriate it subjectively in thought, cannot be again exteriorized, edited by anyone other than by the creator or with his authorization;

Whereas in the present case, Mrs. Heuzé has voluntarily and knowingly reproduced or caused to be reproduced, in the form of a sketch, the creative thought of the owner of the model in question, whose character of originality and novelty is not challenged; whereas if she tries to prove her ignorance of the intellectual property of others, by alleging that she bought said sketches, without discernment, from passing merchants who came to her shop, she fails to prove it;

Whereas the examination carried out by the Court in the council's chambers, in the presence of the parties and their counsels, as well as of the expert, has revealed the two fabrics' character of quasi-slavish copy; whereas with regard to the alleged good faith, Mrs. Heuzé's statements, namely that she bought the offending fabrics from passing merchants and was unaware that they were copies, do not, on their own, suffice to establish good faith, without being substantiated by other reasons; thus it is with good reason that the first judges declared her on this count guilty of the offense of counterfeiting;

On the amount of the damage suffered:

Whereas the attacked infringement consists only in the reproduction, in this case, in the form of fabrics and one design, of the creative idea and that no reproduction in the form of a dress is established, or even alleged;

Whereas, if it is true to say that it is the idea that is protected, it should however be noted that if the couturier has been granted the benefit of the protection of the law of July 19-24, 1793 on "the property rights of authors of all kinds of writings, of music composers, of painters and of designers," that is actually in order to prevent prejudice to be caused to them by the reproduction by others through the effective form of dress of the couturier's model, which would deprive him/her of the legitimate benefit that he/she is entitled to derive from his/her creation;

But whereas no woman dresses herself with a sketch and the damage caused by the infringement in sketching the idea is less serious than the damage caused by the infringement in the form of the dress itself; whereas this is so true that often the couturier, for the purpose of legitimate advertising, himself publishes his/her idea, not for immediate profit, in the form of a design either in ordinary newspapers, or in magazines or technical periodicals;

Whereas it is therefore necessary to take into account the form in which the infringement has been committed in order to assess the damage suffered and its compensation; in this case the Court has sufficient elements to fix it at 1,000 francs;

For these reasons, and for those of the agreeing first judges ...

Confirming, furthermore, for the remainder, the reasons expressed in the said judgment by default, maintains the penalty of 1,000 francs fine pronounced against Mrs. Heuzé;

Reduces to 1,000 francs the amount of damages that Mrs. Heuzé will have to pay to the Bruyère house;

Maintains the amount of damages allocated to the Union of Artistic Protection;

Orders Mrs. Heuzé to pay the costs of the first instance, appeal, and opposition.

Additionally, the Court has rendered 5 judgments against Crab, on request by several fashion houses, on the following terms:

The Court,

Whereas Mr. Crab maintains in support of his appeal that the sole possession of sketches representing original models newly created by fashion houses cannot constitute the offense of counterfeiting of which he is accused, especially since such possession would be justified by a purpose of information and documentation, and that, moreover, that it has never been proved, nor even alleged, that dresses had been made that are the reproduction of the models represented by the sketches in question;

Whereas this appellant claims that, being of American nationality, formerly the owner of a fashion house in New York, he was, at the time of the facts of the proceedings, the representative of various foreign fashion houses; that in this capacity he came periodically to Paris and was instructed to inform the said fashion houses about the novelties presented by Parisian couturiers, by purchasing in particular those whose novelty appeared to him to be the most capable of pleasing foreign customers; whereas he adds that to fulfill the role of informant he had, from the end of 1932, the idea of having recourse to sketches; whereas, for this purpose, he had asked a certain Mr. Schloss, agent of couture, to indicate or to have indicated to him the name of designers capable of providing him with those sketches; that it is thus during a search carried out at the beginning of February 1933, in the room he then occupied at Hotel Atlanta, he had been found in possession of a number of sketches representing new models presented by

Parisian couturiers; whereas it is because of this circumstance that he was wrongly accused of fashion counterfeiting;

Whereas if it is correct to maintain ... that the infringement being the violation ... (same grounds as the judgment above);

For these reasons, and for those of the agreeing first judges,

Confirms.

§ 2.70 THE CREATIVE FASHION INDUSTRY OF THE UNITED STATES REACTS AND TAKES COLLECTIVE ACTION AGAINST RAMPANT COUNTERFEITING, BUT HITS AN ANTITRUST WALL—1941

Feeling helpless in protecting creativity and originality against uncontrolled counterfeiting and piracy, the creative fashion industry of the United States organized a guild that took a series of actions leading to the boycott by the textile industry against those retailers that countered their interests. The Federal Trade Commission did not agree that pursuance of interests in protecting original designs could justify the practice of acts contrary to free competition. The Supreme Court confirmed. It is worth noticing that the guild did not seek to enforce federal statutory rights, like patents, copyrights, or design rights, but engaged in boycotting those engaged in what they viewed as tortious acts of infringement of "original creations." The Court said that even "if copying were an acknowledged tort under the law of every state, that situation would not justify petitioners in combining together to regulate and restrain interstate commerce in violation of federal law."

U.S. Supreme Court

Fashion Originators' Guild of America v. FTC

312 U.S. 457 (1941)

Decided March 3, 1941

Mr. Justice Black delivered the opinion of the Court.

The Circuit Court of Appeals, with modifications not here challenged, affirmed a Federal Trade Commission decree ordering petitioners to cease and desist from certain practices found to have been done in combination and to constitute "unfair methods of competition" tending to monopoly. [note omitted]

Determination of the correctness of the decision below requires consideration of the Sherman, Clayton, and Federal Trade Commission Acts. [note omitted]

Some of the members of the combination design, manufacture, sell and distribute women's garments—chiefly dresses. Others are manufacturers, converters or dyers of textiles from which these garments are made. Fashion Originators' Guild of America (FOGA), an organization controlled by these groups, is the instrument through which petitioners work to accomplish the purposes condemned by the Commission. The garment manufacturers claim to be creators of original and distinctive designs of fashionable clothes for women, and the textile manufacturers claim to be creators of similar original fabric designs. After these designs enter the channels of trade, other manufacturers systematically make and sell copies of them, the copies usually selling at prices lower than the garments copied. Petitioners call this practice of copying unethical and immoral, and give it the name of "style piracy." And although they admit that their "original creations" are neither copyrighted nor patented, and indeed assert that existing legislation affords them no protection against copyists, they nevertheless urge that sale of copied designs constitutes an unfair trade practice and a tortious invasion of their rights. Because of these alleged wrongs, petitioners, while continuing to compete with one another in many respects, combined among themselves to combat and, if possible, destroy all competition from the sale of garments which are copies of their "original creations." They admit that, to destroy such competition, they have in combination purposely boycotted and declined to sell their products to retailers who follow a policy of selling garments copied by other manufacturers from designs put out by Guild members. As a result of their efforts, approximately 12,000 retailers throughout the country have signed agreements to "cooperate" with the Guild's boycott program, but more than half of these signed the agreements only because constrained by threats that Guild members would not sell to retailers who failed to yield to their demands—threats that have been carried out by the Guild practice of placing on red cards the names of noncooperators (to whom no sales are to be made), placing on white cards the names of cooperators (to whom sales are to be made), and then distributing both sets of cards to the manufacturers.

The one hundred and seventy-six manufacturers of women's garments who are members of the Guild occupy a commanding position in their line of business. In 1936, they sold in the United States more than 38% of all women's garments wholesaling at $ 6.75 and up, and more than 60% of those at $ 10.75 and above. The power of the combination is great; competition and the demand of the consuming public make it necessary for most retail dealers to stock some of the products of these manufacturers. And the power of the combination is made even greater by reason of the affiliation of some members of the National Federation of Textiles, Inc.—that being an organization composed of about one hundred textile manufacturers, converters, dyers, and printers of silk and rayon used in making women's garments. Those members of the Federation who are affiliated with the Guild have agreed to sell their products only to those garment manufacturers who have, in turn, agreed to sell only to cooperating retailers.

The Guild maintains a Design Registration Bureau for garments, and the Textile Federation maintains a similar Bureau for textiles. The Guild employs "shoppers" to visit the stores of both cooperating and noncooperating retailers, "for the purpose of examining their stocks, to determine and report as to whether they contain ... copies of registered designs. ..." An elaborate system of trial and appellate tribunals exists for the determination of whether a given garment is in fact a copy of a Guild member's design. In order to assure the success of its plan of registration and restraint, and to ascertain whether Guild regulations are being violated, the Guild audits its members' books. And if violations of Guild requirements are discovered, as, for example, sales to red-carded retailers, the violators are subject to heavy fines.[95]

In addition to the elements of the agreement set out above, all of which relate more or less closely to competition by so-called style copyists, the Guild has undertaken to do many things apparently independent of and distinct from the fight against copying. Among them are the following: the combination prohibits its members from participating in retail advertising; regulates the discount they may allow; prohibits their selling at retail; cooperates with local guilds in regulating days upon which special sales shall be held; prohibits its members from selling

95. Note 3 in the original: "In one instance, a fine of $1,500 was imposed, and the Guild notified its membership that a fine of $5,000 would be assessed in case of future violation."

women's garments to persons who conduct businesses in residences, residential quarters, hotels or apartment houses; and denies the benefits of membership to retailers who participate with dress manufacturers in promoting fashion shows unless the merchandise used is actually purchased and delivered.

If the purpose and practice of the combination of garment manufacturers and their affiliates run counter to the public policy declared in the Sherman and Clayton Acts, the Federal Trade Commission has the power to suppress it as an unfair method of competition. [note omitted] From its findings the Commission concluded that the petitioners, "pursuant to understandings, arrangements, agreements, combinations and conspiracies entered into jointly and severally," had prevented sales in interstate commerce, had "substantially lessened, hindered and suppressed" competition, and had tended "to create in themselves a monopoly." And paragraph 3 of the Clayton Act, 15 U.S.C. § 14, declares

> "It shall be unlawful for any person engaged in commerce ... to ... make a sale or contract for sale of goods ... on the condition, agreement or understanding that the ... purchaser thereof shall not use or deal in the goods ... of a competitor or competitors of the ... seller, where the effect of such ... sale, or contract for sale ... may be to substantially lessen competition or tend to create a monopoly in any line of commerce."

The relevance of this section of the Clayton Act to petitioners' scheme is shown by the fact that the scheme is bottomed upon a system of sale under which (1) textiles shall be sold to garment manufacturers only upon the condition and understanding that the buyers will not use or deal in textiles which are copied from the designs of textile manufacturing Guild members; (2) garment manufacturers shall sell to retailers only upon the condition and understanding that the retailers shall not use or deal in such copied designs. And the Federal Trade Commission concluded, in the language of the Clayton Act, that these understandings substantially lessened competition and tended to create a monopoly. We hold that the Commission, upon adequate and unchallenged findings, correctly concluded that this practice constituted an unfair method of competition. [note omitted]

Not only does the plan in the respects above discussed thus conflict with the principles of the Clayton Act; the findings of the Commission bring petitioners' combination in its entirety well within the inhibition of the policies declared by the Sherman Act itself. Section 1 of that Act makes illegal every contract, combination or conspiracy in restraint of trade or commerce among the several states; Section 2 makes illegal every combination or conspiracy which monopolizes or attempts to monopolize any part of that trade or commerce. Under the Sherman Act "competition, not combination, should be the law of trade." ... And among the many respects in which the Guild's plan runs contrary to the policy of the Sherman Act are these: it narrows the outlets to which garment and textile manufacturers can sell and the sources from which retailers can buy ...; subjects all retailers and manufacturers who decline to comply with the Guild's program to an organized boycott ...; takes away the freedom of action of members by requiring each to reveal to the Guild the intimate details of their individual affairs ...; and has both as its necessary tendency and as its purpose and effect the direct suppression of competition from the sale of unregistered textiles and copied designs ... . In addition to all this, the combination is in reality an extra-governmental agency which prescribes rules for the regulation and restraint of interstate commerce and provides extrajudicial tribunals for determination and punishment of violations, and thus "trenches upon the power of the national legislature and violates the statute." ...

Nor is it determinative in considering the policy of the Sherman Act that petitioners may not yet have achieved a complete monopoly. For "it is sufficient if it really tends to that end, and to deprive the public of the advantages which flow from free competition." ... It was, in fact, one of the hopes of those who sponsored the Federal Trade Commission Act that its effect might be prophylactic, and that, through it, attempts to bring about complete monopolization of an industry might be stopped in their incipiency. [note omitted]

Petitioners, however, argue that the combination cannot be contrary to the policy of the Sherman and Clayton Acts, since the Federal Trade Commission did not find that the combination fixed or regulated prices, parcelled out or limited production, or brought about a deterioration in quality. But action falling into these three categories does not exhaust the types of conduct banned by the Sherman and Clayton Acts. And, as previously pointed out, it was the object of the Federal Trade Commission Act to reach not merely in their fruition, but also in their incipiency, combinations which could lead to these and other trade restraints and practices deemed undesirable. In this case, the Commission found that the combination exercised sufficient control and power in the women's garments and textile businesses

> "to exclude from the industry those manufacturers and distributors who do not conform to the rules and regulations of said respondents, and thus tend to create in themselves a monopoly in the said industries."

While a conspiracy to fix prices is illegal, an intent to increase prices is not an ever-present essential of conduct amounting to a violation of the policy of the Sherman and Clayton Acts; a monopoly contrary to their policies can exist even though a combination may temporarily or even permanently reduce the price of the articles manufactured or sold. For, as this Court has said,

> "Trade or commerce under those circumstances may nevertheless be badly and unfortunately restrained by driving out of business the small dealers and worthy men whose lives have been spent therein, and who might be unable to readjust themselves to their altered surroundings. Mere reduction in the price of the commodity dealt in might be dearly paid for by the ruin of such a class and the absorption of control over one commodity by an all-powerful combination of capital. [note omitted]."

But petitioners further argue that their boycott and restraint of interstate trade is not within the ban of the policies of the Sherman and Clayton Acts, because

> "the practices of FOGA were reasonable and necessary to protect the manufacturer, laborer, retailer and consumer against the devastating evils growing from the pirating of original designs and had in fact benefited all four."

The Commission declined to hear much of the evidence that petitioners desired to offer on this subject. As we have pointed out, however, the aim of petitioners' combination was the intentional destruction of one type of manufacture and sale which competed with Guild members. The purpose and object of this combination, its potential power, its tendency to monopoly, the coercion it could and did practice upon a rival method of competition, all brought it within the policy of the prohibition declared by the Sherman and Clayton Acts. ... Under these circumstances, it was not error to refuse to hear the evidence offered, for the reasonableness of the methods pursued by the combination to accomplish its unlawful object is no more material than would be the reasonableness of the prices fixed by unlawful combination. ... Nor can the unlawful combination be justified upon the argument that systematic copying of dress designs is itself tortious, or should now be declared so by us. In the first place, whether or not given conduct is tortious is a question of state law ... . In the second place, even if copying were an acknowledged tort under the law of every state, that situation would not justify petitioners in combining together to regulate and restrain interstate commerce in violation of federal law. ... The decision below is accordingly

Affirmed.

§ 2.71 UNITED STATES CASE LAW MOVES FORWARD: COPYRIGHT PROTECTION IS AVAILABLE FOR FASHION DESIGNS, BUT THE REQUIREMENT OF ENSURING THAT A NOTICE OF COPYRIGHT IS AFFIXED IN EACH GARMENT MAY BE AN OBSTACLE—1960

The same judge Learned Hand, who, in 1929, admitted that fashion designs were out of protection in the United States (see § 2.67), in 1960 accepted the application of copyright law for that same purpose. The problem in this case was one of ensuring that the copyright notice, as required by the copyright statute, was affixed to every piece of garment. The majority of the Second Circuit understood that such affixation was not always possible and that the burden of proving the ignorance of copyrightability was on the side of the alleged infringers. One judge dissented—the required notice was there or not. If it was not, copyright protection should not be available.

Interestingly, as we have seen in Chapter One, some old French and English statutes, adopted in the context of certification marks, had specific provisions requiring special care in having notices affixed to the cloths in a way that they should not be destroyed when the fabrics were cut or finished. The objectives were, of course, different, but the materiality of the notice was the same.

Also interesting—and very true—is the assertion by dissenting judge Friendly, that, due to the fleeting nature of fashion, "in litigation of this sort the preliminary rather than the final injunction is the thing."

Peter Pan Fabrics, Inc. v. Martin Weiner Corp.

274 F.2d 487 (2d Cir. 1960)

Decided January 27, 1960

Hand, Circuit Judge.

This is an appeal from a preliminary injunction, granted by Judge Herlands, forbidding the defendant to copy an ornamental design, printed upon cloth. The plaintiffs—which for the purposes of this appeal are to be regarded as one—and the defendant are both "converters" of textiles, used in the manufacture of women's dresses. A "converter" buys uncolored cloth upon which he prints ornamental designs, and which he then sells to dressmakers. The plaintiffs bought from a Parisian designer a design, known as "Byzantium," which it registered as a "reproduction of a work of art," (§ 5(h) of Title 17 U.S. Code) and for which the Copyright Office issued Certificate No. H. 7290. This design they print upon uncolored cloth, sold in bolts to dressmakers. The cloth, so "converted," bears upon its edge at each repetition of the design printed "notices" of copyright which are concededly adequate under the Copyright Law. The buyers of the bolts cut the cloth into suitable lengths and use it to make women's dresses; but in doing so, they either altogether cut off the selvage which bears the notices, or else they sew the adjacent edges of the cloth together at the seams in such a way that the notices are not visible unless the seams are pried, or cut, apart, or unless the dress is turned inside out. The appeal raises two questions: (1) whether the defendant has in fact copied so much of the registered design as to infringe the copyright; and (2) whether the design was dedicated to the public, because it was sold without adequate notice of copyright as required by § 10 of the statute.

The test for infringement of a copyright is of necessity vague. In the case of verbal "works" it is well settled that although the "proprietor's" monopoly extends beyond an exact reproduction of the words, there can be no copyright in the "ideas" disclosed but only in their "expression." Obviously, no principle can be stated as to when an imitator has gone beyond copying the "idea," and has borrowed its "expression." Decisions must therefore inevitably be ad hoc. In the case of designs, which are addressed to the aesthetic sensibilities of an observer, the test is, if possible, even more intangible. No one disputes that the copyright extends beyond a photographic reproduction of the design, but one cannot say how far an imitator must depart from an undeviating reproduction to escape infringement. In deciding that question one should consider the uses for which the design is intended, especially the scrutiny that observers will give to it as used. In the case at bar we must try to estimate how far its overall appearance will determine its aesthetic appeal when the cloth is made into a garment. Both designs have the same general color, and the arches, scrolls, rows of symbols, etc. on one resemble those on the other though they are not identical. Moreover, the patterns in which these figures are distributed to make up the design as a whole are not identical. However, the ordinary observer, unless he set out to detect the disparities, would be disposed to overlook them, and regard their aesthetic appeal as the same. That is enough; and indeed, it is all that can be said, unless protection against infringement is to be denied because of variants irrelevant to the purpose for which the design is intended.

The second question is whether the plaintiffs have forfeited their copyright. As we have said, there is no question that the bolts of cloth were adequately marked to comply with § 10, for a notice was "affixed to each copy ... offered for sale"; and, it appeared at intervals along the selvage, so that no one using the cloth could avoid seeing it. However, although the notices served the purpose of advising those who bought, or dealt with, the bolts, they did not give adequate notice to those who bought, or wore, dresses made of the cloth, for, when not altogether cut off, they were so placed as to be most unlikely to be detected. Section 21 of the act provides that the "omission by accident or mistake of the prescribed notice from a particular copy or copies shall not invalidate the copyright"; but the effective suppression of this mark on dresses is neither accidental nor mistaken; and sales with a deliberate omission of notice will forfeit the copyright ... Therefore, if we construe the words of § 10 with relentless literalism, dresses made out of the "converted" cloth may be said to be "offered for sale" without any effective notice. In support of such an interpretation it may be argued that the doctrine, *expressio unius, exclusio alterius,* would apply: that is to say, since Congress made only "omission by accident or mistake" an excuse we must not enlarge the exemption.

On the other hand, it is a commonplace that a literal interpretation of the words of a statute is not always a safe guide to its meaning. Indeed, in extreme situations this doctrine has been carried so far that language inescapably covering the occasion has been disregarded when it defeats the manifest purpose of the statute as a whole. ... We need not go so far in the case at bar. In the first place it is hard to see how "notice" can said to be "affixed" to a "design" when it is incorporated into it; the copyrighted "work" will itself be changed, even though the change be so immaterial as not to impair the aesthetic appeal of the "design."

Be that as it may, we do not hold that in no circumstances will it be possible to "affix notice" upon a "design" which will be still visible when the cloth has been made up into a garment. We do hold that at least in the case of a deliberate copyist, as in the case at bar, the absence of "notice" is a defence that the copyist must prove, and that the burden is on him to show that "notice" could have been embodied in the design without impairing its market value. The defendant asserts that this can be done but it has offered no evidence that it can be. Whatever may be shown at the trial, upon this record we hold that the "design" should be protected, *pendente lite.*

Order affirmed.

Friendly, Circuit Judge (dissenting).

I regret that I cannot join in the judgment of the Court. I would reverse.

Section 10 of the Copyright Act, 17 U.S.C. § 10, provides that "Any person entitled thereto by this title may secure copyright for his work by publication thereof with the notice of copyright required by this title; and such notice shall be affixed to each copy thereof published or offered for sale in the United States by authority of the copyright proprietor." The question is whether plaintiffs met the second requirement.

Admittedly, the notice of copyright is not "affixed to each copy" of the copyrighted design on the dresses manufactured and sold by the purchasers that bought cloth from plaintiffs. Indeed, whether the notice remains affixed to any copy is fortuitous, since, as was conceded at the bar, plaintiffs cannot practically obtain any commitments from the manufacturers in this regard. I do not read the Court's opinion as questioning that the manufacturers make and sell the dresses in this manner "by authority of the copyright proprietor." Such sales were the very purpose of the purchases of the cloth; plaintiffs knew that the notices would generally be cut off; and I read § 10 as using "authority" in the broad sense of permission and not as requiring any technical agency relationship. It is unnecessary to debate whether the conversion of the designs into dresses was a republication; for it was an offer for sale unless we deny those words the sense they have in everyday speech. I take it no one would question that an authorized offer for sale occurred if the purchasers, with plaintiffs' acquiescence, regularly cut off the selvage bearing the copyright notice and sold the cloth in strips; I think there was no less such an offer when the purchasers cut off the selvage and sold the cloth in dresses.

I am not altogether clear whether my brothers say that the sale of the dresses was not an offer for sale with the authority of the copyright proprietor or that it was such an offer but that notice need not be affixed if this was not feasible. The latter construction seems borne out by the suggestion that plaintiffs will be denied a final decree if defendant proves that notice could have been affixed to each copy of the design in the dresses without impairing the market value; for, unless the sale of the dresses is within § 10, plaintiffs are under no requirement to have the notice affixed. In any event the result is plain enough. Plaintiffs receive copyright protection for enabling a multitude of ladies to be caparisoned in the purple of "Byzantium" although the copyright notices, instead of being "affixed to each copy" of the design on the dresses, pile up in the cutting rooms. It is of no moment that the Court now grants protection only *pendente lite.* For the record makes it evident that designs such as plaintiffs' are anything but Byzantine in longevity—indeed, the moving affidavit gives this one but a few months of life—and in litigation of this sort the preliminary rather than the final injunction is the thing.

I could reconcile the majority's result with the language of § 10 if, but only if, there were clear evidence that the dominant intention of Congress was to afford

> the widest possible copyright protection whereas the notice requirement was deemed formal or at least secondary. I find nothing to support such a stratified reading of § 10. The notice requirement goes back to almost the earliest days of copyright under the constitutional grant, Act of April 29, 1802, ch. 36, 2 Stat. 171; its essentiality has been emphasized by the highest authority, ... and when Congress has wished to make an exception, it has known how to do so, *see* 17 U.S.C. § 21. The notice requirement serves an important public purpose; the copyright proprietor is protected so long and only so long as he gives effective warning to trespassers that they are entering on forbidden ground. ... And if the statutory requirement of notice has not been met, it is immaterial whether a particular defendant had actual knowledge of a claim of copyright or not. ...
>
> I realize that the view I hold may seriously impair the use of copyright to prevent piracy in an area where this has been recognized to be rampant for thirty years, ... and probably for much longer, since it may not be practicable to affix the notice to an inside seam on every repetition of the design. It can be argued also that this is to insist on a useless formality since, though there is reason for requiring notice on each copy of a book, one notice on a dress is as good as ten. But, as was held by the Supreme Court in *Dejonge*, it is not for the courts to say that something less than the statutory requirement will serve. Congress has not accompanied the broadening of the subjects of copyright in § 5 with a relaxation of the notice requirement of § 10, except as it has simplified the form of notice for certain subjects in § 19 and has saved against accidental omission in § 21. Nothing gives me warrant for belief that Congress would be content with the proprietor's simply affixing the copyright notice to each copy as it leaves him, when, as here, he knows that almost every notice will be removed before the copyrighted reproductions reach their intended market. As said in *Louis Dejonge Co. v. Breuker Kessler*, 235 U.S. at page 37, "The appellant is claiming the same rights as if this were one of the masterpieces of the world, and he must take them with the same limitations that would apply to a portrait, a holy family, or a scene of war." To be sure, the precise defect held fatal in *Dejonge* is not present here since the notice was on "each copy" as it left plaintiffs, but Mr. Justice Holmes' admonition remains pertinent. ... Perhaps my brothers are right in thinking that Congress wished literal compliance with § 10 to be excused under such circumstances as here; but the voice so audible to them is silent to me.

§ 2.72 THE ONLY INTERNATIONAL AGREEMENT THAT HAS ADOPTED LANGUAGE WITH FASHION DESIGNS AS A SPECIAL TARGET: THE TRIPS AGREEMENT—1994

The section of the TRIPS Agreement that covers industrial designs is not particularly remarkable, except that it pays special attention to designs for textiles. The reason was that the introduction of this section in the Agreement is owed to the initiative of a few GATT Contracting Parties that had particular interests in the fashion industry, namely Switzerland, whose delegation was concerned with the need for providing particular attention to the textile industry of St. Gallen.[96] *The expression of those interests is especially reflected in the language of Article 25.2, which requires an opportunity for the*

96. This piece of information has been provided by Mrs. Thu-Lang Tran Wasescha, who was part of the negotiating team that represented Switzerland in the Uruguay Round negotiations.

textile industry to obtain cheap and expeditious registration if the WTO member accords protection to industrial designs under an industrial property mechanism.[97] *Significantly, the language adopted has not gone as far as a few negotiators had proposed. As the first of the following texts show, Austria was ready to discuss a special regime specifically addressing the fashion industry. The proposed definition of the scope of protection in itself aimed at covering the concerns of the fashion industry, insofar as the protection should "prevent identical reproduction of the appearance of products which differs only in immaterial details or features from that of the protected design"—language that speaks to the little variations introduced in new fashion designs. Switzerland's proposal was not that bold, but it wished nevertheless to have the textile industry specially mentioned in the final text, as a reason for the adoption of a speedy registration system. As said, only the latter proposal has been retained.*

However, industrial property protection for designs does not depend necessarily on registration. The Paris Convention for the Protection of Industrial Property itself has had, since its revision in Lisbon, in 1958, a provision that provides that "Industrial designs shall be protected in all the countries of the Union." without mentioning the need for their registration. What differentiates copyright from industrial property, although the latter tends to depend on formalities, is that the former protects against the copying of ideas, whereas the latter protects against the use of ideas. But copyright can be formal (it was so before the Berne Convention, and in some countries, its enforcement still depends on registration), and industrial property can be informal.

For example, the European Union in 2002 passed a Regulation that provides industrial property protection for non-registered designs. The term of protection is three years from the date of disclosure to the public (understood as a circle of interested persons). The absence of a registration requirement combined with the short term of protection and the loose definition of the novelty requirement (protectable designs are those that are not identical to designs previously made available to the public) could make this mechanism particularly adequate for fashion designs. However, the requirement of "individual character" makes it difficult for the vast proportion of designs produced by fashion houses to benefit from such protection. Only those few designs that stand out from the large mass of uncharacteristic designs could be eligible. Nor is it the intention of the 2002 Regulation to benefit fashion designs in particular. One of the paragraphs of the preamble reads: "A Community design should, as far as possible, serve the needs of all sectors of industry in the Community."

97. The delegation of France, in 1958, in the discussions that led to the introduction of Article 5*quinquies* of the Paris Convention for the Protection of Industrial Property, on the mandatory protection of industrial designs, made a reference to fashion designs, but only in an implicit manner, and without the intention of looking at a sui generis mechanism for their special protection. The delegation, rejecting a proposed definition of industrial designs, stated that national lawmakers should let be free to decide the conditions of protection "in the domain of 'seasonal' creations, whose brevity of protection may have as a compensation a limitation of the formalities and the costs it entails." *See* Bureau International pour la Protection de la Propriété Industrielle, ACTES DA LA CONFÉRENCE RÉUNIE À LISBONNE DU 6 AU 31 OCTOBRE 1958, at 870 (Geneva, 1963). Source: www.wipo.int.

§ 2.72.1 Austria Proposes the Adoption of a Special Regime for the Protection of Fashion Designs—1989

Negotiating Group on Trade-Related Aspects of Intellectual Property Rights, including Trade in Counterfeit Goods

Trade-Related Intellectual Property Rights

Submission by Austria

The following submission has been received from the Permanent Delegation of Austria, with the request that it be circulated to members of the Negotiating Group.

4. Industrial designs ...

4.4 Any future agreement on industrial design should be a tool to prevent identical reproduction of the appearance of products which differs only in immaterial details or features from that of the protected design. ...

4.6 Designs in the field of fashion and textiles have not only a short life cycle, but due to the technological progress information is spread rapidly and copying can start nearly immediately. Therefore a special regime to protect designs in this field should be studied.

§ 2.72.2 Switzerland Proposes the Adoption of a Special Mechanism of Registration for Textile Designs—1990

Draft Amendment to the General Agreement on Tariffs and Trade on the Protection of Trade-Related Intellectual Property Rights

Communication from Switzerland

The attached communication, dated 14 May 1990, has been received from the delegation of Switzerland, with the request that it be circulated to the members of the Negotiating Group.

Sub-section D: Industrial Designs ...

Article 224. Grant, Maintenance, Cancellation of Industrial Design Rights; Other Procedures

(1) Industrial design rights shall be granted within a reasonable time period and at reasonable cost. In particular, the acquisition of industrial design rights in textiles shall not be encumbered by any special requirements such as ex officio examination of novelty before registration, compulsory publication of the design itself or disproportionate fees for multiple users of the registration.

§ 2.72.3 The TRIPS Agreement—1994

Agreement on Trade-Related Aspects of Intellectual Property Rights (TRIPS Agreement)

April 15, 1994

Part II Standards concerning the Availability, Scope and Use of Intellectual Property Rights

Section 4: Industrial Designs

Article 25

Requirements for Protection

... 2. Each Member shall ensure that requirements for securing protection for textile designs, in particular in regard to any cost, examination or publication, do not unreasonably impair the opportunity to seek and obtain such protection. Members shall be free to meet this obligation through industrial design law or through copyright law. ...

§ 2.73 THE CONUNDRUM OF THE PROTECTION OF FASHION DESIGNS: THEIR CONVERSION INTO BUSINESS IDENTIFIERS AND THE NEED TO PROVE SECONDARY MEANING—2000

The following text brings a very important opinion that opens an avenue for the protection of unregistered fashion designs, or part of fashion designs, which consumers have learned to distinguish, as business identifiers. This could be a significant avenue for the protection of those designs and patterns that some fashion houses use with such success that consumers acquire the habit of taking them as signs of identification of the origin, i.e., of the manufacturer of the fashion articles they seek.

However, this opinion deals with unregistered designs. It still leaves open the matter of registered ones. The question is whether the latter could also benefit from the same holding. Wouldn't that be an inappropriate migration of an asset from one field of industrial property to another? Wouldn't that mean the indefinite protection of something that inherently has short-term protection?

The rationale is that, when a designer applies for and obtains the registration of a design, he/she acquires exclusive rights in that design in exchange for (i) its communication to the authority, so that it be disclosed and (ii) upon the expiry of the registration, the design can be used by anyone interested. This second leg of the rationale would constitute an important contribution to the idea of general improvement of social life, in terms of added beauty or, as far as some designs are concerned, of increased efficiency in the use of certain materials.

And that is exactly this second leg that has been the obstacle for the conversion of industrial designs into business identifiers, as in the Lego case *(the European Court of First Instance, 8*th *Chamber, having denied trademark registrability to the Lego's brick*

design). T-270/06, Lego Juris A/S v. OHIM, Judgment of November 18, 2008. Source: < curia.europe.eu >. However, the Lego brick involved a functional design, i.e., a design that was elaborated in such a manner that it was not aimed at simply producing an esthetical impression—a cachet, *as it could be said in French—but mainly at performing a function. This is not the case of fashion patterns such as those of Missoni and Louis Vuitton, just for mentioning two of the best-known designs that have acquired a secondary meaning.*

Anyway, the important avenue opened by the following opinion is that fashion designs can acquire a secondary meaning, in the sense that their symbolic content may migrate from the realm of industrial designs to that of trademarks. In other words, consumers may learn to recognize a design, a color, a visual pattern as an identification of the source of the product, and thus learn to resort to it as a tool for differentiating it from similar products. Above we have seen that already in 1911, a French court had accepted that same understanding (see § 2.65.5).

Supreme Court of the United States

Wal-Mart Stores, Inc. v. Samara Brothers, Inc.

[March 22, 2000]

Justice Scalia delivered the opinion of the Court.

In this case, we decide under what circumstances a product's design is distinctive, and therefore protectable, in an action for infringement of unregistered trade dress under §43(a) of the Trademark Act of 1946 (Lanham Act), 60 Stat. 441, as amended, 15 U.S.C. § 1125(a).

I. Respondent Samara Brothers, Inc., designs and manufactures children's clothing. Its primary product is a line of spring/summer one-piece seersucker outfits decorated with appliqués of hearts, flowers, fruits, and the like. A number of chain stores, including JCPenney, sell this line of clothing under contract with Samara.

Petitioner Wal-Mart Stores, Inc., is one of the nation's best known retailers, selling among other things children's clothing. In 1995, Wal-Mart contracted with one of its suppliers, Judy-Philippine, Inc., to manufacture a line of children's outfits for sale in the 1996 spring/summer season. Wal-Mart sent Judy-Philippine photographs of a number of garments from Samara's line, on which Judy-Philippine's garments were to be based; Judy-Philippine duly copied, with only minor modifications, 16 of Samara's garments, many of which contained copyrighted elements. In 1996, Wal-Mart briskly sold the so-called knockoffs, generating more than $ 1.15 million in gross profits.

In June 1996, a buyer for JCPenney called a representative at Samara to complain that she had seen Samara garments on sale at Wal-Mart for a lower price than JCPenney was allowed to charge under its contract with Samara. The Samara representative told the buyer that Samara did not supply its clothing to Wal-Mart. Their suspicions aroused, however, Samara officials launched an investigation, which disclosed that Wal-Mart and several other major retailers—Kmart, Caldor, Hills, and Goody's—were selling the knockoffs of Samara's outfits produced by Judy-Philippine.

After sending cease-and-desist letters, Samara brought this action in the United States District Court for the Southern District of New York against Wal-Mart, Judy-Philippine, Kmart, Caldor, Hills, and Goody's for copyright infringement under federal law, consumer fraud and unfair competition under New York law, and–most relevant for our purposes–infringement of unregistered trade dress under §43(a) of the Lanham Act, 15 U.S.C. § 1125(a). All of the defendants except Wal-Mart settled before trial.

After a weeklong trial, the jury found in favor of Samara on all of its claims. Wal-Mart then renewed a motion for judgment as a matter of law, claiming, *inter alia*, that there was insufficient evidence to support a conclusion that Samara's clothing designs could be legally protected as distinctive trade dress for purposes of §43(a). The District Court denied the motion, 969 F. Supp. 895 (SDNY 1997), and awarded Samara damages, interest, costs, and fees totaling almost $ 1.6 million, together with injunctive relief ... . The Second Circuit affirmed the denial of the motion for judgment as a matter of law, 165 F.3d 120 (1998), and we granted certiorari, 528 U.S. ___ (1999).

II. The Lanham Act provides for the registration of trademarks, which it defines in § 45 to include "any word, name, symbol, or device, or any combination thereof [used or intended to be used] to identify and distinguish [a producer's] goods ... from those manufactured or sold by others and to indicate the source of the goods ... ." 15 U.S.C. § 1127. Registration of a mark under § 2 of the Act, 15 U.S.C. § 1052 enables the owner to sue an infringer under § 32, 15 U.S.C. § 1114; it also entitles the owner to a presumption that its mark is valid, *see* §7(b), 15 U.S.C. § 1057(b), and ordinarily renders the registered mark incontestable after five years of continuous use, *see* §15, 15 U.S.C. § 1065. In addition to protecting registered marks, the Lanham Act, in § 43(a), gives a producer a cause of action for the use by any person of "any word, term, name, symbol, or device, or any combination thereof ... which ... is likely to cause confusion ... as to the origin, sponsorship, or approval of his or her goods. ..." 15 U.S.C. § 1125(a). It is the latter provision that is at issue in this case.

The breadth of the definition of marks registrable under § 2, and of the confusion-producing elements recited as actionable by § 43(a), has been held to embrace not just word marks, such as "Nike," and symbol marks, such as Nike's "swoosh" symbol, but also "trade dress"—a category that originally included only the packaging, or "dressing," of a product, but in recent years has been expanded by many courts of appeals to encompass the design of a product. ... These courts have assumed, often without discussion, that trade dress constitutes a "symbol" or "device" for purposes of the relevant sections, and we conclude likewise. "Since human beings might use as a 'symbol' or 'device' almost anything at all that is capable of carrying meaning, this language, read literally, is not restrictive." ... This reading of § 2 and § 43(a) is buttressed by a recently added subsection of § 43(a), § 43(a)(3), which refers specifically to "civil action[s] for trade dress infringement under this chapter for trade dress not registered on the principal register." 15 U.S.C. A. § 1125(a)(3) (Oct. 1999 Supp.).

The text of § 43(a) provides little guidance as to the circumstances under which unregistered trade dress may be protected. It does require that a producer show that the allegedly infringing feature is not "functional," *see* § 43(a)(3), and is likely to cause confusion with the product for which protection is sought, *see* § 43(a)(1)(A), 15 U.S.C. § 1125(a)(1)(A). Nothing in §43(a) explicitly requires a producer to show that its trade dress is distinctive, but courts have universally imposed that requirement, since without distinctiveness the trade dress would not "cause confusion ... as to the origin, sponsorship, or approval of [the] goods," as the section requires. Distinctiveness is, moreover, an explicit prerequisite for registration of trade dress under § 2, and "the general principles qualifying a mark for registration under § 2 of the Lanham Act are for the most part applicable in determining whether an unregistered mark is entitled to protection under § 43(a)."

...

In evaluating the distinctiveness of a mark under § 2 (and therefore, by analogy, under §43(a)), courts have held that a mark can be distinctive in one of two ways. First, a mark is inherently distinctive if "[its] intrinsic nature serves to identify a particular source." ... In the context of word marks, courts have applied the now-classic test originally formulated by Judge Friendly, in which word marks that are "arbitrary" ("Camel" cigarettes), "fanciful" ("Kodak" film), or "suggestive" ("Tide" laundry detergent) are held to be inherently distinctive. ... Second, a mark has acquired distinctiveness, even if it is not inherently distinctive, if it has developed secondary meaning, which occurs when, "in the minds of the public, the primary significance of a [mark] is to identify the source of the product rather than the product itself." ...[98]

The judicial differentiation between marks that are inherently distinctive and those that have developed secondary meaning has solid foundation in the statute itself. Section 2 requires that registration be granted to any trademark "by which the goods of the applicant may be distinguished from the goods of others"—subject to various limited exceptions. 15 U.S.C. § 1052. It also provides, again with limited exceptions, that "nothing in this chapter shall prevent the registration of a mark used by the applicant which has become distinctive of the applicant's goods in commerce"–that is, which is not inherently distinctive but has become so only through secondary meaning. §2(f), 15 U.S.C. § 1052(f). Nothing in §2, however, demands the conclusion that *every* category of mark necessarily includes some marks "by which the goods of the applicant may be distinguished from the goods of others" *without* secondary meaning—that in every category some marks are inherently distinctive.

Indeed, with respect to at least one category of mark—colors—we have held that no mark can ever be inherently distinctive. ... In *Qualitex*, petitioner manufactured and sold green-gold dry-cleaning press pads. After respondent began selling pads of a similar color, petitioner brought suit under §43(a), then added a claim under §32 after obtaining registration for the color of its pads. We held that a color could be protected as a trademark, but only upon a showing of secondary meaning. Reasoning by analogy to the *Abercrombie & Fitch* test developed for word marks, we noted that a product's color is unlike a "fanciful," "arbitrary," or "suggestive" mark, since it does not "almost *automatically* tell a customer that [it] refer[s] to a brand," ... and does not "immediately ... signal a brand or a product 'source,'" ... . However, we noted that, "over time, customers may come to treat a particular color on a product or its packaging ... as signifying a brand." ... . Because a color, like a "descriptive" word mark, could eventually "come to indicate a product's origin," we concluded that it could be protected *upon a showing of secondary meaning*. ...

It seems to us that design, like color, is not inherently distinctive. The attribution of inherent distinctiveness to certain categories of word marks and product packaging derives from the fact that the very purpose of attaching a

98. The original note reads: "The phrase 'secondary meaning' originally arose in the context of word marks, where it served to distinguish the source-identifying meaning from the ordinary, or 'primary,' meaning of the word. 'Secondary meaning' has since come to refer to the acquired, source-identifying meaning of a non-word mark as well. It is often a misnomer in that context, since non-word marks ordinarily have no 'primary' meaning. Clarity might well be served by using the term 'acquired meaning' in both the word-mark and the non-word-mark contexts—but in this opinion we follow what has become the conventional terminology.

particular word to a product, or encasing it in a distinctive packaging, is most often to identify the source of the product. Although the words and packaging can serve subsidiary functions—a suggestive word mark (such as "Tide" for laundry detergent), for instance, may invoke positive connotations in the consumer's mind, and a garish form of packaging (such as Tide's squat, brightly decorated plastic bottles for its liquid laundry detergent) may attract an otherwise indifferent consumer's attention on a crowded store shelf—their predominant function remains source identification. Consumers are therefore predisposed to regard those symbols as indication of the producer, which is why such symbols "almost *automatically* tell a customer that they refer to a brand" ... and "immediately ... signal a brand or a product 'source'" ... . And where it is not reasonable to assume consumer predisposition to take an affixed word or packaging as indication of source—where, for example, the affixed word is descriptive of the product ("Tasty" bread) or of a geographic origin ("Georgia" peaches)—inherent distinctiveness will not be found. That is why the statute generally excludes, from those word marks that can be registered as inherently distinctive, words that are "merely descriptive" of the goods, § 2(e)(1), 15 U.S.C. § 1052(e)(1), or "primarily geographically descriptive of them," *see* § 2(e)(2), 15 U.S.C. § 1052(e)(2). In the case of product design, as in the case of color, we think consumer predisposition to equate the feature with the source does not exist. Consumers are aware of the reality that, almost invariably, even the most unusual of product designs—such as a cocktail shaker shaped like a penguin—is intended not to identify the source, but to render the product itself more useful or more appealing.

The fact that product design almost invariably serves purposes other than source identification not only renders inherent distinctiveness problematic; it also renders application of an inherent-distinctiveness principle more harmful to other consumer interests. Consumers should not be deprived of the benefits of competition with regard to the utilitarian and esthetic purposes that product design ordinarily serves by a rule of law that facilitates plausible threats of suit against new entrants based upon alleged inherent distinctiveness. How easy it is to mount a plausible suit depends, of course, upon the clarity of the test for inherent distinctiveness, and where product design is concerned we have little confidence that a reasonably clear test can be devised. Respondent and the United States as *amicus curiae* urge us to adopt for product design relevant portions of the test formulated by the Court of Customs and Patent Appeals for product packaging in *Seabrook Foods, Inc. v. Bar-Well Foods, Ltd.*, 568 F.2d 1342 (1977). That opinion, in determining the inherent distinctiveness of a product's packaging, considered, among other things, "whether it was a 'common' basic shape or design, whether it was unique or unusual in a particular field, [and] whether it was a mere refinement of a commonly-adopted and well-known form of ornamentation for a particular class of goods viewed by the public as a dress or ornamentation for the goods." *Id.*, at 1344 (footnotes omitted). Such a test would rarely provide the basis for summary disposition of an anticompetitive strike suit. Indeed, at oral argument, counsel for the United States quite understandably would not give a definitive answer as to whether the test was met in this very case, saying only that "[t]his is a very difficult case for that purpose." ...

It is true, of course, that the person seeking to exclude new entrants would have to establish the nonfunctionality of the design feature, *see* § 43(a)(3), 15 U.S.C. A. § 1125(a)(3) (Oct. 1999 Supp.)—a showing that may involve consideration of its esthetic appeal ... . Competition is deterred, however, not merely by successful suit but by the plausible threat of successful suit, and given the unlikelihood of inherently source-identifying design, the game of allowing suit based upon alleged inherent distinctiveness seems to us not worth the candle. That is especially so since the producer can ordinarily obtain protection for a design that *is* inherently source identifying (if any such exists), but that does not yet have secondary meaning, by securing a design patent or a copyright for the design–as, indeed, respondent did for certain elements of the designs in this case. The availability of these other protections greatly reduces any harm to the producer that might ensue from our conclusion that a product design cannot be protected under § 43(a) without a showing of secondary meaning.

Respondent contends that our decision in *Two Pesos* forecloses a conclusion that product-design trade dress can never be inherently distinctive. In that case, we held that the trade dress of a chain of Mexican restaurants, which the plaintiff described as "a festive eating atmosphere having interior dining and patio areas decorated with artifacts, bright colors, paintings and murals," 505 U.S., at 765 (internal quotation marks and citation omitted), could be protected under § 43(a) without a showing of secondary meaning ... . *Two Pesos* unquestionably establishes the legal principle that trade dress can be inherently distinctive ... but it does not establish that *product-design* trade dress can be. *Two Pesos* is inapposite to our holding here because the trade dress at issue, the décor of a restaurant, seems to us not to constitute product *design*. It was either product packaging–which, as we have discussed, normally *is* taken by the consumer to indicate origin–or else some *tertium quid* that is akin to product packaging and has no bearing on the present case.

Respondent replies that this manner of distinguishing *Two Pesos* will force courts to draw difficult lines between product-design and product-packaging trade dress. There will indeed be some hard cases at the margin: a classic glass Coca-Cola bottle, for instance, may constitute packaging for those consumers who drink the Coke and then discard the bottle, but may constitute the product itself for those consumers who are bottle collectors, or part of the product itself for those consumers who buy Coke in the classic glass bottle, rather than a can, because they think it more stylish to drink from the former. We believe, however, that the frequency and the difficulty of having to distinguish between product design and product packaging will be much less than the frequency and the difficulty of having to decide when a product design is inherently distinctive. To the extent there are close cases, we believe that courts should err on the side of caution and classify ambiguous trade dress as product design, thereby requiring secondary meaning. The very closeness will suggest the existence of relatively small utility in adopting an inherent-distinctiveness principle, and relatively great consumer benefit in requiring a demonstration of secondary meaning.

We hold that, in an action for infringement of unregistered trade dress under § 43(a) of the Lanham Act, a product's design is distinctive, and therefore protectable, only upon a showing of secondary meaning. The judgment of the Second Circuit is reversed, and the case is remanded for further proceedings consistent with this opinion.

It is so ordered.

§ 2.74 FASHION AND TRADITIONAL TEXTILES: CULTURAL INSPIRATION OR CULTURAL APPROPRIATION?—2000 ONWARDS

Although fashion-related intellectual property law is in great part concerned with creations and concepts that are fleeting in nature, some of its elements are inspired by ideas that last for generations and even become elements of cultural identity of the societies that create them. This has particular relevance as far as handicrafts and traditional textiles are concerned and have a direct translation into a phenomenon generally designated as "cultural appropriation" (or, more exactly, cultural misappropriation)—by which fashion houses inspire themselves in the traditional designs and ornaments that some traditional and indigenous communities make, and have made for generations.

One of the first countries to act on this matter was Panama, where several large indigenous communities have lived for hundreds of years and have created (and continue creating) strong and diverse cultures. The trigger for the piece of legislation that the Legislative Assembly of Panama passed in 2000 for the protection of certain handicrafts—only those that have the meaning of cultural identification are covered—was the abundant making of "molas" (or "dule mor," in native language) by textile producers, who exported them to the United States, where they are much appreciated. "Molas" are a hand-made textile, usually of cotton, that is used by Kuna women in making blouses. They are adorned with very colorful geometrical motives, which were taken from the designs that the Kunas would paint on their bodies before the arrival of the Spanish colonizers.

Traditional communities, with the assistance of the country's industrial property office, lobbied the national assembly for the adoption of a legal mechanism that protected their interests in handicrafts. The result was the first and second texts that follow.

There is, however, an important shortcoming in Panama's initiative, as commendable as it may be. Its scope of application does not go beyond national borders, because there is no international treaty acknowledging (and granting national treatment to) the protection of handicrafts. Panama's law goes as far as according protection to foreign handicrafts provided that the countries where they are originated admit reciprocity.[99] *But, for example, in order to have other countries protecting genuine "molas," Panama had to ensure the registration of a mark of certification—both of origin and of compliance with the traditional standard techniques of the Kunas—in that country. In this manner, the international protection of the certification mark is (to some extent*[100]*) ensured by the Paris Convention, under the national treatment principle—and thus, indirectly, the subject matter of the certification.*

The third of the following texts corresponds to a proposal made in WIPO aiming at introducing in a Treaty on Design Law that has been under discussion for several years, a new requirement for the registration of industrial designs: the acknowledgment by the designer, if that is the case, of the traditional source where the inspiration has come

99. Multilateral treaties on industrial property (namely, the Paris Convention and the TRIPS Agreement) do not accept reciprocal treatment between Contracting Parties. But the case of Panama is different because the protection accorded to traditional handicrafts is beyond the scope of those two treaties.

100. Certification marks are not protected as such by the Paris Convention or the TRIPS Agreement, but only as distinctive marks (either individually or collectively owned) and as geographical indications—where the certification concerns the geographical origin, not the compliance with technical standards.

from. This is a requirement parallel to that being negotiated (thus far unsuccessfully) in the WTO aiming at introducing the obligation to indicate the origin of a genetic resource or piece of traditional knowledge eventually used in the making of an invention for which a patent is applied. Some countries have introduced this requirement in their national statutes. In WIPO, the proposal concerning industrial designs has been introduced by the African Group.

The background of these texts has factual support, even if it is generally closer to matters of cultural perception than to violation of rights. A recent controversy about cultural (mis)appropriation that erupted while this book was being written involved the well-known United States fashion house Tory Burch and the wrong designation of a tunic sweater of unequivocal Portuguese flavor as being "Baja-inspired" (Baja being the abbreviation of the state of Baja California, in Mexico). The tunic, albeit with some minor differences, imitated very closely the design and the ornamental embroideries of a typical sweater that Portuguese fishermen from a village in the North of Portugal (Póvoa do Varzim, a fishing village in the North of Portugal) have used since the beginning of the nineteenth century. Today the garment is seen during local religious events. It is made of white, thick woollen thread, with traditional Portuguese figurative embroideries, in black and red colors. It is sold by local weavers in Póvoa do Varzim for less than 40 euros, whereas Tony Burch's model was priced at 695 euros. This act of cultural (mis)appropriation has generated a strong reaction in the Portuguese media and has been echoed in some international media.[101]
Unlike Panama, Portugal has no intellectual property law that protects Póvoa do Varzim creators and manufacturers against the (mis)appropriation of a design that has been incorporated into the village's cultural heritage.[102] *But even if it had, as said, such protection would be limited to its national territory. It is not even impossible that the same design has been used by Portuguese clothmakers in other parts of the country, which, if true, would destroy the association of the design with its specific geographical and cultural origin.*

In the case of Tory Burch's sweater, the matter is of imitation (given that there were some differences between the two sweaters) and, for some reason that is not very clear, of public deception (to the extent that, initially, the fashion house claimed an association of the sweater's design with a false geographical origin). And yet, at the current stage,

101. The international media more recently reported on another complaint of cultural appropriation. THE TELEGRAPH of June 1, 2021 reported on a letter that the Minister of Culture of Mexico wrote to a number of fashion houses, including Zara and Anthropology, claiming that some of the garments they sold borrowed designs, patterns, and figurative motives created by some Mexican indigenous peoples. According to the report, the Minister is seeking a "public explanation on what basis (those companies) could privatise collective property."
102. In 2002 Portugal's Council of Ministers enacted a Decree-Law (No. 118/2002, of April 18) aimed at the protection of traditional knowledge associated with autochthonous plant varieties. As drafted, the statute is confined to autochthonous plant varieties and their functional uses (medicines, culinary recipes, handicrafts), which means that the use of raw materials that are not autochthonous, such as sheep wool, make the concerned products ineligible for protection. Moreover, the Decree-Law needed to be complemented by a regulation, so that it could be applicable, which it has not been.

there is no intellectual property protection that the designers and manufacturers of Póvoa do Varzim can claim other than, eventually, the protection that applies to geographical indications.

The issue of cultural (mis)appropriation faces two problems—which current intellectual property cannot overcome: the collective nature of the creation, and the absence of time boundaries. Eventually, if some government wished to resort to the industrial design regime to protect traditional textiles, it could pass a statute granting perpetual protection, following the example of article 18 of the law of March 18, 1806, which dealt with the filing of designs with the Council of prud'hommes of Lyon.[103] *But intellectual property is granted to individuals or, in the case of creations generated in an entrepreneurial scenario, to employers. This is exactly one of the problems that traditional communities have in claiming ownership of traditional knowledge and cultural expressions. Those creations are collectively made, which is an obstacle to the acknowledgment of intellectual property in them, given that patents are granted to specifically identified inventors, and copyrights, to specifically identified authors—even if they wish to remain anonymous.*

If the claim of infringement is difficult, if not impossible, to prove in a case like Tory Burch's, which was no less than straight imitation, it will be even more difficult when the fashion house takes a traditional design as a source of inspiration, to which the designer adds his/her own flash of creativity. It is this that explains the reluctance of a large number of WIPO Member States to accept the African Group's proposal.

§ 2.74.1 Panama Adopts a Statute Protecting the Collective Rights of Communities in Traditional Designs (And Other Creations)—2000

Legislative Assembly

Law Nr. 20

June 26, 2000

On the special intellectual property regime of collective rights of indigenous communities, for the protection of their cultural identities and traditional knowledge, and whereby it sets forth other provisions

The Legislative Assembly decrees:

Chapter 1—Purpose

Article 1. The purpose of this law is to protect the collective rights of intellectual property and traditional knowledge of the indigenous communities in their creations, such as inventions, models, drawings and designs, innovations contained in the pictures, figures, symbols, illustrations, old carved stones and others;

103. Protection was granted for one, three, or five years, or perpetually, as designated by the filer. *See supra* § 2.43.4.

likewise, [to protect] the cultural elements of their history, music, art and traditional artistic expressions, susceptible of commercial use, through a special registration system, promotion, commercialization of their rights in order to stand out the value of the indigenous cultures and to apply social justice.

Article 2. The customs, traditions, beliefs, spirituality, religiosity, folkloric expressions, artistic manifestations, traditional knowledge and any other type of traditional expressions of the indigenous communities, constitute part of their cultural assets: consequently, they cannot be the subject of any form of exclusive right of unauthorized third parties under the intellectual property system such as copyrights, industrial models, trademarks, geographical indications and others, unless the application is filed by the indigenous community. However, rights previously recognized under the legislation on that matter will be respected and will not be affected.

Chapter II—Objects Susceptible of Protection

Article 3. The dresses used by the communities of Kuna, Ngobe and Bugle, Embera and Wounaan, Naso and Bre-bre are recognized as traditional dresses of indigenous communities, such as:

Dule Mor. It consists in the combined use of the garment by which the Kuna men and women identify the culture, history, and representation of their community. These are constituted by Morsen, Saburedi, Olassu and Wini.

Jio. It consists of the combined use of the garment by which the Emberas and the Wounaán men and women identify the culture, history and representation of their community. The women use Ua (Paruma), Boró Barí, Dyidi, Kondita, Neta, Parata Kerá, Manía, Soritja Kipará (Jagua), Karichí (achiote), and Kera Patura. The men use the same garments with exception of the Paruma, and also use earflaps, breast straps, Amburá and Andiá.

Nahua. It consists of the garment by which the Ngobes and Buglés identify the culture, history, and representation of their community. This dress is of a single piece. It is wide and it covers half of the leg; it is made with plain cloths of attractive colors, decorated with geometric applications of the cloths of contrasting colors and it includes a wide necklace made with chaquiras. The technical description of these traditional dresses will be contained in their respective registrations.

Article 4. The collective rights of the indigenous communities are recognized in their musical instruments, music, dances or form of performance, oral and written expressions contained in their traditions that constitute their historical, cosmological and cultural expression.

The application for registration of these collective rights shall be filed by the respective general congresses or indigenous traditional authorities, with the General Office for the Registry of the Industrial Property of the Ministry of the Commerce and Industry, hereinafter referred to as DIGERPI, or with the National Copyright Office of the Ministry of Education, depending on the case, for its approval and registration.

Article 5. The collective rights of the indigenous communities are recognized in their working tools and traditional art, as well as the techniques for making them, expressed in the national basic materials, through the elements of the nature, their method or process, elaboration, combination of natural dyes, such as the carved tagua (ivory plant) and wood (cocobolo and nazareno), traditional baskets, nuchus, chaquiras, chacaras and every other cultural expression of traditional aspects of these communities.

The registration of these rights shall be requested by the general congresses or indigenous traditional authorities to the offices mentioned in the previous article.

Article 6. Registrable objects susceptible of protection, as this Law determines to protect their originality and authenticity, are deemed to be [subject to] collective rights.

Chapter III—Registration of Collective Rights

Article 7. The department of Collective Rights and Folkloric Expressions shall be created within DIGERPI, through which, among others, the registration of the collective rights of the indigenous communities will be granted.

This registration shall be requested by the general congresses or indigenous traditional authorities in order to protect their dresses, arts, music and any other traditional rights susceptible of protection.

The registrations of the collective rights of the indigenous communities will not expire, nor will have [limited] duration. The procedure before DIGERPI will not require the service of a lawyer and it is exempt from any payment. The administrative appeals against this registration shall be notified personally to the representative of the general congresses or indigenous traditional authorities.

Article 8. The provisions on collective and certification marks contained in Law nr. 35, of 1996 [the law on industrial property], will be applicable to the present regime, as long as they do not harm the rights recognized in the present Law.

Article 9. DIGERPI will create a position of examiner of indigenous collective rights, for the protection of the intellectual property and other traditional rights of the indigenous communities. This public officer will be in charge of examining all the applications that are filed before DIGERPI related with the collective rights of the indigenous communities, so that the registration be not granted against this law.

Chapter IV—Promotion of the Indigenous Arts and Cultural Expressions ...

Chapter V—Rights of Use and Commercialization

Article 15. The rights of use and commercialization of the art, crafts and other cultural expressions based on the tradition of the indigenous community, shall be governed by each indigenous community's regulation, once approved and registered in DIGERPI or in the National Copyright Office of the Ministry of Education, according to the case. ...

Chapter VI—Prohibitions and Sanctions

Article 17. The literal j is added to the article 439 of the Fiscal Code, as follows:

Article 439. Foreign goods originating from all countries can be imported except the following:

j. *Non-original products, recorded, embroidered, woven, or any other articles that imitate, in whole or in part, the making of the traditional dresses of the indigenous communities, as well as musical instruments and traditional artistic works of these communities.*

Article 18. The numeral 7 is added to the article 16 of the Law 30 of 1984, as follows:

Article 16. The following acts constitute crimes of smuggling:

7. *The possession of non-original, undeclared, or unauthorized goods in transit, under the custom regulation, that imitate in whole or partly, the traditional garments of the Panamanian indigenous communities, as well as the materials and musical instruments and artistic or handmade works of these communities.*

Article 20. The industrial reproduction, either total or partial, of the traditional dresses and other collective rights recognized in this Law, is forbidden, unless it is authorized by the Ministry of Commerce and Industry, with the previous and express consent of the general congresses and indigenous council, and if it is not against the provision established hereon.

Article 21. In the cases not contemplated in the customs law as well as in that on industrial property, the infringement of this Law will be sanctioned, depending on the seriousness of the act, with a fine between one thousand dollars ($1,000.00) and five thousand dollars (B/.5,000.00). In the case of recividism, the fine will be doubled. The sanctions established herein shall apply in addition to the forfeiture and destruction of the products in violation of this law. ...

Article 22. The following authorities are vested with legal power to prosecute the offenders of this Law, to take preventive measures concerning the respective products and goods, and to forward them to the corresponding appointed public officers:

1. The regional governor or the county governor, in case the first one does not exist.
2. The general congress of the respective district. For those effects, traditional authorities may request the cooperation and the support of the Public Force.

Article 23. The small non-indigenous artisans that dedicate themselves to the manufacture, production and sale of the reproduction of crafts belonging to indigenous Ngobes and Buglés that reside in the districts of Tolé, Remedios, San Félix and San Lorenzo of the Province of Chiriqui, are exempt from this law. Those small non-indigenous artisans may manufacture and market those reproductions, but they may not claim the collective rights recognized by this Law to the indigenous group.

Chapter VII—Final Provisions

Article 24. As from the day this law enters into force, the small non-indigenous artisans who dedicate themselves to the elaboration, reproduction and sale of traditional indigenous crafts registered in the General Office of National Craftsmanship, may carry out those activities, with the awareness of the indigenous traditional authorities.

The Ministry of Commerce and Industry, upon the previous verification of the registration date and the issuance of a license, will issue the respective permits and authorizations. However, the Panamanian non-indigenous artisans shall affix, print, write or identify in easily visible way that the product is a reproduction, as well as its origin.

Article 25. For the purposes of the protection, use and marketing of the intellectual property collective rights of the indigenous communities provided for by this Law, the artistic and traditional expressions of other countries are eligible for the same benefits set forth herein, under agreements of reciprocity with those countries.

Article 26. This Law will be regulated by the Executive Branch through the Ministry of Commerce and Industry. ...

§ 2.74.2 Regulation on the Use of the Kuna People's Collective Right—2001

Regulation of the use of the "Mola Kuna Panama" Collective Right

(*Morra* in Kuna language)

Chapter I—Object

Article 1. The purpose of this regulation is to set the conditions and guidelines that must be followed in the use of "Mola Kuna Panama" collective right (from now on Collective Right), as this is an art, a traditional knowledge that belongs to the Kuna indigenous people; therefore, it is the property of the collectivity and not of specific individuals who are part of said people. It has been transmitted from generation to generation, and, therefore, it is the intellectual property of the Kuna people.

Chapter II—Definition

Article 2. It is understood by Mola Kuna Panama or Morra Kuna Panama: Application of a small decorative piece to a larger piece of fabric reversely worked. Combination of canvases with colorful and varied colors. The technique used is based on the artisanal branch of embroidery (applied). They are made manually and contain two or more layers of canvases cut and sewn one on top of the other, so as to show the colors of the lower canvases. The Mola motifs are based on the Kuna people's worldvision, or they simply use designs with geographical or natural motives. The dress of the Kuna woman called "dule mor" is also understood as "mola kuna Panama."

Chapter III—Emblem

Article 3. The "Mola Kuna Panama" Collective Right, in addition to be identified in written form, is presented with the emblem of Kuna origin "Los Kalus," using the design of one of them: "Kalus Tukbis, Art of women." ...

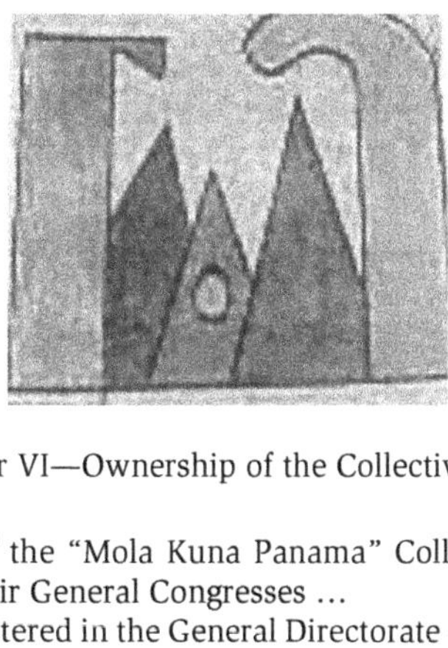

Chapter VI—Ownership of the Collective Right

Article 6: The owner of the "Mola Kuna Panama" Collective Right is the Kuna People, organized in their General Congresses ...

The same are registered in the General Directorate of the Industrial Property Registry (DIGERPI) of the Ministry of Commerce and Industries (MICI).

Paragraph. The owners of the Mola Kuna Panama Collective Right are the members of the Kuna people, especially the Kuna women who make mola.

Article 8. All owners who make mola must write, fix and/or stamp on their products "Mola Kuna Panama" and the emblem (Kalu Ducbis), without prejudice to the fact that organizations or individuals may also use their own distinctive signs. ...

Article 23. Panamanian non-Kuna artisans must fix, print, write or identify in an easily visible way, the identification of their work and the origin and state that they are not made by Kuna hands.

Article 24. The reproduction, stamping, serigraphy or other engravings that imitate the Mola Kuna Panama Collective Right without the owners' authorization, is prohibited.

Article 25. The use of Mola Kuna Panama in industrial reproduction by non-Kuna, must have the consent of the holders of collective knowledge.

§ 2.74.3 Proposal for a Requirement Concerning the Disclosure of Origin of Traditional Designs (To Be Introduced in a Future WIPO Design Law Treaty)—2015

Standing Committee on the Law of Trademarks, Industrial Designs and Geographical Indications

Thirty-Third Session

Geneva, March 16-20, 2015

Industrial Design Law and Practice—Draft Articles

Introduction

1. At its forty-fourth (23rd extraordinary) session, held in Geneva from December 10-12, 2013, the WIPO General Assembly, adopted the following text:

"The WIPO General Assembly:

"(a) requests the SCT to finalize its work on the text of the basic proposal for a Design Law Treaty building upon the outcome of the thirtieth session of the SCT;

"(b) will at the Extraordinary Session of the General Assembly in May 2014 take stock of and consider the text, progress made, and decide on whether to convene a diplomatic conference in 2014 in Moscow. If the Extraordinary Session of the General Assembly in May so decides, a preparatory committee will be held immediately after that session of the General Assembly." ...

14. The following provisions are the subject of alternative options or proposals supported by several delegations:

(i) Article 3(1)(a)(ix), concerning a disclosure requirement in design applications for subject matter using, or directly based on, traditional knowledge, traditional cultural expressions or genetic resources; ...

Article 3 Application

(1) [Contents of Application; Fee] (a) A Contracting Party may require that an application contain some, or all, of the following indications or elements: ...

[(ix) where the subject matter claimed in the industrial design application includes utilization of, or is directly based on genetic resources, their derivatives and the associated traditional knowledge, traditional knowledge, or one or more traditional cultural expressions, each party shall require applicants to: (1) disclose the country of origin, or if unknown, source of the genetic resources or their derivatives, traditional knowledge, or one or more traditional cultural expressions; (2) provide relevant information, as required by the national law of the Intellectual Property Office, regarding compliance with access and benefit-sharing requirements, including prior informed consent; (3) if the source and or country of origin is not known, make a declaration to that effect;][6,7]

Notes:

[6] The following Delegations rejected the proposal by the African Group: the Czech Republic, on behalf of CEBS Group, the European Union, on behalf of the European Union and its twenty-eight Member States, Germany, Japan, on behalf of Group B and on its national capacity, Norway, Republic of Korea, Spain, Switzerland, United Kingdom and the United States of America. They were of the view that the amendment felt outside the scope and objectives of the draft DLT and would not contribute to the harmonization or the simplification of design law formalities.

[7] The African Group rejects the arguments made in the preceding footnote. The African Group considers that the treaty is not finalized yet and that a disclosure requirement is a formality which is essential for the protection against misuse and misappropriation of traditional designs. The proposal was supported by the Delegations of India and Iran (Islamic Republic of) for its inclusion in the text.

Figure 50 Left, Tory Burch's creation, inspired by the traditional woollen sweater from Póvoa de Varzim, Portugal. Right: a sweater created and made in Póvoa de Varzim.

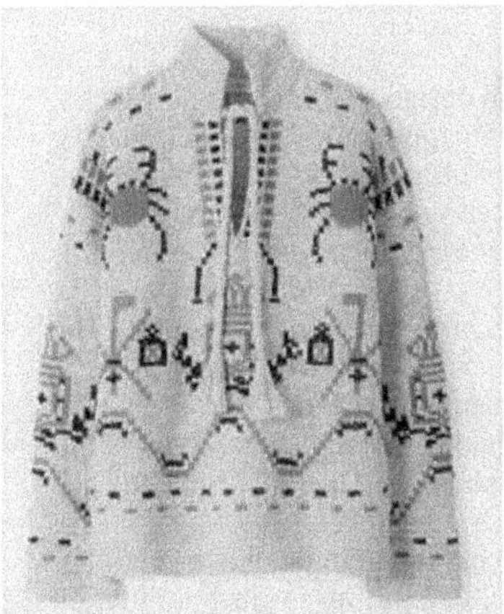

§ 2.75 UNITED STATES CONGRESS RECEIVES A BILL (BUT DOES NOT SUBMIT IT TO VOTE) AIMED AT PROVIDING SPECIAL PROTECTION FOR FASHION DESIGNS—2011

Joining an international movement of according particular attention to fashion designs, whose protection in the United States is, to say the least, inadequate (some commentators would go as far as saying that such protection in practice does not exist), in 2011 a group of representatives introduced in the House a bill aimed at extending copyright protection to fashion designs. The bill has not been submitted to vote. Targeting fashion designs specifically, if approved, the bill would have greatly increased the protection of those designs by proposing, among other measures, to cover designs without the need for registration. The definition of originality was also very broad (but some opponents would say that it was still too strict, because of the requirement that the new design be "nontrivial," which might be read as denying protection to a combination of trivial variations—which is common in fashion designs).

The bill provided for an exception concerning the use of protected designs within the limits of home sewing. This same exception had already been included in the 1352 regulations of Abbeville concerning the mandatory use of marks and strings to identify the cloths made in the city and prohibiting the sale in the city of those cloths without those signs—except the cloths made for dressing the families of their makers (see § 1.06).

The text that follows aimed at consolidating the current provisions of the Unites States Copyright Act (Title 17) and included the most relevant excerpts of the provisions that would be amended or added by the bill—H.R. 2511, of July 13, 2011, "Innovative Design Protection and Piracy Prevention Act." New or modified language appears in italics.

U.S.C. Title 17, Section 1301

(a) Designs Protected.—
  (1) In general.—
  The designer or other owner of an original design of a useful article which makes the article attractive or distinctive in appearance to the purchasing or using public may secure the protection provided by this chapter upon complying with and subject to this chapter. ...
  (4) *Fashion Design.—A fashion design is subject to protection under this chapter.*

(b) Definitions.—For the purpose of this chapter, the following terms have the following meanings:
  (1) A design is "original" if it is the result of the designer's creative endeavor that provides a distinguishable variation over prior work pertaining to similar articles which is more than merely trivial and has not been copied from another source.
  (2) A "useful article" is a vessel hull or deck, including a plug or mold, *or an article of apparel,* which in normal use has an intrinsic utilitarian function that is not merely to portray the appearance of the article or to convey information. An article which normally is part of a useful article shall be deemed to be a useful article. ...
  (7) *A "fashion design"—*

(A) *is the appearance as a whole of an article of apparel, including its ornamentation;*

(B) *includes original elements of the article of apparel or the original arrangement or placement of original or non-original elements as incorporated in the overall appearance of the article of apparel that—*

(i) *are the result of a designer's own creative endeavor; and*

(ii) *provide a unique, distinguishable, non-trivial and non-utilitarian variation over prior designs for similar types of articles.*

(8) *The term "design" includes fashion design, ...*

(9) *The term "apparel" means—*

(A) *an article of men's, women's, or children's clothing, including undergarments, outerwear, gloves, footwear, and headgear;*

(B) *handbags, purses, wallets, tote bags, and belts; and*

(C) *eyeglass frames.*

(10) *In the case of a fashion design, the term "substantially identical" means an article of apparel which is so similar in appearance as to be likely to be mistaken for the protected design, and contains only those differences in construction or design which are merely trivial.*

Rule of Construction.—In the case of a fashion design under this chapter, those differences or variations which are considered non-trivial for the purposes of establishing that a design is subject to protection under subsection (b)(7) shall be considered non-trivial for the purposes of establishing that a defendant's design is not substantially identical under subsection (b)(10) and section 1309(e).

U.S.C. Title 17, Section 1302(5)

Designs not subject to protection

Protection under this chapter shall not be available for a design that is—

(1) not original;

(2) staple or commonplace, such as a standard geometric figure, a familiar symbol, an emblem, or a motif, or another shape, pattern, or configuration which has become standard, common, prevalent, or ordinary;

(3) different from a design excluded by paragraph (2) only in insignificant details or in elements which are variants commonly used in the relevant trades;

(4) dictated solely by a utilitarian function of the article that embodies it; or

(5)(A) embodied in a useful article that was made public by the designer or owner in the United States or a foreign country more than 2 years before the date of the application for registration under this chapter.

(B) *in the case of a fashion design, embodied in a useful article that was made public by the designer or owner in the United States or a foreign country before the date of enactment of this chapter or more than 3 years before the date upon which protection of the design is asserted under this chapter.*

U.S.C. Title 17, Section 1303

Revisions, adaptations, and rearrangements

Protection for a design under this chapter shall be available notwithstanding the employment in the design of subject matter excluded from protection under section 1302 if the design is a substantial revision, adaptation, or rearrangement of such subject matter. Such protection shall be independent of any subsisting protection in subject matter employed in the design, and shall not be construed as securing any right to subject matter excluded from protection under this chapter or as extending any subsisting protection under this chapter. *The presence or absence of a particular color or colors or of a pictorial or graphic work imprinted on fabric shall not be considered in determining the protection of a fashion design under section 1301 or 1302 or in determining infringement under section 1309.*

U.S.C. Title 17, Section 1305(a)

Term of protection

(a) IN GENERAL.—Subject to subsection (b), the protection provided under this chapter—...

(2) *for a fashion design, shall continue for a term of 3 years beginning on the date of the commencement of protection under section 1304.*

(b) Expiration.—

All terms of protection provided in this section shall run to the end of the calendar year in which they would otherwise expire.

(c) Termination of Rights.—

Upon expiration or termination of protection in a particular design under this chapter, all rights under this chapter in the design shall terminate, regardless of the number of different articles in which the design may have been used during the term of its protection.

U.S.C. Title 17, Section 1309

Infringement

(e) Infringing article defined.—

(1) *In general.—As used in this section, an "infringing article" is any article the design of which has been copied from a design protected under this chapter, or from an image thereof, without the consent of the owner of the protected design. An infringing article is not an illustration or picture of a protected design in an advertisement, book, periodical, newspaper, photograph, broadcast, motion picture, or similar medium. ...*

(3) *Fashion design.—In the case of a fashion design, a design shall not be deemed to have been copied from a protected design if that design—*

  (A) *is not substantially identical in overall visual appearance to and as to the original elements of a protected design; or*

  (B) *is the result of independent creation.*

(h) Home sewing exception.—

  (1) *In general.—It is not an infringement of the exclusive rights of a design owner for a person to produce a single copy of a protected design for*

personal use or for the use of an immediate family member, if that copy is not offered for sale or use in trade during the period of protection.

(2) *Rule of construction.—Nothing in this subsection shall be construed to permit the publication or distribution of instructions or patterns for the copying of a protected design."*

U.S.C. Title 17, Section 1310(5)

Application for registration

(a) Time Limit for Application for Registration.—Protection under this chapter shall be lost if application for registration of the design is not made within 2 years after the date on which the design is first made public. R*egistration shall not apply to fashion designs.*

U.S.C. Title 17, Section 1321

Remedy for infringement

...

(2) *Fashion design.—In the case of a fashion design, the owner of a design is entitled to institute an action for any infringement of the design after the design is made public under the terms of section 1310(b) of this chapter. ...*
   (e) *Pleading requirement for fashion designs.—*
      (1) *In general.—In the case of a fashion design, a claimant in an action for infringement shall plead with particularity facts establishing that—*
         (A) *the design of the claimant is a fashion design within the meaning of section 1301(a)(7) of this title and thus entitled to protection under this chapter;*
         (B) *the design of the defendant infringes upon the protected design as described under section 1309(e); and*
         (C) *the protected design or an image thereof was available in such location or locations, in such a manner, and for such duration that it can be reasonably inferred from the totality of the surrounding facts and circumstances that the defendant saw or otherwise had knowledge of the protected design.*
      (2) *Considerations.—In considering whether a claim for infringement has been adequately pleaded, the court shall consider the totality of the circumstances. ...*

§ 2.76 THE UNITED STATES SUPREME COURT HOLDS THAT SOME TWO-DIMENSIONAL FASHION DESIGNS ARE COPYRIGHTABLE—2017

In 2017, the United States Supreme Court made it clear that certain fashion designs are copyrightable, provided they are separable from the utilitarian object in which they are inserted or printed. The Court was referring in particular to ornaments that a manufacturer of cheerleading uniforms printed on those uniforms. The Court understood that the fact that the ornaments were printed on the uniforms did not make of them a utilitarian feature in itself because they existed independently of the uniforms—they could also be applied to other garments.

This decision is somewhat useful for the fashion industry, but still suffers from serious limitations. It could apply to protect certain designs and ornaments that the fashion industry applies to make apparel, shoes, and bags appealing to the consumer's eye. Therefore, new patterns of Louis Vuitton's monogram canvas or Dolce & Gabbana's new floral motives could be copyrighted in the United States, to the extent that they are applied to a large variety of articles, which means that they exist independently from each of those articles.

However, the same would not be true as far as the three-dimensional designs for the dresses, the bags, the shoes, etc., are concerned. In that case, the designs are inseparable from the articles and thus are not copyrightable. Anyway, it is true that a copyright approach to the protection of designs is much more flexible and easy to obtain than the alternative patent protection that is offered by Section 171 of Title 35 of the United States Code.

Supreme Court of the United States

Star Athletica, LLC. v. Varsity Brands, Inc.

March 22, 2017

580 U. S. ____ (2017)

Justice Thomas delivered the opinion of the Court.

Congress has provided copyright protection for original works of art, but not for industrial designs. The line between art and industrial design, however, is often difficult to draw. This is particularly true when an industrial design incorporates artistic elements. Congress has afforded limited protection for these artistic elements by providing that "pictorial, graphic, or sculptural features" of the "design of a useful article" are eligible for copyright protection as artistic works if those features "can be identified separately from, and are capable of existing independently of, the utilitarian aspects of the article." 17 U. S. C. §101.

We granted certiorari to resolve widespread disagreement over the proper test for implementing §101's separate-identification and independent-existence requirements. ... We hold that a feature incorporated into the design of a useful article is eligible for copyright protection only if the feature (1) can be perceived as a two- or three-dimensional work of art separate from the useful article and (2) would qualify as a protectable pictorial, graphic, or sculptural work—either on its own or fixed in some other tangible medium of expression—if it were imagined separately from the useful article into which it is incorporated. Because that test is satisfied in this case, we affirm.

I. Respondents *Varsity Brands, Inc., Varsity Spirit Corporation, and Varsity Spirit Fashions & Supplies, Inc.*, design, make, and sell cheerleading uniforms. Respondents have obtained or acquired more than 200 U. S. copyright registrations for two-dimensional designs appearing on the surface of their uniforms and other garments. These designs are primarily "combinations, positionings, and arrangements of elements" that include "chevrons ..., lines, curves, stripes, angles, diagonals, inverted [chevrons], coloring, and shapes." ...

Petitioner *Star Athletica, L. L. C.*, also markets and sells cheerleading uniforms. Respondents sued petitioner for infringing their copyrights in the five designs. The District Court entered summary judgment for petitioner on respondents' copyright claims on the ground that the designs did not qualify as protectable pictorial, graphic, or sculptural works. It reasoned that the designs served the useful, or "utilitarian," function of identifying the garments as "cheerleading uniforms" and therefore could not be "physically or conceptually" separated under §101 "from the utilitarian function" of the uniform. ... The Court of Appeals for the Sixth Circuit reversed. ... In its view, the "graphic designs" were "separately identifiable" because the designs "and ablank cheerleading uniform can appear 'side by side'—one as a graphic design, and one as a cheerleading uniform." ... And it determined that the designs were "'capable of existing independently'" because they could be incorporated onto the surface of different types of garments, or hung on the wall and framed.

Judge McKeague dissented. He would have held that, because "identifying the wearer as a cheerleader" is a utilitarian function of a cheerleading uniform and the surface designs were "integral to" achieving that function, the designs were inseparable from the uniforms. ...

II. The first element of a copyright-infringement claim is "ownership of a valid copyright." ... A valid copyright extends only to copyrightable subject matter. ... The Copyright Act of 1976 defines copyrightable subject matter as "original works of authorship fixed in any tangible medium of expression." 17 U. S. C. §102(a).

"Works of authorship" include "pictorial, graphic, and sculptural works," §102(a)(5), which the statute defines to include "two-dimensional and three-dimensional works of fine, graphic, and applied art, photographs, prints and art reproductions, maps, globes, charts, diagrams, models, and technical drawings, including architectural plans," §101. And a work of authorship is "'fixed' in a tangible medium of expression when it [is] embodi[ed] in a" "material objec[t] ... from which the work can be perceived, reproduced, or otherwise communicated." *Ibid.* (definitions of "fixed" and "copies"). The Copyright Act also establishes a special rule for copyrighting a pictorial, graphic, or sculptural work incorporated into a "useful article," which is defined as "an article having an intrinsic utilitarian function that is not merely to portray the appearance of the article or to convey information." *Ibid.* The statute does not protect useful articles as such. Rather, "the design of a useful article" is "considered a pictorial, graphical, or sculptural work only if, and only to the extent that, such design incorporates pictorial, graphic, or sculptural features that can be identified separately from, and are capable of existing independently of, the utilitarian aspects of the article." *Ibid.*

Courts, the Copyright Office, and commentators have described the analysis undertaken to determine whether a feature can be separately identified from, and exist independently of, a useful article as "separability." In this case, our task is to determine whether the arrangements of lines, chevrons, and colorful shapes appearing on the surface of respondents' cheerleading uniforms are eligible for copyright protection as separable features of the design of those cheerleading uniforms. ...

B. We must now decide when a feature incorporated into a useful article "can be identified separately from" and is "capable of existing independently of " "the utilitarian aspects" of the article. ...

1. The statute provides that a "pictorial, graphic, or sculptural featur[e]" incorporated into the "design of a useful article" is eligible for copyright protection if it (1) "can be identified separately from," and (2) is "capable of existing independently of, the utilitarian aspects of the article." §101. The first requirement—separate identification—is not onerous. The decisionmaker need only be able to look at the useful article and spot some two- or three-dimensional element that appears to have pictorial, graphic, or sculptural qualities. ...

The independent-existence requirement is ordinarily more difficult to satisfy. The decisionmaker must determine that the separately identified feature has the capacity to exist apart from the utilitarian aspects of the article. ... In other words, the feature must be able to exist as its own pictorial, graphic, or sculptural work as defined in §101 once it is imagined apart from the useful article. If the feature is not capable of existing as a pictorial, graphic, or sculptural work once separated from the useful article, then it was not a pictorial, graphic, or sculptural feature of that article, but rather one of its utilitarian aspects.

Of course, to qualify as a pictorial, graphic, or sculptural work on its own, the feature cannot itself be a useful article or "[a]n article that is normally a part of a useful article" (which is itself considered a useful article). §101. Nor could someone claim a copyright in a useful article merely by creating a replica of that article in some other medium—for example, a cardboard model of a car. Although the replica could itself be copyrightable, it would not give rise to any rights in the useful article that inspired it.

2. The statute as a whole confirms our interpretation. The Copyright Act provides "the owner of [a] copyright" with the "exclusive righ[t] ... to reproduce the copyrighted work in copies." §106(1). The statute clarifies that this right "includes the right to reproduce the [copyrighted] work in or on any kind of article, whether useful or otherwise." §113(a). Section 101 is, in essence, the mirror image of §113(a). Whereas §113(a) protects a work of authorship first fixed in some tangible medium other than a useful article and subsequently applied to a useful article, §101 protects art first fixed in the medium of a useful article. The two provisions make clear that copyright protection extends to pictorial, graphic, and sculptural works regardless of whether they were created as freestanding art or as features of useful articles. The ultimate separability question, then, is whether the feature for which copyright protection is claimed would have been eligible for copyright protection as a pictorial, graphic, or sculptural work had it originally been fixed in some tangible medium other than a useful article before being applied to a useful article.

3. This interpretation is also consistent with the history of the Copyright Act. In *Mazer*, a case decided under the 1909 Copyright Act, the respondents copyrighted a statuette depicting a dancer. The statuette was intended for use as a lamp base, "with electric wiring, sockets and lampshades attached." 347 U. S., at 202. Copies of the statuette were sold both as lamp bases and separately as statuettes. *Id.*, at 203. The petitioners copied the statuette and sold lamps with the statuette as the base. They defended against the respondents' infringement suit by arguing that the respondents did not have a copyright in a statuette intended for use as a lamp base. *Id.*, at 204–205.

Two of *Mazer*'s holdings are relevant here. First, the Court held that the respondents owned a copyright in the statuette even though it was intended for use as a lamp base. *See id.*, at 214. In doing so, the Court approved the Copyright Office's regulation extending copyright protection to works of art that might also serve a useful purpose. ...

Second, the Court held that it was irrelevant to the copyright inquiry whether the statuette was initially created as a freestanding sculpture or as a lamp base. 347 U. S., at 218–219 ("Nor do we think the subsequent registration of a work of art published as an element in a manufactured article, is a misuse of copyright. This is not different from the registration of a statuette and its later embodiment in an industrial article"). *Mazer* thus interpreted the 1909 Act consistently with the rule discussed above: If a design would have been copyrightable as a standalone pictorial, graphic, or sculptural work, it is copyrightable if created first as part of a useful article.

Shortly thereafter, the Copyright Office enacted a regulation implementing the holdings of *Mazer*. ... As amended, the regulation introduced the modern separability test to copyright law:

> If the sole intrinsic function of an article is its utility, the fact that the article is unique and attractively shaped will not qualify it as a work of art. However, if the shape of a utilitarian article incorporates features, such as artistic sculpture, carving, or pictorial representation, which can be identified separately and are capable of existing independently as a work of art, such features will be eligible for registration. ...

Congress essentially lifted the language governing protection for the design of a useful article directly from the post-*Mazer* regulations and placed it into §101 of the 1976 Act. Consistent with *Mazer*, the approach we outline today interprets §§101 and 113 in a way that would afford copyright protection to the statuette in *Mazer* regardless of whether it was first created as a standalone sculptural work or as the base of the lamp. *See* 347 U. S., at 218–219.

C. In sum, a feature of the design of a useful article is eligible for copyright if, when identified and imagined apart from the useful article, it would qualify as a pictorial, graphic, or sculptural work either on its own or when fixed in some other tangible medium.

Applying this test to the surface decorations on the cheerleading uniforms is straightforward. First, one can identify the decorations as features having pictorial, graphic, or sculptural qualities. Second, if the arrangement of colors, shapes, stripes, and chevrons on the surface of the cheerleading uniforms were separated from the uniform and applied in another medium—for example, on a painter's canvas—they would qualify as "two-dimensional ... works of ... art," §101. And imaginatively removing the surface decorations from the uniforms and applying them in another medium would not replicate the uniform itself. Indeed, respondents have applied the designs in this case to other media of expression—different types of clothing—without replicating the uniform. ... The decorations are therefore separable from the uniforms and eligible for copyright protection.[104]

The dissent argues that the designs are not separable because imaginatively removing them from the uniforms and placing them in some other medium of expression—a canvas, for example—would create "pictures of cheerleader uniforms." ... Petitioner similarly argues that the decorations cannot be copyrighted because, even when extracted from the useful article, they retain the outline of a cheerleading uniform. ...

This is not a bar to copyright. Just as two-dimensional fine art corresponds to the shape of the canvas on which it is painted, two-dimensional applied art correlates to the contours of the article on which it is applied. A fresco painted on a wall, ceiling panel, or dome would not lose copyright protection, for example, simply because it was designed to track the dimensions of the surface on which it was painted. Or consider, for example, a design etched or painted on the surface of a guitar. If that entire design is imaginatively removed from the guitar's surface and placed on an album cover, it would still resemble the shape of a guitar. But the image on the cover does not "replicate" the guitar as a useful article. Rather, the design is a two-dimensional work of art that corresponds to the shape of the useful article to which it was applied. The statute protects that work of art whether it is first drawn on the album cover and then applied to the guitar's surface, or vice

104. [Note in the original] We do not today hold that the surface decorations are copyrightable. We express no opinion on whether these works are sufficiently original to qualify for copyright protection, *see Feist Publications, Inc. v. Rural Telephone Service Co.*, 499 U. S. 340, 358–359 (1991), or on whether any other prerequisite of a valid copyright has been satisfied.

versa. Failing to protect that art would create an anomaly: It would extend protection to two-dimensional designs that cover a part of a useful article but would not protect the same design if it covered the entire article. The statute does not support that distinction, nor can it be reconciled with the dissent's recognition that "artwork printed on a t-shirt" could be protected. ...

To be clear, the only feature of the cheerleading uniform eligible for a copyright in this case is the two-dimensional work of art fixed in the tangible medium of the uniform fabric. Even if respondents ultimately succeed in establishing a valid copyright in the surface decorations at issue here, respondents have no right to prohibit any person from manufacturing a cheerleading uniform of identical shape, cut, and dimensions to the ones on which the decorations in this case appear. They may prohibit only the reproduction of the surface designs in any tangible medium of expression—a uniform or otherwise.[105] ...

III. We hold that an artistic feature of the design of a useful article is eligible for copyright protection if the feature (1) can be perceived as a two- or three-dimensional work of art separate from the useful article and (2) would qualify as a protectable pictorial, graphic, or sculptural work either on its own or in some other medium if imagined separately from the useful article. Because the designs on the surface of respondents' cheerleading uniforms in this case satisfy these requirements, the judgment of the Court of Appeals is affirmed.

It is so ordered.

§ 2.77 THE SUPERIOR COURT OF JUSTICE OF BRAZIL ACCEPTS THE APPLICATION OF THE DOCTRINE OF DILUTION TO INDUSTRIAL DESIGNS—2019

Outside the United States, courts continue opening new avenues that permit better protection of the legitimate interests of the fashion industries over their many and varied differentiating assets. This time, a new avenue seems to have been opened in Brazil, whose Superior Court of Justice has accepted that counterfeiting can lead to the dilution (or depreciation, in the Court's own terms) of fashion designs.

Indeed, when we refer to dilution in connection with trademarks, what is diluted—i.e., what is lost or depreciated—is not the trademark in itself, but the distinctive meaning that is associated with it. However, the idea of a distinctive meaning—the symbolism, if you will—can also be obtained from other elements of product differentiation, such as industrial designs and, more broadly, trade dress. This is the very important notion that the Brazilian court, even if it has not elaborated on it, has retained: the imitation of an industrial design which consumers have learned to associate with certain luxury

105. The dissent suggests that our test would lead to the copyrighting of shovels. ... But a shovel, like a cheerleading uniform, even if displayed in an art gallery, is "an article having an intrinsic utilitarian function that is not merely to portray the appearance of the article or to convey information." 17 U. S. C. §101. It therefore cannot be copyrighted. A drawing of a shovel could, of course, be copyrighted. And, if the shovel included any artistic features that could be perceived as art apart from the shovel, and which would qualify as protectable pictorial, graphic, or sculptural works on their own or in another medium, they too could be copyrighted. But a shovel as a shovel cannot.

products, even if it does not affect the trademark, but the design only may cause dilution in the form of loss of prestige.

Superior Court of Justice

Special appeal Nr. 1.332.417—RS (2012/0137220-6)

Appellant: Junior Camilo Fernandes and Other; Respondent: Antonio A. de Freitas

August 20, 2019

This is a special appeal filed by Junior Camilo Fernandes and Other, supported by literals "a" and "c" of the constitutional provision, with the purpose of amending the opinion delivered by the Court of Justice of the State of Rio Grande do Sul, thus summarized (pages 526/527, e-STJ):

> Civil appeal. Obligation to refrain from an act cumulated with damages. Counterfeiting. Registration of industrial design. Improper use of a patented (*sic*) product without due authorization. Duty to compensate. Characterization. When the elements characterizing a particular product are found to have total similarity with the product of another manufacturer, who has a previous right to use, counterfeiting is configured. Hypothesis in which the whole of the evidence set out in the case file demonstrates the defendants' unlawful conduct of manufacturing, selling and exhibiting for sale shoes that incorporate the author's industrial design, duly registered with the National Institute of Industrial Property—INPI, without due authorization, in clear violation of arts 94, 97 and 109 of Law nr. 9,279/96, which justifies the duty to compensate. Judgment upheld.

Material damage. Proof. The counterfeiting of the shoes in question has reduced the sale of the originals manufactured and commercialized by the plaintiff, given they were practically identical to the latter, but [made] with inferior quality and [sold] at negligible prices. In addition, art. 209, *caput*, of Law nr. 9279/96, does not cause the compensation of material damage to depend on the proof of commercialization of the manufactured products, the violation of industrial property rights or the practice of acts of unfair competition being sufficient—hypothesis of the case. Judgment upheld.

Punitive damage. Substantiation. The vulgarization of the product and the depreciation of the trademark owner's commercial reputation, consequences of the practice of counterfeiting, are elements that suffice to harm the image right of the trademark owner, which consequently leads to payment of compensation for punitive damages. Precedents of the Superior Court of Justice and of this Court. ...

[The appellants] argue, in summary, that due to the nullity of the registration of the appealed party's industrial design (sole), and in the absence of "partial nullity (of registration of industrial design)," it should have been recognized "that both the industrial design of the respondent, as well as that of the appellants, could benefit from the same [design], as well as from the combination of known elements in the leathers." They claim that "the fact that there is no illegality in the conduct of the Appellants if fully proved, because they were acting lawfully, in addition to not having been proved, or even described, any damage that may have been suffered by the Respondent." I decide. The appeal is unacceptable. ...

In this regard, the local Court has confirmed that the practice of counterfeiting and unfair competition was characterized, and deemed the conviction of the appellants to the payment of punitive and material damages to be correct. ... Thus, contrary to the appellants' arguments, I understand that their unlawful conduct of manufacturing, selling and exhibiting for sale footwear that incorporates the plaintiff's industrial design duly registered with the National Institute of Industrial Property—INPI has been demonstrated.

Opportunely, the well-founded judgment by the noble first instance judge, Mr. Flavio Mendes Rabello (pages 347/349), [states] *verbis*:

> The lawsuit is based on allegedly unlawful acts of unfair competition and counterfeiting in the face of the "Freeday" trademark and the industrial designs of the "Element" tennis shoes, owned by the plaintiff, practiced by the defendants. The firm Antonio A. de Freitas—ME has a registration of a "configuration applied to shoe soles," certified by the National Institute of Industrial Property (INPI) under number DI6403029-6, and has a registration of an "aesthetic configuration applied to sports shoes," referring to the model of tennis shoes called "Element," certified by the National Institute of Industrial Property (INPI) under number DI6402990-5; it also owns the mixed trademark "Freeday," filed on August 8, 1999 and registered on March 9, 1999 for the term of 10 years, as certified by the National Institute of Industrial Property (INPI) under number 818025557, for apparel and accessories in general and travel articles and clothing. The registration of the industrial design of the plaintiffs precedes those of the defendants. ...

Regarding the INPI administrative process, I understand that, even if it were concluded that there is no imitation of the trademark, due to the fact that "there is no novelty in the design as the defendants allege, the plaintiff's claim would still deserve approval, because, as far as the shoe designs are concerned, substantial imitation and the sale of imitations have taken place. The visual similarities of the products are indisputable, the matter not being just of products that are similar, because all tennis shoes have common characteristics and follow fashion trends that allow the consumer to identify a shoe as being of that kind. The cuts and applications of fabrics and other materials follow the same lines, positions and shapes of the plaintiff's shoes. There are many similarities, which, it seems, go beyond mere coincidences.

What draws attention is the sole of the footwear, which is the same, just not displaying the "Freeday" mark.

I emphasize again, even if the style of the shoe is commonplace, the design of its sole could be different, which is not. ...

So, from what we can see, the imitation of the "Element" tennis shoes, by the defendants, is substantial and conflicts with the industrial designs registered by the plaintiff.

To the holder of the registered industrial design is guaranteed its property (articles 94 and 109 of the applicable Law), which gives him/her the right to prevent its use or reproduction in any way by unauthorized third parties (sole paragraph of art. 109). ...

There is no doubt, therefore, that the elements characterizing the footwear manufactured and commercialized by the defendants are similar to those used by the plaintiff in a product under the same classification, the possibility of consumer confusion being unavoidable. And, although the existence of some distinctive characteristics between the products is not unknown, they are not able to avoid the possibility of confusion between the products, generated by the coincidence of important visual elements.

Thus, the combined use of several coinciding elements, which at the end form the presentation of the product manufactured and commercialized by the defendants, and which characterizes the imitation and the intention of confusing the consumer, gives rise to the finding of counterfeiting.

Moreover, it is important to note that the nullity of Industrial Design nr. 6403029-6 (sole used in tennis in comment) does not represent an offense to the requirements of novelty and originality of Industrial Design nr. 6402990-5 (footwear object of the dispute), as far as that the sole does not represent a design [that is] differential in the final composition of the product—on the contrary, that is the least visible part and draws less attention in both shoes. In addition, under the terms of art. 97, sole paragraph, of Law nr. 9,279/96, the industrial design is deemed original, even when the visual result arises from the combination of known elements. ...

It is obvious that the counterfeiting of the shoes in question has caused the reduction of the sale of the originals manufactured and commercialized by the plaintiff, since they were practically identical to the originals, but [made] with inferior quality and [sold] at insignificant prices. ...

In fact, anyone who would be willing to buy, for a considerable sum, an exclusive product, made by the trademark owner in compliance with various quality, durability and safety standards, would no longer do so if such product were popularized through a generalized counterfeiting.

It is concluded, therefore, that the counterfeiting, in itself, causes a substantial reduction in the revenue to be obtained with the sale of the product distinguished by the registered trademark,[106] which consequently authorizes the compensation for punitive damages.

For these reasons, the upholding of the judgment that condemned the defendants to pay compensation for the material damages suffered is mandatory.

...

The vulgarization of the product and the dilution of the trademark owner's commercial reputation, effects of the counterfeiting, are elements that suffice to damage the right to the image of the trademark owner, which consequently authorizes punitive damages. ...

106. As a consequence of the infringement, the trademark's value may be diluted, but what was actually infringed was not the trademark itself, but the design. And it was the counterfeiting of the design, which consumers apparently had learned to recognize, and its association with poor quality goods sold at low prices that could have led to the dilution of the trademark. So, indirectly, this court has acknowledged the distinctive function of the designs.

Figure 51 Drawings accompanying Industrial Design nr. 6402990-5, for a "Configuration applied to sports shoes" (left) and Industrial Design nr. 6403029-6, for a "Configuration applied to shoe soles" (right). It was the imitation of the design of the shoe's sole that was decisive in persuading the court of counterfeiting. The court also understood that this particular design had become particularly distinctive so as to allow for a finding of dilution. Could in the future this sole be registered in Brazil as a figurative trademark? It seems that the Superior Court of Justice would answer yes.

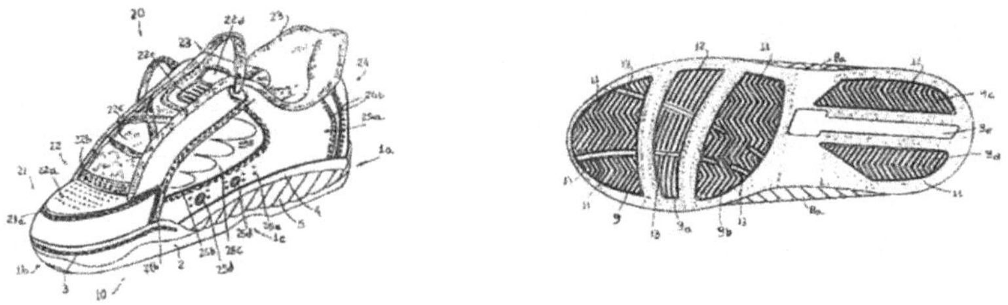

§ 2.78 AN ENGLISH COURT OPENS ANOTHER AVENUE FOR THE PROTECTION OF FASHION DESIGNS: CERTAIN FIGURATIVE ELEMENTS OF APPAREL CAN ASSUME A BRANDING FUNCTION AND THUS BE THE SUBJECT OF PASSING OFF—2020

The following text may be one of the most important texts collected in this book. In a very well reasoned opinion, Deputy Judge David Stone has opened a relevant avenue for the protection of the fashion industry's legitimate commercial interests associated with prestige and reputation: figurative elements, registered or not, can assume the function of branding and, as such, are covered by the passing off doctrine. The Deputy Judge said: "I also note that it does not matter that the trade mark under which the [Defendant's] jeans are sold is different. The rear branding elements which comprise [those of the Plaintiff's] are sufficiently strong and that is what consumers recognise." This is a parallel, if not the same, approach to the notion of admitting that certain ornaments and designs can acquire a branding function through secondary meaning, as suggested above.

High Court of Justice—Business and Property Courts of England and Wales

Intellectual Property Enterprise Court

Freddy Spa v. Hugz Clothing Ltd. and others

November 19, 2020

David Stone (sitting as a Deputy Judge of the Chancery Division)

1. "Body-enhancing" jeans are part of an expanding area of fashion known as shapewear. They can give the appearance of slimmer hips, whilst simultaneously lifting and separating the buttocks. Whilst body-enhancing undergarments have

been popular for centuries, the emergence of shapewear as outer-garments is recent. The Claimant, Freddy SpA, introduced its WR.UP branded jeans in 2012. It says that these were a dramatic departure from what was previously available on the market, attracting significant consumer attention and commercial success. The Defendants, HUGZ Clothing Limited, CC Liverpool Limited and Mr Christopher Kavanagh, have admitted copying the WR.UP jeans and marketing the copies as their own HUGZ branded jeans. Having settled the Claimant's initial complaint in a settlement agreement dated 3 April 2019 (the Settlement Agreement), the Defendants then launched a second version of the HUGZ jeans. In doing so, the Claimant says the Defendants:

i) breached the Settlement Agreement;
ii) infringed the Claimant's European Patent no (UK) 2 666 377 B1 titled "pants, in particular for shaping the female buttocks and hips" (the Patent);[107]
iii) infringed various UK unregistered design rights under the Copyright Designs and Patents Act 1988 (the CDPA); and
iv) engaged in unlawful passing off. ...

9. I have set out the background to the trial in some detail. The lack of engagement from the Defendants since June means that, unusually, issues between the parties have not narrowed before trial. I must therefore determine all the issues in the case, and can do so briefly in some cases. The list of issues set out in a Schedule to HHJ Hacon's order of 19 December 2020 therefore remains apposite, with the exception of the threats counterclaim, which I have struck out: ...

Passing Off

(7) Whether it is customary and conventional for women's jeans to bear branding elements on their rear pockets.
(8) Whether the WR.UP jeans have been promoted by reference to the Freddy Get-Up (as defined—*see* below).
(9) Whether the Claimant owns goodwill in the Freddy Get-Up.
(10) Whether the Second HUGZ Jeans have been promoted by reference to the features set out in paragraph 39 of the Amended Particulars of Claim (*see* below).
(11) Whether it is likely that the Defendants have misrepresented that the Second HUGZ Jeans are connected in the course of trade with the Claimant.
(12) If so, whether it is likely that such misrepresentation has caused the Claimant damage. ...

Passing Off

67. The law of passing off, as set out in *Reckitt & Colman Products Limited v. Borden Inc and Ors* [1990] RPC 341 (*Jif Lemon*) is well known, so I will not set it out here. To succeed in its claim, the Claimant must prove goodwill, a misrepresentation by the Defendants, and damage by reason of the erroneous belief engendered by the Defendants' misrepresentation.

107. The Deputy Judge has found patent infringement. This discussion has been omitted because that was a straightforward question: the patent covers the assemblage of some of WR-UP jeans' components in order to obtain the effects of moulding the woman's hips and buttocks.

Goodwill

68. The Claimant asserted goodwill in the combination of following elements of its WR.UP jeans (referred to in the pleadings as the *Freddy Get-Up*):

i) "a polished metallic badge approximately 15mm high and 15mm wide;
ii) which badge is, save for a narrow border, painted in a pale gloss colour;
iii) which badge features an abstract motif;
iv) which badge is positioned very close to the upper seam of the rear right pocket of the jeans;
v) which badge is positioned close to the outer seam of the rear right pocket of the jeans;
vi) two rear pockets each having two curved seams and one substantially straight seam;
vii) at least one central rear belt loop sewn at an angle to the vertical of approximately 40 degrees; and
viii) a scalloped rear yoke."

69. These elements of the Freddy Get-Up can be described in words, but are perhaps best illustrated by images of the rear of the WR.UP jeans:

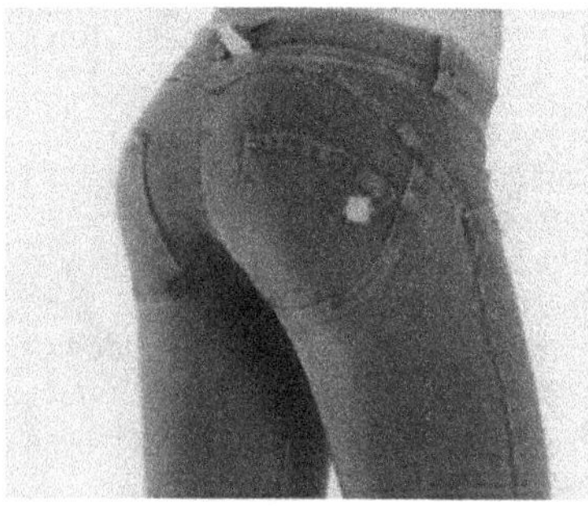

70. The Defendants admitted that the Claimant sold the WR.UP jeans bearing the Freddy Get-Up, however, the Amended Defence averred that the Claimant's jeans are sold by reference only to the brands FREDDY and WR.UP, and that therefore any goodwill and reputation in the UK relates to the FREDDY and WR.UP brands, which the Defendants do not use. The Defendants also put in issue the question of whether it is customary and conventional for women's jeans to bear branding elements on their rear pockets.

71. Ms. Rogan's [expert witness] evidence on the latter issue was clear:

i) Customers expect to see branding on jeans, including as part of the garment itself;
ii) Branding elements are typically added to the back of jeans as this is the largest area to which to add details. The back pocket area is usually highly visible when the jeans are worn. Ms Rogan gave the example of the iconic red tab on Levi's jeans;
iii) Branding elements are often added to the waistband;

iv) The branding elements are to ensure that the jeans are easily recognisable, both to consumers buying their products and also to those seeing people wearing their products;
v) It is important for a brand or designer that customers and potential customers can easily recognise their products on the wearer from a reasonable distance;
vi) Customers want to be seen in particular brands; and
vii) Common branding elements on the rear of jeans include leather or fabric tabs, the shape of pockets, the stitching on the pocket, and metal rivets or bartacks at the corners of pockets.[108]

72. Ms. Rogan also gave specific evidence about the Freddy Get-Up:

In my view, each of these branding elements accords with the tradition of having brand identifiers on the rear of the jeans. As a result, they are likely to be seen by customers as indicating the source of the jeans. However, Freddy's execution through its particular choices of branding elements is unusual and distinctive.

73. Although it is the objective view of consumers that matters, rather than the subjective view of the designer, Ms. Rogan's opinion is also consistent with what Mr Freddi said he set out to do—he gave evidence that he wanted to ensure that someone walking behind a customer wearing WR.UP jeans "would instantly recognise it as being our product."

74. If it was realistically in doubt, it is clear to me from Ms. Rogan's evidence that it is customary and conventional for women's jeans to bear branding elements on their rear pockets. It is also clear to me from the evidence provided by Mr Freddi that the Claimant set out to, and in fact did, market the WR.UP jeans by drawing attention to the Freddy Get-Up. Further, it is clear to me that at the time of the launch of the HUGZ jeans, consumers were aware, through the Claimant's marketing efforts, of the Freddy Get-Up, and had been educated that the Freddy Get-Up on jeans is an indication of origin. The Claimant therefore owns goodwill in the Freddy Get-Up.

Misrepresentation and Damage

75. The Claimant alleged that the Second HUGZ Jeans had been promoted and offered for sale under and by reference to the following get-up (the *HUGZ Get-Up*):

i) "A polished metallic badge of approximately 15mm high and 15mm wide;
ii) Which badge is save for a narrow border, painted in a pale gloss colour;
iii) Which badge features an abstract heart-shaped motif;
iv) Which badge is positioned very close to the upper seam of the rear right pocket of the jeans;
v) Which badge is positioned close to the outer seam of the rear right pocket of the jeans;

108. The pictorial aspects of branding require a certain amount of originality to be accepted as such. They are designs after all. Only designs protectable as designs can acquire the mentioned above secondary meaning, or, as Deputy Judge Stone held, being the matter of passing off, independently from or in addition to the passing off of the trademark itself. It should be added that the Opinion discussed at length whether the ornaments in the back pocket of the Plaintiff's jeans constituted protectable unregistered designs under British law, and concluded affirmatively, in spite of the fact that such protection is not extended to surface decorations. The Judge held that the pocket is not a surface but a three-dimension object. Of course, in other jurisdictions this last discussion might not make sense.

vi) Two rear pockets each having two curved seams and one substantially straight seam;
vii) At least one central rear belt loop sewn at an angel to the vertical of approximately 40 degrees; and
viii) A scalloped rear yoke." ...

77. Counsel for the Claimant suggested that I assess the misrepresentation and damage elements of passing off together. As the Claimant and the First and Second Defendants are competitors, he said, it follows that if the Defendants have misrepresented a trading connection with the Claimant, damage is inevitable. He referred me to the 5th edition of *The Law of Passing Off* by Christopher Wadlow, at paragraph 4-14:

A misrepresentation that the defendant's goods or business are those of the claimant is intrinsically likely to damage the claimant if the fields of business of the claimant and defendant are reasonably close. The fact that virtually every successful passing off action for half a century fell into this category meant that an inquiry as to damages could be granted as a matter of routine if the other elements of the tort were made out.

78. In her report, Ms. Rogan said this:

I noticed that the marketing for both the [Claimant's] jeans and the [Defendants'] jeans focuses on the back of the jeans. This is not unusual; as I mention above, the back of the jeans is a common focus for branding elements. What is unusual, in my view, is that [the Defendants have] adopted the same branding elements as [the Claimant]. As I have said, these are not common features themselves, and my opinion is that they have adopted the same features in order to associate themselves with [the Claimant].

I cannot know the real reasons why they wanted to create this association, but it is clear to me that they wanted consumers to believe either (a) that the two brands are connected in some way, or (b) that a consumer, even if it knows that [the Defendants are] unconnected to [the Claimant] when buying the product, wanted other consumers to believe that the [Defendants'] product was associated with [the Claimant] and its product.

79. Counsel for the Claimant described the former of these two associations as conventional passing off, and I have no hesitation in finding that such passing off is made out in this case. The Second HUGZ Jeans are an obvious rip-off of the WR.UP jeans. The Defendants have clearly adopted very similar branding elements, which, as Ms Rogan says, consumers will recognise as an indication of origin. That is clearly the Defendants' intention—as Ms. Rogan says, the Defendants promote the Second HUGZ Jeans (particularly with on-line sales) by reference to HUGZ Get-Up, which is very similar to the Freddy Get-Up. Whilst there are minor differences (differences in the image on the metallic badge, only one diagonal beltloop), these are insufficient to dispel the misrepresentation caused by the other elements. I also note that it does not matter that the trade mark under which the Second HUGZ Jeans are sold is different. The rear branding elements which comprise the HUGZ Get-Up are sufficiently strong [and] that is what consumers recognise: ... In my judgment, the Second HUGZ Jeans misrepresent, through the HUGZ Get-Up, that there is a connection in the course of trade with the Claimant. As a result, the Claimant has already suffered damage, and will continue to do so whilst the Second HUGZ Jeans remain on sale. That damage includes the lost sales referred to in Mr Freddi's evidence.

80. The position with respect to post-sale confusion is less clear. This is the second type of misrepresentation referred to by Ms Rogan, whereby a consumer knows she is purchasing a knock-off when she buys the Second HUGZ Jeans, but she does so because she wants other consumers to believe that her jeans are associated with the Claimant and its products. ...

132. For the reasons set out above: ...

iv) None of the pleaded designs is commonplace;
v) All of the pleaded designs are owned by the Claimant;
vi) The Second HUGZ Jeans are articles which have been made exactly or substantially to the RSP Design, the Inner Parts Design and the JOTO Design. If the When Worn Design were valid, the Second HUGZ Jeans are articles which have been made exactly or substantially to the When Worn Design;
vii) It is customary and conventional for women's jeans to bear branding elements on their rear pockets;
viii) The WR.UP jeans have been promoted by the Claimant by reference to the Freddy Get-Up;
ix) The Second HUGZ Jeans have been promoted by reference to the HUGZ Get-Up;
x) The Defendants have misrepresented that the Second HUGZ Jeans are connected in the course of trade with the Claimant; ...

133. The Claimant therefore succeeds on its case for patent infringement, unregistered design infringement (other than in relation to the When Worn Design), passing off and breach of the Settlement Agreement.

Credits and Sources of Texts and Illustrations

Texts

§ 1.01. Gustave Fagniez, Documents relatifs à l'Histoire de l'Industrie et du Commerce en France, vol. 1, at 211-212 (Alphonse Picard & Fils, 1898). Source: < gallica.BnF.fr > , 1–2

§ 1.02. A. Giry, Histoire de la Ville de Saint-Omer et des ses Institutions jusqu'au XIVE Siècle, at 502, 517, 547, 553 (F. Vieweg, 1877). Source: Google Books, 2–3

§ 1.03. Gustave Fagniez, Etudes sur l'Industrie et la Classe Industrielle au XIIIe et au XIVe Siècle, at 373-375 (F. Vieweg, 1877). Source: < archive.org > , 3–4

§ 1.04. Decrusy, Isambert and Jourdan, Recueil Général des Anciennes Lois Françaises depuis l'an 420 jusqu'à la Révolution de 1789, vol. 4, 1327-1357, at 452-453 (Belin-Leprieur, 1821). Source: < archive.org > , 4–5

§ 1.05. Calendar of the Patent Rolls, Edward III, 1348-1350, at 27. Source: < archive.org > , 5–6

§ 1.06. Gustave Fagniez, Documents relatifs à l'Histoire de l'Industrie et du Commerce en France, vol. 2, at 287-289 (Alphonse Picard et Fils, 1900). Source: < gallica.BnF.fr > , 6–7

§ 1.07. Owen Ruffhead, The Statutes at Large, From Magna Charta to the End of the Reign of King Henry the Sixth, vol. 1, at 273-274 (Basket, Woodfall, and Strahan, 1763). Source: Google Books, 8

§ 1.08. Eugène Soil, Les Tapisseries de Tournai—Les Tapissiers et Hautelisseurs de Cette Ville, at 355 et seq. and 358 et seq. (Vasseur-Delmée, 1892). Source: < gallica.BnF.fr > , 8–10

§ 1.09. Emilio Motta, *Per la Storia dell'Arte dei Fustagni nel Socolo XIV*, Archivio Storico Lombardo—anno XVII, 140, 144 (1890). Source: < www.omnia.ie > , 10–12

§ 1.10. Augustin Thierry, Recueil des Monuments Inédits de l'Histoire du Tiers État, vol. 2, at 34-35 (Firmin Didot Frères, 1853). Source: < gallica.BnF.fr > , 12–13

§ 1.11. George Espinas, LA DRAPERIE DANS LA FLANDRE FRANÇAISE AU MOYEN-ÂGE, vol. 2, at 941-942 (Auguste Picard, 1923). Source: <archive.org>, 13–14

§ 1.12. Georges Espinas, LA DRAPERIE DANS LA FLANDRE FRANÇAISE AU MOYEN-ÂGE, vol. 2, at 946 et seq. (Auguste Picard, 1923). Source: <gallica.BnF.fr>, 14–16

§ 1.13. Augustin Thierry, RECUEIL DES MONUMENTS INÉDITS DE L'HISTOIRE DU TIERS ETAT, RÉGION DU NORD, vol. 2, at 33-38 (Firmin Didot Frères, 1853), 16–17

§ 1.14. Eugène Soil, LES TAPISSERIES DE TOURNAI—LES TAPISSIERS ET HAUTELISSEURS DE CETTE VILLE, at 365-367 (Vasseur-Delmée, 1892). Source: <gallica.BnF.fr>, 17–19

§ 1.15. Augustin Thierry, RECUEIL DES MONUMENTS INÉDITS DE L'HISTOIRE DU TIERS ETAT, RÉGION DU NORD, vol. 2, at 58, 59 (Firmin Didot Frères, 1853), 19

§ 1.16. Vilevault and Bréquigny, ORDONNANCES DES ROIS DE FRANCE DE LA TROISIÈME RACE, vol. 11, at 11-14 (Imprimerie Royale, 1769). Source: <gallica.BnF.fr>, 20–22

§ 1.17. A.-V. Chapuis, LES ANCIENNES CORPORATIONS DIJONNAISES—RÈGLEMENTS, STATUTS ET ORDONNANCES, at 171-177 (Librairie J. Nourry, 1906). Source: <gallica.BnF.fr>, 22–23

§ 1.18. NOUVEAU RECUEIL DES STATUTS ET RÈGLEMENTS DU CORPS ET MÉTIER DES MAÎTRES-MARCHANDS ET TAPISSIERS-HAUTELICIERS-SARRAZINOIS-RENTRAYEURS-COURTEPOINTIERS-COUVERTURIERS-COUTURIERS-SERGIERS DE LA VILLE, FAUXBOURGS & BANLIEUE DE PARIS, at 1, 8 (Gissey, 1756). Source: <gallica.BnF.fr>, 24–25

§ 1.19. THE STATUTES AT LARGE, FROM THE FIRST YEAR OF KING EDWARD THE FOURTH TO THE END OF THE REIGN OF QUEEN ELIZABETH, vol. 2, at 20-22 (Basket, Woodfall and Strahan, 1770). Source: <archive.org>, 25–26

§ 1.20. THE STATUTES OF THE REALM PUBLISHED BY COMMAND OF HIS MAJESTY KING GEORGE THE III, vol. 2, at 456-457 (Dawsons of Pall Mall, 1816, reprinted 1963). Source: <babel.hathitrust.org>. Pierre Mouton et al., RECUEIL DES STATUTS, ORDONNANCES, RÈGLEMENTS ET PRIVILÈGES, ACCORDÉS EN FAVEUR DES MARCHANDS ORFÈVRES JOUAILLIERS DE LA VILLE & FAUXBOURGS DE PARIS, DONT ILS ONT JOUI DEPUIS L'AN 1435, JUSQU'EN LA PRÉSENTE ANNÉE 1688 (Lambert Rouland, 1688). Source: <gallica.BnF.fr>, 26–28

§ 1.21. Augustin Thierry, RECUEIL DES MONUMENTS INÉDITS DE L'HISTOIRE DU TIERS ETAT, RÉGION DU NORD, vol. 2, at 380-383, 461, 546, 549 (Firmin Didot Frères, 1853). Source: <gallica.BnF.fr>. René de Lespinasse, LES MÉTIERS ET CORPORATIONS DE LA VILLE DE PARIS, VOL. 3, TISSUS, ÉTOFFES, VÊTEMENTS, CUIRS ET PEAUX, MÉTIERS DIVERS, at 23-24 (Imprimerie Nationale, 1897). Source: <gallica.BnF.fr>, 28–31

§ 1.22. René de Lespinasse, LES MÉTIERS ET CORPORATIONS DE LA VILLE DE PARIS, VOL. 3, TISSUS, ÉTOFFES, VÊTEMENTS, CUIRS ET PEAUX, MÉTIERS DIVERS, at 109-110 (Imprimerie Nationale, 1897). Source: <gallica.BnF.fr>, 31–32

§ 1.23. NOUVEAU RECUEIL DES STATUTS ET RÈGLEMENTS DU CORPS ET MÉTIER DES MAÎTRES-MARCHANDS ET TAPISSIERS-HAUTELICIERS-SARRAZINOIS-RENTRAYEURS-COURTEPOINTIERS-COUVERTURIERS-COUTURIERS-SERGIERS DE LA VILLE, FAUXBOURGS & BANLIEUE DE PARIS, at 13-15 (Gissey, 1756). Source: <gallica.BnF.fr>, 32–33

§ 1.24. Maurice Vanhaeck, Histoire de la Sayetterie à Lille, vol. 2, at 6, 12, 13 (Imprimerie Lefebvre-Ducrocq, 1910). Source: <gallica.BnF.fr>, 33–34

§ 1.25. Source: <www.bne.es>, 34–36

§ 1.26. The Statutes of the Realm, vol. 3, at 28, 209-210, 544-545, 854 (Dawsons of Pall Mall, 1817, repr. 1963). Source: Google Books. The Statutes at Large, from the First Year of King Edward the Fourth to the End of the Reign of Queen Elizabeth, vol. 2, at 118 (Basket, Woodfall, and Strahan, 1770). Source: Google Books. The statutes of the realm, Printed by command of his majesty King George the Third, in pursuance of an address of the House of Commons of Great Britain. Edward VI. Source: <catalog.hathitrust.org/>, 36–42

§ 1.27. Augustin Thierry, Recueil des Monuments Inédits de l'Histoire du Tiers Etat, Région du Nord, vol. 2, at 360, 363, 364 (Firmin Didot Frères, 1853). Source: <archive.org>, 42–43

§ 1.28. Recopilacion de las Ordenanças de la muy Noble, y muy Leal Ciudad de Sevilla: de todas las leyes, y ordenamientos antiguos, y modernos; cartas y provisiones Reales, para la buena governación del bien publico, y pacíficio Regimiento de Sevilla y su tierra. Fecha por mandado de los muy altos, y muy poderosos, Catholicos Reyes e Señores, don Fernando, y doña Isabel, de gloriosa memoria, y por su Real provisión, fs. 184-184v., 204-204v. (Andres Grande, 1632). Source: <www.bibliotecavirtualdeandalucía.es>, 44

§ 1.29. Maurice Vanhaeck, Histoire de la Sayetterie à Lille, vol. 2, at 26-27, 35 (Imprimerie Lefebvre-Ducrocq, 1910). Source: <gallica.BnF.fr>, 45

§ 1.30. Alphonse Wauters, Les Tapisseries Bruxelloises—Essai Historique sur les Tapisseries et les Tapissiers de Haute et de Basse-Lisse de Bruxelles, at 144 (Julien Baertsoen, 1878). Source: <gallica.BnF.fr>. Eugène Müntz, A Short History of Tapestry (translated by Miss Louisa J. Davis), at 183 (Cassell & Co., 1885). Source: <archive.org>, 45–46

§ 1.31. René de Lespinasse, Les Métiers et Corporations de la Ville de Paris, vol. 3, Tissus, Étoffes, Vêtements, Cuirs et Peaux, Métiers Divers, at 249-251 (Imprimerie Nationale, 1897). Source: <gallica.BnF.fr>, 47

§ 1.32. Isambert, Decrusy, and Armet, Recueil Général des Anciennes Lois Françaises depuis l'an 420 jusqu'à la Révolution de 1789, vol. 13, 1546-1559, at 374, 377 (Belin-Leprieur, 1828). Source: <archive.org>, 47–50

§ 1.33. Edict du Roy pour une reformation, police, et règlement sur les façons et teintures des draps (Frederic Morel, 1572). Source: <gallica.BnF.fr.>, 50–51

§ 1.34. René de Lespinasse, Les Métiers et Corporations de la Ville de Paris, vol. 3, Tissus, Étoffes, Vêtements, Cuirs et Peaux, Métiers Divers, at 349-350 (Imprimerie Nationale, 1897). Source: <gallica.BnF.fr>, 51–52

§ 1.35. Noel Fail, Mémoires des Plus Notables et Solemnels Arrêts du Parlement de Bretagne (new edition, 1753). Source: <gallica.BnF.fr>, 52–53

§ 1.36. Keith M. Stolte, *How Early did Anglo-American Trademark Law Begin? An Answer to Schechter's Conundrum*, 8 Fordham Int. Prop., Media & Entert. L. J. 2, at 533 and 535 (1997). The original source of these two reports is J.H. Baker & S.F.C. Milsom, Sources of English Legal History—Private Law to 1750, at 615-618 (Oxford Univ. Press, 1986). Source: <archive.org>, 53–54

§ 1.37. The Statutes at Large, From the First Year of King Edward the Fourth to the End of the Reign of Queen Elizabeth, vol. 2, at 681-682 (Basket, Woodfall, and Strahan, 1770). Source: Google Books, 55–56

§ 1.38. Ordonnance du Roi de France et de Navarre, Henry quatrième de ce nom: Sur le fait des marchans futaniers, ouvriers et faisant train et négoce de fustaniers en la ville de Lyon, et par tout le Royaume de France: Contenant le règlement et articles que sa Majesté veut être entretenu et gardé pour l'entretenement dudit art. Publié à Lyon, le 5 Octobre 1595. Source: < gallica.BnF.fr > , 56–57

§ 1.39. Champollion-Figeac, Documents Historiques Inédits tirés des Collections Manuscrites de la Bibliothèque Nationale, vol. 4, at xv (Firmin Didot, 1848), 57–59

§ 1.40. Recueil des Statuts, Lettres Patentes ou Déclarations du Roi, Arrêts du Conseil et du Parlement, Sentences de Police du Châtelet, et Délibérations pour la Communauté des Maîtres Cordonniers de la Ville et Fauxbourgs de Paris, at 7, 14 (Michel Lambert, 1762). Source: < gallica.BnF.fr > , 59

§ 1.41. Antoine Mornac, In Senatu Parisiensi Patroni Observaciones, vol. 4, at 384 (Montalant, 1721). Source: < gallica.BnF.fr > , 59–60

§ 1.42. Reports of Sir George Croke, of the Courts of King's Bench and Common Pleas, of Such Selected Cases as were adjudged during the Reign of James the First (4th ed., Grimston, 1791). Source: < archive.org > , 60

§ 1.43. Nouveau Recueil des Statuts et Règlements du Corps et Métier des Maîtres-Marchands et Tapissiers-Hauteliciers-Sarrazinois-Rentrayeurs-Courtepointiers-Couverturiers-Couturiers-Sergiers de la Ville, Fauxbourgs & Banlieue de Paris, at 95, 110-111 (Gissey, 1756). Source: < gallica.BnF.fr > , 60–61

§ 1.44. Danby Pickering, The Statutes at Large from the Twelfth Year of King Charles II to the Last Year of King James II Inclusive, vol. 8, at 60-67 (Joseph Bentham, 1763). Source: Google Books, 61–62

§ 1.45. Extracted from M. Courtecuisse, *La Manufacture de Draps Fins Vanrobais au XVIIe et XVIIIe Siècles*, in Mémoires de la Société d'Émulation d'Abbeville, vol. 25, at 129 et seq. (F. Paillart, 1920). Source: < gallica.BnF.fr > . Pierre Clément, Lettres, Instructions et Mémoires de Colbert, vol. 2, at 748 (Imprimerie Impériale, 1853). Source: < archive.org > . M. Courtecuisse, *La Manufacture de Draps Fins Vanrobais au XVIIe et XVIIIe Siècles*, in Mémoires de la Société d'Émulation d'Abbeville, vol. 25, at 47-49 (F. Paillart, 1920). Source: < gallica.BnF.fr > . Georges Durand, Inventaire Sommaires des Archives Départementales Antérieurs à 1790—Somme, vol. 2, at 154-155 (Imprimerie Picarde, 1888). Source: < archive.org > . A. Bouillon, Dictionnaire Portatif de Commerce, vol. 2, at 394 (1770). Source: < archive.org > , 62–66

§ 1.46. Recueil des Édits, Déclarations et Lettres-Patentes Enregistrés au Parlement de Metz, vol. 5, at 118, 122-123 (Veuve Antoine & Fils, 1788). Source: < gallica.BnF.fr > , 66–69

§ 1.47. Recueil des Reglements Généraux et Particuliers Concernant les Manufactures et Fabriques du Royaume, vol. 2, at 218 et seq. (Imprimerie Royale, 1730). Source: < gallica.BnF.fr > , 69–71

§ 1.48. Réglement pour la Jurisdiction des Procès et Différents Concernant les Manufactures. Vérifié en Parlement le treizième Août 1669, at 16, 22, 24, 26, 30, 32-33, 37, 43, 56, 65, 81-82, 87 (Philbert Masson, 1707). Source: <gallica.BnF.fr>, 71–75

§ 1.49. Maurice Vanhaeck, Histoire de la Sayetterie à Lille, vol. 2, at 161-163, and 169-171 (Imprimerie Lefebvre-Ducrocq, 1910). Source: <gallica.BnF.fr>, 75–77

§ 1.50. Claude Blondeau and Gabriel Gueret, Journal du Palais ou Recueil des Principales Decisions de Tous Les Parlemens et Cours Souveraines de France, vol. 1, at 901-904 (Denys Thierry & Jean Guignard, 1701). Source: <archive.org>, 78–79

§ 1.51. Colecção Chronologica de Leis Extravagantes Posteriores à Nova Compilação das Ordenações do Reino, Publicada em 1603, vol. 2, at 197 et seq. (Real Imprensa da Universidade, 1819). Source: <www2.senado.leg.br>, 79–81

§ 1.52. Colecção Chronologica de Leis Extravagantes Posteriores à Nova Compilação das Ordenações do Reino, Publicada em 1603, vol. 2, at 262-263 (Real Imprensa da Universidade, 1819). Source: <www2.senado.leg.br>, 81–82

§ 1.53. Source: <gallica.BnF.fr>, 82–84

§ 1.54. René de Lespinasse, Les Métiers et Corporations de la Ville de Paris, vol. 3, Tissus, Étoffes, Vêtements, Cuirs et Peaux, Métiers Divers, at 267-268 (Imprimerie Nationale, 1897). Source: <gallica.BnF.fr>, 84–85

§ 1.55. Recueil des Statuts, Lettres Patentes ou Déclarations du Roi, Arrêts du Conseil et du Parlement, Sentences de Police du Châtelet, et Délibérations pour la Communauté des Maîtres Cordonniers de la Ville et Fauxbourgs de Paris, at 93, 98 (Michel Lambert, 1762). Source: <gallica.BnF.fr>, 85–86

§ 1.56. Nouveau Recueil des Statuts et Règlements du Corps et Métier des Maîtres-Marchands et Tapissiers-Hauteliciers-Sarrazinois-Rentrayeurs-Courtepointiers-Couverturiers-Couturiers-Sergiers de la Ville, Fauxbourgs & Banlieue de Paris, at 140-147 (Gissey, 1756). Source: <gallica.BnF.fr>, 86–87

§ 1.57. Recueil des Principales Ordonnances de Police de Messieurs du Magistrat de la Ville de Lille, at 286 et seq. (Jean-Baptiste Henry, 1771). Source: Google Books, 87

§ 1.58. Rowland Cox, Trade-Mark Cases, at 2-3 (The Riverside Press, 1881). Source: <archive.org>, 88

§ 1.59. The Statutes: Revised Edition—Vol. II, William & Mary to 10 George III—A.D. 1688-1770, at 489-491 (Eyre and Spottiswoode, 1871). Source: Google Books, 88–91

§ 1.60. Recueil des Statuts, Lettres Patentes ou Déclarations du Roi, Arrêts du Conseil et du Parlement, Sentences de Police du Châtelet, et Délibérations pour la Communauté des Maîtres Cordonniers de la Ville et Fauxbourgs de Paris, at 221-223, and 261-264 (Michel Lambert, 1762). Source: <gallica.BnF.fr>, 91–93

§ 1.61. Pierre Vidal, Histoire de la Corporation des Tailleurs d'Habits, Pourpointiers, Chaussetiers, de la Ville de Paris, at 163 et seq. (1923). Source: <gallica.BnF.fr>. Recueil des Statuts, Ordonnances et Règlements de la Communauté des Maîtres et Marchands Chapeliers de la Ville et Fauxbourgs de Paris, at 186-188 (Valade, 1775). Source: <gallica.BnF.fr>. Prost de Royer, Dictionnaire de Jurisprudence et des Arrêts, ou Nouvelle Édition du Dictionnaire Brillon, vol. 3, at 129 (Aimé de La Roche, 1783). Source: <gallica.BnF.fr>, 93–97

§ 1.62. Maurice Vanhaeck, Histoire de la Sayetterie à Lille, vol. 2, at 274, 277-278 (Imprimerie Lefebvre-Ducrocq, 1910). Source: <gallica.BnF.fr>; Jourdan, Isambert, and Decrusy, Recueil Général des Anciennes Lois Françaises depuis l'an 420 jusqu'à la Révolution de 1789, du 31 Décembre 1778 au 3 Mars 1781, at 77 et seq. (Belin-Leprieur, 1826). Source: <gallica.BnF.fr>, 98–101

§ 1.63. Jourdan, Isambert, and Decrusy, Recueil Général des Anciennes Lois Françaises depuis l'an 420 jusqu'à la Révolution de 1789, du 31 Décembre 1778 au 3 Mars 1781, at 357 et seq. (Belin-Leprieur, 1826). Source: <gallica-.BnF.fr>, 101–102

§ 1.64. Jourdan et al., Recueil Général des Anciennes Lois Françaises depuis l'an 420 jusquà la Révolution de 1789, du 3 mars 1781 au 1er janvier 1785, at 245-246 (Belin-Leprieur, 1827). Source: <gallica.BnF.fr>, 102–104

§ 1.65. Jourdan, Isambert, and Decrusy, Recueil Général des Anciennes Lois Françaises depuis l'an 420 jusqu'à la Révolution de 1789, du 3 Mars 1781 au 1er Janvier 1785, at 255-256 (Belin-Leprieur, 1827). Source: <gallica.Bn-F.fr>, 104–105

§ 1.66. Jourdan, Isambert, and Decrusy, Recueil Général des Anciennes Lois Françaises depuis l'an 420 jusqu'à la Révolution de 1789, du 1er Janvier 1785 au 5 Mai 1788, at 103 et seq. (Belin-Leprieur, 1827). Source: <gallica.Bn-F.fr>, 105

§ 1.67. Jourdan, Isambert, and Decrusy, Recueil Général des Anciennes Lois Françaises depuis l'an 420 jusqu'à la Révolution de 1789, du 1er Janvier 1785 au 5 Mai 1788, at 319-320 (Belin-Leprieur, 1827). Source: <gallica.BnF.fr>, 105–106

§ 1.68. John Cutler and Frank. G. Underhay (eds.), Reports of Patent, Design, Trade Mark and Other Cases, vol. 23, at 171-172 (Darling & Son, 1906). Source: <archive.org>, 106–108

§ 1.69. Pouillet et al., Annales de la Propriété Industrielle, Artistique et Littéraire, year of 1937 (January-February-March), at 86 (Bureau des Annales, 1937). Source: <gallica.BnF.fr>, 108–109

§ 1.70. Source: <staging.hcourt.gov.au>, 110–113

§ 1.71. 46 Revista de Direito Mercantil 69 (1982). São Paulo, 114–116

§ 1.72. Source: <www.findlaw.com>, 116-124

§ 1.73. Sources: <curia.europa.eu>; <www.govinfo.gov>, 125–135

§ 1.74. Sources: <law.justia.com>; <www.bger.ch>; <curia.europa.eu>; <clarivate.com/darts-ip/>, 135–154

§ 1.75. Source: <curia.europa.eu>, 154–174

§ 1.76. Source: <casetext.com>, 175–182

§ 2.01. Calendar of Patent Rolls, Henry III, at 138. Source: <sdrc.lib.uiowa.edu/patentrolls>, 183–185

§ 2.02. Calendar of Patent Rolls, Edward III, vol. 2, at 161. Source: <babel.hathitrust.org>, 185–186

§ 2.03. Statutes of the Realm, 11th Edward III c 5. Source: <archive.org>, 186

§ 2.04. Calendar of Patent Rolls, Edward III. Source: <sdrc.lib.uiowa.edu>, 186

§ 2.05. Secousse, Ordonnances des Rois de France de la Troisième Race, vol. 8, at 301-302 (Imprimerie Royale, 1750). Source: <gallica.BnF.fr>, 187–189

§ 2.06. Gaetano Milanesi, Documenti per la Storia dell'Arte Senese, vol. 2, 15th and 16th centuries, at 180, 190-191 (Onorato Porri, 1854). Source: <archive.org>, 189–191

§ 2.07. Luciano Banchi, L'Arte della Seta in Siena nei Secoli XV e XVI—Statuti e Documenti, at 121-122 (L. Lazzeri, 1881). Source: Google Books, 191

§ 2.08. Luciano Banchi, L'Arte della Seta in Siena nei Secoli XV e XVI—Statuti e Documenti, at 124-127 (L. Lazzeri, 1881). Source: Google Books, 191–193

§ 2.09. Gaetano Milanesi, Documenti per la Storia dell'Arte Senese, vol. 2, 15th and 16th centuries, at 209-211 (Onorato Porri, 1854). Source: <archive.org>; S. Borghese and L. Banchi, Nuovi Documenti per la Storia dell'Arte Senese, at 157-158 (Enrico Torrini, 1858). Source: Politecnico di Torino <digit.biblio.polito.it>, 193–194

§ 2.10. J.I. de Brito Rebello, *Alguns traços da vida do Infante D. Henrique*, in O Instituto, Revista Científica e Literária, vol. 41, at 568, 570-571 (Imprensa da Univ. de Coimbra, 1893). Source: <archive.org>, 194–195

§ 2.11. Calendar of Patent Rolls, Edward IV, Edward V, Richard II, 1476-1485, at 342 (Eyre and Spottiswoode, 1901). Source: <archive.org>, 195–196

§ 2.12. Giulio Mandich, *Venetian Patents (1450-1550)*, 30 Journal of the Pat. Off. Soc'y 166, 210, 213, 216 (1948); [short summary; the privileges are described in more detail in] *Roberto Berveglieri*, Inventori Stranieri a Venezia (1474-1788)—Importazione di Tecnologia e Circolazione di Tecnici Artigiani Inventori, at 88-89, and 101-103 *(IVSLA, 1995)*, 196–197

§ 2.13. Alphonse Wauters, Les Tapisseries Bruxelloises, at 133-136 (Imprim. de Ve. Julien Baertson, 1858). <archive.org>, 197–198

§ 2.14. René de Lespinasse, Les Métiers et Corporations de la Ville de Paris, vol. 3, Tissus, Étoffes, Vêtements, Cuirs et Peaux, Métiers Divers, at 112-113 (Imprimerie Nationale, 1897). Source: <gallica.BnF.fr>, 198–199

§ 2.15. Louis Caillet, *Contrat d'apprentissage passé avec Pierre Gobert, drapier de Romans, le 8 juin 1535, par Simon de Despit*, in Nouvelle Revue Historique de Droit Français et Étranger, vol. 35, at 565-568 (1911). Source: <gallica.BnF.fr>, 199–200

§ 2.16. Augustin Thierry, Recueil des Monuments Inédits de l'Histoire du Tiers État, 1ère Série, Région du Nord, vol. 2, at 608, 620 (Firmin Didot Frères, 1853). Source: <gallica.BnF.fr>, 200–201

§ 2.17. Maurice Vanhaeck, Histoire de la Sayetterie à Lille, vol. 2, at 57-59 (Imprimerie Lefebvre-Ducrocq, 1910). Source: <gallica.BnF.fr>, 201–202

§ 2.18. Calendar of Patent Rolls, Elizabeth, vol. 2, 1560-1563, at 336 (H. M. Stationery Office, 1948). Source: <archive.org>; Calendar of Patent Rolls, Elizabeth, vol. 3, 1563-1566, at 235-236 (H. M. Stationery Office, 1960).

Source: <archive.org>; CALENDAR OF PATENT ROLLS, ELIZABETH, vol. 4, 1566-1569, at 157-158, 197-198, 354 (H. M. Stationery Office, 1964); CALENDAR OF PATENT ROLLS, ELIZABETH, vol. 5, 1569-1572, at 17 (H. M. Stationery Office, 1966). Source: <archive.org>, 202–206

§ 2.19. Source: <www.bne.es>, 206–208

§ 2.20. Champollion-Figeac, DOCUMENTS HISTORIQUES INÉDITS TIRÉS DES COLLECTIONS MANUSCRITES DE LA BIBLIOTHÈQUE NATIONALE, vol. 4, at xxxi (Firmin Didot, 1848), 208–209

§ 2.21. Isambert, Taillandier and Decrusy, RECUEIL GÉNÉRAL DES ANCIENNES LOIS FRANÇAISES DEPUIS L'AN 420 JUSQU'À LA RÉVOLUTION DE 1789, vol. 15, 1589-1610, at 283 et seq. (Belin-Leprieur, 1829). Source: <archive.org>, 209–211

§ 2.22. Champollion-Figeac, DOCUMENTS HISTORIQUES INÉDITS TIRÉS DES COLLECTIONS MANUSCRITES DE LA BIBLIOTHÈQUE NATIONALE, vol. 4, at 119-120 (Firmin Didot, 1848), 212–214

§ 2.23. Champollion-Figeac, DOCUMENTS HISTORIQUES INÉDITS TIRÉS DES COLLECTIONS MANUSCRITES DE LA BIBLIOTHÈQUE NATIONALE, vol. 4, at 171 et seq. (Firmin Didot, 1848), 215–217

§ 2.24. Champollion-Figeac, DOCUMENTS HISTORIQUES INÉDITS TIRÉS DES COLLECTIONS MANUSCRITES DE LA BIBLIOTHÈQUE NATIONALE, vol. 4, at 199-200 and 210 et seq. (Firmin Didot, 1848), 217–219

§ 2.25. Maurice Vanhaeck, HISTOIRE DE LA SAYETTERIE À LILLE, vol. 2, at 106-107 (Imprimerie Lefebvre-Ducrocq, 1910). Source: <gallica.BnF.fr>, 219–220

§ 2.26. Eugène Soil, LES TAPISSERIES DE TOURNAI—LES TAPISSIERS ET HAUTELISSEURS DE CETTE VILLE, at 91-92 (Vasseur-Delmée, 1892). Source: <gallica.BnF.fr>, 221

§ 2.27. Source: <www.bne.es>, 221–222

§ 2.28. NOUVEAU RECUEIL DES STATUTS ET RÈGLEMENTS DU CORPS ET MÉTIER DES MAÎTRES-MARCHANDS ET TAPISSIERS-HAUTELICIERS-SARRAZINOIS-RENTRAYEURS-COURTEPOINTIERS-COUVERTURIERS-COUTURIERS-SERGIERS DE LA VILLE, FAUXBOURGS & BANLIEUE DE PARIS, at 371-380 (Gissey, 1756). Source: <gallica.BnF.fr>, 222–224

§ 2.29. Germain Bapst, *Une manufacture de bas de soie à Paris en 1664*, in BULLETIN DE LA SOCIÉTÉ D'HISTOIRE DE PARIS ET DE L'ÎLE DE FRANCE, 11E ANNÉE, 1884, at 60-62 (H. Champion, 1884). Source: <gallica.BnF.fr>; THE STATUTES OF THE REALM, vol. 7, at 98 (1820). Source: Google Books, 224–228

§ 2.30. René de Lespinasse, LES MÉTIERS ET CORPORATIONS DE LA VILLE DE PARIS, VOL. 3, TISSUS, ÉTOFFES, VÊTEMENTS, CUIRS ET PEAUX, MÉTIERS DIVERS, at 290-293 (Imprimerie Nationale, 1897). Source: <gallica.BnF.fr>, 228–229

§ 2.31. Pierre Clément, LETTRES, INSTRUCTIONS ET MÉMOIRES DE COLBERT, vol. 2, at 786-787 (Imprimerie Impériale, 1863). Source: <gallica.BnF.fr>, 229–231

§ 2.32. RECUEIL DES ÉDITS, DÉCLARATIONS ET LETTRES-PATENTES ENREGISTRÉS AU PARLEMENT DE METZ, vol. 5, at 118, 139-141, 142-143 (Veuve Antoine & Fils, 1788). Source: <gallica.BnF.fr>, 231–235

§ 2.33. G.B. Depping, CORRESPONDANCE ADMINISTRATIVE SOUS LOUIS XIV, vol. 3, at 784-785 (Imprimerie Nationale, 1852). Source: <archive.org>, 235–236

§ 2.34. Recueil des Reglements Généraux et Particuliers Concernant les Manufactures et Fabriques du Royaume, vol. 2, at 71 et seq. (Imprimerie Royale, 1730). Source: < gallica.BnF.fr >, 236–237

§ 2.35. Source: < gallica.BnF.fr >, 237–239

§ 2.36. Ebenezer Bain, Merchant and Craft Guilds—A History of the Aberdeen Incorporated Trades, at 255 (J. & J. P. Edmond & Spark, 1887). Source: < archive.org >, 239–240

§ 2.37. Extraordinaire du Mercure Galant, Quartier d'Avril 1678, vol. 2, at 9 (1678). Source: < Google Books >, 240–241

§ 2.38. Maurice Vanhaeck, Histoire de la Sayetterie à Lille, vol. 2, at 199-201 (Imprimerie Lefebvre-Ducrocq, 1910). Source: < gallica.BnF.fr >, 242

§ 2.39. Extracted from Alfred Franklin, Dictionnaire Historique des Arts, Métiers et Professions Exercés dans Paris depuis le XIIIe Siècle, at 543 (H. Welter, 1906). < gallica.BnF.fr >; Mercure Galant (1711), at 195-198. Source: < gallica.BnF.fr >; Extracted from Alfred Franklin, Dictionnaire Historique des Arts, Métiers et Professions Exercés dans Paris depuis le XIIIe Siècle, at 543 (H. Welter, 1906). < gallica.BnF.fr >; G. Touchard-Lafosse, Chroniques de l'Oeil-de Boeuf des Petits Appartements de la Cour et des Salons de Paris, sous Louis XIV, la Régence, Louis XV et Louis XVI, at 237-238 (George Barba, 1874). Source: < gallica.BnF.fr >; Extracted from Edouard Drumont, *Parasols et parapluies*, in La Liberté, January 11, 1875. Source: < gallica.BnF.fr >, 243–250

§ 2.40. Supplément et Suite du Recueil des Règlements Généraux et Particuliers Concernant les Manufactures du Royaume, at 502, 509 (Imprimerie Royale, 1730). Source: < gallica.BnF.fr >, 250–251

§ 2.41. Supplément et Suite du Recueil des Règlements Généraux et Particuliers Concernant les Manufactures du Royaume, at 103, 116-117 (Imprimerie Royale, 1730). Source: < gallica.BnF.fr >, 251–252

§ 2.42. Supplément et Suite du Recueil des Règlements Généraux et Particuliers Concernant les Manufactures du Royaume, at 442-443 (Imprimerie Royale, 1730). Source: < gallica.BnF.fr >, 252–253

§ 2.43. Statuts et Règlement pour la Communauté des Maîtres Marchands, & Maîtres Ouvriers à façon en étoffes d'or, d'argent & de soie, & autres mêlées de soie, laine, poil, fil & coton, de la ville & fauxbourgs de Lyon; & pour la fabrique des dites étoffes. Du 19 Juin 1744. Source: < gallica.BnF.fr >; Arrêt du Conseil d'Etat qui confirme, avec amende & dépens, une Sentence des Juges de la Conservation de Lyon, du 29 Avril 1749. Source: < gallica.BnF.fr >; Jourdan, Isambert, and Decrusy, Recueil Général des Anciennes Lois Françaises depuis l'an 420 jusqu'à la Révolution de 1789, du 1er Janvier 1785 au 5 Mai 1788, at 380-382 (Belin-Leprieur, 1827). Source: < gallica.BnF.fr >; Michel Pelletier, Droit Industriel—Brevets d'Invention, Marques de Fabrique, Modèles et Dessins, Nom Commercial, Concurrence Déloyale, at 380-381 (Baudry et Cie., 1893). Source: < gallica.BnF.fr >, 253–258

§ 2.44. Danby Pickering, The Statutes at Large, From Magna Carta to the End of the Eleventh Parliament of Great Britain, vol. 36, at 260-262 (John Archdeacon, 1787). Source: < archive.org > , 258–259

§ 2.45. D. A. Tompkins, The Cotton Gin. The History of its Invention., at 24, 50-51, 51-53 (self-publication, 1901); source: < archive.org > ; source: < digital-.scetv.org > ; Denison Olmsted, Memoir of Eli Whitney, Esq., at 46 (Durrie & Peck, 1846). Source: < archive.org > , 259–264

§ 2.46. William Carpmael, Law Reports of Patent Cases, vol. 1, at 353-354 (A. Macintosh, 1843). Source: < archive.org > , 264–265

§ 2.47. Nicholas Simon and John Stuart, Reports of Cases Decided in the High Court of Chancery by the Right Hon. Sir John Leach, Vice-Chancellor of England, vol. 1, at 74-76 (J. & W. T. Clarke, 1824), 265–267

§ 2.48. Patents for Inventions—Abridgements of Specifications relating to Sewing and Embroidering, 1755-1866, at 13 (2nd ed., George E. Eyre and William Spottiswoode, 1871). Source: < archive org > ; J. Meyssin, Histoire de la Machine à Coudre—Portrait et Biographie de l'Inventeur, Barthelemy Thimonnier, at 7-8 (Rey et Sézanne, 1867), 267–272

§ 2.49. W.H. Dunbar, George Dingwall Fordyce, and John de Maria, Reports of Cases Decided in the Supreme Courts of Scotland and in the House of Lord on Appeal from Scotland, being a Continuation of the Scottish Jurist, vol. 8 at 321-322 (M. Anderson, 1836). Source: < archive.org > , 272–274

§ 2.50. J. Emerson Tennent, A Treatise on the Copyright for Designs for Printed Fabrics, with Considerations on the Necessity of its Extension, at xi-xv, 67-68, 93, 94, 265-266 (Smith, Elder and Co., 1841). Source: < archive.org > , 274–276

§ 2.51. W. N. Welsby and Edward Beavan, Chitty's Collection of Statutes, with Notes Thereon, vol. 2, at 233, 234, 237 (3rd edition, Sweet, Steven & Sons, 1865), 277–278

§ 2.52. J. Pataille and A. Huguet, Annales de la Propriété Industrielle, Artistique et Littéraire, year of 1857, vol. 3, at 251-252 (Bureau des Annales, 1857). Source: < gallica.BnF.fr > , 278–280

§ 2.53. Patents for Inventions—Abridgements of Specifications relating to Wearing Apparel—Head Coverings, at 164, 184 (2nd ed., George E. Eyre and William Spottiswoode, 1871). Patents for Inventions—Abridgements of Specifications relating to Wearing Apparel—Foot Coverings, at 349-350 (2nd ed., George E. Eyre and William Spottiswoode, 1871). Source: < archive org > , 280–281

§ 2.54. Bulletin des Lois de l'Empire Français, xith series, 1st semester of 1864, vol. 23, at 553 et seq. (Imprimerie Impériale, 1864). Source: Google Books, 281–283

§ 2.55. Rowland Cox, A Manual of Trade-Mark Cases, at 166 (The Riverside Press, 1881), 283

§ 2.56. Source: < www.uspto.gov > , 283–285

§ 2.57. Source: < supreme.justia.com > , 285–287

§ 2.58. James J. Eston, The Law of Patents, Designs, and Trade-Marks As Contained in the Act 46 & 47 Vic. Cap. 57 (Waterlow Bros. & Layton, 1883). Source: < archive.org > , 288–289

§ 2.59. E. Pouillet et al., Annales de la Propriété Industrielle, Artistique et Littéraire, vol. 41, at 152-154 (Arthur Rousseau, 1895), 289–291

§ 2.60. John Cutler (ed.), Reports of Patent, Design, Trade Mark and Other Cases, vol. 14 (1897), at 225 et seq. (Darling & Son, 1897). Source: < archive.org > , 291–292

§ 2.61. E. Pouillet et al., Annales de la Propriété Industrielle, Artistique et Littéraire, vol. 45, at 110-111 (Arthur Rousseau, 1899). Source: < gallica.BnF.fr > , 293–294

§ 2.62. John Cutler and Frank. G. Underhay (eds.), Reports of Patent, Design, Trade Mark and Other Cases, vol. 24 (1907), at 65 et seq. (Darling & Son, 1907). Source: < archive.org > , 294–299

§ 2.63. Hermine Valabrègue, La Propriété Artistique em Matière de Modes, at 66-67 (Libr. Gén. de Droit et de Jurispr., 1935). Source: < gallica.BnF.fr > , 299

§ 2.64. La Revue Judiciaire—Revue Mensuelle, 4th year, No. 3, March 25, 1911, at 89 et seq. Source: < gallica.BnF.fr > ; George Verley (ed.), L'Art et le Droit, at 68-70 (Marchal et Godde, 1912). Source: < gallica.BnF.fr > . George Verley (ed.), L'Art et le Droit, at 304 et seq. (Marchal et Godde, 1912). Source: < gallica.BnF.fr > . Georges Verley and André Lesourd (eds.), L'Art et le Droit, at 82-86 (Marshal et Godde, 1913). Georges Maillard et al., Annales de la Propriété Industrielle, Artistique et Littéraire, vol. 58, at 148-152 (Phily, 1912). Source: < gallica.BnF.fr > . La Gazette du Palais—Jurisprudence et Législation, 1913, 2e Semestre, at 363-364 (1913). Source: < gallica.BnF.fr > , 300–317

§ 2.65. Registration of Designs—Hearings Before the Committee on Patents, House of Representatives, Sixty-Fourth Congress, On the Bills H.R. 6458 and H.R. 13618 Providing for the Registration of Designs, March and April 1916 (Government Printing Office, 1916). Source: < archive.org > , 317–321

§ 2.66. La Liberté, Sunday, December 25, 1921, at 2. Source: < gallica.BnF.fr > . L'Humanité—Journal Socialiste, Thursday, March 17, 1921, at 3. Source: < gallica.BnF.fr > . Vogue, February 1, 1922, at 23. Source: < gallica.BnF.fr > . Le Gard, Wednesday, January 4, 1922, at 1. Source: < gallica.BnF.fr > . Le Rappel, Wednesday, September 19, 1923, at 4. Source: < gallica.BnF.fr > . Être Belle—Supplément d'Art et de Coiffure, No. 263, June 10, 1933. Source: < gallica.BnF.fr > . La Propriété Industrielle—Revue Mensuelle du Bureau International pour la Protection de la Propriété Industrielle, à Berne, September 30, 1934, at 162-163. Source: < gallica.BnF.fr > . Pouillet et al., Annales de la Propriété Industrielle, Artistique et Littéraire, year of 1937 (January-February-March), at 244-249 (Bureau des Annales, 1937). Source: < gallica.BnF.fr > , 322–334

§ 2.67. Source: < www.law.justia.com > , 334–336

§ 2.68. Pouillet et al., Annales de la Propriété Industrielle, Artistique et Littéraire, year of 1936 (January), at 48-55 (Bureau des Annales, 1936). Source: <gallica.BnF.fr>, 336–339

§ 2.69. E. Pouillet et al., Annales de la Propriété Industrielle, Artistique et Littéraire, vol. 81, January-February-March 1939, at 251-256 (Arthur Rousseau, 1939), 340–343

§ 2.70. Source: <supreme.justia.com>, 343–347

§ 2.71. Source: <casetext.com>, 347–350

§ 2.72. MTN.GNG/NG11/W/55, of December 8, 1989. MTN.GNG/NG11/W/73, of May 14, 1990. Source: <www.wto.org>. Source: <www.wto.org>, 350 -353

§ 2.73. Source: <www.law.cornell.edu>, 353–358

§ 2.74. WIPO, *Information on National Experiences with the Intellectual Property Protection of Traditional Knowledge*, WIPO/GRTKF/IC/5/INF/2, of April 4, 2003, Annex III, at 16 et seq. Source: <www.wipo.int>. Source: <www.mici.gob.pa>. SCT/32/2, of January 16, 2015, prepared by the Secretariat. Source: <www.wipo.int>, 358–367

§ 2.75. Source: <www.govtrack.us>, 368–371

§ 2.76. Source: <www.supremecourt.gov>, 371–376

§ 2.77. Source: <clarivate.com/darts-ip/>, 376–380

§ 2.78. Source: <www.bailii.org>, 380–385

Illustrations

Figure 1. Extracted from Livre que fist Jehan Bocace de Certalde des cleres et nobles femmes, 1401-1500, f. 69r. Source: <gallica.BnF.fr>, 2

Figure 2. Extracted from Tacuinum sanitatis (fs. 103r and 103v), manuscript based on an eleventh-century Arabic text by physician and philosopher Ibn Butlan, illuminated in Northern Italy in late thirteenth/early fourteenth centuries. Source: <gallica.BnF.fr>, 5

Figures 3 and 4. Extracted from Eugène Soil, Les Tapisseries de Tournai, 9, 10

Figure 5. Extracted from Emilio Motta, *Per la Storia dell'Arte dei Fustagni nel Socolo XIV*, Archivio Storico Lombardo—anno XVII, 140, 144 (1890). Source: <www.omnia.ie>, 12

Figure 6. Extracted from Le Champion des Dames, by Martin Le Franc, 1440. Source: <gallica.BnF.fr>, 19

Figure 7. Source: Biblioteca Nacional de España, 36

Figure 8. Source: <numelyo.bm-lyon.fr>, 42

Figure 9. Extracted from Eugène Müntz, La Tapisserie, at 362, 365-366 (A. Quantin, 1898). Source: <gallica.BnF.fr>, 46

Figure 10. Source: <gallica.BnF.fr>, 50

Figure 11. Extracted from John Grand-Carteret, L'Enseigne—Son Histoire, Sa Philosophie, Ses Particularités—Les Boutiques, Les Maisons, La Rue, La Réclame Commerciale à Lyon, at 334 (Librairies Dauphinoise and Savoyarde, 1902). Source: <gallica.BnF.fr>, 53

Figure 12. Extracted from Augustin Genoud-Eggis, Vieilles Enseignes Fribourgeoises (J. Guinchard, 1914). Source: < archive.org > , 54
Figure 13. Source: < numelyo.bm-lyon.fr > , 61
Figure 14. Extracted from M. Courtecuisse, *La Manufacture de Draps Fins Vanrobais au XVIIe et XVIIIe Siècles*, in Mémoires de la Société d'Émulation d'Abbeville, vol. 25 (F. Paillart, 1920). Source: < gallica.BnF.fr > , 66
Figure 15. Charles Spindler (1865-1938), illustrator: *Les châtiments utilisés en Alsace au Moyen-Âge: le carcan*. Source: < gallica.BnF.fr > , 69
Figure 16. Source: < gallica.BnF.fr > , 79
Figure 17. Source: < www.britishmuseum.org/collection > , 91
Figure 18. Extracted from Léon Maillard, Les Menus et Programmes Illustrés—Invitations—Billets de Faire Part—Cartes d'Addresse—Petites Estampes du XVIIE Siècle Jusqu'à Nos Jours, at 63 and 71 (G. Boudet, 1898). Source: < gallica.BnF.fr > , 97
Figure 19. Source: < gallica.BnF.fr > , 109
Figure 20. Sources: < www.hautediggitydog.com > ; < myotherbagmexico.com > , 125
Figure 21. Sources: WIPO Global Brand Database; < www.levistrauss.com > , 135
Figure 22. Source: < www.amazon.co.uk > , 154
Figure 23. Source: < curia.europa.eu > , 162
Figure 24. Source: < www.birkenstock.com > , 174
Figure 25. Source: < www.nyfwexperience.com > , 182
Figure 26. Source: < bibliotheque.bordeaux.fr > , 185
Figure 27. Source: < gallica.BnF.fr > , 189
Figure 28. Source: < archive.org > , 198
Figure 29. Source: < www.bne.es > , 208
Figure 30. Source: < gallica.BnF.fr > , 214
Figure 31. Extracted from Le Moniteur de la Maille, at 6, January 1914. Source: < gallica.BnF.fr > , 228
Figure 32. Source: < www.getty.edu > , 231
Figure 33. Source: < gallica.BnF.fr > , 239
Figure 34. Source: < Google Books > , 241
Figure 35. Extracted from M. Gallon, Machines et Inventions Approuvés par l'Académie Royale des Sciences—Planches, Tome Premier, at 173 (Antoine Boudet, 1776). Source: < archive.org > , 246
Figure 36. Extracted from Duhamel, Cabinet des Modes, Huitième Cahier, May 1, 1786. Source: < gallica.BnF.fr > , 248
Figure 37. Source: < gallica.BnF.fr > , 249
Figure 38. © NPdC 2020, 251
Figure 39. Extracted from D. A. Tompkins, The Cotton Gin. The History of its Invention., at 24, 50-51, 51-53 (self-publication, 1901); source: < archive.org > , 264
Figure 40. Extracted from J. Meyssin, Histoire de la Machine à Coudre—Portrait et Biographie de l'Inventeur, Barthelemy Thimonnier, at 7-8, 9 (Rey et Sézanne, 1867). Source: < gallica.BnF.fr > ; Source: Google Patents, 269

Figure 41. Source: Google Patents, 270

Figure 42. Source: <gallica.BnF.fr>, 272

Figure 43. Source: <www.uspto.gov>, 285

Figure 44. Extracted from Le Figaro-Modes—A la Ville—Au Théatre—Arts Décoratifs, No. 24, December 15, 1904, at 18. Sources: <gallica.BnF.fr>; <bibliotheques.specialisees.paris.fr>, 305

Figure 45. Source: <www.parismuseescollections.paris.fr>, 313

Figure 46. Source: <gallica.BnF.fr>, 325

Figure 47. Source: <gallica.BnF.fr>, 331

Figure 48. Extracted from Marie Claire, May 28, 1937, at 10-11, and from The Paris Times, Autumn Fashion Number, Sunday, August 10, 1924. Source: <gallica.BnF.fr>, 334

Figure 49. Source: <gallica.BnF.fr>, 339

Figure 50. Sources: <visao.sapo.pt>; <www.hypnotherapie-net.de>, 367

Figure 51. Source: <www.inpi.gov.br>, 380

Index

A

Abbeville, 6–7, 13, 15, 17, 42–43, 62–66, 368
Abercrombie & Fitch, 132–135, 356
Address cards, 94 (*see also* "Trade cards")
Afonso V, of Portugal, 194
African Group, 360, 361, 367
Aiguillettes, 187–189
Aix-en-Provence, 78
Amiens, 12–13, 16–17, 19, 28–31, 69–71, 84, 200–201
Anticipation, 6, 63, 322, 323
Antitrust, 343–347
Apprenticeship, 72, 198–200, 203, 216, 219, 222, 237
Arcuate, 126, 132–135
Arras, 13–17
Aubusson, 86, 87, 250–251
Austria, 33, 45, 136, 351, 352

B

Bachwitz et autres v. Société Paquin limitée, 316–317
Barthélemy Thimonnier, 267–271
Bartolo da Sassoferrato, 11
Beauvais, 13, 17, 229–231, 250
Béchoff, David et Cie. v. Galeries Lafayette, 300–305
Berne Convention, 351
Birkenstock, 155, 163–174
Blanchard v. Hill, 88
Bon Marché, 300, 303
Bon Ton, Le, 318–321
Bonafusus de Sancta Columba, 183, 184
Braid, 235–236
Brussels, 15, 45–46, 197–198
Bryson v. Whitehead, 266–267
Burberrys, 106–108

C

Calico, 258, 274, 275, 293
Callot Soeurs v. Finkelstein et Gruenwald, 310–313
Canada, 252, 253
Carcassonne, 82, 198
Carpets, 6, 9–10, 18, 19, 24, 32–33, 45, 46, 60, 74, 75, 86, 100, 143, 193–194, 197, 215–219, 221, 222 (*see also* "Tapestries")
Châlons, 4–5, 20
Chamusson et Cie. v. Favier et Beurrier, 313–316
Charles V, of Spain, 46
Charles VI, of France, 22
Charles IX, of France, 52
Châtelet, 47, 56, 187, 188, 222–224, 232–234
Cheney Bros. v. Doris Silk Corporation, 334–336
Chic, Le, 310, 313, 316
Chic Parisien, Le, 316
Cloth Act, 186

Cobblers, 12, 16–17
Colbert, Jean Baptiste, 242
Commercial Revolution, 185
Competition, 93–97, 108–109, 274–276
Conspicuous consumption, 117, 121, 244
Consumerism, 267
Corporatism, 61, 98, 231
Corset, 282, 289–291, 294–299
Cotton gin, 259–264
Council of prud'hommes, 13, 14, 257, 278, 279, 290, 291, 293, 304–306, 310, 311, 316, 317, 332, 361
Countervailing duties, 192
Couso-Brodeur, 268
Cultural appropriation, 358–367

D

Dames Segall et Dodu v. Société Vionnet, 329–331
Damier Ebène Canvas, 155
Débauchage, 72, 215, 273, 283
Demoiselle Jacquet v. Caroline Roux, Rose Descat et autres, 336–339
Dolce & Gabbana, 372
Douai, 1–2
Dilution, 116–118, 120, 123, 124, 132–134, 138, 139, 175, 178, 181, 301, 376–380
Dijon, 22–23
Disruptive technology, 267
Dumping, 191–193
dyers, 9, 19, 23, 30, 35, 48, 49, 51, 57–59, 72, 73, 75, 184, 186, 200, 204, 205, 230, 266, 267, 343, 344

E

Ecuyer de Vizé, 240
Edward III, of England, 5–6, 8, 186
Edward IV, of England, 25–26, 195–196
Edward VI, of England, 36–42
Elbeuf, 102–104
Eli Whitney, 259–264
Elite Styles, 318, 320
Elizabeth I, of England, 55–56, 202–206, 224, 225
Ellie Bonnet, 232–235
England, 5–6, 36–42, 88–91, 185–186, 204, 224–228, 268–269, 288–289
Erhardt v. Durst-Will et autres, 279–280
Espionage, 191–193, 217, 322, 323, 340
European Union, 125–135, 155, 157, 159, 162–174, 351, 367
Exploitation requirement, 215

F

Fashion Originators' Guild of America v. FTC, 343–347
Fashion Week, Inc. v. Council of Fashion Designers of America, Inc., CFDA Foundation Inc., and WME IMG LLC, 175–182
Fast fashion, 300
Felipe II, of Spain, 206
Felipe III, of Spain, 206
Fémina, 338, 339
Fernando and Isabel, of Spain, 34–36, 44
Feuilletin, 250
Flanders, 21, 33, 45, 46, 98, 185, 186, 204, 205, 230
Florence, 191–193, 209
France, 4–7, 27–28, 52–53, 82–84, 105, 198–200, 208–209, 215–219, 224–230, 240–241, 250–253, 255–257, 300–317
François I, of France, 198–199
Freddy Spa v. Hugz Clothy Ltd. and others, 380–385
Furs, 252, 253, 326, 338
Fustians, 56–57

G

Giachetto di Benedetto, 193–194
Grand Chic Paris, Le, 310, 313

H

H&M, 300
Hat makers, 93, 94, 228–229
Henry, the Navigator, 194–195
Henry II, of France, 47
Henry III, of England, 183
Henry III, of France, 94, 229
Henry IV, of France, 14, 48, 57–59, 208–221, 215, 217–219, 225
Henry VIII, of England, 36-42
Heuzé et Dame Heuzé v. Bruyère, 340–343
High loom, 9, 19, 60–61, 70, 220, 221
Home sewing, 6, 368, 370

I

In re Lacy's Patent, 265
In the matter of Bayer's Design, 295–299
Industrial Revolution, 71, 88, 103, 106, 251, 264, 267

J

Jacob W. Davies, 283
Jean Hindret, 224–228
Jean Marius, 243–250
Jehan Fortier, 217, 218
John de Bruyn, 186
John Kempe, 185
John Rutherford v. William Boak, 273–274
Jones v. Hallworth, 292
Juan de Alcega, 206, 207
Judge Adauto Suannes, 114
Judge (deputy) David Stone, 380
Judge Doddridge, 60
Judge Learned Hand, 334, 347

K

Kenzo, 155
Kersies, 55–56
Knitting machine, 202, 224–228
Knitwear, 47, 78, 79, 84–85

L

Lafont et Davasse v. Durst, Wild et Cie., 278–279
Leather, 12–13, 231–235, 272–274
Lego, 154, 155, 353, 354
Levi Strauss, 126, 132–135, 283–285
Liability (personal), 3, 10
Lille, 13–14, 17, 33–34, 45, 46, 75–77, 87, 98–99, 201–202, 219–220, 242, 251–252, 277
London, 6, 40, 41, 54, 60, 84, 91, 107, 125, 186, 203–205, 242, 266, 267, 269
Loragnes, 59–60
Louboutin, 135–152
Louis XIII, of France, 59
Louis XIV, of France, 14, 67, 71, 85, 225, 228–229, 231–235, 243
Louis XV, of France, 82, 252–253
Louis XVI, of France, 98–102, 104–106, 237–239
Louis Hinard, 230
Louis Vuitton, 116–126, 155–162, 300, 354, 372 (*see also* "LVM")
Louis Vuitton Malletier v. OHIM, 156–162
Louviers, 65, 87, 102–104
Louvre, 217, 238, 300, 303
Low loom, 2
LVM, 116–125, 155, 162 (*see also* "Louis Vuitton")
Lyon, 47–50, 56–57, 236–237, 253–256

M

Mango, 300
Mark Foy's, 110–113
Marks of freedom, 101
Maurice Bernard, 300–303, 322
Mercure Galant, Le, 79, 240–241, 244, 247
Merino, 34
Metz, 233
Mini skirt, 290
Missoni, 155, 354
Molas, 359
Monin v. Lanclair, 290–291
Montpellier, 26–28

N

National treatment principle, 359
New York Fashion Week, 175–181
Norfolk, 6, 25–26, 61–62, 283
Norwich, 6, 25, 38, 61–62, 266, 267
Neverfull (bag), 162

O

Olivier de Serres, 212–214
Orvietan, 78

P

Panama, 359–366
Parasitism, 107, 116–118, 152
Parasol, 157, 163, 222–224, 243–252 (*see also* "Umbrella")
Paris, 3–4, 24-25, 28–33, 47, 51–52, 59, 60, 85–87, 91–93, 209–211, 222–224, 228–229, 248–251, 301–303, 313
Paris Convention, 146, 351, 359
Parody, 116–124
Passing off, 3, 29, 34, 37, 59–60, 107, 108, 155, 292, 380–385
Pastel, 47, 59–60, 194–195, 304
Pedro, duke of Coimbra, 194
Pedro II, of Portugal, 81
Peter Pan Fabrics, Inc. v. Martin Weiner Corp., 347–350
Pillory, 37, 41, 88, 90, 91, 300
Pinchinas, 87
Poitiers, 235–236
Portugal, 59, 79–81, 157, 158, 194–195, 206, 251, 360, 367
Position mark, 85, 128–130, 144–147, 170
Póvoa do Varzim, 360, 361
Printemps, 300, 303
printing privilege, 206, 237-239, 240–241

R

Ready-to-wear, 79, 267
Red sole, 135–154
Red tab, 135, 382
Rennes, 52–53
Ribbon, 16, 235–236, 282, 290, 291
Rinaldo di Gualtieri, 189–191
Rodier Frères v. Galeries Lafayette, 306–309
Rose Descat, 336–339
Rouen, 7, 21, 23, 26, 27, 64, 83, 103, 216, 225
Royal Academy of Sciences (France), 229, 232, 243, 245, 246
Rules of origin, 88–91

S

Sabotage, 191–193
Saint-Omer, 2–3
Sandforth's case, 53–54, 60
Saieterie (also sayeterie, sayetterie), 33, 34, 42, 43
Scientific Revolution, 184
Scipion Rozan, 215
Seamstress, 5, 14, 60, 79, 267, 302, 322, 328, 333
Secondary meaning, 118, 126, 136, 141–144, 154, 155, 179–181, 301, 353–358, 380

Sedan, 66–68
Selvage, 64–66, 102–104
Serges, 6, 24, 32, 100, 104, 198, 209, 242
Seville, 34, 44
Sewing machine, 267–272
Shearers, 23, 29, 31–32, 35, 43, 51, 81, 198
Shoemakers, 12, 13, 16–17, 51–52, 59, 85–86, 91–93
Siena, 189–194
Silk, 50, 57–59, 191–193, 198, 221–222, 231
Slippers, 85, 86, 128, 169, 171, 174, 226, 226, 281
Smith v. Nichols, 286–287
Social construction, 110, 243–250
Social value, 243, 259, 267
Société anonyme Valisère v. Tinet-Claverie and F. Claverie, 108–109
Société Madeleine Vionnet et Demoiselle Chanel v. Dame Laniel, 332–334
Socks, 79, 84–85, 187–189, 224–226
Southern v. How, 60
Speedy, 125, 227, 351
Statute of Monopolies, 203, 215, 280
St. Gallen, 350
Star Athletica LLC. v. Varsity Brands, Inc., 372–376,
Stocks, 68, 69, 300, 344
Sui generis, 136
Sumptuary law, 81–82, 186, 209

T

Tailor, 3–5, 14, 19, 30, 54, 60, 79, 93–97, 206–208, 237–240, 267, 268, 296
Tanner, 12, 13, 16–17, 232–234, 273
Tapestries, 46, 60, 86, 87, 189, 190, 197, 215, 216, 230, 250, 251 (*see also* "Carpets")
Technical standards, 1, 3, 5, 29, 32, 44, 50–51, 74, 87, 98, 199, 221
Technology transfer, 184, 217
Toledo, 221–222
Tory Burch, 360, 361, 367
Tournai, 8–10, 17–19, 28, 221
Tours, 27, 255, 257
Trade cards, 53, 94, 97 (*see also* "Address cards")
Trademark Dilution Revision Act (TDRA), 116, 123, 126, 132, 133, 135
Traditional knowledge, 360–362, 365–367
TRIPS Agreement, 136, 350–353
Tub Happy, 110–113
Turkey, 205, 217–219
Turners, 222–224
Turpis causa, 114, 175–182

U

Umbrella, 128, 157, 160, 163, 243–250 (*see also* "Parasol")
United States, 6, 116–144, 175–182, 258–264, 267–270, 284–287, 300, 317–321, 327, 334–336, 340, 343–350, 354–360, 367–376

V

Valisère, 108–109
van Robais, Josse, 62–66
Venice, 196–198, 206
Versace, 126, 155
Vimont v. Yung, 293–294
Vionnet, Madeleine, 322–334
Vogue, 119, 303, 307, 322, 325–327

W

Wal-Mart Stores, Inc. v. Samara Brothers, Inc., 354–358
Weaver, 1–2, 7, 14, 19, 22, 23, 28, 30, 35–36, 38, 39, 42, 44, 48, 51, 55, 56, 62, 80, 81, 102, 184, 185, 192, 197–198, 360

William III, of England, 225, 227–228
William Lee, 202, 224–228, 267
WIPO, 144, 155, 163, 284, 359–361, 366–367
Woolen (woollen) cloth, 22, 51, 58–59, 72–74, 82–84, 102
Worsteds, 25–26, 38–39, 61–62
WTO, 351, 360

Y

YKK, 114–116
Yves Saint Laurent, 136–144

Z

Zara, 300

www.ingramcontent.com/pod-product-compliance
Lightning Source LLC
Chambersburg PA
CBHW071416270226
40258CB00061B/15
9789403537849